THE SCIENCE FICTION REFERENCE BOOK

THE
SCIENCE FICTION
REFERENCE BOOK

A COMPREHENSIVE HANDBOOK AND GUIDE
TO THE HISTORY, LITERATURE, SCHOLARSHIP,
AND RELATED ACTIVITIES OF THE SCIENCE FICTION
AND FANTASY FIELDS

edited by Marshall B. Tymn

STARMONT HOUSE

To Matt—a future fan

Cover and interior illustrations by
Vincent Di Fate
©1981

Library of Congress Cataloging in Publication Data

Main entry under title:

The Science fiction reference book.

Includes bibliographies and index.
1. Science fiction—Handbooks, manuals, etc.
2. Fantastic literature—Handbooks, manuals, etc.
I. Tymn, Marshall B., 1937–
PN3433.5.S33   809.3'876   80–28888
ISBN 0-916732-49-5
ISBN 0-916732-24-X (pbk.)

CONTENTS

BACKGROUNDS

FANDOM

ACADEME

APPENDICES

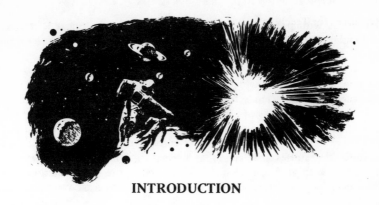

INTRODUCTION

It is time, and past time, that someone should do what Marshall Tymn has done in this book, and that is to put together a guide to the rich resources available for teachers and students of science fiction. I only wish it had been around ten years ago—much misery might have been saved! It is reassuring to look over the list of contributors and find so many names of persons who are not only distinguished in themselves, but to me represent personal friends whose judgment I have every reason to trust—in fact, nearly every name on the contents page is the very name I would have chosen myself, if I had had the wit to conceive of this book and the energy to push it through to completion. I didn't. But Marshall Tymn did, and we are all in his debt.

The Science Fiction Reference Book will be of use to scholars and researchers of all kinds in science fiction. But I suppose it will be read most frequently by teachers, and perhaps that gives me license to say something about how I think science fiction should be taught. Teachers are human beings. Human beings are marvelously diverse; and so each teacher must have his own personal style and concerns. But it seems to me all the same that there are some universals, or should be, and I would like to urge them on anyone about to use the resources of this book to prepare a course.

Since science fiction is a form of literature, I suppose it is inevitable that most teachers of it will come from their English departments, and that they will then bring to it the skills of analysis and criticism that might otherwise be turned on Faulkner or Henry James. Fair enough. But not, I think, extensive enough. One of the ways in which it seems to me that science fiction differs from other fictions is that in it *what* is said is at least as important as *how* it is said.

It must be admitted that, historically, some of the most seminal figures in the development of science fiction were no masters of polished prose. Worse than that. At least half a dozen were clearly deaf to the sound of the English language. They aren't read for style, of course. They are read because they thought things no one had ever thought before, and communicated them to their readers.

Science fiction has become vastly more literate in recent years. Le Guin, Delany and Tiptree, to choose only three at random, are masters of the language.

They use it with precision and grace, in ways that, say, Edgar Rice Burroughs and Stanley G. Weinbaum never could. But I do not think they have more to say.

To come at the same point from another direction, it seems to me that a course in science fiction which limited itself to the writers of the 1970s would miss much of what science fiction is all about. Sf did not begin with *Dune* or *Stranger in a Strange Land,* or even with *Star Trek.* It began almost anywhere you like to say it did—Lucian of Samosata? *Gulliver's Travels?*—but surely it was in full flower with H. G. Wells at the turn of the century. And its real core literature, the stories that represent its maturing into self-awareness as a discrete genre with very special merits, appeared in the science-fiction magazines in the decades just before and after World War II. At least a sampling of these is, I think, a sine qua non. The Science Fiction Writers of America has prepared three volumes of *The Science Fiction Hall of Fame* to preserve that core for us—the best "golden age" stories, as chosen by the corps of science-fiction writers themselves. If I could suggest just one reading assignment for every science-fiction course list, *The Hall of Fame* would be it.

If I were teaching the course, I would then, to be sure, feel obliged to point out that this writer was ham-handed and that one never in his life managed to construct a human character anyone could believe in. But once that disclaimer was out of the way, what a treasure would emerge! Alien creatures, alien worlds. Vast technological change, and its vast impact on human beings. To read science fiction is to stretch the mind. It is not just entertainment. It is technology transfer, and a way to learn what science is all about. It is an opportunity to look at our own world and folkways from outside—what Harlow Shapley called "The view from a distant star"—and to judge objectively our wiseness and our follies. It is, above all, the sovereign prophylactic against future shock; and those core stories of the 1930s, 1940s and 1950s epitomize the qualities that made people pay attention to science fiction in the first place. I cherish them. When I teach a science-fiction course, I delight to share them—and then, of course, Barth and Vonnegut . . . and all the other newer, more graceful science-fiction writers of today.

There was a time when I viewed with alarm the burgeoning of academic interest in science fiction. (There is such a thing as too much respectability!) Perhaps what I have just said is a hangover from that concern; and, anyway, I've been greatly reassured by many of the academics I've met and schools I've visited. It now appears to me that teaching science fiction is not much easier than writing it, and that we all need all the help we can get. This book should lighten the load!

Red Bank
June, 1980

PREFACE

In July, 1975, the first Conference on Teaching Science Fiction was launched at Eastern Michigan University. It is now the largest forum for the exchange of ideas on teaching science fiction in the United States. As director of the conference, I receive many inquiries for core materials, especially those that might serve the needs of the new SF teacher. This volume was compiled as a partial response to those inquiries. Designed primarily as a guide and handbook to science fiction and fantasy, *The Science Fiction Reference Book* contains a variety of background information on the field as a whole, combined with practical information such as reading lists and resource materials. The scope of the volume makes it an ideal introduction to fantastic literature and its activities, not only for the teacher, but for readers of all ages.

I would like to thank the contributors for their fine work in helping to make this book so comprehensive. Special appreciation goes to Vincent Di Fate for his outstanding artwork, to Frederik Pohl for his enthusiastic endorsement, and to Ted Dikty for seeing the volume through to its completion in the face of some discouraging delays.

Marshall Tymn
Fall, 1980

Backgrounds

Thomas D. Clareson

TOWARD A HISTORY OF SCIENCE FICTION

A number of problems hound any attempt to write meaningfully of the history of science fiction. Perhaps the most serious arises from the public's image of the genre as no more than a mixture of spaceships and future societies. This restrictive image has grown out of several of the predominant concerns of the American pulp magazines (elsewhere I have noted that the term "space fiction" was offered in the 1930's as a substitute for science fiction) and the remembered popularity of multimedia heroes like Buck Rogers and Flash Gordon. Such a view would not only limit the potential content of the field, but also would seem to dismiss the fiction of writers like H. Rider Haggard, Frank Stockton, Edgar Rice Burroughs, Arthur Conan Doyle, George Allan England, and Jack London, to name but a few who come easily to mind. Indeed, it overlooks the existence of a body of at least several thousand titles which goes back to early works like Johannes Kepler's *Somnium* (1634), Ludwig Holberg's *A Journey to the World Underground* (1741, 1742), Robert Paltock's *The Life and Adventures of Peter Wilkins* (1751), and Louis Sebastian Mercier's *Memoirs of the Year Two Thousand Five Hundred* (1772, 1802).

Equally troublesome is the perennial debate attempting to distinguish sharply between science fiction and fantasy. So stringently is this issue argued that despite the long-established convention in the stories, there remain those who call a work fantasy if the author permits a spaceship to travel faster than the speed of light. In defining science fiction as "that branch of literature which deals with the human response to changes in science and technology"—a definition which some will find too narrow—Isaac Asimov proposes one of the most plausible criteria for separating sf and fantasy. He asserts both that sf pictures societies differing from the present "entirely because of a difference in science and technology" and that the reader can imagine the "set of continuous changes" transforming the present into the society portrayed in the story: " . . . where no difference in science and technology will suffice to make our society into the society in the book, you have fantasy," as in Tolkien's *Lord of the Rings*.[1] Asimov's position, obviously, is closely akin to that of those individuals who emphasize the extrapolative and prophetic nature of science fiction.

3

A third area of difficulty has occurred because of recent criticism. In an attempt to analyze the nature of sf, some critics have advanced criteria which are as applicable to literary naturalism—also a response to the scientific thought of the nineteenth century—as to science fiction. Perhaps because of the essentially anti-scientific stance, others have stressed the importance (the maturity?) of the dystopian mood so characteristic of the field since mid-century, thus seeing sf as yet another literary expression of man's alienation from the modern world. The latter apparently overlook the fact that despite the importance of the cautionary tale to the genre, even now science fiction has remained essentially optimistic. The seat of this optimism, as Thomas Wymer has pointed out, lies in the fact that much of science fiction has given expression to what is fundamentally an Enlightenment world view.[2] That is to say, sf "has accepted the concept that reason is the highest quality of mind and, as a result, both man and society are perfectable." Moreover, "with reason supreme (and thus the universe itself of a unified, rational nature), all knowledge can be attained. Man must simply persist in his collection of data."[3] Such a generalization becomes translated into the specific when Isaac Asimov says of his own work, "In my stories I always suppose a sane world. I always suppose a world in which there isn't any irrational increase in population, there aren't irrational wars for irrational reasons or causes. . . . In fact in my stories generally the crisis and the resolution results from a confrontation of exponents of the various sides who solve things by their rational discussions."[4]

The ramifications for science fiction are many. The study of character "gives way to the exploration of idea. 'What if' becomes the classic verbalization of the formula. The plot can thus assume the structure of a puzzle or a problem to be solved."[5] In many instances, as in *Beowulf* and the tales of the Arthurian cycle, what the characters *do* assumes a greater importance than what they feel, for they becomes stereotypes—often hero or villain. In this way, at the heart of science fiction may lie a greater potential for the heroic/epic mode than any other form of modern fiction.

The problems cited have arisen in large part because critics and devotees of science fiction, perhaps especially in the last few years, seem to be trying to make the genre a fixed, static form that is somehow instantly recognizable. Ironically, in doing so, they overlook what has become, at least to such individuals as Jack Williamson and Asimov, its central thematic concern: the necessity and inevitability of change. To put the matter another way, surely everyone recognizes the differences, thematically and technically, among Richardson's *Pamela*, Jane Austen's *Emma*, Henry James's *Portrait of a Lady*, and Theodore Dreiser's *Sister Carrie*, but surely no one will deny that all of them are novels. Unfortunately such tolerance does not always exist among students and enthusiasts of science fiction. Their error often results from a lack of, or indifference to, historical perspective.

In terms of intellectual history, science fiction has its chief importance in that it measures the impact of scientific discovery and speculation upon the literary and popular imaginations. In literary terms its lasting importance lies in the creation of both symbolic actions (plots, stories) and of settings (alternate worlds, alternate societies) giving insight into the author's perception of his contemporary world and/or the future of mankind.

Out of the intellectual climate creating the Royal Society, with its emphasis upon the description and exploration of the physical world, came much of the impetus shaping so-called modern fiction. On the one hand, through the isolation of a comparatively few characters in a familiar setting (London, a country estate), the writers undertook a close study of the everyday world. On the other hand, authors like Defoe and Swift adapted to their own ends the so-called "imaginary voyage"—already used by Kepler (*Somnium*, 1634) and Godwin (*The Man in the Moone*, 1638)—a narrative structure going back through the medieval travel books to the *Odyssey* itself. Following the example of Sir Thomas More (*Utopia*, 1516), they used the framework of the voyage to discover a hitherto unknown country whose portrayal allowed them to satirize their own societies. Significantly, these imaginary societies existed in the here-and-now. As I.F. Clarke has shown, apparently the first projection of a future society occurred in the anonymous *The Reign of George VI, 1900-1925* (1763). Indeed, except for a few titles, speculations about the future did not become popular—and therefore a convention—until after the vogue of the utopia in the late nineteenth century. As a matter of fact, the outlining of utopia may not have been the essential factor even then; rather, the writers may well have turned to the future only when they found it necessary to picture an advanced technology. One should recall that Jules Verne drew upon his contemporary world for most of *Les voyages extraordinaires*.

According to Philip Babcock Gove, by the late eighteenth century the imaginary voyage had become the most popular form of fiction. It has remained a staple part of science fiction. Significant to the study of sf in terms of intellectual history, the voyagers' destinations have mirrored the changing topical interests of their contemporaries. For example, citing Marjorie Nicolson, with the advent of Copernican theory came the earliest of those innumerable voyages to the moon, a journey which became a fixed convention for extraterrestrial flight until Schiaparelli's conjectures regarding Martian "canals" in the late 1870's sparked a new controversy which seized and held the public imagination well into the present century. (One has only to turn to the supposedly staid *Atlantic Monthly* to find how often and how furiously the issue was debated; in 1908 *Cosmopolitan* featured H.G. Wells's "The Things That Live on Mars," billed as "a description, based upon scientific reasoning, of the flora and fauna of our neighboring planet, in conformity with the latest astronomical revelations" (44:335). Within another generation the outward voyage had reached galactic proportions. From the comic-strip level of Buck Rogers through the space operas of E. E. "Doc" Smith (*Skylark Three*, 1930), Edmond Hamilton (*Crashing Suns* and *Outside the Universe*, 1929-1930), Jack Williamson (*The Legion of Space*, 1934), and Clifford D. Simak (*Cosmic Engineers*, 1939) to Robert A. Heinlein (the "future history" series of *The Past Through Tomorrow*, 1939-1957; 1967), Arthur C. Clarke (*The City and the Stars*, 1956), Poul Anderson (*Tau Zero*, 1970), and Larry Niven (*Ringworld*, 1970), the core of science fiction dealing with space travel has optimistically proclaimed that the stars are, indeed, man's destination.

One must realize that none of the earlier interests/conventions has disappeared. The effect has been cumulative, thereby enriching sf and allowing each author a wider range to draw from and modify as need be. As Donald Wollheim pointed out, a writer may fit a story into any point of Heinlein's future history without facing the need of elaborate explanation. The conventions—the ever more complex framework—exist. Thus, for example, Arthur C. Clarke may concern himself with either a moon colony which becomes the focus of interplanetary conflict (*Earthlight*, 1951, 1955) or a Martian colony which solves the problem of its survival (*The Sands of Mars*, 1951, 1952), while Heinlein may portray a moon colony in revolt against the Earth, a revolt echoing the American Revolution (*The Moon is a Harsh Mistress*, 1966). Or Larry Niven and Jerry Pournelle may indulge in space opera (*The Mote in God's Eye*, 1974).

Although space flight and extraterrestrial worlds, as noted, have become synonymous with science fiction, this is a serious distortion, for throughout the nineteenth century and well into the twentieth, sf employed a variety of settings mirroring the interests of its contemporaries as they explored the last unknown areas of the Earth. Paltock and Holberg had introduced subterranean locales, but not until after Captain Adam Seaborn (pseudonym of John Cleves Symmes) had published *Symzonia: A Voyage of Discovery* (1820) and the concept of a hollow Earth had filtered down to become, so to speak, public property did the interior world establish itself as a backdrop for a host of novels, ranging from William A. Taylor's utopian *Intermere* (1901-1902) to Frank Powell's melodramatic *The Wolf-Men* (1906) and Marlo Field's didactic *The Astro Bubbles* (1928). Best remembered, of course, is Pellucidar, that seemingly prehistoric world created by Edgar Rice Burroughs. The dream of a Northwest Passage and the obsessive desire to reach the poles, reinforced by such tragedies as those of Franklin and Andrée, peopled the Arctic and Antarctic with the remnants of a variety of ancient peoples: the descendants of the Athenian Greeks in Eugene Shade Bisbee's *The Treasure of the Ice* (1892), the Vikings of Fitzhugh Green's *Z R Wins* (1924), and the "lost tribes" of Arthur W. Barker's *The Light from Sealonia* (1927) among them. Sir H. Rider Haggard opened the interior of Africa to the imaginations of his contemporaries with *King Solomon's Mines* (1885) and *She* and *Allan Quatermain* (1887), an action completed by Edgar Rice Burroughs, whose Tarzan constantly encountered lost tribes in forgotten cities (so much so that some have called Burroughs a "one plot" author).

Increased knowledge regarding pre-Columbian archeology scattered cities of Mayas, Aztecs, and Incas from the Olympian mountains of Washington state (Joseph Badger, *The Lost City*, 1898) and the Grand Canyon (James Paul Kelly, *Prince Izon*, 1910) to Mexico (Juanita Savage, *The City of Desire*, 1930) and South America (Leo Miller, *The Hidden People*, 1920). The Sargasso Sea housed secret places; Atlantis and Lemuria were called up from the vast unknown of prehistory. Increasingly after the First World War, however, writers turned to Asia (where, perhaps, the journey had begun in the medieval travel books) in order to find unknown kingdoms: Indo-China in both Gilbert Frankau's *The Seeds of Enchantment* (1921) and Gilbert Collins' *The Starkenden Quest* (1925); India and Afghanistan in both Harold Lamb's *The House of the Falcon* (1921) and Mark Channing's *King Cobra* (1935); Mongolia in both Lamb's *Marching Sands* (1920) and Rita M. Hanson's *The Desert Road to Shani-Lun* (1939). In Tibet, in James Hilton's *Lost Horizon* (1933) the "lost race" novel found its Shangri-La, which somehow epitomizes the neo-primitivism and rejection of an emerging urban-technological civilization shaping the themes of the motif.

After the Second World War, however, it survived only in an occasional title like Jacquetta Hawkes' *Providence Island* (1959). As the corners of the world became common property, so to speak, the authors turned elsewhere. As early as *The Time Machine* (1895) Wells gave modern form to the theme of time travel. Ray Cummings revived the sub-atomic universe in the stories combined in *The Girl in the Golden Atom* (1923), thereby anticipating the concept of parallel universes so important to contemporary science fiction, as in Clifford D. Simak's "The Big Front Yard" (1958) and Isaac Asimov's *The Gods Themselves* (1972).

An emerging urban-technological civilization—in that phrase lies the key to numerous of the developments in the history of science fiction. For example, no one will question that in *Frankenstein* (1818) Mary Shelley gave form to one of the fundamental themes of sf—science's creation of a monster which it cannot control. It is, of course, a modern rendering of the Faustus myth, in which the scientist seeks knowledge that man should not possess—as innumerable characters have informed literary and filmic audiences. Even though some marvelous power of the new, little-understood electricity brings Frankenstein's creature to life, Mary Shelley looks back toward alchemy and such matters. Nowhere does she give the details of the theory or the process by which the monster is animated: as H.G. Wells said, this phase of the novel is more magical than scientific.[6] Yet she does anticipate the demands of those who insist that the finest science fiction deal with the consequences of some action/situation instead of a mere description of the action or an exposition of its causes.

In contrast stands Jules Verne, who received the adulation of such later figures as Hugo Gernsback. He was no prophet; he simply responded enthusiastically to the accomplishments of the new technology developing in the late nineteenth century. Like so many before him, he adapted the imaginary voyage to his own ends: a celebration of the "hardware" of transportation—balloons, "airships," submarines—and an encyclopedic description of the areas through which his travelers journey, as in *Twenty Thousand Leagues Under the Sea* (1870). He shared his contemporaries' enthusiasm for geology, as perhaps best shown in *A Journey to the Center of the Earth* (1864), and throughout his works he seemed to be in awe of electricity. (One should realize that well into the twentieth century various popularizers were writing books based on the question "What Is Electricity?") His limitation may be best shown by what occurred in *From the Earth to the Moon* (1864); "he spent much of the novel developing a cannon capable of firing a projectile at a velocity of seven miles per second—that is, escape velocity. He later defended this practice while condemning Wells for making use of a metal which negated the law of gravity."[7] In short, he celebrated the machine. He was instantly popular in Britain and America; novels were dedicated to him; the American William H. Rhodes (*Caxton's Book*, 1870) was compared to him; and later Hugo Gernsback was to call him the "father of science fiction."

In the 1970's, amid such problems as pollution and an energy shortage—threats that undermine the very basis of the technology which arose late in the nineteenth century—one perhaps cannot share the dream of inevitable progress having so overwhelming an impact upon those generations between the American Civil War and the First World War. The promise of the earlier Industrial

Revolution seemed to blossom. The electric light, the phonograph, the telephone, the wireless radio, the automobile, the dynamo, the airplane—to say nothing of the "ironclad," the Gatling gun, the submarine—these achievements transformed society within a single lifetime. Writers seized upon each new theory and each new mechanical device. Even the innovations in police work and criminology produced a hero, the "scientific detective," as best exemplified by Arthur B. Reeves' Craig Kennedy, whose monthly adventures first appeared in *Cosmopolitan* in 1910. The inventor and the scientist joined the medical man as heroes of popular fiction. At the juvenile level, the name Tom Swift has become symbolic of that legion of youthful innovators—"The Motor Boys," "The Young Engineers," "The Submarine Boys," "The Automobile Girls"—who used the latest devices to explore the world and bring justice to the oppressed. Countless protagonists sought the "ultimate" weapon. Such ventures took place not in the far-distant future of the space opera but in America here-and-now. One can be certain that this fiction gave the earliest expression to America's love affair with the machine, the "gadget."

In contrast, in Britain, the first nation to achieve industrialization, the machine had become suspect, as in Samuel Butler's *Erewhon* (1872) and W.H. Hudson's *A Crystal Age* (1877). The major voice cautioning his contemporaries against both a belief in inevitable progress and a belief that man is the end-product of evolution belonged to H.G. Wells. Jack Williamson has emphasized Wells's awareness of unending change, Robert Silverberg has asserted that Wells explored in his fiction all of the themes underlying contemporary science fiction, and Mark Hillegas has shown the indebtedness of the great dystopian writers like Zamiatin, Huxley, and Orwell to him. All are correct. He stands antipodal to Verne. The public image of Wells is that of a frustrated old man who, from *A Modern Utopia* (1905), cried out in increasing despair in favor of social and political reform carried out by men of good will. In recent years, however, critics have recognized that his most important work, the early fiction, drew upon biology (rather than technology) in order to dramatize the precarious position of man in a universe which he does not comprehend and which he cannot control. Thus, *The Time Machine* (1895) suggests the conflict in various dichotomies within the Victorian world and climaxes with the vision of that final, reddened twilight of a dying Earth. *The Island of Doctor Moreau* (1897), which can be read as a retelling of the Frankenstein myth, flies in the face of the Enlightenment world view by underscoring man's partial animality and his irrationality. *The War of the Worlds* (1898) again dramatizes man's insecurity by showing that "we cannot regard this planet as being fenced in and a secure abiding-place for Man. . . . " While Verne's appeal may at first be the stronger because of his essentially romantic view of the new technology, once historical events of the twentieth century began to question the concept of progress, writers turned increasingly to Wells.

By 1926, when Hugo Gernsback founded the first of the specialist magazines, *Amazing Stories*, a number of motifs had established themselves within the field of science fiction. What is perhaps most remarkable, one should realize, is that while magazines like *Cosmopolitan*, *Argosy All-Story*, and *Thrill Book* did publish some sf, the great majority of titles were published in hardback editions. Moreover, as critics such as Dorothy Scarborough indicate, it had been accepted as a part of the canon of popular literature.

The categories have historical interest, but more than that some evolved with the field and remain a part of the contemporary scene:

(1) The "lost race, lost lands" novel, beginning with Rider Haggard, was the most popular motif, especially among the British, caught up as they were in the concerns of empire. It developed out of the interests in geology, paleontology, archeology, and exploration. Its themes and literary quality are typified by works like Albert Bigelow Paine's *The Great White Way* (1901), Arthur A. Nelson's *Wings of Danger* (1915), and John Taine's *The Greatest Adventure* (1929). After Haggard and Burroughs, its most lasting achievement occurs in Arthur Conan Doyle's *The Lost World* (1912), which introduces the redoubtable and cantankerous Professor George Challenger. By and large, as noted, the motif became the vehicle expressing the neo-primitivism that objected to (and sought escape from) the developing twentieth century society.

(2) Many writers chose to forego the unexplored areas of the world in favor of prehistory. On the one hand, as in Louis P. Gratacap's *A Woman of the Ice Age* (1906) and Gouverneur Morris' *The Pagan's Progress* (1904), they sought to dramatize the moment of man's emergence as man and thereby capture those static qualities which made him human. On the other hand, they peopled pre-Columbian America with enlightened races resembling the Mound Builders, as in Charles T. Abbot's *The Cliff Dweller's Daughter* (1899), or conjured up the continent of Atlantis, as in Charles J. Cutcliffe Hyne's *The Lost Continent* (1900). Of all the motifs this was the most extravagantly romantic, for, obviously, its writers did not concern themselves with establishing credibility in terms of the familiar, everyday world, as did the writers of the lost race novels.

(3) The interplanetary voyage, already mentioned, served first as a vehicle by which writers of the period sought to reconcile the new science with established religious beliefs. In the preface to *A Journey to Mars* (1894), Gustavus W. Pope asserts that Man must be the same *in Esse* on whatever world he exists because he was created in the image of God; in *Daybreak: The Story of an Old World* (1896), James Cowan goes further when, through the Martian Thorwald, he explains that Christ had been incarnated on Mars as well as Earth so that that world might also be redeemed. One cannot be fully certain where the change to the modern emphasis began. Garrett P. Serviss deserves some of the credit. His *Edison's Conquest of Mars* (1898), a newspaper sequel to Wells's *The War of the Worlds*, pits the evolution of Earth against that of Mars but dismisses technical detail as incomprehensible to his readers and therefore not necessary. His *A Columbus of Space* (1911), although making use of nuclear energy, is satisfied to describe the wonders of Venus and recount a love story. Yet by the publication of Garret Smith's *Between Worlds* in the early 1920's, space opera had been invented.

(4) The most popular motif, quantitatively, resulting from the technology of the period portrayed some future war, as I.F. Clarke has shown. It provided the literary response to the armaments race in Europe, the new military technology, and the imperialistic division of Asia and Africa into spheres of influence. Sir George Tomkyns Chesney began the wildfire with his publication in *Blackwoods Magazine* of "The Battle of Dorking" (1871), a prediction of a successful inva-

tion of Britain by Germans because of the military unpreparedness of Her Majesty's kingdom. As early as 1881 that same concern for unpreparedness showed itself in Park Benjamin's "The End of New York," in which a Spanish fleet bombards the city; he emphasized the humiliation of the defeat by allowing the navy of "an insignificant Republic of South America" (Chile) to relieve the metropolis. More typical of early American treatment of the motif was Frank Stockton's *The Great War Syndicate* (1889), in which private enterprise defeats the British empire. By the First World War, however, America fought off German armies—so deep was the feeling that in 1916 H. Irving Hancock wrote a four-volume juvenile series entitled "Conquest of the United States." By the 1920's the United States struggled against the "yellow hordes" of Asia, a concern going back to Pierton W. Dooner's *Last Days of the Republic* (1880), written in protest against the importation of Coolie labor into California and climaxing in the complete destruction of an independent America. The motif gained one of its most provocative expressions in S. Fowler Wright's *The War of 1938* (1936), the portrayal of conflict between Germany and Czechoslovakia. It survived a thousand galactic wars and has become an important part of the dystopian mood in novels like Joe Haldeman's *The Forever War* (1975).

(5) Utopia may well be a separate genre, but it has long been associated with science fiction, especially in those works, like Chauncey Tinker's *The Crystal Button* (1891) and Hugo Gernsback's *Ralph 124C41+* (1911), which describe future societies perfected by science. Edward Bellamy's *Looking Backward* (1888) set the tone of the many utopian novels at the turn of the century in that it began a long debate on socialism in its various forms. By and large they became essay-like polemics advancing the writer's pet theories, as in William McMasters' *Revolt: An American Novel* (1919), in which he attacked the control that "big money" had over American politics. Robert Herrick's *Sometime* (1933) represents those societies projected into a future when America and often Europe have been destroyed (this time by a new ice age) and the seat of civilization shifted to Africa. Yet so strong has been the dystopian mood for at least a generation that since the outbreak of the Second World War only Austin Tappan Wright's *Islandia* (1942), B.F. Skinner's *Walden Two* (1948), and Aldous Huxley's *Island* (1962) can be regarded as utopian.

(6) Those novels dealing with wonderful inventions and/or wonderful discoveries, as noted, became the special province of the enthusiasts of the new technology. A tunnel is bored from Australia to New York City in Clement Fezandie's *Through the Earth* (1898), synthetic diamonds are produced in Jacques Futrelle's *The Diamond Master* (1909), while both anti-gravity and the ultimate energy are discovered in John Ames Mitchell's *Drowsy* (1917). Nothing seemed impossible. This motif also became the stalking grounds of the "mad" scientist, as early exemplified by William H. Rhodes' *The Case of Summerfield* (1870, 1917), in which the demented chemist threatens to evaporate the oceans of the world unless he is paid a million dollars. Be he hero or villain, the scientist/inventor/engineer (they were synonymous in the public imagination) reigned supreme.

(7) The Gothic tales concerned with madness and mesmerism, as in Poe's fiction, began an interest in abnormal psychology. The classic novel is Robert Louis Stevenson's *Strange Case of Dr. Jekyll and Mr. Hyde* (1886), that study of

dual personality which fostered as many imitations, seemingly, as did *Franken-stein*. Albert Bigelow Paine's *The Mystery of Evelin Delorme* (1894) explores the phenomenon of dual personality; Edward Bellamy's *Dr. Heidenhoff's Experiment* (1880), the first of his novels, introduces an experiment which erases all knowledge of evil from the patient; and Frank Gellett Burgess' *The White Cat* (1907) allows a villainous doctor to summon up the evil alter ego of his patient by means of hypnosis. Ambrose Bierce and Henry James transformed the traditional ghost story into the dramatization of "an anxious state of mind," while in *Questionable Shapes* (1903) and *Between the Dark and the Daylight* (1907), William Deans Howells created the psychologist Wanhope to explain his friends' ghost stories in terms of the psychological theory of the day. For the future development of sf one of the most important works was John Davys Beresford's *The Hampdenshire Wonder* (1911), long celebrated as the first of the "superman" novels, whose young protagonist has a mind far in advance of contemporary man's. From it are descended that legion of mutants, cyborgs, and androids who are *More Than Human,* to cite the title of Theodore Sturgeon's 1953 novel. In its concern for transcendence the motif gave voice to what may be regarded as the first concern for that expanded awareness which has been termed the exploration of "inner space."

(8) The clearest bridge between early science fiction and that of the past generation or so may perhaps be found in the so-called "catastrophe" or "post-catastrophe" motif. Intriguingly, at the same time that literary naturalism depicted the world as the enemy of man, science fiction introduced the idea of some natural disaster which threatens mankind's continued existence. Various stories of Wells established the prototype. Jack London's *The Scarlet Plague* (1915) reduces civilization to barbarism from which there is no escape, while in James Ames Mitchell's *The Last American* (1889), the United States has been destroyed by a climatic change and is explored by a Persian expedition in the thirtieth century. British authors, like Conan Doyle (*The Poison Belt*, 1913), M.P. Shiel (*The Purple Cloud*, 1929), John Wyndham—pseudonym of John Beynon Harris—(*The Day of the Triffids*, 1952), and John Christopher—pseudonym of Christopher Samuel Youd—(*No Blade of Grass*, 1957; *The Long Winter*, 1962; *The Ragged Edge*, 1966), more often used the disaster to cleanse the Earth so that a finer society might emerge or, at least, man might have a second chance. One is tempted to compare these works with *Robinson Crusoe,* where British common sense prevails, for the survivors of the catastrophes win through by a combination of good fortune, courage, and reason to rebuild civilization. Because it dealt with the "ultimate" catastrophe—the destruction of civilization and, often, the world itself, the motif allowed the greatest idealization of the scientist. He was portrayed as a savior; in Garrett P. Serviss' *The Second Deluge* (1912) he built an ark to save a chosen few from a watery nebula that inundated the Earth; in George Allan England's *Darkness and Dawn* trilogy (1914) he awakened from suspended animation to father a new line of humanity in a far-future, devastated world; in Edwin Balmer and Philip Wylie's *When Worlds Collide* (1933) he built a rocket ship and led a chosen few to a new world. In short, throughout the motif the spirit of the Enlightenment prevailed; man triumphed, whatever the odds. Not until after the Second World War when the disaster was no longer natural but man-made, as in Aldous Huxley's *Ape and*

Essence (1948) and Walter M. Miller, Jr.'s *A Canticle for Leibowitz* (1960), did the pattern change.

Significantly, as noted, none of these motifs disappeared. They grew more complex and remained available for the writer to adapt as he saw fit. For example, Max Ehrlich's *The Big Eye* (1949) reflects the growing anxieties of the scientific community after the Second World War; in an effort to gain world-wide unity and bring an end to war, its astronomers announce that a new planet intruding into the solar system will collide with the Earth. In Roger Zelazny's "A Rose for Ecclesiastes" (1964) the dying race is Martian. In Robert Silverberg's *Across a Billion Years* (1969) a team of Earthmen searches for the Mirt Korp Ahm, the so-called High Ones, whose civilization once spread across the galaxy, while in Frederik Pohl's *Gateway* (1977) Earthmen fly the ships they find on the satellite (gateway) left by an ancient and superior race. (The treatment of the alien and his society was to become one of the marked differences between contemporary and early sf.)

Although examples of the various motifs continued to be published in hardback for both adult and juvenile audiences throughout the 1930's, science fiction became identified with the so-called "ghetto" of the specialist pulp magazines. One must understand that this fate was not unique to sf. Publishing exigencies of the mass market created pulps in every field—from *High Seas Adventure, Pirate Stories,* and *Golden Fleece Historical Romances* through innumerable western, detective, and sports titles to *Northwest Romances, Horror Stories,* and *Terror Tales*—during the decade before the Second World War. Secondly, one must remember that many of the individuals who began their careers in the then new specialist magazines are still active. For example, Murray Leinster (pseudonym of Will F. Jenkins), whose earliest stories appeared in *All-Story* and *Argosy* at the time of the First World War, did not die until 1974. John W. Campbell, Jr. edited *Astounding/Analog* from the winter of 1937/1938 until his death in 1971. Consequently some individuals whose entire professional life has been tied to the magazines in one way or another have a strong proprietary feeling toward sf and would separate it from what was published prior to—or, with a few exceptions, outside of—the specialist pulps before the contemporary period. This exclusiveness becomes absurd when one considers such British authors as Olaf Stapledon, whose seminal influence upon the genre everyone acknowledges. Something of a similar problem arises because much of the early material is largely unavailable so that recent criticism, particularly much of the academic criticism, has concentrated upon contemporary figures. Also, of course, for many the historical perspective itself has fallen into disrepute, whatever the reasons.

In 1926, Hugo Gernsback, former editor of *Modern Electrics* and *Electrical Experimenter,* founded *Amazing Stories,* the first magazine devoted exclusively to what Gernsback briefly called "scientifiction." Included in the masthead, a sketch of Jules Verne's tombstone shows a partially veiled figure reaching toward the heavens. Gernsback defined the genre as the "Jules Verne, H.G. Wells, and Edgar Allan Poe type of story—a charming romance intermingled with scientific fact and prophetic vision." Optimism continued unabated. For managing editor he selected the aging son-in-law of Thomas Edison and assigned him, as his chief function, the checking of the accuracy of the science in the stories.

When he lost financial control of *Amazing*, he at once issued *Science Wonder Stories* and *Air Wonder Stories*, which soon merged as *Wonder Stories*. He gathered about him such writers as Jack Williamson, Edmond Hamilton, E.E. "Doc" Smith, Ray Cummings, and Murray Leinster.

His magazines soon lost their place as front-runners, however, to *Astounding Stories*, edited first by Harry Bates and F. Orlin Tremaine and then by John W. Campbell, Jr. While one can see in retrospect that Campbell had certain weaknesses, as shown best in some of his editorials and his obsessive pursuit of an idea like Dianetics, there can be no doubt that for several decades at least he was the moving force shaping the field. His editorship inaugurated what has been called the "Golden Age" of science fiction—that period lasting, roughly, from the late 1930's until the early 1950's. He featured the works of Isaac Asimov, Robert A. Heinlein, A.E. van Vogt, Lester del Rey, Clifford Simak, C.L. Moore and Henry Kuttner (under their various pseudonyms as well as their own names), and Theodore Sturgeon. No one who published with him—from Asimov and Sturgeon to Gordon Dickson and Jerry Pournelle—has anything but praise for the manner in which he worked closely with his writers and guided their efforts. Out of that "Golden Age" came the mythic future history which sees man and his civilization triumphant throughout the galaxies.

Little can be gained by enumerating those few titles which competed, often for but a few issues, with *Astounding* before the Second World War. They were edited by young men like Frederik Pohl and Donald Wollheim, whose influence was to be highly significant at a later date. The magazines themselves were curtailed or killed off by the war. A spate of titles appeared in the 1950's during the so-called "boomlet," a possible result of the public's turning briefly to sf to find simplistic answers to what had happened, for example, at Hiroshima. Two enduring titles did emerge. In the autumn of 1949 Anthony Boucher and Francis McComas launched *The Magazine of Fantasy and Science Fiction*. The element of fantasy is crucial. (*Weird Tales*, around which the Lovecraft cult had gathered since the 1920's, was to die in the 1950's; Campbell had briefly issued a magazine devoted to fantasy, *Unknown*, but it had been a victim of the war.) Not only did Boucher and McComas give the writers a greater latitude within which to work, but they also raised again, for some at least, the question of how well one can distinguish between fantasy and science fiction. The magazine also soon gained a reputation for stressing literary quality. Equally important was *Galaxy*, first published in 1950 and edited by Horace Gold. Samuel R. Delany pinpointed the importance that *Galaxy* was to have in shaping modern science fiction when he emphasized that from the 1950's on the author became free to produce "a completely new world, in which the technological relation to ours is minimal" and to explore "these infinitely multiplied worlds, filled with wondrous things. . . . "[8] In other words, the linear extrapolation from the present world into a possible/probable world of the future (see Asimov's definition insisting that the reader be able to imagine how that future world had emerged from the present) was no longer the iron-clad convention that it had been since late in the nineteenth century. The realism called for was no longer that of making the imaginary world somehow credible in terms of the everyday world (thus the importance of the imaginary voyage, for example, as a narrative structure) but rather in the richness of the texture with which the author created his new world. Delany has called the result "an aim closer to poetry than to any sociological fiction." All that was asked was that the worlds created be consistent within themselves, a characteristic that Jane Mobley, among others, has asked of fantasy. In short, science fiction could now portray worlds capable of carrying metaphor, as in the instances, for example, of Frank Herbert's *Dune* (1965) and Robert Silverberg's *Downwind to the Earth* (1969-1970).

Unlike Delany, in contrasting earlier science fiction with that written since 1950 (or the Second World War), many critics have emphasized utopia and dystopia: a shift from a vision of an earthly paradise to that of an earthly hell. Once again, these views are not mutually exclusive. Wells cautioned his audience against a smug optimism and C.S. Forster warned against technology ("The Machine Stops," 1909), while Keith Laumer's protagonist, Retief of the CDT (Corps Diplomatique Terrestrienne) still manages to keep "full control of the galaxy," as in *Envoy to New Worlds* (1963), in a manner befitting the finest of the old space operas. But a change did take place; perhaps it was first noticeable *quantitatively* in the host of tales soon after the war crying out against the possibility of atomic holocaust. One may choose to date the new mood from Ray Bradbury's *The Martian Chronicles* (1950), in which Earthmen plunder Mars much as Europeans plundered America; or one may begin with Clifford Simak's *City* (1952), in which he underscores man's limitations physically and psychologically and deplores his surrender to a mechanical civilization. What had begun in America as a love affair with technology became disenchantment. The floodgates opened. Kurt Vonnegut, Jr. attacked a society dominated by computerized machines and a managerial elite (but showed man drawn irresistably to the gadget, the machine) in *Player Piano* (1952); Fred Pohl and Cyril Kornbluth satirized a society dominated by advertising corporations in *The Space Merchants* (1953). Nearly twenty years later John Brunner's *The Sheep Look Up* (1972) explored ecological disaster in an America rapidly destroying itself.

The harshest condemnation has undoubtedly come from British writers, especially those who grouped themselves around Michael Moorcock and the magazine *New Worlds*—those to whom Judith Merril, among others, gave the name "New Wave." In referring to them—and the dystopian mood in general—Lester del Rey criticized those individuals who had lost faith in the future. He may well have had some basis for this view when one recalls that Brian Aldiss, whose most experimental and controversial novel remains *Barefoot in the Head* (1970), remarked that he and his colleagues suddenly found themselves living through the dates that Wells had assigned to various utopian events—world congresses and such like. But nothing had changed; indeed, things had grown worse. Far from living in a rational world, they believed themselves in a world growing more irrational, more absurd.

Another important change has occurred in science fiction's romantic concern for transcendence. At the turn of the century in novels like Louis P. Gratacap's *The Certainty of a Future Life on Mars* (1903) and Mark Wicks's *To Mars Via the Moon* (1911), the Earthmen who communicated with the red planet—often with their supposedly deceased friends and relatives—were assured that a better life on a better world awaited them. It was widely suggested at the turn of the century that the next advancement in evolution must be a further development of man's soul. (All such ideas were possible in a world/universe governed by an inevitable linear progression onward and upward.) Even in John D. Beresford's *The Hampdenshire Wonder* (1911), in which almost no one can understand and communicate with the young protagonist and he is killed, one notes the awe with which the narrator regards an advanced and totally rational mind. In the decade before the Second World War the British author, Olaf Stapledon, to whom writers like Arthur C. Clarke acknowledge indebtedness, gave perhaps the fullest expression within the field to the theme of transcendence. In *Last and First Men* (1930), his first novel, he sketched the history of eighteen species of man over a span of two billion years; his last men gain "spiritual maturity and the philosophic mind." In *The Star Maker* (1937) a contemporary Englishman projects his consciousness through all time and space to discover that a Star Maker has created an eternal series of universes, each more perfect than the earlier. He speaks not of a God outside man but rather a kind of life force or consciousness. *Darkness and Light* (1942) unfolds alternate visions of the future. One shows man's extinction; the other, his realization that mankind's function is to produce a mutant race superior to *homo sapiens*.

One could enumerate a legion of supermen and mutants—from Ed Earl Repp's "The Gland Superman" (1938) and A.E. van Vogt's *Slan* (1940) to Keith Roberts' *The Inner Wheel* (1970). In 1953 appeared two novels dealing with the theme, both of which have become classics in the field. In Arthur C. Clarke's *Childhood's End* the alien Overlords intervene in man's affairs to protect him from himself and to act as midwives while the human race evolves psychically in order to unite with the cosmic Overmind. In the climactic sense a single adult watches the children, now combined into a single intellect and long cut off from their parents and mankind because of their psychic powers, undergo a metamorphosis. Not only are they released from their human form, but they dissolve the Earth itself in order to gain the energy needed for the transformation. Mankind will no longer exist except as a part of the Overmind. The second novel was Theodore Sturgeon's *More Than Human*. A number of children, each having unusual psychic ability—ranging from telepathy to teleportation—are brought together to form a single complex organism, *Homo Gestalt*. As a unit the children are able to "blesh"—to blend and mesh together—although retaining their individual identities. Sturgeon's major achievement was not that he created another superior being, but that he found a symbol overcoming the fragmented isolation of individual man.

Although the plot line of these novels demanded a struggle between the supermen and "normal" humanity, as in van Vogt's *Slan*, the authors accepted /advocated the improvement—unless they used the creature(s) to develop the Frankenstein theme. Increasingly, however, the new species was destroyed because it threatened the continued existence of man as he is. Significant in this change are John Wyndham's *Rebirth* (1955) and *The Midwich Cuckoos* (1958). More important for the development of science fiction, however, were those novels in which man denied his humanity. Again Clifford Simak's *City* (1952) is a seminal novel, for given the opportunity, the vast majority of mankind chooses to be transformed into Lopars, a Jovian creature whose perceptions are not so limited as man's. In Silverberg's *Downward to the Earth* (1970), when the protagonist is given the opportunity to be reborn into an alien form, he remarks, "I've tried being human for quite a while. Maybe it's time to be something else."

One may argue that the treatment of the alien has led to the most important thematic change in science fiction. In space opera the alien was merely a displaced Indian in the adaptation of the western to galactic dimensions. For years he was dismissed as the "Bug-Eyed Monster"; the only good alien was a dead alien. Stanley G. Weinbaum broke the stereotype with "Tweel" in "A Martian Odyssey" (1934). For one thing he is more intelligent than his human companion. In "First Contact" (1944) Murray Leinster elevated his aliens to the level of problem-solver when Earthmen and Aliens swap spaceships, thereby supposedly preventing either from following the other to home planet and perhaps destroying it. He again permitted man and alien to cooperate in "Exploration Team" (1956). Yet perhaps not until Philip José Farmer's *The Lovers* (1952, 1961) was the potential of the alien fully realized. The protagonist impregnates a creature (a plant which can assume human form); her death teaches him something of the meaning of love and what it means to be "human," a theme Farmer has explored repeatedly in stories like "Open to Me, My Sister" —retitled "My Sister's Brother" (1960).

There developed an affirmation which denied man's transcendence over other creatures. Naomi Mitchison's *Memoirs of a Spacewoman* (1962) suggests that the diversity of intelligent life forms throughout the universe will be almost unimaginable, while Chad Oliver's *The Shores of Another Sea* (1971) insists that there must be lines of communication among all intelligent beings. James Gunn's *The Listeners* (1972)—at first glance seemingly little more than another celebration of scientists and their persistent efforts to reach a goal—chronicles man's first encounter by means of radio telescope with the computer banks of a long-dead civilization; its open ending implies that mankind will be changed over and over again by such contacts, perhaps without realizing it. At the heart of the affirmation—Simak may be its most consistent spokesman—lies the idea that all intelligence, however diverse its life forms, makes up a unity which is in itself the purpose and meaning of the universe.

Equal in importance to the emergence of this theme has been the creation of totally alien worlds. Because of their scientific accuracy particular praise has gone to Hal Clement (pseudonym of Harry Clement Stubbs) for a novel like *Mission of Gravity* (1954) and to Poul Anderson, among whose successes has been "A Planet Named Cleopatra" (1974), a veritable encyclopedia in its portrayal of that planet. Increasingly, these worlds have made little or no direct reference to the Earth itself, as in Herbert's Dune trilogy. These are the worlds capable of carrying metaphor as the writers immerse their characters (and readers) into exotic societies sharply different from the everyday world in order to comment upon man's ventures, his nature, and his limitations, as in Stanislaw Lem's *Solaris* (1961, 1970). One of the most consistently successful is Ursula K. Le Guin—in many of her short stories and especially in her prize-winning novels *The Left Hand of Darkness* (1969) and *The Dispossessed* (1974). The former in particular had impact upon the field, for only on the planet Gethen (Winter) have humans evolved in a unisexual nature so that they are capable of assuming either the male or female role depending upon their response to another person during estrus. Thus, for example, many individuals have been both father and mother, while the sexual drive is quiescent except during the period of estrus.

Not only does she make the reader question the stereotypes of gender roles in present society, but by implication at least she shows how divisive those roles—and sexuality itself—are to our common humanity.

In its attention to the human condition science fiction has gained a kind of maturity it did not possess as a popular literature celebrating science, the scientist, and progress. It may not always be so entertaining in a melodramatic, "story" sense. Indeed, many current writers are less concerned with story as such, seemingly, than with literary quality and experimentation. In part this results from the influence of the "New Wave" in the 1960's and in part from the efforts of individuals like Harlan Ellison, whose *Dangerous Visions* (1967) was intended to broaden the themes, language, and forms available to the sf writer. One may gain insight into its impact by comparing it with the *Science Fiction Hall of Fame* volumes, edited by Robert Silverberg and Ben Bova, containing those works written before 1965 which the writers themselves through the Science Fiction Writers of America voted as the outstanding examples of sf published in the specialist magazines. One can safely say that after *Dangerous Visions* American science fiction could never be the same. One has only to point to the works of such writers as Joanna Russ, James Tiptree, Gene Wolfe, Thomas Disch, R.A. Lafferty, as well as such works as Sturgeon's "If All Men Were Brothers, Would You Let One Marry Your Sister?" and Philip José Farmer's "Riders of the Purple Wage," both stories by long-established writers published in *Dangerous Visions*.

One might notice other individual efforts. John Brunner has acknowledged that he adapted the narrative techinque of John Dos Passos in *Stand on Zanzibar* (1968), whole Brian Aldiss' indebtedness to Joyce is apparent in *Barefoot in the Head* (1970). Robert Silverberg produced one of the most probing character studies in the genre in *Dying Inside* (1972), in which David Selig, a citizen of a familiar New York City, loses the telepathic power which he was born with. His final cry, "Hello, hello, hello," provides one of the finest symbols of isolated modern man. These writers are using the same techniques as Barth, Barthell, Berger, Coover, and Reed, for example, to explore similar themes. In the sense that it is not merely critical—dystopian—science fiction has turned increasingly to a world that seems incomprehensible, irrational, absurd. Thus, simultaneously, its writers—from Asimov and Niven to Alec Effinger (*What Entropy Means to Me*, 1972) and Samuel R. Delany (*Dhalgren*, 1975)—may dramatize their individual perceptions of the twentieth century—that complex fusion of Enlightenment, romance, and absurdity.

NOTES

1. Excerpted from a taped interview between Dr. Isaac Asimov and Thomas D. Clareson, The College of Wooster, 2 October 1975.

2. Thomas L. Wymer, "Perception and Value in Science Fiction," in *Many Futures, Many Worlds*, ed. Thomas D. Clareson (Kent, OH: Kent State University Press, 1977), pp. 1–13.

3. Thomas D. Clareson, "Many Futures, Many Worlds," in *Many Futures, Many Worlds*, pp. 16-17.

4. Excerpted from a taped interview between Dr. Isaac Asimov and Thomas

D. Clareson, The College of Wooster, 2 October 1975.

5. Clareson, "Many Futures, Many Worlds," p. 17.

6. Robert Philmus, "Science Fiction from Its Beginning to 1870," in *Anatomy of Wonder,* ed. Neil Barron (New York: R. R. Bowker, 1976), p. 31.

7. Clareson, "The Emergence of Scientific Romance, 1870–1926," in *Anatomy of Wonder,* p. 39.

8. Samuel R. Delany, "Critical Methods: Speculative Fiction," in Clareson, *Many Futures, Many Worlds,* p. 289.

Francis Molson

CHILDREN'S FANTASY AND SCIENCE FICTION

Most readers recognize the fame of *Alice in Wonderland* and *Through the Looking-Glass* even if they are unsure that the books are juveniles. Not as many readers, but still a substantial number, know that Lewis Carroll's masterpieces, irrespective of their intended or probable audiences, are outstanding fantasy. But very few readers are aware of the crucial role the two books played in the development of children's literature. Yet the publication of the Alice books, in 1865 and 1871 respectively, marked the first time juvenile fiction was written for the express purpose of "wasting" its young readers' time instead of "improving" it, i.e., of entertaining youngsters instead of teaching or exhorting them as children's fiction of the time was supposed to. Moreover, a case can be made that without Carroll's innovative fantasies a primarily imaginative children's literature might never have developed as it has, or might have been delayed inordinately. That is to say, the making of effective fantasy entails probably more creativity and imaginative force than any other type of children's book. If so, then, the composing of the highly successful and original Alice stories required a very large expenditure of creative energy—so large, as a matter of fact, that Carroll was able to break through the constraints of earnest didacticism, then hemming in and stunting the writing of children's books, and became the first writer of juveniles to enter the realm of the free and untrammeled imagination. Because of Carroll's breakthrough, all subsequent writers of children's books have enjoyed the freedom to be beholden to only their native genius and bent. Surely, then, the historic importance of the Alice narratives deserves to be more widely known.

In any case, it must be admitted that it is especially fitting that two books of fantasy should have been so significantly involved in the history of children's literature inasmuch as works of fantasy have become so prominent among the glories of children's literature. To cite just some, the Alice books themselves, the Grimm and Andersen fairy tales, *The Wind in the Willows* (1908), *The Princess and Curdie* (1883), *Winnie-the-Pooh* (1926), *Charlotte's Web,* (1952), *The Hobbit* (1938), *The Voyage of the Dawn Treader* (1952), and *Tom's Midnight Garden* (1959). Furthermore, to think of children's literature without fantasy would be dismaying: serious, obvious, and too often suffering from the

19

built-in obsolescence of a realism subservient to whatever moral crusade, social issue, or ideology one momentarily dominant pressure group would push until eventually it would be superseded by another pressure group which, in turn, would insist upon its own, purer didacticism. How impoverished, also, would childhood be without the imaginative stimulus all the various kinds of literary fantasy provide. No wonder, then, that in the judgment of many historians and commentators the publication of the Alice books ushered in the first golden age of children's literature.

One of the major ironies of children's literature is that the Alice books, in spite of their originality and brilliance, inspired no large following. There were some books that tried to build directly on what Carroll had done—for instance, Charles Carryl's *Davy and the Goblin* (1886), and Maggie Brown's *Wanted—a King* (1890)—but they are feeble imitations and of only historic import today. Even Carroll's subsequent works—*The Hunting of the Snark* (1876), *Sylvie and Bruno* (1889), and *Sylvie and Bruno Concluded* (1893)—are, frankly, inferior fantasy. Still, the historic importance of the Alice books is huge. If one can borrow from Walt Whitman's description of his debt to Ralph Emerson, the books brought to a boil the cauldron of imagination and creativity then seething in children's literature. What follows, then, is an attempt, first, to describe briefly just that portion of the cauldron, so to speak, out of which the Alice books emerged; second, to suggest the diversity and richness of juvenile fantasy since the publication of Carroll's masterpieces; and third, to present a sampling of contemporary defenses of juvenile fantasy and its role in childhood. It should be stressed that a division into pure and mixed, original and derivative, or any other category of fantasy in order to insure precision or prevent overlapping has not been intended. The categories that will be distinguished merely indicate some of the ways in which juvenile fantasy after Carroll either has developed an emphasis or topic the former utilized or, branching off in new directions, has sought fresh combinations of familiar elements and new subjects or approaches. Finally, it should be noted that authors mentioned and titles cited are representative and are not meant to be exhaustive.

I

Alice in Wonderland and *Through the Looking-Glass*, even though works of great and stunning originality, did not emerge into the world without antecedents. Quite frankly, Carroll could not have written his works nor expected them to be accepted unless there previously existed not only a literary matrix conducive to fantasy but also a potentially receptive audience, created, in part, by the several elements making up the matrix. For instance, a liking for riddle, word puzzles, and other verbal games—nonsense, in other words—already flourished; and readers had had their appetite for nonsense whetted in 1848 by Edward Lear's *A Book of Nonsense*, a work that had come to be enjoyed by adults and children alike. Another element in the matrix was the beast fable. Already become a staple of children's reading fare over the preceding several centuries, and sanctioned by an association with classical times, beast fables like Aesop's unobtrusively but persistently undermined the hegemony the unrelentingly didactic and mildly realistic fiction of the eighteenth and early nineteenth centuries enjoyed in children's literature. Of all the elements in the literary matrix, however, the one that contributed the most to the origin of modern juvenile fantasy was the fairy tale in both its folk and literary forms.

Although they had previously existed for countless years and even collections of them had been made elsewhere, it was not until fairy tales made their appearance in the French court during the late 1700's that they can be said to have entered literature.[1] Charles Perrault is usually accorded the honor of compiling the premier collection of fairy tales, *Tales of My Mother Goose* (1697). Perrault's collection not only brought to the attention of readers, first adults and then children, eight delightfully retold folk tales—among them "Puss and Boots," "Sleeping Beauty," and "Cinderella"—but demonstrated that folk material can be adapted for cultivated tastes without losing its rich imaginative appeal and capacity for lighthearted entertainment. Perrault's tales set a vogue, and others tried their hand at composing literary fairy tales. Most prominent of these were the French aristocratic women, Madame d'Aulnoy (according to the Opies, perhaps the real innovator of the literary fairy tale) and Madame Leprince de Beaumont, the second of whom was responsible for the very famous version of "Beauty and the Beast."

Regardless of the quality of these "court" fairy tales, however, and the witness they provided apropos the value of the imaginative, they did not directly influence Carroll. For, despite their initial popularity, throughout the eighteenth century fairy tales came under attack as hostile to reason and inappropriate in the schooling of children until the tales gradually fell into disfavor. Only the scholarship of the Grimm Brothers in the next century brought fairy tales renewed respectability and popularity. Yet, the court fairy tales are of genuine importance in the development of modern juvenile fantasy since they gave children fortunate enough to hear or read them respite and variety and, thereby, prevented, as was also pointed out concerning the role of beast fables, the complete dominance of a tedious and moralizing realism.

Having a more direct impact on Carroll's work than the court fairy tales were the *Kinder-und Haus-Märchen* of the Grimm Brothers ostensibly collected and retold to preserve the stories as the "art" of the folk, published in three volumes, 1812-1822. Soon translated into English by Edgar Taylor, these tales were quickly taken over by British and other English-speaking youngsters as their special province just as their German counterparts had done earlier. What with their exciting talk of magic, princes and princesses, witches and dark woods, and their plots replete with improbable incidents, occasional violence, and poetic justice, the Grimm tales readily appealed to children's imagination. It is also possible that the tales reminded youngsters of stories they had heard of previously but had been told they should not consider "appropriate" or "good enough." In other words, the Grimm tales per se and by what they suggested made children increasingly dissatisfied with their typical prescribed reading fare and primed for more and more imaginative and exciting reading, perhaps like what they heard and read in the nursery and street.

Hans Christian Andersen not only retold folk tales, following the example of the Grimms, but created his own stories, modeling them, in part, upon the folk tale. So skillful did Andersen become at capturing for his own tales the folk tale's capacity for imaginative appeal that he soon became world famous. His tales, moreover, contributed much to the development of modern juvenile fantasy. For one reason, Andersen demonstrated that writers of fairy tales did not have to depend solely upon authentic folk tales for subject matter, plot, and characters; one could push beyond the old and traditional by either embellishing or out and out inventing. Second, the care, especially a concern for style, Andersen bestowed upon his tales, which he recognized were being read more and more by children, clearly implied a determination to take seriously children and their reading needs, and a conviction that children deserved writing whose style aspired to greatness. Third, certain features of Andersen's tales augmented the technical repertoire available to writers and broadened the range of emotions juvenile fantasy appealed to: the mixing of fairy tale and realistic elements; a fondness for personifying in ways that children and adults alike still find amusing and psychologically supportive; and a willingness to use both sentiment and humor not always completely successfully but never condescendingly nor patronizingly.

II

The collecting and writing of fairy tales did not end with the work of the Grimm Brothers and Andersen. In England, for instance, Joseph Jacob's collection of British fairy tales (1890), and Andrew Lang's various "color" fairy tale books (1889 and subsequent years) gathering stories from all over the world made fairy tales even more accessible to countless readers. Further, writing literary or art fairy tales remained popular throughout the nineteenth century, and only in the current century has their popularity lessened in spite of the example of James Thurber's delightful stories. Important nineteenth century writers of fairy tales were William Thackeray—*The Rose and the Ring* (1855); Robert Southey—"The Three Bears" (1834); John Ruskin—"The King of the Golden River" (1851); and Oscar Wilde—"The Selfish Giant" (1888). Included also should be Christina Rossetti's *Goblin Market* (1864), even though verse, rather than prose, is its medium. In the United States, two authors who achieved success as writers of literary fairy tales were Howard Pyle and Frances Burnett. The former exhibited considerable skill as he imitated the best features of the folk tale in his *Pepper and Salt* (1886) and *The Wonder Clock* (1888), while the latter author, in addition to producing conventional tales such as *The Troubles of Queen Silver-Bell* (1906) and *The Cozy Lion* (1907), proved quite adept in incorporating fairy tale plotting and values in otherwise realistic narratives, e.g., the very popular *Little Lord Fauntleroy* (1886) and *Sara Crewe* (1888).

Victorians also manifested a penchant for novel-length fairy tales.[2] The most prominent and innovative composer of the long juvenile fairy tale was George MacDonald. *The Princess and Curdie* (1883) and *The Princess and the Goblin* (1872) remain today readable and exciting books. In *At the Back of the North Wind* (1871), *The Golden Key* (1867), and *The Light Princess* (1867), moreover, MacDonald broke new ground as he blended fairy tale elements, in particular, the sympathetic bond that exists between nature and human goodness, into the realistic story. The results of MacDonald's blending were twofold. Not only did he assist in originating a new type of juvenile fantasy, mixed fantasy—which today is the dominant form of children's fantasy; but he also deepened and subtilized his fairy tales so that a quasi-mystical strain is readily detected in his most characteristic work. MacDonald's narratives continue in print because his books are intrinsically meritorious and because contemporary writers of the stature of Charles Williams, J.R.R. Tolkien, and C.S. Lewis all have claimed fondness for and affinity with the man and his fantasies.

Howard Pyle, previously mentioned as a skillful practitioner of the brief literary fairy tale form, also attempted to use an amalgam of realism and fantasy in order to express a quasi-mysticism in his thought. The resulting book, *The Garden Behind the Moon* (1895), although not as enticing as MacDonald's work, still merits wider recognition than the usually accorded, casual mention in the history of children's literature. Another American author who wrote lengthy fairy tales but achieved greater results and recognition than Pyle was L. Frank Baum. Interestingly, Baum intended to strip the traditional fairy tale of its violence, potential for frightening youngsters, and its old world associations, and to refurbish the remainder with an American spirit and subject matter, exciting incident, and fresh characters. The immense popularity of both his first "new" fairy tale, *The Wonderful Wizard of Oz* (1900), and his subsequent thirteen other Oz books convincingly testifies to the success of Baum's endeavors.

What with direct imitation of the Alice books proving unsuccessful, it did not take long for writers to suspect that perhaps more fruitful would be emulating Carroll's technique of adapting some of the more distinctive elements of the fairy tale—e.g., the presence of magic, talking animals, or the transformation of the inanimate into the animate—to other genres. In a way, as has been observed, this is what George MacDonald did in weaving realistic elements into his long fairy tales. However, it was Edith Nesbit, destined to become a major figure not only in juvenile fantasy but in children's literature as a whole, who perceived more clearly than any other author of the time, the possible advantages of assimilating fairy tale elements into other genres, in particular, the family story. Already expert in writing the former, Nesbit skillfully blended fairy tale elements and the family story, creating, in the process, what has come to be called mixed fantasy, the most prevalent kind of juvenile fantasy today. Nesbit's most characteristic and best novels—*Five Children and It* (1902), *The Story of the Amulet* (1906), and *The Phoenix and the Carpet* (1904)—aptly demonstrate that an understanding of children and their interests, along with an inventive imagination and a meticulous concern for internal consistency and furnishing explanations, can produce highly entertaining fantasy that never patronizes but invariably challenges and stimulates.

A good number of contemporary writers of mixed fantasy are indebted to Nesbit's fantasies in one way or another. Edward Eager, for example, is an avowed admirer, and his best novels, *Half Magic* (1954) and *Knight's Castle* (1956), are variations, but with enough originality and distinctive humor, of Nesbitean devices and situations, especially the use of a magic talisman. In *The Diamond in the Window* (1962) and its two sequels, Jane Langton adapts for an American setting Nesbit's display of intelligence, respect for her readers, and a concern for providing a plausible and convincing swing back and forth between fantasy and reality. The children of such otherwise disparate fantasies as Alan

Garner's *Elidor* (1967), Penelope Farmer's *The Summer Birds* (1962), and Jean Louise Curry's *Beneath the Hill* (1967) owe a bit to the resourceful surname-less children Nesbit created for her fantasy novels. Finally, Nesbit's innovation of permitting her characters to move into different time dimensions without having to fall asleep or dream made possible the great variety of time travel and time displacement narratives of recent years: to cite just some of the more out-standing examples, Philippa Pearce's *Tom's Midnight Garden* (1959), Julia Sauer's *Fog Magic* (1943), Eleanor Cameron's *The Court of the Stone Children* (1973), William Mayne's *Earthfasts* (1966), and Lucy Boston's several Green Knowe books.

One kind of contemporary juvenile fantasy that cannot be traced directly to Edith Nesbit is heroic or high fantasy. If antecedents for books like Tolkien's *The Hobbit* and Lewis' Chronicles of Narnia, exemplary instances of heroic fantasy for children, are to be distinguished in children's literature, they are not to be found in any one particular writer. Rather, the rise of heroic fantasy can be traced, in part, to the continuing interest of children in saga, myth and legend. Another explanation for the slowly growing popularity of heroic fan-tasy is its endorsement by adults who approve of its concern for dramatizing the individual child's accepting responsibility for the consequences of his or her actions and the individual's participation in an ongoing struggle between Good and Evil, Right and Wrong, and Light and Dark. In addition to the novels of Tolkien and Lewis, other excellent high fantasy is: Curry's *The Sleepers* (1968), Madeleine L'Engle's *A Wrinkle in Time* (1962), Lloyd Alexander's five Prydain novels, Ursula Le Guin's Earthsea trilogy, Susan Cooper's the "rising of the dark" series, and Carol Kendall's *The Gammage Cup* (1959) even if it is relatively lighthearted in tone.

Fantasy centering around animals is a very important type of juvenile fantasy. Surely, the major reason is that children are close to and love animals; hence, one tends to associate childhood with animals. A second reason may be that animals are an essential ingredient of beast fable which constitutes a part of the matrix out of which juvenile fantasy emerged. In particular, descendants of the animals in beast fable which mirror human foibles and temperament have proved to be both attractive and comprehensible to children. The Bremen Town musicians of Grimm, the ugly duckling of Andersen, and the stable of self-sacrificing animals found in folk fairy tales all belong to the beast fable tradition. Not as obviously belonging but still in the same tradition are such animals as the vainglorious lion of Leslie Brooke's *Johnny Crow's Garden* (1903); Toad, Badger, Rat, and Mole of Grahame's *The Wind in the Willows* (1908); the Cowardly Lion of *The Wonderful Wizard of Oz* (1900); Frog and Toad of Arnold Lobel's *Frog and Toad Together* (1972); and even Stuart Little from White's novel by the same name (1945). The "nonsense" animals who descend from the creations of Lear and Carroll are not many but they do exist. Perhaps most notable is Tock, the Watch Dog, of Morton Juster's *The Phantom Toll-booth* (1961), the best example of Carrollian nonsense of recent times.

Legendary and mythic animals also constitute a major segment of fantasy animal narratives. Dragons, unsurprisingly, have been the most interesting and appealing, ranging from the reluctant dragon of Grahame's story by the same name and the various dragons whose exploits are chronicled in E. Nesbit's

The Book of Dragons (1900), to the more seriously rendered dragons of Le Guin's Earthsea trilogy and Ann McCaffery's Pern novels (1976). Other mythic animals abound: the griffin of Frank Stockton's *The Griffin and the Minor Canon* (1887); the unicorn in Garner's *Elidor* (1967); the double-headed creature, the pushmi-pullyu of Lofting's *The Story of Dr. Dolittle* (1920); the sandfairy and Phoenix of Nesbit's novels; the gwythaint and warg which terrify in Alexander's Prydain and Tolkien's Middle-earth respectively; the many "enhanced," talking animals of Lewis' Narnia; the "nightmarish" animals of Maurice Sendak's *Where the Wild Things Are* (1963); and the various gifted animals of Patricia McKillip's *The Forgotten Beasts of Eld* (1974).

Since toys and dolls have always brought pleasure to children, those in animal form bring even additional delight. Presumably, the same is also true of juvenile fantasy concerning toy animals. Surely, the most famous toy animal is the celebrated Winnie the Pooh and his friends created by Milne. A provocative and controversial use of toy animals occurs in Russell Hoban's *The Mouse and His Child* (1967). The author's unrelenting portrait of the violence and absurdity of contemporary life is unsurpassed by any other book in modern children's literature. At the same time, Hoban's almost savage portrait is offset by a display of wit and range of intellectual and cultural allusions not seen in juvenile literature since the appearance of the Alice books.

By far the most numerous of animal fantasies are those featuring animals either living primarily in their own habitat or intermingling with human beings. The former category is represented by the various animals in Rudyard Kipling's *The Jungle Books* (1894, 1895), the deer of Felix Salten's *Bambi* (1928), or, more recently, the rabbits of Richard Adams' *Watership Down* (1972) who, except for the fact that they speak, are allowed to retain virtually all their animality. The latter category—those intermingling with human beings—include Beatrix Potter's Peter Rabbit and company; the captivating animals of Lofting's several Dr. Dolittle narratives; the dogs of Dodie Smith's *A Hundred and One Dalmatians* (1957); the aspiring actress, Jennie, the Sealyham terrier, of Sendak's *Higglety Pigglety Pop!* (1967); the barnyard animals of White's *Charlotte's Web,* (1952); the redoubtable mice of Margery Sharpe's Miss Bianca books; the Peruvian brown bear, Paddington, who cavorts in Michael Bond's many books; the various elephants of Jean De Brunhoff's Babar stories; and the unique animals of Randall Jarrell's *The Animal Family* (1965).

Finally, in addition to stories about toy or stuffed animals, stories about toys and dolls in a variety of shapes and forms are among the most popular and beloved juvenile fantasy—undoubtedly because toys and dolls make up much of the play of childhood. Early in the development of juvenile fantasy, Andersen and Carroll attributed life to inanimate objects, a tin soldier and a pack of playing cards, for example, which attribution parallels that of children to favorite dolls and toys. Collodi's world-famous *Pinocchio* (1880) describes both the animation of a wooden puppet and then its transformation into a real boy. In English-speaking countries surely the most well-known toy-doll story is *Winnie-the-Pooh* (1926). Not as famous but very much loved is Margery Bianco's stuffed rabbit in *The Velveteen Rabbit* (1958) whose capacity to weep a real tear changes it into a real rabbit. Other well-known toy-doll stories are the relatively old but still enjoyable *Racketty-Packetty House* (1906) by Burnett, Rachel Field's *Hitty, Her First Hundred Years* (1929), Pauline Clarke's *The Return of the Twelves* (1963) (about the toy soldiers that supposedly belonged to the Bronte children) and Rumer Godden's *The Dolls' House* (1962) and *Impunity Jane* (1954). An interesting variant of the toy-doll story is *The Secret World of Og* (1962) by Pierre Berton which presents a subterranean world whose inhabitants mimic the behavior of comic and television characters.

III

Science fiction has emerged as a sub-category of juvenile fantasy only within the last thirty years and is already becoming one of its dominant types.[3] As a matter of fact, when mainstream children's literature first recognized the existence of sf and acknowledged its possible attractiveness to young readers is easily dated: the 1947 publication by Scribner of Robert Heinlein's *Rocket Ship Galileo*. Heinlein's skillful amalgam of characters, plot, and subject—a group of teenage boys setting off for the moon in a homemade rocket and their adventures on the moon—not only delighted youngsters but caught the eye of specialists in children's literature. For the latter discovered that sf could be effectively mixed with what was then called the junior novel, and the novel combination would entertain pre-teens and teens as well as meeting their special needs. The success of *Rocket Ship Galileo* both encouraged Heinlein to go on to write other juveniles, the best of which are *Farmer in the Sky* (1950), *Red Planet* (1949), *Citizen of the Galaxy* (1957), and *Tunnel in the Sky* (1955), and induced other authors to try their hand at the "new" genre. Yet, the specialists' recognition of Heinlein's achievement should not be allowed to obscure the fact that juvenile sf did not actually begin with *Rocket Ship Galileo*. Even within the mainstream *The Angry Planet* (1946), by the British author, John Kier Cross, preceded Heinlein's first juvenile. The historic importance of *Rocket Ship Galileo,* to be precise, is not that the novel broke new ground; rather, it is the fact that the novel's merit and its author's prominence forced, so to speak, mainstream children's literature's recognition of sf. Hence, from 1947 on, important review journals of children's books such as *Hornbook* and *School Library Journal* included sf in their purview.

In 1879 Lu Senaren, writing under the pseudonym of Noname, began to churn out some one hundred and eighty stories which narrated the exploits of Frank Reade, Jr., the boy genius, and his many remarkable inventions. Other stories, imitative of the Reade formula, appeared in the Tom Edison, Jr., *Happy Days,* and *Pluck and Luck* series. The Edward Stratemeyer Syndicate, never one to miss out on a possible popular success, published, under the name of Roy Rockwood, a series of adventures patterned after Jules Verne. The eight *Great Marvel* stories, which sent its protagonists to and under the poles and out into space to visit the moon, Mars, and Saturn, remained popular into the 1930's. Far more extensive and popular than the *Great Marvel* series, however, was the Stratemeyer Syndicate's Tom Swift books. Inaugurated in 1910, the series eventually numbered over forty titles; revised and brought up to date as the Tom Swift Jr. books, the series still attracts many readers. In recent years, other series books have been released presumably to take advantage of the interest in sf and to duplicate, if possible, the success of Tom Swift. But none of these—John Blain's Rick Brant or Donald Wollheim's Mike Mars or Carey Rockwell's Tom Corbett—ever matched the popularity of Tom Swift.

In addition to the dime novels and series books from which Heinlein's work descended, other narratives, fantasy and otherwise, contributed to a climate that eventually made possible both juvenile and mainstream acceptance of sf. Very early stories like *Robinson Crusoe* and *Gulliver's Travels* and then later Jules Verne's novels not only became an essential part of children's literature but nurtured a taste for similar adventures. Excessively long and moralizing, *The Water Babies* (1863), by Charles Kingsley, employed fantasy to inform its young readers about the theory of evolution and the means of underwater life. E. Nesbit's *The Story of the Amulet* (1906) utilized time travel and instant language comprehension and described an Utopian London modeled upon the social ideas of H.G. Wells, a close friend of the author. Virtually forgotten books like Pyle's *The Garden Behind the Moon* (1895), in which moonlight acts as a bridge from the moon to earth, or Frances Montgomery's *On a Lark to the Planets* (1904), whose children enjoy a trip into space, kept alive within the mainstream a tolerance for what can best be described as space fantasy, and in this way prepared the way for the possibility of serious sf. More significantly, L. Frank Baum, while creating an indigenous American fantasy, incorporated one of the most exciting scientific phenomena of his time, electricity, into his *The Master Key* (1901). Furthermore, Baum is one of the first authors of juveniles to create a fully rendered robot, Tik Tok, who first appeared in *Ozma of Oz* (1907) and then several years later enjoyed his own book, *Tik Tok of Oz* (1914). Even Lofting, by sending his famous doctor on a trip to the moon, in *Dr. Dolittle in the Moon* (1929), can be said to have assisted in the development of juvenile sf.

Within a decade of the publication of *Rocket Ship Galileo*, at least ninety different additional sf juveniles were released. Absolutely speaking, the number seems insignificant. On the other hand, considering that only ten years earlier both specialists in children's literature and publishers had ignored sf, one must admit the number is impressive. Also, the number does not include any of the series books which continued to sell and enjoy a modest popularity. Obviously, then, more and more youngsters were reading sf and looking for new titles. Furthermore, publishers finally became convinced that juvenile sf was not a passing fad and that a young readership for sf did exist—as youngsters might have testified if only they had been asked or had their tastes consulted. Witness, for example, youngsters' fondness for series books dealing with sf and for sf in the comics, in particular, Flash Gordon and Buck Rogers.

Fortunately, mainstream appreciation of juvenile sf did not fall off after its initial approval of Heinlein. Undoubtedly, two factors in the sustaining of adult approval of sf were the artistry of some of the writers who tried the new genre—e.g., Andre Norton and Alan Nourse—and the Sputnik phenomenon which focused the nation's attention on space and the space program, and brought increasing respectability and credibility to sf and its speculations about space travel. Unfortunately, all of the juvenile sf produced in the 1950's was not up to the level of Heinlein, Norton, and Nourse. The truth is that the majority of the novels were heavy handed, dull or mediocrily written, and deserving of the neglect they have suffered. Historically, authors and publishers have been either prone to incorporate a heavy dose of didacticism into all kinds of children's books, making them, as a consequence, unpalatable or unreadable, or venal, turning out hack work. Not surprisingly, juvenile sf proved to be no exception.

One interesting feature of the juvenile sf published in the 1950's is that about one-third of the titles were written by authors already prominent in adult sf or soon to be: Isaac Asimov writing as Paul French, Robert Silverberg, Donald Wollheim, Poul Anderson, James Blish, Ben Bova, Arthur Clarke, Lester del Rey, Gordon Dickson, Murray Leinster, Jack Vance, and Harry Harrison. Possibly, some of these were forced into the juvenile market for severe economic reasons; without the market they might have been compelled to abandon writing. At least one hopes that economic pressures were intense, for then the motives are understandable and perhaps even forgivable. Otherwise, the hack work some of the name authors produced would be inexcusable. On the other hand, the good work of Bova, del Rey, and Dickson, along with the novels of Heinlein, Norton, and Nourse, not only provided status but constituted a convincing example of what could be done for children without compromising literary quality and writing down to or over their heads. In this way these writers prepared the way for the authors of the next decades when juvenile sf definitely came of age.

Today a reliance on trite subjects appears less often than it used to. For instance, voyages, lunar and otherwise, are no longer the vogue. Yet the occasional contemporary novel that treats of space voyages or expeditions tends to be authentic depiction of the technical requirements of a supposed trip into space, as in Arthur Ballou's *Bound for Mars* (1970), or a gripping portrait of the psychological stress of space exploring, as in Ludek Pesek's *The Earth Is Near* (1974). Today, simplistic and cliche characterization is not as common as before. Hence, lovable cats no longer take off unexpectedly for the moon as did Flyball in *Space Cat* (1952) by Ruthann Todd, and aliens infrequently visit Earth to lecture the human species on its intrinsic destructiveness and pugnaciousness as did the unnamed visitors in Carl Biemiller's *The Magic Ball from Mars* (1953). Rather, cats, as in Andre Norton's *Star Ka'at* (1976), are presented with some subtlety and scientific veracity; and aliens, as in Florence Randall's *A Watcher in the Woods* (1976), are not quick to condemn and slight human beings. Today new subjects are being introduced. The abuses of psychological experimentation are the topics of novels by John Christopher, Sylvia Engdahl, and William Streator. Endurance and resourcefulness in the face of planet-wide disaster are treated convincingly and sometimes movingly in novels like Jay Williams' *The People of the Ax* (1974), Robert O'Brien's *Z for Zacharias* (1975), H.M. Hoover's *Children of Morrow* (1973), and G.K. Kestravan's *The Pale Invaders* (1976). Ecology is popular. James Berry's *Dar Tellum: Stranger from a Distant Planet* (1973) not only argues for conservation but is one of the few sf picture books that present scientific concepts on a level comprehensible to preschool children. Also, Adrien Stoutenberg's *Out There* (1971) is an outstanding investigation of the ecological nightmare brought about by the squandering of earth's resources. Even theological speculation is found in the novels by Alexander Key and Madeleine L'Engle.

Another sign that juvenile sf has matured is that, now convinced of its own seriousness and validity, it can make fun of itself. Thus, Jerome Beatty's Matthew Looney books poke fun at earth's provinciality and chauvinistic understanding of space by transferring these attitudes to the inhabitants of the moon who cannot accept the possibility that life exists on earth since it would be so different and inferior to lunar life. Or *Star Prince Charlie* (1975), by Poul Anderson and Gordon Dickson, mocks both space opera and the conventional novel of youth's coming of age. The most convincing evidence of juvenile sf's maturity, however, is the mainstream's granting its prestigious Newbery Medal—awarded to the outstanding children's book of the year—in 1959 to L'Engle's *A Wrinkle in Time*, concerned with space travel and behavior modification, and in 1972 to Robert O'Brien's *Mrs. Frisby and the Rats of NIMH.*

IV

Juvenile fantasy is thriving at the present in spite of a current emphasis on the new realism which purports to introduce youngsters to the "real" world of sex, drugs, abortion, homosexuality, and similar problems. Authors continue to be drawn to fantasy, and publishers remain, by and large, hospitable although their enthusiasm for animal fantasy may not be as great as it is for high fantasy or sf. Surely, one explanation for the relative strength and good health of the genre is today's relatively sophisticated understanding of literary fantasy and its many advantages for children. This understanding, in turn, stems from the ongoing analysis of fantasy and its role in childhood undertaken by psychologists and educators as well as by the makers of literary fantasy, the writers.

Perhaps the most well-known commentator on fantasy who is also a writer is J.R.R. Tolkien. In his essay "On Fairy-Stories," Tolkien contends at some length that fairy stories ought to be read by adults, but he takes for granted that children read fairy tales and benefit from them.[4] Of the four advantages—fantasy, recovery, escape, and the consolation of the happy ending—Tolkien adduces for reading fairy stories, only two seem particularly germane. His defense of the value of fantasy because it is a basic, although often neglected, power of the mind is just as valid for children as for adults. Also, eucatastrophe, the function of the happy ending of fairy stories to shadow-forth an anticipated joy beyond the world, is readily acceptable to children who find it a complement to the system of poetic justice they so passionately believe in. On the other hand, children, generally speaking, do not require the benefits of recovery and escape since their taste and perceptive faculties are not as jaded as their elders' nor are they as yet overwhelmed by the "banality of the ordinary."

Ursula Le Guin, author of the highly esteemed Earthsea trilogy, has argued for the special appropriateness of fantasy in narratives dealing with the rite of passage or coming of age. She defines, as others have done, coming of age as the time when children must confront and accept the inevitability of their death, the fact of human frailty and evil, and responsibility for their action and their consequences. In "The Child and the Shadow," for instance, utilizing a Jungian symbolism and insight into human consciousness, she explicates an Andersen fairy tale about a young man, his shadow, and a Princess, showing that its plot and imagery symbolize various stages in the development of human personality.[5] And in "Dreams Must Explain Themselves" Le Guin admits that coming of age is an important theme of the Earthsea trilogy.[6] Even the imagery describing Ged, Arha, and Prince Arren's coming of age owes much to Jung. Thus, not only Le Guin's analysis of fairy tales and fantasy but her own imaginative transformation in the Earthsea trilogy of Jungian archetype and insight attest to the function literary fantasy can have in clarifying fundamental stages in human development.

Sylvia Engdahl is one more noted writer of children's books who has championed the importance of fantasy and sf for children. Author of juvenile sf built around the centrality of science in the growth of society, Engdahl has advocated in her non-fiction sf's "missionary" role.[7] That is, juvenile sf will become increasingly essential as it helps children maintain an open mind, if not a hospitable stance, towards the possibility of life existing elsewhere in the universe and inevitability of an encounter between the human race and alien ones. Moreover, juvenile sf, Engdahl points out, is already valuable inasmuch as it keeps youngsters and, through them, the entire country informed about science and technology's growth, challenges, and needs.

In recent years psychologists and educators have been able both to support empirically and to expand the theory underpinning fantasy's claim for preeminence in children's lives. Drs. Evelyn Pitcher and Ernest Prelinger, for example, have demonstrated that most children, because they possess the capacity to fantasize, can devise very brief narratives that boast elements of fantasy.[8] Furthermore, the children, while enjoying making up stories, show a little originality and even wit. Unfortunately, television, with its stultifying effects on the imagination, drastically curtails the child's story-telling ability by ages 7-8. What can be inferred from the Pitcher-Prellinger study is that literary fantasy may be helpful in invigorating or restoring a child's capacity to imagine and fantasize.

The research of Ravenna Helson has already considerably broadened understanding of the sources of juvenile fantasy. In one study Helson points out that different juvenile fantasies thrive at different historical and cultural periods because certain kinds of fantasy enable society to express changing perceptions of itself and its relation to the world at large.[9] For example, the presence of a magical woman or fairy godmother, as in MacDonald's *The Princess and the Goblin*, may reflect Victorian notions concerning the role and worth of the mother which also, on another level, mirror the country's veneration of Queen Victoria. Or, to cite another example, the importance within a fantasy of a group of like-minded comrades, set off from adults or the world, as in Nesbit's *Five Children and It* or Grahame's *The Wind in the Willows*, suggests a revolt against convention and the deterioration of Victorian optimism and certitude.

In another, more provocative study Helson claims to find a close relationship among the sex of writers of fantasy (each sex having uniquely different problems), the circumstances they find themselves in (the varying stages in the process of individuation Jung postulates), and the kinds of fantasy they write.[10] In the case of a middle-aged man, for instance, the freedom and challenge of fantasy allow a venting of the psychological pressure growing old generates within him. While he works out through his writing the problems occasioned by the pressure, distinctive patterns in plot and theme are created; and a particular kind of fantasy gradually may emerge—often times heroic fantasy. While reading the completed fantasy, children respond unconsciously to the distinctive patterns and in this way may find relief from feelings peculiar to their age. Juvenile fantasy, then, can profit both adult authors and young readers. As Helson puts it:

> From a good fantasy then, the child may receive context and expression for his feelings and emotional experiences, while the adult may rework his childhood, become more aware of archetypal relationships, and develop a new, less "ego-centered" self.

The most exciting defense of juvenile fantasy from a psychological perspective is contained in Bruno Bettelheim's *The Uses of Enchantment,* a magisterial study of the contributions fairy tales make in the normal development of children.[11] By a thorough analysis of traditional fairy tales, buttressed by an extensive clinical knowledge of children, Bettelheim uncovers what actually transpires within fairy tales: an introduction to life that is both comprehensible to children and complementary to their view of the world. Furthermore, Bettelheim argues that the internal working of plots of fairy tales may better prepare children for living in the real world than so-called realistic fiction whose usual justification has been that it introduces children to "the way it really is." For example, the tale of the three little pigs does teach that

> we must not be lazy and take things easy, for if we do, we may perish. Intelligent planning and foresight combined with hard labor will make us victorious over even our most ferocious enemy—the wolf! The story also shows the advantages of growing up, since the third and wisest pig is usually depicted as the biggest and the oldest.

Yet the tale teaches not explicitly but symbolically. The three pigs and their houses stand for stages in child development; the wolf, for the hostility a child generates within himself that he does not know how to handle; the wolf's demise, the elimination of the child's guilt in a constructive fashion; and the pig's foraging for food, living in accordance with the reality principle rather than the pleasure principle. Moreover, the fairy tale does not insist what a child must do or even how he should interpret the tale; rather, it leaves all decisions to the reader or hearer including the most important of all decisions—whether to conclude that the tale has a "moral" after all. Thus, the fairy tale leads to genuine maturing instead of underlining the child's immaturity or substituting adult moralizing for a child's freedom to choose.

Another interesting aspect of Bettelheim's defense of fairy tales applies to fantasy as a whole and not just to fairy tales. Bettelheim points out that a significant part of traditional juvenile fiction "provided answers to the crucial questions of how to live the good life" but "did not offer solutions for the problems posed by the dark sides of our personalities." This body of literature may have suggested

> essentially only one solution for the asocial aspects of the unconscious: repression of these (unacceptable) strivings. But children, not having

their ids in conscious control, need stories which permit at least fantasy satisfaction of these "bad" tendencies, and specific models for their sublimation.

Because they are, obviously, fantasy, these specific models may best be furnished by literary fantasy and fairy tale. If Bettelheim is right in criticizing a body of stories that supposedly disseminated right answers and proper values at a time when a common core of ethical and moral values existed, then how much more telling are his observations today when a common core of values has disintegrated and even the very notion of a common core seems untenable!

How ironic it would be if juvenile fantasy, because of its capacity to engage its readers on the preconscious level and, thereby, assist in the formation of values, would come to be recognized as a more effective medium for didacticism than the various realisms that historically have dominated children's literature. Wouldn't Lewis Carroll chortle, if he could return, to discover fantasy, which he utilized to create nonsense so that his young friends might "waste" their time, became the means whereby children could stop "wasting" their reading leisure time on realism and begin "improving" it!

NOTES

1. A recent study of the history of fairy tales that takes a middle position between ponderous scholarship and popularization is Iona and Peter Opie's *The Classic Fairy Tales* (London: Oxford University Press, 1974).

2. Jonathan Cott discusses the rich flowering of fantasy during the Victorian era in *Beyond the Looking Glass: Extraordinary Works of Fairy Tale & Fantasy* (London: Hart-Davis, MacGibbon, 1973).

3. For a more complete discussion of the development of juvenile sf, upon which this section is based, see my "Juvenile Science Fiction" in *Anatomy of Wonder*, ed. Neil Barron (New York: R.R. Bowker, 1976), pp. 302-34.

4. J.R.R. Tolkien, "On Fairy-Stories," *The Tolkien Reader* (New York: Ballantine, 1966).

5. Ursula K. Le Guin, "The Child and the Shadow," *The Quarterly Journal of the Library of Congress*, 32 (April 1975), 139-48.

6. Ursula K. Le Guin, "Dreams Must Explain Themselves," in *Dreams Must Explain Themselves*, ed. Andrew Porter (New York: Algol Press, 1975), pp. 4-15.

7. Sylvia Engdahl, "The Changing Role of Science Fiction in Children's Literature," *Horn Book Magazine*, 47 (October 1971), 449-55.

8. Evelyn Pitcher and Ernest Prelinger, *Children Tell Stories: An Analysis of Fantasy* (New York: International Universities Press, 1963).

9. Ravenna Helson, "Through the Pages of Children's Books," *Psychology Today*, 7 (November 1973), 107-13.

10. Ravenna Helson, "Fantasy and Self-Discovery," *Horn Book Magazine*, 46 (April 1970), 121-34.

11. Bruno Bettelheim, *The Uses of Enchantment: The Meaning and Importance of Fairy Tales* (New York: Alfred Knopf, 1976).

Vincent De Fate

SCIENCE FICTION ART:
SOME CONTEMPORARY ILLUSTRATORS

Venus de Milo.

To a child she is ugly.

When a mind adjusts to thinking of her as a completeness, even though, by physiologic standards, incomplete, she is beautiful.

A hand thought of only as a hand, may seem beautiful.

Found on a battlefield—obviously a part—not beautiful.

But everything in our experience is only a part of something else that in turn is only a part of still something else—or that there is nothing beautiful in our experience: only appearances that are intermediate to beauty and ugliness—that only universality is complete: that only the complete is beautiful: that every attempt to achieve beauty is an attempt to give to the local the attributes of the universal.

—Charles Fort, THE BOOK
OF THE DAMNED

Depending on your definition of it, science fiction is as old as the story of Icarus or as new as the yellowing pages of the April 1926 issue of Gernsback's *Amazing Stories.* Consequently, the art which has accompanied, embellished and illuminated it, is equally as old (or as new) and, as with the literature, has its roots firmly embedded in reality and in the long ago beginnings of the human experience. To chart the course of its development would require many volumes of this size and is, frankly, vastly beyond the range of my personal knowledge and the scope and purposes of this essay. Yet, such a history is of great importance in understanding the full value and vision of science fiction; and made doubly urgent by the fact that no real ground has been broken in establishing that history to date. The books currently available on sf art, though earnest in intent, are more often than not, merely picture books, and almost to a one, directed exclusively at the magazines. Certainly *this* effort, though conscious of the areas outside of magazine publication, will be equally limited in its value, and I look forward eagerly to the day when someone younger, wiser and more patient than I will rise to the challenge and provide us with that much needed background.

Generally, most science fiction art can be found in one of three basic forms. The first to evolve is a type of art which emphasizes the machines, robots, rockets and other tinkerings of science and technology. The "gadget portrait," plain and simple. The second, in chronological order, but not necessarily in importance, is a type which focuses on character portrayal, often interacting with elements of a technological nature, but sometimes depicted in an atmosphere only mildly suggestive of it. The third, frequently combining elements of the first two, derives its principal difference from taking a dimmer view of the wonders of science, and draws much of its inspiration from the surrealists. Because of the need to appeal to a mass audience, a good deal of sf illustration is so ambivalent that it actually defies categorizing, and the artists, often preferring to remain flexible in an ever-changing market, are even harder to pin down. But, these three rough delineations give us a reasonable picture of the development of science fiction art and of the changes in attitude which have occurred among our artists, our authors and our society in general, toward the technological future.

Anthony Frewin, in his book *One Hundred Years of Science Fiction Illustration* (London, 1974) begins his account in 1884 with the publication of *Un Autre Monde*, written (under the pen name of Taxile Delord) and illustrated (as Isidore Grandville) by Jean-Ignace-Isidore Gérard. But where, indeed, does the story of science fiction art begin? With the drawings of tanks, submarines and flying machines by da Vinci in the 15th century, for surely these things were beyond the science of his time? Or with Bosch? Or is it etched into the Plain of Nazca, or in the temple at Copán, or on some cool, soft stone lost in the dust and darkness of Olduvai Gorge? Most sf historians point to the founding of *Amazing Stories* in 1926 as a convenient starting point, for it was there that science fiction first attempted to establish itself as a branch of literature independent from other kinds of fiction. There, too, is where we shall begin, aware nonetheless that, for as long as men have looked up with wonder to the starry night, "speculative" (or "fantastic", or "futurate"—Frewin's term) art has been with us.

The earliest and most highly-touted illustrator of subjects science fictional was Frank R. Paul, who, under the guidance of Hugo Gernsback, established many of

Fall 1931 *Wonder Stories Quarterly*
Art by Frank R. Paul
Copyright © 1931 by Gernsback Publications, Inc.

the conventional themes of sf art and provided a remarkably rich visual vocabulary which would give a striking and distinctive identity to this new literary genre. An Austrian emigrant born in 1880, Paul was trained as an architect and worked briefly as a journalistic illustrator before beginning his long and productive relationship with Gernsback. His work, while often crude and garish by conventional standards, was a marvelous kind of "brain food" for a growing new audience eager to read stories of gadgets and gears and things that go clank in the night. In his austere and economical linear style, often devoid of lighting and atmospheric effects, Paul gave special emphasis to his machines; and those machines endure as a testament to his resourcefulness in matters mechanical, and his unswerving belief in the value of science. Along the diagonal axes is where most of the major elements of his paintings can be found, and this, aided by the linear treatment and the use of large flat areas of saturated color, produces a most dynamic and eye-catching effect. What is most important about his body of work, however, is that it set a trend and instigated a viewpoint about the hardware of the future which, even today, dominates the gadget art of science fiction.

The Polish-born illustrator Hans Waldemar Wessolowski (known to genre readers as simply, Wesso) clearly shows Frank R. Paul's influence, particularly

Astounding Stories, June 1937
Art by Hans Wessolowski
Copyright © 1937 by Street and Smith
Publications, Inc. Copyright © (Renewed)
1965 by the Corde Nast Publications, Inc.

in his early work. Somewhat more adept at painting, Wesso employed a simplified value structure and demonstrated a unique talent for abstract composition in much of his work which set him apart from others who also derived their creative momentum from Paul. While he began his career in science fiction art with *Amazing Stories*, Wesso rose to prominence as the major artist for the Clayton chain's competitive magazine, *Astounding Stories of Super Science*, which began publication in January of 1930. When Clayton Publications went under three years later, *Astounding* was sold to Street and Smith, and Wesso ceased to be a major part of the creative growth of that magazine, though, after a brief absence, he did reappear to produce some fine black and white art, as well as an occasional cover. These later works showed much artistic growth, but whether by personal choice or by circumstances beyond his powers to alter, Wesso's involvement in science fiction was never to return to the level it had once reached.

The work of Robert Fuqua, perhaps even more than Wesso's, shows a Paulesque penchant for gadgets. Although more conscious of atmospheric and lighting conditions, his stylistic use of outlining makes the affinity to Frank R. Paul all the more startling. Even compositionally, Fuqua relied heavily on strong diagonal placements, but in this respect, was a bit clumsy, often forcing "heavy" objects into corners or tottering them on the edge of borders. Still and all, his technical competence and professionalism made him somewhat of an enigma in the early development of gadget art, and for a time he rekindled some of the "sense of wonder" that had endeared Frank R. Paul to so many science fiction readers. By the time he began working for *Amazing Stories* (with the cover of the October 1938 issue) *Amazing* had changed ownership twice and had moved its base of operations to Chicago.

As a result of the first change of ownership in 1929, an illustrator by the name of Leo Morey came to the attention of *Amazing*'s readers. Less preoccupied with hardware, and a better colorist and draftsman than most of his colleagues, Morey was the first to assert some degree of independence from the conventions established by Frank R. Paul. Though Wesso, Fuqua, Paul and the countless others who flocked to this new, growing market had dealt with human and alien characters before, Morey was the first to utilize them in his compositions with any regularity. To be sure, they were there more often than not to indicate scale or model some new kind of rocket belt, and there was never really enough of an emphasis on them to classify Morey with any other group than the gadget people, but nonetheless, the seeds of change were being sown.

Whereas Frank R. Paul is best remembered for creating the momentum of gadget art, Howard V. Brown was the one who seemed to bring it closest to some semblance of perfection. A man of eclectic tastes and talents, Brown carried the trend first suggested by Morey yet a step further by applying mainstream illustrative values to the genre. An excellent colorist and figure painter, yet capable of rendering machines with great facility and imagination, many of Brown's paintings are regarded today as classics of their kind. Who can forget his sinister and otherworldly aliens for Campbell's "The Invaders" (*Astounding Stories,* June 1935) or Lovecraft's "The Shadow Out of Time" (*Astounding,* June 1936), or his gleaming, futuristic spaceships for E.E. Smith's "The Skylark of Valeron" (*Astounding,* August 1934) or Jack Williamson's "The Fortress of Utopia" (*Startling Stories,* November 1939). No one before or since has matched the lushness of his palette or the richness and complexity of his personal vision. There is a spiritual presence in the work of this man that is drawn from the very essence of science fiction.

As the pulp market grew into a major consumer of artwork and science fiction began to manifest itself in various other forms, gadget art became less dominant, but never really faded from its position as the principal identity of the genre. One can clearly see an almost cyclic return to this kind of art every time

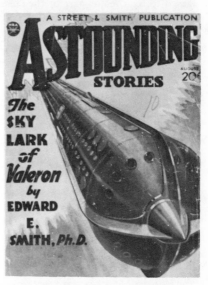

Science Fiction Plus, March 1953
Art by Alex Schomberg

Astounding Stories, August 1934
Art by Howard V. Brown
Copyright © 1934 by Street and Smith
Publications, Inc. Copyright © (Renewed)
1962 by Conde Nast Publications, Inc.

interest in science fiction begins to wane. The gadget image was a good one, one that everyone knew and associated with the field. During this period many fine talents continued to refine and expand the tradition established by Frank R. Paul. Alex Schomberg, Malcom Smith, H.R. Van Dongen, and even Chesley Bonestell kept interest in this kind of art alive while publishers experimented with bug-eyed monsters, scantily clad heroines, and art of a more symbolic type. When the pulps died out in the mid-1950's, a number of artists who had been fairly active in the magazine market carried the gadget tradition into paperbacks.

Most notable of these were Ed Emshwiller (or simply, "Emsh") and Edward Valigursky. Emshwiller's greatest strength was in his ability to handle characters, and we will return to him again elsewhere in this essay, but his versatility extended to virtually every aspect of science fiction illustration and he produced many fine paintings of the nuts and bolts variety. Valigursky, however, is of special interest to us at this point, for though he could render crisp, convincing figures, figures were seldom the main emphasis in his work. With the end of World War II came a renewed optimism about the future and a great streamlining of the traditional methods of illustrating. The realism of artists such as N.C. Wyeth and Maxfield Parrish, which for so long had been the standard of American illustration, was now giving way to a less literal look. In the aeronautics industry, for instance, the meticulous rendering of aircraft sheet by sheet, rivet by rivet, was being replaced by the use of variegated brushwork to suggest detail rather than to clearly define it as had once been the common practice. Valigursky was especially good at utilizing this new paint mannerism and the cleanness and directness of it gave his work a most strikingly futuristic feeling. But

The Magazine of Fantasy and Science Fiction, December 1950
Art by Chesley Bonestell
Copyright © 1950 Mecury Publications, Inc.

IF Worlds of Science Fiction, May 1954
Art by Ed Valigursky
Copyright © 1954 by Quinn Publishing Co.

perhaps even more appealing than its directness was its remarkable sense of motion, for with the application of broad horizontal brush strokes, Valigursky could create a sense of momentum which not only produced an aura of excited activity, but a conviction that his marvelous ships, no matter how fantastic, could actually move. With respect to aerodynamics, one must bear in mind that the bulk of Valigursky's sf art predates manned space flight, and the specifics of what a craft traveling outside of the atmosphere would look like were not really known. Yet, within the context of his paintings, there is no question in the mind of the observer that his ships are real and that they work. Now quite active in the aerospace market, Valigursky is considered somewhat of an expert on the aircraft of World War II.

Occurring simultaneously with the death of the pulps was a shift to photography in the advertising markets which resulted in the elimination of the agency system, although some illustration agencies still exist today. This put a great many illustrators out on the street looking for work, and some of them gravitated to the small but growing paperback field. Sf had been a staple of the pulp industry, and so, many of the early paperback houses maintained some sort of sf list, most of which was reprint material from the magazines (a practice which is still quite common today). The 1950's was a time of great interest in science fiction, what with the development of various and sundry nuclear devices, reports of unidentified flying objects from all over the world, the monster-movie cycle, Sputnik. Some of the old excitment which had drawn artists to the pulps was now taking hold elsewhere. Aside from Freas, Valigursky, Emshwiller, Powers and a few others who distinguished themselves as category specialists, most of the early paperback sf art was being produced by "transients" with no special interest in or knowledge of science fiction. At least two of these

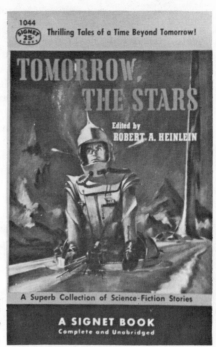

Tomorrow the Stars
Art by Stanley Meltzoff
Copyright © 1952 by The New
American Library, Inc.

"transients," Robert Schulz and Stanley Meltzoff, produced memorable work during their tenure as sf artists. Schulz, primarily a figure painter, worked in every aspect of the field, from westerns (for which he was most widely

Operation Future
Art by Robert Schulz
Copyright © 1955 by Perma-Books, Inc.

known) to mysteries, and did much to shift the emphasis in sf paperback art away from the gadget tradition. Meltzoff, one of the most revered artists of the day, is an amateur ichthyologist and expert spear fisherman, with a remarkable eye for scientific detail. In addition to producing a number of truly impressive covers for *Scientific American*, he executed a series of paintings for Signet's line of Robert Heinlein books which stands as a milestone in the history and development of paperback art. In addition, while working as an instructor at Pratt Institute, he contributed to the artistic development of at least two of sf art's best known practitioners, Paul Lehr and John Schoenherr.

Dean Ellis had spent the early part of his career working in the agencies before turning to free-lance illustration. His first sf assignments were handled with a slightly surrealistic flavor and, as such, are quite atmospheric and effective. In the late '60's however, the release of Stanley Kubrick's motion picture *2001: A Space Odyssey* brought about a renewal of interest in futuristic hardware, and Ellis was among the first with the good sense to capitalize on that interest. Using the props from the Kubrick film as a springboard, Ellis went on to refine his own stockpile of pristine gadgets, from Niven's *Ringworld* to Clarke's *Star Queen*. The penultimate professional, Ellis' crispness and sense of scale and grandeur puts him somewhere very near the top of the long and formidable list of nuts and bolts artists.

The most prominent gadget painter these days is John Berkey, who, after a brief but impressive stint in the paperback sf market, has gone on to blitz the movie ad field, doing advertising art for everything from Irwin Allen's *Towering*

Star Born
Art by Dean Ellis
Copyright ©1972 by Ace Books

Operation Umanaq
Art by Dean Ellis
Copyright ©1973 by Ace Books

2020 Vision, Art by John Berkey, Copyright © 1979 by Avon Books

Inferno to Dino De Laurentiis' *King Kong*. The overwhelming characteristic of his gadget art is his paint mannerism, which, much like Valigursky's, is remarkably fluid and energetic. He, too, shows the influence of *2001*, though many of his spacecraft resemble outboard motors and gumball machines. Despite a deceptively casual look to it, Berkey's work reveals enormous painting strategy and sophistication.

Two airbrush artists round out this brief survey of gadget painters, Christopher Foss and Stanislaw Fernandes. Foss, a devoted realist, paints the most remark-

The Worlds of Fritz Leiber
Art by Christopher Foss
Copyright © 1976 by Ace Books

The Cyberaid
Art by Stanislaw Fernandes
Copyright © 1975 by Avon Books

ably convincing spacecraft I've ever seen. They are veritable plumber's nightmares of access panels, antenna rods, portals, girders and stanchions sedulously rendered by double-zero sables and sparingly dusted with airbrush. Fernandes, a somewhat more voguish painter, is, by contrast, less realistic than surrealistic, and more reliant on airbrush effects for the success of his paintings. An excellent graphic designer as well as illustrator, Fernandes can create a uniquely unified package which makes him quite popular among publishers. Both artists are originally from England and the slightly European flavor of their widely different approaches gives them special appeal in the American market place.

I would be remiss if I did not at least briefly acknowledge the gadget art which manifests itself in various forms outside of the fiction market. Chesley Bonestell, one of the great pioneers of astronomical art, has been hard at work popularizing the concept of manned space travel through and beyond the solar system for the past three decades in his many marvelous book collaborations with such notables as Willy Ley, Wernher von Braun and Arthur C. Clarke. When surveying the achievements of his long and productive career, one hardly knows where to begin to pay him proper tribute. From brilliant architect (the Chrysler Building) to distinguished movie matte painter (*Citizen Kane, Destination Moon*) to revered American painter, Bonestell is perhaps the most beloved visionary

The Magazine of Fantasy and Science Fiction, February 1954. Art by Chesley Bonestell. Copyright ©1954 by Mercury Publications, Inc.

artist of our time. Robert McCall, catapulted into the public eye by the success of *2001* for which he produced a number of impressive posters, has done an extraordinary amount of "speculative" artwork for the aerospace industry. Sidney Mead has been a regular contributor of visionary art, not only to aerospace, but to such other clients as U.S. Steel, Alcoa and RCA, just to name a few. Berkey, in addition to movie art, has utilized his talents for such varied clientele as Otis Elevator, Texaco, and the Department of the Navy.

Clearly, the kind of art which was once deemed suitable only for the pulps, has now infiltrated into every aspect of our society. Record albums, movie posters, automobile and appliance ads, all project their various messages about the size, shape, look and feel of the future, helping us to form a certain set of ideas about our science and technology. Yet gadget art, for all that it does, like the machines it depicts, is a cold and impersonal thing. Somewhere in that vast, throbbing, thumping, churning future there is a man, still striving to define his identity, still struggling to improve his lot, and, let us hope, still the master of his own destiny.

People, in varying degrees, have always been a factor in science fiction art. What was becoming more apparent by the late 1930's however, was a shift in emphasis in some of the magazines to more people-oriented cover art, and the infusion of personality into the main characters. The bug-eyed monster tradition which had begun much earlier was now becoming virtually the sole preoccupation of the cover artists for *Planet Stories, Startling Stories* and *Captain Future*. Universal Pictures, in the early part of the decade, touched off the first American monster movie cycle with the release of such films as *Dracula* 1931), *Frankenstein* (1931), and *The Mummy* (1932). There was little question that monsters provided good box office returns and were of broad appeal. With the exception of *Frankenstein* (whose monster was cobbled together from spare parts of the dead and was brought to life by a bolt of electricity) most of the monsters of this cycle were of supernatural origins. What science could provide was a credible rationale for the existence of these twisted and horrendous beings, and some publishers, eager to milk the monster craze, injected a ghastly procession of malevolent aliens and wretched, misbegotten laboratory accidents onto the pages of the sf pulps. But what self-loathing creature would dare be seen in public without a startled, yet dauntless protagonist to terrorize? In the natural evolution of things, the nubile, near-naked heroine soon joined, and in some instances, replaced the resourceful hero.

The man most associated with the bug-eyed monster (hereinafter referred to as BEM) harried-heroine theme was Earle K. Bergey. To the more serious minded readers, for whom the theme seemed demeaning to science fiction, Bergey was notorious and little objective consideration was given to him. Yet, in point of fact, Bergey was an excellent figure painter, and the background details of his work were every bit as resourceful and imaginative as those of the best of the gadget artists. His principal achievement was to shift the spotlight and put people and aliens above hardware as the major subject matter of his cover art. Moreover, Bergey's people were not just the stiff, clumsy wooden lumps that so many of his predecessors portrayed. Despite their youth and clean cut all-American appearance, they were characters with real identities, capable of conveying fear or compassion, wonder or triumph.

In time, the BEMs began to dwindle and were replaced by the less lecherous variety which had been a mainstay of the serious genre pulps. Such artists as Edd Cartier, Charles Schneeman, H. R. van Dongen, J. W. Scott, Hannes Bok, Robert Jones, Virgil Finlay, Stephen Lawrence, Ed Emshwiller and Frank Kelly Freas developed considerable followings as a result of their abilities to portray intelligent, sympathetic aliens and convincing protagonists of genuine character. The development of this kind of art as an alternative to the gadget tradition was inevitable. Readers, as much as they wanted to read about the marvels of science, also wanted to learn about the reactions of people under stress; how they responded to the alien invasion or the machine gone amuck and how they used their resourcefulness to set things right. These kinds of stories were always the most popular, and now the human element was becoming a major consideration in the packaging of the genre. A number of factors contributed to this; reader interest, the natural evolution of the BEM theme, the influx into the pulp field of artists unfamiliar with sf who resorted to character portrayals to resolve cover assignments. Development beyond the depiction of man in the scientific environment, seemed to be a dead end, though at least two men had the fortitude to try.

One of those men, John W. Campbell, was not an artist at all, but a popular writer and highly influential editor in the genre. From the time that Campbell first came to Street and Smith in 1937 to replace F. Orlin Tremaine as editor of *Astounding Stories*, it was apparent that he had great disdain for the gaudiness which characterized the appearance of many of the magazines in the field. He believed that something which defied scientific understanding would be much more fascinating if you found it under a rock rather than saw it cascading down a mountainside at you. The earliest manifestations of this attitude were

Astounding Science Fiction, October 1940
Art by Hubert Rogers
Copyright © 1940 by Street and Smith
Publications, Inc. Copyright © 1968 (Renewed) by Conde Nast Publications, Inc.

Astounding Science Fiction, October 1939
Art by Hubert Rogers
Copyright © 1939 by Street and Smith
Publications, Inc. Copyright © 1967 (Renewed) by Conde Nast Publications, Inc.

the use of rather sedate looking astronomical paintings and a number of changes in the cover typography and title of the magazine. Consequently, it was a matter of good fortune that a young artist named Hubert Rogers, who had been doing cover paintings for a variety of other Street and Smith pulps, was willing to work for *Astounding*. Rogers, like Howard V. Brown before him, utilized mainstream techniques and aesthetic values, particularly the angular folds and simplified value structures popularized by J.C. Leyendecker, for his work in *Astounding*. Just what exactly Campbell and Rogers were driving toward is not known, but as the years went by, the covers became less overtly science fictional in content and more reliant on symbolism. The covers, every one well executed, are fascinating, but some could just as well have been suited for a mystery magazine or even *The Saturday Evening Post*. Of the more scientific looking ones however, many are revered as classics: E.E. Smith's "Gray Lensman" (October 1939), the merpeople of "Crisis in Utopia" by Norman L. Knight (July 1940), the Venusian underwater city for "Fury" by Henry Kuttner (May 1947), the macabre and symbolic painting for "The Players of Ā" by A.E. van Vogt (November 1948). As an adjunct to his cover work, Rogers would sometimes execute isolated portraits of the main characters in a story rather than illustrate a key action scene. While this was fairly common in the mainstream, Rogers was one of the first to introduce it to the genre and it is today somewhat of a minor tradition in black and white sf art.

Ed Emshwiller was another much beloved sf artist who often used figures in his work. Born in Lansing, Michigan in 1925, Emshwiller studied in Paris and New York after graduating from the University of Michigan in 1949. He began his very active career in sf illustration in 1951, working diligently in the maga-

The Magazine of Fantasy and Science Fiction, August 1958
Art by Ed Emshwiller
Copyright ©1958 by
Mercury Publications, Inc.

zines and, along with Valigursky, dominated the science fiction line of Ace Books until the mid-1960's when he left the field entirely. Unlike Rogers, there was seldom any question about the nature of his cover paintings. Emsh (as he was popularly known) could render virtually any science fiction subject with competence and was especially good at producing works of a horrific or surrealistic nature. In the mid-50's, and largely due to the influence of Richard Powers, Emsh developed an "organic" technology of amorphous shapes which he used occasionally to create a scientific environment as background for his tightly rendered, realistic characters. Today, despite the lamentations of his many fans, Emshwiller is happily engaged in the making of experimental films and is drawing quite a reputation as a pioneer in the use of videotape.

As paperbacks began to take hold, a great many figure artists produced works of a science fictional nature for them. The best known to us, of course, are the ones who developed sf as their area of expertise. Robert Schulz, as mentioned earlier, did some excellent realistic figure art for Pocketbooks, Ace and the New American Library. Dean Ellis, before becoming known as a gadget artist, did some respectable figure work for Bantam, especially for their line of books by Ray Bradbury. A younger Paul Lehr, under the influence of Meltzoff, did some very fine photographically realistic figure art, the most remarkable of which is the cover art for Louis Charbonneau's *No Place on Earth*, which shows Paul and his wife Paula posed as the main characters, fleeing from a futuristic city. Lou Feck, who does every kind of paperback art from gothics to westerns, produces an occasional sf cover in his slick and appealing style for such publishers as

The Time Machine
Art by Richard Powers
Copyright © 1957 by Berkley
Publishing Corporation

Bantam and Warner Books. Fred Pfeiffer, who replaces James Bama (known to sf readers for his super realistic covers for the *Doc Savage* series) as Bantam's contract artist, has produced some excellent sf character studies for the covers of such books as Dean Koontz's *The Flesh in the Furnace* and John Boyd's *The Gorgon Festival*, as well as having done a brief stint as the cover artist for *Doc Savage*. Two artists, Gene Szafran and Robert Foster, are perhaps the best of the figure painters, but the distinctive surrealistic flavor of their work puts them clearly into another category of science fiction illustrators.

After some years of neglect, man at last stood side by side with his technology optimistically surveying the new frontiers, confident in his dominion over his own chattel and eager to explore the corridors of time and the realms of space. The dawn of the Nuclear Age, however, aroused much anxiety and uncertainty about the benefits of scientific research. In the early 1950's, just as paperbacks were growing in strength and numbers, such films as *The Day the Earth Stood Still* (20th Century Fox 1951), *Five* (Columbia 1951), *The Beast from 20,000 Fathoms* (Warner Bros. 1953) and *Them!* (Warner Bros. 1954) were warning movie audiences of the possible consequences of nuclear malfeasance. The decade of the '50's, often called the 'paranoid decade,' saw the outbreak of McCarthyism, the ravages of Korea, the anxieties of the Cold War, the irresponsible spread of nuclear weapons, the growth of automation and the wide-scale application of the computer. It was a time of great discomfort and doubt in our ability to control the unknowable forces which were suddenly at large around us.

For the first time in its history, science fiction art now became the vanguard of a new kind of thinking about scientific progress. While pessimism was not unheard of in sf literature, it would be nearly two decades later before writers

Pstalemate
Art by Richard Powers
Copyright © 1971 by
Berkley Publishing Corporation

would produce, with any regularity, works of a surrealistic or anti-scientific bent. Most important of all, however, was that this new attitude came not from the magazines, which were then a bastion of scientific optimism, but from the paperbacks. The instigator of this "New Wave" art is an American surrealist painter by the name of Richard Powers. Powers, under the guidance and encouragement of publisher Ian Ballantine, executed a number of bizarre and iconoclastic cover paintings which contrasted sharply with the kinds of things readers had come to expect of science fiction art. The result was a minor marketing phenomenon which prompted many illustrators to copy Powers' techniques. In actual fact, there was really no malice intended by Powers by these works, but the use of surrealism, whose ideologies were generally known to be contrary to any kind of institutionalized thinking, created an immediate aura of pessimism and fear. Running the gamut from representational paintings to totally amorphous and non-identifiable works, Powers dredged these fantastic parcels up from the very real estate of the subconscious mind. In so doing, he touches in each of us a sense of repressed anxieties which reaches all the way back to the womb or to half-remembered nightmares. Drawing much of his inspiration from the European surrealists Miro, Tanguy and Matta, he opened a passage to a new and more introspective kind of sf art. To call his work beautiful or ugly is to apply words of little relevance to it. It is alarming and unnerving, powerful and flamboyant, intimidating and occasionally decorative. Like some fantastic beast from the past, or perhaps the future, it is too conspicuous for us to ignore and it speaks to us in a voice all too strangely familiar.

Paul Lehr developed an approach similar to Powers' which is somewhat more decorative and consistently representational. Its main characteristic is a feeling

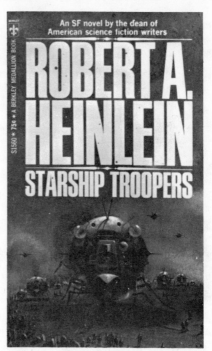

The Best SF Stories From New Worlds
Art by Paul Lehr
Copyright ©1971 by Berkley
Publishing Corporation

Starship Troopers
Art by Paul Lehr
Copyright ©1968 by Berkley
Publishing Corporation

of otherworldliness created by the use of a saturated background color with touches of analogous hues to form a unified color field. The hue or "identity" of a color has a psychological effect on the viewer because of associations we make with objects that exist in nature. Yellow, for instance, is generally thought to be a warm, cheerful color because of its association with the sun, whereas violet, the color of the sky as it deepens into night, is thought to convey a feeling of mystery. By manipulating the relationships of the various aspects of color —hue (identity), chroma (degree of brightness) and value (degree of lightness or darkness)—the artist can create a variety of moods. Lehr is somewhat of a virtuoso at this, and his paintings, usually landscapes, have an eerie sense of atmosphere about them. Born and raised in Armonk, New York, Lehr, now in his late forties, has virtually no interest in science fiction. It is consequently quite remarkable that he is so proficient at creating the proper mood in his work. The landscapes, often populated by miniature shadow figures making meaningful gestures, and strange cities with peculiar egg-shaped domes, sharp spires and flowing ramps, are alive with cosmic wonder. His machines are often fashioned after insects and have such anomalous features as spidery legs, gnashing metal mandibles and leering, translucent eyes. These elements which appeal to the common fears in all of us, are, like the lure of a roller coaster ride, too strong to resist.

A former classmate of Lehr's while at Pratt and an ardent admirer of Powers' science fiction art, John Schoenherr was very active in the field from 1959 to 1967 when his growing interest in wildlife illustration became his major pre-

Analog, December 1967
Art by John Schoenherr
Copyright © 1967 by
Conde Nast Publications, Inc.

Analog, May 1966
Art by John Schoenherr
Copyright © 1966 by
Conde Nast Publications, Inc.

occupation. Using large, looming shapes, dramatically back-lighted and set against twilight skies, Schoenherr's subject matter, whether alien or mechanical, often resembles wildlife of one kind or another. A realistic painter, this reference to natural forms incongruous with the subject gives his work a decidedly surrealistic flavor. A more sedate colorist than Lehr, Schoenherr's usually naturalistic color schemes rely heavily on the middle value range for their penumbral atmosphere. While having done much art for such paperback houses as Ace and Pyramid, he is best known to sf enthusiasts for his work in *Analog* (formerly *Astounding*) where he dominated the covers through the mid-60's, producing many fine paintings.

The Powers influence was taking hold and could be seen lurking in the backgrounds of works by Emshwiller, Gaughan, Ziel, Lewis and scores of others. By the late 1960's, with the wide academic acceptance of science fiction evidenced by the dozens of courses springing up in colleges and universities everywhere, publishers began to reassess the effectiveness of their cover packaging. Generally, sf art up to this point had been thought to appeal to an adolescent audience. Surely, college level readers would be more sophisticated in their tastes, and consequently, surrealism and decorative, non-representational art became the vogue for a time. By the very early '70's however, sf was undergoing a minor recession. "New Wave," though it still exists without the label, failed to be a profitable commercial entity. Packaging in many instances missed the mark entirely, and overestimation of the size of the new college market compelled some publishers to drop their sf lines entirely. By mid-decade, after a return to the old packaging values, science fiction was again enjoying an enormous boom. In that short period of surrealist-dominated art however, much interesting and effective work was done. Many artists, choosing to remain within

Foundation and Empire
Art by Don Ivan Punchatz
Copyright © 1968 by Avon Books

the parameters of representationalism, turned to other European surrealists such as Delvaux, Magritte and Dali for inspiration.

Don Ivan Punchatz, with his distinctive primitive style, executed many excellent and bizarre surrealistic works during this time. His covers for Avon's editions of Asimov's *Foundation* trilogy and Berkley's first printing of Harlan Ellison's controversial *Dangerous Visions* anthology are outstanding for their kind. Though seldom appreciated by the fans, after the collapse, Punchatz moved into other areas of illustration, and now, due to the recent acceptance of surrealism into the mainstream, is considered one of the best graphic designers and illustrators of the day.

Robert Foster, whose startlingly Daliesque realism was very prominent in the paperback market from the late 1960's to the mid-'70's, developed a unique system of working. Relying heavily on photography, Foster would make up his compositions in a darkroom and, having his board photosensitized, would transfer the image onto it in values of a single color. This monochromatic image would function as an underpainting for successive translucent layers of paint until the art was colored to his satisfaction. While most artists would have felt the system confining, Foster obviously found it liberating and used it to bring his work to a unique level of excellence. The remarkable thing was that Foster was such a proficient craftsman, he could actually render objects just as photographically without using the system. In point of fact, he found it a great time saver and diverted his attentions to such considerations as composition and color. As a result, his paintings were almost always quite striking with their

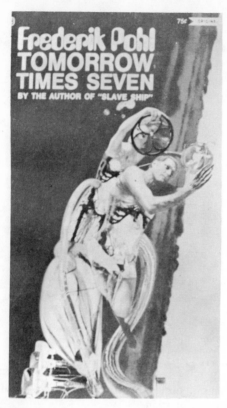

Tomorrow Times Seven
Art by Robert Foster
Copyright © 1969 by
Ballantine Books, Inc.

otherworldly colorfulness and dynamic compositional structures. In the late
'60's and early '70's Foster did a great deal of work for Ballantine Books until
going under contract for Dell. There, as a contract artist, his duties were expanded to include a variety of paperback assignments which he executed with
the same diligence and skill as he had his science fiction work. In 1973, Robert
Foster suffered a stroke which all but ended his career. Recently, after some
years of therapy, he has returned to the field and it is this author's hope, as one
of his most fervent admirers, that he soon regain the proficiency which made
his work a milestone in the annals of science fiction art.

Of the artists who chose a more decorative approach, the most well remembered are Leo and Diane Dillon, who won the art Hugo in 1971 for their covers
on the short-lived but excellent Ace Specials line. Using lush, earthy colors and
well-designed, mosaic-like patterns, the Dillons have developed an adaptation of
commercial surrealism which is all their own. Despite an occasional appearance
on a sf book these days (usually one by Harlan Ellison who has a strong personal
fondness for their work) they are most active in and best known for their delightful children's book illustrations.

Other artists, mostly figure painters, dabbled in the decadent storehouse of
surrealistic ideas. Gene Szafran literally inundated the market with soft, air-
brushed figures in suggestively surrealistic environments, and like a flaming
comet, dropped quickly from sight. Jerry Podwell, who could never quite secure

The Left Hand of Darkness
Art by Leo and Diane Dillon
Copyright©1969 by Ace Books, Inc.

a volume of sf paperback work, has recently found his market doing science fiction art for the men's magazine market. John Holmes, a fine Magritte-inspired surrealist from England, makes occasional appearances in the sf/horror categories, as American tastes permit. Stanislaw Fernandes and Murray Tinkelman, quite active in the field at the moment, might well be marking the beginning of a return to this kind of art.

Perhaps after more than a decade of political assassinations, student riots, racial unrest, unwanted wars in obscure Asian countries, pollution of our environmental resources, hallucinatory drugs and Watergate scandals, we can no longer look with wide-eyed wonder at the vast, wheeling universe. I think not, but certainly a harsh reality has worn away our naivete a bit. At least a little bit. The "New Wave" shows us a grim and distressing vision of ourselves and of our science, a vision perhaps too pessimistic to be valid in itself, but one which we must nonetheless consider.

What lies ahead for sf illustration is not knowable at the moment. Illustration, like other forms of popular art, derives much of its creative momentum from the fine arts, and, at the moment, there seems to be little progress going on anywhere. In 1974, under the guidance of F.C. Durant, the Smithsonian Institution's National Air and Space Museum began expanding its space art collection to include works of a science fictional nature because it was deemed that such works have contributed to the popular acceptance of the concept of interplanetary travel. Such recognition has been long in coming, but it marks the first small step toward respectability. At long last. In time perhaps, the full impact of what our technology can do and how it will change us will be fully known.

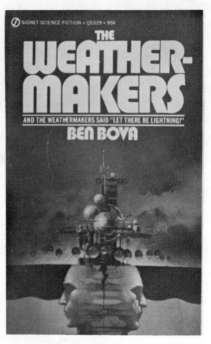

Pstalemate
Art by Gene Szafran
Copyright © 1971 by
G. P. Putnam's Sons, Inc.

The Weather-Makers
Art by Jerome Podwill
Copyright © 1973 by The
New American Library

For now, we have science fiction to show us some of the answers. As a literary genre, despite much growth in the past and much more to come in the future, science fiction will always appeal to a relatively small and selective group of readers. In spite of this fact, its art surrounds us and touches each of us, no matter what our interests, not just at the book racks, but in countless magazine advertisements, package illustrations and billboards, traveling where words cannot to deliver the message of our bright, beautiful, grim tomorrow.

A SELECTED BIBLIOGRAPHY OF WORKS
ON SCIENCE FICTION ART

Aldiss, Brian W. *Science Fiction Art*. New York: Bounty Books, 1975.

Ballantine, Betty, ed. *The Fantastic Art of Frank Frazetta*. New York: Scribner's, 1975.

————. *Frank Frazetta: Book Two*. New York: Peacock Press, 1977.

Batchelor, John. *Mervyn Peake: A Biographical and Critical Exploration*. London: Duckworth, 1974.

Brooks, C.W. *Revised Hannes Bok Checklist*. Baltimore: T-K Graphics, 1973.

Cochran, Russ, ed. *The Edgar Rice Burroughs Library of Illustration: Volume One*. West Plains, MO: Russ Cochran, 1976.

de la Ree, Gerry, et al. *Bok: a tribute to the late fantasy artist, Hannes Bok, on the 60th anniversary of his birth and 10th anniversity of his death*. Saddle River, NJ: Gerry de la Ree, 1974.

—————, ed. *The Book of Virgil Finlay.* Saddle River, NJ: Gerry de la Ree, 1975; rpt. New York: Flare/Avon, 1976.

del Rey, Lester, ed. *Fantastic Science Fiction Art 1926-1954.* New York: Ballantine Books, 1975.

Freas, Frank Kelly. *Frank Kelly Freas: The Art of Science Fiction.* Norfolk, VA: Donning, 1977.

Frewin, Anthony. *One Hundred Years of Science Fiction Illustration 1840-1940.* London: Jupiter Books, 1974; rpt. New York: Pyramid Books, 1975.

Gettings, Fred. *Arthur Rackham.* New York: Macmillan, 1976.

Gilmore, Maeve and Shelagh Johnson. *Mervyn Peake: Writings & Drawings.* London: Academy Editions, 1974; rpt. New York: St. Martin's, 1975.

Hudson, Derek. *Arthur Rackham: His Life and Work.* London: Heinemann, 1960; rpt. London: Heinemann; New York: Scribner's, 1974.

Larkin, David, ed. *Arthur Rackham.* New York: Peacock Press, 1975.

—————. *The English Dreamers.* New York: Peacock Press, 1975.

—————. *Fantastic Art.* New York: Ballantine Books, 1973.

—————. *The Fantastic Art of Charles and William Heath Robinson.* New York: Peacock Press, 1976.

—————. *The Fantastic Creatures of Edward Julius Detmold.* New York: Peacock Press, 1976.

—————. *The Fantastic Kingdom.* New York: Ballantine Books; London: Pan Books, 1974.

—————. *Kay Nielsen.* New York: Peacock Press, 1975.

—————. *Once Upon a Time: Some Contemporary Illustrators of Fantasy.* New York: Peacock Press, 1976.

Nardelli, Fred. *Frank Frazetta Index.* Amsterdam, NY: By the Author, 1975.

Peppin, Brigid. *Fantasy: The Golden Age of Fantastic Illustrations.* New York: Watson-Guptill, 1975; rpt. New York: New American Library, 1976.

Petaja, Emil, ed. *The Hannes Bok Memorial Showcase of Fantasy Art.* San Francisco: Sisu, 1974.

—————, et al. *And Flights of Angels: The Life and Legend of Hannes Bok.* San Francisco: Bokanalia Memorial Foundation, 1968.

Rickard, Dennis. *The Fantastic Art of Clark Ashton Smith.* Baltimore: Mirage Press, 1973.

Sadoul, Jacques. *2000 A.D.: Illustrations from the Golden Age of Science Fiction Pulps.* Chicago: Henry Regnery, 1975.

Watney, John. *Mervyn Peake.* London: Michael Joseph; New York: St. Martin's, 1976.

Vincent Miranda

THE FANTASTIC CINEMA

Perhaps there have never existed less likely bedfellows as fantasy and the film. Fantasy and science fiction have long been the emotional and intellectual playground of a relatively small group. This exclusive audience has easily supported literary fantasy, for an unsuccessful book involves the time of one individual, the author, and a light investment on the part of the publisher. If the book is successful, it can mean a large financial gain for author and publisher; if it fails, the modest investment can be easily borne.

Film has, conversely, been a medium of mass communication. Revolutionary techniques in style, innovative scripts, and unique points of view in perspective and plot have traditionally been a threat to this most commercial of art forms. The average motion picture commands an enormous expenditure in talent and money, tying up hundreds of people, vast production facilities, and mountains of equipment for months at a time. A few days lost in production time can cost hundreds of thousands of dollars. A miscalculation in judgment of the public taste can mean the loss of everything invested in a film. Thus many of the elements that make a successful science fiction or fantasy script are an anathema to the basic tenet of the film. The "formula" is more important to the film industry than to any other commercial endeavor. The repetition of a few popular clichés inside of a standard story line has long been the safest route to follow with film; for among the major studios artistic mediocrity is a small price to pay for financial security. The fantastic film is a gamble. Audiences must assimilate strange new worlds or convoluted visions of their own: societies altered by strange environments, unusual social conditions, or technologies vastly different from ours. All these things must be accepted independently of the drama which must thread its way through its unique surroundings and be resolved within a reasonable running time of ninety to one hundred minutes, the industry's average length for a film.

How does the fantastic film come about? The successful and/or acceptable science fiction and fantasy films have often gained their success as products of an auteur director who has somehow obtained enough money and independence to complete his film without studio or backer interference. Examples of such films are Kubrick's *2001: A Space Odyssey* (1968), Hill's *Slaughterhouse-Five*

56

(1973), Boorman's *Zardoz* (1974), and Roeg's *The Man Who Fell to Earth* (1975). There are also the visions of mainstream studio high adventure which gloss over the fantastic elements and use them as an exotic backdrop for a standard plot; for example, *Journey to the Center of the Earth* (1959), *Fantastic Voyage* (1966), *Logan's Run* (1976), *Damnation Alley* (1977), and *Star Wars* (1978).

In the very early days of the cinema the fantastic was one of the most important sources of material to the filmmaker. Film was a visual medium, a magical one; and although special effects were laughably primitive, the audiences were equally unsophisticated, viewing each cinematic trick with awe. The greatest of the early film fantasists was the Frenchman, George Méliès, who experimented with the work of Verne and Wells, as well as creating films of the supernatural. Audiences, easily jaded, flocked to see fantasies which exploited the more unique and bizarre possibilities of the film medium.

The first major creative center for fantastic film had been France, where early giants such as Méliès, the Lumiere brothers, and Rene Clair mapped out the directions for an entire industry. For at this point, and in their eyes, there was no breakdown of film into genre; the medium *was* the magic they bore. They were reaching for art in film. Their contempt for organization and the lack of a studio system began a gradual decline in the omnipotence of the French filmmaker and soon the scene shifted to Germany, where the great master Fritz Lang (1890–1976) created several very important works, among which were *Sigfried* (1923), *Metropolis* (1926), *Der Frau En Mond* (1928), and *M* (1931). Also came Wiene's *The Cabinet of Dr. Caligari* (1919), Wegener's *Der Golem* (1920), and Murnau's *Nosferatu* (1922).

In these silent days of film there was no language barrier and these films were seen thoughout the world, and to great acclaim. The still-young American film industry took note of their success and began creating the first great American fantastic films, such as *The Lost World* (1925), *Frankenstein* (1931), *Dracula* (1931), and *King Kong* (1933).

Three other things occurred at this time: the commencement of the sound era, the advancements in the increasingly complex technology necessary to keep the public happy, and the advent of the more talented and specialized personnel needed to supply and run that technology. These factors made the basic costs of film production soar. By the beginning of the 1930s most of the great studios had begun their reign, and film had become a hard business. The studios insisted upon one point above all else: that a film bring a solid return for as modest an investment as possible. The comedy, western, suspense, mystery, and romance were all quite popular with the studio heads. Such films required little or nothing in the way of sets or locations out of the ordinary, and a production of acceptable quality could be made for a small investment guaranteeing healthy box office returns. Musicals and costume dramas were riskier productions with their higher budget demands, but a certain standardization of style and plot could reduce the danger of financial loss, and these films were popular with the Hollywood moneymen.

Not so with the fantastic film. By its very nature, good science fiction and fantasy should be innovative and original. Such qualities were avoided by the large studios as a whole. Discounting the Disney organization, one studio that seemed to be at home with the fantastic film was Universal, always considered something of a maverick studio. Begun in 1912 as Universal Film Manufacturing Company, it was by 1915 grinding out films by the hundreds. Their first great successful fantasies were associated with Lon Chaney (1833–1930), who thrilled the filmgoing public with such films as *The Hunchback of Notre Dame* (1923) and *The Phantom of the Opera* (1925).

Realizing the potential of the fantastic film, Universal produced most of the best horror and fantasy of the 1930s and 1940s, including *Dracula* (1931), *Frankenstein* (1931), *The Mummy* (1932), *The Invisible Man* (1933), *The Bride of Frankenstein* (1935), *Son of Frankenstein* (1935), *Dracula's Daughter* (1936), and *The Wolfman* (1941), plus innumerable sequels to tie up loose ends and empty filmgoer's pockets.

In 1945 Universal merged with International Pictures and their fantasy work was put on the back burner for several years until the early 1950s, when producer William Alland and Director Jack Arnold dominated the Universal fantasy outputs with such films as *It Came from Outer Space* (1953), *The Creature from the Black Lagoon* (1954), *Revenge of the Creature* (1955), *Tarantula* (1955), *This Island Earth* (1955), *The Creature Walks Among Us* (1956), *The Mole People* (1956), *Curucu, Beast of the Amazon* (1956), *The Deadly Mantis* (1957), and *The Incredible Shrinking Man* (1957), and nearly dominated the Hollywood fantasy scene as well.

By 1957 Universal science fiction and horror films were being produced cheaply and with an almost incredible lack of production values for a studio with such past generic triumphs. But even as they produced such nonsense as *Monsters on the Campus* (1958) and *The Thing That Couldn't Die* (1958), they also imported from a small company in England called Hammer Films, the first of many great modern British fantasy efforts, such as *House of Dracula* (1958).

Universal managed to produce a long string of successful fantastic films because a good part of their organization was geared to such production. At other studios fantasy and science fiction were of a more specialized nature. At Disney Studios fantasy was, naturally, the staple, although most of their product was primarily on a juvenile level. Disney Studios did produce one monumental science fiction film in 1954, Jules Verne's *20,000 Leagues Under the Sea,* which was a resounding success. This was one of many productions based on Verne; he has been good box office for close to six decades.

Verne's *The Mysterious Island* (1961) is one of the better films of Charles H. Schneer and Ray Harryhausen, a specialized production team. Harryhausen was a student of the masterful Willis O'Brien, who had done the work on *King Kong* (1933), *Son of Kong* (1933), *Mighty Joe Young* (1946), and then a string of decreasingly important special effects film. Harryhausen possessed one thing that O'Brien lacked—a producer. Charles Schneer had seen a market for stop motion film of high quality and controlled budget. Working closely with Harryhausen, Schneer brought forth a number of profitable, high quality, low budget winners that kept many studio auditors alert. These included *It Came from Beneath the Sea* (1954), *Earth vs. the Flying Saucers* (1956), *The 7th Voyage of Sinbad* (1958), the previously mentioned *The Mysterious Island* (1961), *Jason and the Argonauts* (1962), and from the H. G. Wells novel, *The First Men in the Moon* (1964).

H. G. Wells was another keystone of fantastic cinema. He even scripted the classic *Things to Come* (1936), which was the crowning triumph of British science fiction cinema for many years. Two of Wells' books, *The War of the Worlds* and *The Time Machine*, proved to be valuable fodder for George Pal, who, like Charles Schneer, specialized as a producer of fantastic films. The Wells films were made in 1953 and 1960, respectively. Other Pal films included *Destination Moon* (1950), *When Worlds Collide* (1951), *The Conquest of Space* (1955), *Atlantis, The Lost Continent* (1960), *7 Faces of Dr. Lao* (1964), *The Power* (1968), and *Doc Savage, The Man of Bronze* (1975).

Only three really important science fiction films came out in the 1950s as standard studio fare not related to specialized producers or directors. *The Thing* (1951), directed by Howard Hawks and Christian Nyby from RKO, *The Day the Earth Stood Still* (1951), directed by Robert Wise for 20th Century Fox, and *The Forbidden Planet* (1955), directed by Fred M. Wilcox for MGM. All three were high-budgeted top studio talent productions. This handful of films was the cream of the Hollywood crop of fantastic film from a financial standpoint. Literally hundreds of fantastic films had been released throughout the 1940s and 1950s, but almost all had sunk into second or third feature drive-in filler positions, undistinguished and forgotten.

In the 1960s mediocrity prevailed in American fantastic cinema, though American-International kept the torch flickering feebly with a string of outrageously inferior films, often under the helm of Roger Corman, whose greatest successes were loose adaptations of Edgar Allan Poe: *The Pit and the Pendulum* (1961), *The Premature Burial* (1962), *The Raven* (1963), and *Ligeia* (1964).

The rest of the market was dominated by England's Hammer Films, who with a stable of expert fantasy directors, producers, technicians, and actors, recreated the early successes of Universal in color and with explicit spatterings of gore.

Then, in 1968, Stanley Kubrick conned MGM out of the then staggering sum of ten million dollars, and working in England, brought forth the most monumental science fiction film to that date, *2001: A Space Odyssey*. When released, the film caused an uproar. MGM was not sure of how to merchandise such a product and seemed convinced that they had poured their money down the drain. This, along with the film's limited critical approval (soon to be reversed by many critics), seemed to indicate that there was no room for either serious or expensive science fiction on the big screen. But audiences rallied and made *2001* one of the most revered fantastic films of all time, thus setting the stage for the 1970s.

There was born in the 1970s a heightened awareness of technology. We had walked on the Moon, and at the same time we were polluting our planetary environment. Special effects had reached a point of technical brilliance capable of any visual need of the camera. So, in this age, we get a technically superior package for our money. The studios that have survived in a changing Hollywood have shown themselves more receptive to the young experimenter-directors with an interesting fantasy ploy; but the fears still linger.

George Lucas, director of *Star Wars*, offered the film to Universal, which had housed his first success, *American Graffiti* (1973). They turned him down and he found himself creating *Star Wars* at 20th Century Fox. Stephen Spielberg had obtained additional funds from Columbia to re-shoot and re-edit some portions of his *Close Encounters of the Third Kind* (1978) before the studio shut down production as too expensive to continue. The Salkinds sank enormous amounts of capital into *Superman* (1978), hoping that their investment was large enough to support production, and they came close to disaster several times. Saul Bass' *Phase 4* (1974) and George Roy Hill's *Slaughterhouse-Five* (1973), both of which showed poor box office returns in spite of high quality script and talent, were at least brought in under modest budgets.

On the other hand, *Invasion of the Body Snatchers* (1978), a skilled and good-humored sequel to the 1956 Allied Artists classic of the same name, was brought in on a tight budget of about two million dollars and reaped a fortune in box office receipts, thus proving that multi-million dollar productions and constantly stunning special effects are not necessary prerequisites for a successful fantastic film.

2001: A Space Odyssey was the proverbial foot in the door as science fiction/fantasy, and at the same time was a major motion picture. And *Star Wars* seems to have widened the gap, paving the way for what will hopefully be mass public acceptance of the genre and consequently, more and better films of the same ilk. A simple point to be understood in the success of any film is that it must make back approximately twice what was put into it in order to break even. This will cover the initial investment, plus the costs of hyping the product, printing costs, and various other expenses. For the (roughly) ten million dollars it took to bring *Star Wars* to the screen, it has been rewarding for all involved in more ways than one. It has now grossed over 350 million dollars, amply paying off everyone concerned; and this astounding profit margin makes it the highest grossing motion picture in history. *Close Encounters* was also extremely successful, which was the reason the studios were amenable to Spielberg taking more money and re-shooting and elaborating on certain scenes. Richard Donner's *Superman* is doing well at this writing and has been at the top of the list of current highest grossing films.

The flood seems, indeed, to be gaining momentum. Not only are the names of the characters of *Star Wars* on the lips of the average moviegoer, the excitement is there; for the public seems to be accepting the fantastic film. And the studio heads are aware of the fact that if a science fiction/fantasy film is successful, it seems to be phenominally successful; otherwise the list of films in the making or already released at this writing has no other explanation: *Superman II, The Empire Strikes Back, Star Trek,* Disney's *Black Hole, Buck Rogers, Alien, Dracula, Nosferatu, Time After Time,* and others currently being scripted. These films will determine whether or not the fantastic film can once again become a staple of the filmmaker, from both the creative and the business end.

A SELECTED BIBLIOGRAPHY OF WORKS
ON THE FANTASTIC FILM

Agel, Jerome, [ed.]. *The Making of Kubrick's 2001.* New York: Signet, 1970.
Amelio, Ralph J., [ed.]. *Hal in the Classroom: Science Fiction Films.* Dayton: Pflaum, 1974.

Annan, David. *Cinefantastic: Beyond the Dream Machine*. London: Lorrimer, 1974.

—————. *Robot: The Mechanical Monster*. London: Lorrimer, 1976.

Atkins, Thomas R., ed. *Science Fiction Films*. New York: Monarch Press, 1976.

Baxter, John. *Science Fiction in the Cinema*. New York: A. S. Barnes, 1970.

Brosnan, John. *Future Tense: The Cinema of Science Fiction*. New York: St. Martin's, 1979.

—————. *Movie Magic: The Story of Special Effects in the Cinema*. New York: St. Martin's, 1974.

Butler, Ivan. *Horror in the Cinema*. 2nd ed., rev. New York: A. S. Barnes, 1970.

Clarens, Carlos. *An Illustrated History of the Horror Film*. New York: Putnam's, 1967.

Daniels, Les. *Living in Fear: A History of Horror in the Mass Media*. New York: Scribner's, 1975.

De Vries, Daniel. *The Films of Stanley Kubrick*. Grand Rapids, MI: Eerdmans, 1973.

Dillard, R. H. W. *Horror Films*. New York: Monarch Press, 1976.

Edelson, Edward. *Visions of Tomorrow: Great Science Fiction from the Movies*. New York: Doubleday, 1975.

Everson, William K. *Classics of the Horror Film*. Secaucus, NJ: Citadel Press, 1974.

Frank, Alan J. *Horror Movies: Tales of Terror in the Cinema*. London: Octopus, 1974.

—————. *Sci-Fi Now: 10 Exciting Years of Science Fiction from 2001 to Star Wars and Beyond*. London: Octopus, 1978.

Gerani, Gary with Paul H. Schulman. *Fantastic Television*. New York: Harmony, 1977.

Gifford, Denis. *A Pictorial History of Horror Movies*. New York: Hamlyn, 1973.

—————. *Science Fiction Film*. London: Studio Vista; New York: Dutton, 1970.

Glut, Donald F. *Classic Movie Monsters*. Metuchen, NJ: Scarecrow Press, 1978.

—————. *The Dracula Book*. Metuchen, NJ: Scarecrow Press, 1975.

—————. *The Frankenstein Legend: A Tribute to Mary Shelley and Boris Karloff*. Metuchen, NJ: Scarecrow Press, 1973.

Hammond, Paul. *Marvelous Méliès*. New York: St. Martin's, 1975.

Harryhousen, Ray. *Film Fantasy Scrapbook*. 2nd ed., rev. South Brunswick, NJ: A. S. Barnes, 1974.

Hickman, Gail Morgan. *The Films of George Pal*. South Brunswick, NJ: A. S. Barnes, 1977.

Huss, Roy and T. J. Ross, eds. *Focus on the Horror Film*. Englewood Cliffs, NJ: Prentice-Hall, 1972.

Hutchinson, Tom. *Horror & Fantasy in the Movies*. New York: Crescent, 1974.

Jensen, Paul M. *The Cinema of Fritz Lang*. New York: A. S. Barnes, 1969.

Johnson, William, ed. *Focus on the Science Fiction Film*. Englewood Cliffs, NJ: Prentice-Hall, 1972.

Kagan, Norman. *The Cinema of Stanley Kubrick*. New York: Holt, 1972.

Lee, Walt. *Reference Guide to Fantastic Films: Science Fiction, Fantasy, & Horror*. 3 vols. Los Angeles: Chelsea-Lee, 1972–74.

Lenning, Arthur. *The Count: The Life and Films of Bela "Dracula" Lugosi.* New York: Putnam, 1974.

Manchel, Frank. *An Album of Great Science Fiction Films.* New York: Watts, 1976.

————. *Terrors of the Screen.* Englewood Cliffs, NJ: Prentice-Hall, 1970.

Menville, Douglass. *A Historical and Critical Survey of the Science-Fiction Film.* New York: Arno, 1975.

———— and R. Reginald. *Things to Come: An Illustrated History of the Science Fiction Film.* New York: Times Books, 1977.

Moss, Robert F. *Karloff and Company: The Horror Film.* New York: Pyramid, 1974.

Naha, Ed. *Horrors! From Screen to Scream: An Encyclopedic Guide to the Greatest Horror and Fantasy Films of all Time.* New York: Avon, 1975.

Parish, James Robert and Michael R. Pitts. *The Great Science Fiction Pictures.* Metuchen, NJ: Scarecrow Press, 1977.

Phillips, Gene D. *Stanley Kubrick: A Film Odyssey.* New York: Popular Library, 1975.

Pirie, David. *A Heritage of Horror: The English Gothic Cinema 1946–1972.* New York: Avon, 1974.

Rovin, Jeff. *The Fabulous Fantasy Films.* South Brunswick, NJ: A. S. Barnes, 1977.

————. *From Jules Verne to Star Trek.* New York: Drake, 1977.

————. *A Pictorial History of Science Fiction Films.* Secaucus, NJ: Citadel Press, 1975.

Science Fiction Films from 1895 to 1930. London: British Film Institute, 1966.

Shaheen, Jack, ed. *Nuclear War Films.* Carbondale: Southern Illinois University Press, 1978.

Steinbrunner, Chris and Burt Goldblatt. *Cinema of the Fantastic.* New York: Saturday Review Press, 1972.

Strick, Philip. *Science Fiction Movies.* London: Octopus, 1976.

Whitfield, Stephen E. and Gene Roddenberry. *The Making of Star Trek.* New York: Ballantine, 1968.

Willis, Donald C. *Horror and Science Fiction Films: A Checklist.* Metuchen, NJ: Scarecrow Press, 1972.

Marshall B. Tymn

CRITICAL STUDIES AND REFERENCE WORKS

This bibliography does not include handbooks and resource materials intended for use in the classroom, critical anthologies, books on science fiction art and film, or articles in periodicals. Titles were chosen on the basis of their importance to science fiction scholarship and their general availability. The format for this listing is adapted from *A Research Guide to Science Fiction Studies,* edited by Marshall B. Tymn, Roger C. Schlobin and L.W. Currey.

PRELIMINARY SOURCES

Ash, Brian. *Who's Who in Science Fiction.* New York: Taplinger, 1976.

A concise collection of over 400 bio-bibliographical entries of sf writers, editors, artists, and others who have been influential in the development of science fiction from the era of Verne and Wells to the present.

Ashley, Michael. *Who's Who in Horror and Fantasy Fiction.* London: Elm Tree Books, 1977.

A concise collection of over 400 bio-bibliographical entries of writers and editors whose work was primarily in the genre or who exercised influence upon it from the early 18th century to the present.

Briney, Robert E. and Edward Wood. *SF Bibliographies: An Annotated Bibliography of Bibliographical Works on Science Fiction and Fantasy Fiction.* Chicago: Advent, 1972 [paper].

An annotated listing of approximately 100 bibliographies, indices, and checklists, many of which were published in severely limited editions now difficult to locate.

Magill, Frank N. *Survey of Science Fiction Literature.* 5 vols. Englewood Cliffs, NJ: Salem Press, 1979.

The set is comprised of 513 essays representing 280 authors, including about 90 foreign-language titles, written by 72 authors. The works have been carefully chosen; all the award-winners and many of the nominees are repre-

63

sented, and no major work seems to have been omitted. A major reference work which should be acquired by all libraries developing secondary collections.

Nicholls, Peter, ed. *The Encyclopedia of Science Fiction.* Garden City, NY: Doubleday, 1979.

The most comprehensive reference book on science fiction ever published. Covering all aspects of the field, it includes entries on over 1000 authors, editors, illustrators, fan and professional magazines, films and filmmakers, themes, organizations, awards, and much more.

Rock, James A. *Who Goes There: A Bibliographic Dictionary, Being a Guide to the Works of Authors Who Have Contributed to the Literature of Fantasy and Science Fiction, and Who Have Published Some or All of Their Works Pseudonymously.* Bloomington, IN: James A. Rock, 1979.

A checklist of over 1,200 authors and over 2,000 pseudonyms as well as a chronological listing of books published by each author under both pseudonyms and real names. Now the standard work.

SOURCES FOR PRIMARY MATERIALS

A. GENERAL BIBLIOGRAPHIES

Barron, Neil, ed. *Anatomy of Wonder: Science Fiction.* New York: Bowker, 1976.

An annotated bibliography of over 1150 works organized into four historical periods, with an additional category for juvenile titles. A reference section complements the main listing.

Bleiler, E. F. *The Checklist of Science-Fiction and Supernatural Fiction.* Glen Rock, NJ: Firebell Books, 1978.

A revision and enlargement of Bleiler's pioneering *The Checklist of Fantastic Literature,* first published in 1948. Classifies titles according to subject matter. Still the most comprehensive guide to works published during the period 1800–1948.

Burger, Joanne. *SF Published in 1968.* Lake Jackson, TX: Joanne Burger, 1969- [paper].

An annual listing of U.S. hardcover and paperback titles.

Currey, L. W. *Science Fiction and Fantasy Authors: A Bibliography of First Printings of Their Fiction and Selected Criticism.* Boston: G. K. Hall, 1979.

A comprehensive and accurate checklist of book fiction by 215 authors identified with the field from the late 19th century to the present. The checklists are designed to furnish a complete record of all fiction and selected nonfiction published in book, pamphlet, or broadside format through December 1977; and to present descriptions which will enable the reader to identify first printings and any other significant printings or editions. A landmark reference work.

Day, Bradford M. *The Checklist of Fantastic Literature in Paperbound Books.* Denver, NY: Science-Fiction & Fantasy Publications, 1965 [paper]; rpt. New York: Arno Press, 1975.

The only attempt at a complete survey of fantastic literature in paperbound books, and is of value for identifying material from the 19th and early 20th centuries.

—————. *The Supplemental Checklist of Fantastic Literature.* Denver, NY: Science-Fiction & Fantasy Publications, 1963 [paper]; rpt. New York: Arno Press, 1975.

A listing of approximately 3000 titles which supplement those in Bleiler's 1948 checklist.

Derleth, August. *Thirty Years of Arkham House 1939-1969.* Sauk City, WI: Arkham House, 1970.

Contains a brief history of the publishing firm and a bibliography comprising a checklist of publications through 1969 issued under the imprints of Arkham House, Mycroft & Moran, and Stanton & Lee.

Franson, Donald and Howard DeVore. *A History of the Hugo, Nebula and International Fantasy Awards.* [rev ed.] Dearborn Heights, MI: Howard DeVore, 1980 [paper].

This enlarged edition of a work first published in 1971 provides information on the winners and the nominees in each category of the awards, along with historical commentary.

Locke, George, ed. *Ferret Fantasy's Christmas Annual for 1972.* London: Ferret Fantasy, 1972 [paper].

Pages 29-76 comprise an annotated addendum to Bleiler's 1948 checklist and Day's 1963 checklist. The 300 titles cited were published mainly in Great Britain prior to 1948.

—————. *Ferret Fantasy's Christmas Annual for 1973.* London: Ferret Fantasy, 1974 [paper].

Pages 1-27 comprise an annotated addendum to the Bleiler and Day checklists. The nearly 200 titles were published prior to 1948.

Reginald, R. *Science Fiction and Fantasy Literature: A Checklist, 1700–1974 with Contemporary Science Fiction Authors II.* 2 vols. Detroit: Gale Research, 1979.

A listing of 15,884 English-language first editions of books and pamphlets in the field of science fiction, fantasy, and weird supernatural fiction. Also included are 1,443 biographical sketches on living and deceased writers of the modern period. The most comprehensive general checklist ever published, and a major contribution to scholarship in the field.

Schlobin, Roger C. *The Literature of Fantasy: A Comprehensive, Annotated Bibliography of Modern Fantasy Fiction.* New York: Garland, 1979.

An annotated checklist of over 1,000 works covering the period 1858–1979. A necessary tool for fantasy researchers.

Suvin, Darko. *Russian Science Fiction 1956-1974: A Bibliography.* 2nd ed. Elizabethtown, NY: Dragon Press, 1976.

Originally published in 1971, this second edition is an extended, enlarged and corrected version of the only English language checklist of modern Russian science fiction.

Tuck, Donald H. *The Encyclopedia of Science Fiction and Fantasy Through 1968.* 2 vols. Chicago: Advent, 1974, 1978.

Contains brief author biographies and annotated checklists of their writings. The scope of this compilation is immense, and it is likely to remain a standard reference tool for many years.

Tymn, Marshall B., Kenneth J. Zahorski and Robert H. Boyer. *Fantasy Literature: A Core Collection and Reference Guide.* New York: R. R. Bowker, 1979.

A guide to the works of high fantasy published since the end of the Victorian era. The core list contains 240 seminal works with substantive annotations, and a research aids section covers the full range of scholarly and fan activities within the field.

Waggoner, Diana. *The Hills of Faraway: A Guide to Fantasy.* New York: Atheneum, 1978.

A guide to the study of modern fantasy fiction with approximately 1000 annotated entries of which about three-fourths are fiction and the remainder are biographical and critical works.

Wells, Stuart W. III. *The Science Fiction and Heroic Fantasy Author Index.* Duluth, MN: Purple Unicorn Books, 1978.

A checklist of approximately 5000 titles by some 1000 authors published in hardcover and paperback in the U.S. from 1945 through mid-1978. An indispensable work for the period 1969-1978.

B. SUBJECT BIBLIOGRAPHIES

Clarke, I.F. *The Tale of the Future From the Beginning to the Present Day.* London: Library Association, 1961; 2nd ed. 1972 [paper].

The standard work on the tale of the future, which comprises "those ideal satires, ideal states, imaginary wars and invasions, political warnings and forecasts, interplanetary voyages and scientific romances—all located in an imaginary future period." The enlarged edition has been expanded to nearly 2300 entries, covering works published between 1644 and 1970 in the United Kingdom.

Locke, George. *Voyages in Space: A Bibliography of Interplanetary Fiction 1801-1914.* London: Ferret Fantasy, 1975 [paper].

Contains 263 fully annotated entries for books published in the English language before 1915 concerning interplanetary flight and/or descriptions of worlds other than Earth.

Rabiega, William A. *Environmental Fiction for Pedagogic Purposes.* Monticello, IL: Council for Planning Librarians, 1974. Exchange Bibliography 590 [paper].

An annotated bibliography of science fiction and fantasy novels and short stories with themes of ecology and environment.

Silverberg, Robert. *Drug Themes in Science Fiction.* Rockville, MD: National Institute on Drug Abuse, 1974 [paper].

An annotated checklist of approximately 75 novels and short stories with drug themes.

Weinberg, Robert E. and Edward P. Berglund. *Reader's Guide to the Cthulhu Mythos.* rev. ed. Albuquerque: Silver Scarab Press, 1973.

Cites published and unpublished fiction, poetry and non-fiction utilizing or commenting on the mythos.

C. ANTHOLOGY INDICES

Contento, William. *Index to Science Fiction Anthologies and Collections.* Boston: G. K. Hall, 1978.

A comprehensive listing of English-language sf anthologies and single author collections published through June 1977. Lists the contents of more than 1900 titles containing over 12,000 stories by approximately 2500 authors.

Tymn, Marshall B., et al. *Index to Stories in Thematic Anthologies of Science Fiction,* Boston: G. K Hall, 1978.

An index to 181 thematic anthologies of science fiction. Designed as a reference work for teachers constructing thematic units for SF classes, as an aid to acquisitions librarians desiring to add core titles to developing collections, and as a research tool for scholars in the field.

D. MAGAZINE INDICES

Day, Donald B. *Index to the Science-Fiction Magazines 1926-1950.* Portland, OR: Perri Press, 1952.

Indexes the contents of fifty-eight sf magazines from their first issues through December 1950. Only English language magazines are covered, and with the exception of three British titles, all are U.S. publications. A pioneer effort which remains the standard index for sf magazines of the period.

New England Science Fiction Association. *Index to the Science Fiction Magazines 1966-1970.* Cambridge, MA: New England Science Fiction Association, 1971; *The N.E.S.F.A. Index. Science Fiction Magazines: 1971-1972 and Original Anthologies: 1971-1972.* Cambridge, MA: NESFA, 1973 [paper]; *The N.E.S.F.A. Index. Science Fiction Magazines [1973]: and Original Anthologies [1973].* Cambridge, MA: NESFA, 1974 [paper]; *The N.E.S.F.A.*

Index: Science Fiction Magazines and Original Anthologies 1975. Cambridge, MA: NESFA, 1976 [paper] ; *The N.E.S.F.A. Index: Science Fiction Magazines and Original Anthologies 1976*. Cambridge, MA: NESFA, 1977 [paper].

The standard index to the science fiction and fantasy fiction magazines and original anthologies. Since 1966–70 index compiled by Anthony Lewis, issued annually by the New England Science Fiction Association.

Strauss, Erwin S. *The MIT Science Fiction Society's Index to the S-F Magazines, 1951-1965*. Cambridge, MA: The MIT Science Fiction Society, 1965.

Indexes the contents of 100 English language fantasy and science fiction magazines for the period.

SOURCES FOR SECONDARY MATERIALS

A. GENERAL BIBLIOGRAPHIES

Clareson, Thomas D. *Science Fiction Criticism: An Annotated Checklist*. Kent, OH: Kent State University Press, 1972.

A comprehensive guide to the critical literature on the sf genre published in English language books and periodicals prior to 1972. Contains approximately 800 entries arranged into nine sections.

Tymn, Marshall B. and Roger C. Schlobin. *The Year's Scholarship in Science Fiction and Fantasy: 1972-1975*. Kent, OH: Kent State University Press, 1979.

The chronological continuation of Thomas Clareson's *Science Fiction Criticism: An Annotated Checklist*. Annotates all American scholarship, selected British scholarship, and important items from major, established fanzines. Coded entries are arranged into the following categories: general studies, bibliography and reference, author studies and bibliographies, teaching and visual aids.

Tymn, Marshall B., Roger C. Schlobin and L.W. Currey. *A Research Guide to Science Fiction Studies: An Annotated Checklist of Primary and Secondary Sources for Fantasy and Science Fiction*. New York and London: Garland, 1977.

A comprehensive listing of the important research tools published in the U.S. and England through 1977. Contains over 400 annotated entries that span the entire range of sf scholarship including general surveys, histories, genre studies, author studies, bibliographies and indices, and journals. Included also is a special section on Ph.D. dissertations on science fiction.

B. SUBJECT STUDIES AND BIBLIOGRAPHIES

Berger, Harold L. *Science Fiction and the New Dark Age*. Bowling Green, OH: Bowling Green University Popular Press, 1976.

A study of the anti-utopian trend in contemporary science fiction organized into twelve thematic units.

Clarke, I.F. *Voices Prophesying War 1763-1984.* London: Oxford University Press, 1966.

The pioneering study of the literature of futuristic wars and war technology. Appended to the study is the most extensive listing of imaginary war fiction published to date.

Eichner, Henry M. *Atlantean Chronicles.* Alhambra, CA: Fantasy Publishing Company, 1971.

An informal study of theories concerning the location of Atlantis. Its bibliography is the most extensive listing to date of the Atlantis theme in fiction.

Glut, Donald F. *The Dracula Book.* Metuchen, NJ: Scarecrow Press, 1975.

A sketch of the vampire in Western tradition and its manifestation in the arts via the Dracula legend.

––––––. *The Frankenstein Legend: A Tribute to Mary Shelley and Boris Karloff.* Metuchen, NJ: Scarecrow Press, 1973.

The story of the Frankenstein monster in legend, literature, theater, motion pictures, television, radio, and comic books.

Gove, Philip Babcock. *The Imaginary Voyage in Prose Fiction. A History of Its Criticism and a Guide for Its Study, with an Annotated Check List of 215 Imaginary Voyages from 1700 to 1800.* New York: Columbia University Press, 1941; rpt. Arno Press, 1975.

A history of the criticism of the imaginary voyage, with an extensive annotated bibliography of imaginary voyages.

Green, Roger Lancelyn. *Into Other Worlds: Space-Flight in Fiction, from Lucian to Lewis.* London and New York: Abelard-Schuman, 1957; rpt. New York: Arno Press, 1975.

An attempt to describe the outstanding journeys to the moon and the planets in the writings of storytellers from Lucian the Greek near the beginning of the Christian era to C.S. Lewis. Contains a bibliography of works mentioned in the text covering the period 1634 to 1943.

Hillegas, Mark R. *The Future as Nightmare: H.G. Wells and the Anti-Utopians.* New York: Oxford University Press, 1967; rpt. Carbondale: Southern Illinois University Press, 1974.

The first systematic study of 20th century anti-utopian fiction.

Nicholson, Marjorie Hope. *Voyages to the Moon.* New York: Columbia University Press, 1948.

A standard source for analysis and summary of the pre-19th century cosmic voyage as English readers knew it in the 17th and 18th centuries. Appended is an important annotated bibliography of the literature of imaginary flight, plus a checklist of secondary material.

Walsh, Chad. *From Utopia to Nightmare.* New York and Evanston: Harper & Row, 1962; rpt. Westport, CT: Greenwood Press, 1972.

A study of the gradual decline of the utopian novel and its displacement by the dystopian or "inverted utopia."

C. GENERAL SURVEYS AND HISTORIES

Aldiss, Brian W. *Billion Year Spree: The History of Science Fiction.* London: Weidenfeld & Nicolson, 1973; rpt. New York: Schocken Books, 1974 [paper].

A general critical survey of the genre by a leading writer of science fiction.

Amis, Kingsley. *New Maps of Hell: A Survey of Science Fiction.* New York: Harcourt, Brace, 1960; rpt. Arno Press, 1975.

The first full-length study of the genre by a critic from outside the sf community. This study gave direction to current criticism of science fiction by emphasizing its role as an instrument of social diagnosis and warning.

Ash, Brian. *Faces of the Future: The Lessons of Science Fiction.* London: Elek Books, 1975.

A review of a wide-ranging selection of sf works to provide an informal, loosely-constructed account of the development of modern science fiction in its broadest aspects.

—————, ed. *The Visual Encyclopedia of Science Fiction.* New York: Harmony Books, 1977.

A comprehensive guide to the entire field of science fiction divided into four sections: a chronology of important events relevant to the development of the genre, sf themes, essays on science fiction as literature, and sf media and organizations.

Bailey, J.O. *Pilgrims Through Space and Time: Trends and Patterns in Scientific and Utopian Fiction.* New York: Argus Books, 1947; rpt. Westport, CT: Greenwood Press, 1972.

The pioneer critical study of the scientific and utopian romance in English. Emphasis is on fiction published prior to 1914. Still a standard work, its chief value being the thematic arrangement of the material.

Bretnor, Reginald, ed. *Modern Science Fiction: Its Meaning and Its Future.* New York: Coward-McCann, 1953.

One of the earliest comprehensive symposiums on modern science fiction. While partially dated, the essays by writers, critics and editors comprise an important document on science fiction's "golden age."

—————. *Science Fiction, Today and Tomorrow.* New York: Harper & Row, 1974.

An anthology of essays by sf writers about the nature of their genre, art and craft.

Carter, Lin. *Imaginary Worlds: The Art of Fantasy.* New York: Ballantine Books, 1973 [paper].

A historical survey of modern heroic fantasy from William Morris to the present. Includes coverage of major genre authors and analyzes their contribution to and influence on the genre.

Clareson, Thomas D., ed. *Extrapolation: A Science Fiction Newsletter, Volumes 1-10, December 1959-May 1969.* Boston: Gregg Press, 1978.

Reprint of the first ten volumes of the oldest established continuing journal devoted to the study of science fiction.

—————, ed. *Many Futures, Many Worlds: Theme and Form in Science Fiction.* Kent, OH: Kent State University Press, 1977.

A collection of essays approaching the study of science fiction from starting points as diverse as philosophy, mythology, theology, and technology as well as touching upon such established themes as time travel, lost races, and computerized governments.

—————. *SF: The Other Side of Realism: Essays on Modern Science Fiction.* Bowling Green, OH: Bowling Green University Popular Press, 1971.

From a multitude of critical viewpoints the contributors to this pioneer anthology illustrate the many ways in which the study of science fiction may be approached.

del Rey, Lester. *The World of Science Fiction 1926–1976: The History of a Subculture.* New York: Garland; Del Rey Books, 1979.

A survey of American science fiction divided into the major periods of its growth. Intended as an introductory guide to the literature and to those interacting forces which have influenced the development of the genre. ·

Delany, Samuel R. *The Jewel-Hinged Jaw: Notes on the Language of Science Fiction.* Elizabethtown, NY: Dragon Press, 1977.

Critical essays on sf critical theory, writing sf, and author studies. The book's major essay is an extended analysis of Ursula K. Le Guin's *The Dispossessed.*

Franklin, H. Bruce, ed. *Future Perfect: American Science Fiction of the Nineteenth Century.* New York: Oxford University Press, 1966; rev. ed. 1978.

An anthology of 19th century American science fiction with extensive critical commentary by the editor which remains the most perceptive study of science fiction written by American literary figures of the period.

Gunn, James. *Alternate Worlds: The Illustrated History of Science Fiction.* Englewood Cliffs, NJ: Prentice-Hall, 1975; rpt. New York: A&W Visual Library, 1976 [paper].

An informed study of the scientific, social and philosophical climate which brought forth and shaped science fiction from its early beginnings to the present.

Irwin, W.R. *The Game of the Impossible: The Rhetoric of Fantasy.* Urbana: University of Illinois Press, 1976.

An examination of the common characteristics of fantasies written between 1880 and 1957.

Ketterer, David. *New Worlds for Old: The Apocalyptic Imagination, Science Fiction, and American Literature.* Bloomington and London, 1974.

Maintains that because of a common apocalyptic quality and a common grounding in the romance, science fiction and mainstream American literature share many significant features.

Knight, Damon. *In Search of Wonder: Essays on Modern Science Fiction.* Chicago: Advent, 1956; rev. ed. 1967.

Critical book reviews written by Knight for *F&SF* from 1952 to 1955. The revised edition adds material published during 1956-60.

—————, ed. *Turning Points: Essays on the Art of Science Fiction.* New York: Harper & Row, 1977.

Twenty-three essays on science fiction culled from diverse sources spanning nearly three decades of critical statements on the genre.

Kyle, David. *A Pictorial History of Science Fiction.* London: Hamlyn, 1976.

Lacks the scope of Gunn's *Alternate Worlds* but is still one of the best illustrated histories of science fiction.

Lovecraft, Howard Phillips. *Supernatural Horror in Literature.* New York: Ben Abramson, 1945; rpt. Dover, 1973 [paper].

A critical survey of the history of horror fiction by the most important American supernaturalist since Poe.

Lundwall, Sam J. *Science Fiction: An Illustrated History.* New York: Grosset & Dunlap, 1978.

A broad view of the themes, writers, and developments of the genre on an international scale, embracing science fiction in Europe, Latin America, Asia, and Australia, as well as in the United States and Britain.

—————. *Science Fiction: What It's All About.* New York: Ace Books, 1971 [paper].

An informal historical survey of science fiction aimed at the popular market.

Moskowitz, Sam. *The Immortal Storm: A History of Science-Fiction Fandom.* Atlanta: Burwell, 1951; rpt. Atlanta Science Fiction Organization Press, 1954; rpt. Westport, CT: Hyperion Press, 1974.

A personal view of fandom, but still the best picture of this small but influential group of sf activists. Contains much historical data on the fanzines of the 1930s and 1940s unavailable elsewhere.

Mullen, R.D. and Darko Suvin, eds. *Science-Fiction Studies: Selected Articles on Science Fiction 1973-1975.* Boston: Gregg Press, 1976.

Fifty essays selected from *Science-Fiction Studies,* one of the major international scholarly journals devoted to the serious study of science fiction.

—————. *Science-Fiction Studies: Selected Articles on Science Fiction 1976-1977.* Boston: Gregg Press, 1978.

Thirty-eight essays published in SFS during the period.

Nicholls, Peter, ed. *Foundation: The Review of Science Fiction, Numbers 1-8, March 1972-March 1975.* Boston: Gregg Press, 1978.

Reprint of the first eight numbers of the most important British journal on science fiction.

————. *Science Fiction at Large: A Collection of Essays, by Various Hands, About the Interface Between Science Fiction and Reality.* London: Gollancz, 1976; rpt. New York: Harper & Row, 1977.

A collection of lectures delivered at the Institute of Contemporary Arts in London, 1975.

Panshin, Alexei and Cory. *SF in Dimension: A Book of Explorations.* Chicago: Advent, 1976.

Based on a series of essays written by Alexei for *Fantastic Stories,* in which he attempts to define the nature of science fiction as a literary form.

Penzoldt, Peter. *The Supernatural in Fiction.* London: Peter Nevill, 1952; rpt. New York: Humanities Press, 1965.

A survey of English science fiction of the 18th and 19th centuries.

Philmus, Robert M. *Into the Unknown: The Evolution of Science Fiction from Francis Godwin to H. G. Wells.* Berkeley: University of California Press, 1970.

A survey of English science fiction of the 18th and 19th centuries.

Prickett, Stephen. *Victorian Fantasy.* Bloomington: Indiana University Press, 1979.

A critical study of the major writers and works of 19th century fantasy, illustrating how the fantastic flourished in the popular and comic tradition of the period.

Rabkin, Eric S. *The Fantastic in Literature.* Princeton: Princeton University Press, 1976.

An exploration of the nature and uses of the fantastic following from the recognition that it is not the unreal which is fantastic but the unreal in a particular context.

Rose, Mark, ed. *Science Fiction: A Collection of Critical Essays.* Englewood Cliffs, NJ: Prentice-Hall, 1976.

Essays reprinted from various scholarly and academic sources, most of which are highly theoretical.

Rottensteiner, Franz. *The Fantasy Book: An Illustrated History from Dracula to Tolkien.* London: Thames & Hudson, 1978.

An illustrated complement to *The Science Fiction Book.* Less a coherent history than a collection of mini-chapters covering an array of fantasy subjects and themes.

—————. *The Science Fiction Book: An Illustrated History.* London: Thames and Hudson, 1975.

Less a coherent history than a collection of fifty mini-chapters covering an array of sf themes, subjects, and popular writers. Copiously illustrated.

Scholes, Robert. *Structural Fabulation: An Essay on the Fiction of the Future.* Notre Dame: University of Notre Dame Press, 1975.

Based on four lectures delivered at the University of Notre Dame in 1974, this critical and theoretical study of science fiction relates the genre to the literary traditions and to modern intellectual history, arguing for the seriousness of science fiction and its value as literature.

————— and Eric S. Rabkin. *Science Fiction: History, Science, Vision.* New York: Oxford University Press, 1977.

This textbook survey of science fiction offers a synthesis of the historical, scientific and thematic elements that comprise the genre.

Warner, Harry, Jr. *All Our Yesterdays: An Informal History of Science Fiction Fandom in the Forties.* Chicago: Advent, 1969.

A valuable work for its numerous biographical sketches of prominent fans and commentary upon fan activities.

Wolfe, Gary K. *The Known and the Unknown: The Iconography of Science Fiction.* Kent, OH: Kent State University Press, 1979.

A focused critical study which is concerned with the problem of how science fiction images (spaceships, the city, robots, monsters) have developed into "icons," and how these icons are used within specific works and within the genre as a whole.

Wollheim, Donald A. *The Universe Makers: Science Fiction Today.* New York: Harper & Row, 1971.

A personal statement of the place of science fiction in literature via discussions of the most important writers of the genre.

D. MAGAZINE SURVEYS AND HISTORIES

Ashley, Michael, ed. *The History of the Science Fiction Magazine.* 4 vols. London: New English Library, 1974–76; rpt. Chicago: Contemporary Books, 1978.

The first four volumes of a projected five-volume series, each to examine a decade of the sf magazine from 1926 to 1976. More an anthology of science fiction than a history, each volume features ten selections from the magazines, prefaced by a historical essay.

Brown, Charles N. and Dena Brown. *Locus: The Newspaper of the Science Fiction Field, 1968-1977.* Boston: Gregg Press, 1978.

Reprint of the single, most authoritative source of information about the science fiction field. Contains a valuable, comprehensive index to the contents of this ten-year compilation.

Carter, Paul A. *The Creation of Tomorrow: Fifty Years of Magazine Science Fiction.* New York: Columbia University Press, 1977.

A study of the major themes of pulp science fiction. Each theme is amply illustrated with excerpts from the works of the field's major writers.

Rogers, Alva. *A Requiem for Astounding.* Chicago: Advent, 1964.

A nostalgic history of *Astounding Science Fiction* magazine from its birth as *Astounding Stories of Super-Science* in 1930 until its metamorphosis into *Analog* in 1960.

Weinberg, Robert. *The Weird Tales Story.* West Linn, OR: FAX Collector's Editions, 1977.

An informal history of *Weird Tales* (1923-1954), the most influential fantasy magazine of the 1920s and 1930s.

Wertham, Fredric. *The World of Fanzines: A Special Form of Communication.* Carbondale: Southern Illinois University Press, 1973.

An examination of the content, circulation, and methods of production of fanzines, and their influence as a manifestation of creativity apart from "little magazines" and underground newspapers.

E. BOOK REVIEWS

Hall, H.W. *Science Fiction Book Review Index, 1923-1973.* Detroit: Gale Research, 1975.

A complete record of books reviewed in science fiction and fantasy magazines. Beginning in 1970 coverage is extended to include general, library and amateur magazines as well as specialized sources like *Extrapolation.* Annual supplements are issued.

AUTHOR STUDIES & BIBLIOGRAPHIES

A. COLLECTIVE

Aldiss, Brian W. and Harry Harrison, eds. *Hell's Cartographers: Some Personal Histories of Science Fiction Writers.* London: Weidenfield and Nicolson, 1975.

Autobiographical sketches by six post-war sf writers: Bester, Knight, Pohl, Silverberg, Harrison, and Aldiss.

Clareson, Thomas D., ed. *Voices for the Future: Essays on Major Science Fiction Writers.* Vol I. Bowling Green: Bowling Green University Popular Press, 1976.

A collection of critical essays which concern writers whose careers had begun by the end of World War II.

Clareson, Thomas D., ed. *Voices for the Future: Essays on Major Science Fiction Writers.* Vol. II. Bowling Green, OH: Bowling Green University Popular Press, 1979.

A continuation of Clareson's series of critical anthologies on major writers of science fiction. Volume two gives attention to individuals whose careers began in the 1950s.

De Camp, L. Sprague. *Literary Swordsmen and Sorcerers: The Makers of Heroic Fantasy*. Sauk City, WI: Arkham House, 1976.

The evolution of sword-and-sorcery fantasy through biographical sketches of its leading practitioners whose works were central to the growth of the genre.

Hillegas, Mark R., ed. *Shadows of Imagination: The Fantasies of C.S. Lewis, J.R.R. Tolkien, and Charles Williams*. Carbondale: Southern Illinois University Press, 1969; rpt. 1976; new ed. 1979 [paper].

Essays by academic critics on the works of three important fantasists.

Manlove, C.N. *Modern Fantasy: Five Studies*. Cambridge, MA and London: Cambridge University Press, 1975.

A literary analysis of Charles Kingsley, George MacDonald, C.S. Lewis, J.R.R. Tolkien, and Mervyn Peake.

Moskowitz, Sam. *Explorers of the Infinite: Shapers of Science Fiction*. Cleveland: World, 1963; rpt. Westport, CT: Hyperion Press, 1974.

A critical and biographical survey of eighteen early writers from the 17th century to the 1930s.

————. *Seekers of Tomorrow: Masters of Modern Science Fiction*. Cleveland: World, 1966; rpt. Westport, CT: Hyperion Press, 1974.

A companion volume to *Explorers of the Infinite*. Literary profiles of twenty-one authors.

Platt, Charles. *Dream Makers: The Uncommon People Who Write Science Fiction*. New York: Berkley, 1980 [paper].

A collection of 29 biographical profiles of contemporary SF writers based on taped interviews. Bibliographic notes follow each profile. One of the best sources of up-to-date information on some of the field's major practitioners.

Riley, Dick, ed. *Critical Encounters: Writers and Themes in Science Fiction*. New York: Frederick Ungar, 1978.

The keynote volume for Ungar's new "Recognitions" series, which will give serious attention to the literary achievements of well-known SF writers. These essays deal with the works of Asimov, Bradbury, Herbert, Le Guin, Clarke, Delany, Sturgeon, Heinlein, with an essay on four women writers, Joanna Russ, James Tiptree, Jr., Sondra Dorman, and Judith Merril.

B. INDIVIDUAL

(BRIAN W. ALDISS)

Mathews, Richard. *Aldiss Unbound: The Science Fiction of Brian W. Aldiss*. San Bernardino, CA: Borgo Press, 1977 [paper].

An examination of the full span of Aldiss' career, from his earliest fiction to his latest published novel, *The Malacia Tapestry*.

(ISAAC ASIMOV)

Miller, Marjorie M. *Isaac Asimov: A Checklist of Works Published in the United States, March 1939-May 1972.* Kent, OH: Kent State University Press, 1972.

A chronological checklist of Asimov's fiction and non-fiction.

Olander, Joseph D. and Martin Harry Greenberg, eds. *Isaac Asimov.* Writers of the 21st Century. New York: Taplinger, 1977.

Critical essays on the science fiction of Isaac Asimov.

Patrouch, Joseph F., Jr. *The Science Fiction of Isaac Asimov.* Garden City: Doubleday, 1974.

A perceptive study which provides an excellent comparison of Asimov's themes and literary style.

(JAMES BLISH)

Stableford, Brian M. *A Clash of Symbols: The Triumph of James Blish.* San Bernardino, CA: Borgo Press, 1979 [paper].

A discussion of Blish's significant work, from his first published story, "Let the Finder Beware" (1949), to *Black Easter* (1968).

(RAY BRADBURY)

Nolan, William F. *The Ray Bradbury Companion: A Life and Career History, Photolog, and Comprehensive Checklist of Writings With Facsimiles From Ray Bradbury's Unpublished and Uncollected Works in all Media.* Detroit: Gale Research, 1975.

This visually impressive book provides a wealth of data on a writer who has produced what is perhaps the single best-known 20th century science fiction book, *The Martian Chronicles*.

Olander, Joseph D. and Martin Harry Greenberg, eds. *Ray Bradbury.* Writers of the 21st Century. New York: Taplinger, 1979.

Critical essays on the works of Ray Bradbury.

Slusser, George Edgar. *The Bradbury Chronicles.* San Bernardino, CA: Borgo Press, 1977 [paper].

A critical analysis of Bradbury's fiction, useful especially for the synopses of numerous short stories.

(JOHN BRUNNER)

De Bolt, Joe, ed. *The Happening Worlds of John Brunner: Critical Explorations in Science Fiction.* Port Washington, NY: Kennikat Press, 1975.

A collection of interdisciplinary essays which examines Brunner's work for such qualities as technological accuracy and political radicalism as well as literary precedents and style.

(EDGAR RICE BURROUGHS)

Heins, Henry Hardy. *A Golden Anniversary Bibliography of Edgar Rice Burroughs.* West Kingston, RI: Donald M. Grant, 1964.

Still the standard bibliography of the writings of Burroughs. It identifies in detail all the known book and magazine versions of his work, including information for the identification of first editions and reprints of his books.

Lupoff, Richard A. *Barsoom: Edgar Rice Burroughs and the Martian Vision.* Baltimore: Mirage Press, 1976.

A critical study of the eleven works which comprise the Martian cycle.

—————. *Edgar Rice Burroughs: Master of Adventure.* New York: Canaveral Press, 1965; rev. ed. Ace Books, 1968 [paper]; rpt. 1975.

The first book-length study of Burroughs and his work.

Porges, Irwin. *Edgar Rice Burroughs: The Man Who Created Tarzan.* Provo, UT: Brigham Young University Press, 1975.

An extensive, possibly definitive biography of Burroughs.

(ARTHUR C. CLARKE)

Olander, Joseph D. and Martin Harry Greenberg. *Arthur C. Clarke.* Writers of the 21st Century. New York: Taplinger, 1977.

Critical essays on the science fiction of Arthur C. Clarke.

Rabkin, Eric S. *Arthur C. Clarke.* rev. ed. Starmont Reader's Guide No. 1. Mercer Island, WA: Starmont House, 1980.

An introduction to the works of Clarke, containing a biography, chapters on the major works, primary and secondary bibliographies.

Slusser, George Edgar. *The Space Odysseys of Arthur C. Clarke.* San Bernardino, CA: Borgo Press, 1977 [paper].

A complete survey of Clarke's development as an sf writer.

(SAMUEL R. DELANY)

Slusser, George Edgar. *The Delany Intersection: Samuel R. Delany Considered As a Writer of Semi-Precious Words.* San Bernardino, CA: Borgo Press, 1977 [paper].

A critical evaluation of the works of Samuel R. Delany.

(PHILIP K. DICK)

Gillespie, Bruce, ed. *Philip K. Dick: Electric Shepherd.* Melbourne, Australia: Norstrilia Press, 1975 [paper].

A collection of critical essays on the science fiction of Philip K. Dick collected from the pages of *SF Commentary*. Features a checklist of Dick's book and magazine fiction compiled by Fred Patten.

(HARLAN ELLISON)

Slusser, George Edgar. *Harlan Ellison: Unrepentant Harlequin.* San Bernardino, CA: Borgo Press, 1977 [paper].

A literary study of Ellison's fiction and non-fiction.

Swigart, Leslie Kay. *Harlan Ellison: A Bibliographical Checklist.* Dallas: Williams, 1973 [paper].

A descriptive checklist of Ellison's fiction and non-fiction published in English and foreign language books and periodicals through April 1973.

(PHILIP JOSÉ FARMER)

Brizzi, Mary T. *Philip José Farmer.* Starmont Reader's Guide No. 3. Mercer Island, WA: Starmont House, 1980.

An introduction to the works of Farmer, containing a biography, chapters on the major works, primary and secondary bibliographies.

(JOE HALDEMAN)

Gordon, Joan. *Joe Haldeman.* Starmont Reader's Guide No. 4. Mercer Island, WA: Starmont House, 1980.

An introduction to the works of Haldeman, containing a biography, chapters on the major works, primary and secondary bibliographies.

(ROBERT A. HEINLEIN)

Olander, Joseph D. and Martin Harry Greenberg. *Robert A. Heinlein.* Writers of the 21st Century. New York: Taplinger, 1978.

Critical essays on the science fiction of Robert A. Heinlein.

Owings, Mark. *Robert A. Heinlein: A Bibliography.* Baltimore: Croatan House, 1973 [paper].

A checklist of Heinlein's fiction and non-fiction published in books and periodicals.

Panshin, Alexei. *Heinlein in Dimension: A Critical Analysis.* Chicago: Advent, 1968.

The only book-length study of Heinlein's writings published to date.

Slusser, George Edgar. *Robert A. Heinlein: Stranger in His Own Land.* 2nd ed. San Bernardino, CA: Borgo Press, 1977 [paper].

Examines seven of Heinlein's recent novels, from *Double Star* to *Time Enough for Love.*

—————. *The Classic Years of Robert A. Heinlein.* San Bernardino, CA: Borgo Press, 1977 [paper].

Examines Heinlein's classic years, from the publication of "Life-Line" in 1939 to *The Moon Is a Harsh Mistress.*

(FRANK HERBERT)

Miller, David M. *Frank Herbert.* Starmont Reader's Guide No. 5. Mercer Island, WA: Starmont House, 1980.

An introduction to the works of Herbert, containing a biography, chapters on the major works, primary and secondary bibliographies.

(URSULA K. LE GUIN)

DeBolt, Joe, ed. *Ursula K. Le Guin: Voyager to Inner Lands and to Outer Space.* Port Washington, NY: Kennikat Press, 1979.

The first collection of original essays on Le Guin. The contributors to this volume bring a multidisciplinary perspective to the analysis of Le Guin's works.

Olander, Joseph D. and Martin Harry Greenberg. *Ursula K. Le Guin.* Writers of the 21st Century. New York: Taplinger, 1978.

Critical essays on the science fiction and fantasy of Ursula K. Le Guin.

Slusser, George Edgar. *The Farthest Shores of Ursula K. Le Guin.* San Bernardino, CA: Borgo Press, 1977 [paper].

An examination of Le Guin's work, with particular attention to *The Left Hand of Darkness, The Dispossessed,* and the Earthsea trilogy.

(FRITZ LEIBER)

Frane, Jeff. *Fritz Leiber.* Starmont House Reader's Guide No. 8. Mercer Island, WA: Starmont House, 1980.

An introduction to the works of Leiber, containing a biography, chapters on the major works, primary and secondary bibliographies.

(HOWARD PHILLIPS LOVECRAFT)

De Camp, L. Sprague. *Lovecraft: A Biography.* Garden City: Doubleday, 1975.

The first full-length, and to date the most comprehensive, biography of Lovecraft. Extensive checklist of primary and secondary sources.

Owings, Mark with Jack L. Chalker. *The Revised H.P. Lovecraft Bibliography.* Baltimore: Mirage Press, 1973 [paper].

The most comprehensive checklist of writings by and about Lovecraft in English and foreign language books and professional and amateur magazines.

Schweitzer, Darrell. *The Dream Quest of H. P. Lovecraft.* San Bernardino, CA: Borgo Press, 1978.

An assessment of the writings of the best American writer of weird and supernatural fiction since Edgar Allan Poe.

St. Armand, Barton Levi. *The Roots of Horror In the Fiction of H.P. Lovecraft.* Elizabethtown, NY: Dragon Press, 1977.

The first book-length study in English of the greatest writer of supernatural horror fiction of the 20th century.

(ANDRE NORTON)

Turner, David G. *The First Editions of Andre Norton.* Menlo Park, CA: David G. Turner, 1974 [paper].

A chronological checklist of Norton's science fiction and fantasy writings. See also the checklist in *The Many Worlds of Andre Norton,* ed. Roger Elwood (Chilton Books, 1974).

(EDWARD ELMER SMITH)

Ellik, Ronald and William Evans. *The Universes of E.E. Smith.* Chicago: Advent, 1966.

A concordance to the major writings, the Lensman series and the Skylark series. Includes a checklist of Smith's works compiled by Al Lewis.

(JOHN RONALD REUEL TOLKIEN)

Carpenter, Humphrey. *Tolkien: A Biography.* Boston: Houghton Mifflin, 1977.

At present the only source of much biographical data, but Grotta's life should also be consulted (see below).

Foster, Robert. *The Complete Guide to Middle-Earth: From The Hobbit to The Silmarillion.* New York: Del Rey Books, 1978.

Originally published as *A Guide to Middle-Earth* (Mirage, 1971), this essential reference book is a concordance to *The Lord of the Rings,* containing a glossary of all the proper names that appear therein, as well as in *The Hobbit, The Adventures of Tom Bombadil,* and *The Road Goes Ever On.*

Grotta, Daniel. *The Biography of J.R.R. Tolkien: Architect of Middle-Earth.* 2nd ed. Philadelphia: Running Press, 1978.

A readable and accurate biography of Tolkien. The book is of value for its account of Tolkien's literary reputation, the controversy surrounding the publication of LOTR in America, and the growth of the Tolkien cult. Originally published as *J.R.R. Tolkien: Architect of Middle Earth* in 1976.

Kocher, Paul. *Master of Middle-earth: The Achievement of J.R.R. Tolkien.* Boston: Houghton Mifflin, 1972.

An excellent study of Tolkien's major fiction. Especially illuminating are the two chapters which discuss the cosmic order and the races that make up the Fellowship of the Ring.

Mathews, Richard. *Lightning from a Clear Sky: Tolkien, The Trilogy, and The Silmarillion.* San Bernardino, CA: Borgo Press, 1978.

An examination of the entire span of Tolkien's fiction, from his early prequel, *The Hobbit* (1937), to the past posthumous culmination of his work, *The Silmarillion* (1977).

Tyler, J. E. A. *The New Tolkien Companion.* New York: St. Martin, 1979.

A revision of Tyler's *The Tolkien Companion* (1976), which was a compilation of almost every known fact, name, "foreign" word, date, and etymological allusion to appear in Tolkien's history of Middle Earth, with a detailed guide to the various Elvish writing systems, together with explanatory maps, charts, and genealogical tables developed by the compiler. The updated and revised edition incorporates material from *The Silmarillion*.

West, Richard C. *Tolkien Criticism: An Annotated Checklist.* Kent, OH: Kent State University Press, 1970.

A checklist of writings by and about Tolkien.

(JACK VANCE)

Levak, J. H. and Tim Underwood. *Fantasms: A Bibliography of the Literature of Jack Vance.* San Francisco: Underwood/Miller, 1978.

A complete listing of the English-language writings of Jack Vance.

(JULES VERNE)

Chesneauz, Jean. *The Political and Social Ideas of Jules Verne.* London: Thames and Hudson, 1972.

Relates Verne's "voyage extraordinaires" to the political and social theories of 19th-century France.

Costello, Peter. *Jules Verne: Inventor of Science Fiction.* London: Hodder and Stoughton, 1978.

Includes details of Verne's life not enlarged upon by Jean Jules-Verne (see below). Contains numerous plot summaries useful to the researcher not fully acquainted with Verne's work.

Jules-Verne, Jean. *Jules Verne: A Biography.* New York: Taplinger, 1976.

This work by Verne's grandson was originally published in French in 1973 and should be considered the standard biography.

(KURT VONNEGUT, JR.)

Goldsmith, David H. *Kurt Vonnegut: Fantasist of Fire and Ice.* Bowling Green, OH: Bowling Green University Popular Press, 1972 [paper].

An examination of Vonnegut's themes and literary techniques with an assessment of the reasons for his acceptance as a writer of importance.

Klinkowitz, Jerome and John Somer, eds. *The Vonnegut Statement.* New York: Delacorte Press, 1973.

An assessment of Vonnegut the public figure and literary phenomenon and of his writings and literary significance twenty years after the publication of his first book.

Pieratt, Asa B., Jr. and Jerome Klinkowitz. *Kurt Vonnegut, Jr.: A Descriptive Bibliography and Annotated Secondary Checklist.* Hamden, CT: Archon Books, 1974.

The most comprehensive bibliography of writings by and about Vonnegut to date.

(HERBERT GEORGE WELLS)

Bergonzi, Bernard. *The Early H.G.Wells: A study of the Scientific Romances.* Manchester: Manchester University Press, 1961.

A sensitive study of Wells' imaginative development during his formative years.

Hammond, J.R. *Herbert George Wells: An Annotated Bibliography of His Works.* New York: Garland, 1977.

A descriptive bibliography of the works of H.G. Wells and the most comprehensive listing on Wells published to date.

Mackenzie, Norman and Jeanne. *The Time Traveller: The Life of H.G. Wells.* London: Weidenfield and Nicolson, 1973; rpt. as *H.G. Wells: A Biography.* New York: Simon and Schuster, 1973.

An indispensable biography based in part on unrestricted access to the Wells Archive at the University of Illinois at Champaign-Urbana.

Suvin, Darko with Robert M. Philmus, eds. *H.G. Wells and Modern Science Fiction.* Lewisburg: Bucknell University Press, 1977.

Essays on the theme that modern science fiction orginates with Wells. Essential reading for students of Wells.

(ROGER ZELAZNY)

Yoke, Carl B. *Roger Zelazny.* Starmont Reader's Guide No. 2. West Linn, OR: Starmont House, 1979.

An introduction to the works of Zelazny, containing a biography, chapters on the major works, primary and secondary bibliographies.

Fandom

Joe Siclari

SCIENCE FICTION FANDOM
A HISTORY OF AN UNUSUAL HOBBY

INTRODUCTION

In the 1970s, science fiction fandom came of age. Fandom was active on a world-wide scale. It was large, semi-organized, and it carried considerable financial clout in the publishing field. Typical of the scope of current fan activity is the World Science Fiction Convention (worldcon), the highlight of the science fiction fan year. The worldcons are run under the constitution of the World Science Fiction Society (Unincorporated), which consists of all the members of that year's annual convention. In this decade worldcons have been held in five different countries on three continents, with attendance growing from 620 in 1970 at Heidelberg to 6300 in 1978 at Phoenix. The annual Science Fiction Achievement Awards, commonly called the Hugos, are voted on by members of each worldcon and are considered strong selling points by both authors and publishers.

Although it might seem natural to those who now enter science fiction fandom that it exerts a strong influence on the science fiction field through its awards, its conventions and its development of writers and editors, this has not always been true. The current wide range of fan activities is a development of recent years. Previously, fan activities had ranged from that of a normal hobbyist to, at its most concentrated, that of a small sub- or counter-culture in which fans, at times, tried to live the ideals exemplified in the stories they were reading.

This essay is intended as a general outline of science fiction fandom. There exists at present no comprehensive history of the fan movement, although some focused historical treatments have been included in the recommended reading list. Because of space constraints there has been no attempt to include information on fandom outside the United States other than those people and activities which had a direct and major effect in the U. S. It should be mentioned, however, that fandom worldwide, especially in recent years, is as active as that in the United States.

PRE-FANDOM

Just as modern science fiction is normally dated from the publication of the first science fiction magazine, *Amazing Stories* in April, 1926, fandom is normally dated from the issuance of the first fan magazine (fanzine) in 1930. Various claims have been made for the first fanzine but it is generally conceded to be *Comet* (later *Cosmology*) published for the Science Correspondence Club by Ray Palmer (more about him later).

And just as science fiction had its precursers, so did fandom. In his excellent *All Our Yesterdays* (see bibliography), Harry Warner, Jr., cites a variety of near-miss fans who were born too early.

A case could be made for considering the Byron-Keats-Shelly-Wollenstonecraft group, because, from their late-night story tellings came several works, most notably of course the story of the modern Prometheus, *Frankenstein*.

The most famous is Lewis Carroll who, for the amusement of himself and his friends, bound together writings of both a fantastic and a mundane nature in an odd conglomeration of magazines. These sound very much like the familiar contents of today's fanzines. And their titles are reminiscent also: *The Comet, The Rosebud, The Star* and others.

Possibly the most accurate prophecy of the fandom to come was the activities of Howard Phillips Lovecraft and his circle of correspondents. Lovecraft was an avid hobbyist on a wide range of subjects. He wrote about Rome and chemistry and ghosts and astronomy, often publishing these himself by hectograph or even with carbon paper. He naturally became involved in amateur journalism (ayjay). In 1914, he joined the United Amateur Press Association (UAPA), and became a key figure as he plunged into the ayjay political wars of the time. Through UAPA, the Lovecraft circle started as he met such fellow afficianados of fantastic literature as Clark Ashton Smith, W. Paul Cook, Samuel Loveman, Frank Belknap Long and others. They corresponded, wrote articles and fiction, published, feuded, collected and visited each other, engaging in all the activities of later fans.

Lovecraft's correspondence was massive. He hand-wrote thousands of letters, some dozens of pages long, often to would-be writers asking his critical opinion who later became members of the circle. Robert Bloch, Duane Rimel and Robert E. Howard came into the circle in this manner. Lovecraft's most enduring legacy was the creation of the Cthulhu mythos to which others have added. He and the others often wrote each other into their stories, frequently dying brutally under slightly changed names.

Although HPL was the motivating force of the circle, it was more as the leader of a group of peers rather than the glorification he is given by the current Lovecraft fans. If he had lived to participate in the early science fiction cons, HPL would probably have been a central figure. Unfortunately, he died on March 15, 1937. Despite the efforts of August Derleth and Donald Wandrei, with its center gone, the circle began to fade as the members began to gravitate towards other interests.

All of these and others existed without any real relationship to each other or to later fandom, although the Lovecraft Circle did later overlap.

THE BEGINNINGS   1926-1939

In 1926, *Amazing Stories*, published by Hugo Gernsback as the world's first science fiction magazine, began a column of letters from readers with comments on stories, entitled "Discussions." In a short time the letterhacks, as they came to be called, were writing to each other. Soon, they were ready to organize.

The first known science fiction clubs were started in 1929. The first was the Science Correspondence Club, organized by Ray Palmer. As the name implies, the group was organized mainly to discuss science. Its official organ was *The Comet*. Its concentration on science shows the influence of Hugo Gernsback's promulgation that "scientifiction" should primarily promote science rather than adventure.

Early in 1929, Gernsback lost control of *Amazing Stories* and sent out an advertisement announcing the start of a new magazine. In fact, he came out with two new magazines. The first issue of *Science Wonder Stories* is dated June 1929, and the first issue of *Air Wonder Stories* is dated July 1929. Gernsback thereby became the founder of the first competition to the magazine he had started. (In fact, Gernsback was the founder of the first *six* magazines in the field; he also started *Amazing Stories Annual* in 1927, *Amazing Stories Quarterly* in 1928, and *Science Wonder Stories Quarterly* in 1929.)

Through the new *Science Wonder Stories*, several New York City readers came to start the first local fan club, The Scienceers, whose first president was Warren Fitzgerald, the only black in fandom in its formative years. The Scienceers also published a fanzine, *The Planet*, under editor Allen Glasser. Among the members of the Scienceers were Julius Schwartz and Mortimer Weisinger, both later prominent in the comics field. The Scienceers collapsed after only two years, as fan clubs often do. Then in January 1932, Schwartz and Weisinger published the first of the major fanzines, *The Time Traveller*, with Allen Glasser again as editor. *The Time Traveller* lasted only nine issues but it forecast the type of fanzine to come. Its first issue contained a "complete" list of the fantastic films made to that date, compiled by Forrest J Ackerman. It ran indices to the professional magazines, gossip and news about fans, writers and magazines. It started as a mimeographed publication but by the third issue it had changed to a hand-set printed publication when Conrad H. Ruppert gave additional help and loaned his printing press. *The Time Traveller* died in the throes of fandom's first great controversy when Glasser was accused of plagiarism and of stealing a story plot from Weisinger and selling it to *Wonder Stories* in a contest.

In other parts of the country, other fans were also publishing. In Cleveland, Jerome Siegel and Joseph Shuster were publishing an aptly titled zine—*Science Fiction*. Several professionals wrote for *Science Fiction* and its five issues are rare collector's items. This team later was responsible for a more memorable creation; they were the originators of a comic book character named Superman. In California there was also activity. In 1932, Ackerman founded a group called the Fantasy Fans' Fraternity in San Francisco, the first of numerous west coast groups.

In September 1932, several fans, among them Schwartz, Ackerman and Ruppert, joined forces to publish *Science Fiction Digest*. This fanzine started out resembling the better issues of *The Time Traveller* and got better, including in nearly every issue biographies of professionals, reviews, news, discussions of current stories and original fiction by writers such as A. Merritt, Clark Ashton Smith, C. L. Moore, and David H. Keller, M. D. Typical were collaborative or round-robin stories. Most famous is "Cosmos," a novel-length round-robin by A. Merritt, E. E. Smith, Ralph Milne Farley, David H. Keller, Otis Adelbert Kline, Arthur J. Burks, E. Hoffmann Price, P. Schuyler Miller, Rae Winters, John W. Campbell, Jr., Edmund Hamilton, Francis Flagg, Bob Olsen, J. Harvey Haggard, Raymond A. Palmer, Lloyd Eshbach, Abner Gelula, and Eando Binder. In 1934, the name was changed to *Fantasy Magazine* and it continued until 1937.

Another fanzine, *The Fantasy Fan,* was edited by a teenager, Charles D. Hornig, for 18 monthly issues from September 1933 to February 1935. *The Fantasy Fan* was mainly aimed at the weird fiction field and carried poetry and fiction by Lovecraft, Smith, Derleth, Keller and H. Rider Haggard. It is also the zine in which a fan named Bob Tucker made his first appearance. Mainly, however, *The Fantasy Fan* is important because an issue of it was sent to Hugo Gernsbach who, on the basis of this sample, hired the seventeen-year-old Hornig to edit *Wonder Stories.*

Clubs were quickly born and as quickly died in the 1930s. It seemed that nearly anytime two readers met they started a club (and sometimes, one of the two persons was fictitious—a hoax). It was not until Gernsback again showed an interest in his readers that a lasting organization was started. In the May 1934 issue of *Wonder Stories,* The Science Fiction League (SFL) was presented to the readers. This was a full-blown international organization which any reader could join. In a four-page editorial Gernsback called the SFL a "non-commercial membership organization for the furtherance and betterment of the art of science fiction." The magazine would carry club news and membership information so that local chapters could be started. Credit for the SFL is usually given to Hornig; he did manage it at its inception and gave it its voice in *Wonder Stories.*

Fans responded from every part of the country. The first was George Clark, who also started the first local chapter in Brooklyn. Soon other chapters were started, including one in Los Angeles (LASFL). Although most were members in name only, many of the most important fans of the late 1930s and 1940s joined the SFL. Names such as Robert W. Lowndes, Bob Tucker and Raymond Palmer could be found on the rolls.

In New York, William Sykora was director of a group which included Schwartz and Ruppert and newcomers Donald A. Wollheim and John B. Michel. Wollheim and Michel immediately became very active and very controversial figures. They and Sykora were active not only in the SFL but also in the numerous other organizations and publications of the period. They were often critical of both Hornig and *Wonder Stories* and of *Fantasy Magazine,* which they considered only a voice of the professionals. In September 1935, *Wonder Stories* announced their expulsion from the SFL.

All was not quite so serious, however. Many letters to the professional magazines (prozines) complained bitterly of such unimportant details as the rough edges of the pulp size magazines. Bub Tucker, who had to this time been a serious bibliophile, showed a facet of his nature for which he was to become notorious in fan circles. In mock seriousness, he wrote to *Astounding Stories* demanding that the wire staples be replaced by something that reflected the scope of imagination personified in the stories, possibly flavored chewing gum or platinum fasteners. He appointed himself director of the Society for the Prevention of Wire Staples in Scientifiction Magazines (SPWSSTFM).

It must be remembered that most readers of science fiction at this time were young teenagers seeking adventure and escape. So it should come as no surprise to learn that letters poured in and the Staple War ensued. Chief adversary of the SPWSSTFM was the IAOPUMUMFSTFPUSA, or International and Allied Organizations for the Purpose of Upholding and Maintaining the Use of Metallic Fasteners in Science Fiction Publications of the United States of America, led by a High Cocolorum, hight Donald A. Wollheim. Each group put out its own fan publication: Tucker published *D'Journal* and Wollheim's was *Polymorphanucleated Leucocyte*. The war ended when it was pointed out that the *D'Journal* also used wire staples.

An atypical result of the Staple War was the first Tucker Death Hoax. A letter was written and published in *Astounding* stating that Tucker had had an operation and had not recovered. Editor F. Orlin Tremaine accepted this as true and when some fans uncovered the joke, which Tucker denied instigating, Tremaine banned him forever from the magazine's letter column.

Meanwhile, Wollheim was continuing the fight with *Wonder Stories* through the reorganization of the Science Correspondence Club as the International Scientific Association (ISA). Part of Wollheim's conflict with *Wonder Stories* was over non-payment for a story he had written, "The Man From Ariel." In his attempts to get payment, he discovered that other young writers had been similarly slighted. He published his findings and asked fans to boycott the magazine. In 1936, *Wonder Stories* was sold to Standard Magazines and the reorganized magazine, *Thrilling Wonder Stories*, under former fan Mort Weisinger, diminished the activity of the SFL, leaving fan leadership to the ISA.

During the fight for fan leadership, many new fans became active and new clubs were organized. In Philadelphia, a chapter of the SFL was organized and in 1936 it became the Philadelphia Science Fiction Society (PSFS) which still exists today. Members Milton Rothman, John V. Baltadonis, Robert A. Madle and others were prolific fanzine publishers. In Minnesota, artist Morris Scott Dollens started a hectographed zine, *The Science Fiction Collector. The Science Fiction News*, a carbon-copied zine, was published by Dan McPhail, in Oklahoma. *Fantasy Magazine* had remained the dominant fan publication through 1936. In 1937, with Schwartz concentrating on the Solar Sales Agency, the zine was combined with a new impressive *Science-Fantasy Correspondent* from Willis Conover. Unfortunately, the young editor only published three issues and then virtually disappeared from the fan scene for nearly thirty years until he published a very interesting book, *Lovecraft at Last* (Carollton Clark, 1975). Also in 1937 came the start of one of the longest running organizations of fandom, the Fantasy Amateur Press Association (FAPA). This, too, was founded by Wollheim, based on the mundane apas that had been in existence for decades. FAPA was organized as a mutual trading society for the fanzine publishers of the time, eventually becoming a prestigious and limited group.

On October 22, 1936, under the auspices of the ISA, the so-called first science fiction convention was held. At Wollheim's suggestion, a New York contingent including Sykora, Michel, Frederik Pohl and others went by train to meet the Philadelphia fans. At Rothman's home they decided to have a more formal convention in New York the following February to be sponsored by the ISA. The Second Eastern Convention had some 40 attendees, both fans and pros. The precedent set, conventions continued and proliferated until today where there are a hundred or more a year.

In 1937, at the Third Eastern Science Fiction Convention, controversy again appeared when Wollheim read a speech written by Michel proposing that fandom should take a stand against the social ills of the time. This "Michelism" as it was called, was summarized in a resolution favoring a scientific-socialist world state:

> Therefore: Be it moved that this, the Third Eastern Science Fiction Convention, shall place itself on record as opposing all forces leading to barbarism, the advancement of pseudo-sciences and militaristic ideologies, and shall further resolve that science fiction should by nature stand for all forces working for a more unified world, a more Utopian existence, the application of science to human happiness, and a saner outlook on life.

This was backed by a contingent of NY fans, The Futurians, eventually consisting of Pohl, Lowndes, Isaac Asimov, James Blish, David Kyle and others. With the virulent advocacy of the Futurians, "Michelism" evolved into Communism and discussions raged in the fanzines, only to be quieted when the Futurians ceased to support "Michelism" in the fan press.

In 1937, at the Third Eastern Science Fiction Convention, plans were laid for the First National Convention to be held in Newark and run by Sykora and Sam Moskowitz, and for a World Convention to be run by the Futurians, a New York-based fan group, in 1939. By the time of the Newark convention, a feud had developed between Sykora and Wollheim over whether the emphasis of the ISA should be science or science fiction. Since most of the Futurians boycotted the Newark convention and had done nothing to set up the World Convention, Sykora appointed a new committee. The leadership of the World Convention eventually fell to Moskowitz, who organized a national club, New Fandom, with the goal of uniting all of fandom behind him. The Futurians of course vehemently opposed this, claiming that they should be running the con.

The first World Science Fiction Convention was held on July 2–3, 1939. Attending the convention were nearly 200 fans coming from as far away as Los Angeles, which was represented by Forrest J Ackerman and Myrtle Douglas dressed in futuristic costumes. Although the convention was free and open to all, when the Futurians arrived in a group, they were refused entrance because the committee feared they would create a disturbance. The Futurians claimed they would not cause trouble and other attendees agreed they should be allowed to attend. Finally, some of them were allowed admittance but the six Moskowitz considered most dangerous were denied entry. The six were Wollheim, Michel, Pohl, Lowndes, Cyril Kornbluth and Jack Gillespie. During the convention, Dave Kyle announced that the Futurians would have an open house on the last day.

Artist Guest of Honor Frank R. Paul spoke on "Science Fiction, the Spirit of Youth," saying that readers of science fiction remained mentally young and progressive despite their years. Other highlights were the announcement of a new fan-sponsored memorial edition of H. P. Lovecraft's stories, *The Outsider and Others,* and the showing of the film, *Metropolis.* Other speakers included John W. Campbell, Jr., Mort Weisinger, and Leo Margulies.

At the banquet, Paul deferred to Willy Ley for a speech and afterwards groups centered around Ackerman and Ray Bradbury who were showing pictures of Los Angeles fans and around Ley, who discoursed on rocketry. The final day was devoted to a baseball game which had only about 40 participants and spectators.

At the same time the Futurians hosted their open meeting, with about 25 fans in attendance. Discussion naturally centered around the convention and it was generally agreed that it was a good con despite the Exclusion Act. The debate over who was in the right raged in the fanzines, most believing that politics had no part in the fan world but also that the Futurians should have been allowed to attend, at least until they started a fuss. The controversy continued at a con held in Philadelphia in October. Nothing was settled and both sides retreated to the fanzines. The most important decision made was to hold the next world convention in Chicago.

As the 1930s ended, it was easy to see that fandom had reached a major crossroads. The young, isolated fan of the beginning of the decade was getting older. He had changed. From the early Gernsback ideal of the importance of science and scientific experimentation, the fans had become more interested in themselves, their opinions, and their own activities. Indicative of this were the often vitriolic debates in fanzines and the popularity of conventions. From its start in the letter columns of the prozines, fandom had grown to be almost self-perpetuating.

Although fan activity locally and through the mail continued through the 1930s, the major activities in fandom to 1940 centered around the east coast. After the first Worldcon, many fans were disillusioned with all the in-fighting among the New Yorkers. Fans looked to each other for their interests in science fiction and in other things.

In Los Angeles, Forrest Ackerman was leading the Los Angeles Science Fantasy Society (LASFS) into what was hoped to be a fannish Shangri-LA. In Michigan, bombs were dropped on the Michi-fen. The Slan Shack showed fans a new way to live. Degler plunged fandom into a one-sided war with the Cosmic Circle. FAPA ran into trouble with a blitzkrieg. The intellectual VAPA ended in the Futurian Wars and Tucker ran a one-man "renaissance" in Bloomington, Illinois.

GROWTH AND DEVELOPMENT   1940–1949

A characteristic of fandom in the 1940s was a form of bibliomania. Fans were in a slight boom period in science fiction before the war. They were amassing large collections. The *Fantasy Advertiser* had over 1,000 subscribers and paid for articles of interest to collectors. The *Fantasy Commentator* from A. Langley Searles tried "covering the field of imaginative literature" and did a pretty good job with critical articles, bibliographies, and original materials by many famous writers: Merritt, Lovecraft, Kuttner and others. Searles also serialized the first book-length history of fandom, *The Immortal Storm* by Sam Moskowitz. Probably the most massive task ever attempted was a catalog of all the fanzines ever published. It was begun by R. D. Swisher in 1938 and finally published as the *Fanzine Index* by Bob Pavlat and Bill Evans in four parts from 1952 to 1959. It was 141 pages long and listed thousands of titles, editors, and dates of publication to 1952 and it was still not complete to that date. In 1952, another decade-long project was published, *The Index to the Science-Fiction Magazines 1926–1950*, compiled by Donald B. Day. In 185 pages, this index listed every story ever published in a science fiction magazine by title and by author. Other major bibliographic work was done by Evans on the Munsey magazines, Cameron and his classification system, Speer's *Fancyclopedia*, Kennedy's *Fantasy Review* for 1945 and 1946, Boggs' *Fantasy Annual* for 1948, Tucker's numerous indices and yearbooks and many more.

In 1934 the Los Angeles chapter of the Science Fiction League was started. It was an active organization but had little interaction with the rest of fandom. By 1940 the club had grown, changed its name to the Los Angeles Science Fantasy Society (LASFS) and was publicly claiming to be the mecca of fandom. Under the leadership of Ackerman and Morojo (Myrtle Douglas), the LASFS had gotten its own clubhouse and during the war years had numerous visits from fan and pro celebrities traveling through in the armed forces.

During the war years, several major fanzines, Francis Towner Laney's *The Acolyte*, Forrest Ackerman's *Voice of the Imagi-nation* (VOM), the club's own *Shangri L'Affaires* (Shaggy), Phil Bronson's *The Fantasite*, as well as major activity in FAPA gave the LASFS wide-spread publicity and a major voice in fan activities. In 1941 Los Angeles won the right to run the fourth Worldcon, but it was delayed to 1946 because of World War II. By the end of the war, however, the LASFS had changed dramatically. The united front which had been presented to fandom (except for occasional lapses like Heinlein's resignation from the club or T. Bruce Yerke's publication of the cynical "Memoirs of a Superfluous Fan") had broken down as a series of disputes arose over leadership of the club. In 1944 an exodus of major fans including Yerke, Bronson, Laney, Paul Freehafer, and Samuel Russell from the LASFS nearly brought about its extinction. Things calmed down by May, with several members rejoining, but Laney continued his criticism from within even when he was director of the club. He eventually published in 1948 what is perhaps the most famous single article in fan history, "Ah! Sweet Idiocy!," his expose on LASFS.

From the middle of 1944 to late 1947, LASFS was in a renaissance period. The Slan Shackers had arrived from Michigan in late 1945. Burbee brought *Shangri L'Affaires* to the top of the field for 23 issues. The worldcon was revived in 1946. *The Acolyte* was the most popular fanzine of the time. And Laney, Burbee and Ackerman each placed in the top ten fans in polls of the period.

Unfortunately, Morojo had left the club at the end of the war, and Ackerman's interests started shifting from fan to pro. By 1948, instigated by Laney's criticism and Burbee's quips, the Insurgents arose and split the club apart. It took nearly ten years for the LASFS to recover.

His part in the Staple War had brought Tucker wide renown as a humorist in the 1930s. Unfortunately, the effect of the Death Hoax was to drive Tucker to gafia (*get away from it all*) in 1936. His absence from fandom only seemed to whet Tucker's appetite, for when he returned in late 1938, it was with a tremendous burst of activity. In about a year, he published fifteen fanzines, got heavily involved helping the Chicon stay alive, and was writing for many other publications. His humor and wit became legendary both under his own name and under his alias, Hoy Ping Pong. Throughout the 1940s, Tucker was a pungent commentator, comically dispelling many of the delusions fans held about themselves. His *Le Zombie* was one of the "must have" zines for every fan. Begun in 1938, it had published 59 issues by 1944, but slowed down until issue 63 appeared in 1948.

Tucker also started selling stories professionally. In 1941 Fred Pohl accepted "Interstellar Way Station," for *Super Science Novels*; five more stories followed in the next two years. Then, in 1946, Tucker found that he could sell mystery novels and in two years sold *The Chinese Doll, To Keep or Kill,* and *The Dove.* All this professional writing did not keep Tucker from his fanzines. After *Le Zombie* slowed down, he started the *Bloomington Newsletter* at the end of 1945 which ran 28 issues to 1953, midway changing title to the *Science Fiction Newsletter.* Tucker had a second difficult period in 1949 when a young Michifan (from Michigan, of course), after visiting Tucker was inspired by the previous hoax to announce Tucker's death a second time, despite Tucker's admonitions. This time Tucker wasn't banned from any magazines, but he almost lost his regular job when his boss thought he conspired in the hoax as a publicity stunt to sell his books. To the delight of fandom this time Tucker did not gafiate. Robert Bloch, a humorist in his own right as well as the author of *Psycho*, has said that he never had a reason for life until he met Tucker at the 1946 Pacificon; thereafter his purpose was to kid Tucker. This probably best expresses the type of man who has become the most popular fan in history.

Probably Tucker's opposite in fannish regard was Claude Degler. He and his Cosmic Circle comprise an infamous legend in fannish history. Degler first appeared about 1940 as the head of the Cosmic Club of New Castle. He attended Chicon I but did not achieve any notice until Denvention when he expressed a belief in a message from a Martian that was read at the con and started the fanzine *Infinite*.

His surge towards notoriety began in 1943 when Degler started a series of trips which took him around the United States several times leaving behind him a trail of half-formed fan clubs, enemies, adherents and just puzzled fans. At this time he was propagating his idea of the Cosmic Circle, which he claimed would be composed of mutations of cosmic men (Cosmen) that would influence the future.

Over a period of two years, stories built up around Degler, about his abhorrent personal habits, his borrowing money, accusations of books disappearing and yet other reports about his intellectual discussions and his helping other fans. His opponents were vociferous. T. Bruce Yerke actually had a heart attack while trying to throw Degler out of the LASFS. Perhaps part of the Degler legend is perpetuated because his opponents were more strident than his believers. In only two years, Degler built such a reputation that it has lasted over thirty-five years and his name has become a byword for repugnance.

Fans in this period were in almost constant contact with each other. News fanzines (newzines) proliferated. Nearly everyone who was in contact with more than two other fans published a newzine at some time. Besides Tucker's, there were Unger's *Fantasy Fiction Field,* Dunkelburger's *Fanews,* the National Fantasy Fan Federation's *Bonfire,* Taurasi's *Fantasy News* and *Fantasy Times* and many, many others.

Detailed opinions, however, were usually kept in the general fanzines and in the amateur press associations (apas). Besides those already mentioned, there were several fanzines that achieved wide enthusiasm. In the late 1930s and early 1940s two fanzines were very important, *Fantascience Digest* and *Spaceways.* Bob Madle published FD for 14 issues during 1937–41. Madle remained one of the few calm fans of the time and his zine was filled with interesting articles. *Spaceways* was the key fanzine at the turn of the decade. Published by Harry Warner, Jr., its contents ranged from good to excellent with material by Tucker, Ackerman, Jack Speer, Larry Farsaci, and just about all the major fans. Even the fiction it ran was a grade above that of other fanzines and included a round-robin serial about fans. In 1943 a curious fanzine came out of Battle Creek, Michigan. It had a spray-painted cover of a rooster with red pants and was titled *Chanticleer. Chanticleer* was an unusual combination of zany humor (usually supplied by Hoy Ping Pong, Tucker or Editor Walt Liebscher) and serious book reviews. It was one of the most popular and endearing fanzines ever published. Another popular fanzine, *Vampire,* carried a touch of humor. This fanzine came from Joe Kennedy, later to become fairly well known as poet X. J. Kennedy. *Vampire* also carried serious material, such as a debate between Sam Moskowitz and August Derleth over the distribution of Arkham House's *The Outsider and Others,* and a regular column of radio reviews. In 1947 a half-sized, mimeographed fanzine came out of Portland, Oregon. By the third issue, it had reduced to quarter-size, gone offset, and soon became one of the most important fanzines carrying serious and constructive (sercon) material. *The Fanscient* was edited by Don Day for the Portland Science-Fantasy Society. It carried bibliographies and autobiographical sketches by professionals, fiction also often by pros, critical articles and, because it was offset, it ran fine detailed art by D. Bruce Berry, John Grossman and others.

After the generally circulated fanzines, amateur press associations were the favored form of communications among fans. FAPA was the first and remained the premiere apa through the 1940s. But even FAPA had its tribulations. In 1940 the Futurians had become almost inactive and a Philadelphia fan, Jack Agnew, was sending out the mailings. A mailing failed to appear on time. Speer, Rothman and Elmer Perdue drove from Washington to Philadelphia and got the mailing from Agnew and distributed it. They issued a one-shot, *Blitzkrieg,* which gave the operation its name. FAPA entered a revival period and the Brain Trust became an important part of fannish myth. The Brain Trust got its name from several members who discussed serious topics in a mature manner in their zines. Speer, Warner, Rothman, Perdue, Ashley and others who are often engaged in brain-twisting and serious discussions have ever since held that name. In the summer of 1944 a controversy over Claude Degler reached its climax and he was evicted from FAPA. That year the Futurians also regained positions of power in the apa and then resigned en masse to start the Vanguard Amateur Press Association (VAPA). Amid accusations of sabotage, FAPA endured with lesser activity by its members, recovering fully by 1946. Then 1947 brought another crisis. Perdue was late in getting out a mailing so Laney and Burbee held another blitzkrieg to get the mailing. Perdue had the dubious distinction of having been on both sides of a blitz. Despite all its problems, FAPA mailings included some of the best zines of the period. "Ah! Sweet Idiocy!" appeared in 1948; Boggs' *Sky Hook* was always of high caliber, as were Rotsler's *Masque* and zines by Speer, Burbee, Warner, and many others.

Competition to FAPA arose on two fronts. The strongest was VAPA, which was primarily an implement of the Futurians. VAPA was a very intellectual apa and science fiction took a lesser role in many cases than music, poetry, politics, art and other serious topics. The Futurians started to war amongst themselves in 1945 and VAPA suffered although it dragged on to 1950. The destruction of the Futurians occurred in 1945 when Wollheim and Michel decided to cut Lowndes, Blish, Judy Zissman and Virginia Kidd from the group as they previously had cut Asimov, Kornbluth, Harry Dockweiler and Leslie Perri. The rest of the Futurians discovered this plan and kicked them out first with the "X" document which was distributed through FAPA and VAPA. The wording in "X" caused Wollheim to bring a libel suit which never came to court, but it destroyed the Futurians as a viable group.

The only other apa was the Spectator Amateur Press Society (SAPS). It was conceived at a meeting of the Spectators, whence its name, by fans who did not want to have to wait to join FAPA. The original name was to be the Spectator Amateur Press Association, when the inspiration came to change "association" to "society." The change in the acronym to SAPS had a strong effect on the apa as material of a lighter and more humorous nature often appeared, as opposed to FAPA's brain-trusting. SAPS has continued to the present, often with excellent material but has never been a major force in fandom.

One of the topics that occurs constantly in fannish circles is that of a totally fan society. The closest that ideal came to reality was probably the Slan Shack of Battle Creek where a group of fans lived for about two years. Originally the Slan Shack was to have been the start of a larger Slan Center which would be a cooperative home for fans. The Shack started in 1943 when Al and Abby Lu Ashley purchased an eight-room house and shared it with E. E. Evans, Walt Liebscher and Jack Wiedenbeck. The Shack became a goal for every fan who could visit and lasted until they decided to move together to Los Angeles where they eventually split up. Since then, a slan shack has come to mean anyplace where two or more fans share an abode, a very common occurrence.

Almost the opposite of this cooperative effort was the furious activity in the rest of Michigan. In 1939 Martin Alger coined a word which has regretably become a byword when talking about science fiction. He jokingly started the Society for the Prevention of Bug Eyed Monsters (BEM) on the Covers of Science Fiction Publications. The Michigan Science-Fantasy Society was formed and held meetings in members' homes alternating between Detroit and Art Rapp's home in Saginaw. The group was composed of rather colorful and unusual members and soon earned the nickname The Misfits. Big-Hearted Howard DeVore got his name by selling some prozines to fans almost as soon as he learned about fandom. Ray Nelson founded his own club in high school, drew hilariously satiric cartoons and eventually turned pro. Ben Singer feuded with other Michifen, and started his own club which was then black-listed by Detroit for leaving atheistic literature in a public building. Alger sold his vehicle to the State of Michigan which then used it to transport the insane. The FBI even got involved when Singer sent Norman Kossuth an anonymous warning letter and Kossuth turned it over to an FBI agent who visited him on a check of a non-fan friend. In 1948 someone set off a multiple explosion "dago" bomb. And on November 13, 1949 the group's demise was heralded when two Misfits blew in the windows of Art Rapp's house with a bomb that could be heard blocks away.

One of the largest, longest-lived clubs in fandom was started in 1940 and for nearly forty years has remained on the verge of accomplishment. In October, 1940 an article by Damon Knight, "Unite—or Die," appeared in *Fanfare,* the official fanzine of the Strangers Club of Boston. With the demise of the ISA and New Fandom, Knight proposed that a new national organization be set up to supply the fantasy fans of America "with those services which they cannot supply themselves."

The next issue of *Fanfare* carried a proposed constitution and an invitation to join. At the April, 1941 meeting of the Strangers, attended by nine members of the Futurians as well as other fans, the National Fantasy Fan Federation (N3F) was started. The war almost killed the club by drafting nearly all the active members. An older fan, E. E. Evans, eventually became president. He was then apparently taken into service. In actuality, he ran afoul of the law. From November 1942 to spring of 1944, the club was basically in stasis. Then Evans returned, the N3F helped finance Speer's *Fancyclopedia,* and great things appeared to be in store for the club.

The club grew to hundreds of members but never really seemed to get off the ground. Many an active fan joined and then lost interest when the club continued to accomplish nothing. The club did publish some nice things—a 41-page booklet describing "What is Science Fiction Fandom?" in 1944, a Finlay portfolio in 1947, and the first American edition of Dr. David H. Keller's *The Sign of the Burning Hart,* but it could not consistently retain fannish interest. Many N3F members were becoming insular, separating themselves from the rest of fandom and immersing themselves in the club. The N3F started aiming its services at its own members and at new fans (neofen) rather than at the whole of fandom. Despite occasional surges of activity from a few fans, the club has remained at the same level to this time.

Possibly the only activity that kept fannish interest throughout this entire period was the institution of the worldcon as an annual event. When Chicago fan Mark Reinsberg proposed another worldcon, to be held in Chicago, at the Philadelphia Conference, he had gotten support from both of the warring New York factions, the Futurians and New Fandom. The Chicago proposal was accepted unanimously. With Erle Korshak and Bob Tucker, Reinsberg had formed the Illini Fantasy Fictioneers to organize the Chicon. The name Chicon was coined by Forrest J Ackerman who was a fanatical devotee of contracted spelling; he even joined the con as 4SJ and retroactively named the first worldcon the Nycon.

The convention was held on September 1–2, 1940 and was smaller than the one the previous year, with only 128 attendees. The Guest of Honor was Edward E. "Doc" Smith, Ph.D. Bob Tucker gave a welcoming address and probably the most thrilling part of the con was a talk from Doc Smith. In his speech, instead of speaking about science fiction, he talked about the fans, in "What This Convention Means." He stressed the devotion of the fans who paid their own way, unlike normal professional conventions which are paid for by business. This had a tremendous effect on fans, promoting great comeraderie during the con and afterwards. Other major programs included a speech by Ray Palmer, an auction, the premiere of Tucker's "Monsters of the Moon," a film farce made of cuts Tucker had cribbed from his job as a projectionist and the masquerade. The masquerade had good participation with even E. E. Smith coming as C. L. Moore's character, Northwest Smith. Dave Kyle won first prize as Ming the Merciless from the Flash Gordon movie serials. The final item of business of the Chicon was to pick the site of the, by now widely accepted, next annual convention. Denver won and the attendees agreed with Wollheim that Denvention sounded better than Dencon.

The Denvention was again held on the July 4th holiday weekend and the Guest of Honor (GoH) was Robert A. Heinlein, the first of his three GoH appearances. The convention was small, with only 90 die-hard fans attending.

On the first day, Heinlein's speech was about the ability science fiction gave its readers to accept rapid change in society, over thirty years before Alvin Toffler. At the masquerade, E. E. Evans won as a bug-eyed monster. Another interesting costume was Ackerman's Hunchback of Notre Dame with a mask by an LA fan named Ray Harryhausen, who later became the most widely acclaimed stop-motion animator in the film industry. Heinlein attended, sans costume, as Adam Stink, the life-like robot.

The site selection for the next year was exciting, with bids from San Francisco, Washington, D. C., Philadelphia and Los Angeles. LA won. Ackerman named it Pacificon, and plans were started. Then on December 7, 1941, Pearl Harbor was bombed. With a Japanese invasion expected at anytime, the Pacificon was postponed for the duration of the war.

After peace with Japan was assured, it was announced that the Pacificon would be held in 1946. A. E. van Vogt and his wife/collaborator E. Mayne Hull were named as Guests of Honor. The convention started on July 4, but fans, able to travel freely for the first time in years, started arriving the week before. About 130 fans managed to get to Los Angeles for the convention. Unfortunately, much of the speech-making was boring and hard to hear, including van Vogt's speech. Ackerman and Laney, in possibly their only amicable collaboration, presented the attendees with the idea of a Fantasy Foundation. This long-time dream of Ackerman's was to create a library of everything related to science fiction and fantasy and also to put out special publications. Ackerman collapsed immediately after the presentation from what was later diagnosed as intestinal flu complicated by complete exhaustion from his exertions on the con. There were many more programs at the Pacificon than at previous worldcons, but the highlight of the affair was a "Weird Session," run by Laney. It featured a performing story teller the LASFS had discovered, named Theodore and a well-received speech by Samuel Russel on "The Function of Weird in Fiction." Without competition, Philadelphia was chosen for the next worldcon.

Milton Rothman was chairman and the moving force of the Philcon. To organize and run the convention efficiently, he and the Philadelphia Science

Fiction Society (PSFS) created the Philcon Society. Rothman was still the undisputed leader. This direct control over the worldcon caused Moskowitz and Sykora to question Rothman's motives, especially when, in the *Philcon News,* it was suggested that some of the profits go to the PSFS.

The Philcon tried to be the first truly "world" convention but its success was not of its own making. The convention took upon itself the operation of the Big Pond Fund, an idea of Ackerman's to bring a British fan to the United States. Not until 1949, unfortunately, were enough funds accumulated to allow the first recipient, Ted Carnell, early fan turned pro, to come to Cinvention. The convention did have a minor international flavor because Canadians John Millard, "Beak" Taylor and Ned McKeown attended.

Philcon was held over the 1947 Labor Day weekend, August 30 to September 1, at the Penn-Sheraton hotel with John W. Campbell, Jr., as Guest of Honor. Announcements such as these and plans for program items kept the *Philcon News* an eagerly read publication.

The convention started at 1:00 PM Saturday with the introduction of notables, including former Senator Roger Sherman Hoar who wrote science fiction as Ralph Milne Farley. John Campbell's guest of honor speech, based on a book he had just finished, *The Atomic Story,* was about atomic power plants. An editor's panel met with Sam Merwin, Jr. (*Thrilling Wonder Stories, Startling Stories*) and Campbell talking about their magazines, and there was a preliminary business meeting. The most controversial item of business was Jack Speer's condemnation of *Amazing Stories* and editor Ray Palmer for the Shaver Mystery (about which more later). To avoid permanent ill feeling, the resolution was reversed into one of approval of the other magazines. That evening consisted of presentations of future publications from the many small science fiction publishers, including one from Vanguard Records called "Son of Worlds Unseen" by Chan Davis and the auction run by Moskowitz and Erle Korshak. The top price was for a Frank R. Paul *Wonder Stories* cover at $31.00. Big parties developed that night as Tom Hadley of Hadley Publishing Company, Lloyd Eshbach of Fantasy Press and Jim Williams and George O. Smith of Prime Press all had parties open to everyone.

Other programs during the con included De Camp on the occult, Korshak on collecting fantasy, a "Symposium on Interplanetary Travel" with Willy Ley and Dr. Thomas Gardner, and a variety show with Rothman at the piano, Ted Sturgeon and Jerome Stanton in a string duet, Mary Mair singing folk songs, a comedy monologue as William Tenn (Philip Klass) "read his fan mail" and Chandler Davis playing some original piano pieces from his record. Whether or not the parties contributed to their enthusiasm, Jack Speer and Chan Davis definitely attracted the attention of the local constabulary when they set off a box of fireworks on the roof of the hotel.

The final business session divided the $300 profit (of $750 gross) to the N3F, PSFS, the Fantasy Foundation, to buy science fiction for paralyzed fan Joe Suriano, and to the next worldcon. An impromptu bid by the Toronto fans with the motto "To Make the Worldcon Truly International" won overwhelmingly. Early in 1948 the Philcon Committee and the N3F published a *Philcon Memory Book* with photos and con reports.

The 1948 Torcon held several distinctions. In addition to being the first worldcon held outside the United States, it was the last to be held over the July 4th holiday and it was the first of a series of cons that is remembered more for its friendly, party atmosphere than for its program.

The convention was held at the Rai Purdy Studios Hall with attendees staying at three different hotels. Chairman Ned McKeown was absent when the con was started by John Millard, who also introduced the notables, mostly fans, since pros were scarce during the entire convention. McKeown arrived to introduce Robert Bloch for his guest of honor speech, "Fantasy and Psychology," pointing out science fiction as both wish fulfillment and as a source of proposed solutions to the world's difficulties.

Other program items included presentations by the small publishers, extemporaneous speeches by Joe Kennedy (recently voted No. 1 fan) and McKeown on Canadian science fiction magazines, Rothman with a British film on "Atomic Physics." Korshak again presided over the auction with top price going for Virgil Finlay's cover for the June, 1948 *Famous Fantastic Mysteries*, illustrating "The Devil's Spoon" by Theodora du Bois. Tucker presented his "Results of the First Fan Survey," a fannish Kinsey report. The final day of the con consisted of the business session, where, after much closed door politicing, the 1949 con was given to Cincinnati, the banquet, and the final "Fan Entertainment."

The 1949 con was nicknamed Cinvention and was run by the Cincinnati Fantasy Group (CFG). On the stationery, the chairman was Charles R. Tanner but it was an honorary position. The work was done by Don Ford. Cinvention promised that its worldcon would be the best. They had two Guests of Honor: a professional, Lloyd Eshbach, founder of one of the most popular small presses, Fantasy Press, and a fan, Ted Carnell, who had finally received enough money from the Big Pond Fund which Ackerman had almost single-handedly financed. Carnell by this time was also the founder and editor of the British prozine, *New Worlds*.

Cinvention was held over the Labor Day weekend at the Hotel Metropole. Since 1948 the worldcon has been held the same weekend every year it has been in the United States. The only difficulty with the hotel was that some fans could not afford its exorbitant room rates of $3 a night.

A great deal of interest in the worldcon was shown before the con. Editors and writers volunteered their services; there were *five* bids for the next convention (*two* from New York City), plus suggestions for mail balloting so that all members and not just attendees could vote on the location. Harry Moore had lost his New Orleans bid the year before but he arrived early to again promote his Nolacon. Ray Palmer had regained fandom's good graces when he had stopped pushing Shaverism and shocked fans when he announced that he had quit Ziff-Davis to start his own company and science fiction magazine, *Other Worlds*. He had edited *Amazing Stories* and *Fantastic Adventures* since 1938.

There were so many notables attending that two sessions were necessary to introduce them. Tanner then introduced Eshbach for his Guest of Honor speech which consisted of amusing anecdotes. He brought along some old prozines to prove he was a science fiction writer but admitted to being the publisher, rather than author, guest of honor. Lester del Rey spoke on "Sex and Science Fiction," stating that there was none and objecting to stories that intimated that mid-19th century morals would remain forever. He was correct; they did not remain even another quarter century.

Ray Palmer spoke on his life and career, claiming he believed the Shaver Mystery but that it should not appear in science fiction magazines. He would publish it in his new occult fact magazine, *Fate*. Dave Kyle had arrived with a model, Lois Jean Miles, from New York, calling her "Miss Science Fiction." There was a mixed reaction to this; most fans appreciated an attractive woman but deplored the commercialization and hype of the self-acclaimed title. Jack Williamson spoke on "Science and Science Fiction" and Vincent Hamlin talked about his cartoon strip character in "Alley Oop is the Man I'd Like To Be."

The convention received two unusual messages. John W. Campbell telegraphed his apologies for not attending but promised a surprise for fans in the November, 1949 *Astounding*. This was the famous issue he had compiled based on a tongue-in-check letter of comment from 1948 which had praised the stories in the November 1949 issue. The contents included "Gulf" by Heinlein, a Foundation story by Asimov, stories by Sturgeon, del Rey, van Vogt and de Camp, and an article by R. S. Richardson. The second message was a *telephone* call from Sterling Macoboy in Australia!

There was the usual but unmemorable auction and masquerade ball. The business meeting, however, was filled with politics, with many fans scheming to keep the bid away from the controversial, feud-ridden New York. After three ballots, Portland, represented by L. A. fan Ackerman, won.

For the first time, the worldcon received a substantial amount of good press coverage. *The Antiquarian Bookman* devoted an entire issue to science fiction; there was a front page story in the *Cincinnati Post;* Trans Radio Press got coverage from Kyle and TV station WLWT ran a program with 16 con goers. Not related to publicity, but of unusual note was a professional-quality stage backdrop of a robot battling spaceships drawn by two fans, Bill Kroll and John Grossman, in exchange for two $1 memberships. It was at least 9' x 12' and read "7th World Science-Fiction Convention" in large letters. It required the hotel engineering staff to set it up after the two artists had somehow managed to transport it by Greyhound Bus!

The late 1940s included a revival of fannish activity centered on science fiction and publishing. For years the majority of science fiction appeared only in fragile pulp magazines and the paper drives during the war caused a scarcity of many of them. With money and paper reserves finally being released to the public, several fans thought to follow August Derleth's example of Arkham House, by starting private semi-professional publishing houses. Many of these presses lasted only for a book or two, but often, notably Gnome Press, Fantasy Press and Shasta Publishers, reprinted many of the early classics in hardcovers for the first time. By 1950, over a dozen small publishing houses had started. So many books were published that fans often waited a year or more for used prices of $1 for first editions that had originally sold for about $3.

This plethora of science fiction did have two results. The major publishers began to realize that science fiction could be a profitable line and although it did not last long, the first science fiction-oriented book club, The Fantasy Book Club, was started in 1948 by Dave Kyle, offering discounts and special publications.

Fans had grown very serious about their fiction. The critical and biblio-graphical contributions in fanzines and the investment in large libraries of books and even publishing companies were a good indication of the quality of reading matter they expected. When they were disappointed they let the magazine editors know it. They complained about the juvenile quality of Captain Future and Sarge Saturn. Fans were really upset when Palmer started publishing the Richard S. Shaver "dero" stories in 1945 with "I Remember Lemuria." Feelings rose so high that in *Fandom Speaks* Forrest J Ackerman proposed a boycott of *Amazing Stories* until Palmer stopped publishing such trash. Some fans only wanted Palmer to give up trying to convince his readers that the stories were true. Not even the Dianetics controversy in the early 1950s caused as much vitriolic discussion as the Shaver Hoax.

By 1950, fandom had grown into a viable organism. In the postwar period many fanzines were being published, the worldcons were popular and the many small publishers were putting the classic stories into permanent bindings. Fan-dom was about to sprout new offshoots.

BOOM AND BUST   1949–1963

With fandom growing larger at the end of the 1940s, fans were learning about fandom without sharing the same science fictional background. The magazines proliferated with over sixty publishing at some time in the decade, many with fan columns. *Destination Moon* started an avalanche of science fic-tion and monster movies. Television carried *Captain Video, Space Patrol, Tom Corbett—Space Cadet, Tales of Tomorrow* and numerous other series. Comic books were filled with science fiction. Some, like the EC comics and some of the DC, were palatable but most were awful. Even newspaper comic strips carried science fiction, like Jack Williamson's *Beyond Mars* and the Jack Kirby/ Wallace Wood *Skymasters of the Space Force*. Late in this period, the space race affected the field.

1950 started a strange period in fan history. At one and the same time fans were decrying the impersonal growth of fandom and gathering at world-cons nearly 1000 strong. They were publishing sercon journals and creating myths and legends as flambouyant as any fantasy story. While struggling for fannish brotherhood with the TransAtlantic Fan Fund (TAFF), fans were suing each other over WSFS, Inc. There was the Belfast-Savannah Axis and The Cult; there was the Goon Defective Agency and the Enchanted Duplicator, the Boondoggle, the Fort Mudge Steam Calliope Company and Carl Brandon, not to mention Pogo and Roscoe.

Harry Warner believes that the decade of the 1950s was a lighter, friendlier period than any before or since, and that some of the best writers in fandom contributed to this atmosphere by creating legends and elaborating fact into fable. This gave fans with disparate backgrounds a common ground on which to mix.

At its start, *Spacewarp* was almost out of place in the often sercon at-mosphere of the late 1940s. However, it brought a lively atmosphere to fan-dom with its columns and articles, and soon became a central force. Rapp almost singlehandedly created Roscoe, the fannish ghod, who swept fandom with a jihad of mimeo ink. In *Fancyclopedia II*, Dick Eney claims:

> Roscoe is The One True Ghod, incarnate in the form of a beaver. (This
> mystically expresses the fact that all true fen are busy little b's.) . . .
> Roscoe's Mighty Two Front Teeth and Slapping Tail are terrible weapons
> against the evildoer. Holy days are the Fourth day of July ("that's the day
> when Roscoe flies a fiery spaceship in the sky") and Labor Day, the date
> of Roscoe's Birth. Conventions are frequently held to celebrate these
> Sacred Occasions, and fen meeting there quaff libations of beer and other
> beverages in Roscoe's honor.

It was in *Spacewarp* that the fannish propeller beanie was first brought to fandom's attention. Ray Nelson got the idea when taking some fannish pictures in
1947 and then popularized it in numerous cartoons.

When Rapp was inducted into the army a few issues were published by
some temporary editors. Substitutes are rarely as good as the originals but these
replacements were the Los Angeles Insurgents: Burbee, Laney, Boggs, and
Rotsler. Any fanzine whose contents included these four would be of note, but
in these issues of *Spacewarp* they outdid themselves, and with good material
from other BNFs as well, *Spacewarp* was almost a prophecy of what was to
come. It still exists as a SAPS zine.

In 1950, a young fan learned about fandom and within two years became
the most popular faned (fan editor). Lee Hoffman had two unusual characteristics—living in the fannish wasteland of Georgia and being female. There had
been women in fandom before but only Morojo achieved any national prominence and none could be considered influential nationally. Hoffman achieved
this distinction, primarily through her fanzine *Quandry* (*Q*).

Lee started *Q* after seeing a 1940s fanzine from an old-time fan in her
area, Walt Kessel, and reading his *Fancyclopedia*. Early issues were not exceptional but by No. 6, she was getting some good contributors and soon had
Willis, Silverberg, Tucker, Bloch, Shelby Vick, Wilkie Conner, Vernon McCain
and occasionally Laney, Burbee and Ellison writing for her. Fandom was the
general topic in *Q*, fanzines, conventions, fans, fanhistory and myths. Lee was
an adherent of Walt Kelly's comic strip *Pogo* and the possum quickly became a
fannish hero, with fans creating a Pogo mythos. In *Q* first appeared the Fort
Mudge Steam Calliope Company, Hoffman and Willis proprietors, and its negotiations for the development of steam (hot air) with Ken Bulmer's British
conglomerate, the Bulmer Aqueous Vapour Corporation. Willis started his famous column, "The Harp That Once or Twice" in *Q* and Silverberg updated the
numbered fandoms. Lee's own "Lil Peepul" were popular drawings. *Quandry*
became the No. 1 fanzine within a year. It was instrumental in reviving fan
interest in some old-time fans who had mostly gafiated, like Laney, Tucker,
Bloch and Kennedy.

The Hoffman reputation grew but few fen realized that Lee (an ambiguous
name) was female. With the normal, drastic shortage of femmefans of the time,
most assumed that *Q*'s editor was male, and Lee had deliberately kept the
secret. At the 1951 worldcon in New Orleans, the Nolacon, she attended her
first convention. To judge the surprise effect, here is Tucker's version of their
first meeting from *Quandry* No. 15:

Tired weary and disheveled from a long day's drive, I slammed the door of my room, flang the suitcase into a far corner (where it promptly burst open and spilled my cargo of dirty books), stripped off my clothes and jumped into the tub. . . . There came a sound at the door, the peculiar kind of half-hearted knock that could only be caused by a timid fan getting up the nerve to kick the door in. . . . I wrapped a towel around my middle, began searching my luggage for a deck of cards, and yelled a bored invitation to enter.

Three strangers trooped in wearing abashed grins, a girl and two men. The girl looked as if she were desperately searching for better company than the characters trailing her. I silently sympathized, and stared at the trio, the meanwhile dripping soap and water on the rug. The two gentlemen stared at the towel and giggled, while the girl looked at the puddle on the rug.

"Hello," one character said.

"Hello," another character said.

"Hello," the girl echoed.

[The first fan spoke]. "I am Shelby Vick," he explained then in clear, ringing tones.

"The hell you say!" I shot back astounded.

I-am-Shelby-Vick then flicked a finger at his two conspirators. "You know Lee Hoffman, of course?"

Of course. I threw a bored glance at the remaining character and yawned, "Hello, Lee."

"No, no!" contradicted I-am-Shelby-Vick. "Not him . . . HER!"

Mustering what dignity I retained, I picked up my towel from the floor and stalked into the bathroom, flanging shut the door.

Before Hoffman gafiated, *Quandry* lasted for 30 monthly issues that have become legendary. In 1976 in *Fanhistorica No. 1*, Hoffman finally revealed her secrets for publishing a successful fanzine: first, make it legible; second, make it frequent; third, get Walt Willis as lead columnist.

This Willis-Hoffman combination was well known for its legend creation. It was dubbed the Belfast-Savannah Axis for the frequent interaction of the two. They even created their own postal stationery, the poctsarcd. According to Willis, in a letter in *Psychotic No. 17*,

Poctsarcds. Well. At one time when Lee Hoffman and I were in really intensive communication we used to send each other postcards as matters came into our heads because it got so difficult remembering everything when we were writing letters. Once the flow of them dried up for a week or so and I put a postscript on a letter to Lee enquiring what was wrong. Hastily typed, it read: "No poctsarcd?" Lee replied sorrowfully to the effect that she had tried every shop in Savannah but had been quite unable to find any poctsarcds. The poctsarcd situation was serious. They had plenty of pitcuer poctsarcds, but no ordinary poctsarcds. Taking her at her word I ran off a few dozen poctsarcds on the press with Lee's name and address on one side and *POCTSARCD* on the other, and started sending them to her. . . . once you've used a poctsarcd you would never want to go back to old-fashioned postcards.

Probably the best writer of the period and easily the most popular in the United States was Walt Willis. He was an Irish fan whose prolific columns and articles were so highly regarded that Americans donated to a fund to pay for him to come to the United States in 1952 and again in 1962.

Willis was one of the legend makers. His first fanzine, *Slant,* appeared in late 1948. It was small, mostly dedicated to amateur fiction and it was printed on a hand-set letterpress machine. The zine soon turned to more light-hearted contents although it continued to run rather high quality fiction. When *Slant* became too much work, Willis began publishing *Hyphen* with Chuck Harris. "-" is often called the best fanzine of all time. It lasted 36 issues from 1952 to 1965. Besides Willis himself, and Harris, Bob Shaw had a regular column, "The Glass Bushell," and James White, John Berry, Vin¢ Clarke, and William F. Temple were frequent contributors, nearly always well illustrated by ATom (Arthur Thompson).

In addition to his writings for his own fanzine and for *Q,* Willis seemed to be published everywhere, often with "inciteful" satire on fans who took themselves too seriously. Some of his outstanding pieces were fan fiction (fiction about fans, not amateur science fiction). To help pay for his first trip many faneds put out special Willishes (Willis issues) of their zines. For these, Walt wrote installments of "Willis Discovers America," a trip report to America before he ever left Ireland. It is a rapid-fire serial filled with cliff-hanging endings and a pun or three per sentence. Willis brought the pun to a unique peak in fandom and one of his most reprinted articles is a defense of the pun as the highest form of humor.

Perhaps the greatest piece of fannish legend and literature is "The Enchanted Duplicator," the story of Jophan and his journey from the village of Prosaic in the Country of Mundane over the Mountains of Inertia through the wilds of the Realm of Fandom to The Tower of Trufandom to reach the Magic Mimeograph to publish The Perfect Fanzine. This story was written by Willis and Bob Shaw in 1954 and so typifies the ideal of fandom that it has been printed six different times—in 1954, 1962, 1971, 1972–3 in *Amazing* and twice in 1979.

There was a strange fannish magic in Ireland in the early 1950s. There was a tremendous amount of talent in Irish Fandom (IF) totally out of proportion to the number of fans because *every one* of them was talented enough to make legendary characters of the rest. In addition to Willis and Shaw, there was lecherous Chuck Harris, the animal John Berry, and his Goon Defective Agency (GDA), James White, the typical sobersided Irishman, and Madeline Willis the long suffering, who could easily put any of these Wheels of If in their place. Oblique House was the Willis home and gave its name to these bizarre characters, the Oblique Angles. Willis often wrote about Shaw's pointed puns; Shaw described serious, sobersided White and his water pistols; White reverenced the Willis Himself; they all alluded to Harris' lechery; and John Berry created the most popular (fictional) organization in fanhistory, the Goon Defective Agency, whose hero, the Goon, based on Berry's professional police experiences, challenged the villainous Antigoon, among other adventures in his fanzine, *Retribution.* Although not Irish, Arthur Thompson (ATom) was an integral part of all their writing. It was he that usually pinpointed the satire with his many illustrations. One other inspiration came from IF, the game of ghoodminton. Ghoodminton has been described as a game for immortals; unless you were immortal, you might not survive. It was a combination of badminton and mayhem played over a net in the cluttered attic of Oblique House with a normal shuttlecock and bats made from whatever might come to hand. John Berry once found that the cast on his broken arm was a very intimidating bat. One rule was that you could do *anything* to distract your opponents during the game. With reputations like these it is not hard to understand that Willis was not the only Wheel that was appreciated in the United States. Berry, ATom and Shaw were also imported.

Throughout this period, there were numerous good fanzines. Although many seemed to cover the same material with con reports, reviews and fan discussions, most of these fanzines had identifiable personalities and points of view.

In the early 1950s, fannish fanzines following the lead of *Quandry* and *Hyphen* were the most popular. Shelby Vick's *Confusion* fit its name with his ramblings and achieved its peak of prominence when he led the drive for the first Willis trip, 'WAW with the Crew in '52.' Max Keasler published *Fanvariety* (later *Opus*) which was infamous for its numerous and often hysterical typos (typographical errors), its sometimes risque comments, and illos (illustrations). At one point, his local postmaster would not mail an issue and Keasler went to the next town in another state to mail it, claiming the distinction of being the only "border-run fanzine." *Spaceship* was Bob Silverberg's fanzine (which I believe is still extant in FAPA) and had more serious commentary and reviews. *Oopsla* was probably the closest zine to *Quandry* after *Q* died. It contained similar columns and commentary, even continuing Willis' "The Harp That Once or Twice." Ted White and John Magnus published *Stellar*, a zine devoted entirely to fiction about fans, both real and imaginary, including an unfinished serial, "The Death of Science Fiction," inspired by the McCarthy purges of the time. Lee Hoffman reentered fandom in the mid-1950s in FAPA with two unusual fanzines. *Fanhistory* printed important articles on fandom but lasted only four issues. *Science Fiction Five Yearly* caught attention with its publishing schedule and contributors (Bloch, Tucker, White, Ellison and Silverberg). It inspired Bloch to attempt the zine with the longest span between issues, *Science Fiction Fifty Yearly*.

All the good fanzines were not primarily fannish, however. The *Nekromantikon* from Manly Banister was a quality publication filled with amateur fiction, because of Banister's belief that fandom would supply the future science fiction writers. Tucker's *Science Fiction Newsletter* (formerly *Bloomington Newsletter*) was the leading newszine of the day, very similar to the *Locus* of today. It mostly ran news and reviews of the professional field. *Peon* was another quality sercon zine. It ran some fiction from the likes of James White, Jerome Bixby and Harlan Ellison, and regular columns and articles by Terry Carr, Jim Harmon, Robert Bloch and others. Redd Boggs' *Sky Hook* carried critical reviews by William Atheling, Jr. (James Blish). The most unusual fanzine of the time was published by the Elves', Gnomes' and Little Men's Science Fiction, Chowder and Marching Society. Its *Rhodomagnetic Digest* was published half-size offset, sometimes with color covers and often received the criticism that it wasn't really a fanzine. However, it carried criticism, fiction, con reports and fanzine reviews. Its contributors included Arthur C. Clarke, Bob Shaw, Leland Sapiro, Walt Willis, William F. Temple, Jack Vance and Anthony Boucher. Frank Prieto, Ray Van Houten and James Taurasi were so interested in science fiction that when the prozine *Original Science Fiction Stories* folded in 1960, they acquired the rights to publish a mimeographed version. It was basically an amateur publication and only lasted three issues. A club newzine, *EISFA*, was published by Juanita Wellons and Beverly Amer, the founders of the Eastern Indiana Science Fiction Association. Eventually Juanita married Robert Coulson and the fanzine changed from a clubzine with fannish connotations to an intriguing combination of fannish and sercon material. With the 36th issue the title was changed to *Yandro* and today, over 200 issues later, it remains the same.

Immediately after *Quandry*, however, there was no central fanzine that a fan could read. A 14-year-old fan, Joel Nydahl, published *Vega* monthly, improving it with each issue. When he reached one year he decided to pub a special giant issue. It came out in two parts, months late and Nydahl never reached major fanac again. This type of fannish burnout has since been called "Nydahl's Disease."

In 1953, a ditto fanzine began publishing monthly from Portland, Oregon. Richard E. Geis had begun publishing *Psychotic*. Within a year, *PSY* became the fanzine to read. Deliberately carrying much controversial material, fans could keep up with Seventh Fandom, dianetics, and just about all the goings-on in fandom. *Psychotic* carried a regular column by McCain and McLeod, articles by the likes of Tucker, Ellison, Grennell, Gregg Calkins, Silverberg and Bloch, and a letter column which aptly fit its name, "Section Eight."

About the same time that Geis was attracting so many readers to *Psychotic*, another fan, Harlan Ellison, was also attracting attention with Seventh Fandom. Because *Quandry* was so popular, its articles were influential, occasionally more influential than intended. One such article was on "Numbered Fandoms" by Robert Silverberg. The Numbered Fandom Theory was originally presented by Jack Speer in his 1938 article, "After 1939—What?" and in the *Fancyclopedia*. In it, Speer identified periods in fandom based on the primary activities and interests of the fans of the time. In the October 1952 issue of *Quandry*, Silverberg updated that article. He proposed that the current active generation was Sixth Fandom and revolved around *Quandry* and its contributors.

In 1953, the 30th issue of *Q* was sent to fandom with a black border around the cover, announcing the last issue. Harlan Ellison got a bright idea with the issue. He proposed that he and several acti-fans start Seventh Fandom. They created a *7APA*, a newsletter and presented their fait accompli to fandom at the 1953 Midwestcon.

Unfortunately, they disregarded the premise that a numbered fandom is defined by its observed characteristics rather than by declaration. In addition, the 7th fandomites were young and overenthusiastic. When they presented themselves to the rest of fandom, they were ridiculed. Seventh Fandom never achieved any great popularity. Most of the original members never attained any great accomplishments. In the end, Ellison decried fandom's attitude toward Seventh Fandom in the leading fanzine of the day, *Psychotic*, stating that the

Seventh was an ideal that young fans aspired to but that "the mad dogs had kneed it in the groin."

Not all was strife or myth in this period. There were many publications designed to help the fan learn more about science fiction and its fandom. In addition to the Day prozine and the Pavlat-Evans fanzine indices mentioned earlier, there were the 1951 *NFFF Fanzine Checklist,* Guy Terwilleger's *Best of Fandom* anthologies for 1957 and 1958, the hardcover publication of Moskowitz's *The Immortal Storm,* the Tuck *Handbook* which was the original basis for his recent *Encyclopedia of Science Fiction,* the 1957 *Science Fiction Yearbook* from James Taurasi, the 1951 and 1952 *Fanspeak* from N3F, and many reprint fanzines which concentrated on particular topics or writers.

There was also one "private" organization that provided services to fandom. *Operation Fantast* was a combination business and fan club. It was started in 1950 by Ken Slater and those who paid their dues received an annual handbook with lists of fanzines, prozines, clubs, conventions, and a host of other information. They also received a fanzine under the club title with articles, reviews, and letters, use of the lending library, and The Fantasy Art Society. Eventually, Slater gave up *Operation Fantast* and used the knowledge he gained to establish one of the largest fantasy book dealerships in the world, Fantast (Medway) Ltd.

Later in the decade, Richard Eney became one of the most prolific publishers in fandom. He was in most of the apas at the time and published a number of general circulation fanzines (genzines). His many publications can all be identified by the line somewhere in them: "It's Eney's Fault." Two of his publications were among the most ambitious and most interesting in and about fan history. In 1959, after several years work, he published the *Fancyclopedia II,* a comprehensive update of Speer's 1944 version. Three years later, his *A Sense of FAPA* came out. He had compiled a comprehensive historical anthology of nearly 400 pages from the first 100 mailings of *FAPA.*

Fanzines were a major fanac and the apas of the time a major contribution to the total. *FAPA* remained the number one apa with its membership list filled with BNFs and a membership waiting list which involved two years or more of waiting. *SAPS* remained popular and was joined by other imitators; the N3F started its own apa, *N'APA*; the *National Amateur Press Association (NAPA)* used the same name as the mundane ayjay group but only for one mailing before it folded; the aforementioned *7APA* also had a short life.

Two innovative apas appeared and were phenomenally successful. The *Offtrails Magazine Publisher's Association (OMPA)* was modeled on the same tradition as *FAPA* but it was the first apa in the United Kingdom. *OMPA* was established in June, 1954 by Ken Bulmer and Vin¢ Clarke, and the founders clearly stated that it was intended for fun. The name was chosen because its initials sounded like an "echo of a trombone" and should "disperse any stuffiness." In its first year, *OMPA* included many worthwhile items. Willis collected and annotated all the parts of "Willis Discovers America"; Harris produced *Through Darkest Ireland,* and even *Science Fiction Five –Yearly* eventually appeared in *OMPA* although it was first impounded by British customs. Because of the popularity of some of its British and Irish members, *OMPA* achieved much support from the west side of the Atlantic also.

The Cult was an unusual apa. Created by Peter Vorzimer in August 1954, the Cult is a combination of an apa and a correspondence round-robin. The Cult has 13 members, each of whom in turn publish *The Fantasy Rotator* containing all the members' contributions, like a monthly fanzine with the publishing burden divided among the 13 contributors. Response time was quick in this semi-closed apa and controversial discussions were the norm. The privacy available in an apa of this type has proved attractive to many fans and imitators have proliferated.

Local fans and fan groups also flourished. The LASFS revived in the late Fifties and again became a source of good fanzines and good fan gossip. The young Betty Jo Welles became involved in the club, and Bjo became one of the most popular figures in fandom, her artwork appearing all over. Bjo's interest in science fiction art was not limited to drawing. She and her husband, John Trimble, started "Project Art Show" and ran many of the worldcon art shows until 1976.

New York fandom was also active. James Taurasi was a leader in the Fan-Vets. The Lunarians were started and in 1957 ran the first Lunacon. Bill Donahoo published a giant fanzine, *Habbakuk,* of fannish philosophy and happenings about his fannish residences, "The Nunnery" and the "Riverside Dive," which were combinations of slan shacks and beat pads.

A frenzied amount of quality fanzine publishing seemed to revolve around Terry Carr. At various times in this period Carr and Peter Graham published *Vulcan* and *Looking Backward;* Dave Rike and Carr published *Innuendo;* Ron Ellik and Carr came out with *FANAC;* Carr edited *Lighthouse;* and Ted White, Greg Benford, Peter Graham, Carr and others pubbed *Void. Innuendo* was a fannish zine heavily oriented toward fan history. *FANAC* was the major newzine of the late 50s and early 60s. Its biweekly issues were filled with gossip, current happenings, and commentary. *Void* was the fanzine with many heads. Its many editors covered all aspects of fanac—criticism, humor, history and commentary. All were major fanzines.

Carr was also involved in two of the most famous fannish activities, The Tower to the Moon and the Carl Brandon hoax. The Tower was an attempt by Berkely fans to reach the moon before the Russians by building a tower of beer cans in Dave Rike's backyard. In 1953, Carl Brandon started appearing in fanzines. His image as the only black acti-fan drew some attention, but not as much as the quality of his writing. He wrote fannish parodies of well-known works. "The Purple Pastures," "The Catcher of the Rye," "My Fair Femmefan" and "The BNF of IZ" lampooned fannish ideals while also building upon them. At the 1958 worldcon, the Solacon, Carr revealed to fandom that Carl Brandon never existed; he was a combination-fan made up mostly of Carr himself, Rike, Graham, Ellik and "Boob" Stewart. So large had Brandon's fame grown that several fans did not believe him. This was further complicated when shortly thereafter a real Carl Brandon started appearing in fanzines. This one, however, was a blond Swede.

The worldcons of this period reflected the general feelings of the times. They were fun and controversial and for the first time, truly worldwide. The Norwescon was the first worldcon of the 50s and by far the largest to that time. Attendance was 400, double the largest previous world convention. The Portland

Science Fantasy Society was the sponsor and the con came close to disaster when the original chairman and most of the committee resigned. Donald Day became chairman less than six months before the con and with the remaining committee member, secretary Janita Sharp, took over preparations.

The Norwescon was held at the Hotel Multnomah on September 1–4, 1950. The GoH was Anthony Boucher. Boucher's main speech was a talk on science fiction and detective fiction. He was a master of both. Dianetics became a major controversy at the con. Dianetics is a pseudo-psychological theory first presented by science fiction author L. Ron Hubbard in *Astounding.* Some fans wholeheartedly followed Hubbard and editor Campbell's lead into dianetics and later claimed great benefits while others proclaimed it claptrap. When Hubbard later lost control of the Dianetics company, he redesigned it slightly as the Church of Scientology. UFOs also received some attention. The first attempt to start a professional writer's group came at the con. Ted Sturgeon, Groff Conklin, Bob Tucker and Forrest J Ackerman were named to the organizing committee of the Fantasy Writers of America. Other highlights included a special showing of *Destination Moon,* a parody skit on dianetics and religion, an amateur film, *Death Of A Spectator,* starring fans Joe Kennedy, Lloyd Alpaugh and Ron Maddox, and a demonstration by John De Courcey of his matter transmitter. He transmitted his wife from their room to the con hall and she arrived clad only in a towel. The con was also successful financially. So successful, that banquet tickets which cost the committee $1.50 were sold to members for $1 and the con still turned a profit.

The 1951 worldcon was won by New Orleans and became the Nolacon. The convention was held in the St. Charles Hotel, one room of which, No. 770, has become a legend because of the lengthy, riotous party that was held there. It was so famous in fact, that when the hotel was demolished in 1976, Don Markstein included splinters from the building in his fanzines with the reminder that they could possibly be from Room 770.

The 190 attendees were treated to a film program including the premiere of *The Day The Earth Stood Still.* A TV adaptation of Sturgeon's "A Child is Crying" was also shown. Dianetics was again controversial; there was even a discussion on whether it should be allowed at the convention. Other highlights included Sam Moskowitz and E. E. Evans on the history of fandom and an unvoted award to 20th Century Fox, stating that *The Day The Earth Stood Still* was the best science fiction film of the year. The award presentation was filmed and appeared in a Movietone Newsreel, No. 74. At the banquet, Bloch spoke on the derogatory press coverage that worldcons usually receive. The speech may have had some effect, because local coverage was excellent. After two ballots at the business session, Chicago won the right to host the next convention. It was the first time that a worldcon repeated in a city.

Chicon II was chaired by Julian C. May; she was the first chairwoman in worldcon history. Over 1100 persons attended, the record up to that time not to be surpassed until the 1960s. It was here that Hugo Gernsback was honored for his contributions to science fiction.

Gernsback's speech was very controversial. He suggested Federal laws that gave authors some rights to inventions which were based on their science fiction stories. Another speaker was a current celebrity; Gary Davis was the self-styled first "citizen of the world." A (short-lived) professional writers group started, the Science Fantasy Writers of America, with Bradbury as president. Other interesting items included a ballet, *Asteroid,* an expensive but poor banquet, and a bellboy who enjoyed the company of the fans so much that he showed up at a room party with two callgirls whom he had convinced to provide free service. And of course, Willis had been brought over on his first trip. The next con was voted to Philadelphia.

Philcon II faced tragedy before it started when chairman Jim Williams died. Milton Rothman assumed the chair and became the first fan to chair two worldcons. The GoH was Willy Ley, who was the first guest honored for work outside the field of science fiction. Attendance was 750. The Bellevue-Stratford Hotel had booked two other conventions during the same weekend and there were many complaints about hotel service. Ley's speech was on the energy crisis that would arrive as our natural resources were used up. Other programs included a discussion of science fiction in Japan and Great Britain, Philip José Farmer talking about the time he was interviewed for the Kinsey Report and a PSFS skit, "The Game From Outer Space," based on *What's My Line?*

The most important event of the convention was the inauguration of the Hugo awards for the best science fiction of the year. The first year's winners were:

> No. 1 Fan Personality: Forrest J Ackerman
> Interior Illustrator: Virgil Finlay
> Cover Artist: Ed Emshwiller and Hannes Bok (tie)
> Fact Articles: Willy Ley
> New Author or Artist: Philip José Farmer
> Pro Magazine: *Galaxy* and *Astounding* (tie)
> Novel: *The Demolished Man* by Alfred Bester

There were no Hugo awards given in 1954 but they have been given out every year from 1955 on.

The 1954 convention was awarded to San Francisco and the SFCon had 700 attendees at the Sir Francis Drake Hotel under co-chairmen Lester Cole and Gary Nelson. John W. Campbell, Jr. repeated as GoH. The SFCon was a con of bad relations. The hotel and its staff were inconsiderate and inefficient and the fans were poorly behaved. The program included an operetta based on Bradbury's "A Scent of Sarsaparilla," a panel on detective fiction, and a premiere of the amateur film adaptation of Richard Matheson's *Born of Man and Woman,* directed by Alan Nourse. The next con was awarded to Cleveland.

With only 380 attendees, the Clevention in 1955 was a small fannish interlude in worldcons. Co-chairmen were Nick and Moreen Falasca, with Isaac Asimov as GoH. The Clevention re-instituted the Hugo Awards which have since become an institution. They were given out at the banquet on the first night of the con by Tony Boucher. Asimov's speech was on the "Secret Pleasures of Science Fiction" in his usual tongue-in-cheek manner. Other highlights included Tucker comparing a recent survey with his 1948 Torcon report; a skit, "TV3000 A.D.," done by the Cleveland Fan Club, the Terrans; and a skit written by Judith Merril using Dickens' *A Christmas Carol* in a fannish context.

Another fannish institution became established with this worldcon. With the Big Pond Fund and the 1952 Willis Fund, fandom had successfully imported prominent fans to the U. S. In 1955, after two years of planning, fandom successfully implemented the Trans-Atlantic Fan Fund (TAFF) by bringing Ken Bulmer to the Clevention. Plans were laid for alternating trips to the worldcon in the U. S. with trips to England for an American fan.

The 1956 worldcon was held in New York. The NewYorCon or Nycon II as it was later called, was almost as controversial as the first Nycon, but this time a former Futurian was chairman, Dave Kyle. Attendance was up for GoH Arthur C. Clarke with 850 members. Clarke's appearance was eagerly awaited by many fans but the problems at the con almost eclipsed the former fan who had been nicknamed "Ego" Clarke. There were a variety of problems: the air conditioning gave out in the Hotel Biltmore, some fans were not allowed to hear special guest Al Capp's talk at the banquet, the Air Force charged the con for three space-suited mannikins that were stolen (two were later found), the $7.10 banquet had 90 fewer banqueteers than guaranteed and the con had to make up the difference.

Bob Bloch was again the reliable toastmaster, making fun of the ill happenings. And some interesting happenings included believer Campbell failing to get a Heironymous machine working while skeptical E. E. Smith seemed to succeed; a ballet, *Cliché*, starring Olga Ley; and Clarke's critical speech on pseudo-scientific phenomena. London won the 1957 worldcon, and for the first time it went out of North America.

At this convention the first attempt at a permanent worldcon organization, the World Science Fiction Society, Incorporated (WSFS, Inc.) was released upon fandom. For several years fans had talked of a worldcon governing body to help in planning the annual event and at the Clevention a study committee was appointed. Before Nycon II, Kyle, with Art Saha and George Nims Raybin incorporated the organization. Directors were elected at the Nycon, including Ackerman, E. E. Evans, Roger Sims, Taurasi and Nick Falasca.

Between the Nycon II and the Loncon, controversy arose. Kyle, in agreement with Loncon chairman, Ted Carnell, planned a charter flight to carry Americans to England. Part of the trip cost included an emergency fund, which caused the problem, as no plans had been made for use of the money. Some passengers authorized a sum of $5 per person to be used to get newlywed Kyle and his bride Ruth Landis a present. Others contested this and claimed the money belonged to WSFS, Inc., and a lawsuit went to the courts where it dragged on for years and eventually was dissolved and WSFS, Inc. with it.

The first overseas worldcon was held in the Kings Court Hotel, which the committee had booked completely, thereby guaranteeing no complaints from the other guests and no restrictions on parties. Unfortunately, it was under renovation during the con.

The 268 attendees included 70 from North America, including the 55 who came on Kyle's charter. The con started on September 6, deliberately late because of the fannish tradition that nothing starts on time. GoH was John W. Campbell, Jr., for the third and last time.

Although the program was normal for a con there were some British touches: the $2.85 room included breakfast, the banquet included roast duck and a toast to the Queen, and the BBC covered the con extensively. There were also several fannish entertainments: Pete Daniels and his Merseysippi Jazz Band, several fanfilms including *Fanzapoppin,* and a radio show-type tape entitled *The March of Slime.* Overall, it was a very fannish con with a peaceful business session which awarded the next worldcon to another fannish legend—South Gate In '58!

The Solacon was held in Los Angeles with GoH Richard Matheson and 322 attendees. Anna Moffat was chairwoman. A ten-year, one-man crusade came to fruitation with the Solacon. The man was Rick Sneary, who lived in South Gate, a small city outside L.A. He and eventually many others, led by Willis, Hoffman, and ATom had campaigned for "South Gate In '58!" The small city did not have the facilities to host a worldcon so South Gate's mayor convinced L.A. leaders to allow him to temporarily annex the area surrounding the Sola-con's Hotel Alexandria for the duration of the con. So it was "South Gate In '58."

True to its beginnings, the Solacon was very fannish. A slight British in-fluence remained with the tea drinking contest won by Djinn Faine with a measly 23 cups. Other interesting happenings: Jon Lackey, nearing seven feet tall, created a stir in warlock's robes as he strode through the streets; WSFS, Inc. was crushed when Anna Moffat declared the Solacon independent of the controversial organization and was then followed by the fannish reincarnation of Max Keasler, one of the most fannish fans of all time. During the production of *Alice in THRILLING WONDERland,* Sneary proved his endurance by carry-ing a sign: "South Gate Again In 2010." Detroit won the next worldcon.

The 1959 Detention had Poul Anderson as pro GoH, and John Berry, arriving on a special fund as fan GoH. Chairmen for the 371 attendees at the Pick-Fort Shelby Hotel were Roger Sims and Fred Prophet. The con started with the apparently lifeless Howard DeVore being dragged across the stage (he had said that worldcon would only be run in Detroit over his dead body). Anderson's speech, "A Renaissance for Science Fiction," centered on the ability and need for science fiction to entertain. Other program items included Damon Knight on the ability of science fiction to combine fantasy and reality; a fan panel which ran until 4:30 AM, including as much participation from the audience as from the panelists; a successful Auction Bloch, an event at which pros are sold to fans; a drama, "Beyond the Unknown"; and a masquerade. Films were also shown, including several acclaimed shorts by Ed Emshwiller, who is not only a famous science fiction artist, but is so renowned as an ex-perimental filmmaker that NASA hired him to produce some of their films. Bloch again entertained at the banquet and this caused him to award a Hugo to himself for "The Hellbound Train." The E. E. Evans Memorial Award, better known as the Big Heart Award, was given, for the first time, to Bloch. The 1960 con was awarded to Pittsburgh after some backroom negotiations.

After three years of small worldcons, the Pittcon had 568 attendees at the Penn-Sheraton Hotel, under chairman Direce Archer. James Blish was GoH. The Pittcon was generally considered well run but not quite as fannish as the previous few worldcons. The Project Art Show run by Bjo Trimble was ex-cellent. Some of the highlights included the masquerade; beanie-clad singers who eventually became the first giant filk song session (a filk song being a science fiction or fannish related song often written to popular music); an H. P. Lovecraft program at which HPL's long-time friend Frank Belknap Long spoke; and a performance of Terry Carr's "The Purple Pastures," a fannish satire on the obvious *Green Pastures*. Other programs included panels on science fiction art, fanzine publishing and fan clubs. Seattle won for 1961.

Seacon featured Robert Heinlein for his second GoH appearance. Chairman Wally Weder hosted the last small North American worldcon with only 300 attendees. Never again would a worldcon held on this continent have below 500 members and only three below 1400.

Reports on the Seacon are remarkably rare, at least those that talk about the con itself. The con had the normal supply of programs but none of any great note. The masquerade was nice but not very large and Project Art Show repeated its success on a smaller scale and set Bjo on a record-setting run of managing most of the worldcon artshows until her last in 1976. The most publicized event was the fund raising to bring Willis to America ten years after his first trip. Fannishly, this fund succeeded in 1962 and brought Willis and his wife Madeleine to the United States for the 20th Worldcon, again in Chicago, for the third time.

Theodore Sturgeon fascinated his fans and Chairman Earl Kemp and the Chicon committee ran a smooth and enjoyable con. Chicon III may be the best-documented worldcon in history. Jay Kay Klein published the second of his convention annuals with over 250 photos. Advent publishers put out a 200-page proceedings. Willis wrote con reports that totaled over 100 pages and many of the other 950 attendees wrote reports; coincidentally many mentioned the Irish Fan. The con had one of the most extensive programs, including speeches by Jay Holmes from NASA, Ian Ballantine, I. Q. and personality testing and panels on science fiction, fantasy and fannish topics. The masquerade was large with a variety of attractive costumes with additional singing entertainment from Ted Sturgeon, Juanita Coulson and Ted Cogswell. The 1963 con was awarded to Washington, D.C.

The Discon was another large con with 800 attendees. GoH was Murray Leinster. From his experience chairman George Scithers later wrote a worldcon chairman's manual. The opening program was guaranteed to catch attention with Sprague de Camp and Fritz Leiber competing as rival wizards. Other programs included William Atheling's alter ego, James Blish, on the lack of good critics in the field, panels on Burroughs, science fiction editors, author's wives and other regular topics. At the banquet, toastmaster Asimov was for once speechless when he was handed a card which said he had won a special Hugo award for "adding science to science fiction." The first First Fandom award was given to E. E. "Doc" Smith for his long-time contribution to the field and to fandom. The masquerade was particularly well done with numerous excellent costumes.

BUST OR BOONDOGGLE   1964

By 1963, fandom had again reached a peak. The second Willis trip, plus TAFF and the quality of Chicon III and Discon I, good fanzines like *Void*, *Axe*, *Xero*, a revived *Warhoon*, *Fanac*, *Habbakuk* and a revived *FAPA* all contributed to good fraternal feelings. But the pinnacle achieved at Discon held the seeds of the biggest blow-up in fandom's history: The Boondoggle.

At the Discon, the next worldcon was voted to San Francisco for the Pacificon II, which turned out to be the most controversial worldcon. The Pacificon started as ordinarily as every other worldcon. GoH's Edmond Hamilton and Leigh Brackett were announced and plans were laid. J. Ben Stark was chairman. The problems started when early in 1964 an announcement from one of the committee members was circulated to fandom that one particular fan would not be allowed to attend the convention for alleged immoral conduct with children. Never had any fan been so ostracized. Fandom shuddered and split in ire.

On one side were fans who believed the allegations and agreed with the convention committee (concomm). The committee contended that this fan had on more than one occasion done certain things that they considered wrong. They cited several examples. They did not however take any legal action. Aligned against them were the majority of fans who believed that such charges and actions without proof were a slander of character based solely on the dislike of the one fan by certain members of the concomm. Even the parents of some of the children mentioned by the committee repudiated the charges. This controversy dominated the fanzines, major club discussions and the worldcon preparations for the entire year. One group published a fanzine, *The Loyal Opposition* on this Boondoggle and virtually entire issues of other fanzines and apas were filled with vitriolic discussion. The Pacificon committee defended their action but neither they nor the parents involved brought any charges to bear. Suits against the concomm were contemplated but never filed.

The major controversy eventually evolved not into a discussion on the particular individual but into one on whether or not the committee could bar a person from the worldcon without bringing legal action against that person. The opposition organized a boycott of the Pacificon and many fen did not attend. At the convention itself, a disruption occurred when one fan who was visiting friends but not attending the con itself was threatened with expulsion.

RECOVERY: BACK TO BASICS   1964–1967

The Boondoggle disrupted many friendships. The recovery period was a period of insularity. Many active fen semi-gafiated or channeled their fanac into the proliferating numbers of apas or into the specialized fandoms, many of which burst into activity. The specialized fan became prominent until a BNF in one sub-fandom might not even know about a BNF in another. Local activity, clubs and conventions also became popular.

The apas were the first to gather together the remnants of fandom. Much of the popularity of the apas stemmed from their privacy and limited membership. Many apas had distinct personalities and fans tended to gravitate to the ones that attracted them the most. Apas like *The Cult* had unofficial rules on the privacy of members' opinions. *FAPA* and *SAPS* were still the major goals of an apa fan, but many other apas came into existence with frenzied activity. In 1964, *APA-F* was a weekly local apa in New York City. Shortly, *APA-L* followed in Los Angeles. *APA-F* lasted about two years but *APA-L* is still going strong at meetings of LASFS. These two centers of fandom had enough members for local apas but others were also popular. *N'APA* grew larger; the Southern Fandom Press Alliance came into being as did *APA-45* for members born after 1945 and *TAPS*, the Terran Amateur Press Society. The members of *The Cult* were very active and *TAPS* was organized similarly.

There were fanzines of the period. *Riverside Quarterly* was easily the major sercon zine. *Lighthouse, Warhoon* and *Yandro* continued. *Double: Bill* was a good zine from Bill Bowers and Bill Mallardi. *The Double: Bill Symposium* containing the answers of 94 pros to questions on science fiction and writing originated in the fanzine in 1964 and was eventually published independently in 1969. Other good fanzines were *Quark* from Tom Perry, *Niekas* from Ed Meskys, and *Focal Point*, a newzine from Mike McInerny and Rich Brown. A small one-page ditto fanzine started in APA-F but soon evolved into a full-sized genzine. *Algol*, from Andrew Porter achieved its major recognition in its third format as a semi-prozine in the 1970s.

Specialized fandoms had started in the 1950s but with the isolationism in the wake of the Boondoggle, they grew and proliferated. Probably the largest specialization on a single person revolved around Edgar Rice Burroughs. Literally dozens of fanzines were published with ERB and his characters as the focus. These fans even have their own organization, The Burroughs Bibliophiles, which meets annually, usually at the worldcon. One of the best and easily the longest lasting of the ERB-oriented fanzines was *ERB-dom* from Camille Cazedessus. It lasted well into the 1970s, carrying quality articles and reprints of Burroughs material originally published in newspapers and magazines. The media, comics, movies and TV usage of the ERB characters, primarily Tarzan, were also covered. Other prominent zines include *The Barsoomian* and *The Gridley Wave.*

Possibly the largest segment of fandom literally sprang from Dick Lupoff's fanzine, *Xero.* In his fanzine Lupoff ran a column on comic books. It was the instigation needed for such fans as Roy Thomas and Don and Maggie Thompson to start fanzines of their own, dedicated mainly to comics. This sub-fandom has grown so large that it is a distinct entity with its own zines, conventions and even its own apa, CAPA-ALPHA, and would require a history of its own. Some major fanzines over the years include *Alter Ego, RBCC (Rocket's Blast Comic Collector), Witzend, The Comic World, George, Funnyworld, Squa Tront, Spa Fon, Graphic Story Magazine, Newfangels* and *The Buyer's Guide to Comic Fandom.* Many comic publications also covered the newspaper comic strips and some, like the *Menomonee Falls Gazette,* specialized in reprinting many old strips.

In 1965, Lancer Books began publishing Robert E. Howard's Conan saga. This was a long awaited event of a fandom that until then had focused around one fanzine, *Amra. Amra* was published by George Scithers and carried articles, verse, art and fiction by fans and professionals alike, all of whom were fans of REH and other sword and sorcery (S&S) writers. After the paperbacks proved Howard's popularity, many small publishers started reissuing nearly everything he had written. Fanzines proliferated, at first devoted to Howard and then more and more to S&S in general. *The Howard Collector,* from Glenn Lord, then executor of the Howard estate, was particularly interesting. It carried excellent material from Howard's files, letters, unfinished manuscripts, poetry, etc. Howard fandom started slowly and became a giant in the 1970s, even to the start of an apa, REHUPA, The Robert E. Howard United Press Association.

H. P. Lovecraft's name, like Howard's, had been revered by a few afficianados and in the middle 1960s his popularity grew. August Derleth and Arkham House had kept Lovecraft's works in print, and his Cthulu Mythos had been pastisched by many writers after his death. Lovecraftian fans often published special fanzines, most notably *HPL* from Meade Frierson III. Later on a specialized apa, *The Exotic Order of Dagon*, was founded.

One other writer had a fandom created around his works, or rather around one work. J. R. R. Tolkien's popularity all over the United States was preceded by several years by his popularity in science fiction fandom. The Tolkien Society was founded by fans and published its own fanzines.

In 1959, Forrest J Ackerman edited a magazine on horror movies. With the publication of *Famous Monsters of Filmland*, horror movie or "monster" fandom started. Fans had always enjoyed and written about fantastic films, but a large young group of enthusiasts centered around *Famous Monsters*. These soon gained the name "monster" fans because of their interest and sometimes their behavior. Eventually some of these fans grew into serious students of the horror film and a true fandom evolved and published its own fanzines. *Photon* and *Gore Creatures* are two of note.

From California, the home of many strange things, sprang a strange subfandom, Coventry. It started in the 1950s with the creation of the Mariposan Empire, became involved with science fiction, and the scenario of Coventry evolved into that of a spaceship traveling in an alternate universe. The development of this universe caused serious conflict among its participants and eventually it dissolved.

Another organization, the Society for Creative Anachronism (SCA), was not an actual part of fandom but many of its founding (and current) members were fans. The SCA is a medievalist organization whose aim is to recreate and act out the Middle Ages as they were, or as they should have been. They recreate costumes and crafts, and hold jousts and revels. When individual SCA "kingdoms" clash, it has many of the feelings of a major convention.

Many local conventions came into prominence at this time. By the mid-sixties, there were regular conventions in most of the major cities. Boston had Boskone; New York had Lunacon; Philadelphia, Philcon; Washington, D.C., Disclave; Cincinnati, Midwestcon; St. Louis, Ozarkon; and the DeepSouthCon, Southwestercon and Westercon were all traveling regional conventions in their respective areas.

The worldcons remained popular despite the furor over the Pacificon. The 1965 convention was voted to London for the second time. Ella Parker chaired Loncon II which had 350 members, a record for a British convention. GoH was Brian Aldiss. The Mount Royal Hotel was brand new and served excellently as the con hotel. At his GoH speech, Aldiss demonstrated the seriousness of British conventions—he threw a meat pie at Harry Harrison. Bob Bloch was entertaining as usual as the Mystery speaker at the banquet, even though he had been told he would not have to perform. In typical fashion, he told his audience, "I made my peace with God two weeks ago. He surrendered."

Other programs included a speech by John Brunner, a debate between Harry Harrison and Ted White on the then New Wave, and a Transatlantic science fiction quiz which the Europeans won. The site bidding for the next worldcon was very competitive between Syracuse and Cleveland.

The 1966 convention, the Tricon, was held in Cleveland under the chairmanship of Ben Jason. GoH for Tricon was L. Sprague de Camp and the attendance, 850 members, was the highest since the 1962 Chicon. Tricon ran four days, September 2-5, at the Hotel Claremont. *Galaxy* magazine sponsored a special program, a "Galaxy of Fashion" show, which was very popular. Other highlights included an excellent speech by John Brunner, Bjo Trimble's Art Show and a fine masquerade.

The 25th Anniversary worldcon was the first "big" worldcon, with over 1500 attendees. Appropriately, it was held in New York as was the first. Nycon III was held at the Hotel Statler Hilton over the Labor Day weekend. The co-chairmen were Ted White and Dave Van Arnam. One popular pre-con item was the Nycon Comics which were drawn by Jack Gaughan and sent out in addition to the normal progress reports.

Nycon had two GoHs—Lester del Rey, pro, and Bob Tucker, fan. The program was similar to previous worldcons. There was an art show, masquerade, panels and a second "Galaxy of Fashion" show. A Dianetics conference, separate from the worldcon, was held in the hotel the same weekend. The GoH speeches were held at the awards banquet. After a few jokes, toastmaster Harlan Ellison introduced the fan GoH, Tucker, who reminisced on his humorous fannish past. Before the pro GoH speech, Sam Moskowitz spoke for twenty minutes before giving a special award to Edmond Hamilton. As a result, del Rey shortened his speech but still gave an impassioned request for good storytelling as opposed to New Wave style writing. One topic first came to prominence at this worldcon— *Star Trek*—which had created quite a stir during its first year on television. Disregarding the happenings at the last worldcon in Oakland, California, the 1968 convention was voted there again under a new name, Baycon.

SPECIALIZATION AND BIG BUSINESS   1968-1979

Fandom had grown to tremendous proportions. In the 1930s there were perhaps 150-200 fans. In the 1940s the number increased to slightly over 500 and in the 1950s fandom grew to about 2000. The numbers leveled off until the late 1960s and then grew phenomenally. By the end of the decade, over 10,000 called themselves fans and currently the number may be ten times that or more!

By 1967, new fanzines were appearing. U. S. fans were realizing that fandom had dramatically expanded with the 1965 worldcon in London and a strong effort for the first non-English language bid for Heidelberg. In the fifteen years since 1965, five worldcons have been held outside the United States, compared to only one in the previous twenty-five years. Local conventions began attracting 1000 or more attendees, more than worldcons of the previous decade. Some major fanzines reached circulation in the thousands. *Star Trek* and *2001: A Space Odyssey* created a media storm of science fiction which *Star Wars* turned into a super nova. Conventions blossomed all over. Fandom flourished and grew. This growth also created a resentment on the part of the long-time fan who was used to the camaraderie of a smaller fandom but which was impossible in a fandom in which sub-fandoms numbered thousands—more than the total number of fans just a few years before.

Fandom became filled with new phenomena. Giant semi-professional magazines like *Science Fiction Review, Locus* and *Algol* came into being. There was a fannish resurgence visible in the FAAN awards, fan funds and interest in fan history. Many fans even started up small publishing houses again.

In 1967, after a successful worldcon in New York, Richard E. Geis resurfaced in fandom with a thin 16-page issue of *Psychotic No. 21.* It was a forecast of things to come. Within a few issues, Geis again had one of the best fannish fanzines, running articles and columns on fandom, fans, and fandoms past. He also ran film and fiction reviews and *Psychotic* soon grew to over 50 pages, in micro-elite type, of high quality material. Then with issue No. 28, *Psychotic* was changed to *Science Fiction Review,* covering the field in a very controversial and personal manner. Some of his opinionated columnists included Ted White and Piers Anthony, neither of whom held their punches or their opinions. The zine reached a size where it was too large to be a hobby but not large enough to support itself from its subscriptions and so in 1970, it folded. Geis came back with a large personal journal-type zine in 1972 which he wrote completely, except for letters of comment (LoC). It was simply titled *Richard E. Geis,* which soon changed to *The Alien Critic* and finally again to *Science Fiction Review. SFR* is still in existence and fandom is now large enough to make it Geis' main support.

In 1968, a newzine first came to prominence covering the fan and pro field. *Locus* is published by Charles Brown and still exists, although now it covers the professional field almost exclusively and very comprehensively. Because of Brown's relatively serious attitude toward the field, *Locus* has also been the instigator of several other good newzines, mostly fannish in nature. *Focal Point* was published by Rich Brown and Arnie Katz in 1970–71 and, in 1972–73, Katz with his wife Joyce, published *Fiawol.*

Karass, begun by Linda Bushyager in 1972, included news, reviews, and commentary; it lasted five years and often landed her in hot water when her comments pierced sensitive fannish egos. While *Karass* covered fannish matters, Charlie Brown turned *Locus* toward covering the professional field in more detail. When *Karass* became more erratic in its last years, a large void developed in the reportage of fannish events.

Two fanzines finally filled the need, both published in 1978. *File 770* from Mike Glyer reported fan news in great detail. *DNQ* (titled from Do Not Quote) from Victoria Vayne and Taral MacDonald originally started in direct competition with *770* but soon evolved into a zine of commentary and satire with a dollop of news to break up the excitement. There were and are numerous other newzines, good and bad, domestic and foreign, fannish and serious, but none have achieved any prominence in the United States, except for *The Fantasy Newsletter,* which started by announcing forthcoming books and with the 19th issue started printing columns by pros and reviews as well as news. No one can tell for sure because no detailed research has been done and *no one* receives all fanzines in today's fandom, but counting all the sub-fandoms and apas, there could easily be over 5,000 fanzines published annually.

In the late 1960s, with the large numerical expansion of fans, many fans had access to reasonably decent printing equipment. Fewer ditto zines were published; mimeo became the standard and offset printing was not uncommon. With good printing capabilities, with potentially larger numbers of readers and with often highly educated and talented contributors, fanzines entered a new era of excellence. There were still large numbers of bad to medicore zines, but the number of good to excellent zines was very high although the proportion probably remained the same.

In the mid 1960s a fanzine was started in Missouri by Hank Luttrell; a few years later he married Lesleigh Couch and *Starling* became one of the most interesting zines through the next decade. *Starling* was a zine of popular culture and perhaps more than any other single publication showed the breadth of interest and knowledge of fans.

Trumpet was an offset zine started by Tom Reamy in 1965. Its reputation was based on its visual quality, like artist George Barr's adaptation of Poul Anderson's *The Broken Sword* into graphic story form, numerous art folios and illustrated film reviews; but the written articles suffered only in comparison to the graphics. *Trumpet* reached a peak in 1969, but then publication stopped when editor Reamy tried his hand at professional fiction.

Andy Porter's *Algol* was a quality sercon zine in the 1960s carrying interesting but sometimes dull articles on science fiction and also a regular review column, "Lupoff's Book Week." Late in the decade, Porter went offset, improved the quality of the articles and concentrated on the graphics in *Algol*. He eventually expanded the circulation until it could support him. In 1979, *Algol* became *Starship*.

Another 1960s zine, *Double: Bill*, received prominence with the aforementioned Symposium. When it folded, editor Bill Bowers started another zine, *Outworlds*. *Outworlds* achieved nearly a decade of raves as one of the finest and most innovative fanzines of all time. Bowers let his visual senses loose, using mimeo and offset, art, articles, photos and even blank space in a variety of manners. About every other issue the format would change. Bowers did not neglect the quality of his written material while he sought for the perfect fanzine. Columns by Bob Tucker, Robert A. W. Lowndes, Susan Wood and others were interspersed with quality articles and interesting and well-edited letters. *Outworlds* was *the* fanzine while it was published.

Throughout the 1970s a controversy has raged over whether or not zines with circulations of a thousand or more, some of which pay for material and support their publishers, should be considered fanzines. This has particularly affected the Hugo Awards because of its definition of Best Fanzine as best amateur magazine. This controversy has primarily concerned four magazines— *SFR*, *Locus*, *Algol* and *Outworlds*, which dominated the award nominations during this time. *SFR* and *Algol* paid their contributors and both they and *Locus* are profitable ventures. *Outworlds*, on the other hand, reached its height in the normal fannish manner of gratis contributions and still remained in the red. Most fanzine publishers believed that profit-making zines were semi-professional journals and should not be eligible for the Hugo. Eventually, this question became mostly academic; *Outworlds* folded, Brown declared that *Locus* would no longer accept a Hugo nomination and Porter stated that *Algol* was a professional magazine and changed the title to *Starship*, to increase its circulation. Only *SFR* remained eligible and despite combined efforts of fan editors, it again won the award at Seacon in 1979.

Other interesting fanzines included *Granfalloon* from Linda Eyster Bushyager and, for the early issues, Suzle Tompkins; *Energumen* from Michael and Susan Glicksohn; *Prehensile* from Mike Glyer; *Mythologies* from Don D'Ammassa; *The Spanish Inquisition* from Jerry Kaufman and Suzle Tompkins; *Simulacrum* from Victoria Vayne; *Janus* from Linda Bogstad and Jean Gomoll; and *Khatru* from Jeff Smith. *Maya*, a British zine from Rob Jackson, and *SF Commentary*, an Australian zine from Bruce Gillespie, were both of high quality and had large circulations in the United States. In the late 1960s incarnations of *Shangri L'Affaires* from LASFS and *Warhoon* from Richard Bergereon were also popular. This is by no means a comprehensive list.

With the tremendous growth of fandom, many fans longed for the smaller, friendlier fandom of the past. They almost created a sub-fandom of their own. For themselves, they adopted the terms trufan and faan. Two fanzines were almost fanzines from the past and another reprinted articles from past zines. For the past decade, *Mota* from Terry Hughes, has been a thin, fairly frequent zine filled with fan fiction and opinion. It is as close to being a 1950s zine as can be published in the 1970s. *Random* was a short-lived (one year) zine that concentrated on fannish columns, often managing to resurrect gafiated fans to fanac one more time. *Fanhistorica*, from Joe Siclari, concentrated on reprinting quality articles from fandom's past. *Mota* and *Fanhistorica* are still being published. Other fanzines also reprinted old material, often with introductions by Terry Carr in his Entropy Reprint series.

Because fanzines with circulations of 100–300 and unpaid contributions found it impossible to compete equally for a Hugo Award with semi-pro zines which paid their contributors and had thousands of readers, Moshe Feder organized an ad hoc committee and created the FAAN Awards. Besides Feder, the committee included Bushyager, Glyer, Bowers, Warner, Donn Brazier, M. Glicksohn, Sam Long, Jeff Smith, D'Ammassa and Darroll Pardoe. These awards are given in several categories by qualified voters. To be eligible to vote in a category, a voter must have been active in that category, similar to the Academy Awards.

One interesting fannish highlight was the "Flushing in '80" bid for the worldcon. Led by Stu Shiffman, New York fans planned a hoax bid which would use Shea Stadium for the masquerade, program and banquet consisting of ballpark franks, peanuts, popcorn, potato chips and beer. The pro GoH was Bob Tucker, the fan GoH was his alter ego, Hoy Ping Pong and the official Toaster was Susan Wood. Everyone who paid $1 for a presupporting membership was placed on the Concom.

Besides being popular enough to be double GoH at a hoax con, Bob Tucker was also the victim of a fannish deportation plot. In 1975, a special fan fund was organized to send Tucker to the Aussiecon. Bob Shaw, on the other hand, was esteemed highly enough to be imported from Ireland to the Noreascon.

With TAFF going strong for nearly 20 years, and interest in Australian fandom "piquing" with the approach of Aussiecon, The Down Under Fan Fund (DUFF) was developed to ship fans between the U. S. and Australia. In 1972,

Lesleigh Lutrell went to Australia as the first winner. The second winner was Leigh Edmunds who came to the U. S. in 1974; and Rusty Hevelin was shipped to the Aussiecon. Like TAFF, DUFF has been continued over the years.

Two large fannish projects also reached fruitation during this period. Harry Warner, Jr.'s detailed history of science fiction fandom was published. The first volume, *All Our Yesterdays,* was published in 1969 by Advent Publishers and the second volume, *A Wealth of Fable,* was published by Joe Siclari in 1977. In 1979, Richard Bergerson published a giant (600-page) issue of *Warhoon,* which consisted entirely of a retrospective and biography of Walter A. Willis.

Some of the previously mentioned sub-fandoms and some new ones as well grew so large during this period that they could support small publishing houses that catered to their interests. Sword and Sorcery fandom grew so large that Howard books sold out quickly, sometimes within days of publication, and publishers came out with books from many related authors such as Leiber, Karl Edward Wagner and others. Lovecraft was so popular that minutiae, letters, fragments and even notes were put into print.

Star Trek fandom was created with the letter campaign to keep the show on the air for a third year. Unfortunately, considering the overall quality of third year episodes, the campaign was successful. These fans and many, many more eventually started going to conventions and then started their own cons. Attendance at ST cons became phenomenal with thousands crushing into hotels. With this kind of senseless market, commercialization became rampant, with some dealers giving little more than shiny cut silhouettes for a "fan's" money.

Other TV and film fandoms existed but were much smaller. *Star Wars, Logan's Run,* and *Battlestar Galactica* all had followers. These wore uniforms and carried weapons of some sort with which they shot at other, often unknowing, congoers. These received the unflattering appellation of "Jackboot Fandom." The worst of these were the "Runners" and "Sandmen" followers of *Logan's Run* and most were located in California.

Other sub-fandoms centered around Perry Rhodan, Darkover, science fiction films, and Dr. Who. Near the end of the decade, the easy availability of video recorders created its own fandom.

Regional conventions have received little notice in this article because there are too many of them to cover. In this period, there were so many new conventions started that a fan in any part of the United States could find a con within driving distance. A fan with unlimited funds could make a convention every weekend of the year and often have a choice of two or more. To find a local con, all you have to do is get a newzine for a convention listing or read lists in some of the prozines.

The worldcons have changed drastically. Since Nycon III, the only worldcons with under 1000 attendees have been those held in countries for the first time, in Germany and in Australia.

The Baycon was held in Oakland, California at the Hotel Claremont. Co-chairmen Bill Donaho, Alva Rogers and J. Ben Stark were not expecting the 1430 attendees, so many fans had to stay at other hotels some distance from the con. Traveling between hotels was sometimes an adventure because of the student riots in nearby Berkeley. Opinions varied on the Baycon, as with all conventions. In this case, however, opinions were usually extreme with few in the middle. GoHs were Philip José Famer, pro, and Walt Daugherty, fan. The heat in Oakland that Labor Day weekend was extreme and the air-conditioning negligible. At the banquet, the heat became unbearable as Farmer's speech seemed unending. Other programs included special readings by Ellison and Pohl, a medieval program by the Society for Creative Anachronism, and a very large masquerade which *Galaxy* helped finance in place of a "Galaxy of Fashion" show. The masquerade also had three rock bands for additional entertainment. At the business meeting, two fan Hugo awards were added to the list and con site selection was set for two years in advance to allow for better planning. The 1969 worldcon competition between Columbus and St. Louis ended with a St. Louis victory.

The St. Louiscon again set an attendance record with 1534. The GoHs were Jack Gaughan, pro, and Eddie Jones, fan. It was only the second time that an artist had been selected as pro GoH and the first that an artist fan GoH had been chosen. The con gave all attendees a special Gaughan souvenir portfolio. The co-chairmen were Ray and Joyce Fisher. Program items included a comics program, many speeches and panels, the masquerade (at which a fan dressed as comic strip character Charlie Brown broke the movie screen and Harlan Ellison led a collection to pay for the damage), followed by a rock band, and the regular awards banquet. The sites for the next two worldcons were chosen to meet the rule passed at Baycon. Heidelberg, Germany won for 1970, and Boston won for 1971.

The Heicon was the first (and so far only) worldcon held in a non-English speaking country. Con attendance was down to 620 but many Americans did attend, including a plane load of Americans organized and led by Don and Grace Lundry. Heicon was chaired by Manfred Kage and programs were in two languages. Heicon also had more GoH's than any other worldcon. In the pro area GoHs were Robert Silverberg, American, E. C. Tubb, British, and Herbert W. Franke, German. When Elliot Shorter won TAFF, they also named him as fan GoH.

A daily bilingual con newspaper was published, *Fanorama International*, and it included an English translation of Franke's GoH speech, a talk on future technology. The masquerade was very small and a highlight of the con was a boat trip on the Neckar River. The Heicon committee had some minor problems from a left-wing, radical German group that felt that Americans should not attend the con and should get out of Vietnam. At the business meeting, a worldcon rotation system was respecified. Worldcons would be in North America in this order: west area, middle area, east area, and any year a non-North American bid felt it was ready, it could bid. The 1972 site was given to Los Angeles without any competition.

The 1971 Noreascon proved that giant North American worldcons were here to stay. Noreascon had 1600 members and foreshadowed future attendance figures. GoHs were Clifford D. Simak, pro, and Harry Warner, Jr., fan; the chairman was Tony Lewis. The programming was sectioned into three main subjects: "Terraforming the Earth," "Man-Made Man," and "Science Fiction: The Writing on the Wall-Prophecy or Graffiti?" The convention was very smoothly run and reconfirmed the efficiency of the Bostan area fans. There again was a heat problem at the banquet. The air-conditioning quit and the non-diners were allowed into the hall while the meal was still in progress instead of waiting until the start of the program. John W. Campbell, Jr. had died that summer and Lester del Rey gave a eulogy for him. In addition to the regular art show, which was very large, there was a special exhibit of Richard Powers' surrealist paintings which were covers of so many paperbacks in the 1950s and 1960s. Other highlights included a very good masquerade and a dialog between Asimov and Simak. At the business meeting, it was decided that whenever a worldcon was outside North America that a North American Science Fiction Convention (NASFiC) would be held. The 1973 worldcon was voted to Toronto.

The LAcon in 1972 had over 2000 attendees. GoHs were Fred Pohl, pro, and Robert and Juanita Coulson, fans. The co-chairmen of the con were Chuck Crayne and Bruce Pelz. The program was very large, with as many as three program items running simultaneously. One unusual event was a medieval wedding between Steve Goldin and Kathleen Sky. There were panels on energy, fandom, and the space program as well as on science fiction. Ellison talked about professionalism. The film program was very large and well chosen. The banquet had Bloch as toastmaster, short talks by both Coulsons, and a funny anecdotal speech by Pohl. Other highlights were an excellent art show, a Futuristic Fashion Show and a small but very high quality masquerade. At the business meeting, the Best Magazine category was dropped from the Hugo Awards and replaced by Best Professional Editor. Washington, D.C. was selected for the 1974 worldcon.

In 1973, Torcon II established another attendance record with 2900 attendees. They reprised their pro GoH with Robert Bloch who said that since he was GoH at Torcon I 25 years before, he also wanted to be GoH at Torcon III in 1998. Fan GoH was Bill Rotsler. Chairman was John Millard. The Royal York Hotel was under renovation during the con and was also smaller than really needed, but the friendliness of the hotel staff made up for other inconveniences. The programs were not innovative, but were unusually well attended. The banquet sold out and, unfortunately, Lester del Rey had a eulogy for another giant, J. R. R. Tolkien. The art show and masquerade were both small but of high quality. Possibly the added difficulty of bringing things across the border and through customs discouraged those who did not have high confidence in their work. In site selection, Australia easily won over Los Angeles. Los Angeles under Chuck Crayne won the right to put on the first NASFiC.

Dicson II was held in the Sheraton Park Hotel. Chairmen were Jay Haldeman and Ron Bounds and attendance reached 4435, another record. GoHs were Roger Zelazny, pro, and Jay Kay Klein, fan. The programs were well received, especially a "Dialog" between Harlan Ellison and Isaac Asimov, which was really a good-natured insult match. Many program items were on writing. Zelazny's GoH speech was very autobiographical and the con printed 1,000 souvenir booklets of his poems. The banquet was much too long because of toastmaster Andy Offut's extended talking but was very well attended. The art show was the largest ever and included a special show of Chesley Bonestell originals loaned by the Smithsonian. The masquerade was large and much too long. Another highlight was a preview showing of *A Boy and His Dog,* a film based on an Ellison story. The 1976 site bidding was won by Kansas City.

The Aussiecon was the first worldcon to be held in Australia. Chairman was Robin Johnson and GoHs were Ursula K. Le Guin, pro, and Susan Wood, Mike Glicksohn and Donald Tuck, fans. Attendance was 606 and again included a plane load of Americans led by Don and Grace Lundry. The high cost of Le Guin's travel arrangements were paid by the Literature Board of the Australian Council because she also held a writer's conference the week before the con.

The con began on Thursday, August 14, at the Southern Cross Hotel. Much of the program included participation by the Americans attending. The smaller attendance also allowed for more spontaneity, including several fannish programs, such as Susan Wood's interview with Bob Tucker and Tucker instructing the entire convention in the proper fannish procedure used to drink bourbon. The art show and masquerade were both very small in comparison to American cons. The bidding for the 1977 worldcon was won by Orlando.

Chairman Ken Keller and the MidAmeriCon committee in Kansas City were relatively new to worldcon operations and claimed they would have the ultimate worldcon ever, not realizing some of the problems they would face. They tried; parts of the con were elaborate and expensive and sometimes controversial. The GoHs were Robert A. Heinlein, pro, and George Barr, fan. Attendance reached 2800. GoH Heinlein required special consideration during the con and the concomm arranged for the Dorsai (a group of uniformed fans imitating Gordon Dickson's warrior clan) to bodyguard him and to provide for general security. This caused problems. Fans are usually polite and friendly in an amiable, anarchic way, but when placed in opposition to a dictatorial guard, bad feelings arose quickly. Heinlein did insist on one good service which has almost become a tradition; he required the con to stage a blood drive and only those who donated were allowed to meet him.

The program was good, utilizing a nearby convention hall as well as the hotel. Some items were very expensive and did cause budget problems. The con had a professional theater company perform a play, "Sails of Moonlight, Eyes of Dusk," which was well acted, but long and cost $8,000 for one performance. Other unnecessary expenses included beautiful, but very elaborate bases to the Hugo Awards, and a hardbound program book. The art show and masquerade were both among the best ever. The 1978 site was given to another new committee, Phoenix over Los Angeles.

The 1977 SunCon was an unusual bid and a controversial convention. Chairman Don Lundry organized a bidding committee of well-known and experienced fen to bid for the worldcon in Orlando, Florida, near Disney World. Soon after they won, the controversy started. Two key committee members, Rusty Hevelin and JoAnn Wood, resigned, claiming Lundry did not communicate with them. After they were replaced, the original hotel, the only one in Orlando large enough to hold a worldcon, announced bankruptcy. Because of time constraints the site was changed to the Hotel Fontainbleau in Miami Beach without checking with the members of the con. As the con approached, it was noticeable that not having anyone live near the site was a problem.

The con itself had 2050 attendees and ran relatively smoothly. GoHs were Jack Williamson, pro, and Bob Madle, fan. The convention had multitrack programming, which was interesting but too much for the number of attendees since more were expected than had arrived. Highlights included a full track of fan programs, dialogues between several pairs of collaborators and several science programs. The film program was very extensive and of high quality. The art show was large and very good but the masquerade was small and mostly uninteresting. The site for the 1979 worldcon was won by Brighton, England.

For the third year in a row, a worldcon ran into problems before the con itself when Iguanacon's chairman and several key committeemen resigned. The final con chairman was Tim Kyger. At the con itself, with last-minute help from many fans, things went smoothly despite the attendance reaching over 5000, the largest ever. GoHs were Harlan Ellison, pro, and Bill Bowers, fan. Fans premiered *Watership Down* at the con. Harlan Ellison typed a story in a plastic tent in the atrium of the hotel and his speech called for fans to get more involved in social issues. The banquet was also a "roast" of Ellison. The art show was not as impressive as it could have been. The masquerade was impressive but many of the 2500 trying to see it were seated too far away. The site for the 1980 con was voted to Boston.

The last worldcon of the decade was again held in England. The Seacon was held in the resort area of Brighton, August 23–27, 1979. Attendance for the con at the Metropole and several other hotels was 2344. Chairman was Peter Weston and the GoHs were Brian Aldiss, British pro, Fritz Leiber, American pro and Harry Bell, fan. Fans attended from all over the world including several hundred Americans, who cringed at the high prices and found it difficult to find Europeans they wanted to meet. Several American pros were offended when they were ignored by their own British publishers.

The program was adequate but not very innovative. The BBC produced a five-part show on science fiction, partly based on the con. And fans must have had a good time—the bar was always full and 29,000 gallons of beer were sold. Several media personalities were in attendance, including Christopher Reeve (*Superman*), Tom Baker (*Dr. Who*) and Richard O'Brien (*Rocky Horror Picture Show*). A special Dragons Dream art exhibit put on by Roger Dean was impressive as were other parts of the art show. The site selection for the 1981 con was won by Denver over Seattle.

CONCLUDING COMMENTS

Fandom has grown so large and has so many off-shoots that it is impossible for any one fan to participate in all of it or even to keep track of all that is going on. Bit by bit, science fiction fandom has created sub-fandoms which have grown and flourished on their own. Accordingly, science fiction fandom's own flields of interest widen and then shrink, usually because the sub-fandoms attract large numbers of newcomers and collectors who in their turn attract commercial parasites and afterwards branch off on their own.

Now it is no longer outside interests, such as films or the SCA or comics, nor specialized interests, like Burroughs, Lovecraft or Howard, that are swelling fandom. Science fiction, the literature itself, has become respectable and is gaining wide acceptance. For example, while specialized interests might bring even one-third of the attendees to a worldcon, that still leaves nearly 3500 attendees (using Iguanacon figures) who are able to make the annual Big Event.

There are several reasons for the increased amount of participation in fannish activities. There is a larger number of fans, of course, but there is also a larger proportion of highly educated fans often earning higher salaries which enable them to more easily enjoy themselves. Additionally, science fiction is a popular fad because of the highly publicized futurists, both ecologists and technocrats, who recommend science fiction as a prophet of possible trends.

Whether the fannish fandom of the past can ever regain the prominence it once had is a matter of conjecture. It was impossible for the 5000-person mass at the Iguanacon to feel the fraternal atmosphere that permeated fandom through its conventions and fanzines in a smaller, more interactive fandom. Most fans today never even see a fanzine and many believe that the semi-pro publications often filled with dry articles and/or news, are fanzines and vote fan Hugo Awards to them. And most fans do not attend regional cons regularly. From personal experience, I know that fanac requires a tremendous amount of voluntary work; often the only credit received is in the form of blame for the problems which are usually considerable. Fandom will have to confront these problems and find solutions soon or be overwhelmed by the same type of commercialism that dominates some other fields.

Fans have very different ideas on what should be done. Some fanzine fans have tried to retreat into an inner fannish circle whose only entry portal is through the fanzines. Convention fans have plans to create a new WSFS, Inc. to ease the burden and minimize the problems of running conventions that could soon reach 10,000 or more. Still others have retreated into gafia, abhoring the impersonalism which has become prevalent.

Being the amenable anarchy that it is, fandom's future will probably flow with the popularity of the science fiction field, as it has in the past. This will cause idealistic conflicts within itself, but fandom should survive as long as its members want to communicate with each other. Because of its very nature as an anarchy, it is hard to kill. Probably those that want to cling to the fannish spirit of the past will literally create a sub-fandom of the larger more impersonal whole.

RECOMMENDED READING

Asimov, Isaac, *In Memory Yet Green,* and *In Joy Still Felt,* Doubleday & Co., Garden City, N. Y., 11531.

Brown, Brian Earl, *The Whole Fanzine Catalog,* Privately printed: Detroit, 1978–.

Brown, Charles, N., *Locus,* Locus Publications, P. O. Box 3938, San Francisco, California, 94119.

Eney Richard, *Fancyclopedia II,* Mirage Press, 5111 Liberty Heights Ave., Baltimore, Maryland, 21207.

Friend, Beverly, "The Science Fiction Fan Cult," Diss. Northwestern, 1975.

Geis, Richard, *Science Fiction Review,* P. O. Box 11408, Portland, Oregon, 97211.

Glyer, Mike, *File 770*, 14974 Osceola Street, Sylmar, California, 91342.

Knight, Damon, *The Futurians: The Story of the Science Fiction "Family" of the 30's That Produced Today's Top SF Writers and Editors*, New York: John Day, 1977.

Lester, Colin, *The International Science Fiction Yearbook 1979*, Quick Fox, 33 W. 60th Street, New York, N. Y., 10023.

Moskowitz, Sam, *The Immortal Storm: A History of Science Fiction Fandom*, Atlanta: Atlanta Science Fiction Organization Press, 1954; rpt. Westport, Ct: Hyperion Press, 1974.

Nicholls, Peter, *The Science Fiction Encyclopedia*, Doubleday & Co., Garden City, N. Y., 11531.

Pohl, Frederik, *The Way the Future Was*, Del Rey Books, New York, N. Y.,10022.

Porter, Andrew, *Science Fiction Chronicle*, and *Starship*, P. O. Box 4175, New York, N. Y., 10017.

Roberts, Peter, *British Fanzine Bibliography Part One: 1930-50*, Privately Printed: U.K., 1977.

————, *British Fanzine Bibliography Part Two: 1951-1960*, Privately Printed: U. K., 1978.

————, *Guide to Current Fanzines*, 5th ed., Privately printed: U. K., 1978.

Siclari, Joseph, *Fanhistorica*, Joseph Siclari, 4599 N. W. 5th Avenue, Boca Raton, Florida, 33431.

Warner, Harry, Jr., *All Our Yesterdays*, Advent: Publishers, Inc., P. O. Box 9228, Chicago, Illinois, 60690.

————, *A Wealth of Fable*, Joseph Siclari, 4599 N. W. 5th Avenue, Boca Raton, Florida, 33431.

Wertham, Fredric, *The World of Fanzines*, Carbondale: Southern Illinois University Press, 1973.

Willis, Walter, *Warhoon 28*, Richard Bergeron, 1 West 72 Street, New York, N. Y., 10023.

Winston, Joan, *The Making of Star Trek Conventions*, Garden City, N. Y.: Doubleday, 1977.

Harlan McGhan

THE WRITING AWARDS

Introduction

This chapter will cover the yearly awards given specifically for published original works of science fiction, in the various categories for which such awards are given (most usually: novel, novella, novelette, and short story). The limitation to awards for individual works of SF is partly practical. An attempt to cover all SF awards thoroughly—including, for example, awards for fanzines, fan writing, professional editing, dramatic presentations (movies, TV shows), art work, and writer recognition awards ("best new writer," "career achievements") —would make this the project of several lifetimes and many volumes.

Also in part, the limitation to individual works of published original fiction is an expression of my conviction that these are central to all SF activities. The writing endures. The rest is either (like fandom and professional editing) dependent on it, or (like SF art and SF movies) largely derivative from it. The fiction of the past thirty years is very much with us today, still read, still real, vital, and important. Thus, the awards for fiction made throughout this period continue to be of substantial interest. By contrast, there is little to interest most of us any more in knowing, say, the winner of the "best fanzine" award of 1957, or the "best dramatic presentation" award of 1962. (If you do happen to be fascinated by this information, it can be found dutifully recorded for the most important set of awards, the Hugos, in *A History of the Hugo, Nebula, and International Fantasy Awards*, by Donald Franson and Howard DeVore; subsequently referred to as Franson & DeVore.)

Within the restriction to individual works of SF, I have attempted to provide the best possible information about English language awards; and to provide what information I can (often, too little—see the note below) about foreign language awards. In particular, since it is my intention to give the broadest picture I can of the fiction believed to be of interest in any year, I have provided complete lists of nominees for every award, wherever that information has been available to me.

To be nominated at all for an award is an achievement, deserving recognition; and (life being what it is: often unfair) it would be remarkable if the best work always won. Further, to know only what won, without also knowing the competition, is of little real value. (Life being what it is, the fascination lies in seeing what lost to what.) At a minimum, this chapter should provide the most thorough single-source coverage of original science fiction award winners and nominees available in any reference work.

The one category of writing award for original fiction I have systematically excluded from these listings is what I will call "story contests." Typically, a "story contest" is an award for previously unpublished material, with (in many instances) eligibility further restricted by topic or length or both. However, I extend this definition to include any award offered by an individual publisher, the object of which is largely to secure proprietary material for use by that publisher (whether or not the material so secured has previously appeared in print).

The brief objection to all story contests for previously unpublished material is that (1) Awards, by nature, represent a judgment about the relative merits enjoyed by the members of some class of objects; and (2) These awards, by definition, are dealing with the wrong class of objects. Since they do not even pretend to judge published SF, therefore (3) They can tell us nothing about the relative merits of the SF which is being published.

A less facile objection to story contests is that they have the wrong aim. Their objective is never to tell us anything about the state of the art of SF, but always to promote a favored cause. It is true the cause in question may be both innocent and laudable. (Some of these contests have no motive more ulterior than encouraging young writers.) The relevant point is that no award with this sort of target has any discernible relation to quality.

In the first place, the judges of a story contest are restricted to choosing a winner from the manuscripts submitted. But each manuscript submitted comes with the somewhat dubious recommendation that, to date, no one has ever seen fit to publish it (or, if they did, they have no interest in ever publishing it again). The competition, then, however large, is invariably highly artificial. It is by nature insulated from candidates whose prospects in the commercial marketplace are more favorable than the prospects awaiting the contest winner. The easiest races to win are the ones the best runners never enter; but the same circumstance necessarily detracts from the view that victory is a measure of detectable merit.

In the second place, if it is conceded that writing is sometimes done for reasons not entailing an eye to the main commercial chance, it still does not follow that it is the sort of activity one takes up in order to win some contest. In fact—though writers like to win awards as much as anyone (some seem to like it more)—in most instances, the motives which impel someone to write have little to do with the urge to win contests; and, where this is the motive, the results are not likely to be felicitous. Hence, there are no great manuscripts languishing out there, waiting for the incentive of some competition to call them forth. The best a story contest can hope for is to find a winner that will be passable. If, by chance, the winner is more than just passably good, it will have ample opportunity to be recognized by the post-publication awards.

The most notable awards ruled out by the injunction against story contests are those held by publishers, for the purpose of securing proprietary material. Since securing proprietary material to publish is exactly a publisher's business, these contests frequently involve relatively large cash prizes, and they are invariably accompanied by as much publicity as the publisher judges useful. The motives in this sort of case at least have the virtue of being straightforward. A publisher: (A) Needs manuscripts to stay in business. Who knows, there *may* be one or more good unpublished works out there, and this contest just *might* tempt their authors to send them to him first, rather than to some rival. (B) Believes the attendant publicity, whatever the outcome of the contest, will promote his company.

The two best known "bad" examples of what is likely to result from this sort of promotional publisher's contest are both from the fifties. In 1953, *Galaxy* magazine, in combination with the publishing house of Simon & Schuster, offered what they billed as "the richest science fiction novel contest in history." (The "lavishly attractive" sum in question was $6500; actually, pretty good considering the year was 1953. By the standards of that long vanished era, the sums now paid for SF novels are, well, science fictional.) The promising new writer unearthed by this literary talent hunt, over two years after the contest was first announced, turned out to be "Edson McCann," author of a novel titled *Preferred Risk*.

"Edson McCann" later turned out to be somewhat better known under the names Frederik Pohl and Lester del Rey. Evidently, Pohl and del Rey happened to be collaborating at the time on an independently conceived, and already partially written novel, which they had shown to Horace Gold (then editor of *Galaxy*) for possible serialization under their own names. Evidently, Gold at that time was in an increasingly desperate position in his efforts to find a suitable contest "winner." According to Pohl:

> As the deadline approached and he read through the hundreds of entries that blocked every doorway in his apartment, it became clear that there was nothing there that was really outstanding, and an awful lot that was preposterously bad. (*The Way the Future Was: A Memoir*, Ballantine Books, 1978, p. 210)

And so a bargain was struck. Gold would give Pohl and del Rey the prize money for their novel already in process; and they would agree to become "Edson McCann," brilliant but secretive SF discovery. The only real flaw in the plan was that when, after many collaborative difficulties and delays, *Preferred Risk* was finally completed, it turned out not to be a very good SF novel (too).

Thus, the only issue of "the richest science fiction novel contest in history" proved to be hundreds of bad novels (none of which were ever published), one not very good novel (which was being written anyways), and a hoax which failed (after several years).

The same year as the *Galaxy*-Simon & Schuster contest, a second "big money" contest for best original novel was being held by two other publishers: Shasta, a specialty SF hardcover house, in collaboration with the paperback firm of Pocket Books. The "winner" of this contest was Philip José Farmer, for a book titled *I Owe for the Flesh*. That might be regarded as some vindication of story contests, since Farmer really was a brilliant new author, and since the book in question went on to become the "Riverworld" series.

Except, that is, for the facts that, first, Farmer was not discovered by this contest. He had already published his seminal novella, "The Lovers," as well as a number of other excellent stories in 1952 (winning a 1953 Hugo for "best new author" in consequence). Second, judging by subsequent history, Farmer almost certainly would have written the book in question apart from any contest. And third, Shasta shortly fell into serious financial difficulties and expired, without ever paying the prize money or publishing the book.

Thus the only real issue of his contest was to prevent *I Owe for the Flesh* from ever being published (as such); and to deliver a serious financial blow to its author at a vulnerable point in his career.

These are, admittedly, selected examples. To conclude this discussion of the story contests sponsored by publishers on a happier note, at least one significant French language SF award, the Prix Jules Verne, also falls into this category. The "prize" was originated by the French publishing firm of Hachette in 1927, and given annually by them in two discontinuous series. The initial set of awards, which lasted through 1933, went to "novels written in the spirit of Jules Verne"—but was not quite an SF award, in the sense of an award specifically for works of SF, since in 1932 it went to a Western. In 1957 it was revived by the firm (now Hachette and Gallimard), this time strictly as an award for SF novels by contemporary French authors. The second series ran through 1963 before being discontinued for a second and last time.

Both series, however, displayed the critical characteristic which excludes them from listing here. The first owed its inspiration to an effort to find material for a magazine put out by Hachette; and winners of the second were brought out in a special "Rayon Fantastique" edition by H&G. Hence, I am excluding it with equal impartiality, even though—so far as I know—it has never either involved any element of hoax, or paid its winner with less than estimable promptness. (The point is, failings of that sort are not the point.)

Nonetheless, the Prix Jules Verne is by any reckoning an important SF award. There is, thus, no *general* objection to story contests, and I do not mean to imply by my recitation of sad tales from a bygone era that story contests are either unworthy of consideration, or ought to be abolished outright. In fact, they are the oldest sort of SF award made, dating back to the earliest years of the first SF genre magazines. They have maintained an extensive and (largely) honorable tradition since. They surely deserve their own chapter in the history of SF awards. It is just that, with the exception of the preceding remarks, this is not that chapter.

The awards this chapter will concern itself with, then, begin with the International Fantasy Award, first presented in 1951—the first English-language SF award of any consequence for individual works of fiction, which was not a story contest—and run through the newest awards of this description, first presented in 1980. A question worth some consideration, in an introduction to SF awards, is why such awards begin in the early 50s, rather than either earlier or later? What changed, such that before that change there were no SF awards at all, and after it they not only existed, but did so in ever-increasing profusion?

The most significant change that occurred in the relevant period, I think, had to be the introduction of book publishing into SF. Before the late 40s, SF was effectively confined to the genre magazines. These were "pulps," a type of publication more noted for its lurid covers than for its literary qualities; and which enjoyed absolutely no prestige whatsoever. But to give an award for merit necessarily presupposes quality in its object, and always connotes prestige. In an era when SF was synonymous with pulp fiction, then, the idea of a literary award for SF could not help but appear ludicrous. To be sure, in some circles SF is still synonymous with pulp fiction, and the idea of a literary award for it remains ludicrous; but until the start of the 50s the circles were more numerous and much larger, and included everyone but a few fans, hardened to all shame.

Further, as long as SF was confined to the magazines, it was mostly written to the shorter lengths, with novels represented only by the occasional serial. But literary awards for fiction, in any area, are given mostly for novels. All the most famous fiction prizes—the Pulitzer Prize, the National Book Awards (now the American Book Awards), the Newbery Medals—are for novels. The most famous American award for shorter fiction is the O. Henry Memorial Awards. But, asked to name any award for fiction, who would reply "O. Henry"? (For that matter, asked to name any author of fiction, who would name a writer chiefly famous for the shorter lengths?) In an era when SF was mostly done to the novelette length and shorter, then, the idea of a literary award for SF was, if not unthinkable, at least unnatural.

With the advent of book publishing in SF, both these obstacles disappeared, or greatly diminished. Books, unlike pulps, are inherently respectable, and invariably connote prestige (especially hardcovers). The idea of giving a literary award to a *book* is *not* ludicrous. Making, accepting, or paying attention to such an award does not require being hardened to all shame. It is significant, therefore—though the great bulk of SF was still being published in the magazines in 1951—that the first important literary award for SF was given specifically to books.

In addition, the staple of the fiction book industry is the novel, rather than the shorter length. (Shorter lengths are not just hard to get published in book form, but almost always sell poorly and lose money; these are not unrelated.) Hence, once books came to SF, the demand shifted toward novels. And once the SF novel established a real presence in the genre—rather than merely being the occasional aberration—the idea of a literary award for SF became very natural. Since what is natural in the way of ideas tends to get thought of sooner rather than later, and nothing is simpler than implementing an award—essentially, all it requires is an announcement (though a few frills are nice too)—SF awards could not be long in coming. It is significant, therefore, that the first Hugo for fiction—though the great bulk of SF was still being published at the shorter lengths in 1953—was given only in the one category, "best novel." (Also note that, with one exception, every IFA winner or runner-up was a novel, or at least something made to look like a novel.)

To be sure, there is more than can be said on a question as large as why a thing happens at one time rather than another, but this much will have to do for confines of the present chapter. The fact is that, on any explanation, within a few years of the start of noticeable book publishing activity in SF, there was not just one important SF award, but two.

With the exception of noting two potentially troublesome ambiguities in awards' practice, we are now ready to turn directly to the history of the particular award themselves. First, the same award in different years, and different awards in the same year, may use different standards of eligibility for a given category. Given the diversity of categories and awards, and the number of years involved, it is impossible to treat this problem adequately in the space of the present article. A simple warning, then, will have to suffice: At most, the separate categories used in different years should be taken as marking *general* differences of length/time, which tend to shade into each other with some overlapping, rather than hard and fast divisions.

A second ambiguity in awards' practice is more amenable to treatment. Yearly awards are *made* in one year, but they are normally *for* works published the previous year. The awards made at the 1971 World Science Fiction Convention, for example, were for 1970. So how shall we understand the reference of a term like "1971 award"? Is 1971 the year the award was made (so we are actually talking about 1970 science fiction); or is 1971 the year the awarded work was first published (so we are actually talking about an award made in 1972)?

Unfortunately, if we look to current practice with respect to SF awards, we find no resolution of this ambiguity. There are different usages for different awards. Specifically, the two leading awards are split over this issue. Those given by popular vote at the World Science Fiction Convention are dated by the year of the convention; that is, by the year in which they are made. Thus they are called, say, "1979 Hugos," but in reality they are being given for 1978 achievements. In contrast, the awards presented by the Science Fiction Writers of America are dated by the year for which the award is made. Thus, the "1978 Nebulas" are the awards given for 1978 achievements, but in fact they are voted on and handed out sometime during 1979. So the "1979 Hugos" and the "1978 Nebulas" actually cover the same period, the calendar year 1978, and get made in the same year, 1979. They just sound as if they ought to be awards for two different years.

As you can see, the presence of two distinct usages is confusing. Consequently, for the purposes of this chapter, I propose to eliminate one in favor of the other. I will name all yearly awards in the same way, whether or not that is the way they are named by their granting organizations. Besides eliminating any possible confusion on this head, a system of uniform naming will make comparing awards that much simpler.

There is, no doubt, a certain rationality to the Nebula procedure of dating awards by the year for which they are made. However, on balance, it seems best to follow the Hugo practice, and date awards by the year in which they are made. Therefore, I have followed this convention in every case, and named all awards accordingly. Not only does this choice strike me as more direct, but also it is the one sanctioned by standard usage with respect to literary awards generally. In what follows, then, dated yearly awards are made for works first published in the preceding calendar year.

Note on Foreign Awards

Obtaining complete and accurate information on U.S./English-language SF awards is difficult. Obtaining complete and accurate information on foreign SF awards is substantially harder. At any rate, I do not have that information (yet). My ignorance should not be taken as a slight, and I apologize if the very limited treatment I can give these awards makes it seem so. I have been moved to include foreign awards in this article, despite the fact that I cannot begin to do many of them justice, because I judged it better to convey the very sketchy information I happen to have on hand than to risk leaving the impression that

SF is simply or mostly an American/English-language phenomenon. In fact, it is a world-wide enterprise. If what I can provide in this area serves only to give some general sense of the global nature of SF, it will have served its purpose.

General Conventions Used In Listing Awards

Works are listed by the title under which they won the award. Variant titles are listed (in parentheses) only where it seems likely that the work is better known by the alternate name.

The order of finish of nominees in a particular category is indicated by a ranking number to the left of the title. Ties are designated by a "t" added to the ranking number. Thus, two' titles which shared first place honors would both be designated, "1t." Where no number is given to the left of a title, its order of finish, relative to other similarly unranked titles it that category, is not known. I have followed the arbitrary rule in all these cases of listing nominees in alphabetical order by author.

It occasionally happens that a work qualifies for award's consideration, but is withdrawn for some reason by the author: most commonly, in favor of a second title nominated for the same honor; or (less often) as a protest against some action of the awarding organization. I have marked all these titles with an asterisk (*), and appended them out of alphabetical sequence at the end of the particular listing in question.

THE INTERNATIONAL FANTASY AWARD

NOTE ON TERMINOLOGY: In the interests of clarity—since more recent awards containing the word "fantasy" in their title specifically do mean to exclude "science fiction" from consideration—it is worth remarking that "fantasy" is used in "International Fantasy Award!' in a general sense, to delimit the entire field of what is sometimes called "fantastic literature." Hence, both works of "fantasy" and "science fiction" were eligible to win an IFA. (In this chapter, I use "SF" with the same general meaning, to include fantasy.)

The International Fantasy Award is, in every sense, the aristocrat of SF awards. It was the first major English-language award ever to be given specifically for achievements in the general area of SF. It was decided by an elite international "jury" (after the first year). It was awarded at an exclusive dinner, attended by selected SF luminaries (again, after the first year). It lasted only a relatively brief time (so gaining all the charms lent by distance and rarity). It took the form of an elegant "ensemble" (see description below). And, in its day, it was unquestionably the most coveted and prestigious honor in the field (an accolade only slightly diminished by the fact that it was also the only SF award for individual works of fiction in four of the six years it was presented). Such was its authority that the selections made, now twenty-five years ago and more, still carry weight.

The idea of an international "Annual Award for Artistic Merit in Creative Fantasy," as the IFA was officially known, came from four British fans: G. Ken Chapman, Frank A. Cooper, Leslie Flood, and John Beynon Harris (better known under his writing name, "John Wyndham"). While the official justification of the IFA was "to encourage higher standards in SF writing," its actual inspiration appears to have been nothing more profound than the desire to find a new activity for the 1951 national British SF convention held in London. (For the first IFA, "international" meant only that non-British works were eligible for consideration.)

However, the times were right. Whatever the IFA may have lacked in conception was more than compensated for by the enthusiasm with which the notion of such an annual award for SF, once born, was received. Following the tradition of most established literary awards, IFA winners and runners-up were selected by an "expert jury." The first year, this jury was entirely British in composition. But the following year, so successful had the initial award been, it proved feasible to make the selecting body (in addition to the works eligible for consideration) truly international. The 1952 IFA Committee had the following distinguished list of "permanent adjudicators":

BRITISH: John Carnell (editor)
                  Walter Gillings (editor)
                  John Beynon Harris (author & co-founder)
                  J. M. Walsh (author)
                  Fred C. Brown (bibliophile)
                  Walt Willis (Irish fan)

AMERICAN: Everett F. Bleiler, Anthony Boucher, J. Francis McComas (Bleiler a bibliophile & editor, other two editors & writers; all three acting as one)
                  Groff Conklin (editor)
                  August Derleth (editor, publisher)
                  Basil Davenport (reviewer)
                  Willy Ley (science writer)
                  Judith Merril (editor, writer)
                  Wilson Tucker (fan, writer)

FRENCH: Igor Malewski (editor)
                  Georges Gallet (editor, publisher)

SWEDISH: Sigvard Ostlund (bibliophile)

(Despite their title as "permanent adjudicators," it seems reasonable to suppose that members of this committee were not more permanent than members of most such committees. The only name not on this list, that I have ever actually seen instanced as an IFA juror, is P. Schuyler Miller; but there may well have been other persons added to the jury, as well as some persons dropped from it, during the four subsequent years in which awards were made.)

To correspond with this "denationalization" of the award jury, the presentation ceremony was shifted the same year (1952), from the British national SF convention, to a special dinner attended by various prominent SF figures; a tradition maintained until the award itself expired (in 1957). The IFA presented at this dinner was—to quote the rather flowery description of the 1951 awards committee—a "desk ornament in the form of a silver spaceship mounted on an inscribed plinth of polished oak, which also supports a table lighter, the ensemble forming a handsome and valuable example of the highest form of the modelmaker's art." (The cost of this "ensemble" appears to have been borne by The Fantasy Book Centre in London. That organization also undertook the task of publicizing the award, and so, possibly not quite incidentally, themselves.)

Initially there were two categories, one for fiction books (including collections as well as novels), and one for non-fiction books (most likely to be of interest to SF readers, e.g., books about space travel, the planets, lost continents, strange animals, etc.). The non-fiction category was dropped after the first three years. Consideration in both categories was limited to books published during the preceding calendar year.

The single criterion for selecting the fiction winner was the one mentioned in the official title of the IFA: "artistic merit in creative fantasy." The judges obviously took the stipulation that they were looking for "artistic merit" very seriously. The roster of the winners and runners-up for this award is a short list of some of the most impressive SF books published during the early and mid-50s. I have already commented on the continuing influence and prestige enjoyed by the IFA. In large part, this must be attributed to the remarkable sagacity displayed by the judges in their choices: books which shine, if anything, more brightly in the light of a quarter-century of hindsight than they ever could have in the light of the day.

Perhaps, scanning the names of the judges listed above, that is not surprising. The advantage of a jury award must reside in its jurors; who are not constrained to honor what might be less deserving but more popular. It is instructive on this point to compare the IFAs and the Hugos for the two years in which both were made. Unfortunately, the significance of this comparison is diminished by the fact that, during the early years of the Hugo, there were no nominees, and no runners-up in the voting were announced. Thus, while we know that in 1955 *A Mirror for Observers* won the IFA, while *They'd Rather Be Right* won the Hugo; and while it is also now clear that the former is as remarkable a piece of work as the latter is unremarkable; what we don't know is where *A Mirror for Observers,* or any of the IFA runners-up for that year—*Mission of Gravity, One in 300,* or *The Caves of Steel*—might have finished in the Hugo balloting.

What killed the IFA, after an illustrious but relatively brief career, was not bad taste in making selections for it, but the introduction of another and even more important award: the Hugo. Apparently SF, which until 1951 did not have even one award of significance, still was unable in 1956 to support two major awards at the same time.

In any Darwinian struggle between the two, the Hugo had all the advantages of course: it was based in the U.S., the dominant country in SF; it was showcased at the World SF Convention, the premier event of the SF year; and it was democratic in its method of selection, a choice by definition certain to prove popular. In short, if there was only room for one SF award, there was no way for the IFA to compete; and history soon witnessed, for the second time, the surrender of a British aristocrat to an American democrat.

This time, though, there was a late victory, of sorts, by the British. The Hugos began as a "one-shot" awards presentation in 1953, lapsing in 1954, before being reinstituted as a permanent set of annual awards in 1955. Once the Hugos were made permanent annual awards, the IFA evidently was dropped immediately, since no presentation was made in 1956.

But it did not quite go down for the count. By coincidence, the World SF Convention was scheduled to meet in London (England) in 1957. (The first time the World Convention had ever met outside the U.S., not counting Toronto.) Now the World SF Convention happens to control the Hugos, and the host city happens to control the convention. And the Loncon I committee, to which the care of the Hugos was entrusted by the convention, happened to decide not to include any categories for original fiction on the 1957 Hugo ballot. (Indeed, there were only three Hugo categories at all in 1957: best American and best British professional magazine, and best fanzine.)

By another odd coincidence, that same year—the stage, so to speak, being free—the IFA's happened to be revived for a brief farewell presentation. By yet another quirk, the recipient happened to be a British work, which though unquestionably deserving of the highest honors, probably stood no realistic chance of winning a Hugo. (And, if you are interested in one more anomaly, for the first time since the atypical initial IFA, no runners-up were announced).

1957 proved to be the last hurrah of the IFA. The World Convention went back to the U.S. in 1958, and the categories for original fiction were promptly restored (and have enjoyed continuous existence since); and the IFA promptly went back out of existence (this time permanently). By the time the World Convention returned to London in 1965, the IFA was too long cold to be revived, and the Hugos for original fiction too well established to be suspended; and the Nebulas were already looming on the horizon.

The International Fantasy Award, 1951-1957 *(all categories)*

NOTE: Awards are for the previous year, based on first *British* publication. Thus, despite the fact that both 1951 winners saw publication in the U.S. during 1949, each was still eligible for IFA consideration because the British edition did not come out until the following year. All "fiction book" nominees are novels, unless otherwise indicated.

1951: 1st IFA

fiction book
1. *Earth Abides*, George R. Stewart

non-fiction book
1. *The Conquest of Space*, Willy Ley & Chesley Bonestell

1952: 2nd IFA

fiction book
1. *Fancies and Goodnights*, John Collier (collection)
2. *Day of the Triffids*, John Wyndham
3. *The Illustrated Man*, Ray Bradbury (collection)

non-fiction book
1. *The Exploration of Space*, Arthur C. Clarke
2. *Dragons in Amber*, Willy Ley

3. *Rockets, Jets, Guided Missles and Spaceships*, Jack Coggins &
     Fletcher Pratt

1953: 3rd IFA

fiction book
1. *City*, Clifford D. Simak (integrated collection)
2. *Takeoff*, Cyril M. Kornbluth
3. *Player Piano*, Kurt Vonnegut, Jr.

non-fiction book
1. *Lands Beyond*, Willy Ley
2. *Across the Space Frontier*, Collier's magazine symposium
3. *In the Name of Science*, Martin Gardner
     (revised and enlarged edition published as *Fads and Fallacies in the
     Name of Science*)

1954: 4th IFA

fiction book
1. *More than Human*, Theodore Sturgeon (integrated collection)
2. *The Demolished Man*, Alfred Bester

non-fiction book
     category discontinued

1955: 5th IFA

fiction book
1. *A Mirror for Observers*, Edgar Pangborn
2. *A Mission of Gravity*, Hal Clement
3t. *The Caves of Steel*, Isaac Asimov
3t. *One in 300*, J. T. McIntosh

(1956: 6th IFA)

     awards temporarily suspended

1957: 7th IFA

fiction book
1. *Lord of the Rings*, J. R. R. Tolkien

(1958: 8th IFA)

     awards permanently suspended

THE HUGO AWARD

"Hugo" is the popular and common name for any of the official "Science
Fiction Achievement Awards" made by and at the annual World Science Fiction
Convention. The informal term is modeled after the example of the more
famous movie "Oscars" (which were the direct inspiration for the Hugos). The

"Hugo" being honored is Hugo Gernsback, who in 1926 invented science fiction as a distinct literary category (by bringing out the first SF genre magazine to be published in the United States, *Amazing Stories*), and who in 1929 authored the term "science fiction" itself.

Hugos are given in a variety of categories, which have changed more or less drastically at irregular intervals. In the categories of direct interest, here, for the several lengths of original fiction, eight or so different sets of awards have been made during the course of their twenty-seven year history (to date), 1953–79. The particular grouping used in any one year may be noted under the listing for that year. Physically, the award consists of a sleek metal sculpture of a rocket ship, mounted vertically on a wood block base, which is faced with a suitably inscribed plaque detailing the particulars of the given award.

Hugos are decided by a mail ballot, conducted among the registered membership of the year's World Science Fiction Convention. It is not necessary to actually attend the convention in order to vote ("supporting" memberships are available for a reduced fee); and anyone is eligible to buy a convention membership. The Hugos, then, represent the closest existing approximation to a general fan vote on the question: What is the best SF of a particular year?

SF "fandom," a sociological phenomenon unique in all of literature, is a separate topic of its own. What counts here is the point that science fiction fans have a very special relationship to the literature of the field. To mention only one fact, a significant percentage of professional SF authors (and editors and publishers and artists and agents) are "graduates" from the fan ranks. Add to this special relationship the two points that (1) The Hugos are associated with the World Convention, the most important single event of the science fiction year; and (2) The Hugos are the oldest (and hence best established) continuing yearly award for SF; and it is relatively easy to see why: The Hugos are unquestionably the most prestigious SF awards ever made.

It should be mentioned that the "modern era" in Hugo awards did not start until the 1959 convention. Before that, no short list of nominees was chosen (i.e., only one vote was taken, with every work written during the year in the particular category up for consideration); and there was no announcement of runners-up in the balloting. Since no one who actually conducted any of these elections appears to be willing to talk, as a consequence only the names of the winners are known from this period. Further, until 1959, the period of eligibility ran from year's convention to the next, covering parts of two calendar years. As a result, it was possible for two novels published in 1958 to both win Hugos (in different years); and for no novel published in either 1955 or 1957 to win any Hugo.

I have included in the listing below a few notes about rule changes, etc.; but the history of the Hugos is full of irregularities, and no attempt has been made to cover all or even most of these. Those interested in this topic, or in lists of winners and nominees in all the different categories voted (including, e.g., professional magazine, professional artist, fan magazine, fan writer, fan artist, and dramatic presentation), may consult Franson & DeVore for reasonably complete and accurate information.

The Hugo Awards, 1953–1980 (fiction categories only)

1953: 1st Hugo Awards
   (only one fiction category)

novel
1. *The Demolished Man,* Alfred Bester

1954: no awards made
   (Hugos discontinued)

1955: 2nd Hugo Awards
   (Hugos reestablished as a permanent set of awards)

novel
1. *They'd Rather Be Right (The Forever Machine),* Mark Clifton &
   Frank Riley

novelette
1. "The Darfsteller," Walter M. Miller, Jr.

short story
1. "Allamagoosa," Eric Frank Russell

1956: 3rd Hugo Awards

novel
1. *Double Star,* Robert A. Heinlein

novelette
1. "Exploration Team," Murray Leinster

short story
1. "The Star," Arthur C. Clarke

1957: 4th Hugo Awards
   (No Hugos awarded in original fiction categories)

1958: 5th Hugo Awards

novel or novelette
1. *The Big Time,* Fritz Leiber

short story
   (only separate shorter fiction category)
1. "Or All the Seas With Oysters," Avram Davidson

1959: 6th Hugo Awards
novel
1. *A Case of Conscience,* James Blish

   We Have Fed Our Sea (The Enemy Stars), Poul Anderson
   Who?, Algis Budrys
   Have Spacesuit—Will Travel, Robert A. Heinlein
   Time Killer (Immortality Delivered or *Immortality, Inc.),* Robert Sheckley

novelette

1. "The Big Front Yard," Clifford D. Simak

   "Unwillingly to School," Pauline Ashwell

   "Captivity," Zenna Henderson

   "Reap the Dark Tide" (Shark Ship), Cyril M. Kornbluth

   "A Deskful of Girls," Fritz Leiber

   "Second Game" (*Cosmic Checkmate*), Katherine MacLean &
       Charles V. DeVet

   "Rat in the Skull," Rog Phillips

   "The Miracle-Workers," Jack Vance

short story

1. "That Hell-Bound Train," Robert Bloch

   "They've Been Working On . . .", Anton Lee Baker

   "The Men Who Murdered Mohammed," Alfred Bester

   "Triggerman," J. F. Bone

   "The Edge of the Sea," Algis Budrys

   "The Advent on Channel Twelve," Cyril M. Kornbluth

   "Theory of Rocketry," Cyril M. Kornbluth

   "Rump-Titty-Titty-Tum-TAH-Tee," Fritz Leiber

   "Space to Swing a Cat," Stanley Mullen

   "Nine Yards of Other Cloth," Manley Wade Wellman

1960: 7th Hugo Awards

novel

1. *Starship Troopers*, Robert A. Heinlein
2. *Dorsai*, Gordon R. Dickson

   The Pirates of Ersatz (The Pirates of Zan), Murray Leinster

   That Sweet Little Old Lady (Brain Twister), Mark Phillips

   The Sirens of Titan, Kurt Vonnegut, Jr.

short fiction

1. "Flowers for Algernon," Daniel Keyes

   "The Pi Man," Alfred Bester

   "The Alley Man," Philip José Farmer

   "The Man Who Lost the Sea," Theodore Sturgeon

   "Cat and Mouse," Ralph Williams

1961: 8th Hugo Awards

novel

1. *A Canticle for Leibowitz*, Walter M. Miller, Jr.

   The High Crusade, Poul Anderson

   Rogue Moon, Algis Budrys

   Deathworld, Harry Harrison

   Venus Plus X, Theodore Sturgeon

short fiction

1. "The Longest Voyage," Poul Anderson

   "The Lost Kafoozalum," Pauline Ashwell

"Open To Me, My Sister" (My Sister's Brother), Philip José Farmer
"Need," Theodore Sturgeon

1962: 9th Hugo Awards

novel
1. *Stranger in a Strange Land*, Robert A. Heinlein
   Dark Universe, Daniel F. Galouye
   Sense of Obligation (Planet of the Damned), Harry Harrison
   The Fisherman (Time is the Simplest Thing), Clifford D. Simak
   Second Ending, James White

short fiction
1. The "Hothouse" series (5 related stories, published in book form in the
   U. S. as *The Long Afternoon of Earth*), Brian W. Aldiss
   "Monument," Lloyd Biggle, Jr.
   "Scylla's Daughter," Fritz Leiber
   "Status Quo," Mack Reynolds
   "Lion Loose," James Schmitz

NOTE: The rules were subsequently changed to stipulate that only individual
works, and not related series taken as a whole, are eligible for nomination.

special committee award (non-fiction reference work)
   The Handbook of Science Fiction and Fantasy, Donald H. Tuck

NOTE: This is now being published as a three-volume set in a greatly revised
and expanded form, under the title: *Encyclopedia of Science Fiction and
Fantasy.*

1963: 10th Hugo Awards

novel
1. *The Man in the High Castle*, Philip K. Dick
   Sword of Aldones, Marion Zimmer Bradley
   A Fall of Moondust, Arthur C. Clarke
   Little Fuzzy, H. Beam Piper
   Sylva, Vercors

short fiction
1. "The Dragon Masters," Jack Vance
   "Myrrha," Gary Jennings
   "The Unholy Grail," Fritz Leiber
   "When You Care, When You Love," Theodore Sturgeon
   "Where Is The Bird of Fire?," Thomas Burnett Swann

1964: 11th Hugo Awards

novel
1. *Here Gather the Stars (Way Station)*, Clifford D. Simak
2t.*Glory Road*, Robert A. Heinlein
2t.*Witch World*, Andre Norton
4. *Dune World*, Frank Herbert

5. *Cat's Cradle,* Kurt Vonnegut, Jr.

short fiction
1. "No Truce With Kings," Poul Anderson
2. "Code Three," Rick Raphael
3. "A Rose for Ecclesiastes," Roger Zelazny
4. "Savage Pellucidar," Edgar Rice Burroughs

NOTE: "Savage Pellucidar," a newly discovered story of ERB, also received enough nominations in the novel category to qualify there. It was placed with short fiction by the committee, on the grounds that only one-quarter of the material was "new" (first published in 1963).

1965: 12th Hugo Awards

novel
1. *The Wanderer,* Fritz Leiber
   The Whole Man, John Brunner
   Davy, Edgar Pangborn
   The Planet Buyer, (later incorporated into *Norstrilia*), Cordwainer Smith

short fiction
1. "Soldier, Ask Not," Gordon R. Dickson
   "Once A Cop," Rick Raphael
   "Little Dog Gone," Robert F. Young

1966: 13th Hugo Awards

novel
1t. *Dune,* Frank Herbert
1t. *. . . And Call Me Conrad (This Immortal),* Roger Zelazny
   Squares of the City, John Brunner
   The Moon Is A Harsh Mistress, Robert A. Heinlein
   Skylark Duquesne, E. E. Smith

short fiction
1. ""Repent, Harlequin" Said the Ticktockman," Harlan Ellison
   "Marque and Reprisal," Poul Anderson
   "Day of the Great Shout," Philip José Farmer
   "Stardock," Fritz Leiber
   "The Doors of His Face, the Lamps of His Mouth," Roger Zelazny

best all-time series
1. *The Foundation Trilogy,* Isaac Asimov
   the Barsoom novels ("John Carter of Mars"), Edgar Rice Burroughs
   Future History series (*The Past Through Tomorrow*), Robert A. Heinlein
   Lensmen series, Edward E. Smith
   Lord of the Rings, J. R. R. Tolkien

NOTE: This was a special "one-time only" Hugo category. It *may* have resulted from a difficulty over including LotR, which, as a result of its first U. S. paperback edition in 1965, easily received enough nominations to qualify for the novel category; but which was ineligible due to prior hardcover publication.

In any event, LotR is not properly a "series" at all, but one long novel published in three volumes for convenience.

1967: 14th Hugo Awards

novel

1. *The Moon Is A Harsh Mistress*, Robert A. Heinlein

   Babel—17, Samuel R. Delany
   Too Many Magicians, Randall Garrett
   Flowers for Algernon, Daniel Keyes
   The Witches of Karres, James Schmitz
   Day of the Minotaur, Thomas Burnett Swann

NOTE: *The Moon Is A Harsh Mistress* was ruled eligible to compete a second year, on grounds that its serialization took place in parts of both years. The rules for the following year were changed to prevent any further work from competing twice for the same award. (*Flowers for Algernon* was ruled eligible to compete again on grounds that the novel-length version is significantly different from the Hugo-winning shorter version of 1960.)

novelette

1. "The Last Castle," Jack Vance

   "Call Him Lord," Gordon R. Dickson
   "Apology to Inky," Robert M. Green, Jr.
   "The Alchemist," Charles L. Harness
   "An Ornament to His Profession," Charles L. Harness
   "The Eskimo Invasion," Hayden Howard
   "The Manor of Roses," Thomas Burnett Swann
   "For a Breath I Tarry," Roger Zelazny
   "This Moment of the Storm," Roger Zelazny

short story

1. "Neutron Star," Larry Niven

   "Man In His Time," Brian W. Aldiss
   "Delusion for a Dragon Slayer," Harlan Ellison
   "Rat Race," Raymond F. Jones
   "The Secret Place," Richard McKenna
   "Mr. Jester," Fred Saberhagen
   "Light of Other Days," Bob Shaw
   "Comes Now the Power," Roger Zelazny

1968: 15th Hugo Awards

novel

1. *Lord of Light*, Roger Zelazny
2. *The Einstein Intersection*, Samuel R. Delany

   The Butterfly Kid, Chester Anderson
   Chthon, Piers Anthony
   Thorns, Robert Silverberg

novella

1t. "Riders of the Purple Wage," Philip José Farmer

1t. "Weyr Search," Anne McCaffrey
3. "Damnation Alley," Roger Zelazny

"The Star-Pit," Samuel R. Delany
"Hawksbill Station," Robert Silverberg

novelette
1. "Gonna Roll the Bones," Fritz Leiber
2. "Wizard's World," Andre Norton

"Faith of Our Fathers," Philip K. Dick
"Pretty Maggie Moneyeyes," Harlan Ellison

short story
1. "I Have No Mouth, and I Must Scream," Harlan Ellison
2. "The Jigsaw Man," Larry Niven
3. "Aye, and Gomorrah," Samuel R. Delany

special committee award (original anthology)
Dangerous Visions, ed. Harlan Ellison

1969: 16th Hugo Awards

novel
1. *Stand on Zanzibar*, John Brunner
2. *Rite of Passage*, Alexei Panshin

Nova, Samuel R. Delany
Past Master, R. A. Lafferty
Goblin Reservation, Clifford D. Simak

novella
1. "Nightwings," Robert Silverberg
2. "Dragonrider," Anne McCaffrey

"Lines of Power," Samuel R. Delany
"Hawk Among the Sparrows," Dean McLaughlin

novelette
1. "The Sharing of Flesh," Poul Anderson
2. "Total Environment," Brian W. Aldiss
3. "Getting Through University," Piers Anthony
4. "Mother to the World," Richard Wilson

short story
1. "The Beast That Shouted Love At the Heart of the World," Harlan Ellison
2. "All the Myriad Ways," Larry Niven
3. "The Dance of the Changer and the Three," Terry Carr

"The Steiger Effect," Betsy Curtis
"Masks," Damon Knight

1970: 17th Hugo Awards

novel
1. *The Left Hand of Darkness*, Ursula K. Le Guin
2. *Up the Line*, Robert Silverberg

3. *Macroscope*, Piers Anthony
4. *Slaughterhouse-Five*, Kurt Vonnegut, Jr.
5. *Bug Jack Barron*, Norman Spinrad

novella
1. "Ship of Shadows," Fritz Leiber
2. "A Boy and His Dog," Harlan Ellison
3. "We All Die Naked," James Blish
4. "Dramatic Mission," Anne McCaffrey
5. "To Jorslem," Robert Silverberg

short story
1. "Time Considered as a Helix of Semi-Precious Stones," Samuel R. Delany
2. "Passengers," Robert Silverberg
3. "Not Long Before the End," Larry Niven
4. "Deeper Than the Darkness," Gregory Benford
5. "Winter's King," Ursula K. Le Guin

1971: 18th Hugo Awards

novel
1. *Ringworld*, Larry Niven
2. *Tau Zero*, Poul Anderson
3. *Tower of Glass*, Robert Silverberg
4. *The Year of the Quiet Sun*, Wilson Tucker
5. *Star Light*, Hal Clement

novella
1. "Ill Met in Lankhmar," Fritz Leiber
2. "The Thing in the Stone," Clifford D. Simak
3. "The Region Between," Harlan Ellison
4. "The World Outside," Robert Silverberg
5. "Beast Child," Dean R. Koontz

short story
1. "Slow Sculpture," Theodore Sturgeon
2. "Continued on Next Rock," R. A. Lafferty
3. "Jean Dupres," Gordon R. Dickson
4. "In the Queue," Keith Laumer
5. "Brillo," Ben Bova & Harlan Ellison

1972: 19th Hugo Awards

novel
1. *To Your Scattered Bodies Go*, Philip José Farmer
2. *The Lathe of Heaven*, Ursula K. Le Guin
3. *Dragonquest*, Anne McCaffrey
4. *Jack of Shadows*, Roger Zelazny
5. *A Time of Changes*, Robert Silverberg
   *The World Inside, Robert Silverberg

novella
1. "The Queen of Air and Darkness," Poul Anderson

2. "A Meeting With Medusa," Arthur C. Clarke
3. "The Fourth Profession," Larry Niven
4. "Dread Empire," John Brunner
5. "A Special Kind of Morning," Gardner Dozois

short story
1. "Inconstant Moon," Larry Niven
2. "Vaster Than Empires, and More Slow," Ursula K. Le Guin
3. "The Autumn Land," Clifford D. Simak
4. "The Bear With the Knot on His Tail," Stephen Tall
5. "Sky," R. A. Lafferty
6. "All the Last Wars at Once," Geo. Alec Effinger

special committee award (original anthology)
   Again, Dangerous Visions, ed. Harlan Ellison

1973: 20th Hugo Awards

novel
1. *The Gods Themselves*, Isaac Asimov
2. *When Harlie Was One*, David Gerrold
3. *There Will Be Time*, Poul Anderson

   The Book of Skulls, Robert Silverberg
   Dying Inside, Robert Silverberg
   A Choice of Gods, Clifford D. Simak

novella
1. "The Word for World is Forest," Ursula K. Le Guin
2. "The Gold at the Starbow's End," Frederik Pohl
3. "The Fifth Head of Cerberus," Gene Wolfe

   "Hero," Joe Haldeman
   "The Mercenary," Jerry Pournelle

novelette
1. "Goat Song," Poul Anderson
2. "Patron of the Arts," William Rotsler
3. "Basilisk," Harlan Ellison

   "A Kingdom By the Sea," Gardner Dozois
   "Painwise," James Tiptree, Jr.

short story
1t. "Eurema's Dam," R. A. Lafferty
1t. "The Meeting," Frederik Pohl & Cyril M. Kornbluth
3. "When We Went to See the End of the World," Robert Silverberg
4. "And I Awoke and Found Me Here on the Cold Hill's Side,"
      James Tiptree, Jr.
5. "When It Changed," Joanna Russ

special committee award (non-fiction reference work)
   Encyclopedie De L'Utopie Et De La SF, Pierre Versins
   (Note: No English-language translation of this monumental 1000+ page
   encyclopedia has ever appeared.)

1974: 21st Hugo Awards

novel
1. *Rendezvous With Rama,* Arthur C. Clarke
2. *Time Enough For Love,* Robert A. Heinlein
3. *Protector,* Larry Niven

   The People of the Wind, Poul Anderson
   The Man Who Folded Himself, David Gerrold

novella
1. "The Girl Who Was Plugged In," James Tiptree, Jr.
2. "The Death of Doctor Island," Gene Wolfe
3. "Death and Designation Among the Asadi," Michael Bishop

   "The White Otters of Childhood," Michael Bishop
   "Chains of the Sea," Gardner Dozois

novelette
1. "The Deathbird," Harlan Ellison
2. "Of Mist, and Grass, and Sand," Vonda N. McIntyre
3. "Love is the Plan, the Plan is Death," James Tiptree, Jr.

   "The City on the Sand," Geo. Alec Effinger
   "He Fell Into a Dark Hole," Jerry Pournelle

short story
1. "The Ones Who Walk Away From Omelas," Ursula K. Le Guin
2. "With Morning Comes Mistfall," George R. R. Martin
3. "Construction Shack," Clifford D. Simak
4. "Wings," Vonda N. McIntyre

1975: 22nd Hugo Awards

novel
1. *The Dispossessed,* Ursula K. Le Guin

   Fire Time, Poul Anderson
   Flow My Tears, The Policeman Said, Philip K. Dick
   The Mote In God's Eye, Larry Niven & Jerry Pournelle
   The Inverted World, Christopher Priest

novella
1. "A Song for Lya," George R. R. Martin

   "Strangers," Gardner Dozois
   "Born With the Dead," Robert Silverberg
   "Riding the Torch," Norman Spinrad
   "Assault on a City," Jack Vance

novelette
1. "Adrift Just Off the Islets of Langerhans: Latitude 38°54'N, Longitude
   77°00'13"W," Harlan Ellison

   "That Thou Art Mindful of Him," Isaac Asimov
   "Midnight by the Morphy Watch," Fritz Leiber
   "After the Dreamtime," Richard A. Lupoff

"Extreme Prejudice," Jerry Pournelle
"Nix Olympica," William Walling
"A Brother to Dragons, A Companion of Owls," Kate Wilhelm

short story
1. "The Hole Man," Larry Niven

"The Four-Hour Fugue," Alfred Bester
"Cathadonian Odyssey," Michael Bishop
"The Day Before the Revolution," Ursula K. Le Guin
"Schwartz Between the Galaxies," Robert Silverberg

special committee award (non-fiction reference work)
Reference Guide to Fantastic Films, Walt Lee

1976: 23rd Hugo Awards

novel
1. *The Forever War*, Joe Haldeman
2. *Doorways in the Sand*, Roger Zelazny
3. *Inferno*, Larry Niven & Jerry Pournelle
4. *The Computer Connection*, Alfred Bester
5. *The Stochasic Man*, Robert Silverberg

novella
1. "Home Is The Hangman," Roger Zelazny
2. "The Storms of Windhaven," Lisa Tuttle & George R. R. Martin
3. "ARM," Larry Niven
4. "The Silent Eyes of Time," Algis Budrys
5. "The Custodians," Richard Cowper

novelette
1. "The Borderland of Sol," Larry Niven
2. "The New Atlantis," Ursula K. Le Guin
3. ". . . and Seven Times Never Kill Man," George R. R. Martin
4. "San Diego Lightfoot Sue," Tom Reamy
5. "Tinker," Jerry Pournelle

short story
1. "Catch That Zeppelin!," Fritz Leiber
2. "Croatoan," Harlan Ellison
3. "Child of All Ages," P. J. Plauger
4. "Sail the Tide of Mourning," Richard A. Lupoff
5. "Rogue Tomato," Michael Bishop
6. "Doing Lennon," Gregory Benford

special committee award (non-fiction reference work)
Alternate Worlds, James E. Gunn

1977: 24th Hugo Awards

novel
1. *Where Late the Sweet Birds Sang*, Kate Wilhelm

Mindbridge, Joe Haldeman
Children of Dune, Frank Herbert

Man Plus, Frederik Pohl
Shadrach in the Furnace, Robert Silverberg

novella
1t. "Houston, Houston, Do You Read?," James Tiptree, Jr.
1t. "By Any Other Name . . .," Spider Robinson
   "The Samurai and the Willows," Michael Bishop
   "Piper at the Gates of Dawn," Richard Cowper

novelette
1. "The Bicentennial Man," Isaac Asimov
   "The Diary of the Rose," Ursula K. Le Guin
   "Gotta Sing, Gotta Dance," John Varley
   "The Phantom of Kansas," John Varley

short story
1. "Tricentennial," Joe Haldeman
   "A Crowd of Shadows," Charles L. Grant
   "Custom Fitting," James White
   "I See You," Damon Knight

1978: 25th Hugo Awards

novel
1. *Gateway,* Frederik Pohl
2. *The Forbidden Tower,* Marion Zimmer Bradley
3. *Lucifer's Hammer,* Larry Niven & Jerry Pournelle
   Time Storm, Gordon R. Dickson
   Dying of the Light, George R. R. Martin

"Gandalf" Award (best fantasy novel)
1. *'The Silmarillion,* J. R. R. Tolkien
2. *Our Lady of Darkness,* Fritz Leiber
3. *Lord Foul's Bane,* Stephen R. Donaldson
   A Spell for Chameleon, Piers Anthony
   The Shining, Stephen King

novella
1. "Stardance," Spider & Jeanne Robinson
2. "In the Hall of the Martian Kings," John Varley
3. "Aztecs," Vonda N. McIntyre
   "A Snark in the Night," Gregory Benford
   "The Wonderful Secret," Keith Laumer

novelette
1. "Eyes of Amber," Joan D. Vinge
2. "Ender's Game," Orson Scott Card
3. "The Screwfly Solution," James Tiptree, Jr. (as "Raconna Sheldon)
   "Prismatica," Samuel R. Delany
   "The Ninth Symphony of Ludwig van Beethoven and Other Lost Songs,"
      Carter Scholz

short story
1. "Jeffty is Five," Harlan Ellison
2. "Air Raid," John Varley (as "Herb Boehm")
3. "Dog Day Evening," Spider Robinson
   "Lauralyn," Randall Garrett
   "Time-Sharing Angel," James Tiptree, Jr.

1979: 26th Hugo Awards

novel
1. *Dreamsnake*, Vonda N. McIntyre
2. *The White Dragon*, Anne McCaffrey
3. *The Faded Sun: Kesrith*, C. J. Cherryh
   Blind Voices, Tom Reamy
   Up the Walls of the World, James Tiptree, Jr.

honorable mention
   Colony, Ben Bova
   Stormqueen, Marion Zimmer Bradley
   The Far Call, Gordon R. Dickson
   Gloriana, Michael Moorcock
   Stardance II, Spider & Jeanne Robinson

NOTE: This category was added by the SeaCon committee because each of these five novels received over fifty votes on the preliminary nominating ballot—enough to qualify them for the final ballot in most years.

"Gandalf" Award (best fantasy novel)
1. *The White Dragon*, Anne McCaffrey
2. *The Courts of Chaos*, Roger Zelazny
3. *Saint Camber*, Katherine Kurtz
   The Stand, Stephen King
   Gloriana, Michael Moorcock

NOTE: As of 1980, the "Gandalf" for best fantasy novel has been discontinued as a category, on grounds that these works are fully eligible to compete in the "Hugo" novel category.

novella
1. "The Persistence of Vision," John Varley
2. "Fireship," Joan D. Vinge
3. "The Watched," Christopher Priest
   "Enemies of the System," Brian W. Aldiss
   "Seven American Nights," Gene Wolfe

novelette
1. "Hunter's Moon, Poul Anderson
2. "Mikal's Songbird," Orson Scott Card
3. "The Man Who Had No Idea," Thomas M. Disch
   "Devil You Don't Know," Dean Ing
   "The Barbie Murders," John Varley

short story
1. "Cassandra," C. J. Cherryh
2. "Count the Clock That Tells the Time," Harlan Ellison
3. "View From a Height," Joan D. Vinge

   "Stone," Edward Bryant
   "The Very Slow Time Machine," Ian Watson

1980: 27th Hugo Awards

novel
1. *The Fountains of Paradise*, Arthur C. Clarke

   On Wings of Song, Thomas M. Disch
   Harpist in the Wind, Patricia A. McKillip
   Jem, Frederik Pohl
   Titan, John Varley

novella
1. "Enemy Mine," Barry Longyear

   "Songhouse," Orson Scott Card
   "The Moon Goddess and the Son," Donald Kingsbury
   "Ker-Plop," Ted Reynolds
   "The Battle of the Abaco Reefs," Hilbert Schenck

novelette
1. "Sandkings," George R. R. Martin

   "Homecoming," Barry Longyear
   "Fireflood," Vonda N. McIntyre
   "The Locusts," Larry Niven & Steve Barnes
   "Palely Loitering," Christopher Priest
   "Options," John Varley

short story
1. "The Way of Cross and Dragon," George R. R. Martin

   "giANTS," Edward Bryant
   "Unaccompanied Sonata," Orson Scott Card
   "Can These Bones Live?," Ted Reynolds
   "Daisy in the Sun," Connie Willis

THE NEBULA AWARDS

The Nebula awards are given annually by a membership vote of the major association of SF writers, the Science Fiction Writers of America (SFWA). Balloting is done by mail. The awards are announced and presented at a special banquet held in the spring. The Nebulas are the earliest set of SF awards to be distributed, and so serve to inaugurate what has now become a rather lengthy award year. Physically, Nebulas are among the most impressive (and expensive) tokens given for SF writing achievement: consisting of a large block of clear lucite, in which a sizable quartz crystal and a silver glitter spiral nebula are embedded. (Each Nebula is also suitably engraved with the relevant information about its winning author and work, of course.)

The Nebulas originated shortly after the SFWA itself was formed. As with most things, the motivation behind them was mixed. In the first place, they were to provide an alternative to the fan-controlled Hugos, which, it was thought, judged a work more on the basis of popular appeal than any of the more abstract literary merits. In the second place, the award was to offer a formal means by which a writer's achievements could be recognized by his peers. And last, though not perhaps least, the Nebulas were prompted by reasons having more to do with self-promotion than disinterested altruism. (It might be mentioned in this last context that the Nebulas are the only awards to have their own annual anthology, variously edited by different prominent SFWA members, which reprints the winners and selected nominees from the shorter fiction categories.)

Unlike the Hugos and many other sets of awards, from the time of their conception the Nebulas were intended just to honor original fiction. Indeed, the most notable contribution of the Nebulas to the history of SF awards— apart from the fact that they broke the effective monopoly enjoyed by the Hugos, and so indirectly contributed to the award's explosion of the 1970's— was the introduction of an expanded "four-category" system for classifying original fiction: novel (over 40,000 words), novella (17,501 to 40,000 words), novelette (7,500 to 17,500 words), and short story (under 7,500 words). This system has been used for every Nebula award.

The four-category system was clearly an idea whose time had come, for it has since been made more or less standard for other SF awards as well. Most notably, after a certain amount of initial resistance and subsequent back-sliding, it now seems firmly established for the Hugos. (The Hugos never had more than three categories for fiction before 1968—and in 1960 they settled on a two-category system that remained in effect for seven years, that is, until the year *after* the first Nebulas were presented.)

(It is worth remarking that, before 1966, the term "novella" was never, or almost never used to refer to works of SF. Works longer than short stories, but shorter than novels, were invariably called "novelettes." This usage should be kept in mind when considering awards made before 1966: what are now "novellas" were then called "novelettes," and what are now "novelettes" were then often classified as "short stories.")

The four categories of original fiction constituted the entire Nebula ballot until 1974, when a fifth category for "best dramatic presentation" was added (only to be dropped as a regular division in 1978). A sixth and (so far) final category was included in 1975: "grand master," designed to honor the career achievements of distinguished SF authors.

The Nebulas are beyond any reasonable doubt the only current SF awards to seriously rival the Hugos in influence or prestige. As the major gift of SF writers to SF works, they are functionally equivalent to such other important awards (outside SF) as the "Edgars" and the "Oscars." The former award is given by the Mystery Writers of America for the best mystery fiction of the year. It is, incidentally, the example on which the SFWA and its Nebulas are largely based. The latter award is made by the Academy of Motion Picture Arts and Sciences, also mostly to its own members. Certainly the Nebulas are in good company. They cannot fail to be of substantial interest, as the best available indication of the opinion held by SF writers on the question: What is the best SF being written?

Regrettably, the Nebulas have experienced certain practical difficulties in attempting to reach a fair answer to this question. Two of these are worth noting here. (1) The SFWA has been prone to allow very liberal nomination policies. In effect, it has frequently been possible for writers to nominate their own works. Apart from any other objections to this procedure, it tends to produce an extremely long preliminary ballot, with the result that many nominees are not read by many members. In 1976, for example, when the final ballot still offered a hefty 13 different story candidates in the category "best short story," a total of 64 different stories were initially proposed for this honor. Of this total, though, exactly half were nominated by exactly one SFWA member, and 13 more by just two, while only 4 stories were nominated by more than five members.

(2) Although the official membership of the SFWA is impressive, including a probable majority of all the SF writers in the world, a significant portion of the SFWA chooses not to participate in the Nebula elections. The best response has never exceeded 50%, and is often significantly less. Thus, the Nebulas are in fact a minority award, made by a relatively small number of SF writers who bother to vote. Serious doubt exists as to whether this minority fairly represents the larger community of SF writers as a whole—a claim which is essential to their standing as the SF writer's award.

A variety of different rules and procedures have been tried over the years in an effort to eliminate, or at least minimize, these and related problems. Nothing has proved to be entirely satisfactory, however. At the present time, the entire matter is under study again by a special "blue ribbon" committee of the SFWA. In light of the past and continuing importance of the Nebulas to SF, it can only be hoped that a satisfactory resolution of these difficulties will yet be forthcoming.

With this as background, a word of explanation about what the following list excludes may be in order. Since preliminary nomination is extremely easy to achieve, it is of correspondingly dubious worth as an indication of merit. Further, as the aggregate number of works to achieve any Nebula nomination is staggering, in addition to trying the reader's patience for a doubtful end, an attempt to name them all here would extend this article beyond reasonable bounds. Consequently, the following list gives only the final ballot nominees for the several categories from 1967 on; when a distinction was first made between being nominated for a Nebula, and qualifying for the final ballot.

(The initial procedure was to place every item to receive any nomination directly on the final ballot. The listing for 1966 should give you a general idea of what the ballot that leaves you with is like. The reader who does wish to see a complete list of all the works ever to be nominated by anyone for a Nebula, or who wishes further details on past and present Nebula procedures, can find this information in the book by Franson & DeVore cited earlier.)

It may be mentioned in conclusion that the SFWA has also sponsored a special set of retrospective awards, intended to honor works published before 1965. I have not listed these titles, but the shorter works (short story through novella) may be found collected into three volumes under the general title, *The Science Fiction Hall of Fame* (Vol. I, ed. by Robert Silverberg; Vols. IIA and IIB, ed. by Ben Bova).

The Nebula Awards, 1966–1980 (fiction categories only)

1966: 1st Nebula Awards

novel

1. *Dune*, Frank Herbert

   The Star Fox, Poul Anderson
   Nova Express, William Burroughs
   Rogue Dragon, Avram Davidson
   Dr. Bloodmoney, Philip K. Dick
   The Three Stigmata of Palmer Eldritch, Philip K. Dick
   The Genocides, Thomas M. Disch
   The Ship That Sailed the Time Stream, G. C. Edmondson
   A Plague of Demons, Keith Laumer
   All Flesh is Grass, Clifford D. Simak
   The Clone, Theodore L. Thomas & Kate Wilhelm
   The Escape Orbit, James White

novella

1t. "The Saliva Tree," Brian W. Aldiss
1t. "He Who Shapes," Roger Zelazny

   "Rogue Dragon," Avram Davidson
   "The Ballad of Beta-2," Samuel R. Delany
   "The Mercurymen," C. C. MacApp
   "Under Two Moons," Frederik Pohl
   "On the Storm Planet," Cordwainer Smith
   "Research Alpha," A. E. van Vogt & James Schmitz

novelette

1. "The Doors of His Face, the Lamps of His Mouth," Roger Zelazny

   "The Shipwrecked Hotel," James Blish & Norman L. Knight
   "Vanishing Point," Jonathan Brand
   "102 H-Bombs," Thomas M. Disch
   "Half a Loaf," R. C. Fitzpatrick
   "The Decision Makers," Joseph Green
   "At the Institute," Norman Kagan
   "The Earth Merchants," Norman Kagan
   "Laugh Along With Franz," Norman Kagan
   "The Life of Your Time," Michael Karageorge
   "Four Ghosts in Hamlet," Fritz Leiber
   "Small One," E. Clayton McCarty
   "The Adventure of the Extraterrestrial," Mack Reynolds
   "Masque of the Red Shift," Fred Saberhagen
   "Goblin Night," James Schmitz
   "Planet of Forgetting," James Schmitz
   "Maiden Voyage," J. W. Schutz
   "Shall We Have a Little Talk?," Robert Sheckley
   "The Masculinist Revolt," William Tenn

short story

1. ""Repent, Harlequin" Said the Ticktockman," Harlan Ellison

"Eyes Do More Than See," Isaac Asimov
"Founding Father," Isaac Asimov
"Souvenir," J. G. Ballard
"Games," Donald Barthelme
"Lord Moon," Jane Beauclerk
"Uncollected Works," Lin Carter
"A Few Kindred Spirits," John Christopher
"The House the Blakeneys Built," Avram Davidson
"Computers Don't Argue," Gordon R. Dickson
"Come to Venus Melancholy," Thomas M. Disch
"Of One Mind," James Durham
"Inside Man," H. L. Gold
"Calling Dr. Clockwork," Ron Goulart
"Better Than Ever," Alex Kirs
"In Our Block," R. A. Lafferty
"Slow Tuesday Night," R. A. Lafferty
"Cyclops," Fritz Leiber
"The Good New Days," Fritz Leiber
"Though A Sparrow Fall," Scott Nichols
"Becalmed in Hell," Larry Niven
"Wrong-Way Street," Larry Niven
"The Mischief Maker," Richard Olin
"A Better Mousehole," Edgar Pangborn
"A Leader for Yesterday," Mack Reynolds
"Keep Them Happy," Robert Rohrer
"Balanced Ecology," James Schmitz
"Over the River and Through the Trees," Clifford D. Simak
"The Peacock King," Ted White & L. McCombs
"The Eight Billion," Richard Wilson
"Devil Car," Roger Zelazny

1967: 2nd Nebula Awards

novel

1t. *Babel 17*, Samuel R. Delany
1t. *Flowers For Algernon*, Daniel Keyes
3. *The Moon Is A Harsh Mistress*, Robert A. Heinlein

novella

1. "The Last Castle," Jack Vance

    "Clash of Star Kings," Avram Davidson
    "The Alchemist," Charles L. Harness

novelette

1. "Call Him Lord," Gordon R. Dickson

    "Apology to Inky," Robert M. Green, Jr.
    "An Ornament to His Profession," Charles L. Harness
    "The Eskimo Invasion," Hayden Howard
    "This Moment of the Storm," Roger Zelazny

short story

1. "The Secret Place," Richard McKenna

"Man In His Time," Brian W. Aldiss

"Light of Other Days," Bob Shaw

1968: 3rd Nebula Awards

novel

1. *The Einstein Intersection,* Samuel R. Delany

Chthon, Piers Anthony

The Eskimo Invasion, Hayden Howard

Thorns, Robert Silverberg

Lord of Light, Roger Zelazny

novella

1. "Behold the Man," Michael Moorcock

"Riders of the Purple Wage," Philip José Farmer

"Weyr Search," Anne McCaffrey

"Hawksbill Station," Robert Silverberg

"If All Men Were Brothers, Would You Let One Marry Your Sister?," Theodore Sturgeon

novelette

1. "Gonna Roll the Bones," Fritz Leiber

"Pretty Maggie Moneyeyes," Harlan Ellison

"Flatlander," Larry Niven

"The Keys to December," Roger Zelazny

"This Mortal Mountain," Roger Zelazny

short story

1. "Aye, and Gomorrah," Samuel R. Delany

"Earthwoman," Reginald Bretnor

"Driftglass," Samuel R. Delany

"Answering Service," Fritz Leiber

"The Doctor," Theodore L. Thomas

"Baby, You Were Great," Kate Wilhelm

1969: 4th Nebula Awards

novel

1. *Rite of Passage,* Alexei Panshin
2. *The Masks of Time,* Robert Silverberg
3. *Stand on Zanzibar,* John Brunner
4. *Picnic on Paradise,* Joanna Russ
5. *Black Easter,* James Blish
6t. *Do Androids Dream of Electric Sheep?,* Philip K. Dick
6t. *Past Master,* R. A. Lafferty

novella

1. "Dragonrider," Anne McCaffrey
2. "Nightwings," Robert Silverberg

3. "Lines of Power," Samuel R. Delany
4t. "The Day Before Forever," Keith Laumer
4t. "Hawk Among the Sparrows," Dean McLaughlin

novelette
1. "Mother to the World," Richard Wilson
2. "The Sharing of Flesh," Poul Anderson
3. "Final War," K. M. O'Donnell (Barry N. Malzberg)
4. "Once There Was a Giant," Keith Laumer
5. "The Listeners," James E. Gunn
6t. "Total Environment," Brian W. Aldiss
6t. "The Guerrilla Trees," H. H. Hollis

short story
1. "The Planners," Kate Wilhelm
2t. "The Dance of the Changer and the Three," Terry Carr
2t. "Masks," Damon Knight
4. "Sword Game," H. H. Hollis
5. "Kyrie," Poul Anderson
6. "Idiot's Mate," Robert Taylor

1970: 5th Nebula Awards

novel
1. *The Left Hand of Darkness,* Ursula K. Le Guin
2. *Slaughterhouse-Five,* Kurt Vonnegut, Jr.
3. *Bug Jack Barron,* Norman Spinrad

   The Jagged Orbit, John Brunner
   Up The Line, Robert Silverberg
   Isle of the Dead, Roger Zelazny

novella
1. "A Boy And His Dog," Harlan Ellison
2. "Ship of Shadows," Fritz Leiber
3. "Dramatic Mission," Anne McCaffrey

   "Probable Cause," Charles L. Harness
   "To Jorslem," Robert Silverberg

novelette
1. "Time Considered as a Helix of Semi-Precious Stones," Samuel R. Delany
2. "Nine Lives," Ursula K. Le Guin
3. "The Big Flash," Norman Spinrad
4. "Deeper Than the Darkness," Gregory Benford

short story
1. "Passengers," Robert Silverberg
2. "Shattered Like a Glass Goblin," Harlan Ellison
3. "Not Long Before the End," Larry Niven

   "The Man Who Learned Loving," Theodore Sturgeon
   "The Last Flight of Dr. Ain," James Tiptree, Jr.

1971: 6th Nebula Awards

novel
1. *Ringworld,* Larry Niven
2t. *And Chaos Died,* Joanna Russ
2t. *Tower of Glass,* Robert Silverberg
4. *The Year of the Quiet Sun,* Wilson Tucker
5. *Fourth Mansions,* R. A. Lafferty
6. *The Steel Crocodile,* D. G. Compton
   *Downward to the Earth, Robert Silverberg

novella
1. "Ill Met In Lankhmar," Fritz Leiber
2. "The Thing in the Stone," Clifford D. Simak
3. "The Region Between," Harlan Ellison
4. "April Fool's Day Forever," Kate Wilhelm
5. "The Fatal Fulfillment," Poul Anderson
6. "A Style In Treason," James Blish
   *"The Snow Women," Fritz Leiber

novelette
1. "Slow Sculpture," Theodore Sturgeon
2. "Continued on Next Rock," R. A. Lafferty
3. "Asian Shores," Thomas M. Disch
4. "Shaker Revival," Gerald Jonas
5. "The Second Inquisition," Joanna Russ
6. "Dear Aunt Annie," Gordon Eklund

short story
1. NO AWARD
2. "The Island of Doctor Death," Gene Wolfe
3. "Entire and Perfect Chrysolite," R. A. Lafferty
4. "In the Queue," Keith Laumer
5. "By the Falls," Harry Harrison
6. "The Creation of Bennie Good," James Sallis
7. "A Dream at Noonday," Gardner Dozois
8. "A Cold Dark Night With Snow," Kate Wilhelm

NOTE: It is likely that the win in this category by "no award" was the result of a certain confusion over the meaning of that phrase. At least some SFWA members thought that checking this entry meant "no preference," rather than "do not give the award to any story."

1972: 7th Nebula Awards

novel
1. *A Time of Changes,* Robert Silverberg
2. *The Lathe of Heaven,* Ursula K. Le Guin
3. *The Devil Is Dead,* R. A. Lafferty

   The Byworlder, Poul Anderson
   Half Past Human, T. J. Bass
   Margaret and I, Kate Wilhelm

novella
1. "The Missing Man," Katherine MacLean
2. "The Infinity Box," Kate Wilhelm
3. "Being There," Jerzy Kosinski

   "The God House," Keith Roberts
   "The Plastic Abyss," Kate Wilhelm

novelette
1. "The Queen of Air and Darkness," Poul Anderson
2. "Mount Charity," Edgar Pangborn
3. "Poor Man, Beggar Man," Joanna Russ

   "A Special Kind of Morning," Gardner Dozois
   "The Encounter," Kate Wilhelm

short story
1. "Good News From the Vatican," Robert Silverberg
2. "The Last Ghost," Stephen Goldin
3. "Horse of Air," Gardner Dozois
4. "Heathen God," George Zebrowski

1973: 8th Nebula Awards

novel
1. *The Gods Themselves*, Isaac Asimov
2. *When Harlie Was One*, David Gerrold
3. *Dying Inside*, Robert Silverberg

   The Sheep Look Up, John Brunner
   What Entropy Means to Me, Geo. Alec Effinger
   The Book of Skulls, Robert Silverberg
   The Iron Dream, Norman Spinrad

novella
1. "A Meeting With Medusa," Arthur C. Clarke
2. "The Fifth Head of Cerberus," Gene Wolfe
3. "The Word for World is Forest," Ursula K. Le Guin
4. "The Gold at the Starbow's End," Frederik Pohl
5. "With the Bentfin Boomer Boys on Little Old New Alabama," Richard A.
     Lupoff
6. "Son of the Morning," Phyllis Gotlieb

novelette
1. "Goat Song," Poul Anderson
2. "Patron of the Arts," William Rotsler
3. "The Animal Fair," Alfred Bester
4. "The Funeral," Kate Wilhelm
5. "Basilisk," Harlan Ellison
6. "A Kingdom By the Sea," Gardner Dozois
7. "In the Deadlands," David Gerrold

short story
1. "When It Changed," Joanna Russ

2. "And I Awoke and Found Me Here on the Cold Hill's Side," James
   Tiptree, Jr.
3. "Against the Lafayette Escadrille," Gene Wolfe
4. "Shaffery Among the Immortals," Frederik Pohl
5. "On the Downhill Side," Harlan Ellison
6. "When We Went To See The End of the World," Robert Silverberg

1974: 9th Nebula Awards

novel
1. *Rendezvous With Rama*, Arthur C. Clarke

   The People of the Wind, Poul Anderson
   The Man Who Folded Himself, David Gerrold
   Time Enough For Love, Robert A. Heinlein
   Gravity's Rainbow, Thomas Pynchon

novella
1. "The Death of Doctor Island," Gene Wolfe
2. "Chains of the Sea," Gardner Dozois
3. "Junction," Jack Dann
4. "Death and Designation Among the Asadi," Michael Bishop
5. "The White Otters of Childhood," Michael Bishop

novelette
1. "Of Mist, and Grass, and Sand," Vonda N. McIntyre
2. "The Deathbird," Harlan Ellison
3. "The Girl Who Was Plugged In," James Tiptree, Jr.
4. "Case and the Dreamer," Theodore Sturgeon

short story
1. "Love is the Plan, the Plan is Death," James Tiptree, Jr.
2. "With Morning Comes Mistfall," George R. R. Martin
3. "How I Lost the Second World War and Helped Turn Back the German
   Invasion," Gene Wolfe
4. "Wings," Vonda N. McIntyre
5. "A Thing of Beauty," Norman Spinrad
6. "Shark," Edward Bryant

1975: 10th Nebula Awards

novel
1. *The Dispossessed*, Ursula K. Le Guin
2. *Flow My Tears, The Policeman Said*, Philip K. Dick
3. *334*, Thomas M. Disch
4. *The Godwhale*, T. J. Bass

novella
1. "Born With the Dead," Robert Silverberg
2. "A Song for Lya," George R. R. Martin
3. "On the Street of the Serpents," Michael Bishop

novelette
1. "If The Stars Are Gods," Gregory Benford & Gordon Eklund
2. "The Rest Is Silence," Charles L. Grant

3. "Twilla," Tom Reamy
   *"The Women Men Don't See," James Tiptree, Jr.

short story
1. "The Day Before the Revolution," Ursula K. Le Guin
2. "The Engine At Heartspring's Center," Roger Zelazny
3. "After King Kong Fell," Philip José Farmer

1976: 11th Nebula Awards

novel
1. *The Forever War,* Joe Haldeman
2. *The Mote In God's Eye,* Larry Niven & Jerry Pournelle
3. *Dhalgren,* Samuel R. Delany
   A Midsummer Tempest, Poul Anderson
   The Computer Connection, Alfred Bester
   A Funeral for the Eyes of Fire, Michael Bishop
   The Heritage of Hastur, Marion Zimmer Bradley
   Invisible Cities, Italo Calvino
   Autumn Angels, Arthur Byron Cover
   Ragtime, E. L. Doctorow
   The Birthgrave, Tanith Lee
   The Missing Man, Katherine MacLean
   Guernica Night, Barry N. Malzberg
   The Exile Waiting, Vonda N. McIntyre
   The Female Man, Joanna Russ
   The Stochastic Man, Robert Silverberg
   The Embedding, Ian Watson
   Doorways in the Sand, Roger Zelazny

novella
1. "Home is the Hangman," Roger Zelazny
2. "The Storms of Windhaven," Lisa Tuttle & George R. R. Martin
3. "A Momentary Taste of Being," James Tiptree, Jr.
4. "Sunrise West," William K. Carlson

novelette
1. "San Diego Lightfoot Sue," Tom Reamy
2. "A Galaxy Called Rome," Barry N. Malzberg
3. "The Final Fighting of Fion MacCumhaill," Randall Garrett
   "The Warlord of Saturn's Moons," Eleanor Arnason
   "Blooded On Arachne," Michael Bishop
   "The Custodians," Richard Cowper
   "The Dybbuk Dolls," Jack Dann
   "Polly Charms, The Sleeping Woman," Avram Davidson
   "The New Atlantis," Ursula K. Le Guin
   "The Bleeding Man," Craig Strete
   "Retrograde Summer," John Varley

short story
1. "Catch That Zepplin!," Fritz Leiber

2. "Child of All Ages," P. J. Plauger
3. "Shatterday," Harlan Ellison

"Doing Lennon," Gregory Benford
"White Creatures," Gregory Benford
"Utopia of a Tired Man," Jorge Luis Borges
"A Scraping of the Bones," Algis Budrys
"Attachment," Phyllis Eisenstein
"Find the Lady," Nicholas Fisk
"White Wolf Calling," Charles L. Grant
"Sail the Tide of Mourning," Richard A. Lupoff
"Growing Up in Edge City," Frederik Pohl
"Time Deer," Craig Strete

1977: 12th Nebula Awards

novel
1. *Man Plus*, Frederik Pohl
2. *Where Late the Sweet Birds Sang*, Kate Wilhelm
3. *Shadrach in the Furnace*, Robert Silverberg

Triton, Samuel R. Delany
Inferno, Larry Niven & Jerry Pournelle
Islands, Marta Randall

novella
1. "Houston, Houston, Do You Read?," James Tiptree, Jr.
2. "The Samurai and the Willows," Michael Bishop
3. "Piper at the Gates of Dawn," Richard Cowper
4. "The Eyeflash Miracles," Gene Wolfe

novelette
1. "The Bicentennial Man," Isaac Asimov
2. "In the Bowl," John Varley
3. "Custer's Last Jump," Steven Utley & Howard Waldrop

"His Hour Upon the Stage," Grant Carrington
*"The Diary of the Rose," Ursula K. Le Guin

short story
1. "A Crowd of Shadows," Charles L. Grant
2. "Tricentennial," Joe Haldeman
3. "Stone Circle," Lisa Tuttle

"Breath's a Ware That Will Not Keep," Thomas F. Monteleone
"Back to the Stone Age," Jake Saunders
"Mary Margaret Road-Grader," Howard Waldrop

1978: 13th Nebula Awards

novels
1. *Gateway*, Frederik Pohl
2. *In the Ocean of Night*, Gregory Benford
3. *Cirque*, Terry Carr

Moonstar Odyssey, David Gerrold
Sword of the Demon, Richard A. Lupoff

novella

1. "Stardance," Spider & Jeanne Robinson
2. "Aztecs," Vonda N. McIntyre

novelettes

1. "The Screwfly Solution," Racoona Sheldon
2. "A Rite of Spring," Fritz Leiber
3. "Particle Theory," Edward Bryant

"The Stone City," George R. R. Martin
"The Ninth Symphony of Ludwig van Beethoven and Other Lost Songs,"
    Carter Scholz

short story

1. "Jeffty is Five," Harlan Ellison
2. "Air Raid," John Varley (as "Herb Boehm")
3. "The Hibakusha Gallery," Edward Bryant

"Tin Woodsman," Dennis Bailey & David Bischoff
"Camera Obscura," Thomas F. Monteleone

1979: 14th Nebula Awards

novel

1. *Dreamsnake,* Vonda N. McIntyre
2. *The Faded Sun: Kesrith,* C. J. Cherryh
3. *Blind Voices,* Tom Reamy

Strangers, Gardner Dozois
Kalki, Gore Vidal

novella

1. "The Persistence of Vision," John Varley
2. "Seven American Nights," Gene Wolfe

novelette

1. "A Glow of Candles, A Unicorn's Eye," Charles L. Grant
2. "Mikal's Songbird," Orson Scott Card
3. "Devil You Don't Know," Dean Ing

short story

1. "Stone," Edward Bryant
2. "Cassandra," C. J. Cherryh
3. "A Quiet Revolution for Death," Jack Dann

NOTE: Due to an unusually small number of nominations in the three shorter fiction categories, only 8 works total received the number of votes required (=5) to qualify for placement on the final ballot.

1980: 15th Nebula Awards

novels

1. *The Fountains of Paradise,* Arthur C. Clarke

2. *On Wings of Song,* Thomas M. Disch
3. *Titan,* John Varley

   The Road to Corlay, Richard Cowper
   Jem, Frederik Pohl
   Juniper Time, Kate Wilhelm

novella
1. "Enemy Mine," Barry B. Longyear
2. "Fireship," Joan D. Vinge
3. "The Tale of Gorgik," Samuel R. Delany

   "Mars Masked," Frederik Pohl
   "The Battle of the Abaco Reffs," Hilbert Schenck
   "The Story Writer," Richard Wilson

novelette
1. "Sandkings," George R. R. Martin
2. "Options," John Varley
3. "The Ways of Love," Poul Anderson

   "Camps," Jack Dann
   "The Pathways of Desire," Ursula K. Le Guin
   "The Angel of Death," Michael Shea

short story
1. "giANTS," Edward Bryant
2. "Unaccompanied Sonata," Orson Scott Card
3. "The Way of Cross and Dragon," George R. R. Martin

   "Vernalfest Morning," Michael Bishop
   "Red as Blood," Tanith Lee
   "The Extraordinary Voyages of Amelie Bertrand," Joanna Russ

THE WORLD FANTASY AWARD

The World Fantasy Awards, or "Howards," are the invention of the relatively new annual World Fantasy Convention, first held in 1975. In large part, with the indicated change of interest, this convention is modeled after the example of the venerable World Science Fiction Convention, begun in 1939. Whereas both conventions give out an important yearly set of awards, there is an important difference in the two cases. The Hugos of the World Science Fiction Convention are decided by a popular election, with any registered member of the convention eligible to vote. The Howards of the World Fantasy Convention are decided by a distinguished panel of five judges.

Apart from the major difference that one is a "popular" and the other a "jury." award, there are also other, more minor differences of policy. There are only two WFA awards given for original fiction; "best novel" and "best shorter fiction"—and not four. In addition, only the name of the winner is announced in any category, with no indication given as to which of the remaining nominees in that category might have finished 2nd or 3rd.

The familiar name of the World Fantasy Awards, "Howard," is derived from Howard Phillips Lovecraft, the important 1930s writer of weird/horror fiction from Providence, Rhode Island (site of the 1st and 5th conventions). It should be noted that, in the last few years, the name "Howard" has been commonly described as a tribute *both* to Lovecraft and the important 1930s writer of heroic fantasy, Robert E. Howard, from Cross Plains, Texas. The 4th convention, held in Fort Worth, was even dedicated to R. E. H. Nonetheless, I believe this to be an afterthought, based on the fortunate coincidence of names. After all, the tradition has been to use the honored individuals's *first* name for the award, and not his last, as per the example of "Hugo." And then there are the suggestive facts that the inaugural convention was held in Lovecraft's home town, and that the award itself is a bust of Lovecraft.

So far as I can tell, the consensus of opinion is that the WFAs are, by some margin, the most important yearly awards made in the area of fantasy (as opposed to SF). There are several reasons for this. Central among them is the fact that, like the Hugos, the WFAs are associated with a World Convention, the single most important yearly event in the realm of fantasy. That, in itself, lends prestige to them. Partly because they are associated with a Worldcon, they have been able to draw on a very distinguished list of persons to serve as judges, whose connection with the award has added further luster to it. Partly because they are involved with both a Worldcon and prominent individuals, the WFA results have been routinely, widely, and conspicuously reported, a circumstance which has tended to promote their importance even more.

The World Fantasy Awards, 1975–1980 (original fiction categories only)

1975: 1st annual World Fantasy Awards

novel
1. *The Forgotten Beasts of Eld*, Patricia McKillip
   A Midsummer's Tempest, Poul Anderson
   Merlin's Ring, H. Warner Munn

short fiction
1. "Pages From a Young Girl's Journal," Robert Aickman
   "The Events at Poroth Farm," T. E. D. Klein
   "A Father's Tale," Sterling Lanier
   "Sticks," Karl Edward Wagner

1976: 2nd annual World Fantasy Awards

novel
1. *Bid Time Return*, Richard Matheson
   Salem's Lot, Stephen King

short fiction
1. "Belson Express," Fritz Leiber
   "The Barrow Troll," David Drake
   "Born of the Winds," Brian Lumley
   "The Ghostly Priest Doth Reign," Manley Wade Wellman

1977: 3rd annual World Fantasy Awards

novel

1. *Doctor Rat*, William Kotzwinkle
   The Doll Who Ate His Mother, Ramsey Campbell
   The Dragon and the George, Gordon Dickson
   The Sailor on the Seas of Fate, Michael Moorcock
   The Acts of King Arthur and His Noble Knights, John Steinbeck
   Dark Crusade, Karl Edward Wagner

short fiction

1. "There's a Long, Long Trail A-Winding," Russell Kirk
   "The Companion," Ramsey Campbell
   "It Only Comes Out At Night," Dennis Etchison
   "Dark Wings," Fritz Leiber
   "What Is Life," Robert Sheckley
   "Two Suns Setting," Karl Edward Wagner

1978: 4th annual World Fantasy Awards

novel

1. *Our Lady of Darkness*, Fritz Leiber
   The Chronicles of Thomas Covenant The Unbeliever, Stephen R. Donaldson
   in three volumes: *Lord Foul's Bane, The Illearth War, The Power That Preserves*
   The Hour of the Oxrun Dead, Charles L. Grant

short fiction

1. "The Chimney," Ramsey Campbell
   "Loverman's Comeback," Ramsey Campbell
   "Manatee Gal, Ain't Ya Comin' Out Tonight," Avram Davidson
   "Jeffty Is Five," Harlan Ellison
   "When All The Children Call My Name," Charles L. Grant
   "Bagful of Dreams," Jack Vance

1979: 5th annual World Fantasy Awards

novel

1. *Gloriana*, Michael Moorcock
   The Black Castle, Les Daniels
   The Sound of Midnight, Charles L. Grant
   The Stand, Stephen King
   Night's Master, Tanith Lee

short fiction

1. "Naples," Avram Davidson
   "Within the Walls of Tyre," Michael Bishop
   "A Good Night's Sleep" (reprinted under author's title: "Sleep Well of Nights"), Avram Davidson
   "Hear Me Now, Sweet Abbey Rose," Charles L. Grant
   "The Magic Goes Away," Larry Niven (published as a novel, but under 40,000 words)

1980: 6th annual World Fantasy Awards

> Judges: Stephen R. Donaldson, Frank Belknap Long, Andrew J. Offutt, Ted White, Susan J. Wood.

novel

1. *Watchtower,* Elizabeth A. Lynn

> *The Last Call of Morning,* Charles L. Grant
> *The Dancers of Arun,* Elizabeth A. Lynn
> *Harpist in the Wind,* Patricia A. McKillip
> *The Dark Bright Water,* Patricia Wrightson
>> (Appeared in 1978 overseas, but 1979 U. S. edition regarded as first edition available to general fantasy audience.)
> *The Palace,* Chelsea Quinn Yarbro
>> (1978 copyright date, but not released until early 1979.)
> **The Dead Zone,* Stephen King
>> (Withdrawn from contention by author on grounds that novel should be considered SF, not fantasy.)

short fiction

1t. "Mackintosh Willy," Ramsey Campbell
1t. "The Woman Who Loved the Moon," Elizabeth A. Lynn

> "Petey," T. E. D. Klein
> "The Button Molder," Fritz Leiber
> "Saturday's Shadow," William F. Nolan

collection/anthology

1. *Amazons,* ed. Jessica Amanda Salmonson

> *Thieves' World,* ed. Robert Asprin
> *The Year's Finest Fantasy: Volume 2,* ed. Terry Carr
> *Nightmares,* ed. Charles L. Grant
> *Shadows 2,* ed. Charles L. Grant
> *Whispers II,* ed. Stuart David Schiff

Special Addendum: The World Fantasy Award for "Best Collection/Anthology"

note: Of the authors appearing on this list, four are "Life Achievement" award winners: Bloch (1975), Leiber (1976), Bradbury (1977), and Long (1978). Wellman has been a perennial nominee in this category, 1975–79; and Price was nominated in 1977. Carcosa, the operation of owner and editor Karl Edward Wagner, published the Wellman, Price, and Cave volumes (the 1st three books of this publisher). In 1976, Carcosa won in the "Special Award (non-professional)" category; and the illustrator of the Wellman and Cave volumes, Lee Brown Coye, won in the "Best Artist" category both years (1975 & 1978).

1975: 1st annual World Fantasy Awards

1. *Worse Things Waiting,* Manley Wade Wellman

> *From Earth's Pillow,* Basil Cooper

1976: 2nd annual World Fantasy Awards

1. *The Enquiries of Dr. Esterhazy,* Avram Davidson
   Deathbird Stories, Harlan Ellison
   The Early Long, Frank Belknap Long
   Far Lands, Other Days, E. Hoffman Price

1977: 3rd annual World Fantasy Awards

1. *Frights,* ed. by Kirby McCauley
   Long After Midnight, Ray Bradbury
   Cinnabar, Edward Bryant
   Superhorror, ed. by Ramsey Campbell
   The Height of the Scream, Ramsey Campbell
   Flashing Swords #3, ed. by Lin Carter

1978: 4th annual World Fantasy Awards

1. *Murgunstrumm and Others,* Hugh B. Cave
   Cold Chills, Robert Bloch
   Swords and Ice Magic, Fritz Leiber
   The Year's Best Horror Stories: Series V, ed. by Gerald W. Page
   Whispers, ed. by Stuart David Schiff

1979: 5th annual World Fantasy Awards

1. *Shadows,* ed. by Charles L. Grant
   The Redward Edward Papers, Avram Davidson
   Night Shift, Stephen King
   Heroes and Horrors, Fritz Leiber
   The Year's Best Horror Stories: Series VI, ed. by Gerald W. Page
   Night Winds, Karl Edward Wagner

THE JUPITER AWARDS

The Jupiter Awards are a direct result of the relatively sudden and massive interest taken in science fiction by colleges and universities beginning in the 1960s. Along with many other changes in higher education during this turbulent period, went a marked liberalization of attitudes about what was academically important or respectable or acceptable. (The key word of the times was "relevance.") One result of these more liberal attitudes was the widespread inclusion, in regular college curriculums, of what can be termed "popular culture" subjects. One beneficiary of such pedagogical recognition was science fiction.

To many of the older residents of the field, the new academic presence appeared distinctly threatening. The cultured hordes were at the gate, and all the old values were in jeopardy. (The most famous slogan of the 'traditionalists' was, "Let's keep SF in the gutter, where it belongs!") The academics, for their part, were faced with the problem which always confronts any just-arrived group in any established community, of gaining acceptance and status within the larger whole.

The Jupiters were instituted by and on behalf of college teachers, as one way of helping to achieve this end. The idea was to start an award which would take its place, as a third major representative group award (for college teachers), alongside the two already well-known awards of this nature: the Hugos (for fans), and the Nebulas (for writers). The explicitly stated justification behind this idea had two planks. First, it was supposed that the continual yearly growth in the amount of SF being published meant that, by the mid-70's, there was more good writing being done than the combined efforts of the other annual awards could adequately recognize. Second, it was suggested that SF teachers as a group had reached the point in their own growth by the mid-70's, where they existed in sufficient numbers to be considered a large, distinct, special interest faction in SF. Like fans and writers, teachers had their own unique collective viewpoint on what constituted good writing; a viewpoint requiring its own special award for adequate expression. (The claim that, "the reading tastes of instructors is somewhat different from both fans and writers," is, in fact, the thesis of an unpublished paper written at or before the time the Jupiters were conceived by their founder, Dr. Charles Waugh.)

In other words, it was believed likely that, given the opportunity, the teachers would, as a class, nominate and choose a somewhat different set of works than either the fans or writers were doing—and that these other, hitherto unacknowledged works, deserved recognition, too. The point that the teachers were still freshly arrived on the scene, and often regarded by fans and writers alike with a suspicion which ranged up to outright hostility in some cases, was irrelevant. The bottom line was that the teachers were here in force, and to stay. Consequently, they had a right, as legitimate as anyone's, to express their own sense of what works ought to be regarded as outstanding.

The awards are the specific inspiration of Dr. Charles Waugh at the University of Maine. Waugh began in early 1973 by announcing the formation of a new organization, ISFHE, or Instructors of Science Fiction in Higher Education. The sole function of this organization was to award the Jupiters. The first actual Jupiter voting, though, was not held until 1974 (covering the calendar year 1973). Exactly when or why the name "Jupiter" was settled on, I do not know.

Jupiter Awards are given just for original fiction in the four standard length categories: novel, novella, novelette, and short story. To be eligible for nomination and then election in any category, a work must first appear in the calendar year preceding the year of the voting. The eligibility of a work as being "science fiction" is left up to the individual instructors. If enough persons casting nomination ballots think it is SF and vote for it, to qualify it for the final ballot, then it will automatically appear on the final ballot.

The Jupiter Awards, 1974–1979 (complete)

1974: 1st Jupiter Awards
   novel
   1. *Rendezvous With Rama*, Arthur C. Clarke
   2. *Gravity's Rainbow*, Thomas Pynchon
   3. *The Man Who Folded Himself*, David Gerrold

Time Enough For Love, Robert A. Heinlein
Herovit's World, Barry N. Malzberg

novella
1. "The Feast of St. Dionysus," Robert Silverberg
2. "In the Problem Pit," Frederik Pohl
3. "Chains of the Sea," Gardner Dozois
   "The Quincunx of Time," James Blish
   "The Magic Striptease," George Garrett
   "The Hellhound Project," Ron Goulart

novelette
1. "The Deathbird," Harlan Ellison
2. "Everyday Life in the Later Roman Empire," Thomas M. Disch
3. "Flash Crowd," Larry Niven
   "Who Steals My Purse," John Brunner
   "The Girl Who Was Plugged In," James Tiptree, Jr.
   "Survivability," William Tuning
   "The Death of Dr. Island," Gene Wolfe

short story
1. "A Suppliant in Space," Robert Sheckley
2. "A Thing of Beauty," Norman Spinrad
3t. "Direction of the Road," Ursula K. Le Guin
3t. "Of Mist, and Grass, and Sand," Vonda N. McIntyre
3t. "The Village," Kate Wilhelm
   "Shark," Edward Bryant
   "Day of Grass, Day of Straw," R. A. Lafferty
   "The Ones Who Walk Away From Omelas," Ursula K. Le Guin

1975: 2nd Jupiter Awards
 novel
 1. *The Dispossessed*, Ursula K. Le Guin
 2. *The Mote In God's Eye*, Larry Niven & Jerry Pournelle
    All Times Possible, Gordon Eklund
    The Company of Glory, Edgar Pangborn
    Nostrilia, Cordwainer Smith

novella
1. "Riding the Torch," Norman Spinrad
2. "Born With the Dead," Robert Silverberg
3. "A Song for Lya," George R. R. Martin
   "Strangers," Gardner Dozois
   "Assault on a City," Jack Vance

novelette
1. "The Seventeen Virgins," Jack Vance
2. "The Women Men Don't See," James Tiptree, Jr.
3. "Tin Soldier," Joan D. Vinge
   "If the Stars are Gods," Gregory Benford & Gordon Eklund
   "The Horus Errand," William C. Cochrane

short story
1. "The Day Before the Revolution," Ursula K. Le Guin

2t. "An Old Fashioned Girl," Joanna Russ
2t. "The Engine at Heartspring's Center," Roger Zelazny
"Sleeping Dogs," Harlan Ellison
"Blue Butter," Theodore Sturgeon

1976: 3rd Jupiter Awards

No Jupiters presented in 1976 due to a temporary suspension of the awards organization, ISFHE.

1977: 4th Jupiter Awards
novel
1. *Where Late The Sweet Birds Sang,* Kate Wilhelm

novella
1. "Houston, Houston, Do You Read?" James Tiptree, Jr.

novelette
1. "The Diary of the Rose," Ursula K. Le Guin

short story
1. "I See You," Damon Knight

1978: 5th Jupiter Awards
novel
1. *A Heritage of Stars,* Clifford D. Simak

novella
1. "In the Hall of the Martian Kings," John Varley

novelette
1. "Time Storm," Gordon R. Dickson

short story
1. "Jeffty Is Five," Harlan Ellison

1979: 6th Jupiter Awards

No Jupiters presented in 1979 due to a second suspension of the awards organization, ISFHE.

THE JOHN W. CAMPBELL MEMORIAL AWARD

Named in honor of the famous editor of *Astounding/Analog* magazine, John W. Campbell, the award is given each year for the best original science fiction novel. The homage paid to Campbell by this annual award seeks to recognize his overall contribution as the "father of modern science fiction."

The award evidentally had a dual origin. Harry Harrison, who was editing a memorial volume of original stories to Campbell (*Astounding,* 1973), conceived of a memorial award in collaboration with his friend and associate, Brian W. Aldiss. Harrison and Aldiss needed a sponsor, though. As chance would have it, at about the same time the Illinois Institute of Technology, in the person of Leon E. Stover, was looking for some way to honor Campbell. (Campbell had visited IIT in the year preceding his death, and had made a great impression on many influential figures at the Institute.) Since Harrison and Stover were already well acquainted, the natural next step was for the two parties to get together. The result of that collaboration was the John W. Campbell Memorial Award for the best original novel of the year.

The award itself was inaugurated in 1973 (covering calendar year 1972). The initial plan was for an annual award to be sponsored on a permanent basis by IIT. It would be decided by a select jury of five members, with Stover as its chairman, and Harrison and Aldiss as two of its members. The remainder of the committee was comprised of Willis E. McNelly (Professor of English at California State College, Fullerton) and Thomas D. Clareson (Professor of English at Wooster College, Wooster, Ohio). Presentation of the award (a cash prize) would take place at an appropriate formal ceremony, to be hosted by IIT.

Everything was all set—that is, until it came time to choose the winner. The trouble was the first winner of the John W. Campbell Memorial turned out to be *Beyond Apollo,* by Barry N. Malzberg. That created a problem because many people felt *Beyond Apollo* was a novel John W. Campbell would have hated; that it stood for everything he especially disliked in fiction. Those who felt this way had reason, to be sure. After 33+ years as editor of ASF, Campbell's views on good and bad fiction were not exactly secret. There was, of course, no question about the committee's right to choose any work they might favor for an award; or to give it any amount of money they might have; or to represent themselves by any form of hardware they might see fit to hand out. The issue was over the propriety of giving an award, in *Campbell's* name and memory, to a book that could easily be described not just as non-Campbellian, but positively *anti*-Campbellian.

(The whole situation was exacerbated, I imagine, by the fact that one of the year's leading candidates for "best novel" was *The Gods Themselves,* Isaac Asimov's first significant SF novel in many years. Asimov is a writer strongly identified with Campbell and the "Golden Age" of SF at ASF. If there had been a deliberate conspiracy, it would be difficult to produce a more 'appropriate' winner of the very first John W. Campbell Memorial Award.)

The result of these circumstances was that the announcement of the first JWCMA winner was greeted by a storm of protest. Many of Campbell's friends and admirers were outraged. Numerous angry letters were written and published. Even so, the indignation which was aroused by this first award might have had little practical significance—to look on the bright side, at least it seemed to show people were taking the award *seriously*—if it had not been for the awkward point that Leon Stover and the other interested parties at IIT were included in the ranks of the outraged. Stover resigned from the awards committee in protest. IIT withdrew their financial support, and disassociated themselves from any further involvement with the JWCMA (after the first year).

In consequence, for the second year of the award (1974), some changes had to be made in the initial plan. The chairmanship of the committee was assumed by Willis E. McNelly, and the formal awards ceremony moved to his home institution, California State College at Fullerton. The vacancy created by Stover's resignation was more than filled by the appointment of two new members to the select jury: James E. Gunn (like Harrison and Aldiss, a well-known

SF author and editor; but also like McNelly and Clareson, an academic: Professor of English at the University of Kansas), and Mark R. Hillegas (who holds the distinction of having taught what is generally recognized as the first regular credit-bearing class on SF in any college in the U. S., at Colgate in 1962; now a member of the Department of English at Southern Illinois University). Two other, unrelated changes occurred in the second-year jury. Since Aldiss had a novel eligible for consideration that year, to avoid any possible conflict of interest, both he and Harrison were temporarily replaced for the year by Beverly Friend and Peter Nichols.

There was to be no new permanent home for the JWCMA at California State College at Fullerton, though. The third year (1975), the chairmanship was taken over by Harry Harrison (both he and Aldiss were back from their one-year absence). Following the policy of the previous two years, the formal awards ceremony went with the chairman. Interestingly, since the chairman was then in the process of moving to Europe, it ended up being held that year at St. John's College, Oxford. (Like other artists with an eye on tax breaks, Harrison settled in Ireland. Aldiss, however, happens to live in Oxford. I do not know what, if any, connection Aldiss has with St. John's, but I suspect there is one. At any rate, we are not quite done with St. John's yet.)

Besides exporting the award, or rather its chairman and ceremony, to Europe, the other major change of 1975 was in the structure of the committee. Evidently as a result of their experience the previous year, a consensus was reached that henceforth all novels by committee members would be automatically ineligible for consideration. This meant that a "permanent awards committee" could now be officially established. As of 1975, it consisted of six members: McNelly and Clareson, the only two persons to serve all three years; Harrison and Aldiss, the other two remaining members of the original five-person jury; and Gunn and Hillegas, the two 'regular' additions of 1974.

Since 1975, the JWCMA ceremony has remained mostly abroad, and constantly peripatetic. In 1976, the fourth JWCMA was presented at a World SF Writer's Conference, held in Dublin, Ireland. (Harrison was instrumental in organizing this conference.) In 1977, the fifth JWCMA was made part of a formal occasion at the Swedish Author's Organization headquarters, in Stockholm. In 1978, the sixth JWCMA returned to Dublin, for an encore performance at the 2nd (biennial) World SF Writer's Conference. Finally, after an absence of four years, the JWCMA ceremony was returned to the U. S. in 1979. A special two-day "Campbell Award conference" on the teaching and writing of SF, climaxed by an award's dinner, was held at the University of Kansas in Lawrence. This occurred during but was not an official aspect of the summer three-week "Intensive English Institute on the Teaching of Science Fiction" also held there. (By this time, Gunn had become the committee chairman; not exactly by coincidence, he is also Director of the summer Institute.)

The "permanent" awards committee of 1975 has seen some revisions during the last four years, too. By 1978, both Clareson and Hillegas had left the committee. The opportunity was taken to make it more international in character, by appointing first Sam J. Lundwall in 1977, and then Thomas A. Shippey in 1978, as replacements. Lundwall is a Swedish SF author and figure; Shippey is recently a Fellow in English at St. John's College, Oxford, and currently head of the Language and Medieval Department at Leeds University,

England. (It may be recalled that the 1977 awards ceremony was held in Stockholm; and that the third ceremony took place at St. John's.) In 1979, the awards committee was enlarged once again, to a total of seven members, with the addition of Robert Scholes, a Professor of English at Brown University (Providence, R. I.).

The John W. Campbell Memorial Award, 1973–1979

1973: 1st   *Beyond Apollo*, Barry N. Malzberg
       2nd   *The Listeners*, James Gunn
       3rd   *Darkening Island* (*Fugue for a Darkening Plain*), Christopher Priest
               Special award for excellence of writing
                   Dying Inside, Robert Silverberg

1974: 1st   *Rendezvous with Rama*, Arthur C. Clarke
       (tie) *Malevil*, Robert Merle
       2nd   *The Embedding*, Ian Watson
       (tie) *The Green Gene*, Peter Dickinson

1975: 1st   *Flow My Tears, The Policeman Said*, Philip K. Dick
       2nd   *The Dispossessed*, Ursula K. Le Guin

1976: 1st   *Year of the Quiet Sun*, Wilson Tucker*
       2nd   *The Stochastic Man*, Robert Silverberg
       3rd   *Orbitsville*, Bob Shaw

       *The committee felt that no truly outstanding original novel was published in 1975. 1st place, therefore, was a "special retrospective award" made to a truly outstanding original novel which was not adequately recognized in the year of its publication (1970).

1977: 1st   *The Alteration*, Kingsley Amis
       2nd   *Man Plus*, Frederik Pohl
       3rd   *Where Late the Sweet Birds Sang*, Kate Wilhelm

1978: 1st   *Gateway*, Frederik Pohl
       2nd   *Roadside Picnic/Tale of the Troika*, Arkady & Boris Strugatsky
       3rd   *A Scanner Darkly*, Philip K. Dick

1979: 1st   *Gloriana*, Michael Moorcock
       2nd   *And Having Writ . . .* , Donald Benson
       3rd   *Altered States*, Paddy Chayefski

1980: 1st   *On Wings of Song*, Thomas M. Disch
       2nd   *Engine Summer*, John Crowley
       3rd   *The Unlimited Dream Company*, J. G. Ballard

THE LOCUS POLL AWARDS

The Locus Poll is, as its name suggests, a poll, taken among the readers of *Locus,* a semi-professional magazine devoted to news about science fiction. *Locus* is arguably the most important news magazine in the history of science fiction. It is, to mention just one fact, the winner of four Hugos for "best fanzine" over an eight-year period. *Locus* is published by Charles N. Brown. Current paid circulation of *Locus* is in the neighborhood of 4,000 copies/issue. Going by these figures, a reasonable estimate would place its readership at between 10,000–15,000 persons. In the same way the *Wall Street Journal* can be presumed to reach most people with a serious interest in financial matters, this figure can be presumed to include most persons with a serious interest in SF: publishers, writers, editors, agents, teachers, critics, scholars, and the rest.

The Locus Poll was instituted in 1971 (covering the year 1970). It has been held annually ever since. The categories polled vary significantly from year to year: some are placed on the ballot only at occasional intervals, while the rest are subject to invention, discontinuation, subdivision, or amalgamation, as changes in circumstances and interest may suggest.

In those years in which shorter fiction categories have been combined, I have indicated the length of the individual stories as follows: (L) = novella, (M) = novelette, (S) = short story.

The Locus Poll Awards, 1971–1980 (fiction categories only)

1971: 1st Locus Poll, 201 ballots cast
novel
1. *Ringworld,* Larry Niven
2t. *Tower of Glass,* Robert Silverberg
2t. *Year of the Quiet Sun,* Wilson Tucker
4. *And Chaos Died,* Joanna Russ
5t. *Fourth Mansions,* R. A. Lafferty
5t. *Downward to the Earth,* Robert Silverberg
7. *Tau Zero,* Poul Anderson
8. *Tactics of Mistake,* Gordon R. Dickson
9. *I Will Fear No Evil,* Robert A. Heinlein
10. *Star Light,* Hal Clement
11. *Beastchild,* Dean R. Koontz
12. *Deryni Rising,* Katherine Kurtz
13. *Chronocules,* D. G. Compton
14. *The Steel Crocodile,* D. G. Compton
15. *Nine Princes in Amber,* Roger Zelazny
16. *After Things Fell Apart,* Ron Goulart

shorter fiction (one combined category)
1. "The Region Between," Harlan Ellison (L)
2. "The Snow Women," Fritz Leiber (L)
3. "Continued on the Next Rock," R. A. Lafferty (M)

4. "Beastchild," Dean R. Koontz (L)
5. "In the Queue," Keith Laumer (S)
6. "Slow Sculpture," Theodore Sturgeon (M)
7. "Runesmith," Harlan Ellison & Theodore Sturgeon (M)
8. "Brillo," Ben Bova & Harlan Ellison (S)
9. "Asian Shores," Thomas M. Disch (M)
10t. "The Fatal Fulfillment," Poul Anderson (L)
10t. "Dear Aunt Annie," Gordon Eklund (M)
10t. "Entire and Perfect Chrysolite," R. A. Lafferty (S)
13. "The Throwbacks," Robert Silverberg (M)
14. "Ill Met in Lankhmar," Fritz Leiber (L)

1972: 2nd Locus Poll, 330 ballots cast
novel (122 total nominated)
1. *The Lathe of Heaven*, Ursula K. Le Guin
2. *To Your Scattered Bodies Go*, Philip José Farmer
3. *A Time of Changes*, Robert Silverberg
4. *Jack of Shadows*, Roger Zelazny
5. *Dragonquest*, Anne McCaffrey
6. *The World Inside*, Robert Silverberg
7. *The Devil Is Dead*, R. A. Lafferty
8. *The Fabulous Riverboat*, Philip José Farmer
9. *Son of Man*, Robert Silverberg
10. *The Second Trip*, Robert Silverberg
11. *The World Menders*, Lloyd Biggle, Jr.
12. *The Byworlder*, Poul Anderson
13. *Furthest*, Suzette Haden Elgin
14. *Arrive at Easterwine*, R. A. Lafferty
15. *The Forest of Forever*, Thomas Burnett Swann

shorter fiction (one combined category)
1. "The Queen of Air and Darkness, Poul Anderson (M)
2t. "A Meeting with Medusa," Arthur C. Clarke (L)
2t. "All the Last Wars at Once," Geo. Alec Effinger (S)
4. "Wheels," Robert Thurston (M)
5. "The Autumn Land," Clifford D. Simak (S)
6. "Mount Charity," Edgar Pangborn (M)
7. "The Bear with the Knot on His Tail," Stephen Tall (S)
8. "World Abounding," R. A Lafferty (M)
9. "Inconstant Moon," Larry Niven (M)
10. "Dread Empire," John Brunner (L)
11. "A Special Kind of Morning," Gardner Dozois (L)
12. "The Human Operators," Harlan Ellison & A. E. van Vogt (M)
13. "In Entropy's Jaws," Robert Silverberg (S)
14. "Vaster Than Empires and More Slow," Ursula K. Le Guin (S)
15. "All the Way Up, All the Way Down," Robert Silverberg (S)

1973: 3rd Locus Poll, 383 ballots cast

novel (91 total nominated)

1. *The Gods Themselves*, Isaac Asimov
2. *The Book of Skulls*, Robert Silverberg
3. *Dying Inside*, Robert Silverberg
4. *When Harlie Was One*, David Gerrold
5. *A Choice of Gods*, Clifford D. Simak
6. *The Sheep Look Up*, John Brunner
7. *There Will Be Time*, Poul Anderson
8. *The Listeners*, James Gunn
9. *The Guns of Avalon*, Roger Zelazny
10. *The Iron Dream*, Norman Spinrad
11. *The Fifth Head of Cerberus*, Gene Wolfe
12. *What Entropy Means To Me*, Geo. Alec Effinger
13. *The Pritcher Mass*, Gordon R. Dickson
14. *The Brave Free Men*, Jack Vance
15. *Deryni Checkmate*, Katherine Kurtz
16. *Beyond Apollo*, Barry N. Malzberg
17t. *Tunnel Through The Deeps*, Harry Harrison
17t. *Other Days, Other Eyes*, Bob Shaw
19. *Yesterday's Children*, David Gerrold
20. *The Castle Keeps*, Andrew J. Offutt
21. *Beyond the Resurrection*, Gordon Eklund

> *note:* **Cemetery** *World* by Clifford D. Simak received enough votes to make the cut-off point for listing, but was ruled ineligible on grounds it should properly be counted as a 1973 rather than a 1972 novel.

novella (45 total nominated)

1. "The Gold at Starbow's End," Frederjk Pohl
2. "The Word for World is Forest," Ursula K. Le Guin
3. "The Fifth Head of Cerberus," Gene Wolfe
4. "Hero," Joe Haldeman
5. "Midsummer Century," James Blish
6. "With the Bentfin Boomer Boys On Little Old New Alabama," Richard A. Lupoff
7. "The Merchants of Venus," Frederik Pohl
8. "Things Which Are Caesar's," Gordon R. Dickson
9. "334," Thomas M. Disch
10. "Seventy Years of Decpop," Philip José Farmer
11. "What Good is a Glass Dagger?," Larry Niven
12. "The Mercenary," Jerry Pournelle
13t. "Solo Kill," S. Kye Boult
13t. "Collision Course," S. Kye Boult
13t. "Common Denominator," David Lewis
16. "Love is a Dragonfly," Thomas Burnett Swann
17. "In the Ocean of Night," Gregory Benford
18. "Son of the Morning," Phyllis Gotlieb

short fiction (197 total nominated)

1. "Basilisk," Harlan Ellison (M)

2. "Patron of the Arts," William Rotsler (M)
3. "Goat Song," Poul Anderson (M)
4. "And I Awoke And Found Me Here on the Cold Hill's Side," James Tiptree, Jr. (S)
5. "A Kingdom by the Sea," Gardner Dozois (M)
6. "When It Changed," Joanna Russ (S)
7. "The Second Kind of Loneliness," George R. R. Martin
8. "Painwise," James Tiptree, Jr. (M)
9. "The Meeting," Frederik Pohl & C. M. Kornbluth (S)
10. "The Funeral," Kate Wilhelm (M)
11. "Man's Reach," Anthony Boucher
12. "Caliban," Robert Silverberg
13. "On the Downhill Side," Harlan Ellison (S)
14t. "Nobody's Home," Joanna Russ
14t. "When We Went To See the End of the World," Robert Silverberg (S)
16t. "Eurema's Dam," R. A. Lafferty (S)
16t. "The Big Space Fuck," Kurt Vonnegut, Jr.
18t. "Now + n, Now – n," Robert Silverberg
18t. "The Milk of Paradise," James Tiptree, Jr.

1974: 4th Locus Poll, 401 ballots cast
novel (102 total nominated)
1. *Rendezvous With Rama*, Arthur C. Clarke
2. *Time Enough For Love*, Robert A. Heinlein
3. *The People of the Wind*, Poul Anderson
4. *Protector*, Larry Niven
5. *The Man Who Folded Himself*, David Gerrold
6. *Trullion Alastor: 2262*, Jack Vance
7. *The Far Call*, Gordon R. Dickson
   1973 serial version, *Analog*
8. *To Die In Italbar*, Roger Zelazny
9. *Today We Choose Faces*, Roger Zelazny
10. *The Cloud Walker*, Edmond Cooper
11. *Relatives*, Geo. Alec Effinger
12. *Gravity's Rainbow*, Thomas Pynchon
13. *Herovit's World*, Barry N. Malzberg
14. *Hiero's Journey*, Sterling Lanier
15. *The Doomsday Gene*, John Boyd

novella (44 total nominated)
1. "The Death of Dr. Island," Gene Wolfe
2. "The White Otters of Childhood," Michael Bishop
3. "The Feast of St. Dionysus," Robert Silverberg
4. "Sketches Among the Ruins of My Mind," Philip José Farmer
5.. "Chains of the Sea," Gardner R. Dozois
6. "The Defenseless Dead," Larry Niven
7. "Death and Designation Among the Asadi," Michael Bishop
8. "Rumfuddle," Jack Vance
9. "The Safety Engineer," S. Kye Boult

10.   "In the Problem Pit," Frederik Pohl
11.   "Junction," Jack Dann
12.   "My Brother Leopold," Edgar Pangborn
13.   "KJWALLL'EJE'KOOTHAILLL'KJE'K," Roger Zelazny
14.   "Case and the Dreamer," Theodore Sturgeon

short fiction (159 total nominated)
1.   "The Deathbird," Harlan Ellison (M)
2.   "Of Mist, and Grass, and Sand," Vonda N. McIntyre (M)
3.   "Love is the Plan, the Plan is Death," James Tiptree, Jr. (S)
4.   "The Girl Who Was Plugged In," James Tiptree, Jr. (M)
5.   "MS. Found In an Abandoned Time Machine," Robert Silverberg (S)
6.   "The Ones Who Walk Away From Omelas," Ursula K. Le Guin (S)
7.   "Wings," Vonda N. McIntyre
8.   "With Morning Comes Mistfall," George R. R. Martin (S)
9.   "Mud Violet," R. A. Lafferty
10.   "In the Group," Robert Silverberg (S)
11t.   "Many Mansions," Robert Silverberg (M)
11t.   "Field of Vision," Ursula K. Le Guin
13t.   "Barnaby's Clock," R. A. Lafferty
13t.   "The Answer," Terry Carr
13t   "Brothers," Gordon R. Dickson
16.   "The World Is a Sphere," Edgar Pangborn (M)
17.   "Epilog," Clifford D. Simak
18.   "The Women Men Don't See," James Tiptree, Jr.

1975: 5th Locus Poll, 516 ballots cast
novel
1.   *The Dispossessed*, Ursula K. Le Guin
2.   *The Mote In God's Eye*, Larry Niven & Jerry Pournelle
3.   *Flow My Tears, The Policeman Said*, Philip K. Dick
4.   *The Godwhale*, T. J. Bass
5.   *The Unsleeping Eye*, D. G. Compton
6.   *The Inverted World*, Christopher Priest
7.   *Fire Time*, Poul Anderson
8.   *The Forever War*, Joe Haldeman
9.   *The Dream Millenium*, James White
10.   *The Twilight of Briareus*, Richard Cowper
11.   *The Company of Glory*, Edgar Pangborn
12.   *The Domains of Koryphon*, Jack Vance
13.   *The Forgotten Beasts of Eld*, Patricia McKillip
14.   *How Are the Mighty Fallen*, Thomas Burnett Swann
15.   *Total Eclipse*, John Brunner
16.   *The Destruction of the Temple*, Barry N. Malzberg
17.   *Star Gate*, Tak Hallus
18.   *Star Rider*, Doris Piserchia
19.   *A Midsummer's Tempest*, Poul Anderson
20.   *Prince of Annwn*, Evangeline Walton
21.   *Walk to the End of the World*, Suzy McKee Charnas

22. *Icerigger,* Alan Dean Foster
23. *A Knight of Ghosts and Shadows,* Poul Anderson

novella
   1. "Born With the Dead," Robert Silverberg
   2. "A Song for Lya," George R. R. Martin
   3. "Riding the Torch," Norman Spinrad
   4. "Assault on a City," Jack Vance
   5. "Strangers," Gardner Dozois
   6. "The Marathon Photograph," Clifford D. Simak
   7. "The Araqnid Window," Charles L. Harness
   8. "On the Street of the Serpents," Michael Bishop
   9. 'Father," Pamela Sargent
  10. "Tin Soldier," Joan Vinge
  11. "Where Late the Sweet Birds Sang," Kate Wilhelm
  12. "Threads of Time," Gregory Benford
  13. "The East Coast Confinement," Arsey Darnay
  14. "The Kozmic Kid," Richard Snead

novelette
   1. "Adrift Just Off the Islets of Langerhans: Latitude 38° 54′ N, Longitude 77° 00′ 13 ″ W," Harlan Ellison
   2. "The Pre-Persons," Philip K. Dick
   3. "That Thou Art Mindful of Him," Isaac Asimov
   4. "I'm Looking for Kadak," Harlan Ellison
   5. "On Venus, Have We Got a Rabbi," William Tenn
   6. "Twig," Gordon R. Dickson
   7. "Nix Olympica," William Walling
   8. "If the Stars Are Gods," Gregory Benford & Gordon Eklund
   9. "After the Dreamtime," Richard Lupoff
  10. "The Seventeen Virgins," Jack Vance
  11. "The Raven and the Hawk," Bill Rotsler
  12. "Getting Home," F. M. Busby
  13. "Whale Song," Terry Melen
  14. "Catman," Harlan Ellison
  15. "The Gift of Garigolli," Frederik Pohl & C. M. Kornbluth
  16. "Whatever Happened to Nick Neptune?," Richard A. Lupoff
  17. "A Brother to Dragons, A Companion of Owls," Kate Wilhelm
  18. "A Little Something For Us Temponauts," Philip K. Dick
  19. "Gato–O," Don Picard
  20. "A Matter of Gravity," Randall Garrett
  21. "And Keep Us From Our Castles," Cynthia Bunn
  22. "Forlesen," Gene Wolfe
  23. "Under Siege," Robert Thurston

short story
   1. "The Day Before the Revolution," Ursula K. Le Guin
   2. "The Hole Man," Larry Niven
   3. "Schwartz Between the Galaxies," Robert Silverberg
   4. "The Author of the Acacia Seeds and Other Extracts from the Journal of the Association of Therolinguistics," Ursula K. Le Guin

5. "The Engine at Heartspring's Center," Roger Zelazny
6. "The Four Hour Fugue," Alfred Bester
7. "Cathadonian Odyssey," Michael Bishop
8. "Enter a Pilgrim," Gordon R. Dickson
9. "Midnight by the Morphy Watch," Fritz Leiber
10. "Royal Licorice," R. A. Lafferty
11. "We Purchased People," Frederik Pohl
12. "The Stars Below," Ursula K. Le Guin
13. "Do You Know Dave Wenzel?," Fritz Leiber
14. "Mysterious Doings At the Metropolitan Museum," Fritz Leiber
15. "In the House of Double Minds," Robert Silverberg
16. "The Mountains of Sunset, the Mountains of Dawn," Vonda N. McIntyre
17. "Willowisp," Joe Pumilia
18. "Enjoy, Enjoy," Frederik Pohl
19. "Mute Inglorious Tam," Frederik Pohl & C. M. Kornbluth

1976: 6th Locus Poll, 526 ballots cast
novel (105 total nominated)
1. *The Forever War*, Joe Haldeman
2. *The Shockwave Rider*, John Brunner
3. *The Computer Connection*, Alfred Bester
4. *The Stochastic Man*, Robert Silverberg
5. *Dhalgren*, Samuel R. Delany
6. *Imperial Earth*, Arthur C. Clarke
7. *Heritage of Hastur*, Marion Zimmer Bradley
8. *Doorways in the Sand*, Roger Zelazny
9. *Norstrilia*, Cordwainer Smith
10. *The Female Man*, Joanna Russ
11. *Sign of the Unicorn*, Roger Zelazny
12. *Inferno*, Larry Niven & Jerry Pournelle
13. *Showboat World*, Jack Vance
14. *A Funeral for the Eyes of Fire*, Michael Bishop
15. *The Exile Waiting*, Vonda N. McIntyre
16. *Blake's Progress*, Ray Nelson
17. *Warriors of Dawn*, M. A. Foster
18. *Lifeboat*, Gordon R. Dickson & Harry Harrison
19. *Illuminatus!*, Robert Shea & Robert Anton Wilson
20. *The Birthgrave*, Tanith Lee
21. *Missing Man*, Katherine MacLean

novella (47 total nominated)
1. "The Storms of Windhaven," Lisa Tuttle & George R. R. Martin
2. "Home is the Hangman," Roger Zelazny
3. "The Borderland of Sol," Larry Niven
4. "The Silent Eyes of Time," Algis Budrys
5. "Arm," Larry Niven
6. "The Custodians," Richard Cowper
7. "A Momentary Taste of Being," James Tiptree, Jr.

8. "Allegiances," Michael Bishop
9. "Silhouette," Gene Wolfe
10. "Mother and Child," Joan Vinge
11. "Ancient Shadows," Michael Moorcock
12. "Sharking Down," Edward Bryant

novelette (82 total nominated)
1. "The New Atlantis," Ursula K. Le Guin
2. "Down to a Sunless Sea," Cordwainer Smith
3. ". . . and Seven Times Never Kill Man," George R. R. Martin
4. "Retrograde Summer," John Varley
5. "A Galaxy Called Rome," Barry N. Malzberg
6. "For a Single Yesterday," George R. R. Martin
7. "In the Bowl," John Varley
8. "Sandsnake Hunter," Gordon Eklund
9. "The Black Hole Passes," John Varley
10. "Polly Charms, the Sleeping Woman," Avram Davidson
11. "Cambridge 1:58 A.M.," Gregory Benford
12. "San Diego Lightfoot Sue," Tom Reamy
13. "The Venging," Greg Bear
14. "End Game," Joe Haldeman
15. "Blooded on Arachne," Michael Bishop

short story (109 nominated)
1. "Croatoan," Harlan Ellison
2. "The Mother Trip," Frederik Pohl
3. "Child of All Ages," P. J. Plauger
4. "Sail the Tide of Mourning," Richard A. Lupoff
5. "Doing Lennon," Gregory Benford
6. "Sierra Maestra," Norman Spinrad
7. "Rogue Tomato," Michael Bishop
8. "Anniversary Project," Joe Haldeman
9. "Beyond Grayworld," Gregory Benford
10. "Find the Lady," Nicholas Fisk
11. "Catch That Zeppelin!," Fritz Leiber
12. "All the Charms of Sycorax," Alan Brennert
13. "Clay Suburb," Robert Young
14. "Shatterday," Harlan Ellison

1977: 7th Locus Poll, 800+ ballots cast
novel (94 total nominated)
1. *Where Late The Sweet Birds Sang*, Kate Wilhelm
2. *Mindbridge*, Joe Haldeman
3. *Man Plus*, Frederik Pohl
4. *Children of Dune*, Frank Herbert
5. *A World Out of Time*, Larry Niven
6. *Shadrach in the Furnace*, Robert Silverberg
7. *Imperial Earth*, Arthur C. Clarke
8. *Millenium*, Ben Bova
9. *The Hand of Oberon*, Roger Zelazny

10. *Brothers of Earth*, C. J. Cherryh
11. *The Shattered Chain*, Marion Zimmer Bradley
12. *Maske: Thaery*, Jack Vance
13. *Michaelmas*, Algis Budrys
        1976 serial version, F&SF
14. *Triton*, Samuel R. Delany
15. *The Clewiston Test*, Kate Wilhelm
16. *Dragonsong*, Anne McCaffrey
17. *Inferno*, Larry Niven & Jerry Pournelle
18. . *The Dragon and the George*, Gordon R. Dickson
19. *Cloned Lives*, Pamela Sargent
20. *The End of All Songs*, Michael Moorcock
21. *Floating Worlds*, Cecelia Holland
22. *Time of the Fourth Horseman*, Chelsea Quinn Yarbro

novella (49 total nominated)
1. "The Samurai and the Willows," Michael Bishop
2. "Piper at the Gates of Dawn," Richard Cowper
3. "Houston, Houston, Do You Read?," James Tiptree, Jr.
4. "The Anvil of Jove," Gregory Benford & Gordon Eklund
5. "The Eyeflash Miracles," Gene Wolfe
6. "Weather War," William E. Cochrane
7. "Media Man," Joan D. Vinge
8. "Birthdays," Fred Saberhagen
9. "By Any Other Name . . . ," Spider Robinson
10. "The Greenhouse Defect," Andrew J. Offutt
11. "A Thrust of Greatness," Stanley Schmidt
12. "Plutonium," Arsen Darnay
13. "The Crystal Ship," Joan D. Vinge

novelette (80 total nominated)
1. "The Bicentennial Man," Isaac Asimov
2. "The Diary of the Rose," Ursula K. Le Guin
3. "Gotta Sing, Gotta Dance," John Varley
4. "The Phantom of Kansas," John Varley
5. "The Hertford Manuscript," Richard Cowper
6. "The Psychologist Who Wouldn't Do Awful Things to Rats," James Tiptree, Jr.
7. "Custer's Last Jump," Steven Utley & Howard Waldrop
8. "Meathouse Man," George R. R. Martin
9. "Bagatelle," John Varley
10. "Overdrawn at the Memory Bank," John Varley
11. "Woman Waiting," Lisa Tuttle

short story (154 total nominated)
1. "Tricentennial," Joe Haldeman
2. "I See You," Damon Knight
3. "Custom Fitting," James White
4. "The Death of Princes," Fritz Leiber
5. "A Crowd of Shadows," Charles L. Grant
6. "Seeing," Harlan Ellison

7. "Paradise Beach," Richard Cowper
8. "This Tower of Ashes," George R. R. Martin
9. "Mary Margaret Road-Grader," Howard Waldrop
10. "Appearance of Life," Brian W. Aldiss
11. "From A to Z, In the Chocolate Alphabet," Harlan Ellison
12. "The Never Ending Western Movie," Robert Sheckley
13. "Stone Circle," Lisa Tuttle
14. "An Infinite Summer," Christopher Priest
15. "Con Artist," P. J. Plauger

1978: 8th Locus Poll, 700–800 ballots cast
novel (92 total nominations)
1. *Gateway*, Frederik Pohl
2. *In the Ocean of Night*, Gregory Benford
3. *The Ophiuchi Hotline*, John Varley
4. *Time Storm*, Gordon R. Dickson
5. *Michaelmas*, Algis Budrys
6. *A Scanner Darkly*, Philip K. Dick
7. *The Dosadi Experiment*, Frank Herbert
8. *Lucifer's Hammer*, Larry Niven & Jerry Pournelle
9. *Dragonsinger*, Anne McCaffrey
10. *Dying of the Light*, George R. R. Martin
11. *The Forbidden Tower*, Marion Zimmer Bradley
12. *Hunter of Worlds*, C. J. Cherryh
13. *Mirkheim*, Poul Anderson
14. *The Dark Design*, Philip José Farmer
15. *A Heritage of Stars*, Clifford D. Simak
16. *Cirque*, Terry Carr
17. *Moonstar Odyssey*, David Gerrold
18. *Midnight at the Well of Souls*, Jack Chalker
19. *Inherit the Stars*, James P. Hogan
20. *All My Sins Remembered*, Joe Haldeman
21. *The Martian Inca*, Ian Watson
22. *A Little Knowledge*, Michael Bishop
23. *If the Stars Are Gods*, Gregory Benford & Gordon Eklund

fantasy novel (53 total nominated)
1. *The Silmarillion*, J. R. R. Tolkien
2. *Our Lady of Darkness*, Fritz Leiber
3. *The Chronicles of Thomas Covenant The Unbeliever*, Stephen R. Donaldson
4. *The Shining*, Stephen King
5. *The Sword of Shannara*, Terry Brooks
6. *Sword of the Demon*, Richard Lupoff
7. *Heir of Sea and Fire*, Patricia A. McKillip
8. *Book of Merlyn*, T. H. White
9. *A Spell for Chameleon*, Piers Anthony
10. *The Grey Mane of Morning*, Joy Chant
11. *Cry Silver Bells*, Thomas Burnett Swann

12. *Trey of Swords*, Andre Norton
13. *Queens Walk in the Dusk*, Thomas Burnett Swann
14. *Silver on the Tree*, Susan Cooper

novella (22 total nominated)

1. "Stardance," Spider & Jeanne Robinson
2. "A Snark in the Night," Gregory Benford
3. "Aztecs," Vonda N. McIntyre
4. "Auk House," Clifford D. Simak
5. "The Mars Ship," Robert Thurston
6. "In the Hall of the Martian Kings," John Varley
7. "The Family Monkey," Lisa Tuttle
8. "Cold Cash War," Robert Asprin
9. "Joelle," Poul Anderson
10. "The Wonderful Secret," Keith Laumer
11. "Growing Boys," Robert Aickman
12. "Equinoctial," John Varley
13. "Heretic in a Ballon," L. Sprague de Camp

short fiction (114 total nominated)

1. "Jeffty is Five," Harlan Ellison (S)
2. "The Screwfly Solution," Raccoona Sheldon (M)
3. "Air Raid," Herb Boehm (John Varley) (S)
4. "A Rite of Spring," Fritz Leiber (M)
5. "Eyes of Amber," Joan D. Vinge (M)
6. "The Kugelmass Episode," Woody Allen (S)
7. "The Stone City," George R. R. Martin (M)
8. "Particle Theory," Edward Bryant (M)
9. "Ender's Game," Orson Scott Card (M)
10. "The Bagful of Dreams," Jack Vance (M)
11. "The Ninth Symphony of Ludwig van Beethoven and Other Lost Songs," Carter Scholz (M)
12. "The House of Compassionate Sharers," Michael Bishop (M)
13. "The Big Fans," Keith Roberts (M)
14. "The Detweiler Boy," Tom Reamy
15. "Prismatica," Samuel R. Delany (M)
16. "Good-bye Robinson Crusoe," John Varley (M)
17. "Camera Obscura," Thomas Monteleone (S)
18. "Dog Day Evening," Spider Robinson (S)
19t. "Pinnocchio," Stanley Schmidt
19t. "Bitterblooms," George R. R. Martin (M)
21. "A Rain of Pebbles," Stephen Leigh (S)

1979: 9th Locus Poll, approx. 1,000* ballots cast

*In 1980, this figure was reported to be exactly 883.

novel (121 total nominated)

1. *Dreamsnake*, Vonda N. McIntyre
2. *Blind Voices*, Tom Reamy
3. *The White Dragon*, Anne McCaffrey

4. *The Faded Sun: Kesrith*, C. J. Cherryh
5. *Colony*, Ben Bova
6. *Stormqueen!*, Marion Zimmer Bradley
7. *The Far Call*, Gordon R. Dickson
8. *The Avatar*, Poul Anderson
9. *The Courts of Chaos*, Roger Zelazny
10. *Strangers*, Gardner Dozois
11. *The Stars in Shroud*, Gregory Benford
12. *Up the Walls of the World*, James Tiptree, Jr.
13. *The Outcasts of Heaven Belt*, Joan D. Vinge
14. *Sight of Proteus*, Charles Sheffield
15. *The Stand*, Stephen King
16. *Journey*, Marta Randall
17. *Gloriana*, Michael Moorcock
18. *Saint Camber*, Katherine Kurtz
19. *The Faded Sun: Shon'Jir*, C. J. Cherryh
20. *Stardance II*, Spider & Jeanne Robinson
21t. *The Eye of the Heron*, Ursula K. Le Guin
21t. *Hotel Transylvania*, Chelsea Quinn Yarbro
23. *Masters of Solitude*, Marvin Kaye & Parke Godwin
24. *A Different Light*, Elizabeth A. Lynn
25. *Kalki*, Gore Vidal

novella (42 total nominated)
1. "The Persistence of Vision," John Varley
2. "The Watched," Christopher Priest
3. "Seven American Nights," Gene Wolfe
4. "Old Folks at Home," Michael Bishop
5. "Fireship," Joan D. Vinge
6. "The Doctor of Death Island," Gene Wolfe
7. "The Renewal," Pamela Sargent
8. "Insects in Amber," Tom Reamy
9. "The Treasure of Odirex," Charles Sheffield
10. "A Chinese Perspective," Brian W. Aldiss

novelette (90 total nominated)
1. "The Barbie Murders," John Varley
2. "Hunter's Moon," Poul Anderson
3. "Mikal's Songbird," Orson Scott Card
4. "Swanilda's Song," Frederik Pohl
5. "Devil You Don't Know," Dean Ing
6. "In Alien Flesh," Gregory Benford
7. "The Nuptial Flight of Warbirds," Algis Budrys
8t. "The Gunslinger," Stephen King
8t. "The Man Who Had No Idea," Thomas M. Disch
10. "Shipwright," Donald Kingsbury
11. "Black Glass," Fritz Leiber
12. "Starswarmer," Gregory Benford
13. "A Good Night's Sleep," Avram Davidson
14. "The Morphology of the Kirkham Wreck," Herbert Schenck

15.   "Selenium Ghosts of the Eighteen Seventies," R. A. Lafferty
16.   "Within the Walls of Tyre," Michael Bishop

short story (288 total nominated)
1.   "Count the Clock That Tells the Time," Harlan Ellison
2.   "View From a Height," Joan D. Vinge
3.   "Stone," Edward Bryant
4.   "Virra," Terry Carr
5.   "A Hiss of Dragon'" Gregory Benford & Marc Laidlaw
6.   "Cassandra," C. J. Cherryh
7.   "Drink Me, Francesca," Richard Cowper
8.   "A Thousand Deaths," Orson Scott Card
9t.   "SQ," Ursula K. Le Guin
9t.   "Whores," Christopher Priest
11.   "The Very Slow Time Machine," Ian Watson
12.   "Gotcha!," Ray Bradbury
13.   "A Quiet Revolution For Death," Jack Dann

1980: 10th Locus Poll, 854 ballots cast
novel (142 nominees)
1.   *Titan*, John Varley
2.   *Jem*, Frederik Pohl
3.   *The Fountains of Paradise*, Arthur C. Clarke
4.   *Stardance*, Spider & Jeanne Robinson
5.   *On Wings of Song*, Thomas M. Disch
6.   *The Faded Sun: Kutath*, C. J. Cherryh
7.   *The Road to Corlay*, Richard Cowper
8.   *Dragondrums*, Anne McCaffrey
9.   *Engine Summer*, John Crowley
10.   *The Face*, Jack Vance
11.   *Juniper Time*, Kate Wilhelm
12.   *Transfigurations*, Michael Bishop
13.   *Roadmarks*, Roger Zelazny
14.   *Kinsmen*, Ben Bova
15.   *SS-GB*, Len Deighton
16.   *Catacomb Years*, Michael Bishop
17.   *The Web Between the Worlds*, Charles Sheffield
18.   *Mayflies*, Kevin O'Donnell, Jr.
19.   *The Unlimited Dream Company*, J. G. Ballard
20.   *A Planet Called Treason*, Orson Scott Card
21.   *A World Between*, Norman Spinrad
22.   *The Two Faces of Tomorrow*, James P. Hogan
23.   *The Day of the Klesh*, M. A. Foster
24.   *The Ringworld Engineers*, Larry Niven
25.   *Janissaries*, Jerry Pournelle

fantasy novel (86 nominees)
1.   *Harpist in the Wind*, Patricia A. McKillip
2.   *The Dead Zone*, Stephen King

3. *Tales of Neveryon*, Samuel R. Delany
4. *Castle Roogna*, Piers Anthony
5. *The Merman's Children*, Poul Anderson
6. *Fires of Azeroth*, C. J. Cherryh
7. *Watchtower*, Elizabeth A. Lynn
8. *The Last Enchantment*, Mary Stewart
9. *Malafrena*, Ursula K. Le Guin
10. *Death's Master*, Tanith Lee
11. *The Palace*, Chelsea Quinn Yarbro
12. *The Dancers of Arun*, Elizabeth A. Lynn
13. *Kindred*, Octavia Butler
14. *Daughter of the Bright Moon*, Lynn Abbey
15. *The Door into Fire*, Diane Duane
16. *The Sorcerer's Son*, Phyllis Eisenstein
17. *The Drawing of the Dark*, Tim Powers

novella (43 nominees)
1. "Enemy Mine," Barry B. Longyear
2. "Songhouse," Orson Scott Card
3. "Palely Loitering," Christopher Priest
4. "Mars Masked," Frederik Pohl
5. "The Battle of the Abaco Reefs," Hilbert Schenck
6. "The Tale of Gorgik," Samuel R. Delany
7. "The Moon Goddess and the Son," Donald Kingsbury
8. "Ker-Plop," Ted Reynolds
9. "Fireship," Joan D. Vinge
10. "The Story Writer," Richard Wilson
11. "Far Rainbow," Arkady & Boris Strugatsky
12. "Silver Shoes for a Princess," James P. Hogan
13. "Spirals," Larry Niven & Jerry Pournelle
14. "The Dancer in the Darkness," Thomas Monteleone
15. "The Napoli Express," Randall Garrett

novelette (99 nominees)
1. "Sandkings," George R. R. Martin
2. "Options," John Varley
3. "Fireflood," Vonda N. McIntyre
4. "Out There Where the Big Ships Go," Richard Cowper
5. "Galatea Galante," Alfred Bester
6. "Camps," Jack Dann
7. "The Pathways of Desire," Ursula K. Le Guin
8. "The Angel of Death," Michael Shea
9. "The Button Molder," Fritz Leiber
10. "The Things That Are Gods," John Brunner
11. "Phoenix," Mark J. McGarry
12. "The Relic," Gary Jennings
13. "The Ancient Mind at Work," Suzy McKee Charnas
14. "Down and Out on Ellfive Prime," Dean Ing
15. "Prose Bowl," Bill Pronzini & Barry N. Malzberg
16. "The Locusts," Larry Niven & Steve Barnes

17.   "Indifference," Brian W. Aldiss
18.   "The Ways of Love," Poul Anderson
19.   "Some Events at the Templar Radiant," Fred Saberhagen

short story (224 nominees)

1.   "The Way of Cross and Dragon," George R. R. Martin
2.   "giANTS," Edward Bryant
3.   "Quietus," Orson Scott Card
4.   "War Beneath the Tree," Gene Wolfe
5.   "Redeemer," Gregory Benford
6.   "Unaccompanied Sonata," Orson Scott Card
7.   "Wave Rider," Hilbert Schenck
8t. "In Trophonius's Cave," James P. Gerard
8t. "Blood Sisters," Joe Haldeman
10.   "Daisy, in the Sun," Connie Willis
11.   "The Crate," Stephen King
12.   "Rent Control," Walter Tevis
13.   "The Extraordinary Voyages of Amelie Bertrand," Joanna Russ
14.   "The Exit Door Leads In," Philip K. Dick
15.   "Vernalfest Morning," Michael Bishop
16.   "Red as Blood," Tanith Lee
17.   "The Rooms of Paradise," Ian Watson
18.   "Can These Bones Live?," Ted Reynolds
19.   "All the Birds Came Home to Roost," Harlan Ellison
20.   " 'You're Welcome,' Said the Robot . . .," Alan Ryan
21.   "The View from Endless Scarp," Marta Randall

Recent, Minor & Foreign SF Awards
(*for original fiction*)
listings and short descriptions

American
The Balrog Awards

The Hamilton-Brackett Memorial Award

The Prometheus Award

The American Book Awards

British
BSFA Award

British Fantasy Awards

Australian
The Ditmar Awards

The Pat Terry Award for Humour in Science Fiction

Italian
Cometa d'Argento Award

French
Prix Apollo Award

Graoully D'or Awards

German
SFCD Awards

Swedish
The Jules Verne Award

Japanese
Seigunsho (Seiun) Awards

THE BALROG AWARDS

The "Balrog" is the last new award of the 1970's to be started in the general field of SF, with an initiation year of 1979. Like the World Fantasy Award and the Hugo "Gandalf," it is an honor reserved specifically for fantasy: whether fashioned in the Tolkien sub-genre, or 'sword and planet' fantasy *a la* Edgar Rice Burroughs, or 'heroic' fantasy after the mold of Robert E. Howard's Conan the Barbarian, or 'dark' fantasy in the H. P. Lovecraft horror/weird tradition.

The force behind the Balrogs is Jonathan Bacon, the publisher of *Fantasy Crossroads.* They also appear to be tied in some way both to Johnson County Community College, and the Fool-Con, held over April Fool's Day (March 31st to April 2nd). The Fool-Con is where the Balrogs are announced and presented. In addition, the special panel which decides the career achievement Balrog category, is composed of the Guests of Honor and other "special guests" attending the Fool-Con.

The awards of direct interest here are the two Balrogs given for original fiction: "best novel," and "best short fiction." Both of these categories are among the nine Balrogs decided by popular vote rather than by jury decision. Balloting is entirely open. Anyone who wishes to participate in these elections can do so by writing to a specified address and asking for an official ballot. There is no short list of nominees, and only one vote is taken. The clear ambition of the founders is to get the maximum possible participation from the widest possible area. In 1979, 474 ballots were received from 32 different states and 5 foreign countries.

"Balrog," like "Gandalf," is a name taken from J. R. R. Tolkien. (See *The Fellowship of the Ring,* Book Two, Chapter V, "The Bridge of Khazad-dum," for the epic battle between Gandalf and the Balrog.) The award itself is a handsome sculpture of a bas-relief "Balrog" depicted crouching on all fours, mounted in a heart-shaped background evidently representing its wings—the figure raised on an inward-sloping, four-sided base.

The Balrog Awards, 1979–1980 (original fiction categories only)

1979: 1st annual Balrog Awards
   novel
1. *Blind Voices,* Tom Reamy
2t. *The Thomas Covenant Trilogy,* Stephen Donaldson*
      v. 1: *Lord Foul's Bane*
      v. 2: *The Illearth War*
      v. 3: *The Power That Preserves*
2t. *The Stand,* Stephen King
4. *The White Dragon,* Anne McCaffrey

   **The Chronicles of Thomas Covenant The Unbeliever* (to give the trilogy its general name) were first published in a 3-volume hardcover set by Holt, Rinehart & Winston in October of 1977.

short fiction
1. "Death From Exposure," Patricia Cadigan
2. "Jeffty Is Five," Harlan Ellison*
3. "Undertow," Karl Edward Wagner
4. "Conan and the Sorcerer," Andrew J. Offutt

"Jeffty Is Five" was first published in the 7/77 issue of *The Magazine of Fantasy & Science Fiction.*

1980: 2nd Balrog Awards
novel
1. *Dragondrums,* Anne McCaffrey

short fiction
1. "The Last Defender of Camelot," Roger Zelazny

THE HAMILTON-BRACKETT MEMORIAL AWARD

The Hamilton-Brackett Memorial Award began as the Edmond Hamilton Memorial Award in 1977. The idea to honor Hamilton (b. October 21, 1904– d. February 1, 1977) came from Yves de Cargouet, an ardent admirer of his writing. As chance would have it, approximately the same time news of Hamilton's death reached Yves, he happened to be deeply involved in the formation of a new SF convention, "Octocon." (Held in Santa Rosa, CA, in October—again by chance, the month of Hamilton's birth). Since conventions naturally· go with awards, given the initial inspiration plus the work required to put on a convention in any event, and the rest was relatively straightforward.

The theme for the award was contributed by Poul Anderson: to pick the story from the previous year "that created the greatest sense of wonder in the reader." (It is hard to imagine any more fitting notion proposed in memory of Edmond "world wrecker" Hamilton.) Yves then got in touch with Leigh Brackett, and asked her to sanction a memorial award with this theme in honor of her husband. Leigh not only gladly gave her consent, but also agreed to present the first award, at Octocon I in 1977.

When Leigh died early the next year (b. December 7, 1915– d. March 18, 1978; married Edmond Hamilton on December 31, 1946), the award title was revised to honor her memory also. The award theme did not require any adjustment. So, at Octocon II in October of 1978, the second Hamilton-Brackett Memorial Award, though the first under that title, was presented. Leigh and Edmond often collaborated in their writing; it is, perhaps, only fitting that they should be made permanent collaborators *in memorium.*

There was no Octocon in 1979, but the award by this time had become sufficiently vigorous to take on an independent life of its own, and was continued by what would have been the 1979 Octocon Awards Committee, if there had been a 1979 Octocon. But since, without Octocon, it proved impossible to arrange a suitable 1979 presentation site, at Octocon III in 1980 a double ceremony was held, presenting the award to the (previously announced) 1979 winner, and to the new 1980 winner.

The award is administered and financed by a five-person Awards Committee, composed of volunteers drawn from the ranks of "The Spellbinders Inc.", a Sonoma County non-profit organization of SF writers, artists, and fans; the same group which puts on Octocon—when it is held. (Any money earned by Octocon over expenses is contributed to local charities.) The intention, as demonstrated in 1979, is to continue the Hamilton-Brackett Memorial Award whether or not Octocon is held in any future year. Thus, in case Octocon should again fail to go on, arrangements have now been made to see that the award is presented at the Westercon.

The H-BMA is decided by a one-ballot popular vote. Works of any length, with a publication date of the previous calendar year, are eligible; and the single criterion for selection is sufficiently broad that it effectively encompasses the entire field of SF. (At least, so far no work has been disqualified on grounds that it possessed an insufficient "sense of wonder"; though hopefully voters keep this theme in mind when casting their ballot.) Ballots are automatically distributed to the membership of the previous convention, and are available to anyone else who cares to take the trouble to return one. Voting begins in January, and continues until the start of October. Vote totals for the first four years are not available, but may be presumed relatively small (as would be true of any new popular vote award of this sort). Efforts are actively underway at present to increase voter response as much as possible by, e.g., securing a wider distribution of ballots.

Physically, the award consists of a handsome redwood birdseye burl plaque, with a brass plate attached reading: "Hamilton-Brackett Memorial Award, honoring the memory of Edmond Hamilton and Leigh Brackett," with the date, and the name of the winning author and work inscribed below.

Assuming the Octocon continues, as it grows in stature with the passing years—and it is already generally well-regarded on the West Coast, with an attendance substantially in excess of 1,000—the Hamilton-Brackett Memorial award should take on added luster as well. And, quite apart from the fate of Octocon, the Hamilton-Brackett Memorial is certainly a deserving special category award. It unquestionably offers the stiffest possible field of competition, since literally everything published in SF during the entire year is eligible. As knowledge of it becomes more widespread, and participation in the voting increases, it may be hoped that it will come to occupy as special a place in the ever-growing pantheon of SF awards, as the persons it honors do in the ever-growing literature of SF.

The Hamilton-Brackett Memorial Award, 1977–1980

1977: 1st Edward Hamilton Memorial Award

1. *Camber of Culdi*, Katherine Kurtz

   Brothers of Earth, C. J. Cherryh
   Children of Dune, Frank Herbert
   The Triune Man, Richard A. Lupoff
   Dragonsong, Anne McCaffrey

1978: 2nd Hamilton-Brackett Memorial Award

1. *The Forbidden Tower,* Marion Zimmer Bradley

   A Little Knowledge, Michael Bishop
   Time Storm, Gordon R. Dickson
   Moonstar Odyssey, David Gerrold
   "In the Hall of the Martian Kings," John Varley

1979: 3rd Hamilton-Brackett Memorial Award

1. *Midnight at the Well of Souls,* Jack Chalker*

   "Mikal's Songbird," Orson Scott Card
   "The Works of His Hand Made Manifest," Karen G. Jollie
   Saint Camber, Katherine Kurtz
   The White Dragon, Anne McCaffrey

   *A vote for any book in this series was counted as a vote for this book.

1980: 4th Hamilton-Brackett Memorial Award

1. *Titan,* John Varley

   A Planet Called Treason, Orson Scott Card
   The Faded Sun: Kutath, C. J. Cherryh
   The Jesus Incident, Frank Herbert & Bill Ransom
   Harpist in the Wind, Patricia A. McKillip

THE PROMETHEUS AWARD
given for the SF work which best typifies
the values and philosophy of Libertarianism

If the Prometheus Award does not bring any light to bear on the state of SF in general, it might reasonably be expected to generate a little heat. For in this instance, Prometheus comes to SF carrying a political philosophy in one hand, and gold in the other.

The political philosophy is Libertarianism. The Prometheus Award is the narrowest special category award covered in these listings, by some margin. To win it, you need to have written a SF work which promotes Libertarian ideals. To be sure, there is a type of SF which has this sort of flavor (names like Heinlein, Anderson, Pournelle, etc., come to mind); still, it is a good question how many works there are whose theme or point could reasonably be regarded as the promotion of Libertarian ideals.

The evidence seems to indicate there are not too many. Nominations for the award are open, which means that anyone can nominate any work—which means authors can nominate their own works, agents their client's works, publishers their author's works, not to mention all readers their own special favorite works—a procedure, in short, calculated to insure the highest possible number of nominations. Yet only eleven novels were actually nominated for the first Prometheus Award in 1979.

(The 1979 competition was limited to novels. Possibly because of the relatively small number of nominees, the rules were changed for 1980 to allow works of any length to be considered.)

The low nomination total is the more remarkable considering the stakes. The prize for the winning author is $2500 *in gold* (coins—Mexican pesos and Austrian crowns—were used in 1979). That means the prize has a built-in appreciation value: The approximately seven ounces of gold which could be purchased for $2500 early in 1979 had become worth roughly $3000 by the time it was awarded in September, and doubtless will be worth significantly more than $3000 by the time you read this. The Prometheus is an award it pays to win as soon (and as often) as you can. To the best of my knowledge, it is by some margin the most remunerative non-publisher's award ever offered for SF.

The first award was presented during the 1979 annual national convention of the Libertarian Party (Los Angeles, September). The second award was supposed to have been presented at the 1980 national convention (Chicago, July), but evidently plans were changed, since the announcement that nominations were open for the 1980 awards did not even appear until after the convention was over (and, as of the time this is written, late in 1980, no winner has yet been announced).

The Prometheus is decided by a jury or panel called the Prometheus Award Committee. In 1979, this had eleven members. The only names I have seen associated with the committee are L. Neil Smith, who chaired it in both 1979 and 1980; and Robert Anton Wilson, who presented the first award. (The two Wilson's, the one giving and the other receiving the 1979 award, are not related.) The members of the Award Committee select a winner by means of a mail ballot.

To be eligible for the Prometheus, a work must (1) be SF, (2) have been first published during the preceding calendar year, (3) not have been written by a member of the Award Committee, and (4) be nominated by somebody.

I do not know who persuaded the Libertarians to fund this sort of award (or what the argument in its favor was), or exactly where the money for it comes from, or how the judges are chosen; but it all may be presumed to have some official connection with the Libertarian Party apparatus. It is hard to say what, if anything, will issue from the gift of this Prometheus. Perhaps we will soon see awards for SF sponsored by other special interest groups, for the best work promoting socialism, occultism, vegetarianism, or the creative use of hot tubs. Perhaps it is a momentary aberration of the Libertarians, owing more to the hope for (relatively cheap) election year publicity, among a (not insignificant) segment of the voting public thought to be receptive to Libertarian ideas, than to any conviction that SF is the wave of the future, or that an SF award is a rational way to promote a particular political philosophy.

In either case, it is hard to see (apart from the money, which must merit it some consideration, and a warm spot in the heart of authors) what particular importance can reasonably be ascribed to any *ideological* literary award. By definition, the criteria for winning any such award have primarily to do with causes, and only incidentally to do with literature.

Prometheus Award *(one category)*

1979: 1st Prometheus Award

1. *Wheels within Wheels,* F. Paul Wilson
2t. *The Avatar,* Poul Anderson
2t. *The Genesis Machine,* James P. Hogan

1980: 2nd Prometheus Award

    (winner not announced as of 11/80)

THE AMERICAN BOOK AWARDS

The newest (and most short-lived) SF award, first (and last) given in 1980, is also the most newsworthy award for SF to be initiated (and promptly discontinued) in some time. In years past, among the two or three most prestigious literary awards given in the U.S., are the National Book Awards: instituted in 1936 by the book publishing industry (i.e., by organizations like the Association of American Book Publishers, the American Booksellers Association, Inc., and the Book Man Institute, Inc.). In this sense, the NBAs could have been called the "Oscars" of the book business; that is, they were the means by which the book industry both acknowledged and rewarded the achievements of its own members, while at the same time hyping the industry's products.

Until 1980, the National Book Awards remained a relatively cozy affair. Awards were given out in only a few categories. Winners were selected by three-person juries, chosen from members of the prestigious National Institute of Arts and Letters. In simple terms, the NBAs had to do with the literary "establishment," which is to say they had nothing to do with SF.

(Actually, that is not quite right. For example, *The Farthest Shore*, by Ursula K. Le Guin, won the National Book Award for "children's literature" in 1973; and *Gravity's Rainbow*, by Thomas Pynchon, won the National Book Award for "fiction" in 1974. To consider just the latter, you will find *Gravity's Rainbow* listed in these pages as a 1974 finalist for the Nebula (where it lost), for the Jupiter (where it took 2nd), and in the Locus Poll (where it finished 12th out of 15). Readers are free to draw their own conclusion as to what that shows about the relative standards by which SF and "mainstream" literature are judged.)

But on June 27, 1979, by an announcement of the Association of American Book Publishers, all that changed (briefly). The National Book Awards were replaced with the "American Book Awards." Not only were the old NBA categories dramatically expanded for the new ABAs, but the method by which nominees and winners were selected was radically altered as well.

To take these two subjects in order, the ABAs identified thirteen major and three minor award categories for books; included special awards for best book design, hardcover jacket, and paperback cover; and had a "miscellaneous" category besides, for whatever might still deserve an award, but by some circumstance not qualify for consideration under any regular heading. Major book categories were distinguished by the fact that two awards were to be made in each: one to a hardcover, and one to a paperback. Minor book categories got only one award. Science fiction was included among the major categories, as was mystery fiction; while western fiction was relegated to the minor categories, along with poetry and "first novel." That made four major fiction categories, since the "children's" and "fiction" categories of the NBAs were carried over to the ABAs (with the latter now renamed "general fiction"); plus two more fiction categories at the minor level.

So, out of a grand total of 33 awards in all, ten went to fiction books, with two awards specifically reserved for science fiction (and three more for other forms of "generic" fiction). Furthermore, SF was actually eligible for consideration in several other categories. For example, Madeline L'Engle's *A Swiftly Tilting Planet* was not only a 1980 final nominee in the "children's literature" category (paperback division), but won that honor; *Barlowe's Guide to Extraterrestrials* was a final nominee in the Art/Illustrated category; and even an "alternate world" historical novel showed up among the final nominees in the mystery category.

In brief, looked at just from the standpoint of the newly expanded categories for awards, there was every reason for publishers and authors of SF to feel sanguine about the transformation of the NBAs to the ABAs. For the first time, SF was not merely to be recognized, but was given real prominence in the context of a major national literary award.

To turn to the issue of finding a winner for each of these many awards, the reformed selection procedure specified a fairly elaborate three-stage process. First, there was an initial nomination stage, which allowed publishers, for a fee of $25 per title, to put up whichever of their own books they might feel were contenders in the various categories. The only restrictions were (1) the nominating publisher had to be U.S. based, (2) the book had to have a U.S. author, and (3) the book had to have a publication date (in its specific division) of the previous calendar year.

It should be mentioned that there is a clear peculiarity in these rules of eligibility, since they make books eligible for consideration in every division according just to the year of their publication; while at the same time distinguishing paperbacks from hardcovers in the major categories. Thus, a paperback book is eligible if it was first published *as a paperback* in the preceding calendar year, whether or not it happens to be a reprint of some other year's hardcover book. In essence, this gives every book first published as a hardcover, that goes on to enjoy a paperback edition, two chances to win; while original paperbacks, and hardcovers that do not get a paperback edition only have one chance to win. This peculiarity, incidentally, explains the eligibility of both the 1978 hardcovers, *Dreamsnake* and *The Book of the Dun Cow*, in the 1980 SF paperback category.

Second, the nominations received from the publishers were sent to committees of "experts," drawn up one to each category. Committees were composed of persons taken from the ranks of member ABA Academy organizations: representing booksellers, editors, writers, critics, and librarians, with a wild card "specialist" in the particular area thrown in. The basic job of this committee was to pare the rather unwieldy aggregate list of nominees submitted by the publishers down to a manageable list of five finalists (major categories got five finalists in each division, hardcover and paperback). Committees who were so inclined could also add books to the list of nominees received from the publishers, for consideration as possible finalists.

To illustrate the two-step process described so far, the 1980 ABA committee for SF was composed of 11 members: James Baen, Charles N. Brown, Rich Burmeister, James Gunn, Jack C. Haldeman II, David G. Hartwell, Mark Howat, Hazel Potter, David A. Roberts, Robert Silverberg, and Lawrence Walton. A total of 17 hardcover and 20 paperback nominees were received from the publishers (figuring in late additions and subtractions). To this list, the committee added 5 hardcovers and ? paperbacks; the effect, whatever the intention, being to level off the two categories at 22 nominees each. (Only one of the committee's additions, *The Star Spangled Future*, succeeded in making the final cut.)

Third, from the reduced list of five finalists, the winner was to be determined by a vote of 2000 persons, chosen at random off a list of volunteering members from each of the various organizations party to the ABA Academy (with the same 2000 voting the winners of all 33 awards).

On May 1, 1980, in New York, N.Y., at the Seventh Regiment Armory on Park Avenue, the winners of the first American Book Awards, as determined by the process detailed above, were announced. Counting the fact that it began twenty minutes late, the scheduled 65-minute presentation ceremony ran about three hours. (Authors were asked to reminisce about their first publication, and did, at unscheduled length.) The approximately 1300 persons in attendance then proceeded to an unexpectedly late buffet supper. Hosts at the ceremony were John Chancellor and William F. Buckley, Jr.; and presenters included the likes of Lauren Bacall and SF's own Isaac Asimov. Though some of the nominees in SF did attend (Norman Spinrad, Thomas M. Disch, e.g.), neither of the two winning authors—Pohl or Wangerin—was present.

It goes without saying, perhaps, that it was not possible to overhaul so well established an institution as the NBAs in so dramatic a manner, without generating a certain amount of controversy. There were three principal objections raised: (1) The enormous expansion of award categories diminished the value of the "important" awards. To put it another way, the only important fiction award is the one for "general fiction," yet it was now badly outnumbered by the generic fiction awards (none of which were important). (2) Paperbacks were being given undue weight. To put it another way, the only important books are hardcovers, yet in the new scheme paperbacks receive "separate and equal" treatment. (3) Literary awards are no place for democracy. To put it another way, where control of the old NBAs had resided in the hands of the (relatively few) authors and critics, control of the new ABAs had passed into the hands of the (relatively many) publishers, editors, booksellers, and librarians.

In consequence, a hasty boycott of the awards was organized by (some) writers and critics, lead by Alison Lurie, and joined by persons like Norman Mailer, Saul Bellow, Bernard Malamud, Philip Roth, William Styron, Susan Sontag, and others of similar prominence. Mailer, Roth, and Styron all had books in nomination which they requested be withdrawn from consideration. Among publishers, the (hardcover) firm of Farrar, Straus & Giroux said they would not participate in the award, either.

For purposes of the 1980 awards, the ABA board of directors responded to this criticism with a very hard line policy: To be sure, any writer or publisher who did not wish to participate in the ABAs was free to accept neither the award nor the money that went with it. But an award which purports to honor the best of the year in a given category logically must be free to consider every book in that category. Hence, whether a writer's or publisher's book was nominated or not, and won or not, was not up to the book's author and/or publisher, but was an issue to be settled strictly by the ABA selection process itself. The ABA board of directors, and/or the several committees for the different categories, could nominate who and what they liked for whichever honor might be in question (with the publisher's fee paid from a pool of discretionary funds if it came to that); and the voters could vote on it however they saw fit. The request to have certain nominees withdrawn from the voting was, therefore, respectfully declined.

Still, there was denying that there was some justice to criticisms of the new award's structure. Certainly, the three-tiered selection process *is* a bit cumbersome: involving as it does publishers, expert committees, and a selected voting pool. Further, there can be no doubt that the persons who finally vote the winners are not qualified *as a group* in any category. In consequence, winners are selected in every instance largely by ignorance. Put the best face on it you can: Assume every voter is qualified in one or more areas, and actually reads all the nominees in all the categories of most interest to them. The plain truth is still, given 2000 randomly selected persons, that a majority are not likely to be qualified to judge the work in *any* category; and that it is the rare juror indeed who can be supposed to have actually *read* 29 x 5 books preparatory to voting.

The end result of this selection process, therefore, is always liable to be what, in fact, it turned out to be in 1980: when the winning book in nearly every category was simply the best known book among the five finalists—that is to say, the one book whose name a voter who hadn't been reading in that category was most likely to recognize.

Now, if it can be said that there is some point to the objections raised to the 1980 ABAs, it must also be said that the ABA board has not persisted in its policy of hardlining these objections; evidently on the time-honored principal that late is better than never. For 1981, categories have been drastically cut back, to 17. Eliminated, along with some other "too unspecific" categories, are SF, mysteries, and westerns. The grounds offered for eliminating all three categories of generic fiction is that each already has its own set of generic awards. Thus, by official decree of the book publishing industry, the Hugos and Nebulas, the Edgars, and the Golden Spur awards, are elevated to the status of the ABAs.

The roll-back for 1981 in the number of categories undeniably reduces the list of books a voter needs to have read in order to be informed about the choices. It is, however, doubtful that was the object of the exercise, since the entire mechanism of the randomly selected voting pool has also been scrapped. In its place, is a process by which both nominations *and* final choices will be made in future by a panel of judges (a procedure much more in accordance with the one used for the NBAs).

Sic transit SF's brief fling at the big time. The history of SF awards for original fiction is a history of the struggles of SF toward recognition as a form of fiction with serious literary merit. That history begins in 1951, shortly after SF first broke into the book market (see introduction). The thirty-year quest for respectability which has ensued appeared, for a few shining hours in 1980, to have been brought to a climax by the book publishing industry itself, with its official acknowledgment of the legitimacy and place of SF in the ABAs. That sanction has now passed, as abruptly as it came; revealing itself to be not the long-sought full light of recognition, but only a false dawn. It may yet be surmised that SF's day is coming: to judge from the trend chronicled in this chapter, it is inevitable. But the lesson of the ABA's turns out to be, not that SF has finally arrived, but that in 1981, for SF and other forms of generic fiction, there is still no room at the top.

The American Book Awards *(SF categories only)*

1980: 1st ABAs

hardcover
1. *Jem,* Frederik Pohl
   Engine Summer, John Crowley
   On Wings of Song, Thomas M. Disch
   Janissaries, Jerry Pournelle
   Juniper Time, Kate Wilhelm

paperback
1. *The Book of the Dun Cow,* Walter Wangerin, Jr.
   Tales of Neveryon, Samuel R. Delany (integrated collection)
   Dreamsnake, Vonda N. McIntyre
   The Star-Spangled Future, Norman Spinrad (collection)
   The Persistence of Vision, John Varley (collection)

BSFA AWARD

"BSFA" stands for The British Science Fiction Association, Ltd. The BSFA is the national UK SF organization, whose "sole function is to promote and advertise sf activities." It dates from Easter of 1958 when it was formed "to revive UK fandom." Present membership is approximately 500 persons. There is an annual general meeting held at the "Eastercon" where the BSFA Award is presented.

The "Eastercon" is the UK national convention. It was started in 1948 and is held annually at the indicated time in various locales. Present attendance runs around 500 persons. As befits the largest and most important annual British convention, the Eastercon is the site of several award presentations besides the BSFA Award.

The BSFA Award was first presented in 1966 under the title of the "British Fantasy Award." It went to a writer rather than to a specific work until 1970, when it changed names to the "British Science Fiction Award" (or to the BSFA Award). There has been some variation in the rules from year to year, but the general theme has been to stress both British authorship *and* publication. The only regular category is for something like, the "best UK novel newly published in the previous year," but in one year (1972) it went to a one-author collection of stories instead, and in other years "special awards" have been presented to some non-fiction book about SF. It is normally determined by a general (British) fan vote, though that too is subject to exception, and on occasion a select panel of judges has made the choice. The award itself is in the form of a scroll.

The BSFA Award is the oldest and most prestigous British SF award. An incomplete listing of the winners follows.

1970:   *Stand on Zanzibar*, John Brunner

1971:   *The Jagged Orbit*, John Brunner

1972:   *The Moment of Eclipse*, Brian W. Aldiss (a 1970 British collection)

1973:   No award made due to the small number of votes cast.

1974:   *Rendevous with Rama*, Arthur C. Clarke
special award:
Billion Year Spree, Brian W. Aldiss

1975:   *Inverted World*, Christopher Priest

1976:   *Orbitsville*, Bob Shaw

1977:   *Brontomek!*, Michael G. Coney
special award
A Pictorial History of Science Fiction, David Kyle

1978:   *The Jonah Kit*, Ian Watson

1979:   no information

1980:   novel
1. *The Unlimited Dream Company*, J. G. Ballard
   The Fountains of Paradise, Arthur C. Clarke
   On Wings of Song, Thomas M. Disch
   Blind Voices, Tom Reamy
   A. K. A.: A Cosmic Fable, Rob Swigart

short fiction
1. "Palely Loitering," Christopher Priest
   "Camps," Jack Dann
   "Sex Pirates of the Blood Asteroid," David Langford
   "Prose Bowl," Barry Malzberg & Bill Pronzini
   "Crossing Into Cambodia," Michael Moorcock

BRITISH FANTASY AWARDS

The British Fantasy Awards are presented by The British Fantasy Society. The BFS is the national UK fantasy organization (the counterpart of the BSFA). It was founded in March, 1971 as "The British Weird Fantasy Society," evidently with an orientation toward the Lovecraft-style of fiction. (A fact reflected in the original name of the award: August Derleth was Lovecraft's leading disciple and admirer—indeed, he felt so strongly about Lovecraft's writing that he started Arkham Press for the specific purpose of preserving Lovecraft's work, which at the time was to be found almost entirely in the back issues of *Weird Tales* magazine.) In April, 1972, however, the second adjective was dropped from the name. The society now encompasses heroic fantasy, sword and sorcery fantasy, supernatural fantasy, and horror/weird fantasy quite generally.

The first BFA was presented in February of 1972. Originally, the awards were called the "August Derleth Memorial Fantasy Awards;" a name used until July, 1976, when the present more general and descriptive title was adopted. The major fiction prize for best novel is still known as the "August Derleth Award," though. There are currently six award categories: two divisions for original fiction, novel & short story (an omnibus shorter fiction category); plus competitions in film, artwork, small press publications, and comics.

All BFA categories are decided by an individually elected panel of three judges. Only BFS members can vote in the election, but non-BFS members are eligible to serve on the juries. Until 1976, when a statuette by Jim Pitts was adopted, there was no actual physical token of the award given to winners.

In 1975, the BFS organized the first annual "FantasyCon," which is held towards the end of February in various locales (the counterpart of the "Eastercon"). The BFA announcement and presentation now takes place at this convention. What information I have on the original fiction nominees and winners is listed below. The exact period of eligibility is unknown to me, but judging from the titles here, it appears to cover at least parts of the two calendar years preceding the year in which the awards are made.

1972: 1st annual British Fantasy Awards
   no information on any award categories

1973: 2nd annual British Fantasy Awards
   An award was presented to Michael Moorcock at the annual "Eastercon." It may have been for "best novel," but if so, the exact title of the winning work is not known to me.

1974: 3rd annual British Fantasy Awards
   no information on any award categories

1975: 4th annual British Fantasy Awards
   novel
      1.   *The Sword and the Stallion*, Michael Moorcock
      runners-up (may be in order of finish)
         A Quest for Simbilis, Michael Shea
         Shardik, Richard Adams

   short story
      1.   "Sticks," Karl Edward Wagner
      runners-up (may be in order of finish)
         "The Seventeen Virgins," Jack Vance
         "Ghoul's Garden," John Jakes

1976: 5th annual British Fantasy Awards

no information on any award categories

1977: 6th annual British Fantasy Awards

note: This is the first set of awards to actually go by the new name of BFAs—in all previous years, the awards were known as the "August Derleth (Memorial) Awards." (It is also the first year in which actual award statues are handed out.)

novel

1. *The Dragon and the George,* Gordon R. Dickson
2. *Camber of Culdi,* Katherine Kurtz
3. *Interview with a Vampire,* Ann Rice

short story

1. "Two Suns Setting," Karl Edward Wagner
    runners-up (*may* be in order of finish)
    "Der Untergang des Abenlandesmenschen," Howard Waldrop
    "Piper at the Gates of Dawn," Richard Cowper

1978: 7th annual British Fantasy Awards

novel

1. *A Spell for Chameleon,* Piers Anthony
2. *Our Lady of Darkness,* Fritz Leiber
3. *My Lord Barbarian,* Andrew J. Offutt

short story

1. "In the Bag," Ramsey Campbell
2. "The Flight of the Umbrella," Marvin Kaye
3. "The Lady of Finnigan's Hearth," Parke Godwin
4. (title unknown), Harlan Ellison
5. "One Immortal Man," Richard E. Geis

1979: 8th annual British Fantasy Awards

novel

1. *The Chronicles of Thomas Covenant* (3 volumes), Stephen R. Donaldson
2. *The Road to Corlay,* Richard Cowper
3. *Gloriana,* Michael Moorcock
4. *Dying of the Light,* George R. R. Martin
5. *The Quest of the White Witch,* Tanith Lee

short story

1. "Jeffty Is Five," Harlan Ellison
2. "The Big Spell," J. Michael Reaves
3. "The Changer of Names," Ramsey Campbell
4. "The Lady in White," Stephen R. Donaldson
5. "Within the Walls of Tyre," Michael Bishop

1980: 9th annual British Fantasy Awards
novel
1. *Death's Master,* Tanith Lee
2. *Harpist in the Wind,* Patricia McKillip
3. *Sorcerer's Son,* Phyllis Eisenstein

short fiction
1. "The Button Molder," Fritz Leiber
2. "First Make Them Mad," Adrian Cole
3. "Red as Blood," Tanith Lee

THE DITMAR AWARDS

The Ditmars are the major Australian SF awards. They derive their rather odd name from Dr. Ditmar Jenssen, a rather oddly named Australian fan. The Australian tradition—witness also the "Pat Terry" award—appears to be to name awards after locally famous fans; in contrast to the American tradition, which is to name awards after famous pros. (I do not know what Dr. Jenssen is a Dr. of, though I presume medicine, or quite why he is famous in Australian fandom. My impression is that the awards are named for him because he was, in some fashion, instrumental in establishing them.)

Like the Hugos, the Ditmars are a fan-voted honor. In fact, they may well be modeled on the Hugos, which they seem to resemble in many ways, right down to their official title of "Science Fiction Achievement Awards." They are presented annually at a major convention: allegedly, the Australian National Convention held at Easter (like the British national convention, the "Eastercon"). From the information available about sites, however, either the national convention meets at other times of the year, or the awards are also presented at other conventions. (I have given what information I have about particular Ditmar conventions below, with the yearly listing of the awards.)

The only regular Ditmar category besides the ones I have listed below for original fiction is for "best Australian Fanzine." Unlike most other awards, the Ditmars make no distinctions between different lengths of original fiction, so short stories and novels compete against each other—or, rather, they did make no such distinctions until 1978, when the "best Australian SF" category was officially divided into two separate divisions.

1969: 1st annual Ditmar Awards

International SF
1. *Camp Concentration,* Thomas M. Disch

Australian SF
1. *False Fatherland,* A. Bertram Chandler (may be story, not novel)

1970: 2nd annual Ditmar Awards
at 9th annual Australian National Convention, Easter

International SF
1. *Cosmicomics,* Italo Calvino
2. *The Left Hand of Darkness,* Ursula K. Le Guin
3. *Bug Jack Baron,* Norman Spinrad
4. *Stand on Zanzibar,* John Brunner

Australian SF
1. "Dancing Gerontins," Lee Harding
2. "Anchor Man," Jack Wodhams
3. "Split Personality," Jack Wodhams
4. "Kinsolving's Planet Irregulars," A. Bertram Chandler

1971: 3rd annual Ditmar Awards
at 10th annual Australian National Convention, 1 & 2/1971

International SF
1. "no award"
    runners-up (in alphabetical order by author)
    "Time and the Hunter," Italo Calvino
    "The Region Between," Harlan Ellison
    Tower of Glass, Robert Silverberg

Australian SF
1. "The Bitter Pill," A. Bertram Chandler
    special award
    SF in the Cinema, John Baxter

1972: 4th annual Ditmar Awards
at "Syncon II," 8/11–13/1972

International SF
1. *Ringworld*, Larry Niven

Australian SF
1. *Fallen Spaceman*, Lee Harding

1973: 5th annual Ditmar Awards
at Australian National Convention

International SF
1. *The Gods Themselves*, Isaac Asimov

Australian SF
1. "Let It Ring," John Ossian (John Foyster)

1974: 6th annual Ditmar Awards
no fiction awards made

1975: 7th annual Ditmar Awards
at "Syncon"

International SF
1. *Protector*, Larry Niven
2. *The Dispossessed*, Ursula K. Le Guin
3. *Frankenstein Unbound*, Brian W. Aldiss

Australian SF
1. *The Bitter Pill*, A. Bertram Chandler

2. *The Soft Kill,* Colin Free
3. "The Ark of James Carlyle," Cherry Wilder

1976: 8th annual Ditmar Awards

at "Bofcon," August

International SF
1. *The Forever War,* Joe Haldeman

   other nominees (in alphabetical order by author)
   The Indian Giver (The Computer Connection), Alfred Bester
   The Shockwave Rider, John Brunner
   Inferno, Larry Niven & Jerry Pournelle
   "Down to a Sunless Sea," Cordwainer Smith

Australian SF
1. *The Big Black Mark,* A. Bertram Chandler
2. *Way Out West,* Cherry Wilder (may be story not novel)

1977: 9th annual Ditmar Awards

International SF
1. *The Space Machine,* Christopher Priest

   other nominees (*may* be in order of finish)
   A World Out of Time, Larry Niven
   The Hand of Oberon, Roger Zelazny
   "Piper at the Gates of Dawn," Richard Cowper

Australian SF
1. *Walkers on the Sky,* David Lake

   other nominees (*may* be in order of finish)
   "The Ins and Outs of the Hadaya City State," Phillipa Maddern
   "Kelly Country," A. Bertram Chandler
   Future Sanctuary, Lee Harding

   note: "The Ins and Outs of the Hadhya City State" was given an "extra committee award for best Australian short SF."

1978: 10th annual Ditmar Awards

International SF
1. *The Silmarillion,* J. R. R. Tolkien

Australian novel
1. *The Luck of Brin's Five,* Cherry Wilder

Australian short fiction
1. "Albert's Bellyful," Francis Paying

1979: 11th annual Ditmar Awards

International SF
1. *The White Dragon,* Anna McCaffrey

Australian SF
1. *Beloved Son,* George Turner

1980: 12th annual Ditmar Awards

International SF
1.   *The Hitchhiker's Guide to the Galaxy,* Douglas Adams

Australian SF
1.   *Australian Gnomes,* Robert Ingpen

THE PAT TERRY AWARD
FOR HUMOUR IN SCIENCE FICTION

The Pat Terry Award, like the Ditmars, is an Australian award named in honor of a famous Australian fan. Pat Terry—I am told—had at least two distinctions: First, at the time of his death in 1970 at an age somewhere above 80, he was supposedly the oldest active fan in the world. Second, he was noted for his wit. Thus the desire, first, to memorialize him with an award, and the decision, second, to make it a special category award for humor (or for humour, to humor the British spelling).

I have very little hard information about the award itself, beyond what can be gleaned from the very partial listing below—which is just that it is a one-category award, mixing all lengths and even related series of stories together, whose only restriction seems to be the one implicit in the award title. I do know that it is, or was, presented by the "Sydney SF Foundation," but I do not know exactly who or what they are, or were; or how their award happens to be decided; or what it may consist in, if anything.

The first two (possibly three) years it was presented at the Australian National Convention, alongside the Ditmars. In 1978, however, when the winner was an American, it was given at the World Science Fiction Convention in Phoenix during the Hugo awards banquet/ceremony—so the more recent policy may be to take the award to the winner.

1971: 1st annual Pat Terry Award (I guess)
1.   *The Reproductive System (Mechasm),* John T. Sladek

1972: 2nd annual Pat Terry Award
1.   *The Authentic Touch,* Jack Wodhams

1973: 3rd annual Pat Terry Award
1.   *The Falliable Fiend,* L. Sprague de Camp
     runners-up (in alphabetical order by author)
       "Tomb It May Concern," Richard E. Geis
       Mention My Name in Atlantis, John Jakes
       The 'various parodies of John T. Sladek in F&SF'

1974–1977: 4th–7th annual Pat Terry Awards
no information

1978: 8th annual Pat Terry Award
1.   *Callahan's Crosstime Saloon,* Spider Robinson

1979: 9th annual Pat Terry Award
no information

1980: 10th annual Pat Terry Award
1.   *The Hitchhiker's Guide to the Galaxy,* Douglas Adams

ITALIAN SF AWARDS

The most important Italian SF award for original fiction appears to be the "Cometa d'Argento" (Silver Comet) Award, for best SF novel—either domestic or translated—published in Italy during the preceding year. This is sometimes described as the "Italian Nebula," which I assume means that it is selected by an organization or jury of professional writers, editors, etc.

1974: 1st Cometa d'Argento Award
(presented 6/24/74; period of eligibility, 1972-1973)
1.   *Dune,* Frank Herbert
2.   *Bug Jack Baron,* Norman Spinrad

1975: 2nd Cometa d'Argento Award
1.   *A Time of Changes (Il Tempo Delle Metamorfosi),* Robert Silverberg

1976: 3rd Cometa d'Argento Award
no information

1977: 4th Cometa d'Argento Award
no information

1978: 5th Cometa d'Argento Award
(presented at the SFIR, or 'Italian Science Fiction Roundabout,' held in Ferrara—the most important Italian SF convention)
1.   *The Dispossessed (I Reitti Della Altro Planeta),* Ursula K. Le Guin

1979: 6th Cometa d'Argento Award
no information

FRENCH SF AWARDS

The most important current French SF award for original fiction appears to be the "Prix (or Priz) Apollo," for best SF novel—either domestic or translated—published in France during the preceding year. This award is usually referred to as the "French Hugo," which I take is a tribute to its importance rather than a description of its method of selection. It is decided by a jury of ten persons, composed of three authors, three publishers, and four fans (so fans do have an important say, even though there is no general fan vote). The award itself consists of a scroll. The "Apollo" of the title, incidently, is not, as might be thought, the Greek god of prophecy (and also of music, poetry, and medicine); but the space mission Apollo 11. I believe 1972 is the first year of the award.

1972:   *Isle of the Dead*, Roger Zelazny
1973:   *Stand on Zanzibar*, John Brunner
1974:   *The Iron Dream*, Norman Spinrad
1975:   *The Embedding*, Ian Watson
1976:   *Nightwings*, Robert Silverberg
1977:   *Cette Chere Humanite*, Philippe Curval ("This Dear Humanity")
1978:   no information
1979:   *Gateway*, Frederik Pohl

A second, more recent French SF award for original fiction is also worth remarking: the "Graoully D'or." This is the "Grand Prix du Festival de la Science Fiction de Metz." A "Graoully" is supposed to be a type of dragon indigenous to the Metz region of France, so the name of this award could be somewhat loosely translated as, "Golden Dragon." It, too, is for best SF novel, and is decided by a ten member jury, but differs from the Prix Apollo in having a split competition for best foreign and best French writer. The prize is a small hologram, I would guess of a Graoully, inserted in a gold ring. My impression is that 1978 is the first year of the award.

1978:   foreign
        Triton, Samuel R. Delany (trans. Henry-Luc Planchot)
        french
        Transit, Pierre Pelot

1979:   foreign
        A Scanner Darkly, Philip K. Dick
        french
        No Award (no sufficiently outstanding novel published)

        note: An "honororable mention" was given to editor Alain Doremieux for *Les Delires Divergents De Philip K. Dick.*

GERMAN SF AWARDS

I only have a report on one year's awards: by the SFCD, the German National SF Fan Club. (That would presumably make these the "German Hugos.") I would think that awards have been made in other years, too, despite my lack of information about them.

1972:   German novel
        no award

        translated novel
        1. *Test*, Stanislaw Lem
        2. *A Canticle for Leibowitz*, Walter M. Miller, Jr.

3. *The Androdema Strain*, Michael Crichton

4. *The Space Merchants*, Frederik Pohl & C. M. Kornbluth

note: These awards were made in 1972, but I do not know what the period of eligibility was for works to be considered.

SWEDISH SF AWARDS

To the best of my knowledge, there is just one important Swedish SF award for original fiction, "The Jules Verne Award." Fittingly, this is administered by the Jules Verne Society in Sweden (the "Jules Verne Sallakapet"), and was started on the 70th anniversary of Jules Verne's death. But while the society, chaired by Sam J. Lundwall, is an exclusive one, with a 'membership by invitation only' policy, the award is decided by a general fan vote. Since more than 4,000 fans do vote annually, in a sense this is the 'biggest' fan award of the year (if not the most significant or prestigous). In its initial year, 1975, the award was made to individuals for career achievements: the people "felt to have done the most for SF in Sweden." This was evidently changed the next year to the present one category: "best SF book published in Sweden in the preceding year." (Note that it is *not* specifically for the best novel.) The awards presentation usually takes place at "Scancon," the general SF convention of Scandanavia.

1976:   *The Dispossessed*, Ursula K. Le Guin

1977:   *Non-Stop (Starship)*, Brian W. Aldiss

1978:   *Vesna Sveta* ("Spring of Light"), edited by Vladimir Gakov

       note: This volume is an anthology of new Soviet SF. The awards presentatation took place on 2/8/1978, Jules Vernes' 150th birthday.

1979:   no information

JAPANESE SF AWARDS

Japan has a very active and successful SF publishing industry (including a large number of writers), and an equally active and successful fan community. The 'Japanese equivalent of a Hugo' is, in fact, one of the oldest of the foreign SF awards: started in 1970, but replacing a previous set of "Japan SF Fandom Awards." The current series is known as the "Seigunsho" Awards (or the "Seiun" Awards—at least, I think these are one and the same, and not two separate and distinct sets of awards). They are given by The Federation of SF Fangroups of Japan, a national coordinating body which was formed in 1965; at the Japanese National Convention, which was started in 1962. In addition to the four awards listed below for original fiction, there are also awards made in other categories: dramatic presentation, comic art, etc. I believe a full set of awards has been made each year since 1970, though I only have data on two award years.

1971:   *Up the Line*, Robert Silverberg
       no information on any other categories

1978:   novel—translation
       I Will Fear No Evil, Robert A. Heinlein

novel—Japanese
Chikyu: Seishin Bunseki Kiroku, Yamada Masaki ("Record of Psycho-analysis: Earth")

short story—translation
no award

short story—Japanese
"Gorudiasu no Musubime," Komatsu Sakyo ("Gordian's Knot")

No information on any other years.

Howard DeVore

LITERARY AWARDS IN SCIENCE FICTION

When we consider the matter of literary awards in science fiction it is well to remember that fans have always been enthusiastic about their favorite literature and those involved in its production. Science fiction fandom is truly unique in this respect, which is why fans honor their writers perhaps more than they deserve.

This may be due to the fact that more than a few of today's writers rose from the ranks of fandom, and those who did not start as fans often began as steady readers of science fiction.

Since World War II few mainstream writers have produced significant contributions to the genre. A specialized talent is needed to compete successfully, and, considering the limited financial rewards achieved by all but an exceptional few in SF, a writer selling regularly in other fields is not likely to risk his time and ambition to enter new areas.

Since the early thirties fans have taken polls in their amateur magazines and announced that _____ was chosen the No. 1 author, etc.

In most cases nothing further came of it. On occasion they might send the author a copy of the fan magazine and perhaps a handwritten scroll. The first attempt to produce something more enduring was in the early thirties when Raymond A. Palmer announced the creation of the Jules Verne Prize Club. By contributing twenty-five cents fans could enfranchise themselves to vote for their favorite author. The money contributed would be used to buy trophy cups to be awarded the winners. Like many fan projects not much money was collected and the directors have informed me that no trophies were ever presented.

Fans continued to hold polls until 1951, when four British fans decided to present awards at the annual convention in England.

These four were Leslie Flood, John B. Harris, G. Ken Chapman, and Frank A. Cooper. It was truly a "fan" award in that each of these people were active in British fandom, although Harris had been writing professionally since 1934 and is now better remembered under his pseudonym, John Wyndham, while Flood has gone on to become the major professional agent for science fiction in England and Europe.

The awards would be known as the International Fantasy Awards.

That year they were given to George R. Stewart for *Earth Abides,* the

215

fiction winner, and to *The Conquest of Space,* Willy Ley and Chesley Bonestell, for the best non-fiction. In 1952 they invited other prominent fans of respected judgment in the U. S. and Europe, including, among others, Georges Gallet of France, and Donald A. Wollheim, and P. Schuyler Miller of the U. S. to serve as the International Fantasy Award committee.

Through the years this committee's choices were always of major significance. However, the International Fantasy Awards were not well publicized. Clifford D. Simak has recalled that his publisher, Martin Greenberg of Gnome Press, phoned him from New York early in 1953 with the news that his novel *City* had won the IFA. Greenberg was not one to waste dimes, let alone phone calls, and Simak was more impressed by this than by the fact that he had won an award he did not even know existed. Six weeks later the post office advised that it was holding a package addressed to him, which he could claim, upon payment of eighteen dollars import duty. He was much impressed by the trophy but confesses he'd have liked it even more if someone else had paid the duty. The trophy itself was a metal spaceship mounted on a small globe, then mounted on a suitable base.

In all, nine International Fantasy Awards were presented, the last in 1957 to a then little-known, outside his field, philologist, J. R. R. Tolkien for his *The Lord of the Rings.* It is interesting to note that only Arthur C. Clarke, Theodore Sturgeon, and Clifford D. Simak won all three of science fiction's major awards. Of the other IFA winners only L. Sprague de Camp is still alive and writing. It is probable that we will not have another triple winner.

The first two sets of awards were presented at British conventions, therefore they were presented during a formal dinner attended by science fiction personalities. No awards were presented in 1956, and after 1957 the committee quietly folded up and vanished.

Possibly the founders had simply lost interest, more likely their energies were directed elsewhere. By then the Hugo Awards had been established. Perhaps they felt the Hugo Awards had largely replaced the need for their awards.

The Hugo Awards were created for the 1953 (Philadelphia) World Science Fiction Convention. The awards were conceived by Hal Lynch; it was obviously a promotional effort for the convention. They were announced as Science Fiction Achievement Awards in fan and professional magazines several months before the convention. The convention committee listed nominees in a number of categories; by joining the convention fans were entitled to vote on the winners. The Science Fiction Achievement Awards are still referred to by that name on occasion, but early in their history someone nicknamed them Hugos (for Hugo Gernsback, founder of the first SF magazine, *Amazing Stories*) in obvious imitation of the Mystery Writers of America's "Edgar," named, we are told, for Edgar Allan Poe.

Categories for the first awards were Best Novel, Best Magazine, Best Cover Artist, Best Interior Illustrator, Excellence in Fact Articles, Best New Author or Artist, and No. 1 Fan Personality. It is obvious that the awards were heavily slanted toward fan preferences.

Only two awards were presented for fiction, and one of these might have been given for artwork instead. Anything less than novel length was virtually ignored, at that time most SF appeared in magazine form and their editors were considered responsible for everything of lesser length. Fans read the magazines and that's what they voted for.

Willy Ley won the fact article award. In truth he was almost the only person doing such writing on a regular basis in the magazines and it would have come as a shock if anyone else had won.

Philip José Farmer won as Best New Author; his story "The Lovers" had just introduced alien sex into science fiction. Mankind had been fighting bugs for a generation, now he was impregnating them and the fans loved Farmer for it. Forrest J Ackerman won as No. 1 Fan Personality. With the passage of time many fans from the thirties had become writers and/or editors but Ackerman, in spite of numerous and varied professional involvements, has continued even to this day to be known primarily as a fan.

No awards were given in 1954. It should be pointed out that there was not then—and still is not—any continuity of management from one convention to the next. Anarchic though it seems, fans prefer it that way. In 1978 a new constitution for World SF Conventions was proposed and will be approved or rejected in the near future. There is no reason to think that it will be accepted with any more grace than the previous attempts. SF fans do not take easily to any form of regimentation!

Possibly the 1954 (San Francisco) committee had thought awards to be a one-time presentation. If they thought of them at all, they may have decided such awards not worth the pomp and expense; the record is silent. It should be pointed out that in the fifties, conventions were small and done on the cheap. Income was bone-scant and every penny had to be watched for fear the convention would be bankrupt (as indeed happened in 1956). As late as 1958 fans could join the convention and receive all benefits for the sum of one dollar. It should also be noted that most of what income there was, came late in the year. Probably half or more of the committee's final membership would not pay their dollar until they actually arrived at the hotel.

The 1959 convention committee was given thirty-five dollars (the entire profits of the 1958 convention), when they won their bid. In the year that followed, as they prepared for the convention, they would rarely have more than that in the bank.

The 1955 convention was fortunate. Their committee included a member who was capable and willing to do the work of producing the Hugo trophies. Ben Jason made them at a cost of some six dollars each. In the Progress Reports (small bulletins, sent periodically to the membership, describing progress), the committee announced they would present six awards, three for writing, one each for artist, professional magazine, and fan magazine. Without realizing it they were shifting attention away from fan activities and toward professional writing.

The 1956 (New York) convention was planned as a gala affair. In addition to the previous year's categories they added Best Feature Writer, Best Book Reviewer, and restored the category of Best New Writer. Willy Ley won again as Feature Writer, he was still the only individual doing such work on a regular basis. Damon Knight beat out P. Schuyler Miller as Best Reviewer. Miller had been doing reviews consistently (in *Astounding Analog*) for some years but himself admitted that his only criterion was what he liked and disliked, whereas Knight was writing thoughtful in-depth criticism.

Robert Silverberg, who won in the Best New Writer category, and Harlan Ellison, his closest rival for the prize, had each started as fans and were well known for their fine fan magazines. Both had burst out into the professional field the previous year, both were living in the same Brooklyn apartment house and were cordially competitive. They still delight in out-doing each other.

Ben Jason did not produce the trophies in 1956. When the committee investigated costs they discovered that specially made trophies were prohibitively expensive. Ben Jason had used the hood ornament from the Oldsmobile "Rocket" 88 as a model, changing the dimensions but maintaining the basic design. Eventually the 1956 chairman, David A. Kyle, bought several hood ornaments, mounted them on a base, and added a backboard to conceal the hollow on the other side.

It has been stated in many places that the Hugo trophies are always the same, that only the bases vary, according to the whim of the committee. This is simply not true. In desperation (and perhaps for lack of ever having seen a Hugo close up), many committees have been obliged to produce slightly different designs. For some years I was involved in their production, and I know of at least five variations from the original.

While it has no bearing upon this account, it might be noted that the 1956 convention was the first one planned as a Big Event.

It failed to recoup its expenses. At the convention's business meeting it was announced that they were several hundred dollars in debt, and quite literally the hat was passed for donations to cover the deficit. This would affect the thinking of future committees; every effort would be made to hold down expenses. For some years it would limit the number of trophies presented.

The 1957 convention was held in London, England, the first time the affair took place outside the North American continent (despite being billed as "World" since 1939). Perhaps because they also had money problems, the committee limited the Hugos to only three: Best American Magazine, Best British Magazine, and Best Fan Magazine.

For professional SF writers it was a total loss.

In 1958 the categories were increased again. One member of the committee, writer Roger Phillips Graham, had access to a machine shop and was able to produce them at a reasonable price. Held in Los Angeles, movie capital of the world, they added Best Movie, which was won by Richard Matheson's *The Incredible Shrinking Man*. Matheson was also Guest of Honor at the convention.

Best Novel was won by Fritz Leiber, Jr., a California writer. There were raised eyebrows over the fact that local people were winning the trophies. It was the natural result of California fans being the major attendees at a California convention and voting for highly respected writers that happened to live in the area.

Active Fan was reinstated and was won by Walt Willis of Ireland.

For one so isolated, Willis had maintained an incredible amount of fan magazine activity and correspondence for many years.

Relatively poor, there was little hope that he could ever attend an American convention. But in 1952 fans, lead by Shelby Vick, had organized a special fund, inviting contributions to finance his attendance at that year's convention in Chicago. It was done again in 1962, this time by Larry and Noreen Shaw, and they brought over both Walt and his wife Madeline. Beloved by old-time fans, he has since faded away and is now known only as a legend.

The 1959 (Detroit) convention introduced innovations. Until that year the ballot had read "previous year," which could be construed as calendar year, or alternatively it could mean the twelve months immediately prior to the voting. There was considerable confusion, and misunderstanding on the point. Various committees had disqualified stories on the grounds that they hadn't been published within the proper time period. The committee that followed might then apply the rule in such a way that the period being considered overlapped on the period covered by the previous convention's awards, or even worse, might even leave a half-year gap not covered by either committee.

For 1959's awards the criterion of previous calendar year was firmly established, one of the few rules that has never been subsequently fiddled with. The committee also introduced, for the first time, a nomination ballot. Earlier committees had hand-picked the candidates from what *they* considered top contenders. The committee could consist of as few as four people who might well ignore a major piece simply because they were not aware of its publication. Now, everyone was invited to participate, it was not even necessary to join the convention. Hopefully it would increase nominations, but a major reason for this openness was to increase membership in the convention. The committee felt that adding fan participation in the nominating process would give fans an incentive to join the convention, since only convention members could vote on the final ballot, and significantly the final ballot's deadline was several weeks before the convention. If they wanted their votes to count they would have to send their membership fee before the convention, not pay "at the door."

Looking over the list of movies nominated and noting how few nominations there were, the committee added "No Award" to the ballot, another "first" for them. Among their motives was their belief that the few films nominated were all equally wretched.

Their judgment was confirmed when "No Award" came out a hands-down winner. At the banquet, the news was greeted with a rousing cheer.

In their efforts to produce the now obligatory trophies, the committee had obtained a handful of unfinished trophies from Ben Jason. Only six were usable. When only a few nominations were received for the New Author category, they nervously added No Award to that section of the final ballot. To their vast relief NO AWARD won narrowly, and a plaque was given to Brian Aldiss as a close loser, the only time that has been done.

FANAC won the Amateur Magazine award. Previous committees had often stressed the serious side of SF, and the voters had chosen amateur magazines that imitated the professional journals, stressing professional news, etc. *FANAC*, on the other hand, was an energetic chatty journal, completely informal in manner and largely devoted to fannish gossip. Compiled, edited, and published by Ron Elik and Terry Carr, it was beloved by the casual readers. They frequently reported upon their personal plans for a moon trip. Elik and Carr, in their apartment, were piling empty beer cans one on top of another; when it neared the moon they were going to climb up it, hand over hand. Tragically, Ron Elik would die a few years later, only days before his planned marriage and shortly before his first novel was published. Terry Carr went on to become one of the most able and popular of the younger, post-Campbell, editors. Of the six fan magazines nominated, five were of the *FANAC*-type.

The voters that year were discarding formality in favor of fun.

The Pittcon (Pittsburgh, 1960) announced there would be only six awards because they could not produce more than six Hugos.

Ben Jason had agreed to turn over his last remaining castings.

The committee therefore combined Best Novelette and Best Short Story into "Best Short Fiction." They also changed Best Movie into Best Dramatic Presentation, so as to include television drama.

This would develop into a problem shortly thereafter. Rod Serling had just created *Twilight Zone*, an exceptional series that would go on to win Hugos for the next three years. It was soon obvious that no movie or teleplay could compete with a continuing series. When in 1962 a committee was appointed to review rules and recommend changes, this committee quickly agreed that the rules had to be changed in a way that would prevent any series from walking away with the Hugos year after year. This was done; they recommended that only specific episodes of a series could be nominated, not the series as a whole. That rule still stands today, though on one occasion it resulted in five separate episodes from *Star Trek* being pitted against each other.

The previous committee had opened nominating ballots to everyone and allowed fandom at large to reproduce them. This would create a problem in Pittsburgh. Suddenly, they received a package of ballots from England. They were sent by an obscure writer in England, and all ballots nominated him in several categories. He sent a covering letter, saying that these were nominations from friends and relatives who wanted to vote for him. There were perhaps 50 ballots; all bore one of three addresses in a small English town and while the names were all different, they were all in the same handwriting. Sensibly, the committee simply discarded the entire lot and disqualified him. Nobody on the committee had ever heard of the writer, nor the magazines where he claimed the stories had been published, and the entire thing may have been a fannish prank.

The day of the open nominating ballot was almost over. Future committees would limit it to people who had joined the current or previous convention.

1961 would be notable for the fanzine award. Earl Kemp of Chicago was disturbed by the fact that magazine science fiction was on the down-grade; for some time past magazines had been ceasing publication and going out of business. He distributed a questionnaire on the subject to many professional writers and influential fans asking their opinion on the subject. He then issued a report, titled WHO KILLED SCIENCE FICTION?, to the contributors and to 35 members of the Spectator Amateur Press Society. No copies were available to the public but its fame spread and it won the Hugo for Best Amateur Magazine. Most people who voted for it would never see a copy. Not since the days of *Fantasy Magazine* had any amateur publication seen such active professional representation. At the same convention (Seattle '61), new rules were adopted making such an event impossible in the future. Since then, a fan magazine is eligible only if it has published at least four issues and is available to the general public.

1962 (Chicago) would award Robert A. Heinlein his third Hugo, and would spark a controversy when Brian Aldiss won "Best Short Fiction" for a series of connected stories (later published as *The Long Afternoon of Earth*), competing against individual stories by other authors. This was an arbitrary decision by the committee, in response to nominations for virtually all of the stories in the series, itself perhaps a unique event. Immediately the rules were again changed to prevent this happening. It would seem that over the years committees had failed to see many of the possibilities, but at least a subsequent convention always corrected prior mistakes.

It was also notable for the nomination of *The Two Worlds of Charlie Gordon*, a TV drama based on the short story, *Flowers For Algernon*. Basically the same story, it appeared in a different category and was once more eligible. It did not win but would make yet a third appearance a few years later as the movie *Charly*.

The committee would present three special awards: to Cele Goldsmith for reviving the corpse of *Amazing Stories* and *Fantastic*; to Donald Tuck for his monumental work, *Handbook of SF & Fantasy* (currently available as *The Encyclopedia of SF & Fantasy*—Advent, 3 volumes; and to Fritz Leiber and the Hoffman Electronic Corporation who were using short SF stories as part of their advertising campaign. It was easy to see that once special awards were begun, it was a powerful temptation for each convention committee to present them.

The 1963 convention would present no major surprises. Dramatic Presentation was voted "No Award." Special awards went to P. Schuyler Miller, who had been reviewing for *Astounding/Analog* for many years with understanding and compassion. They also presented a special award to Isaac Asimov for his popular science articles.

Baycon (San Francisco, 1964) received so few nominations for Drama that they dropped it from the final ballot completely, replacing it with a new category, Best Book Publisher. Paperbacks now dominated the field and paperback publishers appeared on the final ballot, hardcover publishers being virtually ignored.

It seems that no committee could leave the rules and definitions alone. In 1965 the committee decided to simply drop the Special Drama award and it did not appear on the nomination ballot.

At that point fans did a reversal. They complained strongly to the committee and many wrote in nominations on their ballot. The committee tallied the write-ins and placed two movies on the final ballot, later declaring *Dr. Strangelove* the winner.

Before the 1966 nomination ballots were sent out, the Science Fiction Writers of America had announced that they would be issuing their own annual awards. For the first time there would be competition for awards and there can be no doubt that this would have a vast effect on future voting.

There can be no doubt that the Nebula awards have influenced the Hugo awards. The Nebula awards are presented approximately four months before the Hugo awards. Fans would be aware of the stories on the Nebula ballot and would read them before making their own independent choice for the Hugo awards. The history of the Nebula awards must, of course, be presented in this chapter. However, it seems preferable to cover it at the end of the chapter to avoid confusion. In drawing comparisons it must be noted that a different dating system is used for the Hugo and Nebula awards. Nebula awards are dated for the year in which the story appeared, Hugo awards are always dated one year later.

Although *Dune World* had been nominated in 1965 as a novel, the 1966 (Cleveland) committee declared that its publication, in expanded and extended form (as *Dune*) as a hardcover book merited special consideration and it appeared on the ballot once more. The committee announced later that this story and *Call Me Conrad* received almost an identical number of votes and declared a tie. Once more fans voted against Best Dramatic Presentation and it failed to appear on the final ballot.

The committee added another new category, Best All Time Series.

Lord of the Rings (Tolkien) had recently appeared in paperback form and was attracting wide attention. It had been nominated in both novel and series categories. Arbitrarily the committee declared it to be a series. The Burroughs fans were out in force, they were being urged to vote in a block for Burroughs-centered material.

Best Artist was won by Frank Frazetta, who was doing the Burroughs covers for Ace books, and Best Fanzine was won by *Erb-Dom,* a fanzine centered around Edgar Rice Burroughs. They also managed to get Burroughs' Barsoom series nominated for Best Series, but failed to sweep that one. Isaac Asimov has, over the years, built a tremendous popularity with SF fans as a writer and as a person. His Foundation series managed to swamp the Burroughs fans.

As an example of how few votes influence there awards, the 1966 committee admitted that only 160 nominating ballots were returned of the 6000 ballots mailed out. Until the 1970s the voting was always very small; with an expanding membership this has been partially overcome.

In the dear, dead years most members of a convention tried to read all of the major stories before voting. Now, many dedicated old-time fans admit that they cannot read even a fair portion of the published material and many do not vote. The Science Fiction Writers of America face the same problem with their Nebula awards.

The 1967 convention, in New York, would find *Flowers For Algernon,* now expanded into a novel, nominated in yet a third category.

Unfortunately, it was competing against Robert A. Heinlein's *The Moon Is A Harsh Mistress.* This story had been nominated in 1966 and there was considerable controversy over its being nominated in two separate years. As a magazine serial, most portions had appeared in 1966 and the committee allowed it to compete. It won easily. Best Magazine competition was somewhat slanted since some of the committee members served on the editorial staff of F & SF, therefore they had disqualified it from contention. As for Dramatic Presentation it was *Star Trek* time and the Trekkies were out in force, three of the five contenders were *Star Trek* episodes. The committee presented a special award to CBS for "21st Century."

Convention memberships were rising and this was reflected in the fact that the 1967 committee received 279 nominating ballots.

The Science Fiction Writers of America had recently added Novella (17,500 to 40,000 words) to their Nebula awards and after the Hugo nomination ballots were mailed out the Baycon (San Francisco 1968) committee, without consultation, decided to add this category to the awards.

Some stories originally nominated as "novelettes" were listed on the final ballot in this category. Only three titles appeared on the final ballot in the short story classification, the committee announced that although they received many nominations these were the only titles to attract significant attention. *Star Trek* dominated Dramatic Performance, all contenders being from the TV series. It is also significant that the taboo bender, *Dangerous Visions* (anthology) had appeared and many stories from it appeared as nominated stories. To demonstrate the influence that these titles had the committee presented special awards to Harlan Ellison, editor of *Dangerous Visions,* and to Gene Roddenberry for directing *Star Trek.*

St. Louis (1969) had few surprises, the movie *Charly* (screen version of *Flowers For Algernon*) was nominated for the fourth year, but failed to win. A Special Award was presented to Armstrong, Collins, and Aldrin for "Best Moon Landing Ever." As it was the first moon landing, there really wasn't much competition.

Again in 1970 (Boston) there were no significant moves. Wilson Tucker won as "Best Fan Writer" after almost forty years of continuous fan activity. Dramatic Presentation went to general news coverage of Apollo 11.

1971 was significant only for the fact that the fiction awards for Hugos were identical with the Nebula results for that year.

In 1972 (Los Angeles), Philip José Farmer's *To Your Scattered Bodies Go* won the novel category after a delay of many years.

Special committee awards went to Harlan Ellison for editing *Again Dangerous Visions,* and to French and Spanish publishers for excellence in book and magazine productions.

1973 (Toronto) saw Isaac Asimov win his first award for published fiction, an unusual arrangement where alternate sections of his novel appeared in issues of *Galaxy* and *If,* an obvious effort to boost their faltering circulation. "Special Award" went to Pierre Versins for his encyclopedia of sf (no relation to the similar book published by Advent), published in the French language.

One report has it that nobody on the convention committee could read French and that it was given on the basis of what other fans had said of it. 1973 also saw the first John W. Campbell Memorial Award and this one needs some special explanation.

The award is *not* a Hugo trophy. It is a plaque, presented by Conde Nast publications to the "Best New Writer" in memory of John W. Campbell. Nominations appear on the Hugo ballot through special arrangements with the committee but the convention committee has no control over it, other than counting the ballots.

During the 1973 World Convention, word was received that J. R. R. Tolkien had died. Lin Carter, prominent fantasy author and editor, immediately contacted the publishers of Ballantine Books and before the convention ended had announced the creation of the Gandalf Award. In an arrangement similar to the Campbell award, the Gandalf Award would appear on the 1974 (and subsequent) Hugo ballot and a plaque presented to some master of fantasy, as distinguished from science fiction. While a new writer is certainly eligible it is almost certain to be given to some writer who has spent many years building his reputation for fantasy writing.

1974 would see the Novella award go to James Tiptree, Jr., a rising new writer who appeared reluctant to meet his fans and who operated from a P. O. Box in Virginia. Three years later it would be revealed that "he" was a sixty-year-old woman who had already established herself as a major writer, under her own name, in another field. Most nominees for the Campbell Memorial award had established themselves as fans before trying professional writing. In 1974 it resulted in a tie between Lisa Tuttle and Spider Robinson. As might be expected, the first Gandalf award was presented posthumously to J. R. R. Tolkien and a special award was presented to Chesley Bonestell for a generation of meticulous astronomical illustrations.

The 1975 convention, held in Australia, presented no surprises at all. Special awards were presented to Donald A. Wollheim, of DAW books, as "The Fan Who Has Done Everything," culminating a thirty-five year career as fan and professional, and to Walt Lee for his massive reference book on SF and fantasy films.

1976 (Kansas City, Mo.) again reflected the burgeoning attendance and the expanding interest in science fiction. Almost 1600 Hugo ballots were cast. At long last the committee was receiving a truly significant number of votes. James Gunn received a special award for his *Alternate Worlds,* an illustrated history of science fiction. Arthur B. Cover and Tanith Lee were nominated for the Campbell Memorial award but it was almost immediately discovered that they both had published professionally before 1976, and were therefore disqualified. They were replaced by M. A. Foster and Joan Vinge.

In 1977 Joan Vinge was nominated again for the Campbell award but this time it was her turn to be disqualified on the basis of prior publication. In many cases fans will fail to notice a rising star's first few appearances, and will nominate authors in categories where he/she/they are not eligible. Special committee award went to George Lucas for his *Star Wars*, an indication that fans still like the old-time Space Opera when it is done with love and care.

Iguanacon (Phoenix 1978) received 540 nominating ballots and 1246 fans cast their final ballots to present Hugo awards almost identical with the earlier Nebula awards, the lone exception being Joan Vinge, who beat out Raconna Sheldon (James Tiptree, Jr.) in the Best Novelette category. As the year drew to a close, a study group was re-writing the constitution of the World Science Fiction Society, a mass of fourteen pages of microscopic rules and regulations. I've been informed that they plan no changes regarding the Hugo awards, however, this author has been involved with the design and the production of the Hugos and several times has been appointed to committees involved with rules changes. I have no reason to think that fan personalities or politics has changed and I'm willing to bet that the next year will see further scrambling of the awards.

Marshall B. Tymn

SCIENCE FICTION AND FANTASY PERIODICALS

Amateur and professional magazines have been published in the science fiction and fantasy fields in countless numbers by scores of clubs, organizations, and individuals for several decades, and the phenomenon shows no sign of abating. This chapter will mention only major titles which are issued regularly.[1] Fiction-only magazines are not included in this survey. For additional listings of science fiction periodicals, see *The International Science Fiction Yearbook 1979* (Quick Fox, 1978) and *The Science Fiction Encyclopedia,* ed. Peter Nicholls (Doubleday, 1979). For a comprehensive list of fantasy periodicals, see my *Fantasy Literature: A Core Collection and Reference Guide* (R. R. Bowker, 1979).

Science fiction and fantasy periodicals come in three general types: fan magazines, professional magazines, and scholarly journals. The first American appearance of a fan magazine devoted exclusively to science fiction was the May 1930 number of *The Comet,* the official organ of the newly-formed Science Correspondence Club. Many of the big names of the day were regular contributors, including the then-unknown German fan Willy Ley, who wrote a column on rockets and space.[2] Fanzines, as they are commonly called in SF circles, have been published in record numbers ever since. As Elizabeth Calkins and Barry McGhan point out in *Teaching Tomorrow*:

> The creation and publication of amateur SF magazines . . . consume a great deal of the time, energy, and money of the more avid science fiction readers. Although most fanzines cost their publishers more than sales bring in, they continue to spew out of basement ditto machines, mimeographs, and off-set presses in bewildering numbers. Most often, a publication appears on the scene for a while and then disappears just as suddenly, when the publisher/editor runs out of money, time, things to say, or whatever.

> The contents of these magazines (some of which are lavishly done, with printed copy, art work, and photos) include articles about authors and their works, debates about trends within the field, extensive letter columns, news items, stories, poetry, and drawings. Many professional writers saw their first work printed in a fanzine.[3]

Most fanzines fade away after a few issues; some, however, manage to stay in print for several years, becoming relatively stable fixtures on the scene. The following fanzines have endured the test of time and can be recommended for their overall fine quality and excellent coverage of the field: *Fantasy Crossroads* (1974) publishes fiction, verse, and articles on heroic fantasy, with an emphasis on contemporary authors. *Fantasy Newsletter* (1978) reports on recent and forthcoming events and publications of interest to fantasy fans. Very thorough in its coverage, this attractively illustrated publication nicely complements the fantasy coverage in *Locus*. The latter magazine, subtitled *The Newspaper of the Science Fiction Field* (1968), is an indispensible publication for those who desire regular coverage of science fiction and fantasy on all levels, including everything needed to keep up with activities and publications in the field.[4] *Mythlore: A Journal of Fantasy Studies* (n. d.) contains articles and reviews on J. R. R. Tolkien, C. S. Lewis, Charles Williams, and other writers. *SF Commentary: The Independent Magazine about Science Fiction* (1969) is distinguished for its quality reviews and special issues on individual authors. *Science Fiction Review* [formerly *The Alien Critic*] (1972) features author interviews, book reviews, lengthy editorials, miscellaneous commentary, and extensive letter columns. *The Science-Fiction Collector* (1976) is the major fanzine for the collector and bibliographer, and is an important source for checklists, indexes, and other bibliographic items.[5] *Thrust: Science Fiction in Review* (1972) contains articles, interviews, regular columns, and extensive book reviews. *Vector: The Journal of the BSFA* (1958) is the official publication of the British Science Fiction Association, and contains criticism, fiction, reviews, letter columns, and information about the British science fiction scene. *Xenophile* [combined with *The Fantasy Collector*] (1974) is a collector's magazine featuring extensive want lists and dealer's lists, indexes and bibliographies, and articles.

A small number of science fiction periodicals can be classified as professional. These periodicals have several characteristics which separate them from fanzines: (1) they pay their contributors, (2) they are distributed at newsstands and/or by SF book dealers, (3) the format (quality of paper, printing, art work) is considerably upgraded, and (4) they are often associated with a small press. The following professional magazines serve a variety of needs within the field: *Cinefantastique* (1970), the finest magazine on the fantastic film, it features major articles on recent films, as well as studies on the works of film directors; additional content includes film reviews and previews. *Future Life* features author interviews and articles on science fiction themes; it appeals to a younger audience and has enjoyed immense popular success. *Starship: The Magazine about Science Fiction* [formerly *Algol*] (1963), one of the best magazines of comment on science fiction, includes articles by science fiction writers and critics, interviews, regular columns, and book reviews. A companion publication, *Science Fiction Chronicle* (1979), is a monthly review of current events in the field.

The field is currently without a review magazine. *Delap's F & SF Review* (1975), edited by Richard Delap, lasted thirty issues, ceasing publication in 1978. During its time it was a fine review magazine, serving the science fiction and fantasy fields well with its comprehensive coverage. *Science Fiction &*

Fantasy Book Review replaced *Delap's* in 1979 as the only publication devoted exclusively to reviewing current works of fiction and criticism. It folded in February, 1980 after thirteen issues.

At the present time there are four scholarly journals published in the English language on the topic of science fiction. Founded in 1959, *Extrapolation* was the first academic journal devoted to science fiction. Under the editorship of Thomas D. Clareson, it has established itself as a wide-ranging publication with a diverse audience. It is published quarterly by the Kent State University Press.[6] *Foundation: The Review of Science Fiction,* a British critical journal, is noted for its scholarly reviews of new books and its series on the craft of science fiction. Edited by Malcolm Edwards, *Foundation* has been publishing three times a year since 1972.[7] *Science-Fiction Studies,* established in 1973 by then editors R. D. Mullen and Darko Suvin, has since become an important international journal, though with a small audience; it emphasizes theoretical and bibliographic studies. SFS is published three times a year at McGill University.[8] *Science Fiction: A Review of Speculative Literature,* was founded in 1977 to promote the works of Australian science fiction writers, although British and American writers are also the subject of discussion. Edited by Van Ikin, the journal is published semi-annually at the University of Sydney.

An associational item is the *SFRA Newsletter,* published ten times a year by the Science Fiction Research Association, and available to its members only. This publication features regular reviews of all critical studies and reference works published in the field, as well as notices of science fiction activities of particular interest to academics.

Another associational item is the special science fiction and fantasy issue of scholarly and educational journals. The following is a comprehensive listing of recently published issues, listed in chronological order: *Colloquy: Education in Church and Society* (May 1971); *Journal of Popular Culture* (Spring 1972); *Journal of the American Studies Association of Texas* (1973); *Ontological Thought* (April 1973); *The Shaw Review* (May 1973); *Studies in the Literary Imagination* (Fall 1973); *Journal of General Education* (Spring 1976); *Wisconsin English Journal* (April 1976); *Publishers Weekly* (June 14, 1976); *Mosaic: A Journal for the Comparative Study of Literature & Ideas* (Winter 1977); *The CEA Critic* (January 1978); *Literature/Film Quarterly* (Fall 1978); *Media & Methods* (November 1979); and *Mosaic* (Spring/Summer 1980).

NOTES

[1] This chapter does not discuss all-fiction magazines such as *Analog, F&SF,* etc., nor general content magazines with the one exception of *Future Life.*

[2] Details of fanzine publishing history and additional titles of fanzines can be found in Fredric Wertham, *The World of Fanzines* (Southern Illinois Univ. Press, 1973); Colin Lester, ed. *The International Science Fiction Yearbook* (Quick Fox, 1978); Harry Warner, Jr., *All Our Yesterdays* (Advent, 1969) and *A Wealth of Fable* (Fanhistorica Press, 1976–77); Beverly Friend, "The Science Fiction Fan Cult" (Diss. Northwestern, 1975); Peter Roberts, *Guide to Current*

Fanzines and *British Fanzine Bibliography* (38 Oakland Dr., Dawlish, Devon, UK); and Brian Earl Brown, *The Whole Fanzine Catalog* (16711 Burt Rd., No. 207, Detroit, MI 48219).

[3] *Teaching Tomorrow: A Handbook of Science Fiction for Teachers* (Dayton, OH: Pflaum/Standard, 1972), p. 37.

[4] A two-volume reprint edition of this authorative source of information about the science fiction field, covering the years 1968–77, is now available from Gregg Press.

[5] Beginning with issue No. 9, *Science-Fiction Collector* has combined with *The Age of the Unicorn,* an advertising magazine, under a new title, *Megavore: The Journal of Popular Fiction.*

[6] The first ten volumes of *Extrapolation,* long unavailable, have been reprinted by Gregg Press. The reprint edition carries the subtitle, *A Science Fiction Newsletter,* which was subsequently changed to *A Journal of Science Fiction and Fantasy,* which was dropped with the volume 20, number 1 issue (Spring 1979).

[7] Gregg Press has reprinted the first eight numbers of *Foundation,* covering the period 1972–75, during which time Perer Nicholls was the editor.

[8] Two volumes of selected essays from *Science-Fiction Studies* have been reprinted by Gregg Press. The first contains fifty essays published in SFS during the period 1973–75; the second contains thirty-eight essays appearing during the period 1976–77.

Addresses of Periodicals Mentioned

Cinefantastique. Ed. Frederick S. Clarke. Box 270, Oak Park, IL 60603.

Extrapolation. Ed. Thomas D. Clareson. Box 3186, College of Wooster, Wooster, OH 44691.

Fantasy Crossroads. Ed. Jonathan Bacon. 7613 Flint, No. A, Shawnee Mission, KS 66214.

Fantasy Newsletter. Ed. Paul C. Allen. Box 170A, Rochester, NY 14601.

Foundation. Ed. Malcolm Edwards. North East London Polytechnic, Longbridge Road, Dagenham, Essex RM8 2AS, England.

Future Life. Ed. Eds. Naha and Robin Snelson. 475 Park Ave. South, New York, NY 10016.

Locus. Ed. Charles N. Brown. Box 3938, San Francisco, CA 94119.

Mythlore. Ed. Gracia Fay Ellwood. 2011 Rose Villa St., Pasadena, CA 91107.

SF Commentary. Ed. Bruce Gillespie. GPO Box 5195AA, Melbourne, Victoria 3001, Australia.

Science Fiction. Ed. Van Ikin. English Dept., University of Sydney, New South Wales 2006, Australia.

Science Fiction Chronicle. (see *Starship*).

Science Fiction Review. Ed. Richard E. Geis. Box 11408, Portland, OR 97211.

The Science-Fiction Collector [now *Megavore*]. Ed. J. Grant Thiessen. c/o Pandora's Books Ltd., Box 86, Neche, ND 58265.

Science-Fiction Studies. Eds. Marc Angenot, Robert M. Philmus, and Darko Suvin. Arts Bldg., McGill University, Montreal, Que., H3A 2T6, Canada.

Starship. Ed. Andrew Porter. Box 4175, New York, NY 10017.

Thrust. Ed. Douglas Fratz. 11919 Barrel Cooper Ct., Reston, VA 22091.

Vector. Ed. Christopher Fowler. 72 Kenilworth Avenue, Southgate, Reading RG3 3ND, England.

Xenophile. Ed. Nils Hardin. 26 Chapala No. 5, Santa Barbara, CA 93101.

Academe

James Gunn

FROM THE PULPS TO THE CLASSROOM: THE STRANGE JOURNEY OF SCIENCE FICTION

Science fiction has traveled a strange road from isolation, in part self-imposed, to critical and academic acceptance. From the marvelous adventures of Edgar Allan Poe through the extraordinary voyages of Jules Verne to the scientific romances of H.G. Wells, under whatever name science fiction has passed over the century and a half during which it has existed, it always has seemed like an un-welcome relative at the feast of literature.

Even its creators looked down on it. Poe preferred his mood stories and. his tales of ratiocination to his more science fictionish pieces. Wells thought more highly of his contemporary novels of manners than the pessimistic scientific romances of his early days. Wells' admirers, Joseph Conrad and Henry James, much as they liked his scientific romances, kept after him to give up his journal-istic ways with a story and devote himself to high art, but Wells "was disposed to regard a novel as about as much an art form as a market place or a boule-vard." I have no evidence to support the notion, but I would not be surprised if evidence should appear that Jules Verne liked *Mathias Sandorf* and *Michael Strogoff* better than *Journey to the Center of the Earth* and *From the Earth to the Moon*.

There may be an illuminating irony in the fact that in almost every case the science fiction has endured and the rest has faded. At the time they were writ-ten, poor relation to literature or not, prototypical science fiction passed in the great society of books as fiction of only small difference from the rest, perhaps more popular than some, perhaps less artistic than others, but part of the general spectrum of literature.

But the creation of the mass magazines in the latter part of the Nineteenth Century, the development of the all-fiction pulp magazines beginning in 1896 with *Argosy*, and the creation of the category pulp magazines starting with *Detective Story Magazine* in 1915 encouraged the separation of a species into genera and genera into families, and in each closed environment the families of fiction began to evolve separately. In 1926 science fiction split off the parent stock with the founding of *Amazing Stories* and began its evolutionary struggle toward some ideal form.

When science fiction enclosed itself in what would later be called a ghetto, it dropped out of critical view. As late as 1914, Sam Moskowitz has pointed out, the *New York Times* was reviewing books such as Edgar Rice Burroughs' *Tarzan of the Apes.* By 1926 not only were such reviews unlikely, science fiction was scarcely being published in book form, and what was published—stories from the early pulp magazines, books by Burroughs and A. Merritt, the strange and wonderful speculations of Olaf Stapledon—was not available in libraries.

A great deal of fantasy was available in book form during this period, and it was reviewed. Fantasy always has enjoyed a better critical acceptance than science fiction, perhaps because it was less concerned with reality and therefore less threatening, certainly because it was more traditional and thus yielded to existing critical techniques, but most of all because fantasy could not be subtracted from the history of literature without stripping literature of origins and half its substance.

Science fiction, however, was ignored by publishers and critics. It was a late comer, a product of the Industrial Revolution and the Age of Reason and the scientific enlightenment, and to overlook it was the act of a gentleman and a connoisseur. Science fiction was brash and crude; it smelled of oil and hot metal; and where science fiction was brashest and crudest and most typical, in the science fiction magazines, was where it was ignored by everyone except its fans, those strange new creatures that Hugo Gernsback discovered when he published *Amazing* and called by name in his third issue. Books to come out of this environment—real science fiction with the smell of the pulp magazines still on them—had to wait until the middle Forties, mostly until the two big 1946 postwar anthologies, Groff Conklin's *The Best of Science Fiction* and Raymond J. Healy and J. Francis McComas's *Adventures in Time and Space*, and the fan presses that began preserving for posterity the immortal words of H. P. Lovecraft and E. E. Smith.

Twenty years, almost to the day, science fiction spent in its pulp ghetto, and almost another twenty years elapsed before the critics noticed that something new had emerged from that period of isolation. It is that period and that process, those years between 1946 and the present, that I wish to describe here, because it has helped to shape the present situation of science fiction and we can move on more confidently in the academic consideration of science fiction if we know where we have been and where we are and how we got there.

By 1946, of course, Donald A. Wollheim had already edited a couple of science fiction books, one for Pocket Books, one for Viking, J. Berg Eisenwein and Phil Stong had edited even earlier anthologies, August Derleth had founded Arkham House and published Lovecraft's *The Outsider, and Others,* and J. O. Bailey had completed his pioneer dissertation, *Pilgrims Through Space and Time* (the preface to the 1947 Argus book was dated December 1945). A few critical studies had been published before Bailey's, such as Philip Babcock Gove's *The Imaginary Voyage in Prose Fiction,* which would be followed in 1948 by Marjorie Hope Nicholson's *Voyages to the Moon.* But Bailey's was the first critical study actually to concern itself with science fiction, even if he refers to it throughout his book as scientific fiction.

The most important books in the critical appreciation of science fiction, however, were the Conklin and Healy and McComas anthologies. I know what they represented to me---a World War II veteran returning after three years to finish up his final year of college; they provided an overview and understanding of the recent accomplishments of science fiction that I could not have obtained by a perusal of all the science fiction magazines published between 1926 and 1946, even if they had been available anywhere west of Sam Moskowitz and east of Forrest J Ackerman. Groff Conklin's and John Campbell's introductions to Conklin's anthology were particularly helpful; I like to think of them as the opening wedge of critical understanding that later would allow science fiction to slip into the tunnel vision of the mainstream. Another pioneer book of criticism, the slim, red volume called *Of Worlds Beyond*, edited by Lloyd A. Eshbach and published by his Fantasy Press, came along in 1947 as another revelation.

Conklin followed his epic collection with other anthologies, which not only made stories from the magazines more broadly available but continued his critical and taxonomical approach to the field. He was joined by others, particularly Derleth, whose anthologies for Pellegrini & Cudahi beginning in 1948 and culminating for me in the 1950 collection, *Beyond Time and Space*, were unusually helpful in tracing a literary genealogy for science fiction back to Plato. A double handful of fan presses would follow Arkham House in keeping science fiction books in print until the commercial publishers caught on to the sudden new surge of interest, just as Advent Press was virtually alone in publishing science fiction criticism until the past couple of years.

Other contributions to a critical consideration of science fiction would follow: my master's thesis was completed in 1951 and some 20,000 words of it were published in *Dynamic Science Fiction* in 1952---probably the only thesis ever serialized in a pulp magazine, thanks to Robert Lowndes. Reginald Bretnor edited an exciting and important collection of essays about science fiction, *Modern Science Fiction*, for Coward-McCann in 1953. Rumors of other studies and dissertations floated around; about this time Jack Williamson was working on his study of Wells which eventually would find its way into Leland Sapiro's *Riverside Quarterly*, about the only place to find serious literary criticism of science fiction, and then into a book, *Critic of Progress*, published by Mirage Press. Other consciousness-raising reviews and essays by Damon Knight and James Blish appeared in fan magazines and later were collected into *In Search of Wonder* and *The Issue at Hand* in 1956 and 1964 respectively. But all of these efforts were largely missionaries talking to the already converted.

The emergence of science fiction from its exile was represented in the Fifties by the interest of the occasional literary figures such as Basil Davenport and Clifton Fadiman. Both were associated with the Book of the Month Club; Davenport wrote an introduction or two, edited anthologies, and wrote *An Inquiry into Science Fiction* in 1955; Fadiman edited *Fantasia Mathematica*; and both (if I remember correctly) allowed themselves to appear on the back cover of the *Magazine of Fantasy and Science Fiction* saying something in praise of science fiction and the magazine. Unlike other magazines, *Fantasy and Science Fiction* tried to broaden its base of readership, extending pseudopods into the mainstream by reducing reliance upon conventions, insisting on skillful writing and a greater concern for the complexities of character and of language, by associating science fiction with more literary works in the fantasy tradition, by reprinting stories from the experimental mainstream, and by critical or biographical headnotes. And their backcover ads consciously tried to attract non-science fiction readers.

Then the critical situation for science fiction began heating up. In the publishing field conditions were not promising: the big magazine boom of the early Fifties had collapsed, dragging some old standards down with it, the surge of new science fiction writers which always seems to accompany magazine booms had slowed as well, Tony Boucher had retired as editor of *Fantasy and Science Fiction* and Horace Gold was in his last couple of years as editor of *Galaxy*, the early enthusiasm created by the founding of Ballantine Books had dwindled, such path-pointing books as Vonnegut's *The Sirens of Titan* and Miller's *A Canticle for Leibowitz* had not yet been published; in fact, conditions were pretty much as usual for science fiction—lousy. But I did get a letter from my agent, Harry Altshuler, that Bantam Books was looking for some new writers and shortly after that they accepted *Station in Space*. Some vibrations were making themselves felt, perhaps, but little was happening except that some college professors led by the late Professor Scott Osborn of Mississippi State University organized the first Conference on Science Fiction under the Modern Language Association. That was 1958; a year later the first academic journal in the field, *Extrapolation*, was founded.

Meanwhile something extraordinary was happening at Princeton. Kingsley Amis, a recognized English poet and author, presented a series of lectures for the Christian Gauss Seminar in Criticism in the spring of 1959, and in the lectures he proclaimed his long-time admiration for science fiction. A year later the lectures appeared in book form as *New Maps of Hell*, and various surprised popular media, reviewing the book, began to reconsider their own policy of consistently ignoring or denigrating the science fiction which had somehow reached their desks. *Time Magazine*, which previously had mentioned only to ridicule, started publishing an occasional favorable review, included one retrospective look, as I recall, at Richard Matheson's *I Am Legend*, which had been published only in paperback, and other magazines and newspapers began to include articles about science fiction, authors, and individual works, including the *New York Times* (which still has not published a major review on a science fiction book, unless one includes the review about Stanislaw Lem, as it has on a mystery), the *New Yorker*, the *Christian Science Monitor*, the *Wall Street Journal*, *Publishers Weekly*, and many others, although some of them would not discover science fiction until much later.

One small event in the real world might have been a precipitating factor: in 1957 the U.S.S.R. launched its first satellite, *Sputnik*. With that event space travel became plausible and with it the fiction that had dealt so consistently with space flight.

Other major critics were making themselves heard: Bruce Franklin's study of Nineteenth Century American science fiction, *Future Perfect*, was published by Oxford University Press in 1966, which also published Mark Hillegas's *The Future as Nightmare* in 1967, and I. F. Clarke's *Voices Prophesying War* in 1966. C. S. Lewis's essay, "On Science Fiction," was presented as a talk to the Oxford University English Club in 1955, and his "Unreal Estates" was recoded as a discussion in 1962, but they did not get into print, apparently, until the latter was published in *SF Horizons* in 1964 and both were published in *Of Other Worlds* in 1966.

The most recent voices raised in behalf of science fiction have been those of Leslie Fiedler and Robert Scholes, professors of English at the State University of New York at Buffalo and at Brown University, respectively. Oddly enough, their views have been expressed in essays with similar titles: Fiedler's "Cross the Border, Close the Gap" and Scholes's "As the Wall Crumbles" in *Nebula Award Stories Number Ten*. Both have other critical works about science fiction, in particular Fiedler's historical-critical anthology, *In Dreams Awake*, and Scholes's *Structural Fabulation*.

I met Fiedler first. At the Science Fiction Research Association meeting in Toronto in 1971 he seemed a novice at science fiction, as eager to learn as he was to teach, but he was a quick study, and by the Nebula Award Day in New York the following spring, where I invited him to speak, he had much to say. For too long, he said there, critics had been trying to tell readers why they should like what they don't like; what they ought to be doing, he said, is trying to find out why people like what they like. Why, for instance, has H. Rider Haggard's *She*, in spite of its artistic deficiencies, never been out of print since its publication in 1886?

Fiedler seemed to like science fiction not because it was good but because it was vulgar—no, that's not quite right, because vulgar, or pop, literature is good. In "Cross the Border . . . " he wrote, "We have . . . entered quite another time—apocalyptic, anti-rational, blatantly romantic and sentimental; an age dedicated to joyous misology and prophetic irresponsibility; one distrustful of self-protective irony and too-great self-awareness." The answer, he wrote, is to turn frankly to pop forms, such as the western, science fiction, and pornography. In New York he asked for a cross-fertilization of science fiction and pornography such as he saw in some of the work of Philip José Farmer. One wonders where Fiedler's desire to break new critical trails begins and his attempts to shock his readers into new awarenesses leaves off.

In his anthology, *In Dreams Awake*, Fiedler wrote that science fiction writers, often accused of "slapdash writing, sloppiness, and vulgarity," cannot learn from "the floggers of a dead avant-gardism, capable of creating neither myth nor wonder, only parody and allusion. No, it is precisely out of 'slapdash writing,' 'sloppiness,' and especially 'vulgarity,' as exemplified in, say, Shakespeare, Cooper, Dickens, and Twain, that myth is endlessly reborn, the dreams we dream awake."

Being loved by Leslie Fiedler is a bit like being loved by a lion; we aren't sure we're being appreciated for the right reasons.

On the other hand, we feel more comfortable with Robert Scholes—at least I do—because he relates us to the rest of literature rather than setting us off because we're different. Scholes is a leading critic of contemporary literature, particularly that branch of contemporary fiction for which he supplied a name in his book *The Fabulators*.

I met Scholes at a science fiction gathering, too—the World Science Fiction Convention in Washington, D.C., in 1974—and later asked him to contribute an essay to the recent volume of *Nebula Award Stories* that I edited. In "As the Wall Crumbles," he put the literary position of science fiction this way: "Pleasure in fiction is rooted in our response to narrative movement—to story itself. This is a fundamental kind of pleasure, almost physical, and closely connected to physical sensations like those of motion and sex."

Much "mainstream" fiction, he went on, is so overburdened with a weight of analysis and subtle refinement of consciousness that we do not get from it the pure fictional pleasure that lies at the heart of our need for narration. "One result of this situation is that many people may resort, more or less guiltily, to 'lesser' forms of fiction—outside the mainstream of serious literature—for a narrative 'fix,' a shot of joyful story-telling. . . . What most people need in fiction is something that satisfies their legitimate desire for the pleasures of story-telling, without making them feel ashamed of having some childish and anti-social impulse. We need recreational texts, good stories that leave us refreshed without any feeling of guilt. We need stories that are genuinely adult in their concerns and ideas while satisfying our elemental need for wonder and delight. Science fiction at its best answers this need better than any other form of contemporary fiction. And it does more. . . . "

Now, as a science fiction writer and reader, I say, "That's more like it!"

Scholes also speaks the more esoteric language of academia. That is a valuable asset, because it allows him to attack the stronghold of scorn and indifference with its own weapons. In *Structural Fabulation*, which is not only the name of his book but the name he gives science fiction, Scholes traces science fiction to the romance (in the traditional division of fiction between realism and romance); he divides the romance into pure romance (sublimation with minimal cognition, sometimes called "escapism") and the didactic romance (or fabulation, as in allegory, satire, fable, and parable); the didactic romance he divides, in turn, into speculative fabulation (or romances of science, such as More's *Utopia*) and dogmatic fabulation (romances of religion, such as Dante's *Divine Comedy*); speculative fabulation he divides, at last, into pseudo-scientific sublimation (space opera, and so forth) and structural fabulation.

Structural fabulation, or science fiction, is "the tradition of More, Bacon, and Swift, as modified by new input from the physical and human sciences." And Scholes restates the message of "As the Wall Crumbles" in more academic language: "We require a fiction which satisfies our cognitive and sublimative needs together. . . . We need suspense with intellectual consequences, in which questions are raised as well as solved, and in which our minds are expanded even while focused on the complications of a fictional plot." And he goes on, "In works of structural fabulation the tradition of speculative fiction is modified by an awareness of the nature of the universe as a system of systems, a structure of structures, and the insights of the past century of science are accepted as fictional points of departure."

Scholes has other pleasant things to say about science fiction: the Hugo award is at least as reliable an indicator of quality as, say, the Pulitzer Prize for fiction; and, the most appropriate kind of fiction that can be written in the present and the immediate future is fiction that takes place in future time. But most of all he urges his "fellow teachers and makers of curricula to open their courses to the literature of structural fabulation and allow it to contribute to that critical revaluation of our literary past which functions so powerfully to keep that past alive."

Other critics have worked within the field itself, struggling with definitions and classification, strengthening our internal structures. I could mention names like Tom Clareson and Darko Suvin and Dale Mullen and Robert Philmus, as well as Joanna Russ and Samuel Delany, who are critics as well as writers of fiction, but I am primarily concerned here with the ways in which the outside world—the *mundane* world, the science fiction fan language would call it—has become reconciled to science fiction.

The process of reconciliation, of acceptance, of discovery continues. And that continuing process of opening the science fiction treasure house to an unsuspecting and up-to-now largely unappreciative non-science-fiction-reading public is the condition of science fiction criticism today.

Meanwhile the concept that science fiction was a branch of literature which could be taught to the better understanding and appreciation of students began occurring to a few teachers here and there. Sam Moskowitz has conducted an unrelenting quest for encyclopedic knowledge of science fiction and pre-eminence in the science fiction fan world, a quest recorded in his history of fandom, *The Immortal Storm*, whose fruits are the biographies of science fiction authors and editors published first in Ziff-Davis magazines in the late Fifties and early Sixties and then in the books *Seekers of Tomorrow* and *Explorers of the Infinite*. He tells about organizing an evening course in science fiction for City College of New York in 1953 and 1954. But the first course taught within the official curriculum of a college is believed to be Mark Hillegas's course at Colgate in 1962. Jack Williamson began teaching a course at Eastern New Mexico University in 1964, and Tom Clareson was not far behind at Wooster.

My own science fiction teaching began in 1969. About the same time Robin Scott Wilson began his Science Fiction Writers Workshops at Clarion and Stanford launched a summer Science Fiction Institute. Courses have burgeoned since then. Jack Williamson's last survey in 1972 counted some 240 college courses. Judging by a little experience and a lot of intuition, I would say that there is scarcely a college in the nation that does not have at least one science fiction course a year, and if a college doesn't have a course it is because the faculty can't find anyone to teach it rather than that they believe it is beneath them.

At the University of Kansas the single annual course that I began teaching in 1971 to as many as 165 students has increased by two courses offered at the sophomore level, six sophomore courses in fantasy (eight in the spring), a course in the writing of science fiction, and a summer program for teachers. There are special reasons for such growth at Kansas, of course, but I suspect that similar developments are occurring at other places around the nation: junior colleges, four-year colleges, universities—at last count the nation had some two thousand colleges and universities, and it may be a reasonable estimate that they are teaching some two thousand science fiction courses.

What began as an attempt by a few pioneers to teach students what the teachers themselves found uniquely fascinating and what they were uniquely equipped to teach changed into a kind of self-preservation in the late Sixties when student power became an issue and relevance became a byword, and in the Seventies when vocationalism began diverting students away from the humanities toward business, journalism, engineering, social work, and the social and behavioral sciences. The question of jobs became the issue, not just for the students but for the faculty as well; the end of automatic enrollment increases and the beginning of enrollment drops made the attractiveness of course offerings a subject for concern in English departments everywhere.

I do not like to think, nor would I suggest, that colleges have taken up science fiction only in response to the need for inducing students to take some kind of English course, but it may not be unfair to propose that the pioneers were not so much trailbreakers for the wagon trains of settlers that would follow as the first scouts for a pack of migrating lemmings.

The question of qualified teachers was raised early. I began to think about it in 1969, when a combination of circumstances that I have related elsewhere led me to consider the development of a series of lecture films featuring science fiction writers and editors talking about those aspects of science fiction that they knew best. Basically I hoped to provide help for teachers who felt unprepared, unqualified, unable to cope with their new assignment. There were many of them in the early Seventies. When I was president of the Science Fiction Writers of America in 1971-72, I received one or two plaintive letters a week from teachers saying that they had been assigned this science fiction class, they had never read science fiction before, and could I send them a list of what to teach and suggestions about how to teach it.

It was enough to make a professor go write a book. I didn't—not about the teaching of science fiction—but others wrote or compiled such books. I'll get to them a little later, and to the book I did write.

That science fiction lecture series developed more slowly than I ever could have imagined. It was an education for all of us in the difficulties and costs of making films. But we now have eleven films in the series, in color, ranging in length from twenty to forty minutes; and three more are being edited toward availability. They have been seen all over the world—two institutions in Australia have standing orders for all the films we produce—and it is a source of considerable satisfaction to me that students, wherever they are, have the opportunity to hear the history of science fiction from the lips of Damon Knight and Isaac Asimov, its ideas from Fred Pohl, its techniques from Poul Anderson, its themes from Gordon Dickson, its film history from Forrest Ackerman, its relation to the mainstream from John Brunner, and its new directions from Harlan Ellison, as well as Jack Williamson describing the early days of the magazines, Clifford Simak reminiscing about his career, and Harry Harrison and Gordon Dickson discussing with the late John Campbell a story idea that later developed into an *Analog* serial.

During the period that science fiction was spreading like a plague from space through colleges and universities, it also was beginning to swim upstream—to mix the metaphor—into high schools and junior high schools and even primary schools. The secondary schools had different motivations from the colleges. Some of them want to provide incentives for poor readers, and discovered that some students could graduate from television cartoons to comic magazines to science fiction stories; anything was legitimate that got students interested in reading. At the other end of the academic spectrum, gifted students often were bored with the pace of secondary education, and science fiction, with its concern for ideas and themes, kept their attention and their involvement.

In addition, the loosening of academic disciplines in secondary schools—perhaps part of the same movement toward relevance which may be responsible for the increasing difficulties with the written language that students are bringing into college—provided a place in the secondary curriculum for a spreading system of elective mini-courses. Among the mini-courses, almost always, was a science fiction option; administrators soon found that science fiction courses were always over-enrolled. Meanwhile, teachers in disciplines other than English discovered that through science fiction they could get students to consider the human aspects of science, sociology, politics, philosophy, religion, and other intellectual areas to which they might come unwillingly, or without understanding, in the abstract.

Whatever the reasons—I do not pretend that my list is comprehensive—science fiction courses have proliferated in high schools until they may rival woodworking or home economics.

All of this movement of science fiction into the academic curriculum has had its inevitable reactions: delight, sometimes mixed with disappointment, on the part of students; consternation and bewilderment and sometimes a sigh of relief on the part of teachers; and disapproval, in general, on the part of the science fiction community. Writers and editors and readers saw science fiction threatened by the same hand that had, they thought, throttled the life out of Shakespeare and beat the dickens out of Dickens, and by the same dessicating mouth that had turned history into dust. Moreover, they thought, the hand and the mouth weren't even prepared; they had no idea what science fiction even felt like, much less what it was really about.

People such as Lester del Rey and Ben Bova and Harlan Ellison saw in the new academic interest disaster for science fiction. Teachers were using science fiction merely as a stepping stone for their ambition; they were riding the winds of popularity; they were liking science fiction, if they did, for the wrong reasons; and they would turn students off to science fiction faster than the authors and the magazines were turning them on.

Much of this resentment of the science fiction community against academia seemed to come to a focus at a two-day meeting at Kean College of New Jersey in the spring of 1974. There I heard writers complaining bitterly about what was being taught and who was teaching the courses. Harlan Ellison had horror stories about his campus visits and what teachers were doing to science fiction there, and even the reasonable Fred Pohl viewed with alarm.

Phil Klass, who wrote so many magnificent stories under the name of William Tenn, had described the situation even before that 1974 meeting. In a "Science Fiction and the University" issue of the *Magazine of Fantasy and Science Fiction* for May, 1972, he wrote an article entitled "Jazz Then, Musicology Now" in which he worried about the impact on science fiction of academic responsibility. Then Ben Bova published an editorial in the June, 1974, *Analog* raising more serious questions about the preparation of teachers and the academic exploitation of science fiction. He asked why the Science Fiction Research Association was not setting and demanding professional qualifications among science fiction teachers; and he feared "a variation of Gresham's law in which the bad teaching and schlock movies and TV shows will drive out the good ones."

In rebuttal in the November, 1974, issue of *Analog* for which Ben should be given credit—when I dropped into his office after the Kean College conference he asked me to write it; even better, he offered to pay me for it—I tried to respond to the fears that Ben's editorial had voiced. I said, in brief: 1) science fiction's fear of outsiders is part of the ghetto mentality; 2) our history of booms and busts make us paranoid about booms; 3) every new subject or discipline goes through a period when its teachers are unqualified; 4) professional organizations, at least in the academic disciplines, do not determine qualifications; in colleges, at least, this is done by departments; 5) all of us, including writers and editors, use science fiction for our own ends, and none of us is truly innocent of exploitation; 6) science fiction needs sophisticated criticism and should welcome academic critics; 7) science fiction will stand out as an oasis in a desert of required courses, no matter how poorly taught; 8) the teachers who volunteer for science fiction courses tend to be the better, more experimental teachers; 9) college and high school classes provide an opportunity unparalleled since the founding of *Amazing Stories* to create new readers; I cited evidence that it was doing so; and 10) in any case, only the stories can turn people on, and we should be devoting our concerns toward writing them better and with broader appeals.

You will note that I have given the rebuttal more space than the argument, but that's always the case when one participant in a debate is absent.

That editorial had an amusing sequel. Lester del Rey wrote a rebuttal to my remark, and that of others, about science fiction as a ghetto. In the March, 1975 issue of *Galaxy*, he began his article by saying it wasn't a ghetto at all, that he had always read and written extensively outside the field; and he ended his piece by saying, "Stay out of my ghetto."

So much for ghettos.

One of the problems I didn't mention in my guest editorial in *Analog* was the difficulty with teaching tools. I'm not talking about scholarship here, although scholarship clearly contributes to teaching through insights and through the education of teachers. I am talking about the books the students handle and hopefully read, the textbooks and the anthologies and the novels.

Although Bruce Franklin's *Future Perfect* was published in 1966, it was concerned with Nineteenth Century science fiction, a topic more scholarly than teachable, particularly in the introductory classes most of us teach. The first teaching anthologies, Robert Silverberg's *Mirror of Infinity* and *Science Fiction Hall of Fame*, the second because of its contents and selection process, by the authors themselves, and Richard Ofshe's *Sociology of the Possible*, were not published until 1970. The last never had a cheap edition, I think, and the first two were not available in paperback until a year or two later. Sam Moskowitz's books of biographical sketches, *Explorers of the Infinite* and *Seekers of Tomorrow*, were published before 1970 but, though useful, were not really teachable, and in any case were not available in paperback (or in any other form, for a while) until the recent Hyperion Press reprint. The same is true of his fascinating studies of early science fiction, *Science Fiction by Gaslight* and *Under the Moons of Mars*.

Tom Clareson's *SF: The Other Side of Realism*, with its useful reprints of scholarly and popular articles, and Dick Allen's *Science Fiction: The Future*, were published in 1971. Don Wollheim's personal history, *The Universe Makers*, was published in 1971, and Clareson's academic anthology, *A Spectrum of Worlds*, in 1972; neither has appeared in paperback. It is instructive about the youth of our field that a standard such as Harrison and Pugner's *A Science Fiction Reader* did not appear until 1973; the first thorough history of the field, Brian Aldiss's *Billion Year Spree*, appeared the same year, although Sam Lundwall's *Science Fiction: What It's All About* was published in 1971. Two books for high school teachers, Calkins and McGhan's *Teaching Tomorrow* and Hollister and Thompson's *Grokking the Future*, came out in 1972 and 1973, Beverly Friend's *Classroom in Orbit*, in 1974. The discursive symposium, Reginald Bretnor's *Science Fiction, Today and Tomorrow*, appeared in 1974, paperback in 1975.

My own illustrated history, *Alternate Worlds*, was originally scheduled for 1972, could have been published in 1973, but various problems including complexity and a change in editors delayed it until fall, 1975. The hardcover edition cost a prohibitive (for a college text) $29.95, but it is now available from A&W Visual Library for $8.95; and it has become a requirement for many science fiction classes, including my own Science Fiction Institute. I don't think any science fiction teacher worthy of the name should be allowed to teach without the book in his or her personal library; but that may be my particular bias.

By the summer of 1975 I could prepare for the students in my Institute a list of fifty-five books of academic interest or usefulness just from those I could see on my shelves.

I would like to return for a moment to the matter of price and format: these are serious matters, particularly at the college level where a semester's course may involve ten to fifteen novels or short story collections. With this many required texts, none of them can be expensive; they must be in paperback—and in print. Being published in paperback in our field means that the books go out of print rapidly as they become available. A case in point is Jack C. Wolf and Gregory Fitz Gerald's useful anthology *Past, Present, and Future Perfect*, which was published by Fawcett in 1973 and has been unavailable ever since. My own three-volume historically-organized anthology for Mentor Books, *The Road to Science Fiction*, has been an attempt to remedy this situation.

The problem of availability has been even a greater problem in the science fiction books themselves. Paperback publishers traditionally have been geared to the rhythm of the newsstands. The publishers throw a big printing of books onto the stands for a period which may last from a month to three months; at that point the newsstand proprietors replace the old books, tear off their covers, and return the covers for credit. Nor all your piety nor wit will get a reorder out of such a publisher; he doesn't have the warehouses or the mechanism. The books will be out of stock or out of print until the next printing, if any. I have often received notices from the university book store that one-third to one-half of my book orders were out of stock or out of print. Teachers of science fiction got used to scrambling for replacements, or, if we were more sophisticated, to ordering fifty percent more books than we intended to use. The latter solution, though it had the psychological advantage of cynicism, often left us with two or more books serving the same purpose.

Even this situation is easing a bit as paperback publishers become educated to the fact that science fiction is not the same as mysteries, westerns, nurse novels, and gothics, which may well be interchangeable. The publishers are keeping science fiction books in print and in stock longer; I have received special educational flyers recently from Ballantine, Bantam, New American Library, and Dell listing their science fiction for the classroom. If nothing else, teachers may have helped the science fiction community achieve a momentary victory in its long campaign to convince publishers that science fiction books sell year after year and should be kept in print.

Four publishers have brought old "classics" back into print, beginning with Hyperion and followed by Arno, Gregg, and Garland, Hyperion and Gregg coming out with second series, and Gregg with what seems like a continuing series. The price of the books, however, as well as their antiquity make them additions to scholarly resources rather than to classroom teaching, although the Garland series did include a number of titles from the so-called Golden Age. Students, at least, can find the books in the library.

Avon Books started a Rediscovery series that it said was "dedicated to making important and influential works of science fiction available once more—and on a continuing basis—to discerning readers." That promising dedication would be even more promising were it not for the suspicion that these "important and influential works" are also those books that happen to be available, either because the rights belonged to Avon already or because the rights had been reverted to the author by the original paperback publisher. Unfortunately even for this limited value, the series has been cancelled.

What else lies ahead for the science fiction teachers? Jack Williamson has edited a book for teachers of science fiction; it will be published by Mirage Press under the title of *Science Fiction: Education for Tomorrow*. Tom Clareson has edited a book for teachers of science fiction; it will be published by Owlswick Press under the title of *Science Fiction: Education for Tomorrow*. Tom Clareson has edited a collection of essays about the science fiction writers of the Thirties and Forties; by the time this piece sees print Bowling Green University Popular Press will have published the first couple of a continuing series. A book about the writing of science fiction, *The Craft of Science Fiction*, edited by Reginald Bretnor and published by Harper & Row, appeared in 1976. *Writer's Digest* published a 1976 book called *Writing and Selling Science Fiction and Fantasy*, for G.K. Hall & Co. Through the efforts of Martin Greenberg, Joseph Olander, and Patricia Warrick, SFWA and SFRA have combined forces, put together teams of ten science fiction writers and ten teachers, two by two like Noah and the Ark, to produce an anthology called *Science Fiction: Contemporary Myth Makers, the SFWA-SFRA Anthology*, to be published by Harper & Row. Oxford University Press has published a critical edition of H.G. Wells's *The Time Machine* [and] *The War of the Worlds*, edited by Frank D. McConnell, and Robert Scholes and Eric S. Rabkin's *Science Fiction: History, Science, Vision*, and have contracted for a series of critical studies on individual science fiction writers under the general editorship of Robert Scholes. Martin Harry Greenberg and Joseph Olander have been editing a series of collections of essays focused on individual writers. And two companies are making back issues of the old magazines available once more, in microfilm, one edited for Greenwood Press by Tom Clareson.

Back in the late Sixties, Arthur C. Clarke made a comment that was picked up by the Science Fiction Writers of America as a motto: "The future isn't what it used to be." It has been a strange journey for science fiction from the pulps to the classroom, but for science fiction teachers I suggest that the best is yet to come.

Roger C. Schlobin

MASTERPIECES OF MODERN FANTASY:
AN ANNOTATED CORE LIST[1]

The reading of fantasy and the examination of its nature are increasingly popular activities in contemporary society. The successes of J. R. R. Tolkien's *The Lord of the Rings* and Richard Adams' *Watership Down*—both in books and films—have made fantasy a common preoccupation and interest. What was once an esoteric activity occupying a few academics and initiates now fills classrooms to overflowing, generates millions of dollars at box offices, and enriches once-impoverished publishers and authors beyond their wildest expectations. This popular acclaim should be no surprise. As J. R. R. Tolkien points out, "Fantasy is a natural human activity,"[2] and fantasy yields significant benefits to its readers. Only those who are so pitifully bound to the "everyday"—the embracers of "hard reality"—fail to appreciate the deep core of humanity that fantasy touches and choose to deny that essential portion of man that Harvey Cox so appropriately calls *"homo fantasica."*[3] So basic is fantasy and the ability to fantasize to the psyche that it is inappropriate to limit fantasy with the labels "literature" and "genre." Rather, it does, like a "bar of light,"[4] blaze across the full spectrum of literary types[5] and experience. Everyone, in one form or another, is an accomplished fantasist. In dreams—both sleeping and waking—all deny fact and the empirical, sublunar world through flights of imagination and fancy. In these normal human diversions is the psychological and, sequentially, the literary nature of fantasy: it is, according to what the individual knows of the corporeal world, the creation or apprehension of what could never have been, cannot be, and can never be. This appears to be a relativistic definition, and one that belies other, more complex analyses. However, without an understanding of how fantasy is recognized within its social, cultural, and historical context, there is a great danger of turning fantasy literature into a universal panacea, offering solutions to whatever the twentieth-century mind finds unbelievable, regardless of its origins. Without the understanding that the recognition and existence of fantasy depends in major part on the reader's ability to recognize it as fantasy,[6] the unicorns, dragons, and other creatures included in the classical and medieval encyclopedias and bestiaries are seen as the products of fancy rather than the examples of natural history that they are. The use of this illustration should not, however, be construed as indicating that fantasy has not been around for a long, long time in literature. In fact, C. G. Jung[7] and Erich Neumann[8] have demonstrated that fantasy is an essential part of the

246

creative process. The works of Aesop (sixth century B.C.), Aristophanes (fifth century B.C.), and Lucian (first century A.D.) are ample evidence of fantasy's antiquity, and the fact that most great writers have tried their hands at writing fantasy is support for its essential role in the creation of fiction.[9]

Yet, it is the reader's ease of apprehension of fantasy that is the very factor that makes it so difficult to study and intellectually understand. As with all deeply human reactions and emotions, fantasy is easily felt, but seldom explained well. Essentially, in its literary form, it evokes wonder. This wonder may range "from crude astonishment of the marvellous, to a sense of 'meaning-of-the-mysterious' or even of the numinous."[10] When the reader participates in the "advanced imagining"[11] and highly disciplined journeys of fantasy, he or she travels, as a god, on a road where the world is created *"ex nihilo,"* out of nothing;[12] experiences rare dreams and sensations for the first time;[13] breaks traditions[14] and violates rituals; opens non-empirical doors;[15] and finds that, as the journey continues, the mind expands and is enriched by the exercise of its own capacities. In the fantastic experience in literature, man and emaginative culture transcend "the limits both of the naturally possible and of the morally acceptable."[16] Moreover, as the mythopoetic force that is, fantasy shares myth's capacity to impinge upon "the awesome ultimate mystery which is both beyond and within himself [mankind] and all things. . . . "[17] Intellectually, it is the state from which words turn back,[18] where "mythological symbols touch and exhilarate centers of life beyond the reach of vocabulary of reason and coercion";[19] it is subtle, self-luminous,[20] impulsive, and non-causal. Fantasy encloses its readers in a place where archetypes and primordial images come alive[21] through participation in the racial or collective unconscious[22] and rejection of everyday concerns and preoccupations. Thus, fantasy lures its readers into an examination of their own natures and the seminal truths of their existence.

These realms of fantasy are not, as easily could be expected, a full denial of or departure from the normal, work-a-day world. If only because they are dependent on semantics, they must be transmitted by language, and fantasy is bound by contrast to empirical and causal expectation. Fantasy creation and its concrete manifestations in art may not be, as Eric S. Rabkin asserts, a full one-hundred-eighty-degree turn from the "ground rules" of the everyday,[23] but they clearly depend on a movement from learned, traditional, and ritualistic expectations. This places a certain responsibility on the reader if appreciation is to occur. This mental movement or leap has been variously labeled. Samuel Coleridge called it the "willing suspension of disbelief," a term adopted by T. S. Eliot and one which has gained wide acceptance; J. R. R. Tolkien calls it the "literary belief" in "sub-creation";[24] E. M. Forster, "acceptance";[25] Tzvetan Todorov, rational "uncertainty" or "hesitation";[26] and W. R. Irwin, "credence,"[27] All of these labels or tags point to a detachment from the ordinary and a union with a fiction that Robert Scholes has identified as fabulation: " . . . fiction that offers us a world clearly and radically discontinuous from the one we know, yet [which] returns to confront that known world in some cognitive way."[28] Through this shift, the fantastic demands that its readers enter into a "complex and dynamic relationship"[29] in which inner realities are paradoxically made manifest, the internal is externalized and made visible through art,[30] and the "physical body is left behind and an imaginary body, often differing markedly from the physical one, takes over."[31]

However, while fantasy literature is a sustained metaphor for the release of the mind and psyche from its empirical bonds and intellectual restrictions, at its best it is never chaotic or irrational. Even in the creation of an absolute fantasy world, particularly in fully supernatural fantasy that Robert H. Boyer and Kenneth J. Zahorski call "high fantasy,"[32] fantasy is contingent upon reality[33] and does maintain its link with the normative perspective. The more astute critics have noticed this, and in the process have given new meaning to the time-worn attack that fantasy is simply escapism. The various substantive elements of fantasy—its archetypal and mythic content—are controlled and shaped by the laws of play and game. As such, it should be "continuous and coherent"[34] and consistent in its underlying principles no matter how far they may deviate from expectation. Thus, while fantasy rejects or ignores what the intellect knows, its playfulness requires the active working of the intellect.[35] Just as the involvement in the release of festivity and holiday operates by the lawful reversal of everyday, so too fantasy conforms to its own strictures, and the resultant liberation generates purposeful and joyful play, allowing the mind to seek and explore its own capacities for apprehension.

It is in the arena of play that the value of fantasy is found. C. G. Jung explains that fantasy is the essential unifying element of the psyche[36] and the director of its energy flow.[37] As such, it is the basic principle of artistic creation[38] and invention; it supplies the will with needed content,[39] purpose, and focus. Without fantasy, man and his society would be cut off from the "visceral fonts of renewal"[40] and would be denied the spiritual union with past and future. In the conflict between creation and social, religious, and cultural restrictions, fantasy maintains man's sense of himself and his capacities, denying the separation from self that must result from purely external determinants of behavior and thought. Within the state of enchantment[41] and wonder that it creates, fantasy ignores the immediate and embraces the elemental and the whimsical, rejects the cultural and moralistic and confronts the essential and universal potentialities of art and mind. Since it is reality formed both in and out of the mind, fantasy confronts and materializes the non-effectable and, as it transcends mundane limitations, it becomes more and more irreducible, always promoting growth and enhancing existence, forming an interface with basic historical and human realities.

This introduction has been designed to acquaint the reader with the basic concepts of fantasy and fantasy literature and to introduce the major scholarly discussions of its nature. What is most important, however, is how these theories and thoughts test out against the novels, collections, and anthologies that are cited, by first edition, in the annotated bibliography that follows. The bibliography is offered as a core list of readings for those teachers, librarians, scholars, and fans who would like to explore the rich and varied expressions of fantasy in literature. The majority of the works have been purposefully selected from the modern era, for at no other time has there been such a proliferation of quality writing. As man's understanding and knowledge of himself, his customs, behavior, conventions, and world have grown, his ability to gain the insights necessary to quality fantasy has increased correspondingly and become more profound and mature. For the time being, at least, now is the golden age of fantasy!

In addition to the first edition citation and because of the mercuric life span of fantasy paperbacks, the bibliographic entries that follow also include references to library reprints. All series are listed in reading order.

NOTES

1. Portions of this bibliography also appear in the author's *The Literature of Fantasy: An Annotated Bibliography of Fantasy Fiction* (New York: Garland Publishing, 1979).

2. J. R. R. Tolkien, "On Fairy Stories," *The Tolkien Reader* (New York: Ballantine, 1966), p. 55 [82]. See also Harvey Cox, *The Feast of Fools: A Theological Essay on Festivity and Fantasy* (New York: Harper & Row, 1970), p. 8.

3. Cox, p. 11.

4. E. M. Forster, *Aspects of the Novel and Related Writings* (1927; rpt. London: Edward Arnold, 1974), p. 74.

5. W. R. Irwin, *The Game of the Impossible: A Rhetoric of Fantasy* (Urbana: University of Illinois Press, 1976), p. 8.

6. Gary K. Wolfe, "Symbolic Fantasy," *Genre*, 8 (1975), 197.

7. C. G. Jung, *Psychological Types*, trans. H. G. Baynes, rev. R. F. C. Hull (Princeton: Princeton University Press, 1971), pp. 58, 115, 433; C. G. Jung, *The Archetypes and the Collective Unconscious*, 2nd ed., trans. R. F. C. Hull (Princeton: Princeton University Press, 1968), p. 78.

8. Erich Neumann, *The Origins and History of the Consciousness*, trans. R. F. C. Hull (1954; rpt. Princeton: Princeton University Press, 1970), p. 11.

9. Philip Van Doren Stern, ed., "Introduction," in *The Moonlight Traveler: Great Tales of Fantasy and Imagination* (Garden City, NY: Doubleday, Doran, 1943), p. xv.

10. C. N. Manlove, *Modern Fantasy: Five Studies* (Cambridge: Cambridge University Press, 1975), p. 7.

11. Cox, p. 62.

12. Ibid., p. 59.

13. C. S. Lewis, "On Science Fiction," in *Of Other Worlds: Essays and Stories,* ed. Walter Hooper (New York: Harcourt, Brace & World, 1966), p. 70.

14. Robert Scholes and Robert Kellogg, *The Nature of Narrative* (London: Oxford University Press, 1966), p. 14.

15. Cox, p. 12.

16. Northrop Frye, *The Anatomy of Criticism: Four Essays* (Princeton: Princeton University Press, 1971), p. 127.

17. Joseph Campbell, *The Masks of God: Creative Mythology* (1968; rpt. New York: Penguin, 1976), p. 6. This is the basis for the omission of horror fiction in the bibliography. Fantasy mirrors the wonder of the mind's creative power; horror violates and distorts creation. For additional amplification of this distinction, see Manlove, p. 9.

18. Campbell, p. 6.

19. Ibid., p. 4

20. Ibid., p. 649.

21. Jung, *The Archetypes and the Collective Unconscious*, pp. 66–67; Jung, *Psychological Types,* p. 52.

22. Jung, *The Archetypes and the Collective Unconscious*, p. 155.

23. Eric S. Rabkin, *The Fantastic in Literature* (Princeton: Princeton University Press, 1976), pp. 12, 14–15, 41, 42.

24. Tolkien, pp. 36–37 [63–64].

25. Forster, p. 75.

26. Tzvetan Todorov, *The Fantastic: A Structural Approach to a Literary Genre,* trans. Richard Howard (1970; rpt. Ithaca, NY: Cornell University Press, 1975), pp. 25, 31.

27. Irwin, p. 66.

28. Robert Scholes, *Structural Fabulation: An Essay on Fiction of the Future,* University of Notre Dame Ward-Phillips Lectures in Language and Literature, No. 7 (Notre Dame: University of Notre Dame Press, 1975), p. 29. In fantasy, the return to the normal world is the reader's responsibility, and whether he returns with cognitive wisdom depends on the reader and the nature of the fantasy; cognitive return is not a requirement for the existence of the fantastic experience. Those who cannot maintain the duality—believing in the fantasy world but maintaining awareness of the normal world at the same time— are those unfortunates who frequently are committed to insane asylums.

29. Irwin, p. 55.

30. Neumann, p. 369.

31. Cox, p. 73.

32. Robert H. Boyer and Kenneth J. Zahorski, eds., *The Fantastic Imagination: An Anthology of High Fantasy* (New York: Avon, 1977), p. 2.

33. Jane Mobley, "Toward a Definition of Fantasy Fiction," *Extrapolation,* 15 (May 1974), 118.

34. Irwin, p. 9.

35. Ibid., p. 60.

36. Jung, *Psychological Types,* p. 52.

37. Ibid., p. 433.

38. Ibid., p. 115.

39. Ibid.

40. Cox, p. 69.

41. Tolkien, p. 54 [81].

MASTERPIECES OF FANTASY: AN ANNOTATED CORE LIST

A. NOVELS AND COLLECTIONS

EDWIN A[BBOTT] ABBOTT

Square, A., pseud. *Flatland: A Romance of Many Dimensions.* London: Seeley, 1884.

A two-dimensional being ponders the possibility of a one-dimensional realm and attempts to share his knowledge of the three-dimensional "spaceland" with his doubting fellows. The classical mathematical fantasy, which is also a satire on women and education.

RICHARD ADAMS

Shardik. London: Allen Lane, 1974.

The principal character, Kelderick, is saved from death by a bear. He believes that the bear is a god, whom he names Shardik, and adopts it as his totem. Through this and a series of circumstances, he becomes his people's leader and spends most of the novel as a pawn to political and social forces. Ultimately, he escapes these external pressures and discovers that his metaphysical and religious beliefs are not the true perspective on himself and his society. Instead, he adopts a more successful rational and realistic view in his search for truth.

Watership Down. London: Rex Collings, 1972.

In this unique fantasy, a beast epic, a group of rabbits search for their own utopia and their particular joys. Filled with excellent anecdotal and epic digressions as the "rabbit's eye" view lends unusual perspectives and identifies its own special brand of heroes and villains.

BRIAN ALDISS

The Malacia Tapestry. London: Faber & Faber, 1976.

A highly descriptive and picaresque tale that is set in a fantastic city, Malacia, in which humans, soothsayers, strange beings, and dinosaurs roam about amid splendor and squalor. It focuses on the career of an itinerant actor, Perion de Chirolo, and his quest for love, fame and wealth and culminates with his final confrontation with a "devil jaw" on his paramour's estate and the resolution of his quests. Strongly reminiscent of the 18th-century picaresque novel and the engravings of Hogarth in its description and characterization.

POUL ANDERSON

The Broken Sword. New York: Abelard-Schuman, 1954; rev. ed. New York: Ballantine, 1971 [paper].

Set in Elfland, a classic fantasy about a changeling's attempt to reconcile his humanity with his training and conditioning as an elf prince. Valgard the changeling—originally stolen by Imric, Elf earl, and replaced by a necromantically conceived elf-troll—continually doubts his own value as he judges himself in relation to the graceful and magical elves, but he does find his true value through his final confrontation with the evil and perverse elf-troll who replaced him in the human realm.

A Midsummer Tempest. Garden City, NY: Doubleday, 1974.

A pseudo-historical novel based on the premise that Shakespeare was a historian recording actual events and personages in his plays. Prince Rupert of the Rhine battles against Charles I of England, Oberon and Titania lament the coming of science and Christianity, Puck sorrows under the "wintry" faith of Puritanism, and Ariel and Caliban continue their conflict as the aging Caliban searches for his lost Miranda. Anderson adds his patent creative anachronisms (e.g., Rupert avoids a conflict with the Puritans by escaping on a steam engine) in this stylistic *tour de force* that captures the content and the flavor of Shakespeare's settings and characters.

Operation Chaos. Garden City, NY: Doubleday, 1971.

In a realm where magic is an everyday, mundane reality, a werewolf and a witch meet in the army during wartime while they are utilizing their special talents to combat an equally magical enemy. After the conflict is over, they are mustered out of their special "corps" and marry. Shortly after, they must harrow Hell to recover their stolen child. A humorous and ingenious fantasy with a very well-conceived setting that utilizes such things as "rune keys" to start cars and open locks. Many of the minor characters, particularly the denizens of hell, are delightfully drawn.

Three Hearts and Three Lions. Garden City, NY: Doubleday, 1961.

One of the better examples of the sword and sorcery sub-genre of fantasy. Drawn from Medieval French, Danish, and Arthurian legends and using the concepts of the parallel universe and the eternal hero, this is the tale of a 20th-century man who becomes a knight in a magical realm, allies himself with a wereswan and a dwarf, and battles a werewolf, a dragon, and the evil Morgan le Fay. Sadly, when his tasks are done, he must return to his own mundane world, leaving behind a legend promising his return. For a comparable work, see Robert Heinlein's *Glory Road*, 1963, below.

PIERS ANTHONY (See PIERS ANTHONY DILLINGHAM JACOB)

PETER S[OYER] BEAGLE

A Fine and Private Place. New York: Viking, 1960.

Beagle's first novel and a strong initial indication of his delightful ability to combine the everyday and the fantastic. In a Bronx cemetery, the barrier between life and death is eliminated to accommodate some very different love affairs. A special comic role is played by a sardonic, foul-mouthed raven.

The Last Unicorn. New York: Viking, 1968; rpt. Boston: Gregg, 1978.

The poignant quest of the last unicorn for her ensorcered fellows that is filled with wonder, magic, emotion, and Beagle's own touch of "matter-of-factness." The characterization of the unicorn's companions—Molly Grue the tavern wench and Schmendrick the magician—is particularly well done.

JOHN BELLAIRS

The Face in the Frost. London: Macmillan, 1969.

Roger Bacon and Prospero seek to ward off evil and protect the original spell that binds the four elements together and maintains order in the world. Set in the 20th century and suitable for juveniles.

JAMES BLISH

The After Such Knowledge Tetralogy

Doctor Mirabilis. New York: Dodd, Mead, 1971.

Black Easter or Faust Aleph-Null. Garden City, NY: Doubleday, 1968.

The Day After Judgment. Garden City, NY: Doubleday, 1971.

A Case of Conscience. New York: Ballantine, 1958 [paper].

In the "Afterword" to *The Day After Judgment,* Blish points to a speech in the novel which explains the rationale of his loosely connected tetralogy: " 'maybe,' Baines said, 'A large part of the mystic tradition says that the possession and use of secular knowledge—or even the desire for it—is in itself evil, according to Ware [the archmage]' " (p. 103). Within this philosophic premise, the series operates within a wide variety of settings and circumstances. *Dr. Mirabilis* is a fictional biography of Roger Bacon that is a vivid portrait of thirteenth-century attitudes and beliefs. *Black Easter* focuses on the activities of a master sorcerer and his client, a materialistic industrialist. Together, they conspire to release a number of devils and demons upon the world and, as a result, bring about Armageddon. In *The Day After Judgment,* the direct sequel to *Black Easter,* the world has ended and the remnants of mankind and its armies struggle against Satan and his minions as the city of Dis comes to Earth. In *A Case of Conscience,* a space-faring Jesuit priest must decide if an alien race is totally good or totally evil since it appears that the aliens have avoided original sin.

ANTHONY BOUCHER (See WILLIAM ANTHONY PARKER WHITE)

ERNEST BRAMAH (See ERNEST BRAMAH SMITH)

JOHN BRUNNER

The Traveler in Black. New York: Ace, 1971 [paper].

A series of stories centered on the traveler in black, a mysterious, godlike figure who moves about the land bringing order out of chaos. His physical identity varies, but his nature is always the same: in bringing order, his pronouncements and actions are both just and ironic, offering surprising truths to the mistakenly self-righteous. Contents: "Imprint of Chaos," "Break the Door of Hell," "The Wager Lost by Winning," and "Dread Empire."

EDGAR RICE BURROUGHS

The Mars or Barsoom Series
A Princess of Mars. Chicago: A. C. McClurg, 1917.
The Gods of Mars. Chicago: A. C. McClurg, 1918.
The Warlord of Mars. Chicago: A. C. McClurg, 1919.
Thuvia, Maid of Mars. Chicago: A. C. McClurg, 1920.
The Chessmen of Mars. Chicago: A. C. McClurg, 1922.
The Master Mind of Mars. Chicago: A. C. McClurg, 1928.
A Fighting Man of Mars. New York: Metropolitan, 1931.
Swords of Mars. Tarzana, CA: E. A. Burroughs, 1936.
Synthetic Men of Mars. Tarzana, CA: E. A. Burroughs, 1940.
Llana of Gathol. Tarzana, CA: E. A. Burroughs, 1948.
John Carter of Mars. New York: Canaveral, 1964.

Although traditionally considered science fiction, this series lacks the necessary ingredient of extrapolation that would make it part of that genre. Rather, it is a rationalized fantasy, and Burroughs has used occasional scientific pretenses to ease the reader's willing suspension of disbelief. Moreover, it would be impossible to measure the influence of this series on the development of contemporary sword and sorcery fantasy. In the series, an earthman, John Carter, is astrally transported in answer to the appeal of a beautiful princess. He uses his superior earthly muscles and his cunning to become warlord of Mars and marries the princess. Throughout the series, John Carter, his wife, family, and companions are continually involved in bizarre adventures, most of which involve the divergent races and constant warfare of Mars.

JAMES BRANCH CABELL

The Biography of the Life of Manuel

Beyond Life: Dizain des Demiurges. New York: McBride, 1919.

Figures of Earth: A Comedy of Appearances. New York: McBride, 1921.

The Silver Stallion: A Comedy of Redemption. New York: McBride, 1926.

The Witch Woman: A Trilogy About Her. New York: Farrar, Straus, 1948.

The Soul of Melicent. New York: Frederick A. Stokes, 1913; rev. ed. as *Domnei A Comedy of Woman-Worship.* New York: McBride, 1920.

Chivalry. New York: Harper, 1909; rev. ed. New York: McBride, 1921.

Jurgen: A Comedy of Justice. New York: McBride, 1919 [paper].

The Line of Love. New York: Harper, 1905; rev. ed. New York: McBride, 1921.

The High Place: A Comedy of Disenchantment. New York: McBride, 1923.

Gallantry: An Eighteenth Century Dizain in Ten Comedies with an Afterpiece. New York: Harper, 1907; rev. ed. as *Gallantry: Dizain des Fetes Galantes.* New York: McBride, 1922.

Something About Eve: A Comedy of Fig-Leaves. New York: McBride, 1927.

The Certain Hour (Dizain des Poetes). New York: McBride, 1916.

The Cords of Vanity: A Comedy of Shirking. New York: Doubleday, Page, 1909; rev. ed. New York: McBride, 1920.

From the Hidden Way: Being Seventy-five Adaptations. New York: McBride, 1916; rev. ed. New York: McBride, 1924.

The Jewel Merchants: A Comedy in One Act. New York: McBride, 1921.

The Rivet in Grandfather's Neck: A Comedy of Limitations. New York: McBride, 1923.

The Eagle's Shadow. New York: Doubleday, Page, 1904; rev. ed. New York: McBride, 1923.

The Cream of the Jest: A Comedy of Evasions. New York: McBride, 1917; rev. ed. New York: McBride, 1922.

The Lineage of Lichfield: An Essay in Eugenics. New York: McBride, 1922.

Straws and Prayer Books: Dizain des Diversions. New York: McBride, 1922.

Cabell's twenty-volume Life of Manuel is the most massive series in a genre that has a great affection for multi-volume works. Combining poetry and prose, the series has three major themes: chivalry, gallantry, and poetry itself. Set in the mythic, neo-medieval kingdom of Poictesme, and often starkly realistic in its treatment of human nature, the major focus is on the rise, life, fall, and deification of its central figure. The most acclaimed volumes are *Figures of Earth,* concerning the early adventures of Manuel and the formation of a group of comrades, the Fellowship of the Silver Stallion; *The Silver Stallion,* examining the reactions of the various members of the Fellowship of the Silver Stallion to Manuel's death and his deification; and *Jurgen,* concerning a journey through various bizarre environments and various amorous encounters with unusual women, such as Mrs. Satan.

ITALO CALVINO

Il Cavaliere Inesistente and Il Visconte Dimezzato [American title: *The Non-existent Knight and The Cloven Viscount*]. Torino: Giulio Einandi, 1957.

Il Cavaliere Inesistente: The being Agilulf is a white suit of armor with nothing inside it. A paladin in Charlemagne's army, he exists because he remains constantly aware of himself and his virtue. In juxtaposition, his squire, an idiot, is constantly in personal peril because he is completely unaware of himself. For example, he nearly drowns in a bowl of soup because he's not sure if he's to eat the soup or if the soup is to eat him. This farcial adventure is loosely unified by Agilulf's absurd quest to confirm the virginity of a woman he saved from rape many years prior.

Il Visconte Dimezzato: A viscount is halved by a cannonball. One half after being sealed with pitch, returns to his estate and establishes a reign of macabre terror. The other half, containing all the virtuous qualities, arrives later, saves a young maiden from the evil half, and fights a fantastic duel with the evil half. A delightful parody of the psychomachia traditionally associated with the fantasy genre.

LEWIS CARROLL (See CHARLES LUTWIDGE DODGSON)

ANGELA CARTER

The Infernal Desire Machines of Doctor Hoffman [American title: *The War of Dreams*]. London: Rupert Hart-Davis, 1972.

Machines driven by sexual desire create macabre and total delusion for an entire population in this grotesque fantasy. The protagonist, a civil servant, finally destroys the machines and his own innocence amid a kaleidoscope of shifting identities and allegiances.

ROBERT W[ILLIAM] CHAMBERS

In Search of the Unknown. New York: Harper and Brothers, 1904; rpt. Westport, CT: Hyperion, 1974.

A time-lost fantasy by the author of the classic horror collection *The King in Yellow* (1895). A young scientist enters a realm where prehistoric creatures have survived and have maintained unexpected and charmingly bizarre personalities.

JOY CHANT

Red Moon and Black Mountain: The End of the House of Kendreth. London: Allen & Unwin, 1970.

Oliver Powell and his younger brother and sister are summoned to "The Starlit Land" to confront Fendral, the fell enchanter and perverter of the ethereal star magic. Oliver becomes Li'vanh, Lord of Warriors, and is allied with the High King Kiron, the Princess In'serinna, and their human and animal following. An excellent epic fantasy that concludes with Oliver facing the necessity of human sacrifice with him as the victim. Suitable for juveniles.

G[ILBERT] K[EITH] CHESTERTON

The Man Who Was Thursday: A Nightmare. New York: Dodd, Mead, 1908.

A very atypical work that successfully treads the fine line between absurdity and seriousness. Mutability and the nature of the cosmos are the themes as six philosophic London spies unwittingly form a council of anarchists that they believe they are actually infiltrating. Little do they realize that the seventh and final member of their group is the only true anarchist, the awesomely enigmatic Sunday.

DONALD CORLEY

The House of Lost Identity. New York: McBride, 1927.

A fine collection of charming and whimsical tales that are paragons of Cabell's assessment in his introduction to the book: the unique "property of magic is its pleasing ability to coerce 'nature' . . . . " Contents: "The House of Lost Identity," "The Price of Reflection," "The Daimyo's Bowl," "Figs," "The Manacles of Youth," "The Ghost-Wedding," "The Glass Eye of Throgmorton," "The Legend of the Little Horses," "The Tale that the Ming Bell Told," "The Book of Debts," and "The Song of the Tombelaine."

F[RANCIS] MARION CRAWFORD

Khaled: A Tale of Arabia. 2 vols. New York: Collier, 1890.

A djinn is allowed to become a man but can only gain a soul and the true paradise of Allah if he wins the love of a self-centered and petulant princess. Interesting for its action and pseudo-orientalism.

AVRAM DAVIDSON

Peregrine: Primus. New York: Walker, 1971.

A picaresque sword and sorcery novel that was to be the first in a trilogy that has yet to be continued. It is the episodic and loosely connected quest by the young bastard of a pagan king for his brother. Set in a society gone dogmatically Christian, the novel is chiefly distinguished by the protagonist's traveling companions: Atilla the Fourth, king of a horde of about eleven warriors; Stingy Gus, caesar of a city-state; Eudoxia, a madame; Claud, who acts the idiot; and Appledore, philosopher and sorcerer.

The Phoenix and the Mirror [or The Enigmatic Speculum]. Garden City, NY: Doubleday, 1969.

Vergil Magus, a sorcerer, is commissioned to construct a major speculum —a virgin mirror that reveals more than just reflection—to discover the whereabouts of a kidnapped maiden. The excellent alchemical adventure of the construction of the speculum almost overshadows Vergil's love quest for the maiden and his final confrontation with the legendary Phoenix.

L[YON] SPRAGUE DE CAMP

The Fallible Fiend. New York: Signet, 1973 [paper].

A fiend from a parallel plane is summoned by magic. Delightful episodes occur as the fiend misunderstands his commands and tries to function in a totally alien environment, which is, of course, quite normal for the reader. Deteriorates somewhat at the end as the fiend becomes a hero and saves civilization.

The Goblin Tower. New York: Pyramid, 1968 [paper].

A highly episodic sword and sorcery fantasy that is part of de Camp's loosely connected novels that focus on the device of alternate planes of existence. As is typical of de Camp's fiction, this is filled with fine secondary characters: a lusty girl, a doddering sorcerer, and a strong lout. The novel reaches an effective dénouement as the young king who has fled his kingdom to avoid a ritual beheading and his companions deliver a chest of magic scrolls that has become incidental in light of the happenings along the way.

The Clocks of Iraz. New York: Pyramid, 1971 [paper].

The sequel to *The Goblin Tower* (see above) and the continued adventures of the fugitive king and jack-of-all-trades Jorian. He still cannot overcome his attraction to the least attractive member of his former harem and continues to search for her. As is expected in de Camp's fiction, there are many fine moments of magic, action, and characterization.

L[YON] SPRAGUE DE CAMP and FLETCHER PRATT

The Incomplete Enchanter Series
The Incomplete Enchanter. New York: Henry Holt, 1941.
The Castle of Iron: A Science Fantasy Adventure. New York: Gnome, 1950.
The Wall of Serpents. New York: Avalon, 1960.

Harold Shea and his companions learn that they can transport themselves to various literary realms through a combination of magic and mathematics. In *The Incomplete Enchanter*, the characters journey first into Norse mythology and then into Edmund Spenser's *Faerie Queene*. In *The Castle of Iron*, the setting is Ariosto's *Orlando Furioso*. *The Wall of Serpents* collects two earlier short stories—"Wall of Serpents" (1953) and "The Green Magician" (1954). They are set in the realms of the *Kalevala* and Irish mythology, respectively. Throughout the series, a comic tone is maintained as characters lose their memories, inadvertently change into wolves, confront awesome sorcerers and beasts, and, in *The Incomplete Enchanter*, are even present for Ragnarok, the final battle of Norse mythology when the gods and all things are destroyed. An omnibus volume, *The Compleat Enchanter: The Magical Adventures of Harold Shea* (Garden City, NY: Nelson Doubleday [The Science Fiction Book Club], 1975), contains *The Incomplete Enchanter* and *The Castle of Iron* but omits *The Wall of Serpents.*

GORDON R[UPERT] DICKSON

The Dragon and the George. Garden City, NY: Nelson Doubleday [The Science Fiction Book Club], 1976.

A fine fantasy romp concerning a maiden who is lost in an oppressively mundane everyday world and found in a world of magic, wonder, and knighthood. Her boyfriend's mind is projected into the body of a talking dragon to effect her rescue, and the company he accumulates on his quest and their often burlesque adventures make this one of the most pleasing examples of rationalized fantasy.

CHARLES LUTWIDGE DODGSON

Carroll, Lewis, pseud. *Alice's Adventures in Wonderland.* London: Macmillan, 1865.

─────. *Through the Looking Glass and What Alice Found There.* London: Macmillan, 1872 [actually released in 1871].

Through the artistry of Walt Disney, the adventures of Alice have become enormously popular, and it is rare to find someone who is not aware of her journeys through Dodgson's "fairy tale" settings. However, examination of the two books from an adult and/or scholarly point of view reveals that Alice's adventures often are excursions into the darker portions of human consciousness, and that *Alice's Adventures in Wonderland* with its major theme of change and *Through the Looking Glass* with its structural model of the chess game are dark narratives focusing on a repressed Victorian child overwhelmed and intimidated by capricious and illogical adults and authority figures. Dodgson uses this repressive situation to illustrate the essential honesty and straightforwardness of children.

DIANE DUANE

The Door Into Fire. New York: Dell, 1979 [paper].

Despite an overly cute "Overture" by David Gerrold, Duane's first book publication effectively combines a diverse number of elements with a sword & sorcery frame. Herewiss is the first male in eons to possess an internal magical flame of awesome power. However, the various instruments that the females use to focus and control their flames shatter whenever Herewiss attempts to use them. He does find initial help through a carnal relationship with a goddess and through a friendship with a fire elemental. Ultimately, he finds true control when his friends are threatened by a primeval being that Herewiss releases from a portal in an enigmatic city. Interwoven into the plot are Duane's excellent handling of the homo- and heterosexual triangles among Herewiss, his friend Prince Freelorn, and Segnbora, a woman who is also trying to control her flame. In addition, Duane's characterization of the humanization of the fire elemental brings a strong poignancy to the novel.

LORD DUNSANY (See EDWARD JOHN MORETON DRAX PLUNKETT)

E[RIC] R[UCKER] EDDISON

The Worm Ouroboros: A Romance. London: Jonathan Cape, 1922.

A psychomachia that is set on an imaginary Mercury and fought by the forces of Demonland and Witchland. Considered by many to be an allegory of the fall of Lucifer (the sorcerer-king of Witchland) and to be one of the best examples of a non-extrapolated environment. As its title—a major symbol of the eternal cycle—indicates, the novel has no resolution but ends with the realization that struggle must continue for eternity.

PHILIP JOSÉ FARMER

Night of Light. New York: Berkley, 1966 [paper] ; rpt. New York: Garland, 1975.

John Carmody, a vicious criminal, is transformed into a priest by the miraculous "night of light" (a periodic solar flare) and fathers a new god to replace the one he'd slain in his previous evil existence. This, like other Farmer novels, is distinguished by the mixture of the real and the unreal, the mystical and the mundane.

The World of Tiers Series

Maker of Universes. New York: Ace, 1965 [paper] ; rpt. New York: Garland, 1975.

Gates of Creation. New York: Ace, 1966 [paper] .

A Private Cosmos. New York: Ace, 1968 [paper] .

Behind the Walls of Terra. New York: Ace, 1970 [paper] .

The Lavalite World. New York: Ace, 1977 [paper] .

The World of Tiers series, also known as the Pocket Universe series, focuses on a race of superior beings who created totally new universes for their personal toys. Jadawin, also known as Robert Wolff, has created the pocket universe that most of the action takes place in. Humanized by his contact with mankind, Jadawin is converted from a typical scheming, arrogant, and uncaring "Lord" to a more involved and compassionate individual. Much of the action of the series is generated by Jadawin's conflicts with Kickaha the Trickster, also known as Paul James Finnegan and probably a Farmer self-portrait, as the two struggle for control of Jadawin's desirable pocket universe. This is a complicated and fascinating series in which Farmer explores the nature of artistic and literary creation, often expressing his views through the female Lord Anana, Jadawin's sister.

CHARLES G[RANDISON] FINNEY

The Circus of Dr. Lao. New York: Viking, 1935.

The inhabitants of Abalone, Arizona, are entertained by the wonders of Dr. Lao's circus: a medusa, a chimera, a werewolf, and a satyr, all authentic. The circus' finale is a ritual offering to an ancient and unknown god, and each spectator experiences an ironic, personal, and horrible vision of self during the ceremony.

"The Magician Out of Manchuria." In *Unholy City and Magician Out of Manchuria*. New York: Pyramid, 1968 [paper].

Finney's magician is a lazy and dishonest brigand and con man who sheds his skin at various inopportune intervals because of his serpent lineage. Along with a queen made beautiful by magic, an ass, and an assistant, the magician is involved in adventures and hairbreadth escapes. His dalliances and rescue of the Queen of Lust are among the best moments in this novelette which also includes such items as the magician's paraphrase of James Joyce's *A Portrait of the Artist as a Young Man* to the ass. Funny, often esoteric, and a heavy-handed criticism of socialism.

GEORGE U. FLETCHER (See FLETCHER PRATT)

ALAN GARNER

The Weirdstone of Brisingamen. London: Collins, 1960.

Although considered primarily as a juvenile, this is one of the few books that evokes a sense of wonder comparable to Tolkien's Trilogy (see below). Two 20th century children and the immortal Merlin seek a talisman that is essential to the safety of the world and to the preservation of the sleeping King Arthur.

The Moon of Gomrath. London: Collins, 1963.

The sequel to *The Weirdstone of Brisingamen* which continues Garner's excellent amalgamation of Western and Northern European mythology and the geography of his hometown Alderley in Cheshire. Susan, one of the young protagonists, finds herself the focus of the yet undefeated evil forces due to a magical bracelet she wears. The episodes involving the Wild Hunt and the "Old Magic," the seemingly ill-advised powers that the children summon, comprise two of the most effective portions of the book.

RANDALL GARRETT

Too Many Magicians. New York: Doubleday, 1966; rpt. Boston: Gregg, 1978.

An excellent whodunit set in an alternate universe where the Plantagenets still rule and magic is an honored profession. The main thrust of the novel is the solving of a seemingly sorcerous murder that takes place at a magicians' and sorcerers' convention. For a comparable work, see James Gunn's *The Magicians* below.

JANE GASKELL (See JANE LYNCH)

KENNETH GRAHAME

The Wind in the Willows. London: Methuen, 1908.

A classic among contemporary beast fables with an adventuresome toad, a mole, a water rat, and a badger as its well-characterized protagonists. In a variety of ways, the novel is the celebration of the English countryside and an examination of the relationships between the worlds of man and nature. While the toad's adventures have been more frequently remembered than the other protagonists', such episodes as how mole learns to love the river, rat's infatuation with the life of a sailor, mole's night in the Wild Wood, and the vision of Pan on the river bank are of equal, if not greater, value.

NICHOLAS STUART GRAY

The Stone Cage. London: Dobson, 1963.

An amplification of the Brothers Grimm tale of Rapunzel. The child Rapunzel is taken by guile from her parents by a witch who attempts to raise the child as a witch. With the protection of a cynical cat, Tomlyn, and an idealistic raven, Marshall, Rapunzel grows to womanhood unaffected by the spells and machinations of the witch, Mother Gothel. However, before the beautiful maiden can be united with her beloved prince, she, Tomlyn, and Marshall, with the aid of the wizard Macpherson, must defeat the witch and endure a necromantic exile to the dark side of the moon.

ROGER LANCELYN GREEN

From the World's End. A Fantasy. Leicester, U.K.: Edmund Ward, [1948].

A dark tale of two lovers who spend a night in the house on the edge of the world. They are separated and drawn into the unacceptable extremes of caritas and cupiditas by visitations from the fairy folk. The book parallels C. S. Lewis' use of the celestial and earthy Venus in *That Hideous Strength* (1946) and is distinguished by Green's knowledge of Celtic and Welsh mythology.

JAMES GUNN

The Magicians. New York: Scribner's, 1976.

A fantasy-mystery set in the 20th century in which a detective joins forces with a fetching sorceress and a mathematical wizard to discover the true name of the leader of a magical "covention." Only by gaining the control of the true name can the three protagonists defeat the evil wizard's plan to unleash Satan and his minions on the world.

H[ENRY] RIDER HAGGARD

The She Trilogy

Wisdom's Daughter: The Final and Love Story of She-Who-Must-Be-Obeyed. London: Hutchinson, [1923].

She: A History of Adventure. New York: Harper & Brothers, 1886 [paper].

Ayesha: the Return of She. London: Ward Lock, 1905.

While the style and devices of these 19th-century lost-race romances are a bit difficult for the 20th-century reader, the She Trilogy continues to maintain an unusual appeal through its immortal white goddess and her search for the reincarnation of her long-dead lover, Kallikrates, plus its invariable true-blue, confused male protagonists. While *Wisdom's Daughter* is published last, it is the background novel for the series and recounts Ayesha's origin, youth, and murder of her lover. A related novel is *She and Allan* (New York: Longmans, Green, 1921; rpt. Van Nuys, CA: Newcastle, 1976). In this combination of two of Haggard's most popular protagonists, Allan Quatermain journeys into the spirit world in search of his dead wife and meets Ayesha. Although he rejects Ayesha's offer of immortality, he does aid her in putting down a revolt against her rule.

H[ENRY] RIDER HAGGARD and ANDREW LANG

The World's Desire. New York: Longmans, Green, 1890.

A continuation of the *Odyssey* in which Odysseus, finding everyone at home dead of a plague, travels to Egypt in search of the world's desire, the immortal Helen of Troy. Odysseus' cunning is overcome by Pharaoh's wife and sister, the sorceress Meriamun, and by court intrigue. He and Helen find their love thwarted by death and the fates.

ISIDORE HAIBLUM

The Tsaddik of the Seven Wonders. New York: Ballantine, 1971 [paper].

A farcical yiddish fantasy that must contain every cliché ever associated with the Jewish stereotype. A Hebrew wise man and time traveler, the tsaddik, and his homunculus, Greenburg, join forces with a dimensional civil servant and combine their magic and technology to close an inter-dimensional rift caused by a greedy, interplanetary real estate agent.

ROBERT A[NSON] HEINLEIN

Glory Road. New York: Putnam, 1963.

In this robust sword and sorcery adventure, a disenchanted and purpose-less Oscar Gordon is recruited by the devastatingly attractive empress of the twenty universes and takes to heroing and the glory road. The characters are frolicsome, and there is a constant interchange between the practical and the philosophical, the flesh and the spirit. The flesh wins frequently. Uniquely Heinlein in its combinations of romanticism and scepticism, magic and science, gruffness and sentimentality.

"Magic, Inc." In *Waldo and Magic, Inc.* Garden City, NY: Doubleday, 1950.

A matter-of-fact look at magic as a business in a realm that accepts magic shops as easily as supermarkets. As in any business community, there is competition and crime. The protagonist must deal with a protection racket run by the devil, and to do so, he enlists the help of an erudite African witch doctor, a charming old witch, and a government agent.

FRANK HERBERT

The God Makers. New York: G. P. Putnam's, 1972.

What begins as a straight-forward science fiction novel soon becomes a mystical and religious fantasy as a young explorer dies, undergoes rites of passage, and is reborn as a god of awesome power.

WILLIAM HOPE HODGSON

The Nightland: A Love Tale. London: Nash, 1912; rpt. Westport, CT: Hyperion, 1976.

A far-future novel centered on the dying remnants of humanity and the quest of a strangely transported 19th-century man to rescue a girl who is the reincarnation of his previous lost love. His journey between the only two remaining havens of humanity in a land gone dark and evil is the most effective portion of the book; the return trip with the girl dissolves into an exposé of Victorian sexual inhibitions and urges. There is a revised and condensed version, titled *The Dream of X*, which was printed in paperback by Harold Page of New York to protect Hodgson's American copyright (1912). It includes thirteen of Hodgson's poems that are not in the first edition and has been reprinted by Donald Grant (West Kingston, RI, 1977).

ROBERT E[RVIN] HOWARD

The Conan Series & Related Volumes by Other Authors

Conan the Conqueror: The Hyborean Age. New York: Gnome, 1950.

The Sword of Conan. New York: Gnome, 1952.

King Conan. New York: Gnome, 1953.

The Coming of Conan. New York: Gnome, 1953.

Conan the Barbarian. New York: Gnome, 1954.

Tales of Conan with L. Sprague de Camp. New York: Gnome, 1955.

Conan with L. Sprague de Camp and Lin Carter. New York: Lancer, 1967 [paper].

Conan of Cimmeria with L. Sprague de Camp and Lin Carter. New York: Lancer, 1969 [paper].

Conan the Freebooter with L. Sprague de Camp. New York: Lancer, 1968 [paper].

Conan the Wanderer with L. Sprague de Camp and Lin Carter. New York: Lancer, 1968 [paper].

Conan the Adventurer with L. Sprague de Camp. New York: Lancer, 1966 [paper].

Conan the Buccaneer by L. Sprague de Camp and Lin Carter. New York: Lancer, 1971 [paper].

Conan the Warrior. Ed. L. Sprague de Camp. New York: Lancer, 1967 [paper].

Conan the Usurper with L. Sprague de Camp. New York: Lancer, 1967 [paper].

Conan the Conqueror. Ed. L. Sprague de Camp. New York: Lancer, 1967 [paper].

Conan the Avenger with Björn Nyberg and L. Sprague de Camp. New York: Lancer, 1968 [paper] [expansion of Howard, Nyberg, and de Camp's *The Return of Conan*. New York: Gnome, 1957].

Conan of Aquilonia by L. Sprague de Camp and Lin Carter. New York: Ace, 1977 [paper].

Conan of the Isles by L. Sprague de Camp and Lin Carter. New York: Lancer, 1968 [paper].

Immensely popular, Howard's sword and sorcery novels and collections featuring the barbarian Conan have had significant influence on the development of contemporary popular fantasy. These adventures pit the barbaric and guileless warrior and his broad sword against wizards, ghouls, sorceresses, mad kings, beasts, gods, and mortals. Most of Howard's Conan tales were written in the mid 1930's, but since the 1950's, other authors—most notably L. Sprague de Camp and Lin Carter—have completed unfinished Howard manuscripts or adopted the barbarian as their own. There is even a parody of Howard by Poul Anderson, "The Barbarian," in the May, 1956, issue of *Fantasy and Science Fiction*. Most recently, Karl Edward Wagner has been editing the tales as they originally appeared in *Weird Tales* for Berkley Publishing, 1977 [paper].

The Solomon Kane Collections

The Moon of Skulls. New York: Centaur, 1969 [paper].

The Hand of Kane. New York: Centaur, 1970 [paper].

Solomon Kane. New York: Centaur, 1971 [paper].

Written in the late 1920's and the early 1930's, these are the tales of Howard's other heroic figure, and Solomon Kane, an oppressively puritan character, was Howard's first sword and sorcery protagonist. The stories are set in a sixteenth-century locale complete with black magic, fiends, monsters, and, for the virtuous Kane, maidens-that-must-be-denied.

C[HARLES] J[OHN] CUTCLIFFE [WRIGHT] HYNE

The Lost Continent. New York: Harper; London: Hutchinson, 1900 [simultaneous publication?].

A young Atlantean returns to his homeland to find a heartless and evil usurper on the throne. His initial attempt at revolt fails and his beloved is buried alive. Seven years later he returns, tries to lead another revolt, and restores his beloved to life. However, the virtuous priesthood realizes that the evil queen, Phorenice, cannot be destroyed by force and that they must destroy the entire island to rid the world of her insanity. A few of the valiant rebels are sent off on an ark with the accumulated wisdom of Atlantis to found a new world. A highly descriptive work that enjoyed significant popularity when it was serialized in *Pearson's* in 1899.

PIERS ANTHONY DILLINGHAM JACOB

Anthony, Piers, pseud. *A Spell for Chameleon.* New York: Ballantine, 1977 [paper].

Everyone in the magical realm of Xanith has a sorcerous talent except Bink of the North Village. Bink's seeming weakness is the cause of his exile. His search for his own spell or magic embroils him and his comrades in a quest to the evil magician Trent and in numerous conflicts with elves, dwarves, krakens, dragons, and a sphinx. A charmingly human tale that is distinguished by three of the better female characterizations in contemporary fantasy: Iris, Chameleon, and Franchon.

JOHN JAKES

The Last Magicians. New York: Signet, 1969 [paper].

A tale of wonder and psychomachia that centers on Cham, the last of the evil red magicians, who has denounced his final vows to the fell god of his order, "The Unborn." Trapped within a new order that is antithetical to magic and to him, he is forced to confront his past master to survive in the new world. The characterization of Cham and his dilemma is unusually well done. For comparable works that feature an evil protagonist, see Michael Moorcock's Elric series and Karl Edward Wagner's Kane series below.

JAAN KANGILASKI

The Seeking Sword. New York: Ballantine, 1977 [paper].

An unusual combination of fantasy and horror featuring a stone age shaman who has placed his soul in a sword. Controlling all who handle it, the sentient sword has survived through the ages successfully seeking revenge on all the descendants of an enemy tribe. The action in the novel is set shortly after the shootings at Kent State University and contains many topical allusions. The modern characters are particularly realistic, and their attempts to cope with the sword's bloody acts are well delineated and pointedly human.

CHARLES KINGSLEY

The Water Babies: A Fairy Tale for a Land Baby. London: Macmillan, 1863; rpt. New York: Garland, 1976.

A young chimney sweep is aided by the fairy queen in escaping his tormentors and his dirt. He is transformed into a water-baby (a water sprite) and is gradually purged of his rough humanity through the wonder of his experience and his new friends. Particularly noteworthy for its settings, characters, and involved incidents which reflect Kingsley's ability to create a well-developed fantasy realm.

KATHERINE KURTZ

The Deryni Series

Camber of Culdi: Volume IV in the Chronicles of the Deryni. New York: Ballantine, 1976 [paper].

Saint Camber: Volume II in the Legends of Camber of Culdi. New York: Ballantine, 1978.

Deryni Rising: Volume I in the Chronicles of the Deryni. New York: Ballantine, 1970 [paper].

Deryni. Checkmate: Volume II in the Chronicles of the Deryni. New York: Ballantine, 1972 [paper].

High Deryni: Volume III in the Chronicles of the Deryni. New York: Ballantine, 1973 [paper].

In this sword and sorcery series, a royal house is defended by a young king, Kelson, and his father's trusted advisor, Morgan, a member of the half-human, persecuted, and sorcerous Deryni race. Kelson and Morgan must battle rival Deryni through powers arcane, resolve the rift between the human and Deryni races through social and psychological reform, unify the state and the church through politics, and Kelson must ultimately come to terms with his own Deryni powers. While the affairs of state do occupy a large portion of the series, there are also a number of poignantly human moments: the wedding night of the discovered Haldene heir, Kelson's ancestor who has been living the religious life as a monk, is accomplished with great beauty in *Camber of Culdi,* and the tragic love of Bronwyn and Kevin in *Deryni Checkmate* displays Kurtz's ability to characterize human emotion and personal tragedy. It should be noted that while *Camber of Culdi* is billed as the fourth volume in the series, it is actually the background novel for the chronicle. It occurs two hundred years before Kelson's coronation and is a biography of the Deryni patron saint, Culdi, and the history of the reinstatement of Kelson's royal line, the Haldene kings. This is one of the better series in all of contemporary fantasy and successfully rivals Andre Norton's Witch World and Roger Zelazny's Amber series (see below). It is complex without being confusing, effectively narrated, and based on the theme of the resolution of prejudice through rites of passage. It does, however, have an unsatisfying arcane resolution.

R[APHAEL] A[LOYSIUS] LAFFERTY

The Devil Is Dead. New York: Avon, 1971 [paper] ; rpt. Boston: Gregg, 1977.

A meandering and difficult narrative of a sea journey on a ship captained by what appears to be the devil. The prose and plot are involved and convoluted, and the major theme of appearance and reality constantly distorts the meaning of the action, making it difficult to understand. The ultimate question of the novel raised is not whether the captain is the devil or, when the captain dies, if the devil is really dead. Rather, it is the following paradox: if the devil should die, then, would not evil be unrestrained and be far worse than it normally is?

SANDERS ANNE LAUBENTHAL

Excalibur. New York: Ballantine, 1973 [paper].

A modern Arthurian romance in which the Pendragon comes to 20th-century Mobile, Alabama, to recover Excalibur from a pre-Columbian ruin. Includes all the trappings of the legend, including a grail quest, and an excellent cast of good and evil female characters, including Morgan le Fey and Morgause of Orkney.

TANITH LEE

Night's Master. New York: DAW, 1978 [paper].

A loosely connected series of tales interconnected by the often strange and "unhuman" interests of Azhrarn, Prince of Demons and Night's Master. His machinations among the affairs of men and women produce bizarre and ironic dramas that compare favorably with Jack Vance's

Dying Earth tales and Sylvia Townsend Warner's *Kingdoms of Elfin.* The semi-sequel to this volume—*Death's Master.* New York: DAW, 1979 [paper] —focuses on Uhlume, Death's Master, and also produces macabre and gothic tales as human kind attempts to win its way to immortality through hoax and wit.

The Birthgrave Trilogy

The Birthgrave. New York: DAW, 1975 [paper] .

Vazkor, Son of Vazkor. New York: DAW, 1978 [paper] .

Quest for the White Witch. New York: DAW, 1978 [paper] .

> A two-generation, mother and son, fantasy. A young woman awakes in a volcano suffering from amnesia in *The Birthgrave.* Forced into a world she neither knows nor understands, she experiences life as the mate of Vazkor, a sorcerer and conqueror. She finally discovers her true identity as an immortal and is able to use her magical powers. In *Vazkor, Son of Vazkor,* her son, who she abandoned to be raised as the son of a nomad chief, discovers his origin and goes in search of his albino mother, who he believes has ruthlessly slain his father. The search is completed in *Quest for the White Witch,* as the son comes to his full power as an immortal. The series ends with one of the few examples of justifiable incest in all of literature.

URSULA K[ROEBER] LE GUIN

The Earthsea Trilogy

A Wizard of Earthsea. Berkley: Parnassus, 1968; rev. ed. London: Victor Gollancz, 1971.

The Tombs of Atuan. New York: Atheneum, 1971.

The Farthest Shore. New York: Atheneum, 1972.

> Le Guin's tales of the wizard Ged are among the most highly acclaimed of contemporary fantasies. Her epic and human chronicle of the training, maturation, and final days of the archmage is a well-paced narrative filled with well-researched magical lore and marked by serious explorations of the questions of identity, power, and ethics. In addition, her characterization of the sorcerous and world-wise dragons is one of the best in all fantasy. Suitable for juveniles.

FRITZ LEIBER

Night's Black Agents. Sauk City, WI: Arkham House, 1947.

> This collection is Leiber's first book, and, while its fantasy content is restricted to three of its ten short stories—"The Man Who Never Grew Young" and two Fafhrd and the Gray Mouser tales, "The Sunken Land" and "Adept's Gambit"—it is important for the often clumsy, but very enlightening, statements of Leiber's philosophy and opinions. For example, his contempt for the insulating and restrictive nature of excessive civilization is made very clear. The other stories in the collection are quite correctly labeled horror in the table of contents: "Smoke Ghost," "The Automatic Pistol," "The Inheritance," "The Hill and the Hole," "The Dreams of Albert Moreland," "The Hound," and "Diary in the

Snow." The 1978 paperback reprint (New York: Berkley) adds two horror stories that did not appear in the first edition: "The Girl with the Hungry Eyes" and "A Bit of the Dark World." Both editions contain an interesting foreword in which Leiber explains the birth of the Fafhrd and the Gray Mouser series (see below).

The Fafhrd and the Gray Mouser Series

Two Sought Adventure: Exploits of Fafhrd and the Gray Mouser. New York: Gnome, 1957.

Swords and Deviltry. New York: Ace, 1970 [paper] ; rpt. Boston: Gregg, 1977.

Swords Against Death. New York: Ace, 1970 [paper] ; rpt. Boston: Gregg, 1977.

Swords in the Mist. New York: Ace, 1968 [paper] ; rpt. Boston: Gregg, 1977.

Swords Against Wizardry. New York: Ace, 1968 [paper] ; rpt. Boston: Gregg, 1977.

The Swords of Lankhmar. New York: Ace, 1968 [paper] ; rpt. Boston: Gregg, 1977.

Swords and Ice Magic. New York: Ace, 1977 [paper] ; rpt. Boston: Gregg, 1977.

Rime Isle. Chapel Hill, NC: Whispers Press, 1977.

These collections and one novel (*The Swords of Lankhmar*) are among the most popular examples of sword and sorcery fantasy. The series is pure fun as the northern barbarian Fafhrd and the diminutive thief the Gray Mouser fight, connive, and love their ways through quests, adventures, and dilemmas. Leiber offers the best description of the series in "Adept's Gambit" (see *Night's Black Agents* above): "Material relating to them has, on the whole, been scattered by annalists, since they were heroes too disreputable for classic myth, too cryptically independent ever to let themselves be tied to a folk, too shifty and improbable in their adventures to please the historian, too often involved with a riff-raff of dubious demons, unfrocked sorcerers, and discredited deities—a veritable underworld of the supernatural."

C[LIVE] S[TAPLES] LEWIS

The Space Trilogy

Out of the Silent Planet. London: Lane, 1938.

Perelandra [occasionally titled *Voyage to Venus: Perelandra* in later editions]. London: Lane, 1943.

That Hideous Strength: A Modern Fairy-Tale for Grown-Ups. London: Lane, 1945; abr. ed. as *The Tortured Planet.* New York: Avon, [1958] [paper].

Sometimes called the Ransom Trilogy after its protagonist, this is an examination of the nature of creation, life, and ethics. In the first two volumes, Ransom travels to Mars and Venus to witness the advent of life and intelligence. In the third volume, Ransom returns to Earth, and, as the Arthurian pendragon, he successfully confronts a major threat to Man, God, and existence. The series is distinguished by its extensive mythological and theological content as Lewis gives his substantial intellect full rein. Its major theme is that Man must be in accord with divine creation and elemental law if he is to be successful and happy, and throughout the series, it is made quite clear that science and technology lead Man away from his individual and cosmic destiny.

DAVID LINDSAY

A Voyage to Arcturus. London: Methuen, 1920; rpt. Boston: Gregg, 1977.

A vivid and difficult novel that at times seems to defy understanding. However, it never denies wonder, and its parallel between biological alternations and perceptions is one of the most unusual in all fantasy. The excellent description of the planet Tormance, a place where physical change is a way of life, and the protagonist Maskull, an Earthling who has been persuaded to travel to this metamorphic environment, are well integrated as alien visitor and alien place try to come to terms in the arena of truth and perception, godhood and humanity. A classic of macabre imagination with a unique ending as Maskull dies and is reborn.

H[OWARD] P[HILLIPS] LOVECRAFT

The Dream-Quest of Unknown Kadath. Buffalo, NY: Shroud, 1955 [paper].

Originally written in 1926 and not published separately until this edition, this is one of Lovecraft's rare excursions outside of the realm of the horror genre, although it does contain elements of horror and certainly uses portions of the Cthulhu mythos. It is written very much in the style of Lord Dunsany (see Plunkett below) and utilizes Lovecraft's frequent protagonist, Randolph Carter. It concerns Carter's "dream-quest" through a fantastic metropolis where he meets a number of horrible and pleasing creatures. Ultimately, the traveler confronts one of the most despicable of the Cthulhu dieties, Nyarlathotep, eventually falls back into his waking world, and discovers that he has been traveling through his native Boston.

JANE LYNCH

The Atlantis Series

Gaskell, Jane, pseud. *The Serpent.* London: Hodder and Stoughton, 1963.

————. *Atlan.* London: Hodder and Stoughton, 1965.

————. *The City.* London: Hodder and Stoughton, 1966.

An involved series with significant political content and intrigue. All the volumes are cliff-hangers, as the princess, Cija, spends her first seventeen years in cloistered isolation and then strikes out into the world. She becomes involved in white and black magic, marriage to a semi-human overlord, many wars and battles, court politics, and numerous relationships. After many years as a wanderer, she discovers her semi-human overlord, falls in love with him, and shares his conquest of Atlantis. Rewarding for the reader who will persevere in spite of the often overly dense prose and excessive melodrama.

GEORGE MACDONALD

Phantastes: A Faerie Romance. London: Smith, Elder, 1858.

An allegorical journey through fairyland filled with all the wondrous temptations and challenges of the quest for love and self. Anodos, the protagonist, wanders in a shadow land governed by magic, and in the course of his travels, he lives a wondrous life, dies, and is reborn to more fully experience the fairy world. Despite numerous opinions to the contrary, MacDonald's prose is not so difficult, and this adventure, amid reality and illusion, good and evil, perfection and fallibility, does share a sense of participation with the reader.

PATRICIA A. MCKILLIP

The Forgotten Beasts of Eld. New York: Atheneum, 1974.

A highly imagistic and descriptive setting surrounds the innocent Sybel, the child and protege of a wizard who, at his passing, left her a company of semi-legendary beasts, all excellent creatures. However, her ideal world is doomed to pass, and, torn between her love for a fosterling child and a knight, she is introduced to the outside world and its treachery and deceit.

The Riddle Master of Hed Trilogy

The Riddle-Master of Hed. New York: Atheneum, 1976.

Heir of Sea and Fire. New York: Atheneum, 1977.

Harpist in the Wind. New York: Atheneum, 1979.

This trilogy focuses on Morgan, prince of the provencial and agrarian land of Hed, and Raederle, his betrothed. In *The Riddle-Master of Hed,* Morgan, thinking himself only the leader of farmers, becomes the most successful student in the College of Riddle-Masters (seekers and interpreters of ancient wisdom) in the far-distant capital. Assuming a quest of awesome dimensions, he leaves the capital, becomes estranged from his agricultural heritage and his family, and solves a seven-hundred year old riddle, a key to ancient knowledge and sorcerous power. In *Heir of Sea and Fire,* the focus shifts to Raederle, Morgan's beloved, as she seeks to discover what has happened to Morgan who has journeyed to confront the enigmatic High One on Erlenstar Mountain. Morgan is accompanied on his quest for an understanding of the forces that bind his world together by the mysterious Harper who seems both his friend and enemy. At the conclusion of the second volume, Raederle must attempt to come to terms with a new Morgan, one who has been tormented, tempered, and transformed into a god-like figure after his stay with the High One, a being other than what anyone had expected. Morgan, too, must adjust to his new-found powers and seek peace for himself and his people. In *Harpist in the Wind,* Morgan must confront his final destiny. Joining himself to the land-magic of all the realms in his world and finally discovering the true nature of High One, Morgan discovers that it has fallen to him to harp the wind and to replace the dying god through a series of mythic and archetypal trials and quests.

DAVID MASON

The Deep Gods. New York: Lancer, 1973 [paper].

The mind and personality of a twentieth-century man are transmigrated into the dead body of a man who existed long before recorded history.

This pre-Edenic world of the far-distant past is teetering on the edge of destruction, and the commonality that binds all nature together before the Fall is in grave danger. The protagonist must confront the tragedy and deal with the deep gods—whales—as one of their wisest fellows has gone mad and threatens all creation.

WILLIAM MAYNE

A Game of Dark. London: Hamish Hamilton, 1971;

A psychological fantasy in which a boy, haunted by a dream of a destructive dragon, flees his own lack of sympathy for his ill father and his disinterest in his parents' morality. In his medieval dream world, he is trained by a lord and finally faces the dreaded white worm (dragon). Violating his chivalric training, he destroys the worm by reason rather than by combat. It is this commitment to reason that allows him to leave his dream world and return to cope with his actual life.

A[BRAHAM] MERRITT

The Ship of Ishtar. New York: G. P. Putnam's Sons, 1926.

A tour-de-force by one of the early masters of fantasy. Description, event, setting, and characterization are well handled as an American adventurer is drawn into a parallel world while staring at what seems to be an intricate and detailed ship model. On board the strange "Flying Dutchman," the Ship of Ishtar, he finds the deck evenly divided into black and white and discovers an eternal battle between the forces of good and evil as they each try to extend their portion of the ship and achieve complete sovereignty.

MICHAEL MOORCOCK

The Elric Series

Elric of Melniboné. London: Hutchinson, 1972 [No. 1]. A 1972 Lancer edition was entitled *The Dreaming City.*

Elric: the Return to Melniboné. Brighton-Seattle, WA; Unicorn, 1973 [paper] [not seen].

The Dreaming City. New York: Lancer, 1972 [paper] [No. 6?].

The Jade Man's Eyes. Brighton-Seattle, WA: Unicorn, 1973 [paper]. Later revised in *The Sailor on the Seas of Fate.*

The Stealer of Souls and Other Stories. London: Spearman, 1963 [No. 2].

The Sleeping Sorceress. London: New English Library, 1971 [No. 3]; abr. ed. New York: Lancer, 1972.

The Singing Citadel. Frogmore, UK: Mayflower, 1970 [paper] [No.5].

Stormbringer. London: Jenkins, 1965 [No.4].

The Revised Elric Series

Elric of Melniboné. New York: DAW, 1976 [paper].

The Sailor on the Seas of Fate. New York: DAW, 1976 [paper]. Includes the revision of *The Jade Man's Eyes.*

The Weird of the White Wolf. New York: DAW, 1977 [paper] . Revision of
   The Sleeping Sorceress.

The Vanishing Tower. New York: DAW, 1977 [paper] .

Stormbringer. New York: DAW, 1977 [paper] .

The Bane of the Black Sword. New York: DAW, 1977 [paper] .

> Moorcock's original series grew without too much attention to series
> coherency, and the reader should appreciate that the original Elric books
> listed above do not necessarily reflect a reading order based on internal
> chronology, nor can they since the original series does skip about and
> overlap. Unless the reader is a very serious Moorcock fan or scholar, the
> revised and clarified DAW series is recommended. However, Moorcock's
> Elric should not be neglected; he is one of the most unusual characters in
> all of fantasy, not just of sword and sorcery fantasy. Elric, the last in the
> line of a race of eldrich sorcerer-kings, wanders about in a world increas-
> ingly dominated by man, a race he views as short-lived and contemptible
> in their magic and ambitions. An albino and congenitally weak, Elric must
> depend on Stormbringer, his black rune blade, to drink souls and give
> him strength. Elric's powers, adventures, dark melancholy, fatalism, and
> tendency to drink the souls of those he loves best make him both a tragic
> and an alien figure, at once admirable and repulsive.

C[ATHERINE] L[UCILE] MOORE

Jirel of Joiry. New York: Paperback Library, 1969 [paper] .

> This collection would be noteworthy if only for the occurrence of one of
> the few female protagonists in fantasy in general and sword and sorcery
> fantasy in particular. It is, however, more than just that. Jirel's admirable
> courage in the face of horror and helplessness make her an exciting and
> dynamic figure, and Moore's description, settings, and dark devices are
> striking and original. "The Black God's Kiss," in which Jirel carries a very
> ironic gesture of affection for an enemy, is a particularly fine example of
> Moore's ability to endow her character with both human and superhuman
> characteristics. All of the short stories in this volume originally appeared
> in *Weird Tales* from 1934 to 1939 and first appeared in book form in
> *Shambleau and Others* (New York: Gnome, 1953) and *Northwest of
> Earth* (New York: Gnome, 1954). One of them, "Quest of the Starstone,"
> was written in collaboration with her husband, Henry Kuttner.

WILLIAM MORRIS

The Well at the World's End. Hammersmith: Kelmscott Press, 1896.

> Long considered Morris' masterpiece and considered by many one of the
> greatest fantasy novels ever written. A young boy flees his home and
> comes to manhood as a ruler and a warrior in a medieval realm. Along the
> way, he loves two women: one gives him suffering, the other joy. His
> greatest challenge comes at the end of the book when he must confront
> the power that can be his if he drinks from a magical well.

H[AROLD] WARNER MUNN

King of the World's Edge. New York: Ace, 1966 [paper].

The Ship From Atlantis [with Emil Petaja's *The Stolen Sun*]. New York: Ace [Double], 1967 [paper].

Merlin's Ring. New York: Ballantine, 1974 [paper].

> *The Ship from Atlantis* is the sequel to *King of the World's Edge* and *Merlin's Ring* utilizes the same characters without sustaining the plot of the first two novels. In *King of the World's Edge,* Myrdhinn and a few Britons escape the fall of the round table, journey to the New World (North American), and establish a settlement in opposition to the Toltecs and Mayans. In *The Ship from Atlantis,* Myrdhinn's (Merlin's) godson sails off on an Odyssey-like adventure and discovers a ship from destroyed Atlantis. On the ship is one of the more unusual female protagonists in fantasy, Corenice, a sorceress made of metal. Both *King of the World's Edge* and *The Ship from Atlantis* are reprinted in an omnibus volume, *Merlin's Godson* (New York: Ballantine, 1976), and it should be noted that *King of the World's Edge* made its first appearance in magazine form in 1939, some twenty-eight years before its sequel. *Merlin's Ring* is a vast epic fantasy that spans the age of Atlantis to the sixteenth century. Merlin's godson, Gwalachmai, uses his uncle's ring to endure through time and continually be reunited with his beloved, Corenice.

JOHN MYERS MYERS

Silverlock. New York: Dutton, 1949.

> A fantastic jaunt through a realm called The Commonwealth. The protagonist, a transported Earthling, accompanied by his multi-named guide (Taliesin), meets a homosexual Beowulf, Circe, the Green Knight, King Arthur, the Houynyhms, and Satan among others as he journeys through a series of experiences and realms that seem to be drawn from all that is wondrous in myth, legend, and literature.

ANDRE NORTON

The Witch World Series: Simon Tregarth and Family

Witch World. New York: Ace, 1963 [paper]; rpt. Boston: Gregg, 1977.

Web of the Witch World. New York: Ace, 1964 [paper]; rpt. Boston: Gregg, 1977.

Three Against the Witch World: [Beyond the Mind Barrier]. New York: Ace, 1965 [paper]; rpt. Boston: Gregg, 1977.

Warlock of the Witch World. New York: Ace, 1967 [paper]; rpt. Boston: Gregg, 1977.

Sorceress of the Witch World. New York: Ace, 1968 [paper]; rpt. Boston: Gregg, 1977.

The Witch World Series: Wereriders

The Crystal Gryphon. New York: Atheneum, 1972.

The Year of the Unicorn. New York: Ace, 1965 [paper]; rpt. Boston: Gregg, 1977.

The Jargoon Pard. New York: Atheneum, 1974.

The Witch World Series: Miscellaneous

Spell of the Witch World. New York: DAW, 1972 [paper]; rpt. Boston: Gregg, 1977.

Trey of Swords. New York: Grosset & Dunlap, 1977.

Zarsthor's Bane. New York: Ace, 1978 [paper].

> Andre Norton's Witch World series is one of the most celebrated in contemporary fantasy. Set in a matriarchial world governed by a cult of witches, it explores the human elements of fear, self-concept, ambition, greed, and power. While all of the tales are set in this realm, the series is subdivided into three categories. The major one, comprised of five novels, focuses on the transported Earthling Simon Tregarth and his family. Saved by the Siege Perilous, a magical transporter, from certain death on Earth, he marries one of the normally virginal witches, and they discover to their delight that her powers unexpectedly remain intact. Battling resurrected adepts from the past of Witch World, struggling against the dreaded scientific Kolder, and daring the threat of the witches themselves, they and their two sons and daughter defend themselves and their world and, at the same time, unravel many of its long-buried mysteries. The Wererider or shapechanger subdivision is more romance or love oriented than the main Tregarth division, and it is principally concerned with the discovery of self and the tolerance of uniqueness. The two miscellaneous short story collections deal with isolated activities outside the concerns of the other two divisions. Throughout the series, the wide and varied character of Norton's well conceived world is continually demonstrated. Well plotted and humanly characterized, all the works have an excellent spirit of adventure and romance, magic and science, and humanity and necessity.

MERVYN PEAKE

The Gormenghast Trilogy

Titus Groan. London: Eyre and Spottiswoode, 1946.

Gormenghast. London: Eyre and Spottiswoode, 1950.

Titus Alone. London: Eyre and Spottiswoode, 1959.

> Peake's Gormenghast Trilogy, long one of the more curious fantasies, centers on the labyrinth of Castle Gormenghast, its inhabitants, and its 77th Lord, Titus. Darkly Gothic, fatalistic, and ritualistic, it chronicles Titus' youth, rebellion, adventures and rite of passage as he discovers that, no matter how far he travels, he cannot escape his birthplace and domain. The 1968 Eyre and Spottiswoode edition of *Titus Groan* has a brief introduction by Anthony Burgess.

EDWARD JOHN MORETON DRAX PLUNKETT

Dunsany, Lord, pseud. *The King of Elfland's Daughter.* London: G. P. Putnam's Sons, 1924.

> A major influence on many contemporary fantasy authors—notably L. Sprague de Camp, Fritz Leiber, and H. P. Lovecraft—and considered

Dunsany's greatest novel. Alveric, an adventurous prince from of the Vale of Erl, takes an elf-princess as his bride. However, she can no more remain in the lands of men than a flower can live in ice. After bearing Alveric a son, Orion, she returns to the land of fairy. Alveric, armed with a magical sword formed from seventeen thunderbolts, pursues her. Thwarted by elfin magic, his love nonetheless proves to be the greater power, and finally his father-in-law reunites the lovers by making Erl part of fairyland. While Dunsany's prose is often difficult, there are moments of glowing description, and the themes of alienation, love, and the effect of alien knowledge are given effective shape through the language and the characters.

JOHN COWPER POWYS

Morwyn: or, The Vengeance of God. London: Cassell, 1937; rpt. New York: Arno, 1976.

A retired army captain falls in love with the daughter of a vivisector. When all three are struck by a divinely directed meteor, the father is killed and the two lovers are transported to Hell. While in Hell, the two lovers are befriended by the ancient Welsh poet, Taliesin. They need his protection as they are accosted by first the ghost of the father and then the spirits of all the sadists and vivisectors in Hell. The onslaught becomes so dire that they must awaken Merlin, who visits their own sins on the ghosts. They are then joined by Socrates and one of the ancient judges of the Golden Age, free one of the ancient Titans from his suffering, and return home. One of the few examples of didactic fantasy.

FLETCHER PRATT

Fletcher, George U., pseud. *The Well of the Unicorn.* New York: William Sloane, 1948; rpt. New York: Garland, 1975.

Considered one of the classics of contemporary fantasy, in this sword and sorcery adventure, Airar Avarson and the enchanter Meliboë together weld the free fishers, the star captains, and the Imperial Children of the Well into a strong force that repels the invading Vulkings and preserves democratic rule. At the end of the book, Airar and Meliboe come to the magical well and must decide if the peace a draft of its water promises is worth the price that it demands.

FRED SABERHAGEN

The Broken Lands Trilogy
The Broken Lands. New York: Ace, 1968.
The Black Mountains. New York: Ace, 1971 [paper].
Changeling Earth. New York: DAW, 1973 [paper].

As this trilogy opens, science and technology are suppressed and, in fact, negated by an ancient device to prevent another nuclear holocaust. Magic reigns supreme, and society has returned to a pre-industrial level. The conflict between science and magic and the rediscovery of the scientific past form the nucleus of most of the action, and finally the world is re-enlightened, the suppressive device destroyed, and magic banished.

CARL SHERRELL

Raum. New York: Avon, 1977 [paper].

Raum, an earl of Hell, is summoned by a wizard. When the wizard is slain, Raum is free to walk the earth. Initially cutting a path of blood and conquest through the world, he seeks Camelot and Merlin to discover the true nature of himself, the world, Satan, and Hell. As he experiences the world and life, he becomes more and more human and less demonic. As the novel progresses, he finds both love and despair as his demonic nature is totally erased. A swashbuckling work that is also marked by a strong element of tragedy and poignancy.

ROBERT SILVERBERG

The Book of Skulls. New York: Charles Scribner's Sons, 1972.

Four students, inspired and directed by the rediscovery of a long-lost manuscript, "The Book of Skulls," go in search of immortality, knowing full well that two of them must die.

CLIFFORD D[ONALD] SIMAK

The Enchanted Pilgrimage. New York: Berkley, 1975.

A pilgrimage of marvels and a search for knowledge. Mark Cornwall joins forces with a rafter goblin, a figure called the Gossiper, his true love Mary, a motorcyclist, and various other mythical creatures to journey to the Misty Mountains and find the Old Ones. While the end result is not what Mark expects as a scholar (and sadly not what the reader is lead to expect), the quest is in itself charming and more than compensates for the inappropriate ending.

ERNEST BRAMAH SMITH

Bramah, Ernest, pseud. *The Wallet of Kai Lung.* London: Grant Richards, 1900.

—————. *Kai Lung's Golden Hours.* London: Grant Richards, 1922.

—————. *Kai Lung Unrolls His Mat.* London: Grant Richards, 1928.

—————. *The Return of Kai Lung.* New York: Sheridan, 1937.

—————. *Kai Lung Beneath the Mulberry-Tree.* London: Grant Richards, 1940.

—————. *Kai Lung: Six: Uncollected Tales from Punch.* Ed. William White. Tacoma, WA: Non-Profit Press, 1974.

—————. *Moon of Much Gladness: Related by Kai Lung.* London: Cassell, 1932 [not seen].

All of the witty and comic Kai Lung volumes are structurally arranged as tale collections, much like *The Thousand Nights and One Night* and *The Canterbury Tales.* They are all set in a completely fictional China inhabited by dragons, maidens, adventurers, and magicians. Much of the charm of the tales is created by the conversion of supposed oriental homelies, tales, and parables into the English idiom.

NANCY SPRINGER

The Book of Suns. New York: Pocket Books, 1977 [paper] .

A well-told narrative in which two youths, a prince and a peasant, become blood brothers in a magical, medieval setting. They become the leaders of the fairy folk and scattered bands of virtuous people in a tyrannized and poisoned kingdom and overthrow the prince's evil father. In the process, they come to terms with their own mystical destinies, their loves, and their unexpected common parentage.

THOMAS BURNETT SWANN

Day of the Minotaur. New York: Ace, 1966 [paper] .

Most of Swann's fiction is set in ancient mythical or legendary lands and adopts their figures as characters. This novel is drawn from Cretan mythology and describes the final, fatal confrontation between intelligent beasts and man. The romance between the minotaur, Eunostos, and the half-woman, half-dryad, Thea, forms a poignant sub-plot.

Lady of the Bees. New York: Ace, 1976 [paper] .

Set in fictional Latium, this is the tale of how the dryad Mellonia (the eternal dryad who appears with Aeneas in Swann's *Green Phoenix.* New York: DAW, 1972 [paper]) and her companion, the young faun Sylvan, assist Remus and Romulus in regaining their usurped throne. An enlargement of the novelette "Where is the Bird of Fire?" (1962).

The Not-World. New York: DAW, 1975 [paper] .

Dierdre, an invalid and a novelist, finds unexpected adventures in the Not-World, a wooded remnant of the Celtic past peopled with things and creatures ancient and magical. Her quest for the imprisoned and seemingly youthful adventurer Dylan leads her to revelations of the mind and soul, the active verses the passive life, in this last bastion against the creeping mechanization of the oncoming Industrial Revolution. As always in Swann's fiction, science, technology, and civilization are seen as evil threats to wonder and magic.

J[OHN] R[ONALD] R[EUEL] TOLKIEN

The Lord of the Rings

The Hobbit or There and Back Again. London: Allen and Unwin, 1937; rev. ed. London: Allen and Unwin, 1951; 2nd rev. ed. London: Allen and Unwin, 1966.

The Fellowship of the Ring. London: Allen and Unwin, 1954. 2nd ed. Boston: Houghton Mifflin, 1967; rev. ed. New York: Ballantine, 1965 [paper] .

The Two Towers. London: Allen and Unwin, 1954. 2nd ed. Boston: Houghton Mifflin, 1967; rev. ed. New York: Ballantine, 1965 [paper] .

The Return of the King. London: Allen and Unwin, 1955. 2nd ed. Boston: Houghton and Mifflin, 1967; rev. ed. New York: Ballantine, 1965 [paper] .

Tolkien's Lord of the Rings series stands as the uncontested masterpiece of contemporary fantasy. Its struggle between good and evil; its focus on the diminutive heroes Frodo and Samwise; its brilliantly drawn sorcerer, Gandolf, and master necromancer, Sauron; and its many villains, noble king, magical characters, geography, description, characterization, and created languages and songs make the series a work of high moment and rich experience. *The Hobbit* is the background work for the Trilogy that comprises the main action. In it, Bilbo discovers the one ring, the powerful talisman that is the stake in the later struggle between the fell and the virtuous.

HENRY TREECE

The Green Man. London: Bodley Head, 1966.

Set in 6th century Northern Europe and inspired by Danish chronicle, this is one of the most brutal, barbaric, and savage fantasies ever written. Much of the reason for this is that Treece rejects the symbolism of ritual and returns to actualities. For example, instead of a fertility ritual in which the queen blesses the fields, in this work the queen is stripped nude and dragged across the fields by horses. Distinctive features, aside from the blood and brutality, are the appearances of the senile Beowulf and King Arthur and a most unusual conclusion.

"JACK" [JOHN HOLBROOK] VANCE

The Dying Earth. New York: Hillman, 1950 [paper].

A collection of six loosely connected tales that appear here for the first time. Unified by their common setting—Vance's vision of the Earth in the far distant future when the sun is going dark and mankind has lost its vitality—these short stories focus on various protagonists as they move through a world assured of its doom. Indulgent and decadent, they seek their strange pleasures and live out their eldritch lives amid magic, degenerate science, monstrosities, beauty, and cruelty.

The Eyes of the Overworld. New York: Ace, 1966; rpt. Boston: Gregg, 1976.

A semi-sequel to *The Dying Earth* through its setting. Composed of seven interrelated short stories (five of which were originally published in *The Magazine of Fantasy and Science Fiction* in 1965 and 1966) that have as their protagonist Cugel the Clever. Cugel, a master thief and sorcerer, seeks a magic lens and doles out suffering and cruelty to all he meets as he travels to his goal. He considers everyone a dupe until his own ironic end.

A[LFRED] E[LTON] VAN VOGT

The Book of Ptath. Reading, PA: Fantasy Press, 1947; rpt. New York: Garland, 1975.

An army captain, transported to Gondwanaland in the distant future, becomes a demigod. He falls under the evil control of the goddess Ineznia, but after completing seven magical tasks, his full powers are awakened and he destroys her. Originally published in *Unknown* (October 1943), this edition is the first book released by the Fantasy Press.

KARL EDWARD WAGNER

The Kane Series

Darkness Weaves With Many Shades. Abr. ed. Reseda, CA: Powell, 1970 [paper].
  Cmpt. ed. New York: Warner, 1978 [paper].

Death Angel's Shadow: [Three Tales of Kane]. New York: Warner, 1973 [paper].

Bloodstone. New York: Warner, 1975 [paper].

Dark Crusade. New York: Warner, 1976 [paper].

Night Winds. New York: Warner, 1978 [paper].

> Like Michael Moorcock's Elric and Carl Sherrell's Raum (see below), Wagner's protagonist Kane is at least partially evil. In these sword and sorcery adventures, his redemptive quality is that his selfishness and greed bring about the destruction of greater evils than himself.

SYLVIA TOWNSEND WARNER

Kingdoms of Elfin. New York: Viking, 1977.

> A collection of sixteen short stories that chronicles the history, geography, and life of the often cruel and capricious elves and their human changelings. A fine example of the creation of "un-human" and alien beings.

T[ERENCE] H[ANBURY] WHITE

The Once and Future King Series

The Sword in the Stone. New York: G. P. Putnam's Sons, 1938.

The Witch in the Wood [retitled "The Queen of Air and Darkness" in *The Once and Future King*]. New York: G. P. Putnam's Sons, 1939.

The Ill-Made Knight. New York: G. P. Putnam's Sons, 1940.

The Once and Future King. London: Collins, 1958.

The Book of Merlyn: The Unpublished Conclusion to "The Once and Future King." Austin: University of Texas Press, 1977.

> The best contemporary treatment of the Arthurian legend, far exceeding the pseudo-historical treatments by Mary Stewart, *The Crystal Cave* and *The Hollow Hills.* White's characterization and modern view of the lives of Arthur, Merlin, and all the other figures of Camelot is filled with humor, joy, sadness, cruelty, pathos, and tragedy. His use of contemporary psychological explanations and his introduction of modern anachronisms give a unique perspective, none more striking than Merlin, the wizard who is living backwards, remembering the future and forgetting the past. *The Once and Future King* is an omnibus volume, collecting revisions of *The Sword in the Stone* (with two new chapters), *The Witch in the Wood* (retitled "The Queen of Air and Darkness"), *The Ill-Made Knight,* and adding a new section, "The Candle in the Wind." *The Book of Merlyn* was written in 1940–1941 and supposedly not published because of paper shortages during World War II. However, there is more credence to the view that neither White nor his publisher thought enough of this heavily political and bitter attack on mankind to pursue its publication.

CHARLES WILLIAMS

All Hallow's Eve. London: Faber and Faber, 1945.

> The fictional biography of Simon the clerk and the tale of his attempt to become a mage and control matter and essence, life and death, through sorcery and alchemy. Williams' last novel.

"JACK" [JOHN STEWART] WILLIAMSON

Darker Than You Think. Reading, PA: Fantasy Press, 1948; rpt. New York: Garland, 1975.

> Probably the best werewolf tale ever told. The young and confused protagonist, the startlingly alluring heroine, and the gothic allusions to an ancient battle between mankind and a race of sorcerous shapechangers give this novel considerable impact as the shape changers—homo superiors —begin to rise again. First published in *Unknown,* December 1940.

ROGER ZELAZNY

Jack of Shadows. New York: Walker, 1971.

> A highly mythic work that combines magic and science as Jack of Shadows, a sorcerer or "power" and a dark-side dweller on a world with no rotation, uses both computers and sorcery to gain revenge against his fellow darksiders. Destroying the machinery and magic that holds the world still, he dramatically changes the world order.

The Amber Series

Nine Princes in Amber. New York: Doubleday, 1970.

The Guns of Avalon. New York: Doubleday, 1972.

The Sign of the Unicorn. New York: Doubleday, 1975.

The Hand of Oberon. New York: Doubleday, 1976.

The Courts of Chaos. New York: Doubleday, 1978.

> Zelazny's popular Amber Series focuses on mythical patterns, magic, political intrigue, and the nature of reality. The only true reality is Amber, whose ruling family creates all other places, "shadow," with their minds. When Oberon, the family's patriarch, disappears, the various children plot against each other for the crown. Corwin, the protagonist, finds himself one of the prime candidates and struggles against his kin. However, it soon becomes clear that Amber's struggle is not within but without as the mysterious Courts of Chaos threaten Amber's order and the primeval pattern that is its unifying essence. The series draws heavily on the Tarot cards and the Grail legend (from Jesse Weston's *From Ritual to Romance*) for much of its material.

B. ANTHOLOGIES

JONATHAN BACON and STEVE TROYANOVICH, eds.

Omniumgathum: An Anthology of Verse by Top Authors in the Field of Fantasy. Lamoni, IA: Stygian Isle Press, 1976 [paper].

This fan publication is the only volume of collected fantasy verse. Includes poetry by Manly Wade Wellman, A. Merritt, H. P. Lovecraft, H. Warner Munn, Hannes Bok, Mervyn Peake, Stanley Weinbaum, Andre Norton, Robert E. Howard, Michael Moorcock, Poul Anderson, Clark Ashton Smith, William Hodgson, Frank Belknap Long, Emil Petaja, August Derleth, Roger Zelazny, and Brian Lumley.

ROBERT H. BOYER and KENNETH J. ZAHORSKI, eds.

Dark Imaginings: A Collection of Gothic Fantasy. New York: Dell, 1978 [paper].

A classroom-oriented anthology that treads the fine line between horror and fantasy. It is divided into two sections: Gothic high fantasy (1) and Gothic low fantasy (2). Contents: (1) George MacDonald, "Cross Purposes"; A. Merritt, "The Woman of the Wood"; Robert E. Howard, "The Mirrors of Tuzun Thune"; C. L. Moore, "Werewoman"; Clark Ashton Smith, "The Enchantress of Sylaire"; Fritz Leiber, "The Unholy Grail"; Poul Anderson, excerpt from *Three Hearts and Three Lions*; and Ursula K. Le Guin, "Darkness Box." (2) Arthur Conan Doyle, "The Brown Hand"; William H. Hodgson, "The Inhabitants of the Middle Islet"; H. Rider Haggard, "Smith and the Pharaohs"; Algernon Blackwood, "The Dance of Death"; H. P. Lovecraft, "The Haunter of the Dark"; T. H. White, "The Troll"; Ray Bradbury, "The Crowd"; and Peter Beagle, "Lila the Werewolf."

The Fantastic Imagination: An Anthology of High Fantasy. New York: Avon, 1977 [paper].

A well-conceived selection of "high fantasy"—fantasy dealing with cosmic issues and characters of high stature—that contains both short stories and self-contained excerpts from novels. Along with Jane Mobley's *Phantasmagoria* (see below), this is one of the two best anthologies in paperback that is currently available. Contents: Johann Ludwig Tieck, "The Elves"; Lord Dunsany, "The Sword of Welleran"; George MacDonald, "The Light Princess"; John Buchan, "The Grove of Astaroth"; James Branch Cabell, "The Music From Behind the Moon"; Frank R. Stockton, "The Accommodating Circumstances"; H. E. Bates, "The Peach Tree"; Alexander Grin, "The Loquacious Goblin"; J. R. R. Tolkien, "Riddles in the Dark" (from *The Hobbit*); C. S. Lewis, "The Magician's Book" and "The Dufflepuds Made Happy" (both from *The Voyage of the Dawn Treader*); Mark Van Doren, "The Tall One"; Lloyd Alexander, "The Foundling"; Peter S. Beagle, "Come Lady Death"; Ursula Le Guin, "The Rule of Names" (one of the seed stories for *The Wizard of Earthsea*); and Sylvia Warner Townsend, "Beliard."

The Fantastic Imagination II: An Anthology of High Fantasy. New York: Avon, 1978 [paper].

The companion volume to *The Fantastic Imagination* that is somewhat expanded in its coverage to include examples of sword & sorcery fantasy. Contents: George MacDonald, "The Golden Key"; Barry Pain, "The Glass of Supreme Moments"; Frank R. Stockton, "Old Pipes and the Dryad"; Lord Dunsany, "The Kith of the Elf-folk"; Kenneth Morris, "Red-Peach-Blossom Inlet"; Selma Lagerlöf, "The Legend of the Christmas Rose"; Evangeline Walton Ensley, "Above Ker-Is"; Eric Linklater, "The Abominable Imprecation"; C. L. Moore, "Jirel Meets Magic"; David H. Keller, "The Thirty and One"; Ursula K. Le Guin, "April in Paris"; Joan Aiken, "A Harp of Fishbones"; Lloyd Alexander, "The Smith, the Weaver, and the Harper"; Patricia McKillip, [from] "The Throme of the Earl of Sherill"; Sylvia Townsend Warner, "Elphenor and Weasel"; and Vera Chapman, "Crusader Damosel."

TERRY CARR, ed.

New Worlds of Fantasy. New York: Ace, 1967 [paper].

All of the Carr collections cited here reprint short stories that are mixtures of fantasy, horror, and science fiction; very few of them are pure fantasy. Contents: Roger Zelazny, "Divine Madness"; John Brunner, "Break the Door of Hell"; Jorge Luis Borges, "The Immortal"; R. A. Lafferty, "Narrow Valley"; Ray Russell, "Comet Wine"; Katherine MacLean, "The Other"; Mildred Clingerman, "A Red Heart and Blue Roses"; Terry Carr, "Stanley Toothbrush"; Thomas M. Disch, "The Squirrel Cage"; Peter S. Beagle, "Come Lady Death"; Curt Clark, "Nackles"; J. G. Ballard, "The Lost Leonardo"; Keith Roberts, "Timothy"; Avram Davidson, "Basilisk"; and Alfred Gillespie, "The Evil Eye."

New Worlds of Fantasy No. 2. New York: Ace, 1970 [paper].

Contents: Robert Sheckley, "The Petrified World"; Keith Roberts, "The Scarlet Lady"; Avram Davidson, "They Loved Me in Utica"; Jorge Luis Borges, "The Library of Babel"; B. J. Bayley, "The Ship of Disaster"; Joanna Russ, "Window Dressing"; Harry Harrison, "By the Falls"; Kris Neville, "The Night of the Nickel Beer"; David Redd, "A Quiet Kind of Madness"; Roger Zelazny, "Museum Piece"; Terry Carr, "The Old Man of the Mountains"; Britt Schweitzer, "En Passant"; Wilmar H. Shiras, "Backward, Turn Backward"; Thomas M. Disch, "His Own Kind"; Katherine MacLean, "Perchance to Dream"; Leonid Andreyeff, "Lazarus"; R. A. Lafferty, "The Ugly Sea"; and Robert Bloch, "The Movie People."

No. 3: New Worlds of Fantasy. New York: Ace, 1971 [paper].

Contents: Peter S. Beagle, "Farrell and Lila the Werewolf"; R. A. Lafferty, "Adam Had Three Brothers"; Avram Davidson, "Big Sam"; Edgar Pangborn, "Longtooth"; Fritz Leiber, "The Inner Circles"; Victor Contoshi, "Von Goom's Gambit"; Zenna Henderson, "Through a Glass—Darkly"; Roger Zelazny, "The Stainless Steel Leech"; Terry Carr, "Sleeping Beauty"; Robert Bloch, "The Plot is the Thing"; Jorge Luis Borges, "Funes the Memorious"; J. G. Ballard, "Say Goodbye to the Wind"; and William M. Lee, "A Message from Charity."

LIN CARTER, ed.

Discoveries in Fantasy. New York: Ballantine, 1972 [paper].

A historical anthology of neglected fantasy originally published from 1900 to 1931. Contents: Ernest Bramah, "The Vision of Yin" and "The Dragon of Chang Tao"; Richard Garnett, "The Poet of Panopolis" and "The City of Philosophers"; Donald Corley, "The Bird With the Golden Beak" and "The Song of the Tombelaine"; and Eden Phillpotts, "The Miniature."

Flashing Swords! No. 1. Garden City, NY: Nelson Doubleday [Science Fiction Book Club], 1973.

This series contains stories written by an informal collection of writers known as The Swordsmen and Sorcerers' Guild of America, "S.A.G.A." While Andrew Offutt's *Swords Against Darkness* series contains more sword and sorcery tales, these volumes contain more quality. Contents: Fritz Leiber, "The Sadness of the Executioner"; Jack Vance, "Morreion"; Poul Anderson, "The Merman's Children"; and Lin Carter, "The Higher Heresies of Oolimar."

Flashing Swords! No. 2. Garden City, NY: Nelson Doubleday [Science Fiction Book Club], 1973.

Contents: L. Sprague de Camp, "The Rug and the Bull"; Michael Moorcock, "The Jade Man's Eyes"; Andre Norton, "The Toads of Grimmerdale"; and John Jakes, "Ghoul's Garden."

Flashing Swords! No. 3: Warriors and Wizards. New York: Dell, 1976 [paper].

Contents: L. Sprague de Camp, "Two Yards of Dragon"; Andre Norton, "Spider Silk"; Fritz Leiber, "The Frost Monstreme"; Lin Carter, "The Curious Custom of the Turjan Seraad"; and Avram Davidson, "Caravan to Illiel."

Flashing Swords! No. 4: Barbarians and Black Magicians. New York: Dell, 1977 [paper].

Contents: Jack Vance, "The Bagful of Dreams"; Poul Anderson, "The Tupilak"; John Jakes, "Storm in a Bottle"; Katherine Kurtz, "Swords Against the Marluk"; and Michael Moorcock, "The Lands Beyond the World."

Great Short Novels of Adult Fantasy. Vol. 1. New York: Ballantine, 1972 [paper].

An anthology of fantasy originally published from 1856 to 1953. Contents: Fletcher Pratt and L. Sprague de Camp, "Wall of Serpents" (see de Camp and Pratt, *The Incomplete Enchanter* above); Anatole France, "The Kingdom of the Dwarfs"; Robert W. Chambers, "The Maker of Moons"; and William Morris, "The Hollow Land."

Great Short Novels of Adult Fantasy. Vol. II. New York: Ballantine, 1973 [paper].

Four novellas published from 1858 to 1923. Contents: George MacDonald, "The Woman in the Mirror"; Robert W. Chambers, "The Repairer of Reputations" (from *The King in Yellow*); Ernest Bramah, "The Transmutation of Ling"; and Eden Phillpotts, "The Lavender Dragon."

Kingdoms of Sorcery. Garden City, NY: Doubleday, 1976.

A historically and thematically arranged anthology containing short stories and novel excerpts that is divided into five sections: (1) The Forerunners of Fantasy, (2) Fantasy as Saga, (3) Fantasy as Parable, (4) Fantasy as Anecdote, and (5) Fantasy as Epic. Contents: (1) Voltaire, "The History of Babouc the Scythian"; William Beckford, "The Palace of Subterranean Fire"; and George MacDonald, "The Witch Woman." (2) William Morris, "The Falla of the Mountain Door"; E. R. Eddison, "A Night-Piece on Ambremerine" (from *Mistress of Mistresses);* Fletcher Pratt, "Dr. Melibo̊ĕ the Enchanter" (from *The Well of the Unicorn,* see above); Fritz Leiber, "The Two Best Thieves in Lankmar" (from *Swords Against Wizardry,* see above). (3) Edgar Allan Poe, "Shadow and Silence"; Clark Ashton Smith, "Fables from the Edge of Night"; and Robert H. Barlow, "The Tomb of the God." (4) T. H. White, "Merlyn and Madame Mim" (from *The Once and Future King,* see above); L. Sprague de Camp, "The Owl and the Ape"; and Lin Carter, "The Twelve Wizards of Ung." (5) C. S. Lewis, "Deep Magic from the Dawn of Time" (from *The Lion, the Witch, and the Wardrobe*); J. R. R. Tolkien, "The Bridge of Khazad-Dum (from *The Fellowship of the Ring,* see above); and Richard Adams, "The Story of the Blessing of El-Ahraihad" (from *Watership Down,* see above).

See the companion volume, *Realms of Wizardry,* below.

The Magic of Atlantis. New York: Lancer, 1970 [paper].

A group of short stories that focuses on the many wonders of Atlantis as it lived and died. Contents: Robert E. Howard, "The Mirrors of Tuzun Thune"; Henry Kuttner, "The Spawn of Dagon"; L. Sprague de Camp, "The Eye of Tandyla"; Lin Carter, "The Seal of Zoan Sathla"; Edmond Hamilton, "The Vengeance of Ulios"; Clark Ashton Smith, "The Death of Malygris"; and Nictzin Dayalhis, "The Heart of Atlantan."

New Worlds for Old. New York: Ballantine, 1971 [paper].

A gathering of late-nineteenth and twentieth-century makers of imaginary worlds. Contents: William Beckford, "Zulkaïs and Kalilah"; Edgar Allan Poe, "Silence: A Fable"; George MacDonald, "The Romance of Photogen and Nycteris"; Oscar Wilde, "The Sphinx"; Lord Dunsany, "The Fall of Babbulkund"; H. P. Lovecraft, "The Green Meadow"; Gary Myers, "The Feast in the House of the Worm"; Lin Carter, "Zingazar"; George Sterling, "A Wine of Wizardry"; Robert E. Howard, "The Garden of Fear"; C. L. Moore, "Jirel Meets Magic"; Clifford Ball, "Duar the Accursed"; Clark Ashton Smith, "The Hashish-Eater"; Mervyn Peake, "The Party at Lady Cusp-Canine's"; and Lin Carter, "The Sword of Power."

Realms of Wizardry. Garden City, NY: Doubleday, 1976.

As in its companion volume, *Kingdoms of Sorcery* (see above) the selections are thematically arranged into five subdivisions: (1) Fantasy as Legend, (2) Fantasy as Satire, (3) Fantasy as Romance, (4) Fantasy as Adventure Story, and (5) New Directions in Fantasy. Contents: (1) Lord Dunsany, "The Hoard of the Gibbelins"; H. P. Lovecraft, "The Doom That Came to Sarnath"; Robert Bloch, "Black Lotus"; and Gary Myers, "The Gods of Earth." (2) Richard Garnett, "The City of Philosophers";

James Branch Cabell, "Some Ladies and Jurgen"; and Donald Corley, "The Book of Lullume." (3) H. Rider Haggard, "The Descent Beneath Kor"; A. Merritt, "The Whelming of Cherkis" (from *The Metal Monster*); and Hannes Bok, "How Orcher Broke the Koph" (from *The Sorcerer's Ship*). (4) Robert E. Howard, "Swords of the Purple Kingdom"; Clifford Ball, "The Goddess Awakes"; and C. L. Moore and Henry Kuttner, "Quest of the Starstone." (5) Jack Vance, "Liane the Wayfarer" (from *The Dying Earth*, see above); Michael Moorcock, "Master of Chaos"; and Roger Zelazny, "Thelinde's Song."

The Year's Best Fantasy Stories. New York: DAW, 1975 [paper].

An annual series with a sword and sorcery emphasis; readers should be cautioned that the selections only partially represent a selection of the "year's best." A number of the stories in each volume are specially commissioned and have not appeared elsewhere. Each volume contains an appendix surveying the year's best fantasy. Contents: Marion Zimmer Bradley, "The Jewel of Arwen"; Lloyd Alexander, "The Sword Dyrnwyn"; Robert E. Howard, "The Temple of Abomination"; Clark Ashton Smith, "The Double Tower"; Fritz Leiber, "Trapped in the Shadowland"; Lin Carter, "Black Hawk of Valkarth"; Hannes Bok, "Jewel Quest"; L. Sprague de Camp, "The Emperor's Fan"; Pat McIntosh, "Falcon's Mate"; Charles R. Saunders, "The City of Madness"; and Jack Vance, "The Seventeen Virgins."

The Year's Best Fantasy Stories: 2. New York: DAW, 1977 [paper].

Contents: Tanith Lee, "The Demoness"; Thomas Burnett Swann, "The Night of the Unicorn"; Pat McIntosh, "Cry Wolf"; Fritz Leiber, "Under the Thumbs of the Gods"; Paul Spencer, "The Guardian of the Vault"; L. Sprague de Camp, "The Lamp from Atlantis"; Gary Myers, "Xiurhn"; Lin Carter, "The City in the Jewel"; Walter C. DeBill, Jr., "In'Ygiroth"; Clark Ashton Smith and Lin Carter, "The Schroll of Morloc"; C. A. Cador, "Payment in Kind"; and Avram Davidson, "Milord Sir Smith, the English Wizard."

The Year's Best Fantasy Stories: 3. New York: DAW, 1977 [paper].

Contents: L. Sprague de Camp, "Eudoric's Unicorn"; Gardner F. Fox, "Shadow of a Demon"; Pat McIntosh, "Ring of Black Stone"; George R. R. Martin, "The Lonely Songs of Laren Dorr"; Karl Edward Wagner, "Two Suns Setting"; Clark Ashton Smith, "The Stairs in the Crypt"; Raul Garcia Capella, "The Goblin Blade"; C. J. Cherryh, "The Dark King"; Lin Carter, "Black Moonlight"; Gary Myers, "The Snout in the Alcove"; and George R. Saunders, "The Pool of the Moon."

The Young Magicians. New York: Ballantine, 1969 [paper].

An excellent representation of contemporary heroic fantasy writers. Contents: William Morris, "Rapunzel"; Lord Dunsany, "The Sword of Welleran"; E. R. Eddison, "In Valhalla"; James Branch Cabell, "The Way of Ecben"; H. P. Lovecraft, "The Quest of Iranon" and "The Cats of Ulthar"; Clark Ashton Smith, "The Maze of Maal Dweb"; Lin Carter, "The Whelming of Oom" and "Azlon"; A. Merritt, "Through the Dragon

Glass"; Robert E. Howard, "The Valley of the Worm"; L. Sprague de Camp, "Heldendammerung" and "Ka the Appalling"; Jack Vance, "Turjan of Miir" (from *The Dying Earth,* see above); J. R. R. Tolkien, "Once Upon a Time" and "The Dragon's Visit"; and C. S. Lewis, "Narnian Suite."

L[YON] SPRAGUE DE CAMP, ed.

The Fantastic Swordsmen. New York: Pyramid, 1967 [paper].

The selections stress sword and sorcery fantasy and horror. Contents: Robert Bloch, "Black Lotus"; Lord Dunsany, "The Fortress Unvanquishable Save for Sacnoth"; Robert E. Howard and L. Sprague de Camp, "Drums of Tombalku"; John Jakes, "The Girl in the Gem"; Henry Kuttner, "Dragon Moon"; H. P. Lovecraft, "The Other Gods"; Michael Moorcock, "The Singing Citadel"; and Luigi de Poscailis, "The Tower."

The Spell of Seven: Stories of Heroic Fantasy. New York: Pyramid, 1965 [paper].

An excellent sword and sorcery anthology. Contents: Fritz Leiber, "Bazaar of the Bizarre"; Clark Ashton Smith, "The Dark Eidolon"; Lord Dunsany, "The Hoard of the Gibbelins"; L. Sprague de Camp, "The Hungry Hercynian"; Michael Moorcock, "Kings in Darkness"; Jack Vance, "Mazirian the Magician"; and Robert E. Howard, "Shadows in Zamboula."

Swords and Sorcery: Stories of Heroic Fantasy. New York: Pyramid, 1963 [paper].

Contents: Poul Anderson, "The Valor of Cappen Varra"; Lord Dunsany, "Distressing Tale of Thangobrind the Jeweller"; Robert E. Howard, "Shadows in the Moonlight"; Henry Kuttner, "The Citadel of Darkness"; Fritz Leiber, "When the Sea King's Away"; H. P. Lovecraft, "The Doom That Came to Sarnath"; C. L. Moore, "Hellsgarde"; and Clark Ashton Smith, "The Testament of Athammaus."

Warlocks and Warriors. New York: G. P. Putnam's Sons, 1970.

Another example of de Camp's ability to select strong heroic fantasy. Contents: Ray Capella, "Turutal"; Lin Carter, "The Gods of Niom Parma"; Robert E. Howard, "The Hills of the Dead"; Henry Kuttner, "Thunder in the Dawn"; Fritz Leiber, "Thieves' House"; C. L. Moore, "Black God's Kiss"; Lord Dunsany, "Chu-bu and Sheemish"; Clark Ashton Smith, "The Master of the Crabs"; H. G. Wells, "The Valley of Spiders"; and Roger Zelazny, "The Bells of Shoredan."

DONALD M. GRANT, ed.

Swordsmen and Supermen. New York: Centaur, 1972 [paper].

An outstanding group of five new and reprinted examples of sword and sorcery fantasy. The Crombie tale, concerning a questing shape-changer, is a particular treat. Contents: Robert E. Howard, "Meet Cap'n Kidd"; Jean D'Esme, "The Death of a Hero"; Darrel Crombie, "Wings of Y'vrn"; Arthur D. Howden Smith, "The Slave of Marathon"; and Lin Carter, "How Sargoth Lay Siege to Zaremm."

DAMON KNIGHT, ed.

The Dark Side. Garden City, NY: Doubleday [Science Fiction Book Club], 1965.

Selections stress the gothic element of heroic fantasy. Contents: Ray Bradbury, "The Black Ferris"; Robert A. Heinlein, "They"; James Blish, "Mistake Inside"; H. L. Gold, "Trouble with Water"; Peter Phillips, "c/o Mr. Makepeace"; Avram Davidson, "The Golem"; H. G. Wells, "The Story of the Late Mr. Elvesham"; Theodore Sturgeon, "It"; Anthony Boucher, "Nellthu"; Richard McKenna, "Casey Agonistes"; T. L. Sherred, "Eye for Iniquity"; and Fritz Leiber, "The Man Who Never Grew Young."

The Golden Road: Great Tales of Fantasy and the Supernatural. New York: Simon and Schuster, 1973.

A strong overview of the fantasy genre. Contents: John Collier, "Are You Too Late or Was I Too Early"; R. A. Lafferty, "Entire and Perfect Chrysolite"; Kate Wilhelm, "Jenny with Wings"; H. G. Wells, "The Truth About Pyecraft"; C. M. Kornbluth, "The Words of the Guru"; Robert Arthur, "Postpaid to Paradise"; Arthur Machen, "The White People"; Mark Twain, "Extract from Captain Stormfield's Visit to Heaven"; Alfred Bester, "Will You Wait?"; Stephen Vincent Benét, "The King of Cats"; Ursula K. Le Guin, "The Word of Unbinding"; Robert A. Heinlein, "Magic, Inc."; Zenna Henderson, "Anything Box"; Heywood Broun, "Artist Unknown"; Venard McLaughlin, "The Silence"; H. P. Lovecraft, "The Dream Quest of Unknown Kadath"; Algis Budrys, "The Weeblies"; Oliver Onions (pseud. for George Oliver), "Phantas"; and Larry Niven, "Not Long Before the End."

JANE MOBLEY, ed.

Phantasmagoria: Tales of Fantasy and the Supernatural. Garden City, NY: Anchor-Doubleday, 1977 [paper].

Along with the Boyer and Zahorski volume (see above), this is one of the two best fantasy anthologies available. Its two sections—(1) The Wondrous Fair and (2) The Passing Strange—include magical fantasy and the supernatural, respectively. Contents: (1) Anon., "Arthur and Gorlagon"; George MacDonald, "The Fortress Unvanquishable Save for Sacnoth"; Theodore Sturgeon, "The Silken Swift"; Robert Bloch, "The Dark Isle"; Jorge Luis Borges, "The Rejected Sorcerer"; Nicholas Stuart Gray, "According to Tradition"; Andre Norton, "The Gifts of Asti"; Ursula K. Le Guin, "The Rule of Names"; Sylvia Warner Townsend, "Winged Creatures"; and Peter S. Beagle, "Sia." (2) J. Sheridan Le Fanu, "An Account of Some Strange Disturbances in Aungier Street"; Algernon Blackwood, "Confessions"; Oliver Onions (pseud. for George Oliver), "The Beckoning Fair One"; M. R. James, "Oh, Whistle, and I'll Come to You, My Lad"; Peter S. Beagle, "Come Lady Death"; Elizabeth Jane Howard, "Three Miles Up"; and Doris Betts, "Benson Watts is Dead and in Virginia."

ANDREW J. OFFUTT, ed.

Swords Against Darkness [I]. New York: Zebra, 1977 [paper].

Although the quality of the selections in this series of sword and sorcery anthologies is uneven, they are noteworthy because they are one of the few places where original stories are appearing in book form. Contents: Robert E. Howard and Andrew Offutt, "Nekht Semerkeht" (represented as Howard's last story); Poul Anderson, "The Tale of Hauk"; George W. Proctor, "The Smile of Oisia"; Bruce Jones, "Pride of the Fleet"; Manly Wade Wellman, "Straggler from Atlantis"; Richard L. Tierney, "The Ring of Sef"; Raul Garcia Capella, "Lararut's Bane"; David Drake, "Dragon's Teeth"; and Ramsey Campbell, "The Sustenance of Hoak."

Swords Against Darkness II. New York: Zebra, 1977 [paper].

Contents: Andre Norton, "The Sword of Unbelief"; Ramsey Campbell, "The Changer of Names"; Manly Wade Wellman, "The Dweller in the Temple"; David M. Harris, "The Coming of Age in Zamora"; Richard L. Tierney, "The Scroll of Thoth"; Tanith Lee, "Odds Against the Gods"; Dennis More, "On Skellig Michael"; and Andrew Offutt, "Last Quest."

Swords Against Darkness III. New York: Zebra, 1978 [paper].

Contents: Ramsey Campbell, "The Pit of Wings"; Richard L. Tierney, "The Sword of Spartacus"; Wayne Hooks, "Servitude"; David C. Smith, "Descales' Skull"; Tanith Lee, "In the Balance"; David Madison, "Tower of Darkness"; David Drake, "The Mantichore"; Kathleen Resch, "Revenant"; Jon DeCles, "Rites of Kings"; Robert E. Vardeman, "The Mating Web"; Manly Wade Wellman, "The Quest of Dzinganji"; Darrell Schweitzer, "The Hag"; Geo. W. Proctor, "A Kingdom Won"; M. A. Washil, "Swordslinger"; and Poul Anderson, "On Thud and Blunder."

ERIC S. RABKIN, ed.

Fantastic Worlds: Myths, Tales, and Stories. New York and Oxford: Oxford University Press, 1979.

Also available in paperback, this anthology is the most varied currently available with its international scope and wide-ranging historical perspective. Contents: "Genesis"; "Blackfoot Genesis"; "The Eye of the Giant"; Amos Tutuola, "How I Brought Death Into the World"; Ovid, "The Myth of Actæon," "The Myth of Narcissus," and "The Myth of Philomela"; "The Ghost Wife"; "The Magic Swan Gesse"; Chinua Achebe, "Why the Tortoise's Shell is Not Smooth"; Joel Chandler Harris, "How Mr. Rabbit Was Too Sharp for Mr. Fox"; Esther Shepherd, "Paul Bunyon on the Columbia"; Jacob and Wilhelm Grimm, "Little Red-cap,"; "The Sleeping Beauty," and "Hansel and Grethel"; Hans Christian Andersen, "The Tinderbox"; George MacDonald, "The Tale of Cosmo"; J. R. R. Tolkien, "Leaf by Niggle"; Joseph Addison, "Our Ideas of Time"; E. T. A. Hoffmann, "Ritter Gluck"; Edgar Allan Poe, "The Oval Portrait"; Lewis Carroll, "The Garden of Live Flowers"; James Thurber, "The Secret Life of Walter Mitty"; Norton Juster, "The Royal Banquet"; E. T. A. Hoffmann, "The Sandman"; Edgar Allan Poe, "The Black Cat"; H. P. Lovecraft, "The Picture in the House"; Joseph Sheridan Le Fanu, "The Hand"; Ambrose Bierce, "The Moonlite Road"; M. R. James, "Lost Hearts"; William Morris, "Golden Wings"; Lord Dunsany, "The Sword of Welleran"; Sylvia Townsend Warner, "The Five Black Swans"; Edgar

Allan Poe, "The Facts in the Case of M. Valdemar"; Nathaniel Hawthorne, "The Birthmark"; H. G. Wells, "The Star"; Kurt Vonnegut, Jr., "Epicac"; Jack Finney, "The Third Level"; Arthur C. Clarke, "The Star"; Franz Kafka, "The Judgment" and "A Common Confusion"; Bruno Schulz, "Cockroaches"; Jorges Luis Borges, "Pierre Menard, Author of the Quixote"; Julio Cortázar, "Axolotl"; Tommaso Landolfi, "Pastoral"; Italo Calvino, "All at One Point"; Peter Bichsel, "There Is No Such Place as America"; Donald Barthelme, "The Piano Player"; Richard Berautigan, "Homage to the San Francisco YMCA"; Robert Coover, "The Marker"; and Spencer Holst, "The Zebra Storyteller."

HANS STEFAN SANTESSON, ed.

The Mighty Barbarians: Great Sword and Sorcery Heroes. New York: Lancer, 1969 [paper].

A presentation of the major heroes in contemporary heroic fantasy: Fritz Leiber's Fafhrd and the Gray Mouser in "When the Sea King's Away," L. Sprague de Camp's Suar Peial in "The Stronger Spell," Henry Kuttner's Elak in "Dragon Moon," Lin Carter's Thongor in "Thieves of Zangabol," and Robert E. Howard's Conan in "A Witch Shall Be Born."

The Mighty Swordsmen. New York: Lancer, 1970 [paper].

Like its predecessor, *The Mighty Barbarians,* this is a showcase for sword and sorcery heroes: Lin Carter's Thongor in "Keeper of the Emerald Flame," Roger Zelazny's Dilvish the Damned in "The Bells of Shoredan," John Brunner's Mazda in "Break the Door of Hell," Robert E. Howard's Conan in "Beyond the Black River" and in Björn Nyberg's adaptation "The People of the Summit," and Michael Moorcock's Elric in "The Flame Bringers."

GAHAN WILSON, ed.

First World Fantasy Awards. Garden City, NY: Doubleday, 1977.

Fantasy and horror honored by the First World Fantasy Awards (1975), "The Howards"; a number of the panel discussions and speeches that occurred at the awards convention; and an essay, "Toward A Greater Appreciation of H. P. Lovecraft," by Dirk Mosig. Fiction Contents: Robert Bloch, "The Bat Is My Brother" and "Beatles"; Patricia McKillip, from *The Forgotten Beasts of Eld* (see above); Robert Aickman, "Pages from a Young Girl's Journal"; T. E. D. Klein, "The Events at Poroth Farm"; Sterling E. Lanier, "A Father's Tale"; Karl Edward Wagner, "Sticks"; Manly Wade Wellman, "Come Into My Parlor" and "Fearful Rock"; Fritz Leiber, "The Bait"; Dave Drake, "The Shortest Way"; Dennis Etchison, "The Soft Wall"; Joseph Payne Brennan, "The Abandoned Boudoir"; H. Warner Munn, "Cradle Song for a Baby Werewolf"; Walter Shedlofsky, "Guillotine"; and David Riley, "The Farmhouse."

DONALD A. WOLLHEIM, ed.

Swordsmen in the Sky. New York: Ace, 1964 [paper].

Sword and sorcery fantasy set in a science fiction frame. Contents: Poul

Anderson, "Swordsman of Lost Terra"; Andre Norton, "People of the Crater"; Leigh Brackett, "The Moon That Vanished"; Otis Adelbert Kline, "A Vision of Venus; and Edmond Hamilton, "Kaldar, World of Antares."

DONALD A. WOLLHEIM and GEORGE ERNSBERGER, eds.

The Avon Fantasy Reader. New York: Avon, 1969 [paper].

This volume and its successor (see below) reprint selections from Wollheim's Avon Fantasy Reader series (1947–1951). Contents: Robert E. Howard, "The Witch from Hell's Kitchen"; C. L. Moore, "Black Thirst"; Algernon Blackwood, "A Victim of Higher Space"; Nictzin Dyalhis, "The Sapphire Siren"; William Hope Hodgson, "A Voice in the Night" (from "Men of Deep Waters"); Thorp McClusky, "The Crawling Horror"; and Manly Wade Wellman, "The Kelpie." The selections in this volume and the one below represent both horror and fantasy.

The 2nd Avon Fantasy Reader. New York: Avon, 1969 [paper].

Contents: Robert E. Howard, "The Blonde Goddess of Bal-Sagoth"; C. L. Moore, "Shambleau"; Zealia Brown Bishop, "The Curse of Yig"; Clark Ashton Smith, "Ubbo-Sathla"; Donald Wandrei, "The Painted Mirror"; Edward Lucas White, "Amina"; Robert Bloch, "The Black Kiss"; Laurence Manning and Fletcher Pratt, "The City of the Living Dead"; and Sax Rohmer, "The Curse of a Thousand Kisses."

Joe De Bolt

OUTSTANDING SCIENCE FICTION BOOKS: 1927–1979

With the special assistance and contributions of
Dr. John R. Pfeiffer, Professor of English, Central Michigan University

Why another choice list of science fiction? After all, the list of Hugo awards provides the choices for best works of the SF community, while the Nebula awards do the same for the Science Fiction Writers of America. *Anatomy of Wonder* gives critical, popular, and historically important works, while many other SF reference works contain additional lists of recommended science fiction. Yet every list is a function of its selection process and bears the stamp of its creator. Thus, lists vary one from another; such pluralism is good for the SF reader; for it allows her or him a wider scope of choice, and it is good for the SF researcher, as well, for it aids in filling in the total picture of the genre.

The present list is, I believe, unique among the others. It was generated on the basis of the number of reviews works received. This was made possible by the appearance of H. W. Hall's excellent and important work, *Science Fiction Book Review Index, 1923-1973*, (Detroit, MI: Gale Research, 1975), and the subsequent annual supplements. As Hall points out: "This book review index provides access to science fiction and fantasy book reviews which appeared in the science fiction magazines from 1923 through 1973 [and for each year afterward in the annual supplements]. From 1970-1973 [and onward to the present] coverage of magazines is somewhat broader. In addition to the science fiction magazines, a number of general magazines, library magazines, and amateur magazines (fanzines) were indexed, both to give the index more utility, and to provide a broader variety of viewpoints than might be found in only the science fiction magazines. The primary criterion for choice of non-science fiction magazines for indexing was the established fact that the magazine carried reviews of science fiction books." (p. 9 ix, Hall, 1975).

Taking Hall as the data base, a card file was made which collected the reviews each work received, both from the large, 1975, Hall volume and its annual supplements. Every effort was made to control for variations in titles, so that a work that appeared under different titles received the total reviews

291

for all of them. Also, novels that appeared in omnibus works were given proportional review credit; for example, if three novels that were published independently were collected in a single volume which got one review, one-third of a review was added to the totals for each of the novels.

Finally, lists of works published each year were compiled and ordered by the number of total reviews each work had received. In order to control somewhat for variations in the number of works published and review sources open to science fiction in different years, the percentages of works accepted for the final lists were adjusted over time. Generally, a larger percentage of early works were included than later works. That the number of early works is still smaller than that of later works is not surprising when one recalls the more or less continual expansion of SF book publication. Groff Conklin reported that 250 SF books appeared from 1946 to 1952, but by the 1970s, according to *Locus*, this number or more of new works was appearing every year, with highs of 528 in 1978 and 685 in 1979.

Why start the list with 1927? That was an arbitrary decision; 1927 was about the time that reviews of SF became numerous enough to allow works to be differentiated, and, when this project began, it gave an exact 50-year time span. (The time needed for the project has now extended that span to 52 years). Of course, 1927 was the year after the founding of *Amazing*. Fritz Lang's *Metropolis* had just appeared, and the first stories had appeared, or were about to, by the likes of Edmond Hamilton, David Keller, Stanton Coblentz, and Jack Williamson. "Doc" Smith was beginning his great space opera, while Phil Nowland was launching Buck Rogers. Genre labeled SF was being created about this time, so this starting date does have some historical importance, as well.

But isn't the use of reviews to generate such a list just a gimmick? No, for it does produce a list of works that differs from others, and thereby surfaces a number of items that have been overlooked. Moreover, by using accumulated reviews one weights a work not only in terms of the attention it received upon its original publication, but includes weights for the reviews it garnered in any subsequent editions and reprintings. This produces a weight for a work that combines both its contemporary impact and its posterity's, as well. Of course, there are many variables that influence a work being reviewed or not, and most could not be controlled in this project. And just having a review does not indicate whether a work is good or bad. But the assumption here is that the summed reviews of a work are a measure of the work's importance to the field; review space is always limited, and the trivial gets ignored in favor of the significant. A writer's stature also must affect frequency of reviews, but, again, the works of the more important writers tend to receive the larger number. Note that since the emphasis here is upon single SF books, the total works included in this list for an author cannot always be taken as an accurate indicator of an author's importance. The relative absence in this list of works by Gordon Dickson is a case in point; my personal critical selections would have included many more, but the review numbers did not come out that way. These cautions are intended to warn against using this list for invidious comparisons.

Other criteria used for finalizing this choice list are: only works of science fiction are included (fantasy works are included in another section of this volume); works are listed under their year of original book publication, or the year of their most representative edition in book form: only English language works or works translated into English have been included; in the case of translations, their first English language appearance in book form determines the year in which they are listed; since many reviews appear long after a book's publication, and many more after a paperback edition, the lists for 1978 and 1979 must be taken as especially tentative relative to other years. The year 1979 has a short list, since many reviews for books from that year didn't appear until 1980, and Hall's volume for 1980 was not available.

The list itself is divided into years; the more total reviews a work received, the higher its rank within its year. The most reviewed book, or books in the case of ties, is listed first in each year and is marked with an asterisk (*). The remaining selected works are listed in descending order of total number of reviews; they were not given rank numbers—such a procedure would imply more significance to often closely ranked works than would be prudently warranted—and ties, which are frequent in the body of many years, are listed alphabetically by author.

The completion of this project, which required much more time and labor than expected, involved significant help from several sources. These include Denise De Bolt, Joseph De Bolt, Jr., Michelle De Bolt, and, from the Central Michigan University Library, David Ginsberg. Marshall Tymn also contributed by drafting a number of the annotations. I thank all these persons, for, without their help, this task would not have been completed.

And Dr. John R. Pfeiffer . . . what can be said of his altruism and support? His selfless help, like an older brother's, has been essential for the completion of my project. He has been Reich to my D'Courtney.

Finally, here is the list. It may not include all the best SF works, nor all the most important ones, and compilations of future reviews will certainly alter it, but its more than 300 annotated entries are certainly among science fiction's most outstanding books. They are all worth reading.

1927

*Karel Capek
The Absolute at Large
New York: Macmillan

A humorous satire by a major Czech writer, this novel describes the social upheaval resulting from the invention of an atomic engine that releases God, "in chemically pure form," as a by-product of its energy production. Scientist Rudy Marek invents this "Perfect Karburator" to save the world from the energy crisis of 1943, when the coal mines have played out. Chaos results as people become religious from the contaminating God force and—as the force spontaneously turns to over-production—commerce dies, economies fail, and nations, inflamed by religious conflicts, go to war. As Marek says, "I believe that He once did really create the laws of Nature . . . [but] our modern industry commerce, that I swear He did not create, for He simply doesn't know a thing about it."

1928

*Abraham Merritt
Seven Footprints to Satan
New York: Boni Liveright

A mysterious arch-criminal, calling himself Satan, manipulates the world through his control of its leaders. Satan tries to recruit the handsome adventurer, James Kirkham, to his cause, but Kirkham only pretends compliance until he and the beautiful Eve Demerest, another of Satan's victims, can escape. The plot turns through fantastic settings, secret passages, conspiracies and intrigues until the stalwart hero uncovers the secret of Satan's powers. A distillate of pulp and Fu-Manchu-type fiction, this was nót Merritt's best novel, but it may have been his most popular; made into a successful film.

1929

*Sydney Fowler Wright
The World Below
London: Collins

Two men are lost thousands of years in the future, and George, armed only with woodman's axe and clasp-knife, is sent in search of them. He finds a dangerous but beautiful alien earth peopled by two sentient humanoid species, the furry aquatically-adapted Amphibians and the giant subterranean Dwellers, both of whom regard humanity as animals, inferior in biology and culture. This work's first half appeared earlier as *The Amphibians* (1924).

Sir Arthur Conan Doyle
The Maracot Deep and Other Stories
Garden City, NY: Doubleday, Doran

A deep sea expedition, led by Professor Maracot, is lost under five miles of water in the Atlantic deeps. Instead of death, the expedition finds the descendants of lost Atlantis, sunk below the waves 8,000 years earlier as punishment for its decadence.

Although Vernian in its science, this short novel, written in Doyle's old age, also includes a strong mystical element in its use of a war between good and evil as background; the Atlantian God, Lord of the Dark Face, must be bested by Professor Maracot in order to save the city's few remaining survivors. The original printing also included three short stories: "Spodegue's Dropper," "The Disintegration Machine," and "When the World Screamed."

Floyd Phillips Gibbons
The Red Napoleon
New York: Cape and Smith

After Stalin's assassination in 1932, a new U. S. S. R. dictator, the part Mongoloid Ivan Karakhan, launches a second world war to defeat racism and make racial amalgamation state policy. With the help of the peoples formerly dominated by the Europeans, he soon conquers Europe and Asia, and turns to the U. S. and Canada. Military actions are detailed in realistic maps. Although read by some as an early anti-racist work, others see this as Gibbons' (a famous war correspondent) personal plug for strong air and sea power against the "yellow-peril."

Otis Adelbert Kline
The Planet of Peril
Chicago: A. C. McClurg

Venus is a world of super science and medieval society peopled with brave warriors, fair maidens, and fierce monsters. Robert Grandon hews his way across this planet of pulp conventions, not only in this novel, but in two sequels as well: *The Prince of Peril* (1930) and *The Port of Peril* (1949). The author, founder of a very successful literary agency, was a competitor of Edgar Rice Burroughs for space in the magazines, and these works, along with two related novels set on Mars, are very much in the Burroughs mode.

1930

*William Olaf Stapledon
Last and First Men: A Story of the Near and Far Future
London: Methuen

With magnificent vision, but a heavy style, the author, a British philosopher, sketched the evolution of humanity over millions of years in this, his first novel: international wars wrack the 20th Century, the U. S. emerges the victor and a world state appears, new forms of humanity emerge, the Martians invade, the moon falls toward the earth and humanity settles Venus and Neptune. Finally, an abnormal star bathes the solar system with poisoning radiation, and dying humanity seeds the universe with its spore. Stapledon's goal: ". . . to attempt to see the human race in its cosmic setting, and to mould our hearts to entertain new values." A related work is *Last Men in London* (1932).

Eric Temple Bell (as John Taine)
The Iron Star
New York: E. P. Dutton

Intrigued by the case of a missionary with strange drug-addiction-type symptoms and his wife, who has apparently degenerated into an ape-like animal, the Chicago physician, Dr. Colton, leads a party of two physicists and a young girl into the African Congo. They discover the gigantic remains of an ancient meteorite whose opium-like emanations change humans into beasts. The author, a Cal Tech mathematician, peppered the novel with the scientific speculations and social opinions of his day.

Philip Gordon Wylie
Gladiator
New York: Knopf

Professor Abednego Danner injects his pregnant domineering wife with his new discovery, a chemical which will give their child super strength and invulnerability to knives and bullets. After birth, Hugo Danner's unhappy life is traced through childhood, love affairs, and World War I, as he is torn between his desire to keep his super powers secret and his need to use them to justify his existence. Although written in 1927, this first novel was withheld from the market until 1930 by its author, later a noted U. S. writer. It served as the basis for a disappointing farcical film, and, more appropriately, as the alleged proto-type of the well-known *Superman* comic strip.

1931

*Raymond King Cummings
Brigands of the Moon
Chicago: A. C. McClurg

Originally published in *Astounding* in 1930, this is a tale of space war and piracy, as Earth and Mars compete for potent lunar radium deposits. The heroes then confront alien space invaders in a sequel, *Wandl the Invader* (1932). Enter-taining space opera by a major U. S. pulp writer.

*Abraham Merritt
The Face in the Abyss
New York: Horace Liveright

In the story's first part (originally published as "The Face in the Abyss" in 1923), a young mining engineer, Nicholas Graydon, and three other men seeking lost Incan treasure deep in the Andes enter a lost world, the surviving remnant of an ancient advanced culture. Only Graydon survives, saved by a beautiful woman, Suarra, whom he befriends, while his companions, driven by greed, are destroyed before a giant evil stone face. In the second part (originally "The Snake Mother," 1930), Graydon returns to the lost land, Yu-Atlanchi, to aid the half-woman, half-snake Adana in her battle against Nimir, Lord of Evil, and to win Suarra as his bride.

1932

*Aldous Leonard Huxley
Brave New World
London: Chatto & Windus

About 600 years in the future, a world state provides total material security to a stable society controlled by genetic engineering, conditioning, a hedonistic philosophy, elimination of the family, and censorship; material need, pain, and even worry have been largely eliminated. Bernard Marx, a social malcontent, and the woman, Lenina Crowne, for whom he has a socially un-healthful possessiveness, go on holiday to the isolated Savage Reservation in New Mexico, where Indians follow their traditional ways. There they find John, the accidental offspring of a woman from their own society; an unsocialized person, John is returned to civilization for scientific observation. Finding the modern world empty and loveless, he rejects it and is finally driven to escape by suicide. Bernard is exiled to an isolated island. A classic dystopian novel by a noted British author.

1933

*Edwin Balmer and Philip Gordon Wylie
When Worlds Collide
New York: Stokes

Two approaching planets threaten earth, the smaller, Beta, by a near miss which will cause disastrous tidal effects and the larger, Alpha, by a catastrophic direct hit. Earth's leading scientists desparately plan space ships which will carry a few hundred survivors to Beta. In the U. S., Dr. Hendron's two ships take shape with the help of his daughter, Eve, her boyfriend, Tony Drake, and a South African pilot, Dave Ransdell. Overcoming social disorder and rampaging nature, they escape only hours before the final collision. A sensational novel in its day, it later served as the basis for a successful film by George Pal (1951). Sequel: *After Worlds Collide* (1933).

1934

Herbert George Wells
Seven Science Fiction Novels of H. G. Wells
New York: Knopf

Collection of seven of Wells'—and the genre's—major SF novels. The works are presented chronologically: *The Time Machine* (1895), which carries its inventor into the future, to the time of the depraved Morlocks and innocent Eloi, and beyond; *The Island of Dr. Moreau* (1896), where experiments in changing animals into humans end in catastrophe for the doctor and his assistant, Montgomery; *The Invisible Man* (1897), Griffin, whose selfish misuse of his marvelous discovery costs him dearly; *The War of the Worlds* (1897), in which the mighty Martian invaders are defeated by Earth's lowliest defenders; *The First Men in the Moon* (1901), which depicts a lunar voyage powered by an antigravity device; *The Food of the Gods* (1903), in which a new food causes its consumers to become giants; and *In the Days of the Comet* (1906), when a passing comet's gasses so change human behavior that Earth becomes a utopia. Several other major SF novels by Wells are *not* included: *When the Sleeper Wakes, A Modern Utopia, The World Set Free, Men Like Gods* and *The War in the Air.*

Edgar Rice Burroughs
Pirates of Venus
Tarzana, CA: E. R. Burroughs

Carson Napier blasts off from Guadalupe Island for Mars, but an error in calculation brings his huge spaceship to Venus instead. There, on the island of Vepaja, he falls in love with the lovely but unattainable Duare, who views his love for her, a princess, as an insult. Soon, adventures sweep them across the planet. First work in Burroughs' Venusian series; other include *Lost on Venus* (1933), *Carson of Venus* (1938), *Escape on Venus* (1946), and "The Wizard of Venus" (1964). Generally considered inferior to the author's Tarzan and Martian series.

1935

*William Olaf Stapledon
Odd John: A Story Between Jest and Earnest
London: Methuen

A British doctor and his bovine wife give birth to a mutant child. John Wainwright, who first exhibits super intelligence, later develops super control over his psychological processes and finally exhibits super-parapsychological powers. "Odd" John's life is traced through his prodigious childhood, his founding of a colony of similar stigmatized mutants on a distant Pacific island, and his and the colony's ultimate suicide by atomic bomb in the face of intervention by several governments. Confident of his innate superiority, he sees his kind as aloof from mere human norms and values, and, at times, steals from, kills, and variously manipulates normal humans.

1936

*Karel Capek
War With the Newts
Prague: Fr. Borovy

A classic comic satire on western society and Nazism which traces the history of a species of intelligent salamanders from their first discovery and exploitation by humanity, through their adoption of human culture, to their war and ultimate victory over humankind by the aquaforming of the continents. The "Chief Salamander" turns out to be a renegade human named Andreas Schultze, a veteran of World War I, who broadcasts his demands in a "dreadful croaking voice." The Nazis were not amused. The work was the cause, some say, of Capek's failure to receive the Nobel Prize for Literature.

Festus Pragnell
The Green Man of Kilsona
London: P. Allan

A scientist induces a mind switch between his brother and an ape-like man with green hair inhabiting a sub-atomic world. Macroscopic and microscopic worlds operate on different time scales; so, although only a brief time had passed for the experimenter, his brother passes thirty years in the ape-man's body. Originally published in *Wonder Stories* as "The Green Man of Graypec" (1935). A better work than its general neglect in science fiction would indicate.

1937

*William Milligan Sloane
To Walk the Night
New York: Farrar

The mysterious death of Professor Le Normand sets Jerry Lister, his former student, and Bart Jones, Jerry's best friend, on the search for its cause.

They meet Le Normand's new wife, whose beauty and strangeness fascinate Jerry and the two soon marry. But Selena's alienness becomes more apparent; perhaps she is an entity from another time, another world, the possessor of the body of a missing retarded girl. Finally, Jerry, too, must die to protect her secret; but, tragically, Selena, a being of cold intellect, had discovered love with Jerry. Despite its dated setting, a compelling and chilling novel.

1938

*Ayn Rand
Anthem
London: Cassell

A dystopian vision of collectivism carried to its ultimate extreme. Following a cataclysmic war, society is reduced to a simple agrarian base. The collectivist victors operate entirely through committees, and, under such slogans as "What is not done collectively cannot be good," repress *all* individualism, even the use and memory of first person pronouns. A nonconforming young man, Equality 7-2521, is assigned work as a streetsweeper despite his great talent for science. Acting in secret, he rediscovers the electric light, only to be punished rather than rewarded for his efforts. Equality 7-2521 flees to the uncharted forest, followed by his secret and illicit love, Liberty 5-3000. There they find a house preserved from the "Unmentionable Times" of the past and in its library they rediscover such words as "I" and "My." Taking the name "Prometheus," the young man vows to rebuild the lost world of freedom. Written by the founder of Objectivism, this novel is especially pertinent in today's world of growing socialism.

1939

*Robert Cedric Sherriff
The Hopkins Manuscript
London: Victor Gollancz

The diary of Edgar Hopkins, a very ordinary British gentlemen, which describes the events surrounding the Moon's collision with Earth. Low-keyed and stiff-lipped, the British prepare for the disaster, which, when it comes, wraps the world in floods, storms, and earthquakes. Although badly shaken, civilization survives; but the Moon's fortuitous plunge into the North Atlantic sets off suicidal warfare among the European nations over this new territory. Eventually, Selim, a Persian fanatic, leads an invading horde of former colonial peoples that wipes out the remnants of Europe. The author, well known as a screen writer and playwright, also wrote the noteworthy anti-war play, *Journey's End.*

*Stanley Grauman Weinbaum
The New Adam
Chicago: Ziff-Davis

Edmond Hall, born of ordinary middle-class parents in Chicago, is a mutant gifted with an unemotional, powerful dual mind, but suffers physical stigmata such as physical frailness and abnormally jointed fingers. Made lonely through life by his appearance, feelings of superiority, and inability to accept human society, Hall finds no fulfillment in power, wealth, or knowledge; even his discovery of Sarah, a mutant like himself who bears his child, cannot satisfy him. Rather, he finds himself emotionally dependent on his lovely human wife, whose sexuality becomes his paramount satisfaction and his ultimate death. A flawed novel, but still worthwhile as an interesting variant on the superman myth.

1940

*Herbert Best
The Twenty-Fifth Hour
New York: Random House

Warfare aimed at the homefront had triggered the collapse of civilization in Europe, and, without high technology, social conditions are sliding into anarchy and cannibalism. In the isolated U. S., economic collapse and wild inflation have taken hold, to be followed by a plague, probably from germ warfare. Against this background, the stories of two persons unfold; Hugh Fitzharding, a British Army officer, and Ann Shillito, an American woman. Eventually they find each other and a home in a revitalized Egypt. A very graphic and fascinating extrapolation of the world war then brewing in Europe.

1941

*Lyon Sprague de Camp
Lest Darkness Fall
New York: Holt

The author employs his extensive background in technology and history in this classic time travel tale, which has Martin Padway, American archaeologist, zapped by lightning back to the Rome of 535. Armed with his wits and little else, Padway not only survives and prospers, but sets about defeating the invading armies of Justinian and preventing the decline of the West into the Dark Ages. Sixth Century society is vividly depicted, as are Padway's realistic problems in developing such innovations as the brandy still, the semaphore telegraph, modern political procedures, the zero, and the printing press. The author's wit and humor sparkle throughout.

Philip Duffield Stong (ed.)
The Other Worlds
New York: Wilfred Funk

This anthology is noteworthy as one of the earliest to use stories from science fiction magazines. It contains twenty-five science fiction and horror stories and introductory notes by the editor, who, by the way, was the author of *State Fair*. Includes stories by del Rey, Sturgeon, Binder, Leinster, Lovecraft, Wellman, Derleth, and Kuttner, among others.

1942

*William Olaf Stapledon
Darkness and the Light
London: Methuen

A fictional future history, more tract than novel, with a twist. The narrator is allegedly given two views of the future, one where "the light" predominates, the other with forces of "darkness" in ascendancy. The turning point lies shortly in the future, when, except for Tibet, the world is divided into two great empires, the Russian and the Chinese. Tibet develops "a sort of religious communism." In the "dark" history, those beliefs are destroyed, in part by a successful "synthetic" religion preaching acquiescence, cruelty, and suffering. Eventually, China rules the world and, over millenia, the human species undergoes degeneration and becomes extinct. In the "light" history, Tibet survives, successfully spreading its vision to undermine Russia and China. Eventually, a new world order emerges, the "Federation of Mankind," and, following various travails, humanity dies off after developing a new, super human being, one "capable of greater power of intelligence and sensibility, and also spiritual insight." They pass into their own, unseen destiny. A tedious, sketchy exercise, but one instructive about the author's beliefs.

Clark Ashton Smith
Out of Space and Time
Sauk City, WI: Arkham House

Chosen by the author himself, this first collection contains twenty fantasy and science fiction stories from 1922 to 1939, most from the pages of the legendary *Weird Tales.* Included are the noteworthy "The End of the Story" (1930), "The City of the Singing Flame" (1931) and an introduction, "Clark Ashton Smith: Master of Fantasy" by August Derleth and Donald Wandrei.

Austin Tappan Wright
Islandia
New York: Farrar & Rinehart

A highly praised utopian work by a law professor who died in 1931, this massive book represents only a fraction of the detailed material about his fantasy land, Islandia, which the author compiled over many years. A young American diplomat, John Lang, takes up his post in Islandia, an agricultural society on the continent of Karain, to further economic development with the industrial world. Islandia is divided between those wanting such "progress" and those favoring the retention of its natural harmony and beauty, both physical and cultural. The conservatives win, and Lang, enraptured by Islandia, makes it his new homeland. Additional background on Islandia is contained in *An Introduction to Islandia* (1942) by Basil Davenport.

1943

*Eric Frank Russell
Sinister Barrier
Kingswood, Surrey, UK: World's Work

Based on the works of Charles Fort, this novel illustrates the Fortean conclusion that humanity is the property of someone else. Famous scientists are dying, seemingly by natural or accidental causes, but Bill Graham, American intelligence agent, discovers a common link: all had discovered that aliens, normally invisible floating energy spheres, surround humanity. These Vitons, Graham learns, are somewhat telepathic and manipulate humans, thereby causing the social problems that always have plagued humanity. Then, they feed off the resultant negative human emotions. Faced with exposure, the Vitons goad the East into a destructive war with the West. As the West crumbles, scientists secretly search for a weapon effective against their alien overlords. Crudely written, but still an engrossing thriller. The U. S. edition (Fantasy Press, 1948) is considerably longer than the British first edition. Published initially in the first issue of *Unknown* in 1939.

1944

*Thomas Calvert McClary
Rebirth: When Everyone Forgot
New York: Bartholomew House

Disgruntled with the evil capitalist world of 1958, a socialist scientist induces universal amnesia, reducing humanity to mental infancy so it can develop a new, superior society. Mass destruction and death results as people, at first unable even to feed themselves or walk, recapitulate with amazing rapidity the author's view of sociocultural evolution. Some of the characters retain their pre-amnesia "instinctual" bent, while others, freed from cultural restraints, blossom new talents. Soon, the turmoil subsides and, inexplicably, a communistic utopia emerges. First published in *Astounding* in 1934, the novel's psychology and sociology are highly implausible today, but some still consider it a science fiction classic.

1945

*Stanton Arthur Coblentz
When the Birds Fly South
Mill Valley, CA: Wings Press

Although best known for his satirical novels, the author, also a poet, creates here a sensitive love story set in a fascinating lost world. While climbing "The Mountain of Vanished Men" in Afghanistan for a closer view of a giant female-shaped rock formation, Dan Prescott, an American geologist, becomes lost and is abandoned by his party. He is rescued by the beautiful Yasma, member of a self-isolated people, the Ibandru, and is taken to her home in the hidden valley of Sobul at the foot of the stone woman's mountain. The Ibandru are a wholesome and happy people who worship the goddess Yulada, whose figure they see in the mountain, and Dan makes a new life among them. But each fall the Ibandru mysteriously disappear, apparently migrating south like the birds, and return in the spring. Despite his best efforts, Dan cannot follow them. Do they disappear into thin air? Do they transform into the hidden birds whose lovely song Dan hears at migration time? Eventually Dan convinces Yasma, whom he deeply loves, to marry him despite the warnings of disaster by the soothsayer, and he promises to let her go each fall. But the winter's loneliness is too dreadful for Dan, and he stops Yasma from leaving. Her inner compulsion denied, Yasma weakens and dies. The prophecy is fulfilled and the tormented Dan returns to the outside world.

1946

*Alfred Elton van Vogt
Slan
Sauk City, WI: Arkham House

Slans, distinguishable by the golden tendrils that grow among their head hair, are believed to be an evil race of machine-produced mutants who secretly plot to rule Earth. Their telepathic, physical, and intellectual powers are feared and they are alleged to turn human babies into monsters. In response, Earth's dictator, Kier Gray, his chief of secret police, John Petty, and Earth's human billions persecute slans and plan their genocide. Reminiscent of the terror of Jews in Nazi Germany, the novel's effective opening chapters have the young slan, Jommy Cross, fleeing the mob as his mother is shot down on the city streets. Knowing that he must survive to adulthood to aid the slan cause through the use of a super weapon developed by his murdered father, Jommy allies himself with Granny, a decrepit old junk peddler, who uses him to steal for her. But slans are pacific by nature, and Jommy, rejecting revenge, turns instead to a search for a non-violent end to human/slan hostility. His complexly plotted quest eventually leads him to the truth, that slans are actually natural mutations and represent humanity's next evolutionary step. Originally published in *Astounding* in 1940, this was the author's first novel, and is considered by many to be a SF classic.

Edward Elmer Smith and Mrs. Lee Hawkins Garby
The Skylark of Space
Providence, RI: Hadley

Originally published in 1928 in Gernsback's *Amazing Stories,* this grand-sire of *Star Wars* helped pioneer galaxy-spanning space opera. Richard Seaton, morally upright scientific genius, discovers an atomic energy source of limitless power. He and his friend, the young multimillionnaire and aviation engineer, Martin Crane, form a company to develop the process and build the first spaceship. However, the evil but brilliant Marc DuQuesne, in the pay of the unscrupulous giant World Steel Corporation, steals part of the secret, and in an effort to get Seaton to reveal the remainder, kidnaps Seaton's fiancee, Dorothy Vaneman, and flees into deepest space. The chase is on as Richard and Martin launch their own spaceship, Skylark, in pursuit; there follow rescues, adventures, aliens, and space wars, as heroes, heroines, and villains zip from star to star and from crisis to crisis. Among other things, Seaton's alien allies provide the body for a new Skylark, one made from Arenak, a substance 500 times as strong as the best steel. Finally, Richard, Dorothy, Martin, and Margaret Spencer (another of

DuQuesne's kidnap victims) return to Earth, but not before both couples are married in an alien ceremony on the world of Osnome. The unrepentant "Blackie" DuQuesne escapes to do evil another day. Despite this novel's dreadful writing, the imagination of SF fans was kindled and three sequels followed: *Skylark Three* (1930) *Skylark of Valeron* (1934), and *Skylark DuQuesne* (1965).

Eric Temple Bell [as John Taine]
The Time Stream
Providence, RI: Buffalo Book Company and G. H. E.

An awe-inspiring tale of time travel and super science in which civilizations rise and fall, planets are shattered, and San Francisco experiences its greatest earthquake and fire. It all begins simply enough as a company of nine friends in their favorite San Francisco tavern find their reality of 1906 shattered by the sound of a watch's mainspring snapping. Gradually they remember that they are men with a mission: to explore time in an attempt to prevent a marriage. In some great distant time, a people have established a utopia based on controlled atomic energy, a libertarian social order, and eugenics. One couple, however, insist on marrying even though their offspring will destabilize society and destroy their Eden. Despite heroic acts by the stalwart band as they swim the time stream, that "continuous, unchanging record of everlasting existence" that constantly flows past us, the lovers have their way and catastrophe follows. This 1931 *Wonder Stories* novel by a well-known mathematician shows its age, but is considered by some to be the author's best.

Raymond John Healy and Jesse Francis McComas (eds.)
Adventures in Time and Space
New York: Random House

This giant anthology of 997 pages contains thirty-three stories, two science articles, and an editors' introduction. The stories largely date from the late 30s to the mid 40s and represent an excellent sampling of early modern science fiction, which was born during those years. Especially noteworthy are Heinlein's "Requiem," "The Roads Must Roll," and "By His Bootstraps," (the last one as Anson MacDonald); Campbell's "Forgetfulness" and "Who Goes There?" (as Don A. Stuart); Asimov's "Nightfall"; van Vogt's "Black Destroyer," "Asylum," and "The Weapons Shop"; del Rey's "Nerves"; Boucher's "Q. U. R."; Fredric Brown's "The Star Mouse"; Harry Bates' "A Matter of Size" and "Farewell to the Master"; Henry Hasse's "He Who Shrank"; Lewis Padgett's "The Twonky"; and P. Schuyler Miller's "The Sands of Time." Other notable authors include Eric Frank Russell, Raymond Z. Gallun, Cleve Cartmill, Alfred Bester, Ross Rocklynne, Robert Moore Williams, L. Sprague de Camp, Raymond F. Jones and S. Fowler Wright. Due to the timing of its publication, its superior contents, and its great commercial success, this work is one of science fiction's two most influential anthologies—the other being Harlan Ellison's *Dangerous Visions* (1967).

1947

*George O. Smith
Venus Equilateral
Philadelphia: Prime Press

The ten stories of the 1942–1945 *Astounding Science Fiction* series about a radio relay station built into an asteroid and put into a trojan position with Venus. Extrapolating from the science of his day, the author, himself an electronic engineer, showcases the social and technical consequences of such a station through a series of suspenseful and often comic adventures. Includes an introduction by John W. Campbell, Jr. on the extrapolative nature of SF.

Alfred Elton van Vogt
The Weapon Makers
Providence, RI: Hadley

When Neelan returned to Imperial City, Earth, from prospecting meteorites, he was only seeking the cause of death of his telepathically-linked twin. Yet he was soon enmeshed in a complex web of intrigue surrounding the libertarian Weapon Shops (whose slogan, "The right to buy weapons is the right to be free," symbolizes their enduring resistance to Earth's ruling Isher empire), the Empress herself, and the immortal Robert Hedrock, superscientist creator of the Weapon Shops and founder of the ruling dynasty. No less than humanity's destiny hangs in the balance, as Hedrock struggles to free interstellar flight from its official proscription. First published in *Astounding* in 1943 and later revised to make it the sequel to *The Weapon Shops of Isher* (1949).

David Henry Keller, M. D.
*Life Everlasting and Other Tales
of Science, Fantasy, and Horror*
Newark, NJ: The Avalon Company

Contains a long introduction by Sam Moskowitz, the title novel, ten short stories (mostly from the 1930s), and a Keller bibliography. In the novel, which first appeared in 1934, a utopia results from the discovery and mass distribution of a "serum" that cures every physical and mental ailment, prevents crime and evil behavior, and bestows immortality. But sterility also results, and women, facing a completely liberated but babyless life, choose to have their babies and the bad old days restored through the distribution of an "anti-serum." Several of the short stories are excellent terror tales, especially "The Thing in the Cellar" (1932), in which a young boy is forced to confront what his parents believe to be an imaginary terror lurking in the basement. The author's medical and psychiatric background is reflected in many of these works.

John Stewart Williamson [as Jack Williamson]
The Legion of Space
Reading, PA: Fantasy Press

Fresh from Legion Academy, young John Ulnar is assigned to the bodyguard of beautiful Aladoree Anthar, who holds the secret of AKKA, a powerful weapon upon which rests the security of the solar system. But treachery is afoot, and John is duped by his relative and superior officer, Eric Ulnar, who has recently returned from an expedition to Barnard's Star where he has enlisted the aid of the alien Medusae to restore him to the Imperial throne once held by the Ulnars. Aladoree is captured, and John and three fellow Legionnaires, Jay Kalam, Hal Samdu, and Giles Habibula are off to the rescue. Needless to say, the plot is foiled, and the young hero is given the name John Star in recognition of his achievement. A major space opera of its time, this 1934 *Astounding* novel (revised in 1947) was followed by two sequels: *The Cometeers* (1936) and *One Against the Legion* (1939). Cleanly written and entertaining.

1948

*John Wood Campbell, Jr.
Who Goes There? Seven Tales of Science Fiction
Chicago: Shasta

Contains seven of the author's "Don A. Stuart" stories, published in the mid 30s, and an introduction in which SF is described as "an effort to predict the future on the basis of known facts, culled largely from present-day science laboratories." In the title story, a scientific expedition to Antarctica discovers a monstrous alien frozen in the ice for 20 million years. Yet the alien lives, and its thawing at camp unleashes a ferocious killer able to read minds and change shape to resemble any living thing; soon the members must decide which among them are really human, and which the monster's creations. This chilling mystery served loosely as the basis for the 1951 film, *The Thing*. In "Twilight" a time traveler recounts his experiences seven million years in the future. Despite its machine-created utopia, humanity, having lost its "instinct for curiosity," is dying; in "Night," a sequel, an aviator testing an antigravity device is thrown billions of years into the future to find humanity dead and the universe dying. Neptune still harbors a civilization of "curious machines," but they, too, await final extinction; there remains nothing about which to be curious. The remaining stories are "Elimination," "Dead Knowledge," "Frictional Losses," and "Blindness."

Theodore Hamilton Sturgeon
Without Sorcery
Philadelphia: Prime Press

A collection of thirteen stories, originally published between 1939 and 1947, and a brief introduction by Ray Bradbury which praises the author, one of modern SF's prime originators of non-technologically oriented SF of superior literary merit. Outstanding stories include "Bianca's Hands," a tale of horror and love in which a young man becomes obsessed with the beautiful hands of an ugly imbecilic girl, and "Microcosmic God," in which a scientist creates a race of tiny, time-accelerated beings whom he tortures into developing fantastic inventions. Also noteworthy are "Ether Breather," the author's first published story, "It," and "Shottle Bop." Eight of these stories are reprinted in *Not Without Sorcery* (1961).

Alfred Elton van Vogt
The World of A̅
New York: Simon & Schuster

Apparently heavily influenced by Count Korzybski's General Semantics, this novel traces the adventures of Gilbert Gosseyn (pronounced "go sane") as he uses his non-Aristotelian consciousness and an "extra brain" to foil an alien plan to conquer Earth. This author's work has been characterized by some as "the extensively recomplicated plot," by others as "hard-SF dreams," and by yet others as the product of a "pygmy who has learned to operate an overgrown typewriter." All these observations are reflected in this 1945 *Astounding* novel— a plot that is difficult to follow, and contains magical science, and flaws of writing and characterization—yet it retains the power to capture readers with such visions as a super computer, the Games Machine, which picks Earth's leaders on the basis of their semantic training, duplicates bodies which Gosseyn can sequentually occupy when he is killed, and the struggles against wily and brutal invaders from the stars who have insinuated themselves into the very heart of Earth's major institutions. A sequel, "The Players of Null-A" (alternately titled *The Pawns of Null-A*), appeared in 1948.

1949

*Stanley Grauman Weinbaum
A Martian Odyssey and Others
Reading, PA: Fantasy Press

The basic collection of Weinbaum's short fiction. Noted for his alien landscapes and beings which transcended the SF of his day, Weinbaum is at his best in the title story. Dick Jarvis of the first Mars expedition crashes; as he struggles to return to the mothership, he meets Tweel, an ostrich-like alien. Together they confront a menagerie of bizarre life forms—a silicon creature that lives for centuries expelling bricks which it assembles into pyramids, a hallucination-producing tentacled blob, walking grass blades, and barrel-like creatures who rush to and fro pushing little carts. In a sequel, "Valley of Dreams," Jarvis visits Tweel's city which is now partially deserted and decaying. Yet he finds that Tweel's species had once been great and had visited Earth where they were worshipped as the Egyptian God, Thoth. Jarvis gives them atomic power which may help them progress again. Another set of stories involves the adventures of Ham Hammond: in "Parasite Planet," Ham struggles to master the wet, moldering biology of Venus. He meets his future wife, Patricia, and together they continue the exploration of Venus in "The Lotus Eaters," then move on to Uranus in "The Planet of Doubt." Alien life forms also steal the show in "Mad Moon"; the balloon-headed "loonies" of Jupiter's moon, Io, seem of little help to Grant Calthrope as he and a castaway girl flee the malevolent and intelligent rat-like "slinkers." Another outstanding story is the chilling "The Adaptive Ultimate"; a new drug not only restores a woman dying from tuberculosis, but gives her super powers to adapt to any condition. She threatens to rise to world domination until her doctor, who loves her, manages to destroy her power, and her beauty with it. This collection was combined with another, *The Red Peri* (1952), plus additional material and reissued as *A Martian Odyssey and Other Science Fiction Tales* (Hyperion Press, 1974). When Weinbaum died in 1935, he was only thirty-three years old; his exceptional SF-writing career had lasted only fifteen months.

Fredric William Brown
What Mad Universe
New York: E. P. Dutton

Out of an infinity of universes there must be one that mirrors the adolescent SF fan's fantasies, complete with the trappings of SF pulpdom. And that is exactly where SF editor Keith Winton finds himself in this zany first novel by one of SF's best comedic writers. Although similar to L. Sprague de Camp and Fletcher Pratt's *The Incomplete Enchanter* (1941), in that the hero is miraculously tossed into a mythic world, Brown's version differs in that it is a very real post-WW II America with the addition of occasional SF conventions, such as bug-eyed monsters and invading aliens. In a sense, Brown anticipated Ursula K. Le Guin's *The Lathe of Heaven* (1971); ironically, his work is dismissed as clever light comedy while hers is probed for deep philosophic meanings.

Robert Anson Heinlein
Red Planet
New York: Scribner

Set on the Mars of Percival Lowell and carefully accurate in the science of its day, this juvenile novel relates the adventures of Jim Marlowe and Frank Sutton, two colonial boys, and Willis, Jim's friend/pet, a soccer ball-shaped Martian animal, capable of simple speech and of perfectly parroting any sounds it hears. Mars, under the control of the Earth-based Mars Company, is administered by corrupt officials. The boys, off at Company boarding school, learn of a Company plot against the colonists. They run away to tell their parents, but, despite flight by ice skates on the frozen canals, the harsh environment almost kills them. The sentient Martians, giant, contemplative and mysterious, save the boys. Rebelling against the Company, the colonists win their independence, only to find the Martians, now fed up with the Earthmen, demanding that they leave. Only Jim's and Willis's friendship causes the Martians to relent.

Robert Anson Heinlein
Sixth Column
New York: Gnome Press

The U. S. has just been overrun by the PanAsians, when Major Ardmore of military intelligence arrives at the Citadel, a supersecret science lab buried deep in the Rocky Mountains. By an unfortunate coincidence, the lab itself has just undergone a catastrophe; an experiment has gone awry, and only six men remain alive—a mathematician, a bio-chemist, a physicist, and three enlisted men. Vowing to liberate America, Ardmore uses his meager resources of men and equipment to develop new weapons of unrivaled power. But how can seven men overthrow the crushing yoke of millions of PanAsian troops? Ardmore calls on his civilian skills in advertising to design a phony religion, the worship of the great god "Mota." The PanAsians see religion as a way of controlling the conquered, and Ardmore's men recruit priests and build congregations under the very noses of the enemy. Their new weapons are disguised as religious paraphernalia, and the temples are stockpiled against the coming day of rebellion. Despite its too obvious coincidences of plot, this story remains intriguing for its use of an underground pseudo-religion based on science. Fritz Leiber's *Gather Darkness* (1950) makes an interesting parallel read. This Heinlein novel has also appeared under the title *The Day After Tomorrow.*

Edward Elmer Smith
Skylark of Valeron
Reading, PA: Fantasy Press

The third in the four-volume Skylark series, this novel again pits nefarious "Blackie" DuQuesne and his evil henchmen against the upright Richard Seaton, Martin Crane, and their wives. While on a voyage to explore another galaxy, the Seaton party is set upon by substanceless projections of pure intelligence, and escape into the fourth dimension just as their two-mile long ship, Skylark Three, is destroyed. Meanwhile, DuQuesne, plying the stars in search of Seaton, tricks Seaton's alien friends on Norlamin into building him a super-science spaceship on the pretense that he will attempt Seaton's rescue. Blackie uses his new weapons—volatilization rays and force beams that lift Earth's navies out of the seas—to conquer Earth, the first step on his conquest of the universe. But Seaton, finding ever more advanced knowledge, survives and returns to Earth in a new Skylark armed with even more powerful super super-science. Blackie is converted into one of the immortal pure intellects and exiled to the ends of the universe, while Earth receives a utopian government, a "government of right instead of by might." Originally published in *Astounding* in 1934.

John Stewart Williamson [as Jack Williamson]
The Humanoids
New York: Simon & Schuster

Williamson's novel is far more important for its influence than for its intrinsic quality. The "humanoids" are a population of robots created to function as servants and protectors of the human species. They do this, unfortunately (or so it seems), to a fault, smothering human initiative and creativity. But the inhibiting influence of the robots is deliberately designed to force mankind to transcend its limits and to develop paranormal powers. The rebel, Forester, the first to do so, becomes the first success of the humanoids' purpose. The sequel, *The Humanoid Touch* (1980), picks up the theme and identifies a new species of human that can leave the robots behind. This second work is far more crisply written. An associated work is Williamson's classic novelette, "With Folded Hands" (1947), while John Brunner's story, "Thou Good and Faithful" (1953), seems to be an interesting spin-off. At the heart of these stories is the pressing question for an age of rapidly developing automating technology. What is the good/use of it? Answer: to free man to do something really constructive with his inner being and fundamental nature.

1950

*Henry Kuttner and Catherine Lucile Moore (as Henry Kuttner)
Fury
New York: Grosset & Dunlap

In the 27th Century, 600 years after humanity's forced exile from a destroyed Earth, the human race survives securely, but stagnantly, in "impervium"-domed cities beneath the seas of a Venus in the throes of a vicious Jurassic age. This slide into decadence and decay is reversed by events set in motion when Blaze Harker, a member of the "immortal" ruling caste, vindictively has his baby son physically altered to resemble a normally-lived "commoner." Raised in ignorance of his true heritage, Sam's frustrated abilities are directed into a cutthroat, devious drive for power, which culminates in his leading a renewed assault to pacify the planet's surface. Intrigue and action abound, as humanity struggles again to ascend the path of progress. The authors, husband and wife, were among the most influential and prolific of SF's Golden Age writers, often, singularly or together, writing under such pseudonyms as Lewis Padgett and Lawrence O'Donnell. A prequel to *Fury*, "Clash by Night," appeared in *Astounding* in 1943.

Robert Anson Heinlein
The Man Who Sold the Moon
Chicago: Shasta

Six of the stories that chronologically initiate Heinlein's famous Future History series. In "Life-Line," Dr. Pinero's invention of a machine that can accurately foretell the time of an individual's death creates shockwaves as society comprehends its implications; eventually, the good doctor is murdered and his machine smashed, perhaps a comment both on humanity's ambivalence about knowing the future and on the dangers to those, such as the author, who endeavor to provide such knowledge. "Let There Be Light" involves a young pair of scientists who invent a cheap, clean, efficient and safe solar energy cell; entrenched vested interests try to suppress their discovery, but the couple make their process a gift to the world (reserving a nominal royalty, of course). These solar cells seem to be powering the massive moving beltways that have replaced automotive transportation in "The Roads Must Roll," in which a rebellion breaks out among the para-military technicians that maintain this essential system. Heinlein raises the problem, still unsettled today, of how to select and train the dedicated, dependable personnel needed to operate our increasingly complex and dangerous technology. This is explored further in "Blowups Happen," where the technicians working in nuclear plants must be aided by psychologists in handling the stress produced by the constant concern over nuclear accidents.

In the title story, entrepreneur D. D. Harriman cons, cajoles, and coerces reluctant humanity into realizing his dream of space flight to the moon. Ironically, Harriman is prevented from leaving Earth by the need to remain behind to keep the space program operative. In a powerful sequel, "Requiem," Harriman finally finagles his way to the moon, only to die there from the exhaustion of his voyage; this is Heinlein at his most sublime. Most of these stories, plus others from the Future History series, are collected in Heinlein's *The Past Through Tomorrow* (1967).

Raymond Douglas Bradbury
The Martian Chronicles
Garden City, NY: Doubleday

The most famous single volume of SF in the modern development of the genre. Titled *The Silver Locusts* in the first British edition and translated into many languages, it may be the best selling SF work of modern times as well. Assembled from previously published stories, it recounts the gradual colonization of Mars by men from Earth. Its thematic analogue is the actual colonization of the New World by Europeans—and their rape and destruction of the indigenous Amerind culture. Mankind finally succeeds in becoming "Martians," but not without many ordeals. A television mini-series of *Chronicles* was finally aired in early 1980, but it barely captured the beauty of Bradbury's prose and the elegance of his imagery.

Judith Merril
Shadow on the Hearth
Garden City, NY: Doubleday

The upper-middle-class life of the Mitchell family in suburban lower Westchester is shattered at 1:19 P.M., Monday, May 3, when the U. S. suffers nuclear attack. Husband Tom is in New York on business, and that blasted area is sealed off, leaving wife Gladys and her two daughters, Ginny, five, and Barbie, fifteen, to face survival at home. Slowly their normal assumptions about life tumble; a new, ominous shadow—nuclear radiation—threatens them. Her traditional role has hardly prepared Gladys for the emergency, yet she bravely carries on. Unlike other nuclear war stories of the time, such as Philip Wylie's *Tomorrow* (1954) and Pat Frank's *Alas, Babylon* (1959), Merril's suburban setting and use of an ordinary housewife's point of view add an unusual depth of insight and sympathy to the story. However, her nuclear was is over in five days, the U. S. victorious, the road to recovery likely; the reality of nuclear war today would be many times worse.

Isaac Asimov
I, Robot
New York: Gnome Press

This famous collection of nine robot stories from the 1940s is known to almost two generations of American public school students. It features as a common motif the almost equally famous "three laws of robotics"—equivalent to a sort of Sermon on the Mount for sentient machines—designed to protect the machine as well as the men they serve. Indeed, the machines are in some ways better than men, both morally and ecologically. Many stories feature conflicts in the robots' service to men in spite of the seemingly all-inclusive laws designed to avoid such problems. For example, in the notable "Liar!" a mind-reading robot, Herbie, is trapped in the bind of either hurting people if it lies and tells them what it knows they want to hear, or of hurting them if it tells truths which it knows they don't want to face; poor Herbie goes insane. More robot stories are collected in *The Rest of the Robots* (1964).

Robert Anson Heinlein
Farmer in the Sky
New York: Scribner

Another of Heinlein's excellent "juvenile" novels. Billy Lerner and his family are immigrant homesteaders on Jupiter's moon, Ganymede. The quality of pioneering, even in a future of advanced technology, is captured by Heinlein: the long voyage; the lack of needed supplies; the need for intelligence, dedication, and labor by the pioneers. Family stresses must be managed or they can be as disruptive as the tidal effects of Jupiter's satellites when they are aligned. As usual, Heinlein posits tension between the homesteaders and the wrong-headed administrators of the home world. The establishment of scouting on Ganymede is detailed, as are the techniques for farming this alien world. A good read.

Fritz Reuter Leiber, Jr.
Gather, Darkness!
New York: Pellegrini & Cudahy

Golden Age science fiction tended to celebrate science and technology simplistically, but not always. The forties and fifties saw Western man grapple with the conflict of science and the humanities, reason and faith. *Darkness* comes to grips with this conflict cogently, reminiscent of the themes of the quite different mainstream fiction of C. P. Snow. In a future dark age, the remnants of past high science and technology, dressed in the religious garb of miracles, are used by a rigid theocracy to reinforce its social control and stifle progress. An underground of "witches," the Darkness, has formed and uses science, similarly disguised, to attack the Hierarchy's grip.

1951

*Robert Anson Heinlein
The Puppet Masters
Garden City, NY: Doubleday

Heinlein's own working of the story better known in Jack Finney's *The Invasion of the Body Snatchers*. Slug-like creatures attach themselves to people and threaten humanity until a way to destroy them is found. The story was popular and inferior, but something in the psyche of readers of the early fifties apparently drew them to this sort of piece.

Lyon Sprague de Camp
Rogue Queen
Garden City, NY: Doubleday

The planet Ormazd is populated by tall pink-skinned egg-laying humanoids who, for the past several hundred years, have developed a sex-caste society similar to that of bees. Numerous autonomous bronze age communities exist, each built around a single, fertile queen served by a few male drones and numerous non-sexually functioning female workers. The arrival of a spaceship from Terra is seen as an opportunity for the leaders of one community, Elham, to gain military help against their enemies, but interplanetary law forbids such intervention. However, Iroedh, an Elham worker, blackmails a crew member, Winston Bloch, to help her rescue her good friend, Antis, a drone about to be culled. Later, the outcasts, Iroedh and Antis, team up with Bloch and his wife, Dulac, to fight through attacks by rogue drones while on a mission for the ship. In the process, they discover that diet is the basis for workers' nonsexuality. Love and marriage again come to Ormazd, ending centuries of cultural stagnation. The contrast in sexual patterns produces humorous misunderstandings on the part of the Ormazdians, and serves to satirize our romantic conventions. Also contains a glossary of Ormazdian words. Part of the author's "Viagens Interplanetarias" series.

Raymond Douglas Bradbury
The Illustrated Man
Garden City, NY: Doubleday

The second most famous of Bradbury's SF works, it is constructed much as *Martian Chronicles*—of previously published stories. Here the "frame" is the completely tatooed body of a man, each tatoo giving rise to a story. The metaphor is brilliant. The stories are varied. Perhaps the most famous of them is "The Veldt," which tells of a pair of disinterested parents of the future who buy their children a playroom that can "realize" anything the imaginations of the two kids can think of. In their rage at being ignored, the children imagine an African veldt, complete with hungry lions, who devour the parents when they come to find the kids. The novel was made into a very fine motion picture starring Rod Steiger.

Austin Hall and Homer Eon Flint
The Blind Spot
Philadelphia: Prime Press

First published in *Argosy* in 1921, this is, in the words of Lester del Rey, "either the first major story to deal with travel between alternate universes or one of the most powerful novels of strange occult powers." The Blind Spot is an occasional opening between our Earth and another; through it, strange personages, such as the benign Rhamda Avec and the evil Bar Senestro, have arrived to seek a mysterious jewel. Although designated a venerated classic by some, Damon Knight calls it a chuckleheaded book of jumbled plot and garbled prose. A sequel, "The Spot of Life," appeared in 1932.

Clifford Donald Simak
Time and Again
New York: Simon & Schuster

The novel is in effect a sort of "Bible" written by its protagonist Asher Sutton, who has traveled through thousands of years of history, meeting, understanding, and loving an almost infinite variety of life forms and cultures. As in his more famous work, *City,* mankind is found less than dominant in the universe. Simak's concern with history and the fictional opportunities of the time travel effect run through many of his novels—even to the very recent potboiler, *Mastodonia* (1978).

Arthur Charles Clarke
Prelude to Space
New York: World Editions

A bridge between the earlier romantic and later realistic tales of the first moon voyage, this novel portrays the preparation for the launch as observed by Dirk Alexson, a historian chosen to document the event. Eventually, the *Prometheus* springs into space, and a new era for humanity dawns. A work refreshing in its confidence in science and technology, it is probably the first fiction to advocate the use of comsats (Clarke first advanced the concept in 1945).

Arthur Charles Clarke
The Sands of Mars
London: Sidgwick & Jackson

Newsman and former SF writer Martin Gibson travels to colonial Mars. There he finds the new settlement struggling to make the planet self-sufficient and, thereby, a permanent home for humanity. Along the way, Martin discovers his long-lost illegitimate son, Jimmy, among the spaceship's crew, makes friends with a likable little Martian, Squeak, and becomes converted to a strong pro-Martian settlement viewpoint. Technical details of space flight, domed Martian city life, and the exploration of Mars abound. An optimistic view of humanity's future.

Robert Anson Heinlein
The Green Hills of Earth
Chicago: Shasta

The second volume of Heinlein's Future History stories, which reflect the optimistic realism of the U. S. of the 1940s. Contains "Delilah and the Space-Rigger," "Space Jockey," "The Black Pits of Luna," "Gentlemen Be Seated," "Ordeal in Space," "It's Great to be Back," "The Green Hills of Earth," "—We Also Walk Dogs," "Logic of Empire," and "The Long Watch." Although grounded in the beliefs that people act on the basis of their own self-interest and that human reason and technical know-how will pull us through, these stories also exalt the potential for self-sacrifice and discipline in humanity, as in the remarkable title story about Rhysling, the Blind Singer of the Spaceways, who created the folk music of a space-going society and who sacrificed his life in order to save a spaceship and its passengers from radioactive death. Heinlein's people have something for which to live—and, therefore, if necessary, for which to die.

John Wyndham Parker Lucas Beynon Harris (as John Wyndham)
The Day of the Triffids
Garden City, NY: Doubleday

One of the classic invasion-of-Earth stories so perversely obsessive to the early fifties readers. The "Triffids" are plant creatures who threaten the existence of men. At story's end no way to stop them has been found—a metaphoric message to readers uneasy with the "progress" of mid-twentieth-century civilization. Harris would do it again with *The Midwich Cuckoos* (1958). *Triffids* was made into a fairly effective horror film.

1952

*Clifford Donald Simak
City
New York: Gnome Press

Assembled from short stories, in this novel Simak countered the themes of inevitable progress and ascendancy to dominance prevalent in the science fiction of the fifties by telling a tale of a mankind doomed to die of boredom and sterility of spirit, to be survived by his robots and "best friends," the specially-mutated dogs. Both "species" are sentient and spend their time as caretakers of sepulchered Earth remembering the last days of their human masters. The novel won the International Fantasy Award.

John Wood Campbell, Jr.
The Astounding Science Fiction Anthology
New York: Simon & Schuster

Excellent anthology of twenty-two stories and one article from SF's greatest magazine. "Classic" stories are numerous, and include Heinlein's "Blowups Happen," Asimov's "Nightfall," Leinster's "First Contact," Sherred's "E for Effort," Sturgeon's "Thunder and Roses," Schmitz's "The Witches of Karres," and van Vogt's "Vault of the Beast." Also represented are Williamson, de Camp, Padgett, O'Donnell, Pierce, Russell, Tenn, Neville, Simak, del Rey, Piper, and others. These stories exhibit the qualities that made *Astounding—* and Campbell's editorship—so unique and outstanding in modern SF.

Leigh Brackett
The Starmen
New York: Gnome Press

Michael Trehearne learns that he is not an Earthman, but a descendant of the Vardda, the only species physically capable of star travel. The Vardda have been genetically altered to withstand space travel, and they guard their secret jealously, for it gives them a lucrative monopoly on interstellar trade. Still, an underground exists which hopes to rediscover the lost genetic secret and make it known to other species. Michael, sympathetic to the rebels, finds the secret and tries to tell the galaxy. Entertaining space opera, but not Brackett's best. An abridged version of this work appeared as *The Galactic Breed* (1955), but the Gnome edition has been reprinted as *The Starmen of Llyrdis* (Ballantine, 1976).

Isaac Asimov
The Currents of Space
Garden City, NY: Doubleday

In a far future of galactic intrigue, Rik is found naked and mindless. With the help of the peasant girl, Lona, he sets out to find his identity, and, with it, the cause of his amnesia. The planet Florina faces destruction from its sun, which is about to go nova, a fact wiped from Rik's mind, along with the rest of his memories. A minor Asimov novel.

Arthur Charles Clarke
Islands in the Sky
Philadelphia: John C. Winston

Sixteen-year-old Roy Malcolm, a contestant on the Aviation Quiz Program, wins a trip to anywhere on Earth. He chooses a two-week visit to Earth's space station, where further adventures carry him around the moon. A weak plot serves as a pretense for this nuts and bolts tour of 21st-century space exploration, but its still a good juvenile novel.

Everett Franklin Bleiler and Thaddeus Eugene Dikty (eds.)
The Best Science-Fiction Stories: 1952
New York: Frederick Fell

The fourth volume in SF's first annual reprint anthology series. Contains eighteen stories chosen by the editors as among the past year's best. Especially noteworthy are Alfred Bester's "Of Time and Third Avenue," Bradbury's "The Pedestrian," Kornbluth's "The Marching Morons," and William Tenn's "Generation of Noah." The editors claim to seek stories combining literary craftsmanship and artistic insight.

Groff Conklin (ed.)
Invaders of Earth
New York: Vanguard

Twenty-two stories on the theme of alien visitations to Earth, selected by one of SF's most respected anthologists. Contains the script of Orson Welles' famous radio drama under the title of "Invasion from Mars" (Howard Koch's adaptation of H. G. Wells' *The War of the Worlds*); other stories of interest include Fredric Brown's "The Waveries," Mildred Clingerman's "Minister Without Portfolio," Edgar Pangborn's "Angel's Egg," and Sturgeon's "Tiny and the Monster." Stories are predominantly from the 1940s and late 1950s and range from horror to humor.

Kurt Vonnegut Jr.
Player Piano
New York: Scribner

In his many novels Vonnegut consistently conveys at least one message: that mankind's philosophies and ideologies can never satisfy him. Indeed, perhaps human endeavors are ultimately meaningless. In *Piano* he explores the phenomenon in the conflict of the team-oriented corporate commercial behavior that lock-steps people, who then revolt and destroy the system, only to wish for its return when standing in the ruins produced by the rebellion. The message repeats the Vonnegut works of the seventies.

James Benjamin Blish
Jack of Eagles
New York: Greenberg

One of many paranormal-powers-emerging yarns written in the fifties and sixties. It happens to Danny Caiden. For a time he is on the run from the law as well as the lawless. He survives and lives happily. Similar stories are Frederik Pohl's *Drunkard's Walk* (1960), Wilson Tucker's *Wild Talent* (1954), and Frank Robinson's *The Power* (1956). Such works captured the imagination as variations of starry-eyed, "gee whiz" power fantasy, but were a broad initial prospectus for more probing, less simplistic explorations of psi powers in the sixties and seventies.

Judith Merril (ed.)
Beyond Human Ken
New York: Random House

The second anthology by SF's leading woman anthologist. It contains twenty-one stories from the 1940s and early 1950s. Outstanding works include Padgett's "A Gnome There Was," del Rey's "Helen O'Loy," and Boucher's "The Compleat Werewolf"; there are also stories by Tenn, Russell. Blish, Heinlein, Leinster, Clifton, Christopher, and Sturgeon.

1953

*Theodore Hamilton Sturgeon
More Than Human
New York: Farrar, Straus and Young

Much of Sturgeon's science fiction concentrates on the latent power in humanity to transcend its miserable state and take control of its destiny— frequently through recognition that it is essentially a social organism wherein the individual must see that he must find harmony with and even love for his brothers. *More Than Human* won the International Fantasy Award for a story that portrays the birth of several people who have potentially superhuman talents, not to be realized until they travel their separate courses, meet, recognize each other, and merge into a single sentient entity "more than human." The story, with its portrayal of the agony and pain prerequisite to realization of new and superior identity, along with its final optimism, has worn well over the years.

Arthur Charles Clarke
Against the Fall of Night.
New York: Gnome Press

A richly imaginative fantasy of a man's quest for the stars. Alvin, the protagonist, explores his billion-year-old city and the stars above it in a quest for understanding of his universe and himself. An expanded version, *The City and the Stars,* was published in 1956.

Cyril M. Kornbluth
The Syndic
Garden City, NY: Doubleday

Vonnegut was sadly bemused by the predicament of corporate man in such works as *Player Piano*. Kornbluth's analysis in this novel is not much more hopeful, but the story he tells is tipped slightly in favor of the ability of capital interests to give order to the chaos of mankind's culture and history—if only intermittently. In the 1960s and 1970s, of course, in the works of such writers as John Brunner, big business takes heavy criticism.

Ward Moore
Bring the Jubilee
New York: Farrar, Straus and Young

It was the South who really won the Civil War. However, Hodgins McCormick time-traveled back and accidently changed history; so the victory is not part of the history of the real present. Alternate history stories done well, as this one is, make the processes of history come alive. Moore's novel is followed in later decades by Walter Miller's *A Canticle for Leibowitz* (1960)—really about the past and not the future; Keith Roberts' *Pavane* (1968); Jack Finney's *Time and Again* (1970); and Kingsley Amis' *The Alteration* (1977). In fact, extrapolation of the past from the present appears to yield aesthetically stronger novels than stories of extrapolation of the future.

Frederik Pohl and Cyril M. Kornbluth
The Space Merchants
New York: Ballantine

In addition to its prestige among science fiction readers, the novel had something of a cult status among left-leaning readers of the period. It satirizes aggressively the Madison Avenue advertising machinery that combines with big capital to forge and manipulate a consumer civilization. The central conflict surrounds the attempt of the ad-makers to exploit Venus. The story is a benchmark for SF attacks on unscrupulous business that would burgeon in the 1960s and 1970s, especially in the works of John Brunner.

Frederik Pohl (ed.)
Star Science Fiction Stories
New York: Ballantine

Fifteen original stories representing such authors as C. M. Kornbluth, Lester del Rey, Fritz Leiber, Clifford D. Simak, John Wyndham, Isaac Asimov, Robert Sheckley, Murray Leinster, Henry Kuttner and C. L. Moore, and Arthur C. Clarke. The pioneer original SF anthology series.

Alfred Bester
The Demolished Man
Chicago: Shasta

This novel is a landmark because it won the first Hugo Award. It offers an arch-criminal pursued by a telepathic detective in a story that weds the SF tale with the tale of detection. The two protagonists are portrayed with a complexity that far outdistanced most of the other SF written at the time.

Raymond Douglas Bradbury
The Golden Apples of the Sun
Garden City, NY: Doubleday

Golden Apples ranks in prestige just behind *The Martian Chronicles* and *The Illustrated Man* as among the best collections of Bradbury's short fiction. The mix of fantasy and science fiction among the twenty-two stories includes "The Pedestrian" and "A Sound of Thunder." The first is a sad inspection of a media-anesthesized (by television) middle-American population. The second summons the Emersonian perception of a universe so integrated in its parts in time and space that a butterfly killed by a time traveler to the past alters the present to which he will return.

Arthur Charles Clarke
Childhood's End
New York: Ballantine

This work is the basis of Clarke's fame and popularity in science fiction. With its wide inclusion as required reading in SF college courses, it continues to be the most read of all of his novels. Human civilization is in trouble. The divine overmind of the universe sends agents of a superspecies to force humanity to serenize and turn the evolutionary corner that will allow its "children" and progeny to mutate, grow up, and join the cosmic overmind itself—a special destiny in which not even the members of the agent super race can participate. The work amply echoes the Judeo-Christian proposition that mankind needs a Messiah for "salvation." No doubt this accounts for the novel's enormous popularity. Clarke infused the script of Kubrick's *2001: A Space Odyssey* with a similar message.

Robert Anson Heinlein
Starman Jones
New York: Scribner

One of the best of the juvenile novels Heinlein wrote for Scribner's during the 1940s and 1950s. An Ozark farm boy who has the ability to remember verbatim everything he has ever read, and becomes the acting captain of a star-traveling liner.

Henry Kuttner and Catherine Lucile Moore (as Lewis Padgett)
Mutant
New York: Gnome Press

From the "Baldy" stories of the late 1940s and early 1950s Kuttner assembled this story as one of the contributions to the science fiction novel dealing with the emergence of psi powers in mankind.

Fritz Reuter Leiber, Jr.
The Green Millennium
New York: Abelard Press

The popular, if latent, wish for messianic deliverance from a badly screwed-up world is humorously granted in this yarn about alien cats who come to our planet and literally bring "peace on Earth" through the effect the odor of the cats has on humans. There will be no more war. An upbeat, corny balm to Americans who were digging bomb shelters in their backyards.

1954

*Edgar Pangborn
A Mirror for Observers
Garden City, NY: Doubleday

No science fiction novel has produced a better account of mankind's age-old search for and identification of "the truly good man." In this story Martians, optimistic for the eventual moral maturation of humanity, secretly aid in the preservation of a man who can begin a great epoch of moral growth for the cultures of Earth.

Harry Clement Stubbs (as Hal Clement)
Mission of Gravity
Garden City, NY: Doubleday

This work is principal among those works by Clement that set an early standard for the writing of science fiction that adhered rigorously to science and known physics. The story describes and analyzes the indigenous species and the problems of the human explorers who visit these "people" on a planet where gravity is sometimes as high as seven hundred times that of Earth.

James Murdoch Macgregor (as J. T. McIntosh)
One in Three Hundred
Garden City, NY: Doubleday

The title is McIntosh's gloss of the Darwinian theory of natural selection applied to the survival rate of humans when the sun goes nova and they must winnow their numbers to colonize Mars and face the rigors of making a new home for themselves on the red planet.

Isaac Asimov
The Caves of Steel
Garden City, NY: Doubleday

A murder mystery combining robotics and sociology, and introducing the characters Elijah Baley, a human detective, and his robot assistant, R. Daneel Olivaw. An exploration of the relationship between man and machine, with a detailed and realistic portrayal of a future New York City.

Everett Franklin Bleiler and Thaddeus Eugene Dikty (eds.)
The Best Science-Fiction Stories: 1954
New York: Frederick Fell

One of the annual volumes in the excellent "year's best" series begun by the editors in 1949. Contains an introduction by Fritz Leiber, an index of the series' contents up to that time, and thirteen stories. Of special note are Alfred Bester's "Time Is the Traitor," Leiber's "A Bad Day for Sales," J. T. McIntosh's "One in Three Hundred," Walter M. Miller's "Crucifixus Etiam," and Ward Moore's "Lot." After this volume, Dikty edited the annual alone until the series ended in 1958.

Symmes Chadwick Oliver (as Chad Oliver)
Shadows in the Sun
New York: Ballantine

Backward Earth surrounded by a fabulously advanced civilization—of which humanity is unaware—is the familiar Golden Age science fiction setting of *Shadows*. One Earthman learns that a Texas town is a galactic outpost. Contact made, he sets about the task of bringing mankind to readiness for participation in the interstellar community. Oliver's credentials as an anthropologist drive his science fiction and make his work from the 1950s to the 1970s milestones of excellence in humans-meet-aliens narratives.

James Murdock Macgregor (as J. T. McIntosh)
Born Leader
Garden City, NY: Doubleday

An Earth dying from radiation that had leaked from atomic power plants and engines has sent a colony to a new planet fourteen light-years away. Beautiful Mundis is peaceful with no indigenous animals, only benign plants, a comfortable year-round constant temperature, no storms, oceans, or mountains; socially the colony resembles its environment, emphasizing a cooperative, idyllic and nearly stagnant life. A democratic council rules under a constitution that forbids atomic energy and requires strict rules of eugenic exogamy for various sub-groups. But this calm is shattered by two forces: Rog Foley, born on Mundis and a natural leader, mobilizes the youth to force change; the Clades, a later colony which left during Earth's brutal final throes, attempt the conquest of Mundis. Their bleak world, a neighbor to Mundis, is cold and mountainous, a fitting home for a people turned autocratic, militaristic, and sexist with a social structure based entirely on competition; they do not tolerate the family, individualism, religion or beauty. The Mundans have cannibalized their starship, have no weapons, and the older generation has been conditioned against the use of atomic energy. But the apparent weaklings are really the stronger, for they have a free society and Rog to lead it. Without struggle there is no progress, but for humans the most muscular are not always the fittest.

Edward Shepherd Mead
The Big Ball of Wax
New York: Simon & Schuster

Again big business is under attack, this time in its particular capacity to trivialize and subvert the distribution and use of inventions and discoveries whose wise understanding might provide real progress for mankind. The mood of this narrative is glibly and even nonsensically comic, but the anticipation of the somber treatise novels such as John Brunner's *The Sheep Look Up* (1972) is clear and explicit.

1955

*Philip Kindred Dick
Solar Lottery
New York: Ace

Dick takes on the whole agenda of big business, totalitarianism, syndicated crime, terrorism, and the possibility of the deliverance from these plagues by the moral heroism of individuals, who will fight against all of these agencies' attempts to "fix the game." Good wins out in this one, though it will fight to a draw or lose altogether in Dick's later novels.

Leigh Brackett
The Long Tomorrow
Garden City, NY: Doubleday

One of the fine earlier post-catastrophe novels. It concentrates on the struggle to resurrect reason and science amid the superstition of the survivor culture that has come to regard these as the cause of the disaster. Brackett had all the storytelling art and understanding of human character to provide a moving examination of this age-old human conflict.

Arthur Charles Clarke
Earthlight
New York: Ballantine

An enlargement of a novelette that appeared in *Thrilling Wonder Stories* in 1951. Takes place on the Moon in the 22nd century; realistic portrayal of conditions on the Moon.

Isaac Asimov
The Martian Way and Other Stories
Garden City, NY: Doubleday

A collection of four stories: "The Martian Way," "Youth," "The Deep," and "Sucker Bait," which originally appeared in *Galaxy, Space Science Fiction,* and *Astounding Science Fiction.*

Raymond Douglas Bradbury
The October Country
New York: Ballantine

The principal brilliance of Bradbury as a short story writer is again represented in this mix of fantasy and science fiction tales.

Cyril M. Kornbluth
Not This August
Garden City, NY: Doubleday

The McCarthy pogrom against Communism in the late 1940s fired the imagination of a number of writers and lots of readers through the cold war fifties. Heinlein's *Sixth Column* (1949) had featured the conquest of the U. S.

as a *fait accompli.* Kornbluth's novel has the U. S. conquered by Russia and China. But the heroic rugged individualism of Billy Justin, in a guerrilla counter-attack, recaptures America. Another SF novel read widely well beyond fandom.

Issac Asimov
The End of Eternity
Garden City, NY: Doubleday

Barrington J. Bayley's "Chronotic Empire" novels of the 1970s, and numerous others in between, owe much to Asimov's vintage examination of one of the major problems of time travel: If you can change the past to improve the present, should you do it? Here, in a spritely, if simplistically galvanized adventure of a single man's ability to change the policy of the use of time-travel technology, Asimov answers, you should not!

James Benjamin Blish
Earthman, Come Home
New York: Putnam

The third volume in the Cities in Flight series, which is composed of four novelettes written between 1950 and 1953: "Okie" (1950), "Bindlestiff" (1950), "Sargasso of Lost Cities" (1953), and "Earthman Come Home" (1953). The stories were combined to form the volume *Earthman, Come Home* after extensive revision. New York City and its mayor, John Amalfi, confront other rogue cities throughout the galaxy; eventually New York flees to the Greater Magellanic Cloud to found New Earth.

Robert Anson Heinlein
Tunnel in the Sky
New York: Scribner

An overcrowded Earth reduces its surplus population by colonizing distant planets, instantly transporting people through interstellar gates. To qualify for good jobs on this new frontier, students must take a survival course with test conditions that include "any planet, any climate, any terrain" and "no rules, all weapons, any equipment"; passing means living through the test. Rod Walker and some of his classmates from Patrick Henry High are sent to a savage jungle planet for their test, along with students from other high schools and colleges. Unfortunately, a nova disrupts gate travel, stranding the young people, who, under Rod's leadership, come together to found their own community. In overcoming their obstacles, Rod and the other youths come of age. In addition to its adventure, this juvenile novel abounds in ethical and social issues.

David McIlwain (as Charles Eric Maine)
Timeliner
London: Hodder & Stoughton

First presented as a BBC play, "The Einstein Way," (1954), which in turn was revised from "Highway i" (*Authentic,* 1953). The complications of time travel and a murder.

Harold Mead
The Bright Phoenix
London: Michael Joseph

The particular nightmare of the "utopian" totalitarian state, anchored classically in Orwell's *1984*, is given an alternate treatment here. A highly centralized and technologically sophisticated enclave of civilization has survived world war three, but fails in its attempts to extend its hegemony to other regions of war-torn and backward Earth.

Theodore Hamilton Sturgeon
A Way Home
New York: Funk & Wagnalls

A collection of eleven stories, including "Unite and Conquer," which proposes that national emnities on Earth will dissolve in the face of a threat from alien invaders. Vintage Sturgeon.

1956

*Alfred Bester
Tiger! Tiger!
London: Sidgwick & Jackson

One of the two novels with which Bester lead the field in the Golden Age of science fiction in the 1950s. This is the story of a spacer who reaches deep into his being under the ultimate test: he will die if he doesn't transcend his normal humanity and become a superman. Moreover, he is able to set a prospectus for the rest of competent humanity to follow. An emerging superman story elevated by the wit and shrewd analysis of what is wrong with the present conduct of human culture. A revised U. S. edition appeared as *The Stars My Destination* (1957).

Christopher Samuel Youd (as John Christopher)
The Death of Grass
London: Michael Joseph

A film version ran rather successfully in the ecology-hysterical 1970s. *Grass* is one of a cluster of disaster stories written by Christopher, and perhaps his best-known. A plague destroys the grasses of Earth (corn, wheat, rice) and causes a famine that radically reduces the population of the planet. Christopher is at his best describing the adventures and ordeal of the few survivors and the changes they must make in their values when "civilization" collapses. U. S. title: *No Blade of Grass*.

Robert Anson Heinlein
Double Star
Garden City, NY: Doubleday

This Hugo winner reads rather woodenly in the 1980s. In it an actor is forced to take an unmanagable politician's place. The politician dies; so the actor carries on—to realize the constructive goals the kidnapers wished to prevent. A perhaps dangerous endorsement of the proposition that the end justifies the means.

Judith Merril (ed.)
S-F: The Year's Greatest Science-Fiction and Fantasy
New York: Gnome

Eighteen stories, with an introduction by Orson Welles. Authors represented include Avram Davidson ("The Golem"), James E. Gunn ("The Cave of Night"), Walter M. Miller, Jr. ("The Hoofer"), Theodore Sturgeon ("Bulkhead"), Algis Budris ("Nobody Bothers Gus"), Isaac Asimov ("Dreaming Is a Private Thing"), and Damon Knight ("The Country of the Kind"). Also included is "The Year's Best S-F," a summation by the compiler. Merril launched what came to be a highly respected year's best anthology series, emphasizing literary quality as well as ideas.

Robert Anson Heinlein
Time for the Stars
New York: Scribner

One of the juvenile novels Heinlein wrote for Scribner's during the 1940s and 1950s. The story concerns a rivalry between telepathic twins, one of whom is aboard an interstellar exploratory ship and the other is on Earth.

Frank Patrick Herbert
The Dragon in the Sea
Garden City, NY: Doubleday

Also known by its alternate titles, *21st Century Sub* and *Under Pressure*, this was the author's first SF novel. America and the Eastern Powers are locked in a finely balanced protracted war. Short of oil, America is pirating it from wells secretly drilled in enemy territory using mini-nuclear subs (subtugs) towing huge plastic undersea barges (slugs) that can hold up to one hundred million barrels. But twenty of the last twenty missions have failed, the subtugs and crews lost, and Ensign John Ramsey, psychologist and electronics expert, is assigned to the next mission to solve the mystery. The other three crew members of the teardrop-shaped Hell Diver Class subtug, *Fenian Ram*, are the captain, Commander Sparrow, a Bible-quoting borderline psychotic, Lieutenant Commander Leslie Bonnett, who harbors deep insecurity feelings, and engineering officer Joe Garcia, a suspected spy. Together in the small sub they battle the sea, the enemy, and each other while under intense psychological pressure that generates paranoia. Detailed descriptions of the subtug, the slug, and underwater warfare.

Stanley Bennett Hough (as Rex Gordon)
No Man Friday
London: Heinemann

The solitary survivor of the first Martian expedition adapts to living conditions on the planet; a detailed portrayal of his struggle for survival. U. S. title: *First on Mars*.

Anonymous editors
Sometime, Never
London: Eyre & Spottiswoode

The tale of interest in this three-story collection is Golding's "Envoy Extraordinary." It is the novella version of his play *The Brass Butterfly*, recounting the frustratingly temporary, perhaps even meaningless effects of the inventions of a genius in the civilization of ancient Rome. He makes a steam engine, a paddlewheel ship, explosives, and what not. But the Emperor thinks of them as amusing gadgets. Human civilization simply rejects the knowledge it is not ready for, much as aborigines can not see the picture on a television set. Also included are John Wyndham's "Consider Her Ways" and Mervyn Peake's "Boy in Darkness."

James Benjamin Blish
They Shall Have Stars
London: Faber & Faber

The first of four novels (chronologically, second in order of publication) of the *Cities in Flight* tetralogy, featuring the adventures in interstellar travel of whole cities, equipped with faster-than-light drives. In *Stars* the drive is perfected.

Lester del Rey
Nerves
New York: Ballantine

The novelized version of a story published in 1942 depicting the breakdown of a nuclear power plant. The story is flimsy and the science is vague, but the prediction has proved uncannily accurate for real events of the 1970s.

Philip Kindred Dick
The World Jones Made
New York: Ace

A man with the power to see a year into the future causes major changes in society. This messianic figures runs throughout Dick's works as an important subsidiary theme, and can be seen elsewhere in *The Three Stigmata of Palmer Eldritch* (1964), *Do Androids Dream of Electric Sheep?* (1968), and *A Maze of Death* (1970).

Evan Hunter (as Hunt Collins)
Tomorrow's World
New York: Avalon

An elaboration of "Malice in Wonderland," published in *If* in 1954. Concerns a future in which drug-addict cults seek to destroy the United States. Published as *Tomorrow and Tomorrow* by Pyramid Books in 1956.

1957

*Arthur Charles Clarke
The Deep Range
New York: Harcourt, Brace

Clarke's non-fictional writing on oceanographic topics pays dividends in this adventure story of sea-life and man and the conflicts between commercial exploitation and preservation of the ecology and life forms of Earth's oceans. Commerce loses. Looks forward to Robert Merle's *Day of the Dolphin* (1969).

*Symmes Chadwick Oliver (as Chad Oliver)
The Winds of Time
Garden City, NY: Doubleday

Deals with the awakening of interstellar visitors, held in suspended animation since crashing on Earth 15,000 years ago, their fate, and that of the human protagonist.

Isaac Asimov
The Naked Sun
Garden City, NY: Doubleday

Sequel to *The Caves of Steel*; the exploration of the man-machine relationship is continued, here broadened to examine opposing varieties of human frailty exposed in an interstellar murder investigation.

Stanton Arthur Coblentz
Hidden World
New York: Avalon

This story first appeared in the mid-1930s, and is several levels of sophistication above the space opera and gadget stories of the time. It satirizes war, politics, and commerce, along with the additional agenda of foolishness and viciousness that dogs human culture. The metaphor is a squabbling netherworld, transparently representative of European and American powers that would fight World War II. Reissued as *In Caverns Below* (1975).

John Wyndham Parkes Lucas Benyon Harris (as John Wyndham)
The Midwich Cuckoos
London: Michael Joseph

The "Cuckoos" are the women of the English village of Midwich made pregnant by an extraterrestial superspecies. They bear children who grow up to take over the world. The great power of the story is the success with which it evokes the folk-tale religious superstition of the women impregnated by the devil with an "incubus." *The Village of the Damned*, a film version of the novel is a regular TV late-movie confection.

Harry Edmund Martinson
Aniara: A Review of Man in Time and Space
Stockholm: Bonnier

The story in 102 poems of the spaceship *Aniara*, which collides with meteors on her way to Mars and passes into interstellar space. The poems tell the story of the people on the ship and on Earth. Made into an opera in 1959, with much success all over Europe.

Alfred Elton van Vogt
Empire of the Atom
Chicago: Shasta

The first five of the "Gods" series in novel form. The other work in the series is *The Wizard of Linn* (1962). Adventures of a mutant genius in a barbaric future culture.

Fred Hoyle
The Black Cloud
London: Heinemann

The works of Hoyle the astronomer are at least as notable as the works of Hoyle the SF writer. In this story of the descent of a cloud of interstellar gas upon the solar system he combines astrophysics and fiction in a yarn that is both educational and entertaining. The cloud turns out to be both intelligent and benign.

John Holbrook Vance (as Jack Vance)
Big Planet
New York: Avalon

An Earth agent pursuing a megalomaniac is stranded on a low-density world on which a great variety of social systems co-exist. Adventure and intrigue as only Vance can portray it.

James Benjamin Blish
The Seedling Stars
New York: Gnome Press

The tale of cybernetic and biological alteration of humans has long since come to the fore in science fiction, especially in Martin Caidin's *Cyborg* (1972), Frederik Pohl's *Man Plus* (1976), and George Turner's *Beloved Son* (1978). This Blish work includes his "Pantropy" stories, the best of which is the famous "Sunface Tension," revealing the physical and cultural problems of colonizing distant worlds with a seed form of the human species biologically changed to survive in alien environments.

Walter Braden Finney (as Jack Finney)
The Third Level
New York: Rinehart

A collection of short stories, most of which deal with the problems of history and time travel, by the author of the horrific *The Body Snatchers* (1955) and the exquisitely detailed *Time and Again* (1970), his magnum opus time-travel novel.

Catherine Lucile Moore
Doomsday Morning
Garden City, NY: Doubleday

Conspiracy and revolution against COMUS (Communications of the U. S.) in a near-future setting.

Frederik Pohl
Slave Ship
New York: Ballantine

The Vietnamese, improbably, conquer the Orient. Western powers line up against them. The search is on for the weapon that can tip the scales for the war that seems inevitable—a weapon that is in fact a species of alien. But the weapon is a two-edged sword. The war is not fought. Compare this with yarns of Oriental conquest by Heinlein in *Sixth Column* (1949) and by John Hersey in *White Lotus* (1965).

1958

*Brian Wilson Aldiss
Non-stop
London: Faber & Faber

Aldiss makes use of the setting of the enormous starship continuing its voyage over centuries, the generations of the life and history of its passengers forming the materials out of which he erects a thesis that humanity as a culture-making species may decline. However, its most gifted members will lead mankind again to control the direction of its destiny. Issued in the U. S. as *Starship* (1959).

Algirdas Jonas Budrys (as Algis Budrys)
Who?
New York: Pyramid Books

The preoccupation with the Cold War between the U. S. and Russia continues in this work about a genius physicist, who, damaged by a lab accident, is picked up by Russia and repaired with metal facial features. Returned to the U. S., he can no longer be trusted—as a matter of policy in a conflict ordered by institutionalized paranoia.

Arthur Charles Clarke
The Other Side of the Sky
New York: Harcourt, Brace

A collection of twenty-four stories containing the pre-1960s fiction that Clarke thought memorable. Includes "The Nine Billion Names of God," "The Star," "Venture to the Moon," "The Other Side of the Sky," and "The Songs of Distant Earth."

Robert Anson Heinlein
Methuselah's Children
Hicksville, NY: Gnome Press

The fourth work in Heinlein's Future History series. A race of near-immortals conflicts with the rest of human society and is forced to flee to the stars. The story is continued in *Time Enough for Love* (1973), which focuses on the life of Lazarus Long, a major character in the earlier novel.

Edmund Cooper
Deadly Image
New York: Ballantine

A decadent future society dependent on androids is threatened with a revolt. Set in a realistically depicted post-holocaust society.

Richard Burton Matheson
A Stir of Echoes
Philadelphia: Lippincott

A hypnotist removes inhibitions from a subject's mind, who then develops extra-sensory powers which prove a curse to the victim.

James Benjamin Blish
The Triumph of Time
New York: Avon

The concluding volume of the *Cities in Flight* series, in which the end of the physical universe is depicted. British title: *A Clash of Symbols.* The first three volumes of the series are *They Shall Have Stars* (1956), *A Life for the Stars* (1962), and *Earthman, Come Home* (1955). The series concerns itself with the future history of the human race, following the career of New York City, which has been liberated from the surface of the Earth by means of anti-gravity devices.

Robert E. Sheckley
Immortality Delivered
New York: Avalon

An attempt to deal with psychic survival (life after death) in science fiction. A man dying in an automobile accident has his mind drawn to the year 2110, where immortality has been achieved. Good social and philosophical comment. Released as *Immortality, Inc.* by Bantam in 1959.

1959

*Robert Anson Heinlein
The Unpleasant Profession of Jonathan Hoag
Hicksville, NY: Gnome Press

A collection of six science fiction and fantasy stories: "The Unpleasant Profession of Jonathan Hoag" (*Unknown*, 1942), "The Man Who Travelled in

Elephants," "'All You Zombies,'" "They," "Our Fair City," and "'He Built a Crooked House.'"

Frederik Pohl and Cyril M. Kornbluth
Wolfbane
New York: Ballantine

Aliens physically capture Earth from its orbit and manipulate mankind in a process to manufacture food for themselves. With a struggle, the humans free themselves. In the Cold-War Paranoia over spies and fifth-column activity of the 1950s, this sort of story got the same obsessive reception as Heinlein's *The Puppet Masters* (1951) and Finney's *The Body Snatchers* (1955).

Isaac Asimov
Nine Tomorrows
Garden City, NY: Doubleday

A collection of nine stories and two poems, including "Profession," "All the Troubles of the World," and "The Ugly Little Boy."

Poul William Anderson
Virgin Planet
New York: Avalon

An enlarged version of a novelette which originally appeared in *Venture* magazine in 1957. The story concerns a man who lands on a planet occupied only by women descended from survivors of a space wreck several hundred years earlier. Part of Anderson's Psychotechnic series.

Kurt Vonnegut, Jr.
The Sirens of Titan
New York: Dell

Ever wonder what the real reason for the development of the beer can opener, the "church key," is? The answer is wound through the turbulently sad wittiness of *Sirens*. A ship of the immortal superspecies, the Tralfamadorians, lies out of order on a moon of Jupiter. It needs a single part to repair it. To obtain the part the Tralfamadorians cause the rise of the human race, who build a civilization with a culture that can produce such a part. We must admit there is no dearth of beer can openers on Earth. What did *you* think the meaning of human existence was?

Algirdas Jonas Budrys (as Algis Budrys)
The Falling Torch
New York: Pyramid

Human colonists have built an empire based in the Centauri star system, but Earth has been conquered by "Invaders." The son of the President-in-exile of Earth, Michael Wireman, an unprepossessing twenty-six year old, finds the gumption within himself to galvanize a resistance on Earth and retake it. Such is the potential force of individual human will.

Edmund Cooper
Seed of Light
London: Hutchinson

Based on the "travelling ark" theme, ten survivors from Earth travel in a starship to find a new planet on which to settle.

Robert Anson Heinlein
Starship Troopers
New York: Putnam

One of four of Heinlein's Hugo Award-winning novels, *Starship Troopers* recounts the life and early career of a cadet at a space academy of the future. The macho male culture and right-wing political philosophy that characterize much of Heinlein's fiction are present in this story which is suitable for, if not deliberately pitched at, youthful readers.

Mordecai Marceli Roshwald
Level Seven
London: Heinemann

Cast in the form of a narrative of a survivor waiting for the end in a fortified bomb shelter after the world has been virtually destroyed by war, this novel is not very original either in plot or execution. But it gained fame because it was read and recommended by such luminaries as Bertrand Russell and Linus Pauling.

Robert Silverberg
Starman's Quest
Hicksville, NY: Gnome Press

A juvenile that deals with the relationship of twins, one of whom travels in a starship and hence ages more slowly than the other.

Manly Wade Wellman
The Dark Destroyer
New York: Avalon

Revised from the story "Nuisance Value," which appeared in *Astounding Science Fiction* in 1938. An adventure in which human survivors fight a rear-guard action against the snail-like Cold People who have conquered Earth.

1960

*Algirdas Jonas Budrys (as Algis Budrys)
Rogue Moon
Greenwich, CT: Fawcett

Reprinted again and again since its first publication, the intensely focused action of *Rogue* concerns the attempt to explore an alien architectural construct discovered on the moon. Maze-like, the construct kills the human investigators again and again with every additional portion of it they penetrate.

The ploy and metaphor of the novel's apparatus, however, provides a matter transmitter as a means of transportion of the explorers to the moon. In the process, the man sent also remains behind. A "copy" of him travels, and is killed. The "copy" remaining behind experiences the successive deaths. The existential tension is excruciating, and classic.

*Harry Maxwell Harrison
Deathworld
New York: Bantam

Another notable work illustrating science fiction's assimilation of Darwinist theory. Life on "Deathworld" mutates to fight human colonizers, who, in sequels, *Deathworld 2* (1964) and *Deathworld 3* (1968), themselves mutate to continue to colonize successfully. Essentially adventure narratives.

Mark Clifton
Eight Keys to Eden
Garden City, NY: Doubleday

Clifton was the co-author of *They'd Rather Be Right* (1957) with Frank Riley, winner of the Hugo Award in an earlier edition in 1955 and not otherwise mentioned in this list of works. *Eden* features a group of explorers who go to a new planet as pre-colonizers and find such mystical peace and harmony on it that they forget Earth almost completely. A very satisfying example of the type of story in which mankind transcends his material bonds and joins the cosmic oversoul. There is a similar theme in *They'd Rather Be Right*.

Philip José Farmer
Strange Relations
New York: Ballantine

Farmer is well-known for his part in breaking down the barriers to treatment of sexual topics in SF. This handful of stories is calculated to strike at the nerve of the most piously and traditionally held sexual beliefs, especially when inspected in alien behaviors untroubled by human biases. Consider only the implications of the title of the key story, "Open to Me, My Sister," to catch the mood of the rest.

Robert P. Mills (ed.)
The Best from Fantasy and Science Fiction, Ninth Series
Garden City, NY: Doubleday

The first of a series of anthologies edited by Mills during his association with *The Magazine of Fantasy and Science Fiction*. Contains sixteen stories, eight poems, and six "Feghoot" vignettes, including such writers as Keyes, Goulart, Heinlein, Tenn, Knight, Bester, and Sturgeon.

Brian Wilson Aldiss
Galaxies Like Grains of Sand
New York: New American Library

A collection of eight stories, all of which appeared between 1957–58, and connecting sections that sketch the future history of our galaxy: "Out of Reach"; "All the World's Tears"; "Who Can Replace a Man?"; "O Ishrail!"; "Incentive"; "Gene-Hive"; "Secret of a Mighty City"; "Visiting Amoeba." Such scope is awe-inspiring; as our universe dies, the precursor of the next, speaking in "Visiting Amoeba" says: "Tell them again what a galaxy is . . . galaxies like grains of sand, each galaxy a cosmic laboratory for the blind experiments of nature . . . this laboratory is closing. A newer one, with more modern equipment, is opening just down the street." Derived from, but superior to Aldiss' earlier British collection, *The Canopy of Time* (1959).

Lyon Sprague de Camp
The Glory That Was
New York: Avalon

A combination of time travel and history, in which an eccentric archaeologist recreates Periclean Athens as the setting for various adventures.

Walter Michael Miller, Jr.
A Canticle for Leibowitz
Philadelphia: Lippincott

No work in science fiction has received more praise for consummate fusion of story and art. It won a Hugo Award. Few science fiction courses fail to make it required reading. The story is of events, after World War III nearly wastes earth, surrounding the rise of the Abbey of the Monks of Leibowitz, "bookleggers," through another twenty centuries that recapitulate in the future the actual history of the world that we all know, centering on the dark ages, the rise of the age of science of reason, and, once again, the nuclear age—with the threat of World War IV. Brilliant wit, character study, command of the principle issues of history, philosophy, art and economics are balanced in one of the few SF novels that is polished from beginning to end.

Theodore Hamilton Sturgeon
Venus Plus X
New York: Pyramid

The explicit treatment of sex in science fiction took a long time to reach a status where it stopped raising eyebrows—if not much more serious consternation. This treatment of all kinds of sexual permutations and possibilities was inherently wholesome and executed with great sensitivity. As the forerunner of such works as Gerrold's *The Man Who Folded Himself* (1973), it has not only worn well; it continues to be superior to later works.

1961

*Robert Anson Heinlein
Stranger in a Strange Land
New York: Putnam

Heinlein has indicated he wrote *Stranger* in an attempt to write a novel that would capture the popular mood and be a commercial success. It is unique among his works. Successful far beyond the ghetto readership of SF, it became a cult book. Charles Manson, leader of the Sharon Tate murders commune, apparently took something of the inspiration for his life-style from the novel. College instructors read it in Freshman composition courses as they read J. D. Salinger's *Catcher in the Rye* and William Golding's *Lord of the Flies*. It features Valentine Michael Smith, a human brought up with Martian culture and enhanced by Martian parapsychological powers. Smith comes to Earth, and in spite of the assistance of Jubal Harshaw (the central voice of the novel), commences a Christ-figure career, is martyred, and is apparently resurrected in a dream-vision of Jubal, who, in spite of his aging body, seems sexually revitalized by the experience. In all, a very very popular mish-mash of power fantasy, free love, and blank check mysticism comparable to Bach's *Jonathan Livingston Seagull.*

*Zenna Henderson
Pilgrimage: The Book of the People
Garden City, NY: Doubleday

For the rightly disposed reader, Henderson's "People" stories have an undeniably inspirational quality. This novel and its sequel, *The People: No Different Flesh* (1967) are assembled from individually published stories with linkage added. The People are human in every respect, except that they are extraterrestrial in origin, are apparently in a morally "unfallen" state, and have a whole panoply of parapsychological powers that they never use except with wholesome intent. When their own sun went nova, survivors became castaways on Earth. Persecuted by human beings, they live in remote places. Each story tends to feature the contact of one or a few Earth humans with the People, usually to the benefit of the Earthlings. Major characters in the stories are women or girls and boys, never men.

Theodore Hamilton Sturgeon
Some of Your Blood
New York: Ballantine

A non-SF study of a blood-drinking psychotic. A brilliant revision of the vampire theme.

Kingsley William Amis and Robert Conquest (eds.)
Spectrum
London: Victor Gollancz

The first of a series of five anthologies published between 1961–66 which were influential in popularizing science fiction in England. *Spectrum* contains ten stories by Pohl, Simak, Budrys, Tenn, Barr, Berryman, Elliott, Sheckley, MacLean, and Heinlein.

Arthur Charles Clarke
A Fall of Moondust
New York: Harcourt, Brace & World

The "dust" fell on a vehicle full of tourists sight-seeing on the moon. The story is of their rescue, carefully scientific and thoughtfully psychological. Paul Gallico would do it later in the non-SF novel *The Poseidon Adventure*. Clarke's work joins the many SF tales that perform the useful task of encouraging an attitude of great care in dealing with the products and situations made possible by advanced technology.

Daniel Francis Galouye
Dark Universe
New York: Bantam

With nuclear war inevitable, seventeen groups of people were sealed below ground to insure humanity's survival. Generations later, their descendants have returned to the now safe surface. But not those in U. S. Survival Complex Number Eleven. Early on an earth shift had caused their lights to fail and the people to move deeper into their caverns, forgetting their origins, except for myths of an ancient paradise, and reverting to simple technology and tribal society. This is the world of Jared Fenton, a young man who seeks the ultimate meanings of Darkness and Light—which now have taken on the religious connotations of evil and good—in a society where even the word "seeing" has been replaced by "smelling" and "hearing." People perceive by echo and smell in tunnels where giant mutated carnivorous bats prey upon them and poisonous spiders lurk in out of the way places. For Jared and his people the basic rule is survival. When help finally comes from the surface, the rescuers are mistaken for monsters, or perhaps the devils of Cobalt or Strontium themselves. Details of social life in total darkness are well worked out, as are the mythology and ritual patterns that carry the history of the group, but which have developed purely metaphysical and symbolic meanings.

James Edwin Gunn
The Joy Makers
New York: Bantam

Gunn picks up the Huxlian attack on mankind's pursuit of physical happiness. The narrative is much more interesting than Huxley's.

Harry Maxwell Harrison
The Stainless Steel Rat
New York: Pyramid

The first of three novels, *The Stainless Steel Rat's Revenge* (1970) and *The Stainless Steel Rat Saves the World* (1972), which are broad but incisive satires of space opera science fiction. In this first novel Slippery Jim Di Griz, an interstellar-criminal-turned-law-enforcer, is forced to join the Special Corps.

Alan Edward Nourse
Tiger by the Tail and Other Science Fiction Stories
New York: McKay

A collection of nine stories from the 1950s. The author, a medical doctor, draws on his own profession as background for the humorous "The Coffin Cure," in which a cure for the common cold also causes supersensitivity to smells, and "Family Resemblance," which argues compellingly (with tongue in cheek) that humanity descended from pigs, not apes. Medicine is also involved in "Nightmare Brother," where an astronaut is given life-threatening fantasies to prepare him to face the horrors of alien worlds, and "The Native Soil," in which a pharmaceutical company gets bogged down trying to harvest Venusian mud, a powerful antibiotic, which the natives use as food. Other stories include "Love Thy Vimp," that has invading, pesky, ape-like aliens defeated by being loved; "Problem," where aliens trick humanity out of Earth; "Brightside Crossing," about an exploring party's trek across the "hot side" of Mercury; "Letter of the Law," in which a con-man must tell the biggest lie to win his trial on a planet of liars; and the title story, about a woman's handbag that is an entrance to another dimension.

1962

*Brian Wilson Aldiss
The Long Afternoon of Earth
New York: New American Library

Reminiscent of the somber forecast of Simak's *City* (1952), *Long Afternoon* also predicts the decline and end of humanity, its few remaining representatives dwelling on an Earth whose rotation has literally stopped. Like the symbolism of a clock wound down, the metaphor of a stopped Earth works. Such a vision counters the bright-eyed dream of progress that filled much Golden Age SF. Received a Hugo Award. Expanded for its U. K. edition, *Hothouse* (1962).

Philip Kindred Dick
The Man in the High Castle
New York: Putnam

What would the world be like if Germany and Japan had won World War Two? The answer is the frame and setting of this alternate world novel that won a Hugo Award. It is, in addition, a novel-within-a-novel—the inner novel itself an alternate world story of how it would be if the U. S. and allies had won the war. Neither "novel" is, as it happens, an account of reality. In a complex work Dick reasserts the classical Aeschylean theme that in war all are defeated.

John Anthony Burgess Wilson
A Clockwork Orange
London: Heinemann

The career, influence, and success of *Clockwork* is legend, culminating in 1971 with a movie version by Stanley Kubrick. Released first as an "X" rated production, some of its violence was very quickly cut and the film finished much of its first run with an "R" rating. It addresses something of the nightmare possibilities of Crichton's *The Terminal Man* (1972)—though *Terminal* is a feeble effort in comparison to *Clockwork*. In the near future, illustrating the sinister and Draconian devices of totalitarian government aided by advanced neuroscience, a rapist is conditioned as a punishment for his crime to the degree that he grows nearly catatonically ill at the mere suggestion of violent behavior. Perhaps more powerful is the picture of Burgess' future, classic in the category of Orwell's *1984* and Huxley's *Brave New World.* Burgess' nearly equally obsessive but less well-known SF novel of overpopulation, *The Wanting Seed,* appeared in 1963.

Horace Beam Piper
Little Fuzzy
New York: Avon

The racism, anthropomorphism, and species chauvinism of mankind are apparent to reflective people. When the "Fuzzies" are discovered, they are almost victimized by the willingness of commercial profiteers to ignore their sentience and make a fast buck. This sprightly story and its sequel, *The Other Human Race* (1964), participate in the growing mood in America of the 1960s to guarantee the civil rights of the relatively helpless minorities.

Robert Silverberg
Recalled to Life
New York: Lancer

Investigates the moral and social issues arising in response to a method of restoring the dead to a full and healthy life.

James Graham Ballard
The Wind from Nowhere
New York: Berkley

The works of Ballard bear a stamp that clearly transcends the art and resonance of most science fiction. Among his several works of ecodisaster *Wind* may be part of an earth, air, fire, and water quartet (note *The Drowned World* (1962); *The Burning World* (1964), expanded as *The Drought,* (1965); and perhaps *The Crystal World* (1966). In *Wind* a gale of many hundreds of miles per hour scours the face of Earth. Even the shelter fortress of a millionaire falls before it. When the Earth is a wasteland, the wind stops. No clear reasons are provided. Humanity and all its works are sand before the inscrutable and elemental force of nature. The obvious debts to works such as Conrad's *Typhoon,* and even Melville's *Moby Dick,* have often been noted.

John Kilian Houston Brunner
Times Without Number
New York: Ace

Three sections with original titles comprise Brunner's "Society of Time" series, which deals with variations on the theme that nothing in time should be tampered with.

Arthur Charles Clarke
Tales of Ten Worlds
New York: Harcourt, Brace & World

A collection of fifteen stories, the most notable of which is "I Remember Babylon."

Naomi Margaret Haldane Mitchison
Memoirs of a Spacewoman
London: Victor Gollancz

This add-a-pearl, episodic yarn by a friend of Aldous Huxley transcends its narrative defects with its sensitive vignettes of the many possible alien points of view humans may someday have to appreciate. The lessons for individual human relationships are obvious and wise.

1963

*Kurt Vonnegut, Jr.
Cat's Cradle
New York: Holt, Rinehart and Winston

Vonnegut's bleakly humorous satire on the Manhattan Project that produced the atomic bomb. Here the invention is "ice-9," a molecule that freezes well above the temperature of "normal" ice. Moreover, it transforms all of the ordinary water it contacts into more ice-9. The result is that very soon after its release, all of Earth's water, and life, becomes frozen. The analogue for nuclear radioactivity is obvious. Vonnegut's wit is vintage in this work.

Robert Anson Heinlein
Orphans of the Sky
London: Victor Gollancz

The last of Heinlein's "Future History" series, containing two novelettes, "Universe" (1941) and "Common Sense" (1941), which deal with the theme of the generation-starship.

Paul Myron Anthony Linebarger (as Cordwainer Smith)
You Will Never Be the Same
Evanston, IL: Regency

A collection of eight stories including "Scanners Live in Vain," and "The Game of Rat and Dragon," which form a part of Smith's famous "Instrumentality of Mankind" series.

John Kilian Houston Brunner
Castaways' World
New York: Ace

First novel in The Zarathustra Refugee Planets series, comprising, in addition, *Secret Agent of Terra* (1962) and *The Repairmen of Cyclops* (1965). The fight for survival of two refugee parties under different leadership from the human-colonized planet, Zarathustra, who fled their planet when its sun went nova. Published as *Polymath* in 1974.

Walter Tevis
The Man Who Fell to Earth
Greenwich, CT: Fawcett

The novel was made into a major movie in 1976 which never received much fanfare. It may be that its message is too close to the bone. A man from another planet comes to Earth to seek help for his ancient and wise, but dying species. His strategy is to become human, contact Earth's leadership and get them to work on his species' revitalization. He becomes "human," but finds inexorably that humanity is racist, is xenophobic, to the degree that it not only repudiates and defeats him, but will also very likely destroy its own posterity.

John Holbrook Vance (as Jack Vance)
The Dragon Masters
New York: Ace

Perhaps the principal strength of Vance's science fiction is his brilliant evocation of the exotic flora and fauna of alien worlds. Here dragons and men join as a weapons system in one more way to prosecute war. Anne McCaffrey would exploit and elaborate the men and dragons motif into the rich tapestry of her "Dragonriders of Pern" series.

James White
Star Surgeon
New York: Ballantine

A novel in the "Sector General" series, which deals with an interstellar space hospital for alien life forms.

1964

*Edgar Pangborn
Davy
New York: St. Martin

The setting is right and the character is right to identify this SF novel with Henry Fielding's eighteenth-century classic *Tom Jones,* a serio-comic account of an intelligent, lusty young man making his way in the world. In Pangborn's novel the world is a post-holocaust one; nevertheless, the character study is nearly as fresh as Fielding's.

Fritz Reuter Leiber, Jr.
The Wanderer
New York: Ballantine

The scenario of Earth hit or narrowly missed by a comet, asteroid, moon, or planet has worn exceptionally well in science fiction historically. Niven and Pournelle's *Lucifer's Hammer* (1977) is the most popular recent example.

Leiber's Hugo Winner did the job nicely, too. In this version a planet/spaceship gobbles up the moon for fuel, leaving destruction in its wake—a wake traveled by a pursuing "planet," with neither "planet" ever identified.

Poul William Anderson
Trader to the Stars
Garden City, NY: Doubleday

More adventures of Nicholas Van Rijn, trader-entrepreneur extraordinary, as he keeps the practice of free enterprise lively in a far-future universe. Capitalism advocacy SF stories would fall out of favor through the 1960s and the early 1970s, but would begin to get a stronger reception in the late 1970s.

Robert Ervin Howard
Almuric
New York: Ace

Although best known for his Conan the Barbarian sword-and-sorcery stories, Howard here tells the tale of Esau Cairn, twentieth-century American social misfit, who is inadvertently transported to Almuric, a Barsoomian-like world, where he must struggle to survive. His strength and courage earn him a place among the Gura, tribal ape-men, and he finds that he can fit in on barbaric Almuric. A man's true nature is to battle for existence. First published as a 1939 *Weird Tales* serial.

Harry Clement Stubbs (as Hal Clement)
Close to Critical
New York: Ballantine

More adventures of Mesklinites on their planet of awesome gravity, classically originated in Clement's *Mission of Gravity* (1954). Not quite a sequel.

1965

*Sam Moskowitz (ed.)
Modern Masterpieces of Science Fiction
Cleveland: World

A companion volume to the editor's *Seekers of Tomorrow* (1966), which profiles twenty-one writers whom he believes to be the most influential in modern science fiction. Each author is represented here with a "superior example" of his or her fiction. Especially noteworthy stories include Williamson's "With Folded Hands," Sturgeon's "Microcosmic God," Simak's "Huddling Place," Leiber's "Coming Attraction," and Farmer's "Mother." Other writers represented are Smith, Campbell, Leinster, Hamilton, Wyndham, Russell, de Camp, del Rey, Heinlein, van Vogt, Asimov, Moore, Kuttner, Bloch, Bradbury and Clarke. In an introduction the editor, a long-time SF fan, surveys modern science fiction from 1938 to the early 1960s, with an emphasis on the influence of Campbell.

Philip Kindred Dick
The Three Stigmata of Palmer Eldritch
Garden City, NY: Doubleday

This is Dick's much-admired new scripture via the "Barbie-Doll" doll-house toy/LSD craze of the tripped-out 1960s. People play dolls and drugs in masturbatory drug dreams until Eldritch brings them "Chew-Z," a drug that really alters reality instead of people's perception of it. Eldritch, as part of the vision of these real trips, is a new "Christ." The trips are real; transubstantiation is real—as orthodox Christianity has insisted in its age-old doctrine. You can't return from them. The world is forever changed with the use of "Chew-Z"; tragic for some, sublimely fulfilling for others. The novel is the best of those in which Dick works through perhaps the major concern of his fiction—distinguishing between illusion and reality.

Brian Wilson Aldiss
Best Science Fiction Stories of Brian Aldiss
London: Faber & Faber

Fourteen stories, including "Who Can Replace a Man?" "Psyclops," "The New Father Christmas," and "The Impossible Star." Published in the U. S. as *Who Can Replace a Man?* (1966).

John Kilian Houston Brunner
The Squares of the City
New York: Ballantine

This is the first of Brunner's major novels dealing with totalitarianism, human rights, and the nature of political processes in the Western world. The story is of two men who play a game with people, based on an actual chess match Brunner dug up to structure his plot.

Frank Patrick Herbert
Dune
Philadelphia: Chilton

Dune and its sequels, *Dune Messiah* (1969) and *Children of Dune* (1976), have been wonderfully popular. The attraction and superior quality of the trilogy is set in the first and best, *Dune*, which is a painstakingly worked out presentation of a planetary environment and system of cultures much like that which would be present on Earth if it had almost no water. The question of how life might evolve upon such a planet at all is easily set aside while one enjoys the work's imaginative accomplishment. *Dune* won both the Hugo and Nebula Awards.

1966

*Ursula Kroeber Le Guin
Rocannon's World
New York: Ace

The first of Le Guin's "Hainish" novels, which include *Planet of Exile* (1966), *City of Illusions* (1967), *The Left Hand of Darkness* (1969), and *The Dispossessed* (1974), which comprise a literate and philosophically profound future history in which people from the planet Hain originally seeded the habitable worlds of our part of the galaxy with human life. *Rocannon's World* is set against the background of a galactic war.

Ursula Kroeber Le Guin
Planet of Exile
New York: Ace

The second work in Le Guin's "Hainish" series, in which survivors of an Earth colony on a far world revolt against alien enslavement.

James Graham Ballard
The Crystal World
London: Jonathan Cape

This novel must be regarded as the best of Ballard's consistently excellent canon of SF stories and novels. A primordial force from the depths of the universe plays upon Earth turning all things organic that it touches to beautiful —but dead—crystal forms. An expedition to the African region where the effect is taking place returns nothing but a deepening of the physical mystery and the evidence for the appalling conviction that humanity is utterly powerless in the utterly dispassionate sweep of the processes of the cosmos. The presentation of the obsessed, personal experience of this condition in the story's protagonist is the extraordinary achievement of the work.

James White
The Watch Below
New York: Ballantine

Generally well-known for his speculative medicine science fiction, White in this novel may have been at his best with a non-medicine related story. In World War II five people are trapped in the hold of a cargo ship that sank. Incredibly, their progeny survive for 100 years and are rescued. A timely event since Earth is being visited by a water world species and needs diplomats with a real sympathy for the desires of the invaders. An agreement to share Earth's oceans is struck. The account of the undersea entombment is particularly persuasive. The novel deserves more recognition than it has received.

Roger Joseph Zelazny
This Immortal
New York: Ace

Zelazny broke sensationally on the science fiction scene with this Hugo-winning first novel. It transforms the traditional post-nuclear-holocaust Earth SF setting into an opportunity for the ingenious use of mythical personalities and powers. Earth has become a museum-zoo for superior aliens. Myth-charactered, mutant humans are the fauna. An "immortal" Earthman represents what is left of mankind in dealing with an alien visitor who can change the destiny of apparently dead-ended humanity. The elements of fantasy with a rationalized base are here and will typify Zelazny's major work.

1967

*John Kilian Houston Brunner
Quicksand
Garden City, NY: Doubleday

Brunner continued to hone the art for character analysis that would invest his major works in this study of the realtionship of a psychologist and an anonymous girl, a patient who believes she is from a decadent utopian future. It leads to tragedy for both. A bleak reversal of the upbeat *Pygmalion* story.

Harlan Jay Ellison (ed.)
Dangerous Visions
Garden City, NY: Doubleday

One of the most influential anthologies ever published in the science fiction field, containing thirty-three original stories by New Wave writers. Followed by *Again, Dangerous Visions* (1972).

Samuel Ray Delany, Jr.
The Einstein Intersection
New York: Ace

Zelazny's trick of capturing human character in the personality forms of mythic characters and radically mutated "human" creatures is wonderfully executed in this Nebula Award winner by Delany. With a fascinating cast of characters wending their way through a world of the far future, Delany explores the meaning of history, of personal experience, of identity and love in the eternally converging timescape of an Einsteinian universe. The human mind and spirit have always known a Euclidian universe makes no sense. Perhaps a relativity universe does.

Helen Woods Edmonds (as Anna Kavan)
Ice
London: Owens

A character study of a young woman and her tragic fate in the terrible weather of an approaching ice age. The personal tragedy of Kavan herself is a poignant backdrop to retrospective appreciation of this work.

William Francis Nolan and George Clayton Johnson
Logan's Run
New York: Dial

A totalitarian government of the future by statute requires death at an early age (21 years?). But there is an underground that provides an alternative to this jazzed-up, unoriginal, illogical, imitation of the world of the infinitely better *1984* by George Orwell. The movie was popular, too. All kinds of things of no fundamental quality were popular in the permissive late 1960s in the U. S. There are two sequels and a couple of seasons of TV series in the "Logan" package.

Roger Joseph Zelazny
Four for Tomorrow
New York: Ace

Four novelettes: "The Furies" (1965), "The Graveyard Heart" (1964), "The Doors of His Face, the Lamps of His Mouth" (1965), and "A Rose for Ecclesiastes" (1963).

1968

*Samuel Ray Delany, Jr.
Nova
Garden City, NY: Doubleday

Again Delany writes an adventure novel with a biologically fanciful cast of characters. This one is set in a future containing a frenetic Earth culture and involves a quest/contest for a valuable element used as an energy source. The fun is in the portrayal of the characters who find that friendship and love transcend biology. The serious theme comes in the epic effort and intensity of the quest; ships must dive through exploding stars to recover the elements.

Leslie Purnell Davies
The Alien
London: Jenkins

The British government has a problem. A seriously injured man, John Maxwell, is brought to a hospital where he is found to have non-human blood, a heart on the right side, yellowish skin, strange scars on temples and chest, and blond hair streaked with white. Moreover, he has false credentials and a large bank account, both of which are only a year old. Is he an alien dropped from a recently reported UFO, or a saboteur of a major research lab working on synthetic tissue? Set in the Britain of 2016, the story unwinds as government agents and a second, mysterious group of men trail Maxwell after his release from the hospital. A spy-counter-spy novel which turns on the future development of techniques for radically altering personality.

Raphael Aloysius Lafferty
Past Master
New York: Ace

A *roman a clef* featuring St. Thomas More, sixteenth-century author of the classic *Utopia*, who is brought forward in time to a fraying utopia of the future to give it new life. More meets the same fate he met in real history— martyrdom. His effect on the future utopia is also mixed, as it was before.

John Kilian Houston Brunner
Stand on Zanzibar
Garden City, NY: Doubleday

Brunner's major achievement in the science fiction novel. It introduced a variety of story-telling experiments in a major SF work. Highly influential. Set in the near future, focusing on America and its influence on the world, it provides a bleak analysis—often in a mood of black humor—of the influence of multi-national corporations and the problem of overpopulation in making the planet Earth less and less fit for habitation. Within its episodes Brunner orchestrates an encyclopedic knowledge of the natural and physical sciences and their very latest developments in genetics and artificial intelligence in particular.

Keith John Kingston Roberts
Pavane
Garden City, NY: Doubleday

A wonderfully executed alternate history novel that in content and quality should be recognized as comparable to the heralded Walter Miller's *Canticle for Leibowitz* (1960). An atomic war wastes mankind, but its history repeats itself. Here the Spanish Armada has won and the world of the 1960s is a Roman Catholic religious hegemony. The fruits of scientific discoveries have been suppressed and the inquisition continues, but a new atomic war has not happened. Roberts is brilliant at creating the detail of the culture and civilization he erects.

Joanna Russ
Picnic on Paradise
New York: Ace

Russ' very rational feminism is once again at work in *Picnic*. Here a time-travel company plucks a woman from ancient Greece to serve as the rescuer of a group of tourists stranded on "Paradise," a tourist planet. In the rugged survival exercise, the women prove more competent than the males in the group. The analysis of the individual characters is the novel's strength.

1969

*Ursula Kroeber Le Guin
The Left Hand of Darkness
New York: Walker

The first of Le Guin's novels that won both the Hugo and Nebula Awards, and likely still the best of all her works. In the universe of her Hainish empire a lone human ambassador, Genly Ai, travels to the planet "Winter" to work the diplomacy that will let the newly-discovered planet join the loose federation of worlds. Genly and the Winterite Estraven travel and suffer together in a story that reveals through the complications of a relationship with a physiologically ambisexual species a long catalogue of insights into the nature of relationships between human men and women.

Roger Joseph Zelazny
Isle of the Dead
New York: Ace

Zelazny's ascendent reputation probably carried this work to more critical attention than it deserved from the reviewers. Myths and men, the stuff of the earlier successes, plus the intriguing proposition of the opportunity for a man to play God, are shuffled and redealt in this one.

Kurt Vonnegut, Jr.
Slaughterhouse Five
New York: Delacorte

Mainstream critics find this Vonnegut novel the best of his several famous ones. In it World War II veteran of the American bombing of Dresden, Billy Pilgrim, moves from past to Babbit-like present to future before the all-seeing vision of the Tralfamadorian superspecies that seems to control and trivialize human destiny—or at least lift no hand to make the human experience meaningful. Outrage at the bombing of Dresden is particularly pertinent because it was not a meaningful military target and the war was virtually over anyway.

Harry Maxwell Harrison
Captive Universe
New York: Putnam

The enormous world-carrying starship of Heinlein and Aldiss is restaged to carry this account of the decline and revitalization of a number of exemplary Earth cultures on an interstellar journey. The starship "universe" is much too small for the growth of an authentic humanity. Moreover, men must have the opportunity to know their environment, or they will go mentally moribund.

Michael John Moorcock
The Ice Schooner
London: Sphere

Future Earth is frozen in a globe-spanning ice age. The remnants of humanity have culturally adapted to the ice with fine technological and psychological precision; their wind-driven ice ships ply the Matto Grosso ice plain to hunt the land-whales and trade between the ice cliff cities. But disaster may threaten their way of life; are the land-whales migrating south to escape slowly rising temperatures? Perhaps the legendary Ice Mother in her lost city of New York has the answer; young captain Konrad Arflane and crew set sail in the *Ice Spirit* in quest of Her. They find the truth, but its cost is their deep faith in "the ice eternal, the doctrine that all must grow cold, that the Ice Mother's mercy is all that allows us to live." The icescape and ecology of this world are well-developed, the human cultures plausible; approaches Herbert's *Dune* (1965) and Le Guin's *The Left Hand of Darkness* (1969).

Anne Inez McCaffrey
The Ship Who Sang
New York: Walker

One of the most hyperbolic and, at the same time, most sensitive treatments of cybernetic extrapolation in science fiction, this story features the wedding of a young woman's nervous system and a space ship, who become "Helva." It is the personality of the singing Helva that is so attractive in the story that follows.

Michael John Moorcock
Behold the Man
London: Allison & Busby

Through a time travel effect Karl Glogauer travels from the 20th century and becomes the Christ of the Gospels. The boy he replaces is a moron. Karl has sex with Mary. He is the public figure of the stories. He is killed but he doesn't rise from the dead. A grim parody and debunking of the mythic material upon which Christianity and the Western world have built a culture.

Robert Silverberg
To Live Again
Garden City, NY: Doubleday

In a near future U. S., a kind of immortality is possible. A successful person can have his personality "taped" during life for resurrection after his death as a subsidiary sentient in the mind of another. Thus, a person if rich enough to afford this expensive purchase, can add the deceased's special abilities to his own. When the economically powerful Paul Kaufmann dies, the availability of his recorded psyche, or "soul" sets off an intensive struggle for its possession by two irreconcilable rivals, the nouveau riche John Rodris, and Mark, Paul's nephew, scion of the Kaufmann dynasty. But in such high circles of power treachery may lurk anywhere—among your business colleagues, your family, or even in your own mind where an adopted personality can, if strong enough, oust its host and take command. A study of power, corruption, and betrayal.

Roger Joseph Zelazny
Damnation Alley
New York: Putnam

In a post-nuclear war America, only California and New England survive as more or less organized entities, and they are harrassed by roving gangs, disease, and other destructive aftereffects. Between the coasts lies a social and environmental jungle, once the heartland of the U. S., now a damnation alley for anyone seeking to cross it. When New England is stricken by a plague, criminal Hell Tanner is offered a pardon in return for taking them the cure across this zone of death; setting off in an armored car, he confronts dangers ranging from radiation and giant mutated animals to outlaw gangs. Not generally considered one of Zelazny's best novels, it is still more inventive and exciting than its 1977 movie adaptation.

1970

*Poul William Anderson
Tau Zero
Garden City, NY: Doubleday

This story epitomizes the implications of Einsteinian relativity physics. The universe literally ends and begins again for the passengers of a space ship accelerated to just short of the speed of light, necessary to save the ship from destruction. Good traditional science fiction with a ruggedly enterprising hero. It looks ahead in theme to Robert Forward's wonderful exposition of the temporal relativistics of a pulsar in *Dragon's Egg* (1980).

*Stanislaw Lem
Solaris. Trans. Joanna Kilmartin and Steve Cox.
London: Faber & Faber

Like Ballard's *Crystal World* (1966), Lem's novel presents an inexplicable physical effect—an ocean covering a whole planet out of which lift the shapes and forms that can obsess the imaginations of men. It is the most famous and likely the best of the novels written by this Polish author whose reputation developed grandly throughout the 1970s. First published in Poland in 1961.

Robert Silverberg (ed.)
Science Fiction Hall of Fame. Vol. I.
Garden City, NY: Doubleday

Due to its wide adoption as a text in the thousands of college level SF courses in the 1970s this may well be the most commercially successful SF anthology of all. Stories are included according to votes cast by the Science Fiction Writers of America association. For its time it represents a very credible and valid best-of-the-best collection. It is succeeded by Volumes IIA and IIB (Ben Bova, 1973), which present over twenty novellas. Only Harlan Ellison's *Dangerous Visions* anthologies (1967, 1972) rival the *Hall of Fame* anthologies in popularity and success. *Hall of Fame*, Volume One contains stories by Asimov, Bester, Bixby, Blish, Boucher, Bradbury, Brown, Campbell, Clarke, del Rey, Godwin, Heinlein, Keyes, Knight, Kornbluth, Leiber, Leinster, Matheson, Merril, Padgett, Simak, Smith, Sturgeon, van Vogt, Weinbaum, and Zelazny.

Robert Anson Heinlein
I Will Fear No Evil
New York: Putnam

This excursion into the possibilities of a wedding of science fiction and pornography received wide attention only because Heinlein wrote it. In it the standard Heinlein hero and central intelligence is a very old and very rich lecherous fellow who manages to get his brain transplanted to the freshly dead body of his beautiful, young, female secretary. The ensuing odyssey analyzing the ramifications of a change not only of bodies but of sexual psychology never inspires but is sufficiently prurient to reward readers who take time for this sort of thing in the first place.

Ira Levin
This Perfect Day
New York: Random House

But it's not "perfect"; it is another totalitarian utopia in the mood of *1984* and *Brave New World*. This time to get free of it, the hero has to wreck the computer that controls the civilization. Levin is better known by far in the mainstream for *Rosemary's Baby* (non-SF) and the slick *The Stepford Wives* (1972), both of which are better novels.

Robert Silverberg (ed.)
The Mirror of Infinity: A Critic's Anthology of Science Fiction
New York: Harper & Row

An excellently designed anthology of thirteen superior stories primarily from the 1940s, 1950s, and 1960s. Each story is prefaced by a brief description of its author and its critic, followed by a critical foreword by a major SF scholar. Contents include H. G. Wells' "The Star," Campbell's "Twilight," Asimov's "Nightfall," Lewis Padgett's "Private Eye," Clarke's "The Sentinel," Robert Sheckley's "Specialist," James Blish's "Common Time," Cordwainer Smith's "The Game of Rat and Dragon," Heinlein's "All You Zombies—," J. G. Ballard's "The Subliminal Man," Ellison's "I Have No Mouth, and I Must Scream" (a 1968 Hugo Winner), P. A. Zoline's "The Heat Death of the Universe," and Borges' "The Library of Babel." In an introduction, the editor briefly overviews the history of SF and credits it as containing ". . . the governing myths of the dawning age of galactic man." Weak on coverage of non-English language SF, but highly readable, both in the classroom or out.

Nikolai Mikhailovich Amosov (as N. Amosoff)
Notes from the Future. Trans. George St. George.
New York: Simon & Schuster

The fictional diary of Ivan Nikolaevich Prokhoroff, a Russian scientist working on the cybernetic modeling of human physiological processes, who learns he has leukemia and tries to save his life by undergoing anabiosis (suspended animation). Set around 1969, the novel's first half details, with copious technical information, Ivan's race to develop anabiosis; of equal importance is his soul searching as he tries to come to terms with a life laced with tragic love affairs and limited by a scientist's narrow concerns and with his probable death by either his disease or by the dangerous anabiosis process itself. In the novel's second half, Ivan's gamble succeeds; he is awakened in 1991, his leukemia cured. Now philosophical and psychological elements loom large as he faces a brave new world where great technical advances have occurred, where all people are better off materially, and where capitalism and socialism have effected a compromise and war is considered a thing of the past. A superior mixture of hard SF, utopia, and a realistic view of science in the U. S. S. R., all infused with the convoluted introspections of the central character.

Ralph Blum
The Simultaneous Man
Boston: Little, Brown

Along with the cloning of bodies, the cloning of minds or memories offers fascinating puzzles as well as probing metaphysical problems in the science fiction of the 1970s. Blum's *Man,* about the replication of a man's memory in another man and the resultant conflicts that arise, anticipates John Varley's heroine protagonist—of many bodies and memories—in *The Ophiuchi Hotline* (1977).

Robert Silverberg
Tower of Glass
New York: Scribner

Science fiction novels of awesome artifacts accrete impressively in the 1970s. *Glass* is an awesome-artifact-aborted story. A magnate and his robots commence building an immense tower for communication with distant aliens. However, the theologically structured relationship between the man and his robots breaks down and the tower is destroyed. Obvious associations with the Biblical "Tower of Babel" story. Just one of the great number of consistently good pieces Silverberg would produce across the 1970s.

1971

*Ursula Kroeber Le Guin
The Lathe of Heaven
New York: Scribner

A low-budget public television film version of *Lathe* of some merit was aired in early 1980. The story is about a man whose dreams change reality and of the analyst who tries to control him. Rightly read, one suspects it is an effective metaphor for the individual's problem of deciding what is real as well as for the relationship of the world's power elite to the great mass of mankind. Le Guin has explicitly acknowledged her debt for the illusion versus reality theme of the novel to Philip K. Dick.

Lester del Rey
Pstalemate
New York: Putnam

A now routine paranormal-powers-emerging story by one of the most popular Golden Age SF writers. One twist here provides the future self of the hero with the power to time-travel back to his early development to show him how to escape the madness that seems inevitable.

James Benjamin Blish
. . . And All the Stars a Stage
Garden City, NY: Doubleday

Medical advances that give parents the choice of sex of their children have resulted in an overabundance of males which, in turn, has caused the rise of women to social, economic, and political domination. Jorn Birn, one of society's numerous superfluous males desperate for employment, takes a job with a new interstellar exploration program just as it is learned that the sun will nova. Desparately, a small fleet of ships is built and, under attack by the multitude to be left behind, launched in search of a new home. But the search seems neverending as planet after planet proves inhospitable. Interestingly, shipboard life soon spells the death of the Matriarchy.

Robert Silverberg (ed.)
New Dimensions I
Garden City, NY: Doubleday

Of the fourteen stories in this first volume of one of the field's best original anthology series, there were three award nominees: Gardner Dozois' "A Special Kind of Morning," R. A. Lafferty's "Sky," and Ursula K. Le Guin's "Vaster Than Empires and More Slow." Especially successful in its first five years, *New Dimensions* averaged 3.2 award nominees per volume; three of these won Hugos: Le Guin's "The Ones Who Walk Away from Omelas," Tiptree's "The Girl Who Was Plugged In," and Lafferty's "Eurema's Dam." Beginning with volume II, Silverberg retires as editor, to be replaced by Marta Randall.

William Hjortsberg
Gray Matters
New York: Simon & Schuster

One of the most subtly terrifying threats to modern man is the possibility that our civilization might succeed in homogenizing us to a point so complete that we are anonymous prisoners of it—indistinguishable from one another, virtually from birth. This nerve is touched in this novel of a "utopia" that preserves brains for life in new bodies, taking the opportunity to shape the brains with more enriched values while they wait. Some brains resist such "washing," preferring their powerfully neurotic individualities. One man escapes this utopia, and dies for it. But there is a triumph in his act of freedom.

John Keith Laumer
Dinosaur Beach
New York: Scribner

Agent Ravel of Nexx Central moves out from his base, Dinosaur Beach, in the Jurassic period to correct the time continuum disturbed by humanity's meddlings. But sinister forces are at work as Ravel loses girl and gets girl, is manipulated toward hidden ends, faces increasingly complex deadly technologies, and experiences quantum leaps in consciousness. Time-traveling space opera on a cosmic scale, fast-paced and entertaining, and all elegantly tied together by novel's end.

Robert Silverberg
The World Inside
Garden City, NY: Doubleday

Stories of overpopulation and the solutions to overpopulation are a staple of science fiction over the years. Silverberg explores the degree of success in one utopian solution in this novel. The urban population lives hive-like in enormous buildings. The agrarian population lives in statically existing tribes. There is the appearance of happiness; but it's not real. In the very manicured condition of the open land between building, is represented the moribund corsetting such a civilization must put, as well, on the individual. ·

Gordon Rupert Dickson
Sleepwalker's World
Philadelphia: Lippincott

"One day we'll all be gods . . . All of us. Not yet. We're still men and women now. I resent it, but it's a fact." So says Rafe Harold, cosmonaut, the most perfect man in mind and body in the world. Or so it seemed until sinister events began on Earth. Interstellar flight is being unaccountably delayed; Rafe's old friend, the top biophysicist, Abner Leesing, disappears; human vitality is being sapped as people are forced into a mind-disturbing sleep each night, the by-product of broadcast power stations that draw on the Earth's hot core for energy and which cannot be shut down without pushing Earth's huge population into starvation. In search of Leesing, Rafe, along with Leesing's crippled sister, Gaby, and her protector, a talking wolf, Lucas, find themselves confronting the power behind Earth's visable government. This is Shaitan, a grotesque giant with a child's head, who uses specialized types of broadcast power and his psychic ability to control the "zombies," the few people immune to the power stations, and strange shadow-men; these hold the government in thrall. But Shaitan's destruction reveals an even greater power behind him. In pursuit, Rafe and his two allies fly to the island of Havn where, in the presence of the captive Leesing, they confront the ultimate power—the Old Man, a superman who has manipulated humanity for centuries and who now feeds on the nightmare emotions of the sleepers. In destroying this Satan, Rafe and Lucas die; yet, paradoxically, they still live. Humanity's, and the Universe's, potential is still unfolding.

Thomas Michael Disch (ed.)
The Ruins of Earth: An Anthology of Stories of the Immediate Future
New York: Putnam

Sixteen dystopian stories, six original to this book, on the theme of ecological catastrophe. The editor contributes an introduction, "On Saving the World," and insightful or ironic quotes before most stories. Better stories include Vonnegut's "Deer in the Works" (not SF), Dick's "Autofac," Harrison's "Roommates," Ballard's "The Cage of Sand," Daphne du Maurier's "The Birds," and Gerald Jonas' "The Shaker Revival." In the final story, "America the Beautiful" by Fritz Leiber, a sensitive young British poet flees a U. S. domestically perfect but soul-sick from its constant militarism and hatred against the Communist East: "America is beautiful, the great golden apple of the Hesperides, hanging in the west like the setting sun. But there's a worm in the core of that apple, a great scaly black dragon."

1972

*Harlan Jay Ellison (ed.)
Again, Dangerous Visions
Garden City, NY: Doubleday

Like the first *Dangerous Visions* (1967), an anthology of original stories supposedly too hot for regular publication. Of the forty-six stories here, two won Hugos, Le Guin's "The Word for World is Forest" and Wolfe's "Against the Lafayette Escadrille," and one a Nebula, Joanna Russ' "When It Changed." Stories ranged from excellent to silly, traditional to avant garde. The title of Vonnegut's contribution, "The Big Space Fuck," more or less sums it up. The editor has been at work on a final *Dangerous Visions* since the second volume appeared.

Isaac Asimov
The Gods Themselves
Garden City, NY: Doubleday

Asimov, in spite of his enormous influence and popularity in science fiction, had not won the Hugo Award for a novel. *Gods* received the award, not so much for its individual quality, but for Asimov's achievement as a whole. Its story was timely enough—about the discovery of an apparently inexhaustible energy supply that turns out to hurt the balance of a hitherto unsuspected parallel universe. There is no free lunch in our universe; nor is there likely to be one between universes.

Michael Crichton
The Terminal Man
New York: Knopf

This novel moved into the limelight on the heels of the enormous popularity of Crichton's *The Andromeda Strain* (1969). Its story of a man whose brain is controlled with neurosurgically-implanted electrodes is basically unoriginal in science fiction. But it probably served the general reading public well in alerting them to the threat of manipulation of the human brain that the story depicts.

John Kilian Houston Brunner
The Sheep Look Up
New York: Harper & Row

Perhaps the best constructed of Brunner's four or five major "awful warning" stories set in America. This one anatomizes the ways in which the advanced industrial civilizations of the twentieth century, through irresponsible ignorance of polluting by-products, are quickly poisoning Earth's biosphere.

Robert Silverberg
Dying Inside
New York: Scribner

The enormous popularity and art of Daniel Keyes' classic *Flowers for

Algernon (1966) earlier puts this excellent Silverberg novel in perspective, the story of the ebb and flow, the growth and death of consciousness and intelligence in a human individual. In *Dying Inside* David Selig begins life as a telepath, exploits the power, loses it, and learns to live as a normal man. This may be Silverberg's finest work.

Norman Richard Spinrad
The Iron Dream
New York: Avon

In this work Spinrad suggests that we entertain the proposition that if Hitler had written a novel, this would be it. It is the nightmarish power fantasy that incorporates all of the perverse elements of the Nazi-facist histrio-myth in a yarn set in a post-nuclear holocaust world. It was nominated for a Nebula Award, and deserves the distinction for its fine control of its book-within-a-book architechtonics. But Spinrad's best work remains his 1969 blockbuster, *Bug Jack Barron*.

Isaac Asimov
The Early Asimov or, Eleven Years of Trying
Garden City, NY: Doubleday

A collection of Asimov's previously uncollected early pulp fiction. The twenty-seven stories span 1940, with Asimov's amateurish first published story, "The Callistan Menace," to 1949 and, "Mother Earth," an *Astounding* story of an engineered defeat of Earth so that the thirst for revenge will cause it to progress and eventually become superior to its interstellar neighbors. Although some are entertaining, these are hardly Asimov's best; the gems from this period, such as "Nightfall," the robot stories, and the "Foundation" stories, appear elsewhere. Still, the book is an extraordinary documentation of Asimov's development as a writer; surrounding the stories are numerous fascinating notes by Asimov on his publishing history and relationship with John W. Campbell, Jr.

Lester del Rey (ed.)
Best Science Fiction Stories of the Year
New York: E. P. Dutton

Premier volume in an annual year's best series edited by a veteran SF writer. In a foreword which discusses the problem of defining science fiction, the editor claims that "probably it can best be defined as a fiction which attempts to deal entertainingly with alternate possibilities." The stories selected were those the editor said he enjoyed reading the most during the preceding twelve months. There are fifteen stories, ten from the major SF magazines and five from original anthologies. Outstanding stories include Silverberg's "Good News from the Vatican" (a 1971 Nebula winner), Sturgeon's "Occam's Scalpel," Farmer's "The Sliced-Crosswise Only-on-Tuesday World," Anderson's "A Little Knowledge," and David M. Locke's "The Power of the Sentence." The book concludes with "The Science Fiction Yearbook," del Rey's review of SF in 1971, which overviews the SF magazines, book publishing, authors, major changes in the field, and other news: "In sum, science fiction has never previously been as active, healthy or generally accepted as it is now." A superior collection of fairly traditional science fiction.

Arthur Charles Clarke
The Wind from the Sun
New York: Harcourt Brace Jovanovich

A collection of the short stories Clarke wrote in the 1960s, all science fiction, including the lovely account of the interplanetary "yacht" race by craft fitted with immense sails to catch the solar wind for propulsion, in the title story.

Harry Maxwell Harrison
Tunnel Through the Deeps
New York: Putnam

In this alternate world, there was no Catholic victory in Moorish Spain, Britain has been world leader for centuries, and the U. S. revolution was lost, with George Washington hanged as a traitor and America still a British colony. Hoping to compensate for his family's disgrace two hundred years earlier, Augustine Washington is chief engineer on a great building project, a tunnel from Long Island to Land's End in England. Of course Gus has his problems, such as those with his girl's father, the tunnel designer, who is suspicious of Washington's new-fangled engineering techniques, and with those who would stop the tunnel's construction. A fine melodramatic, fake Victorian novel, full of humor and insight into the British character. A kind of parody of science fiction's oh-so-serious awesome artifacts story.

James Benjamin Blish
Midsummer Century
Garden City, NY: Doubleday

Twentieth-century scientist John Martels falls down an experimental radio telescope and lands in a disembodied brain, the Qvant, thousands of years in the future. On a planet turned tropical, humanity, mostly reduced to primitive tribes, looks to the Qvant for guidance in its losing battle against sentient birds with ESP. Martels' only hope of returning to his own time is reaching a colony of people in Antarctica who still possess high technology. From then on things get complicated. A strange uneven novel, perhaps done tongue-in-cheek, perhaps simply poorly done.

1973

*Arthur Charles Clarke
Rendezvous with Rama
London: Victor Gollancz

Clarke's great prestige as an SF writer—based principally on *Childhood's End* (1953) and his contribution to *2001: A Space Odyssey* (film)—was finally recognized with the Hugo Award to *Rama*, a good, but not great, super-race, stupendous-artifact yarn. In it a vast space-ship enters the solar system. It contains a complete world that pulses into life as it approaches Earth's sun. Human explorers investigate its very interesting mechanism and contents for the time of its passage. But much remains a mystery as the inhabitants, if any, are never met and the exploration team must leave the ship as it departs the solar system to continue its puzzling interstellar journey.

Robert Anson Heinlein
Time Enough for Love
New York: Putnam

The novel is a late-typical Heinlein smorgasbord of sex, genetics, power fantasy, libertarianism, theory of history, social criticism, slick narrative pace, and mono-character wrapped in the life and adventures of the nearly immortal Lazarus Long. Heinlein is much pre-occupied with the ways of beating death and preserving the capacity to enjoy sex and great wealth in a world where the human condition and human expectation provide far less for the average man.

Brian Wilson Aldiss
Frankenstein Unbound
London: Jonathan Cape

Nuclear war in space has triggered a rupturing of the space/time infrastructure, and reality is breaking down; timeslips are juxtaposing different times and territories on the Earth's surface. From his time of 2020 and his house in Texas, Joe Bodenland drives his car into an adjacent timeslip and finds himself trapped near Geneva, Switzerland in the year 1816. But this is a mythic world; he meets Victor Frankenstein and his monster. In an effort to learn more of the Frankenstein myth in order to save the falsely convicted Justine Moritz from hanging, Joe seeks out Mary Shelley. He finds her, along with Lord Byron and Percy Shelley, only to discover that she has yet to complete her novel. Returning to Frankenstein's world, he tries to prevent the scientist from creating a bride for his monster. Failing this, he kills Frankenstein and pursues the monster and his bride to kill them, too. As did Frankenstein in Mary Shelley's novel, Joe, along with his own age, shares a similar fate: "by seeking to control too much, we have lost control of ourselves." A polemic against the modern age of science and a support of the author's argument, in *Billion Year Spree* (1973), of the significance of Mary Shelley's novel.

Benjamin William Bova (ed.)
The Science Fiction Hall of Fame, Volumes IIA and IIB
Garden City, NY: Doubleday

Retroactive Nebulas are awarded for these twenty-two novellas by a vote of the Science Fiction Writers of America. All stories were published before 1965, when the Nebula Awards were originated, and most are from the 1940s and 1950s. Every work is classic; a basic library of excellent science fiction. Volume I, short stories, was edited by Robert Silverberg (1970).

David Gerrold
The Man Who Folded Himself
New York: Random House

As the probability that people will be cloned comes closer and closer to realization in the last decades of the twentieth century, this novel reminds readers that the old time-travel paradox physics accomplished the same effect and the same parable of identity crises. Through a time-travel belt, its owner replicates himself in both male and female form, again and again, meeting himself, loving himself, hating himself, as members of the same and the opposite sex. The story's logic is dazzlingly irresistible, even as its propositions shock the reader with answers to the most fundamental questions of the meaning and identity of an individual human being. This from the man who engineered the *Star Trek* episode, "The Trouble with Tribbles," the cuddly creatures who would not stop multiplying.

Stanislaw Lem
The Invincible. Trans. Wendayne Ackerman.
New York: Seabury

A space ship, *Invincible,* visits a planet and is immobilized, its crew driven crazy, by a highly evolved machine species. The ship goes to discover what happened. But like all of Lem's superficially simple stories, there is more to this one than a familiar SF situation. It questions the very possibility that mankind has any destiny at all in the universe, beyond relatively early demise. Originally published in Poland in 1964.

Sterling E. Lanier
Hiero's Journey
Radnor, PA: Chilton

It is 7476 A.D., long after technological civilization has been destroyed by nuclear war, and North America has reverted to a wilderness filled with mutated life. Many animals are highly intelligent, some have telepathy, as do most of the surviving humans. Among the remnants of Canada, a society of priest/scientists are trying to rediscover the lost knowledge of the nearly legendary past; they face threats from the Unclean, the Dark Brotherhood of mutated humans, who live to the south. Per Hiero Desteen, Secondary Priest-Exorcist, Primary Rover and Senior Killman, is sent south to explore the ancient city ruins for the secrets of the awesome and mysterious computer and other lost weapons of the past. Astride his bull morse (a mutated moose) named Klootz, Hiero's journey leads him through forests and swamps and across the vast inland sea of the drowned Great Lakes, where he encounters monsters and murderous tribesmen. Along the way he rescues a maiden who becomes his companion and also takes up with a telepathic and charming bear named Gorm. Lusty high adventure in a continually surprising and fascinating ecology.

Peter Dickinson
The Green Gene
New York: Pantheon

White parents in England begin having black babies, the result of a re-emergent gene operating to combat cancer in the species. Unfortunately, racist attitudes make people too stupid to understand this. The result is a race war.

This kind of SF story fits the mood of the late 1960s and early 1970s when racism in the Western world was getting enormous attention, though by 1973 the heightened sensitivity was petering out.

George Alec Effinger
Relatives
New York: Harper & Row

Complex novel composed of three stories which are interspersed among each other; each story is set in an alternate Earth, but each has a similar character—Ernest Weinraub, Ernst Weinraub, and Ernst Weintraub—who is taken through his daily routine. One is a worker in an urban dystopia, the second an ineffectual intellectual drinking himself to destruction in a decadent world dominated by Europe, and the third is a hard-core communist struggling in an oppressive world ruled by a "Jermany" that has won the First World War. Their drab lives are drably unfolded in drab prose. The author's point, if any, escapes many; still, others find the work powerful.

Roger Elwood (ed.)
Future City
New York: Trident

Theme anthology on the city of the future by one of science fiction's most controversial and prolific editors of the late 1960s and early 1970s. Contents include a foreword by Clifford Simak and an afterword by Frederik Pohl, three poems (by Thomas Disch, D. M. Price, and Virginia Kidd), and nineteen generally downbeat but interesting stories. Authors include Ben Bova, Barry Malzberg, Dean R. Koontz, Frank Herbert, Robert Silverberg, Thomas F. Monteleone, Harlan Ellison, and Miriam Allen de Ford.

Howard Melvin Fast
A Touch of Infinity
New York: Morrow

A collection of fine stories by the author of the far more popular *Spartacus* (non-SF). Virtually all of Fast's best fantasy and science fiction stories are collected in *Time and the Riddle* (1975), in which Fast speaks of the influence upon him of Zen—an influence apparent in many of his stories.

Barry N. Malzberg
Herovit's World
New York: Random House

Malzberg is in a class with Philip K. Dick when it comes to writing yarns of complex metaphysical meaning and social satire employing the most unlikely materials. Here he has spun a story that self-consciously examines the lives and motives of SF writers and SF fandom. This is a feat only the most elegantly cerebral of writers can bring off. Malzberg succeeds. Richard Lupoff will do another in *Space War Blues* (1978), employing SF story tropes.

Michael Allen Rogers
Mindfogger
New York: Knopf

A Hip, With-it electronics genius named Niles Spindrift (sic), working for a Reactionary Big Bad Business, is on the threshhold of a major Breakthrough on Mind research. Smelling a Profitable Weapons Contract, the Company takes an interest, and, to keep his work out of the Oppressor's hands, Spindrift Drops Out and goes Underground in the Counter-Culture. Eventually, he perfects his gadget, the Mindfogger, which has the Power to Cloud Men's Minds, and give them a Rush, too. Striking out against the Establishment, Spindrift uses his gadget for Good by sabotaging an Evil Defense Factory, causing Production to fall. Caught, and as quickly escaped, Sprindrift hides in the mountains where his really Big Breakthrough occurs—the Power was in his Mind all the time, and not in the Machine. Oh yes, he has a girl who tags along, and they have sex. Stereotypic, simplistic, and pointless, but probably a Blast for California counter-culture nostalgia buffs.

Robert Silverberg (ed.)
Deep Space
New York: Nelson

An anthology of eight stories from 1944 to 1968 that catches science fiction's traditional sense of wonder. A. E. van Vogt's "Far Centaurus" tells of the first interstellar voyage, taken at sub-light speeds with its crew in suspended animation, which arrives at Alpha Centauri only to find that humanity has meanwhile developed faster than light travel and is already there to greet them. In Jack Vance's "Noise" a spaceman is marooned on a planet where red, blue, silver, green, and gold suns illuminate long consecutive days, and diaphanous mirages seem to take increasingly substantial form. Also includes stories by Chad Oliver, a young Harlan Ellison, Damon Knight, Gordon Dickson, Terry Carr, and Silverberg. Science fiction as it ought to be.

Arkadi Natanovich Strugatski and Boris Natanovich Strugatski
Hard to Be a God. Trans. Wendayne Ackerman.
New York: Seabury

The English translation of the Russian novel published first in 1964, this work put the Strugatskis high on the list of 1970s novelists. They have been prolific since. The story is of the manipulation of the culture of a medieval-level Earth colony on a new planet by a team of people from the advanced civilization of original Earth. The colonists deal with the team as "Gods." But the human "gods" are no more successful at the job than other "gods" in human history have been.

1974

*Ursula Kroeber Le Guin
The Dispossessed: An Ambiguous Utopia
New York: Harper & Row

The second of Le Guin's double prize-winning SF novels (*The Left Hand of Darkness* also won both the Hugo and Nebula awards), *Dispossessed* is a novel of utopia versus transparently real present-day human culture inspired by the wisdom of balances inherent in Taoist thought. Shevek, the physics genius, grows up on rugged, enlightened Anarres, planet of banishment of the populations who revolted on the rich and fertile planet Urras, wherein a wasteful, culturally moribund and politically repressive establishment holds sway. Inventor of the "ansible," a device that makes instant communication between the stars possible, Shevek goes to Urras to be honored with its greatest science prize. Thus the stage is set for examining the contrasts in culture between the two planets in the alternating chapters of the novel. Beautiful thoughts in often beautiful language—a hallmark of Le Guin.

Laurence van Cott Niven (as Larry Niven) and Jerry E. Pournelle
The Mote in God's Eye
New York: Simon & Schuster

This writing team has been extraordinarily successful from the middle to the late 1970s. Their *Inferno* (1976) earned award nominations; and their *Lucifer's Hammer* (1977) was a mainstream best-seller. *Mote,* as the first of three great successes, is the neo-space operatic extravaganza of an expedition to a remote world of unlikeable aliens. It received lots of big prize nominations.

Christopher Priest
Inverted World
London: Faber & Faber

Men move a city across two continents and through an equally problematical Einsteinian temporal/spatial continuum. The story provides a stunning metaphor for the on-going conflict between beliefs in the need for technological progress and the need to concentrate on strictly human affairs. The first want the city to keep moving; the latter want it to halt. The novel won the British Science Fiction Award.

Philip Kindred Dick
Flow My Tears, the Policeman Said
Garden City, NY: Doubleday

Once again, as in *Eye in the Sky* (1957), Dick tells a story of someone coerced by someone else's reality. Here the victim is a television star. He has an affair with the decadent, drug-dreaming daughter of the police chief of a totalitarian state. The generally high regard in which Dick has been held through the 1970s by academic SF critics makes it easier to understand why this novel won the 1975 Campbell Memorial Award.

Joseph W. Haldeman
The Forever War
New York: St. Martin

In the last years of the 20th century, William Mandella is drafted into an army to fight the "Taurans." Armies move instantaneously among stars by means of "collapsars," causing time dilation effects that force soldiers returning "home" to Earth hundreds of years into the future of the "present" they departed. The war lasts over a thousand Earth years. Mandella is the only soldier to survive from the beginning. Beyond its intrinsic merits as an elaborate adventure yarn, the novel is a wonderful parody of SF clichés: The war is a tragic mistake; Mandella's last battle turns out to be critical, even though fought with clubs, swords and arrows; Mandella and his beloved marry and live happily; humanity is cloned from a telepathic corporal and conquers the galaxy. The narrative is almost as clean as that of the Hemingway who taught writers such as Haldeman how to make it. The novel put Haldeman in the limelight and won both the Nebula and the Hugo awards.

Stanislaw Lem
The Futurological Congress, from the Memoirs of Ijon Tichy
Trans. Michael Kandel.
New York: Seabury

Once the translation of his works was in full swing, Lem's reputation soared among influential critics in England and America. Here he joins the likes of Malzberg, Dick, and Lupoff in writing a satirical attack on the phenomenon of the futurists convention. The scene becomes a battleground of all the most frenetic and savage behaviors and decadence emerging in modern society. Originally published in Poland in 1971.

Robert Silverberg
Born With the Dead
New York: Random House

Three novellas that deal with death. "Born With the Dead," which won a Nebula in 1974, depicts a time when the dead, if not too damaged, can be resurrected or "rekindled," but without the zest of the living. A man obsessively pursues his "rekindled" wife into the self-segregated world of the dead; finally annoyed, she and her "rekindled" colleagues kill him. God seems to exist in "Thomas the Proclaimer," where a professional prophet calls forth the miracle of stopping the Earth from rotating for a day; but if God exists, must not evil, too? "Going" tells of the decision by a healthy, talented and successful man over 130 years old to take his own life despite the possibility of living much longer. Downer stories, well written, but not likely to satisfy readers seeking action plots.

Arthur Wilson Tucker
Ice and Iron
Garden City, NY: Doubleday

A time-space slip makes possible a tenuous contact between a present threatened with a new ice-age and a future dominated with a female-directed totalitarianism, suggesting that the good news of survival into any future must likely be tempered with the observation that that future might be worse than the present. Tucker's best novels deal with the agendas of human history, past and future, through devices of suspended animation and time travel. Revised for the 1975 paperback edition.

1975

*Arthur Charles Clarke
Imperial Earth: A Fantasy of Love and Discord*
London: Victor Gollancz

A detailed tour of humanity's condition in the year 2276. Duncan Makenzie, the clone of the clone of Malcolm Makenzie, the engineer and founder/ruler of the human colony on Titan, travels to Earth to (a) give a speech before Congress, on the occasion of the United State's fifth centennial, (b) make the contacts on Earth needed to preserve his family's power on Titan, (c) get himself cloned to continue the Makenzie line, and (d) look up an old flame, Calindy. It is the time of civilization's full flowering on Earth; social problems seem to have been reduced to their absolute minimums, and freedom, equality, peace, and prosperity abound. Yet decadence may arrive with the next generation. As Duncan works out his own problems, he also discovers a new goal for humanity—one that might stave off civilization's decline—the search for other intelligence in the universe. An optimistic, pro-science and pro-technology novel that fascinates futurists. Also contains a brief note in which Clarke acknowledges the origins of some of the ideas developed in the book.

Ursula Kroeber Le Guin
The Wind's Twelve Quarters
New York: Harper & Row

Seventeen pieces by perhaps the premier writer of both fantasy and SF in the 1970s. Some of the stories belong to the world of her "Earthsea" trilogy. Others belong to the SF novels of her "Hainish" universe series, including the beautiful accessory tale to her *The Dispossessed* (1974), "The Day before the Revolution."

John Kilian Houston Brunner
The Shockwave Rider
New York: Harper & Row

Brunner discussed the inspiration for this novel with Alvin Toffler, the author of *Future Shock*. Set in America, civilization of the near future is threatened with the tyranny of a nation-wide computer data net. The net is neutralized by the genius of the novel's hero, Nicholas Halflinger, who can screw up the computer net with a self-devouring program, thus giving civilization a reprieve to recover the freedom it needs so that human culture can progress and survive. *Shockwave* is the fifth of Brunner's major novels of social criticism.

Samuel Ray Delany, Jr.
Dhalgren
New York: Bantam

Set in a radically deteriorated future America, the novel is very much a poetic magnum opus among Delany's works. The vicissitudes in the lives of the cast of characters stumbling through their days in the near rubble of a major metropolis is one more presentational account in fiction of the "decline of the West." Delany's narrative releases a highly-polished orchestration of stream-of-consciousness, straight narrative, purple prose, bizarre characters, and an abiding pessimism. Critics have divided in finding it either marvelous or substantially overblown.

Joanna Russ
The Female Man
New York: Bantam

Russ has been a fine and rational speaker for feminism in SF. This novel is her most substantial statement. It contrasts an "Earth" of the future ruled entirely by women with the world of the present, presenting one example after another of the perversity and destruction to wholesome human values of a male chauvinist culture.

Robert Silverberg
The Stochastic Man
New York: Harper & Row

Lew Nichols is a professional forecaster, using data, statistics, and intuition. Believing that knowing the future can enable one to change it and make it better, he gives his help to Paul Quinn, a young liberal politician, to make him mayor of New York as a steppingstone to the Presidency. Meanwhile, he has problems with his beautiful wife, who leaves him and joins a fatalistic cult, and Martin Carvajal, an infallible forecaster, who actually has ESP and can see the future to the point of his death. But it appears that the future is fixed, and a knowledge of it cannot be used to make changes. Another of Silverberg's later, more philosophical works; proves that stochasticism doesn't engender warm feelings in the reader.

Alfred Bester
The Computer Connection
New York: Berkley

Bester's prestige for his Golden Age classics *Demolished Man* (1953) and *The Stars My Destination* (1957) no doubt carried this rather mediocre novel to the attention it received. Supermen fight a supercomputer and win, to preserve for mankind the opportunity to become super. It is derivative of *Destination* and retrograde in its lickity-split Heinleinian narrative that slap-dashes character, stitches action like a sewing machine, and wraps up its agenda in auld lang syne, nostalgia SF, tie-off-all-the-open-plot-arteries, happily-ever-after ending. The British edition is titled *Extro*.

Benjamin William Bova
Notes to a Science Fiction Writer
New York: Scribner

Written by the then editor of *Analog,* this popularly written textbook for the developing SF writer uses four of the author's own stories as demonstrations. Each story is prefaced by a section on the theory of one of the main elements of a short story writing—character, background, conflict, and plot—and followed by a section on practice which shows how the theory was applied in that story. The first three stories have appeared in the author's *Forward in Time* (1973): "Fifteen Miles," one of the author's Chet Kinsman stories, in which the astronaut must hike to safety across the open lunar surface burdened physically by a wounded Jesuit scientist and mentally by his guilt over his past killing of a female Soviet cosmonaut (sequel to the story "Test in Orbit"); "Men of Good Will," a joke story about a Soviet and U. S. gun battle on the moon which leaves a cloud of bullets in a lunar orbit with "periluna" at the antagonists' bases; "Stars, Won't You Hide Me?" in which humanity has been destroyed for its past sins by vengeful aliens who pursue the last man to the end of the universe. In "The Shining Ones," a young boy dying from leukemia runs away from home to seek a cure from an alien spacecraft which has suddenly appeared.

John Crowley
The Deep
Garden City, NY: Doubleday

The flat world model of popular medieval cosmology (the esoteric Ptolemaic model notwithstanding) and the feudal, myth-driven cultures that inhabited it are endlessly fascinating in real history; so Crowley erects in this novel another of the awesome artifact stages (most popular forerunner is Niven's *Ringworld*, 1970) upon which to weave his tale. On a plate-shaped world, perched upon a fabulously tall column, people live their lives, capriciously manipulated by agencies and creatures beyond their understanding. The "Deep" is the seemingly infinite mysterious universe around them. The novel was welcomed by SF writers and critics alike.

Lester del Rey
Early del Rey
Garden City, NY: Doubleday

Twenty-four mostly uncollected del Rey stories from his first in 1938 to the beginning of his professional writing career in 1951. Similar to *The Early Asimov* (1972), del Rey contributes biographical notes, and the volume ends with a bibliography of early works. Although mostly minor del Rey stories, they are generally entertaining and, like much pulp fiction, surprisingly moving. Note "Though Dreamers Die," "The Faithful," "The Smallest God" and "Anything."

Robert Carroll O'Brian
Z for Zachariah
New York: Atheneum

A young farm girl, Ann Burden, is the sole survivor in a Pennsylvania valley that fortuitously escapes the death of an atomic war. Suddenly her solitude is broken by the appearance of a man; a chemist, engaged in plastics research, he is wearing the only copy of an experimental radiation-proof suit. Unfortunately, he is mentally unstable, and attacks the girl; to escape him, she eventually steals the suit and goes in search of another safe valley. Published as a novel for young adults, its excellence and maturity recommend it highly for adults.

Kate Wilhelm
The Infinity Box: A Collection of Speculative Fiction
New York: Harper & Row

Nine well-crafted stories, four from *Orbit,* of small screen SF, mostly with realistic settings in the present or near future, with emphasis on characterization and a liberal/left orientation. In the title story, a man discovers he can possess the mind of a woman he knows; as his power over her grows, so does his corruption. As another example, in "The Village" a U. S. Vietnam military force finds itself suddenly (and inexplicably) in a typical American town; carnage follows. Also includes Wilhelm's well-known "The Funeral."

1976

*Laurence van Cott Niven (as Larry Niven)
A World Out of Time
New York: Holt, Rinehart & Winston

Action abounds in this space operish tale of Jerome Branch Corbell, a frozen down cancer victim awakened in the 22nd century in the body of a mind-wiped criminal. This is the method used by the all-powerful State to get people to do their dirty work. Corbell is given the choice of piloting a sub-light ship on a one-way mission to seek planets for future colonization, or he, too, will be "wiped," and another frozen patient's mind given his adopted body. Faking agreement, Corbell steals a ship and escapes to the galactic core, only to find it collapsing in a giant black hole. He uses the hole for traveling back to Earth, but in doing so he is thrown three million years into the future. The sun is a red giant and Earth now circles Jupiter; a mighty war between immortal pre-adult Boys and Girls have wrought great changes and destruction. In searching for answers amid Earth's ruins, Corbell discovers an evil old woman who may have the secret of immortality. After numerous plot turnings and twistings, all ends well, and Corbell lives happily ever after.

Joseph W. Haldeman
Mindbridge
New York: St. Martin

Jacque Lefavre can make contact with the groupmind species, "The L'vrai," but others cannot, unfortunately. The L'vrai are one of a super-intelligent group of races in the universe, far advanced over relatively brutal humanity whose opening era of spaceflight will ultimately threaten them. In the knick of time mankind learns to develop rapport with the L'vrai, thus signifying its maturity. Humanity needs help and guidance from a superior intelligence or it will not survive. *Mindbridge* has been widely read because of the excellent reputation of the prizewinning *The Forever War* (1974).

Kate Wilhelm
Where Late the Sweet Birds Sang
New York: Harper & Row

When humanity poisons itself, the extended Sumner family survives as the result of an elaborate preparation for the disaster. Time passes and sterility among the people appears. Selected members are cloned as a solution. But cloning does not prove a solution. The clones are in effect a separate species whose rapport with the individual humans and survival competence prove insufficient, resulting in the extinction of the clones and the biogenetic technical knowhow that created them. A conventional humanity survives in a very simple agrarian civilization. The novel is too short for its potential contents, but the principal strength of Wilhelm, the analysis of human relationships, both exotic and ordinary, in the temporary but doomed clone and human individual culture is fascinating. This work won the Hugo Award. Wilhelm deserves the award for consistent excellence over a number of her works.

Frank Patrick Herbert
Children of Dune
New York: Berkley

Like the first work in the series, *Dune* (1965), this third work became a mainstream best-seller. In it the dream of Paul Atreides is being realized. The ecology of Dune is being transformed from desert to a life-supporting ecology. But Leto, child of Paul, foresees the dangerous consequences of a too precipitate manipulation of the planet's ecology. As he comes to the throne, he intends to lead his people back to a culture that preserves an interdependent relationship with the planet—avoiding ecological as well as psychological imbalance.

Frederik Pohl
Man Plus
New York: Random House

Roger Torraway's body is cybernetically enhanced so he can live on Mars, the first of a new species of "humans" intended to populate a Martian colony of survivors after mankind destroys itself on Earth. The body of the story analyzes the changing psychology of Roger as he learns his new body. At the end we learn the whole enterprise of the cyborg/martian project has been engineered by the machine intelligence of the computers created by mankind, linked together and sentient, and desiring to survive even if humanity is too stupid to do other than destroy itself. Roger is, in fact, part animal and part computer. Pohl tells this tale with clear narrative in a richly comic mood.

Barry N. Malzberg
Scop
New York: Pyramid

Despite its compact prose, complex structure, multiple narrators, and interconnectedness with other Malzberg works, *Scop* is still one of the author's more straightforward works. Scop—named after a truth drug, Scopolamine—is obsessed with the assassinations in the U. S. of the 1960s; he feels they have bequeathed his own brutal world of 2040 and that he must return to the past, prevent the assassinations, and, thereby, destroy his own time. The "Institute" lets him time travel back, although its agents also work to hinder his efforts. After repeated attempts, Scop finds that he cannot change things; indeed, his actions all seem to strengthen the inevitability of the events. As usual, many of Malzberg's interests are represented—the assassinations replayed again and again, a sexually hung-up neurotic and ineffectual leading character, inept bureaucracy, a preoccupation with intercourse, even in machine-like metaphors, and so on. Actually, Malzberg may be said to have written only a single work—an exploration of the body and soul of the U. S. in the 1960s and early 1970s, when an entire culture went nuts and did its best to kill itself at the height of its golden age. Malzberg's exploration is among the best, and someday will receive the attention it deserves.

Robert Silverberg
The Best of Robert Silverberg
New York: Pocket Books

The author himself selected these ten stories from his output up to 1971; in addition, he provides commentaries on the writing of each story. An excellent collection, it contains the Hugo-winning "Nightwings"; the Nebula-winning "Good News from the Vatican" and "Passengers"; and "Sundance" and "Hawksbill Station." Barry Malzberg provides an introduction. This collection has been reissued by Gregg Press, along with a new second volume which contains Silverberg's better later short fiction, such as "Born with the Dead," "When We Went to See the End of the World," and "Schwartz Between the Galaxies." These volumes are a basic library of Silverberg's short fiction.

Roger Joseph Zelazny
Doorways in the Sand
New York: Harper & Row

Another of Zelazny's sparkling action stories. A peculiar character, Fred Cassidy, is a perpetual student taking advantage of his uncle's will which supports him until graduation; of course, his knowledge is vast after years of study, while for recreation he climbs the outside of buildings. Fred's halcyon days are shattered when he is suspected of stealing a peculiar artifact, the "star-stone." The stone is of great value, the legacy of a long-lost race, and is cyclically loaned among the various members of the interstellar community; interestingly, the "star-stone" is really a life form, and communicates with Fred through ESP. But not everyone in the galaxy wants the newly contacted Earth as a competitor, so some peculiar alien agents try to sour the deal by copping the stone, while still other peculiar aliens, cosmic cops of a sort, try to prevent them; strangely, these aliens take the form of Earth animals as disguises, for example as a wombat and a kangaroo. And if these complications weren't enough, Fred falls into an alien machine and gets himself molecularly reversed. Fast-reading fun.

Alfred Bester
The Light Fantastic
New York: Berkley

Collection of seven stories by a science fiction master. Includes the classic, "Fondly Fahrenheit," involving an android that inexplicably commits bloody murder and the strange mental miasma that engulfs both it and its master, and "The Men Who Murdered Mohammed," a unique view of time travel as a subjective experience wherein those who kill their past really kill only their own future. A companion collection of Bester stories, *Star Light, Star Bright* (1976), has also appeared; it includes such well-known stories as "Oddy and Id" and "The Pi Man." Bester laces both collections with extensive commentaries on the stories and science fiction. Both volumes are combined by Doubleday in *Starlight: The Great Short Fiction of Alfred Bester* (1976).

Samuel Ray Delany, Jr.
Triton
New York: Bantam

This novel may be a much better disciplined transformation of Delany's widely reviewed and very controversial *Dhalgren* (1975). The Neptunian moon Triton is a *Walpurgisnacht* of experimental life styles, especially those expressive of the problems of sexual identity and political ideology. This time the self-conscious ruminations of the writer at work writing a SF novel are collected in two appendices at the end of the story. Delany demands a lot from his readers. He is almost always intelligent.

Anne Inez McCaffrey
Dragonsong
New York: Atheneum

Another of the works accessory to McCaffrey's very successful "Dragonriders of Pern" series, featuring the cooperation of humans and time-traveling dragons to keep their planet from destruction. *Dragonsong* is one of three issued with the Atheneum imprint, presumably aimed at a pre-adult readership. In any case it develops at least one more major character in the series—Menolly, whose genius is for music.

Christopher Priest
The Space Machine: A Scientific Romance
London: Faber & Faber

A tribute to H. G. Wells, it borrows his Victorian style and characterization and the settings of his *The Time Machine* and *The War of the Worlds,* and blends these with the greater scientific sensibility of modern SF. The hero and heroine inadvertently trigger the time machine, which lands them on Mars. Marooned there, their Victorian values are severely put to the test as they discover that the human-like Martians are the slaves of the blob Martians. Worse yet, the blobs are planning an invasion of Earth! The couple escape, but find themselves in the leading wave of invasion ships. Landing in England, they watch the English countryside being devastated by the Martian invaders; they are joined by a young observer busily recording these catastrophic events; his name is H. G. Wells. Humorous, entertaining, fascinating, and well crafted, this excellent work deserves more attention than it has received.

Kate Wilhelm
The Clewiston Test
New York: Farrar, Straus & Giroux

Anne Clewiston, a brilliant young scientist, has discovered a pain-suppressing chemical. The pharmaceutical company, for which she and her co-scientist husband, Clark, work, is rushing the drug to market despite violent side effects in some test animals. Bedridden from a car crash, Anne struggles to stop human trials of the drug. In addition, she begins to realize that her marriage is not the equal relationship she once imagined. Is her growing resistance due to the drug—self-administered to relieve her intense pain—or is she maturing into independence? The novel provides a study of sex roles and of the development and testing of new drugs.

1977

*John Herbert Varley
The Ophiuchi Hotline
New York: Dial

Earth's sciences and culture flourish with the enrichment of messages of information from the stars, the "Ophiuchi Hotline." In the new technology the clones of Lilo live out lives that reveal and foreshadow the destiny of humanity—certainly not to dominate galactic civilization. That domination is reserved for the mysterious "Invaders" who want and will take the solar system for their own habitation. Mediating this eventuality are the "traders," the senders of the hotline information, who in exchange merely want to live as humans for awhile, finding change of this sort necessary in their millions of years of nomadic existence in the galaxy. Varley's feel for the implications of science and the aspirations of the human spirit are wrapped in a fine storytelling talent. His *Persistence of Vision* (1978) and *Titan* (1979) are equally rewarding.

Frederik Pohl
Gateway
New York: St. Martin

Just when humanity is at the very limits of its planet's ability to support it, the Heechee civilization is discovered—artifacts on the solar planets and "Gateway," an asteroid spaceport with ships that can carry men virtually anywhere at translight speeds. But you don't know what your destination is until you try it once. The rewards are enormous. The mortality rate is high. "Prospectors" tend to die or wind up millionaires. The hero is Robinette Broadhead, foodminer, who hits in the lottery and gambles all to get to Gateway, and prospecting, and the big money. He succeeds. The novel is interchaptered with post hoc psychoanalytical sessions between Broadhead and his computer analyst.

The discovery of supercivilization can, messiahlike, refresh the flagging spirit of humanity. Nice balance of clear narrative and engaging (only slightly campy) humor. Has a sequel in *Beyond the Blue Event Horizon* (1980).

Algirdas Jonas Budrys (as Algis Budrys)
Michaelmas
New York: Berkley

Laurent Michaelmas, the most popular media commentator of the late 20th century, has secret access to the world's data banks and communication channels through his sentient computer, Domino. This makes Michaelmas the secret manager of the world, as he selflessly manipulates information to prevent wars, hunger, and chaos. Suddenly, the inexplicable happens; a U. S. astronaut picked for a sensitive mission, but dead in a crash, is suddenly announced to be alive, allegedly saved at a mysterious medical center in the Alps. Michaelmas reasons that this can mean only one thing, that aliens are trying to affect humanity, and, therefore, will be after him. He must find and stop this influence within eighteen hours. Despite these fascinating story elements and the author's great craft, this novel remains basically unsatisfactory and uninvolving. Who cares about God's problems, even if he is a TV celebrity?

Gregory Benford
In the Ocean of Night
New York: Dial

The story is of the character of Nigel a super-scientist of the 21st century who must choose between the security of Earth and the preservation and exploration of clues and artifacts that come from an extraterrestial species. His choices permit damage to Earth and confuse his relationship with two women, but Earth survives and Nigel, bringing his moral dilemmas and enormous knowledge of science and man into some kind of balance, learns from the extraterrestial that human meaning will not be complete until it encompasses and relates to all that is in the universe. The novel has been almost unanimously acclaimed by major critics.

Laurence van Cott Niven (as Larry Niven) and Jerry E. Pournelle
Lucifer's Hammer
Chicago: Playboy

A meteor hits Earth and destroys most of civilization and mankind. The survivors manage to put it together again in a convincing and harrowing story that is an excellent extrapolation of how it would be after a worldwide catastrophe. The astrophysics and geology is textbook accurate and beautifully exposited. The Niven/Pournelle team also produced *The Mote in God's Eye* (1974), *Inferno* (1976) and are clearly masters of the "disaster" tale that has fetched great popular reader interest.

Philip Kindred Dick
A Scanner Darkly
Garden City, NY: Doubleday

The major novels of Dick have never failed to raise the persistent metaphysical question. What is man? What is an individual identity? He does so in *Three Stigmata . . .* and in *Flow My Tears. . . .* In *Scanner* he has written a story against the use of drugs, describing in inexorable detail the horror and agony of people who use them. Nevertheless, Dick's account winds around a central character who is both drug pusher as well as the substance abuse police agent determined to stop the pusher he himself, in alter ego, is. This Jekyll/Hyde confluence perfectly mirrors the motives of self-preservation and self-hate and destruction that war in addicts of all descriptions.

Joseph W. Haldeman
All My Sins Remembered
New York: St. Martin

The story is assembled principally from the institutional records of an agent assassin sent from world to world as part of the killer arm for a policy that often calls for diplomacy by murder. Bioform change and memory and personality transformation are part of the portfolio. But the supersophisticated tactics of savagery require their price in an unbearable agony of individual conscience. Here, in an unrelieved serious mood, Haldeman continues his fictional case against human brutality in all forms most prominently begun in *The Forever War* (1975).

1978

*Vonda N. McIntyre
Dreamsnake
Boston: Houghton Mifflin

Snake, the healer, loses her "dreamsnake," a species of viper brought to Earth from another planet and very hard to breed. To replace it she travels far and is tested by excruciating pain and threat of death. She triumphs by finding not only more snakes but also how to breed them, thus making it possible for the guild of healers to multiply their numbers and spread their compassionate service to all of the cul-de-sacs of human survivors in the era following nuclear holocaust on Earth. The work's excellence lies in the poetically negotiable authenticity of Snake's ordeal. McIntyre burst upon the SF scene in the late 1970s. *Dreamsnake* is unquestionably one of the more enduring Nebula/Hugo winners.

Alice B. Sheldon (as James Tiptree, Jr.)
Up the Walls of the World
New York: Berkley

Best known as one of SF's finest short story writers, this is Sheldon's first novel. It is structured as three separate but related stories treated in round-robin chapters. One, set on Earth, tells of a group of people caught in a government parapsychological experiment. The second involves alien flying beings living in the atmosphere of a gas giant; these are being disturbed by another alien, a vast galaxy-cruising, star-destroying entity, in the third section.

All three threads intertwine ever more closely until a final resolution ties them completely together. Many good short scenes, effective aliens on the gas giant, but still not of the quality associated with the author's shorter fiction.

Tom Reamy
Blind Voices
New York: Berkley

Tom Reamy's novel may gain something in its enthusiastic reception because people in the SF establishment liked him well. His death in 1977 left the same frustration in eager readers that fans felt over the early death of Stanley Weinbaum who died at 35. *Voices* is a virtuous superman-emerging story, set in depression years Kansas, involving the members of a traveling circus and the people of the small town it visits. The show's owner has parapsychological powers and is evil. "Angel" is one of his side-show attractions, who exhibits the power of levitation, shy and fearful of his boss. With the help and inspiration of one of the several girls from the town who visit the show, Angel matures and triumphs over the evil owner. The story deals in at least two kinds of nostalgia. The first is the way in which it makes depression-deprived small-town America seem attractive. The second way is in the refurbishing of the traditional moral proposition that the morally good will survive the morally evil, even when the morally good person begins at a grave disadvantage.

Donald R. Bensen
And Having Writ . . .
New York: Bobbs-Merrill

A first novel by a SF editor, but a good one anyway. Four humanoid aliens about to crash on Earth use a one-time-only escape device, which puts them in a parallel universe. Now, instead of causing a big bang over Siberia, they fall into the ocean, are picked up, and arrive at San Francisco during Teddy Roosevelt's presidency. In order to escape this backward planet, they decide to speed up the growth of its science. Edison is elected President, but foils the aliens' plans by keeping them in the U. S. They escape, and with the help of a newspaperman, travel through Europe trying to stir up a World War, a prerequisite, their social science tells them, to rapid scientific development. Many "real" persons turn up as characters, including the Kaiser, the Czar, and H. G. Wells. A highly inventive and humorous tale.

Virginia Kidd (ed.)
Millennial Women
New York: Delacorte

An anthology of six original stories by women about women. Ursula Le Guin contributes the longest, "The Eye of the Heron"; in it a society founded on non-violence must come to terms with its invasion by an aggressor, while a young woman finds that she must reject her society's traditional definition of female behavior. Other authors are Cynthia Felice, Elizabeth Lynn, Diana Paxson, Joan Vinge, and Cherry Wilder.

Anne Inez McCaffrey
The White Dragon
New York: Ballantine

The mainstream best-selling latest in the "Dragonriders of Pern" series. This one tells the story of the birth and adventures of a dwarf dragon, and her exceptional rapport with the young aristocrat Jaxom, in the continuing effort to preserve the planet Pern from destruction.

Robert E. Sheckley
Crompton Divided
New York: Holt, Rinehart & Winston

Alistair Crompton is cured of a rare disease by having his personality split up, parts of which are placed in android bodies and sent to frontier planets. But Crompton wants to reintegrate himself, and sets off on a planet-hopping odyssey across the galaxy. Along the way he encounters flamboyant planets, including one with a continual sex orgy and another modeled after California, and aliens. Ron Goulart-type action in a humourous light novel part satire, part farce. British title is *The Alchemical Marriage of Alistair Crompton*.

Poul Anderson
The Avatar
New York: Berkley

The author's most ambitious work. Earth is being closed to space exploration by liberal welfare politicians just at the time that the first contact with other intelligent life has occurred. This has been made possible by the presence of space-warping gates which open up interstellar travel; these are the gift of the mysterious "Others," a super race that helps other intelligences without destroying their initiative. Daniel Brodersen, an inventive and courageous entrepreneur, sets out to end this politicians' barrier to further human progress, but in running their blockade his ship and crew are cast into the unknown depths of the galaxy. Struggling blindly from gate to gate, Brodersen and crew view the wonders of the universe, finally ending at the home of the "Others," themselves. Philosophy, politics and science are blended with interesting characterizations in this paean to human freedom.

Damon Knight (ed.)
Orbit 20
New York: Harper & Row

The last volume of science fiction's most influential original anthology series; from its founding in 1966 through *Orbit 20* it produced twenty-two Nebula nominees and four winners. Best known for its literary rather than traditional SF stories, *Orbit* fared much worse in the fan-voted Hugos, producing only eight nominations and no winners. Its predominant tone was set by its most frequently occurring authors— R. A. Lafferty, Kate Wilhelm, and Gene Wolfe. In this final volume all three appear, along with several less well-known writers. Wolfe's fine story, "Seven American Nights," is a fair exemplar, being the diary of a cultured youth from a future affluent Persia who is visiting a decayed, dying America. As the youth tells of his pursuit of a romantic relationship, the reader is treated to views of the U. S.'s crumbling national monuments and of the people of Washington, D. C. going about their business as if their empire was not collapsing. Wolfe seems preoccupied with decaying societies, a popular theme of Western science fiction of the late 1960s and 1970s.

John Herbert Varley
The Persistence of Vision
New York: Dial

The first collection of stories by one of SF's best new writers. These nine stories, five from *Fantasy and Science Fiction,* were first published between 1975 and 1978. Six have received award nominations: "The Phantom of Kansas"; "Air Raid"; "Retrograde Summer"; "In the Bowl"; "In the Hall of the Martian Kings"; and "Gotta Sing, Gotta Dance." The 1978 title story won both a Hugo and Nebula. In it a man fleeing declining American culture finds his way to a commune populated by the deaf and blind; they seem to be achieving a special kind of transcendence, which the visitor sacrifices his hearing and vision to achieve. Soft rather than hard SF.

Kate Wilhelm
Somerset Dreams and Other Fictions
New York: Harper & Row

Collection of SF/mainstream blended stories, half of which first appeared in the original anthology series, *Orbit*. Stories are characterized by literary emphasis; other critics refer to them as talky, oblique and elusive. Better examples include "State of Grace," "The Encounter" and title story, in which a woman anaesthesiologist returns to her dying home town where, as part of a dream research project, she dreams that she is back in the wonderful town of her childhood.

Chelsea Quinn Yarbro
False Dawn
Garden City, NY: Doubleday

Ecological disaster has swept the world. A mutated woman who can regenerate parts of her flesh survives and journeys through a blighted California; she meets a man, once the leader of a gang, and they rely on each other to survive. Captured by a gang, the woman is brutally raped but she and the man escape. Their journey continues, each new contact a let down, each potential haven really a danger; there appears to be no better future. A bitter, violent story.

1979

*Arthur Charles Clarke
The Fountains of Paradise
London: Victor Gollancz

This novel won the Nebula and Hugo Awards. By the late 1970s, Clarke had become an SF patriarch. This is a very competently told awesome artifact story—lots of them in the 1970s. This time the big project is building an elevator to a synchronously orbiting space station to make interplanetary travel cheaper and more convenient. It works; time passes; a marvelously maturing humanity makes contact with aliens from the stars. The future is wide open with opportunity. Science fiction needs optimistic visions. *Fountains* is welcome, but routine.

John Herbert Varley
Titan
New York: Berkley

Varley burst upon the SF scene in the late 1970s. This novel is widely acclaimed. It is an awesome artifact story reminiscent of Clarke's *Rendevous with Rama* (1973), with a difference. Clarke's interstellar spaceship world was empty. Varley's *Titan* world is a fully flora-ed and fauna-ed terrarium, vast in scale, run by a "goddess" who watches TV re-runs from Earth and suffers from *ennui*, so the expedition from Earth discovers. Everything turns out happily in the end.

Frederik Pohl
Jem
New York: St. Martin

In the late seventies the new success of Pohl, one of the deans of modern SF, has been little short of incredible. *Man Plus* in 1976 and *Gateway* in 1977 won fistsful of awards for the novel. *Jem* might have received its nominations on the critical inertia of these preceding successes. In *Jem* a new Earth-type planet is found just in time to become a substitute home for humanity which shortly ruins Earth in a world war. Pohl unrolls his story as an analysis of the dynamics of three valued resources: people, the food to feed them, and the energy to drive the civilizations they can build. The representatives of each of these interests anchor colonies on Jem, colonies who look, respectively, for hospitality from the three species indigenous to Jem. The Earth colonists almost destroy Jem, but don't. Pohl's hope for the survival of human culture has worn very thin here.

Michael Bishop
Catacomb Years
New York: Berkley

Shortly after the beginning of the third millennium, the U. S. in decline, major cities dome themselves over and lock out the world and its problems. In Atlanta, Georgia, the events for the next three-quarters of a century—the domed city's catacomb years—are depicted in terms of major happenings and individual vignettes. The novel is actually a series of previously-published stories, among the most noteworthy of which is "The Samurai and the Willows," and original connective material. Life inside the dome sinks into individual escapism and heightened state control, and change becomes anathema. Eventually this system crumbles due to scientific development and outside events. *A Little Knowledge* (1977) is a related work. Emphasis is on the social life and its meaning under the dome; the engineering is skirted. Although billed as a future history, it has little value as such.

Spider Robinson and Jeanne Robinson
Stardance
New York: Dial

The polite rock script is informal, laid back; a woman bursting with talent, bulges and height, is told she is too tall to dance. Rather than giving up, she strives to perfect her talent. Still, success eludes her until she becomes the girl of a rich man who takes her to his orbiting space station; there, she perfects her new, breakthrough dance form, free-fall choreography. Her sister aids her, and all is filmed by the side-kick cameraman, who is telling the tale. Suddenly, aliens from deep space appear; are they a threat? The dancer dances, the aliens dance, and they like us. Eventually, the dance troop moves on to transcendental rebirth. The tall, buxom free-fall dancer is played by Sharra Drummond. Her loyal sister is Norrey Drummond. The video-man side-kick, a crippled ex-dancer, is Charlie Armstead. The rich man, a heavy, is Bryce Carrington. The pretty firefly-like aliens play themselves. A less than successful expansion of a Hugo and Nebula winning novella; a must for those dance fans who would rather read the description of a dance than see one. The authors were after something important, something special, but couldn't quite find it.

Charles Sheffield
Sight of Proteus
New York: Ace Books

A first novel, by a president of the American Astronautical Society, highly inventive, complexly plotted, and Niven-like in its impact. As a future Earth sways under a burden of population and consumption beyond its carrying capacity, it becomes possible for people who can afford it to change their bodies into many other forms using computer-assisted techniques. Behrooz Wolf, with the Office of Form Control, must regulate this process and defend against its abuse. Good, traditional SF.

Elizabeth Cummins Cogell

SCIENCE FICTION AND FANTASY COLLECTIONS
IN U. S. AND CANADIAN LIBRARIES

The recent proliferation of science fiction research activity and the popular interest in the field as a whole has prompted academic libraries to develop systematic science fiction collections. The first attempt to compile a listing of such collections was Hal Hall's preliminary list in the April 1972 issue of the *SFRA Newsletter,* in which thirty-five American, four Canadian, and two British collections were identified. Hall updates this listing in his chapter on "Library Collections of Science Fiction and Fantasy" in *Anatomy of Wonder.*

This inventory lists nearly one hundred significant collections, the majority of which are in college and university libraries, although a few city libraries are noted. No individually owned collections are included. The information is accurate as of May 15, 1977.

The purpose of this listing is to guide scholars in locating and using not only the major author and thematic collections but also the several collections within a given geographical area. Therefore, detailed information is furnished for small (at least 200 books), medium, and large collections. Entries are arranged alphabetically by state and then by supporting organization. Each entry includes general information about the library and its collection, followed by an analysis of both primary and secondary books, magazines, and manuscripts. An author index is included.

Two professional organizations should be acknowledged for their support of library science fiction collections. The Science Fiction Research Association, through its annual meetings and monthly newsletter, has helped disseminate information; and *Extrapolation,* a scholarly journal which serves SFRA, has published articles on library research collections. Science Fiction Writers of America has established a Regional Depository System, whereby publisher donated books are made available to libraries in selected geographic areas in the United States and Canada.

The largest collections remain in the hands of private individuals, although the number of these collections is dwindling as they are purchased by research libraries and science fiction book dealers. One of the world's most complete collections is owned by Forrest J. Ackerman, a noted science fiction fan, literary agent, film consultant, editor, and bookseller. His 200,000 piece collection is housed in a special Fantascience Museum in Hollywood, California.

I am grateful to the librarians who completed the questionnaires for this listing; they were helpful, encouraging, and forthright. Any corrections or additions to this list would be appreciated and should be sent to the compiler so that the list can be periodically updated.

EXPLANATION OF ENTRIES

I. A typical entry

[1]ID1. [2]IDAHO STATE UNIVERSITY   [5]Director: Eli M. Oboler
   [3]University Library   [6]Hours: 8am-11pm, M-Th; 8am-
   [4]Pocatello, ID 82309   5pm, Fri.; 9am-5pm, Sat.; 2pm-
   11pm, Sun.

[7]Collection Title: None
[8]Person to Contact: Douglas Birdsall, Humanities Librarian
[9]Location: With the general collection.
[10]Restrictions: None
[11]Index/Catalog: None
[12]ILL: Yes
[13]Origin: NA

[14]Holdings — Magazines:
[15]Primary: ca. 156   [16]Secondary: ca. 12
[17]Subscriptions: ALG; FSF; SFST

[18]Title	[19]Prim/Sec	[20]Dates	[21]Condition
ALG	S	On order	Original
FSF	P	1976-Date	"
SFST	S	1976-Date	"

[22]Holdings — Books:
   [23]Primary: ca. 200 [24](95%; 5%)   [25]Secondary: ca 30
   [26]Current: Yes
   [27]Specialized: No

[28]Holdings — Miscellaneous:
Cassette holdings include several lectures and panel discussions, as well as individual works, such as *The Martian Chronicles.*

II. Description of individual, numbered items

1. *CODE SYMBOL.* Entries are alphabetized by state, then by name of the organization; the code consists of the state's zip code letters, followed by a number identifying the entry's alphabetical order within the listings for that state.
2. *NAME OF ORGANIZATION.* Name of city, university, college, or trust which sponsors the library.
3. *NAME OF LIBRARY.*

4. *ADDRESS*. Mailing address of the library, which may be different than the address of the organization.
5. *DIRECTOR*. Administrative head of the library.
6. *HOURS*. Hours and days when the library is open.
7. *COLLECTION TITLE*. Phrase or letters by which the library identifies its special holdings; sometimes this title includes more than just sf (e.g. Special Collections) or less than the total field of sf (e.g. Imaginary Voyages).
8. *PERSON TO CONTACT*. Individual most knowledgeable about the use of the collection.
9. *LOCATION*. Section of the library where the collection is housed; if it is not housed separately, it is shelved with the general holdings.
10. *RESTRICTIONS*. Limitations on the use of the collection.
11. *INDEX/CATALOG*. Description of a card catalog, shelf list, or other type of index for sf holdings, separate from the main library catalog. In addition to this index, nearly all libraries have entered sf in standard form in the library's main card catalog.
12. *ILL*. Availability of individual items through interlibrary loan.
13. *ORIGIN*. Date and conditions under which the collection was initiated and developed.
14. *MAGAZINE HOLDINGS*. Periodicals relating to the sf field; if a number immediately follows this heading, it is the total number of issues (not titles) held by the library.
15. *PRIMARY*. Number of periodical issues which contain primarily fiction.
16. *SECONDARY*. Number of periodical issues which contain primarily essays, interviews, and information about sf; includes scholarly journals, book review magazines, and fanzines (amateur publications by sf fans).
17. *SUBSCRIPTIONS*. Magazines currently subscribed to; abbreviations are identified elsewhere in this appendix.
18. *TITLE OF THE MAGAZINE*. Individual titles which the library holds; abbreviations are identified elsewhere in this appendix.
19. *PRIMARY/SECONDARY*. Classification of the individual title according to the criteria stated in No. 15-16.
20. *DATES*. Volume numbers or years of the issues held by the library; if a run is incomplete, that is specifically noted.
21. *CONDITION*. The state of the issues held by the library, i.e., original copy or microfilm.
22. *BOOK HOLDINGS*. Volumes relating to the sf field; if a number immediately follows this heading, it is the total number of volumes held by the library.
23. *PRIMARY*. Number of volumes which contain primarily fiction, poetry, or drama.
24. *CONDITION OF BOOKS*. First number refers to % of the collection in hardback; second number refers to % of collection in paperback.
25. *SECONDARY*. Number of volumes which contain primarily essays, interviews, and information about sf; includes indexes, bibliographies, history, criticism, and other standard reference books.
26. *CURRENT*. Whether the collection is static or up-to-date.

27. *SPECIALIZED.* Whether or not the book holdings include a specialized collection (e.g. by author, motif, or historical period).
28. *MISCELLANEOUS HOLDINGS.* Material which cannot be classified as magazine or book; entries are alphabetized by the nature of the material (e.g. art, cassettes, letters, manuscripts, papers).

ABBREVIATIONS USED IN THE APPENDIX

ALG	*ALGOL*
AMZ	*AMAZING SCIENCE FICTION/AMAZING STORIES* *AMAZING SCIENCE FICTION STORIES* *AMAZING STORIES FACT AND SCIENCE FICTION*
AMZQ	*AMAZING STORIES QUARTERLY*
ASF	*ANALOG SCIENCE FACT AND FICTION/ANALOG SCIENCE FACT-SCIENCE FICTION* *ANALOG SCIENCE FICTION – SCIENCE FACT* *ASTOUNDING SCIENCE FACT AND FICTION/ASTOUNDING SCIENCE FICTION*
AST	*ASTOUNDING STORIES OF SUPER SUPER SCIENCE*
AUT	*AUTHENTIC SCIENCE FICTION SERIES*
BFF	*BEYOND FANTASY FICTION/BEYOND FICTION*
ca	Approximately
CIN	*CINEFANTASTIQUE*
CTL	*CTHULHU CALLS*
DFSF	*DELAP'S FANTASY & SCIENCE FICTION REVIEW*
ERB	*ERBDOM*
EX	*EXTRAPOLATION: A JOURNAL OF SCIENCE FICTION AND FANTASY*
FAD	*FANTASTIC ADVENTURES*
FAN	*FANTASTIC/FANTASTIC SCIENCE FICTION STORIES* *FANTASTIC STORIES OF IMAGINATION*
FAU	*FANTASTIC UNIVERSE SCIENCE FICTION*
FBK	*FANTASY BOOK*
FDN	*FOUNDATION: THE REVIEW OF SCIENCE FICTION*
FFM	*FAMOUS FANTASTIC MYSTERIES*
FSF	*FANTASY AND SCIENCE FICTION* *MAGAZINE OF FANTASY AND SCIENCE FICTION*
FUT	*FUTURE COMBINED WITH SCIENCE FICTION STORIES* *FUTURE SCIENCE FICTION*
GAL	*GALAXY MAGAZINE/GALAXY SCIENCE FICTION*
HOR	*HORIZONS*
ISF	*IMAGINATION STORIES OF SCIENCE AND FANTASY* *IMAGINATION SCIENCE FICTION*
JIR	*JOURNAL OF IRREPRODUCIBLE RESULTS*

JLN	*JACK LONDON NEWSLETTER*
LM	*LUNA MONTHLY*
LOC	*LOCUS*
M	Midnight
ML	*MYTHLORE*
MSF	*MARVEL SCIENCE FICTION*
MSS	*MARVEL SCIENCE STORIES*
mss	manuscripts
MT	*MARVEL TALES*
N	noon
NA	Not Available/Not Applicable
n.d.	no date given
NEB	*NEBULA SCIENCE FICTION*
NWB	*NEW WORLDS/NEW WORLDS SCIENCE FICTION*
OSF	*ORBIT SCIENCE FICTION*
OW	*OUTWORLDS*
OWS	*OTHER WORLDS SCIENCE STORIES*
PLA	*PLANET STORIES*
RQ	*RIVERSIDE QUARTERLY*
sf	science fiction
SFA	*SCIENCE FICTION ADVENTURES*
SFBRI	*SCIENCE FICTION BOOK REVIEW INDEX*
SFM	*SCIENCE FICTION MONTHLY*
SFRA	*SCIENCE FICTION RESEARCH ASSOCIATION NEWSLETTER*
SFRE	*SCIENCE FICTION REVIEW*
SFS	*SCIENCE FICTION STORIES/ORIGINAL SCIENCE FICTION STORIES*
SFST	*SCIENCE FICTION STUDIES*
SFT	*SCIENCE FICTION TIMES*
SFWA	*SCIENCE FICTION WRITERS ASSOCIATION BULLETIN*
SPW	*SPACEWAY/SPACEWAY SCIENCE FICTION*
SSM	*SPACE SCIENCE FICTION MAGAZINE*
SSS	*SUPER SCIENCE STORIES*
STL	*STARTLING STORIES*
SUP	*SUPERNATURAL STORIES*
TWS	*THRILLING WONDER STORIES*
UNI	*UNIVERSE SCIENCE FICTION*
VEN	*VENTURE SCIENCE FICTION*
W	Winter
WIF	*IF, WORLDS OF SCIENCE FICTION/WORLDS OF IF*
WNL	*WHAT'S NEW ABOUT LONDON, JACK*

WOF   *WORLDS OF FANTASY*
WOT   *WORLDS OF TOMORROW*
WRT   *WEIRD TALES*
WST   *WONDER STORIES*

AZ1. UNIVERSITY OF ARIZONA   Director: W. David Laird
     University Library   Hours: (Spec. Coll.): 9am-5pm,
     Tucson, AZ 87521   M-F; 9am-12N, Sat.

Collection Title: None
    Person to Contact: Ross McLachlan, Special Collections; Karen S. Seibert.
    Location: Special Collections Department, C-2; Central Reference, A-2.
    Restrictions: Spec. Coll. is a closed stack area. Patrons must fill out a
    charge-out form; materials must be used in the immediate area.
    Index/Catalog: Yes; Spec. Coll. maintains separate files for all sf holdings,
    cataloged and uncataloged.
    ILL: No; but photocopying, microfilming, and photographing facilities
    are available at the patron's expense.
    Origin: Late 1960's — Margaret Brown collection was purchased; definite
    effort made to keep the collection current. 1975 — Anthony Boucher
    library was acquired, which doubled the collection.

Holdings — Magazines: 2972
    Primary: NA   Secondary: NA
    Subscriptions: ALG; ASF; DFSF; EX; FAN; FSF; GAL; LM; RQ; SFST

Title	Prim/Sec	Dates		Condition
ALG	P	1973-Date		Original
AMZ	P	1928-71 (incomplete)		"
ASF	P	v. 11-Date	"	"
EX	S	v. 1-Date	"	"
FAN	P	v. 1-Date	"	"
FFM	P	v. 1-14	"	"
FSF	P	v. 1-Date	"	"
GAL	P	v. 1-Date	"	"
PLA	P	v. 1-6		"
SFST	S	v. 1-Date		"
STL	P	v. 1-32	"	"
WIF	P	v. 1-Date	"	"
WRT	P	v. 5-46	"	"

The above are the longer runs from a large collection of 91 pulps; numerous
fanzines are not yet cataloged.

Holdings — Books:
    Primary: 5013 (47%; 53%)   Secondary: 89
    Current: Yes
    Specialized: Yes; 60 authors whose complete works are being collected;
    includes first editions of Hugo and Nebula Award winners.

Holdings — Miscellaneous:
  Manuscripts: A number of uncorrected proof copies of works by major
    sf authors.
  Papers: Several boxes of Anthony Boucher's clippings and memorabilia.

CA1. CALIFORNIA STATE
UNIVERSITY
  University Library
  Fullerton, CA 92634

Director: NA
Hours: NA

Collection Title: NA
  Person to Contact: NA
  Location: Special Collections and with the general collection.
  Restrictions: NA
  Index/Catalog: Special Collections has a separate card catalog.
  ILL: NA
  Origin: NA
  Holdings — Magazines: 1350
    Primary: NA   Secondary: NA
    Subscriptions: NA

Title	Prim/Sec	Dates	Condition

Information on individual titles or representative titles is NA.

  Holdings — Books: over 2800
    Primary: NA   Secondary: NA
    Current: Yes; SFWA Depository
    Specialized: NA
Holdings — Miscellaneous:
  Manuscripts: Manuscripts, papers, and documents of 30 sf writers, including
    Philip K. Dick, Harry Harrison, Frank Herbert, Norman Spinrad, Robert
    Moore Williams.
  Tapes: Over 30 taped interviews and speeches of sf personalities.

CA2. CITY OF SAN DIEGO
  San Diego Public Library
  820 "E" Street
  San Diego, CA 92101

Director: Marco Thorne
Hours: 10am-9pm, M-Th; 9:30 am-
5:30pm, F-Sat.

Collection Title: None
  Person to Contact: Literature & Languages Section.
  Location: Lit. & Lang. Sect.`
  Restrictions: Reference books & periodicals do not circulate.
  Index/Catalog: None for the general sf collection; a small mystery and sf
    reference collection of books and periodicals has an author/title catalog '
    in Lit. & Lang. Sect.
  ILL: Yes; circulating material only.
  Origin: n.d. — Gift.

Holdings — Magazines:
    Primary: 870   Secondary: NA
    Subscriptions: ALG; ASF; FSF; GAL

Title	Prim/Sec	Dates	Condition
ALG	S	11/73-Date	Original
ASF	P	8/60-Date (Incomplete)	”
FSF	P	1966-Date ”	”
GAL	P	1953-Date ”	”

The above 4 runs contain ca. 520 issues; there are an additional 350 issues of other titles; individual information NA.

Holdings — Books:
    Primary: 1800 (NA)   Secondary: NA
    Current: NA
    Specialized: No; the special reference collection consists of 400 books and
        magazines.

CA3. CITY OF SAN FRANCISCO   Director: NA
      San Francisco Public Library   Hours: 9am-9pm, M-Th; 9am-6pm,
      Civic Center   F-Sat.
      San Francisco, CA 94199

    Collection Title: McComas Collection of Fantasy and Science Fiction
    Person to Contact: Dennis L. Maness, Lit. Dept.
    Location: Literature Dept.
    Restrictions: None as to type of user; require deposit of identification.
    Index/Catalog: Yes; a card catalog in Lit. Dept.
    ILL: No.
    Origin: 1960's — Gift of core collection by Frances McComas, founder and
        editor of FSF; purchase of magazines.
    Holdings — Magazines:
        Primary: NA   Secondary: NA
        Subscriptions: AMZ; ASF; DFSF; EX; FAN; FSF; GAL; LOC; SFST

Title	Prim/Sec	Dates	Condition

NA. This massive collection includes complete runs of 92 titles, beginning with AMZ in 1926; all original.

    Holdings — Books:
        Primary: ca. 1300 (85%; 15%)   Secondary: ca. 50 in the general
                                              collection
        Current: Yes
        Specialized: No

CA4. CITY OF SANTA ANA   Director: Howard Samuelson
      Santa Ana Public Library   Hours: 10am-9pm, M-F; 10am-
      26 Civic Center Plaza   6pm, Sat.; 2pm-5pm, Sun.
      Santa Ana, CA 92701

Collection Title: Science Fiction Collection
  Person to Contact: Audrey Eilts
  Location: First floor; also a separate collection in Boys and Girls and in
    Young Adult Section.
  Restrictions: None
  Index/Catalog: Yes; sf shelf list of all books is kept at the Reader Advisor
    desk.
  ILL: Yes
  Origin: 1960
  Holdings — Magazines: None
  Holdings — Books:
    Primary: 1550 (85%; 15%)   Secondary: 50
    Current: Yes
    Specialized: Includes ca. 300 titles in Young Adult and Boys-Girls Col-
      lection; includes a fair selection of first editions; complete collections
      by best authors (i.e., Asimov, Bradbury, Heinlein, Sturgeon, etc.);
      includes good collection of bibliographies, criticism, history.

CA5. THE HUNTINGTON LIBRARY,   Director: James Thorpe
     ART GALLERY AND   Hours: 8:30am-5pm, M-Sat.
     BOTANICAL GARDENS
     Henry E. Huntington Library
     1151 Oxford Road
     San Marino, CA 91108

Collection Title: None
  Person to Contact: Carey S. Bliss, Curator of Rare Books; Jean F. Preston,
    Curator of Manuscript Dept.; Reader Services Librarian (for the refer-
    ence collection).
  Location: Closed stacks.
  Restrictions: For scholars only; application for reading privileges should
    be made to Reader Services Librarian; letters of recommendation may
    be required.
  Index/Catalog: None; there is a mineographed list of one special collec-
    tion: Philip Durham, "The Huntington Library Collection of Beadle's
    Dime Novels," 1954.
  ILL: No
  Origin: NA
  Holdings — Magazines: No long runs.
  Holdings — Books:
    Primary: NA   Secondary: NA
    Current: No
    Specialized: Rare books and manuscripts are not identified by subject. Sf
      scholars should be aware of the following:
        Beadle's Dime Novels Collection (1531 titles).
        English Literature Before 1900 (includes 70% of all titles printed
          in England before 1641 and 95% of all plays and masques
          before 1641).

American Literature Before 1900 (one of the largest collections of Am. fiction; includes most of the early editions of writers of consequence).

English and American Literature Since 1900 (limited to complete works of 400 authors).

Holdings — Miscellaneous:

Manuscripts: Sf scholars should particularly note mss items for the following authors: Ambrose Bierce, Nathaniel Hawthorne, Jack London, Mary Shelley, Jonathan Swift, Mark Twain.

CA6. LOS ANGELES SCIENCE   Director: Jim Glass
     FANTASY SOCIETY, INC.   Hours: 7:30pm., Th.
     11360 Ventura Blvd.
     Studio City, CA 91604

Collection Title: LASFS Library
   Person to Contact: Jim Glass, Librarian.
   Location: Freehafer Hall, 11360 Ventura Blvd., Studio City, CA 91604.
   Restrictions: Public may browse; only members may borrow items.
     LASFS membership is $5; lending privileges only to members in or near Los Angeles.
   Index/Catalog: Yes; will be computerized in future; sorted lists of holdings and new acquisitions will be published.
   ILL: No
   Origin: 1937 — donations by members.
Holdings — Magazines: ca. 2900
   Primary: NA   Secondary: NA
   Subscriptions: None; rely on donations

Title	Prim/Sec	Dates	Condition

NA; an extensive collection of ca. 2000 pulps and digest-sized prozines, as well as ca. 900 fanzine issues. Fanzine holdings include LASFS publications since 1938 (*Imagination, Vom, Shangri L'Affaires, Apa L*, etc.).

Holdings — Books:
   Primary: 2000 (20%; 80%)   Secondary: 40
   Current: Yes
   Specialized: Includes autographed copies of books by Pournelle and Niven and other authors who are members of the Society.
Holdings — Miscellaneous:
   Art: Some original prozine art.
   Manuscripts: Some original mss.

CA7. SAN DIEGO STATE UNIVERSITY   Director: Louis A. Kenney
     San Diego State Univ. Library   Hours: 7:30am-11pm, M-Th; 7:30
     San Diego, CA 92182   am-5pm, F; 10am-5pm, Sat.; 1pm-
                                     10pm, Sun.

Collection Title: The Chater Collection
1977.

> Person to Contact: Louis A. Kenney, Director of Library Services; Gordon Samples, Librarian in Charge of Special Collections, Bernice Barclay, Subject Bibliographer for Science Fiction.
>
> Location: Rare, first editions housed in Spec. Coll.; Chater Collection will be housed in Spec. Coll.; remainder in general collection.
>
> Restrictions: None for general collection; remainder do not circulate and must be used in Spec. Coll.
>
> Index/Catalog: Only for the Chater Collection; Mrs. Chater has maintained her personal catalog, by author only, which will be given to the Library and will remain with the Collection.
>
> ILL: Yes, for books in the general collection; photocopies of periodical articles are available.
>
> Origin: 1965 — Professor Elizabeth Chater, science fiction writer and teacher at San Diego State Univ., gave the library duplicate copies from her collection. May 1977 — Professor Chater presented her entire personal library of 3600 volumes to the Library. Comprehensive in nature, it includes many first editions, rare books and posters.

Holdings — Magazines:

> Primary: 175   Secondary: 175
>
> Subscriptions: ASF; EX; FDN; FSF; RQ; SFST

Title	Prim/Sec	Dates	Condition
ASF	P	v. 74, 1964-Date (v. 62, 1962, incomplete)	Original
EX	S	v. 11, 1969-Date	,,
FDN	S	no. 4, 1973-Date,(incomplete)	,,
FSF	P	v. 45, 1973-Date	,,
RQ	S	v. 1, 1964-Date	,,
SFST	S	v. 2, 1975-Date	,,
SFBRI	S	1970-Date	,,

Holdings — Books:

> Primary: General Coll. — 1750 (15%; 85%)   Secondary: 14
>   Spec. Coll. —   90 (20%; 80%)
>   Chater Coll. — 3600 (25%; 75%)
>
> Current: Yes
>
> Specialized: No; collection is comprehensive covering all aspects—fictional, critical, artistic.

Holdings — Miscellaneous:

> Slides and phonodiscs: *Science Fiction: Jules Verne to Ray Bradbury*, 240 slides in color and 3 phonodiscs, Center for Humanities, 1974. *Science Fiction Sound Effects Record*, Folkways Records, 1958.
>
> Cassettes: Bradbury, Ray, *A Dramatization of the Martian Chronicles; Science Fiction at Its Best*, Living Literature, 1970, Chater, Elizabeth, *The Fantastic Experience in Literature*, Speech, 1976.
>
> M.A. Theses: Ardagna, Mark A., *Stronghold: A Novel*, 1976; Blake, Stephen B., *Those Now Among Us*, 1975; Randles, Dale E., *The Programmed Universe*, 1970.

CA8. UNIVERSITY OF CALIFORNIA   Director: James V. Mink
University Research Library   Hours: 9am-5pm, M-Sat.
Los Angeles, CA 90024

Collection Title: Nitka Collection of Fantastic Fiction
Person to Contact: Reference Librarian, Dept. of Special Collections.
Location: Dept. of Spec. Coll.
Restrictions: Yes; must be used in the Spec. Coll. reading room under the usual supervision.
Index/Catalog: Yes, with an author or title arrangement; the shelf list brings it together.
ILL: No
Origin: 1967 — purchase of the Nitka Collection; a small amount of material has been added since then.
Holdings — Magazines:
Primary: ca. 6500   Secondary: NA
Subscriptions: FSF; a number of fanzines, but records are incomplete.

Title	Prim/Sec	Dates	Condition
FSF	P	Complete run	Original

A large collection of sf pulp magazines, but titles and dates are NA; fanzines are primarily 1950-65.

Holdings — Books:
Primary: 9000 (66%; 34%)   Secondary: 25
Current: No
Specialized: No
Holdings — Miscellaneous:
Art: Ed Valigursky, 2 original watercolors for *If,* 1954.
Bradbury material: 3 boxes of manuscripts, correspondence, books, and ephemera by and relating to Ray Bradbury; "The Dogs That Eat Sweet Grass," typescript, 1965; "Interview of" unedited transcript, 1961; "Moby Dick. Screenplay by Ray Bradbury," not final shooting script, Nov. 14, 1956.
Letters: A few items from Clark Ashton Smith and L. Sprague de Camp.
Manuscripts: Franz Leiber. "The Silver Eggheads," 1958; Ward Moore. "Greener Than You Think," n.d.; G. Edmondson. "The Ship That Sailed the Time Stream," ca. 1963; Margaret St. Clair. "The Fungus Hunters," n.d.; Henry Kuttner. "A Gnome There Was and Other Tales of Science Fiction and Fantasy by Lewis Padgett," ca. 1950.
Transcripts: Van Vogt, "Reflections of A. E. van Vogt," Interview.

CA9. UNIVERSITY OF CALIFORNIA   Director: Eleanor Montague
RIVERSIDE   Hours: NA
University Library
P.O. Box 5900
Riverside, CA 92507

Collection Title: Eaton Fantasy and Science Fiction Collection
   Person to Contact: Clifford Wurfel
   Location: Special Collections Dept.
   Restrictions: Select items cannot be checked out; all items available to
      researchers.
   Index/Catalog: Yes; separate card catalog with author, title, subject
      access; complete listing by Robert Reginald to be published by Gale
      Research Co., 1978.
   ILL: Yes
   Origin: 1970 — purchased as a collection of 7000 titles from widow of
      Dr. Lloyd Eaton of Berkeley, Calif.
Holdings — Magazines:
   Primary: NA   Secondary: NA
   Subscriptions: ALG; AMZ; ASF; DFSF; EX; FSF; GAL; LM; and others.

Title	Prim/Sec	Dates		Condition
AMZ	P	1926-Date	(incomplete)	Original
ASF	P	1930-60	(scattered)	,,
		1960-Date	(incomplete)	,,
EX	S	1959-Date	,,	,,
FSF	P	1949-Date	,,	,,
GAL	P	1950-Date	,,	,,
STL	P	1939-53	,,	,,
WIF	P	1952-74	,,	,,

The above are longer runs from a large collection of over 140 titles.

Holdings — Books:
   Primary: 9000 (85%; 15%)   Secondary: NA
   Current: Yes
   Specialized: Dr. Eaton's holdings were especially strong in early and scarce
      items published from 1870-1930 by British and American authors;
      collection includes the following definable subject areas, although
      volumes are not housed together by these themes: fantasy, utopia,
      horror, occult, gothic, speculative fiction, science fiction. Strong
      holdings for the following authors: Edgar Rice Burroughs, George
      Griffith, H. Rider Haggard, Will F. Jenkins, David H. Keller, H. P.
      Lovecraft, A. Merritt, Talbot Mundy, E. E. Smith, Jules Verne, S.
      Fowler Wright.

CA10. UNIVERSITY OF CALIFORNIA   Director: NA
         SANTA CRUZ   Hours: NA
            University Library
            Santa Cruz, CA 95062

   Collection Title: NA
      Person to Contact: NA
      Location: Special Collections
      Restrictions: NA
      Index/Catalog: NA

ILL: NA
Origin: NA
Holdings — Magazines: 0
Holdings — Books:
    Primary: NA   Secondary: NA
    Current: NA
    Specialized: Yes, published books by Robert A. Heinlein only.
Holdings — Miscellaneous:
    Manuscripts, notes, and correspondence of Robert A. Heinlein. About 60 mss are available for use; correspondence is sealed and not usable.
    Manuscripts and associated material by Eric Temple Bell.

CA11. UNIVERSITY OF SOUTHERN   Director: Roy L. Kidman
           CALIFORNIA   Hours: 8am-12M, M-Th; 8am-5pm,
           University Library   F.; 9am-5pm, Sat.; 1pm-12M, Sun,
           University Park
           Los Angeles, CA 90007

Collection Title: None
    Person to Contact: Reference Department.
    Location: With the general collection in the general library and branch libraries.
    Restrictions: Non-USC patrons may use the material in the library.
    Index/Catalog: None
    ILL: Yes, books only.
    Origin: NA
Holdings — Magazines:
    Primary: 243   Secondary: 7
    Subscriptions: SFST

Title	Prim/Sec	Dates	Condition
ASF	P	12/1934-1/1959	Original
FSF	P	Fall, 1949-7/1969	"
GAL	P	12/1950-8/1965	"
SFST	S	Vol. 2, 1975-Date	"

Holdings — Books:
    Primary: NA   Secondary: 4
    Current: NA
    Specialized: American Literature Collection has very complete collections of Ambrose Bierce, Edgar Rice Burroughs, August Derleth, Jack London, Ray Bradbury, Kurt Vonnegut; other branches have works of Isaac Asimov, Jules Verne, Robert Heinlein; library will be happy to check particular authors and titles.
Holdings — Miscellaneous:
    The Cinema Library: 25 vol. on sf/f films
                         10 publ. screenplays of sf/f films
                         75 unpubl. screenplays of sf/f films

25 teleplays and other production material from the
Star Trek television program

12 taped interviews with Ray Bradbury

American Literature Collection: Ambrose Bierce — 34 letters; 1 correspondence; 7 documents; clippings of newspaper and periodical con-
trib. August Derleth — 17 letters; 4 correspondences. Jack London —
33 mss; 28 letters; 23 correspondences; 103 documents.

Mss and letters of many other American writers; write for specifics.

CO1. CITY OF DENVER   Director: Henry Shearouse
     Denver Public Library   Hours: 10am-9pm, M-Th; 10am-
     1357 Broadway   5:30pm, F-Sat.
     Denver, CO 80203

Collection Title: None
Person to Contact: JoAnne McBride, Literature & Language Librarian.
Location: With general fiction in Literature & Language Division.
Restrictions: None
Index/Catalog: None
ILL: Yes
Origin: NA
Holdings — Magazines:
     Primary: 24   Secondary: 2
     Subscriptions: ASF; FSF; LOC

Title	Prim/Sec	Dates	Condition
ASF	P	1/1976-Date	Original
EX	S	v. 1-10	"
FSF	P	1/1976-Date	"
LOC	S	12/1976-Date	"

Holdings — Books:
     Primary: ca. 2935   Secondary: ca. 60
     Current: Yes
     Specialized: No
Holdings — Miscellaneous:
Reference copy of each script of the original *Star Trek*.

CO2. COLORADO STATE UNIVERSITY   Director: LeMoyne W. Anderson
     Colorado State Univ. Libraries   Hours: 8am-12M, M-Th; 8am-5pm,
     Fort Collins, CO 80523   F; 9am-5pm, Sat.; 12N-12M, Sun.

Collection Title: Imaginary Wars Collection
Person to Contact: John Newman, Special Collections Librarian
Location: Spec. Coll. Dept.
Restrictions: Rare titles do not circulate
Index/Catalog: Yes; separate main-entry and shelf list files and various
tabular lists; annotated bibliography of American imprints published

in *Extrapolation,* vol. 16, numbers 1 and 2 (December 1974 and May 1975), "America at War," John Newman.
ILL: Yes; for easily replaced titles only.
Origin: 1968 — result of staff and faculty interest in the subject.
Holdings — Magazines:
Primary: No significant holdings   Secondary: NA
Subscriptions: None
Holdings — Books:
Primary: ca. 600 (80%; 20%)   Secondary: None
Specialized: The entire collection deals with fictional or future wars involving a known society or a close parallel to a known society. Also included are fictionalized outcomes of real wars. Collection seeks to be comprehensive and complete within these definitions.

CO3. UNIVERSITY OF COLORADO   Director: Leo Cabell
      University of Colorado Libraries   Hours: NA
      Boulder, CO 80302

Collection Title: None
   Person to Contact: Leo Cabell
   Location: With the general collection
   Restrictions: None
   Index/Catalog: None
   ILL: Yes
   Origin: Gradually built up.
   Holdings — Magazines:
   Primary: NA   Secondary: NA
   Subscriptions: All standard magazines

Title	Prim/Sec	Dates	Condition
ASF	P	1960-Date	Original
FAN	P	1931/32-1943	"

Individual information on additional titles NA.

   Holdings — Books:
   Primary: ca. 3000 (90%; 10%)   Secondary: ca. 100
   Current: Yes
   Specialized: No

DC1. SMITHSONIAN INSTITUTION   Director: Catherine D. Scott
      National Air and Space   Hours: 10am-5:15pm, daily
      Museum Library
      6th & Independence Ave., S.W.
      Washington, DC 20024

Collection Title: None
   Person to Contact: Reference Librarian
   Location: With the general collection

Restrictions: Yes; no individual borrowing

Index/Catalog: None for science fiction; there is a booklet available which describes the major holdings: Catherine D. Scott, "National Air and Space Museum Library," Sept. 28, 1976.

ILL: Yes

Origin: 1972 — through donations and interested curatorial staff.

Holdings — Magazines:

Primary: 96   Secondary: None

Subscriptions: ASF

Title	Prim/Sec	Dates	Condition
ASF	P	v. 64, 1969-Date	Original

Holdings — Books:

Primary: 200   Secondary: None

Current: Selectively

Specialized: No

Holdings — Miscellaneous:

Star Trek film: "Where No Man Has Gone Before" (Not for release or showing, archival film only)

Remarks: Researchers should know that the NASM Library consists of over 21,000 books; 4,600 bound periodicals; 500,000 technical reports. Special Collections include:

Bella Landauer — aeronautical sheet music collection and children's book collection

Institute of Aeronautical Sciences historical collection

William A.M. Burden — early ballooning books and scarce aeronatica

Samuel Pierpont Langley — Largest ms collection in NASM; includes correspondence, order books, financial accounts, work schedules, experimental notebooks, diaries, scrapbooks.

Stephen M. Balzer — Papers on development of the Balzer-Manly engine

Major photographic collections, including Sherman Fairchild's aeronautical collection; balloons, airships, personalities, aircraft.

DC2. UNITED STATES CONGRESS   Director: NA
     The Library of Congress   Hours: NA
     Washington, DC 20540

Collection Title: None

Person to Contact: Jean C. Sansobrino, Acting Head, Reference Section, Serial Division; Kay Rodgers, Reference Librarian, Science & Technol. Div.; John C. Broderick, Chief, Manuscript Division.

Location: With the general collection.

Restrictions: Vary with each Division; many of the pulp fiction magazines are housed in a separate storage area and must be requested at least 24-48 hours in advance.

Index/Catalog: Special files for individual collections such as the pulp fiction collection.

ILL: NA

Origin: NA

Holdings — Magazines:

Primary: NA   Secondary: NA

Subscriptions: LC receives copies of all copyrighted publications and retains many of them.

Title	Prim/Sec	Dates	Condition

NA; LC has a collection of pulp fiction magazines which includes many sf titles.

Holdings— Books:

Primary: NA   Secondary: NA

Current: Yes; LC receives copies of all copyrighted publications and retains many of them.

Specialized: No

Holdings — Miscellaneous:

It is probable that a search through the LC manuscript collections would reveal letters from science fiction writers to individuals whose papers are kept in LC.

FL1. FLORIDA INTERNATIONAL   Director: Howard Cordell
     UNIVERSITY   Hours: 8am-10pm, M-Th; 8am-
        University Library   5pm, F; 8:30 am-5pm, Sat.; 2pm-
        Tamiami Trail   9pm, Sun.
        Miami, FL 33199

Collection Title: None

Person to Contact: Clifford Dawdy or Dottie Rosenthal

Location: With the general collection

Restrictions: None

Index/Catalog: None

ILL: Yes

Origin: 1971 — as part of the regular acquisitions program

Holdings — Magazines:

Primary: ca. 420   Secondary: 2

Subscriptions: None

Title	Prim/Sec	Dates	Condition
AMZ	P	Apr. 1926-Dec. 1945	Microfilm
AMZQ	P	W 1928-Fall 1934	,,
EX	S	1959-74	,,
FAD	P	May 1939-Oct. 1945	,,
PLA	P	Nov. 1939-Fall 1945	,,
WST	P	June 1929-Apr. 1936	,,

The above are the longer runs of the collection of 15 titles.

Holdings — Books:

Primary: 36 (95%; 5%)   Secondary: 2

Current: Yes

Specialized: No

Holdings — Miscellaneous:

Motion picture: *The Day the Earth Stood Still*

FL2. FLORIDA STATE UNIVERSITY   Director: Charles E. Miller
        University Library   Hours: 8am-12M, M-Sat; 2pm-12M,
        Tallahassee, FL 32306   Sun.

Collection Title: None
   Person to Contact: NA
   Location: With the general collection
   Restrictions: None
   Index/Catalog: No
   ILL: No
   Origin: n.d. — as a part of the Undergraduate Library which has been
      absorbed in the regular collection
   Holdings — Magazines:
      Primary: 0   Secondary: 8
      Subscriptions: SFST

Title	Prim/Sec	Dates	Condition
SFST	S	v. 1, 1973-Date	Original

   Holdings — Books:
      Primary: 420 (NA)   Secondary: 50
      Current: NA
      Specialized: No

GA1. UNIVERSITY OF GEORGIA   Director: Warren N. Boes
        Ilah Dunlap Little   Hours: 8am-12pm, M-Th; 8am-
          Memorial Library   6pm, Fri; 9am-6pm, Sat; 2pm-
        University of Georgia Library 12M, Sun.
        Athens, GA 30602

Collection Title: None
   Person to Contact: Science Fiction Bibliographer
   Location: With the general collection
   Restrictions: Periodicals do not circulate
   Index/Catalog: None
   ILL: Yes
   Origin: 1968 — purchase of an extensive retrospective collection
   Holdings — Magazines:
      Primary: 3150   Secondary: 23
      Subscriptions: EX; SFST

Title	Prim/Sec	Dates	Condition

NA; library has approximately 120 separate magazine titles, primarily American, e.g. ASF; EX; FAN; GAL; LOC; SSM; WIF; WOF; all original
   Holdings — Books:
      Primary: 3000 (75%; 25%)   Secondary: 150
      Current: Yes
      Specialized: No

ID1. IDAHO STATE UNIVERSITY
      University Library
      Pocatello, ID 83209

Director: Eli M. Oboler
Hours: 8am-11pm, M-Th; 8am-
5pm, F; 9am-5pm, Sat; 2pm-
11pm, Sun.

Collection Title: None
    Person to Contact: Douglas Birdsall, Humanities Librarian
    Location: With the general collection
    Restrictions: None
    Index/Catalog: None
    ILL: Yes
    Origin: NA
Holdings — Magazines:
    Primary: ca. 156   Secondary: ca. 12
    Subscriptions: ALG; FSF; SFST

Title	Prim/Sec	Dates	Condition
ALG	S	On order	Original
FSF	P	1963-Date	"
OW	S	1976-Date	"
SFST	S	1976-Date	"

Holdings — Books:
    Primary: ca. 200 (95%; 5%)   Secondary: ca. 30
    Current: Yes
    Specialized: No
Holdings — Miscellaneous:
    Cassette holdings include several lectures and panel discussions, as well as
    individual works, such as *The Martian Chronicles*.

IL1. CITY OF CHICAGO
      Chicago Public Library
      425 N. Michigan
      Chicago, IL 60611

Director: David L. Reich
Hours: 10am-9pm, M-Th; 10am-
6pm, F; 10am-5pm, Sat.

Collection Title: None
    Person to Contact: J. W. Reginald Scurr, Literature and Philosophy
        Division.
    Location: With the general collection in the main library and branch
        libraries.
    Restrictions: None
    Index/Catalog: None
    ILL: Yes
    Origin: NA
Holdings — Magazines:
    Primary: ca. 239   Secondary: ca. 53
    Subscriptions: ASF; FSF; GAL; LM

Title	Prim/Sec	Dates	Condition
ASF	P	v. 85 (1970)-Date	Original
FSF	P	1955-Date (incomplete)	”
GAL	P	v. 9-15; 33-36; 1972-Date	”
LM	S	No. 8 (1970)-Date	”

Holdings — Books:
  Primary: NA   Secondary: NA
  Current: Yes
  Specialized: No, to serve the general reading public; includes 61 vol. Arno
    Press series.

IL2. KISHWAUKEE COLLEGE   Director: Patsy Lundberg
        Kishwaukee College Library   Hours: 8am-9:30pm, M-Th; 8am-
        Malta, IL 60150   4pm, Fri.

Collection Title: None
  Person to Contact: Patsy Lundberg
  Location: With the general collection
  Restrictions: None
  Index/Catalog: None
  ILL: Yes
  Origin: n.d. — Purchases to accommodate sf course; 1976 — 119 titles
    purchased with Title 6 grant funds.
  Holdings — Magazines:
    Primary: 0   Secondary: ca. 67
    Subscriptions: EX; LM

Title	Prim/Sec	Dates	Condition
EX	S	1959-74;	Microfilm
		1975-Date	Original
LM	S	1972-Date	”

Holdings — Books:
    Primary: ca. 250 (25%; 75%)   Secondary: NA
    Current: NA
    Specialized: No
  Holdings — Miscellaneous:
    Cassettes: 6 tapes — Isaac Asimov Cassette Library
                 6 tapes — Ray Bradbury Cassette Library

IL3. NORTHERN ILLINOIS   Director: NA
        UNIVERSITY   Hours: 8:30am-5pm, M-F.
        No. Illinois University Libraries
        DeKalb, Il 60115

Collection Title: Science Fiction Magazine Collection
  Person to Contact: Anthony Bliss, Head, Department of Rare Books and
    Special Collections.

Location: Spec. Coll. Dept.
Restrictions: Rare Book reading room use only.
Index/Catalog: Computer print-out list by title, with holdings indicated.
ILL: None
Origin: ca. 1969 — purchase of a complete collection
Holdings — Magazines:
    Primary: ca. 1500-2000   Secondary: NA
    Subscriptions: AMZ; FAN; FSF; GAL

Title	Prim/Sec	Dates	Condition
AMZ	P	v. 1, 1926-Date	Original
ASF	P	1930-Date	”
FAD	P	1939-53	”
FAN	P	1952-Date	”
FAU	P	1953-60	”
FFM	P	1939-53	”
FSF	P	1950-Date	”
GAL	P	1950-Date	”
PLA	P	1939-55	”
STL	P	1939-55	”

The above titles are the longer runs in the collection of 100 titles.

Holdings — Books:
    Primary: NA   Secondary: NA
    Current: General acquisitions
    Specialized: No; Lovecraft collection of first and early editions in process.
Holdings — Miscellaneous:
    Currently in process, an H.P. Lovecraft Collection, including some mss.

IL4. SOUTHERN ILLINOIS   Director: Sidney E. Matthews
      UNIVERSITY, CARBONDALE   Hours: 7:45am-12M, M-Th;
        Morris Library   7:45am-6pm, F; 9am-6pm, Sat;
        Carbondale, IL 62901   2pm-12M, Sun.

Collection Title: None
    Person to Contact: Alan M. Cohn, Humanities Librarian
    Location: Humanities Division
    Restrictions: None
    Index/Catalog: None
    ILL: Yes
    Origin: Part of the general development of the collections.
Holdings — Magazines:
    Primary: ca. 200   Secondary: ca. 225
    Subscriptions: CIN; EX; FSF; ML; RQ; SFST

Title	Prim/Sec	Dates	Condition
CIN	S	1975-Date	Original
EX	S	1959-Date	”
FSF	P	1960-Date	”

ML	S	1973-Date	"
RQ	S	1964-Date	"
SFST	S	1973-Date	"

Holdings — Books:

Primary: ca. 2000 (90%; 10%)   Secondary: ca. 150
Current: Yes
Specialized: No

IL5. UNIVERSITY OF ILLINOIS   Director: NA
      AT URBANA-CHAMPAIGN   Hours: (Rare Book Room): 9am-
      University Library   12N, 1pm-5pm, M-F; 9am-12N Sat.
      Urbana, IL 61801

Collection Title: Wells Collection
Person to Contact: N.F. Nash, Rare Book Room Librarian
Location: Rare Book Room
Restrictions: Yes; material must be used in Rare Book Room.
Index/Catalog: Wells materials listed in vol. 11 of the *Catalog of the Rare Book Room, University Library, University of Illinois,* Boston, MA: G.K. Hall & Co., 1972.
ILL: Yes, for a few items; xerox copies of letters, etc. can be obtained.
Origin: 1953/54 — purchased Wells Collection from Bertram Rota, Ltd., London; negotiated by Prof. Gordon Ray.
Holdings — Magazines: NA
Holdings — Books:

Primary: ca. 1000   Secondary: NA
Current: Yes
Specialized: H. G. Wells' works in many languages and editions; includes his books, books to which he contributed, an almost complete file of English editions inscribed or corrected by Wells, 1883-1945, and ca. 150 vols. from Wells' library, many inscribed to him.

Holdings — Miscellaneous:

Bibliography: 1. Two, to books and short pieces, begun by Mrs. G.P. Wells; project currently continued.
                    2. Typewritten copies of letters written by HGW; filed chronologically, 1880-1915; project currently continued.
                    3. Chronology of HGW's life; project currently continued.
Correspondence: 1. General: letters to HGW, wife, secretary, etc.; ca. 60,000, 1888-1946. Filed alphabetically by signer and chronologically.
                    2. Correspondence: letters from HGW, wife, secretary, etc.; ca. 1500, 1880-1946. Alphabetized by recipient and filed chronologically.
Documents: 1. HGW personal documents include the following: business affairs (taxes, investments, pass-books, real estate, receipts, account books, inventories,

law suits, etc.); diaries, journals, passports, diplomas, drawings, juvenilia (mss of "newspapers" and tales), address books and phone directory, publication records, etc.

2. Family documents of Amy Catherine Robbins Wells and Francis C. Wells.

Manuscripts:

1. Book mss: mss and/or proofs of work published in book or pamphlet form. Alphabetized by title of first publication by HGW. Includes 40 novels, 37 sociological books, 11 pamphlets.

2. Periodical mss: mss, typescripts and/or clippings of ca. 500 unreprinted serial publications.

3. Speeches: chronological list of mss of published speeches, giving location in Archive.

4. Prefaces to others' books: filed according to book title.

5. Unpublished material: mss and/or typescripts of pieces for which publication has not been traced; ca. 150, filed by type and chronology.

Pictures:

Photographs, snapshots, etchings, prints; filed by subject, when known. Includes 4 albums of photographs given to the Library in 1964 by Frank Wells, HGW's younger son.

Secondary Material:

Clippings about HGW from periodicals.

IL6. WHEATON COLLEGE
   Wheaton College Library
   501 East Seminary Ave.
   Wheaton, IL 60187

Director: NA
Hours: 9am-5pm, M-F; 9am-12N, Sat.

Collection Title: The Marion E. Wade Collection
   Person to Contact: Dr. C.S. Kilby, Curator; or Barbara J. Griffin, Librarian
   Location: NA
   Restrictions: Non-circulating
   Index/Catalog: Cataloging in process
   ILL: No
   Origin: 1965
Holdings — Magazines:
   Primary: NA   Secondary: NA
   Subscriptions: All are either of the mythopoeic type (*Mythlore, Mythprint, Unicorn, Mallorn*) or more in the order of bulletins (*The New York C.S. Lewis Society Bulletin, Portland Society Bulletin, The Lamp-Post, The Sayers Review, The Chesterton Review*).

Title	Prim/Sec	Dates	Condition

NA; includes ca. 75 titles which are concerned with modern mythology; hundreds of early periodicals pertaining to G.K. Chesterton.

Holdings — Books:

Primary: NA   Secondary: NA

Current: NA

Specialized: Yes; the collection contains books and articles by and about 7 authors: Owen Barfield, G.K. Chesterton, C.S. Lewis, George Mc-Donald, Dorothy Sayers, J.R.R. Tolkien, Charles Williams; includes many first editions, as well as later editions, of Lewis, McDonald, Tolkien, Williams.

Holdings — Miscellaneous:

Correspondence: Letters of the 7 authors, including:

Lewis — 1115 original, mainly unpublished letters and 375 copies of letters by Lewis.

Williams — 950 holograph letters by Williams

Critical papers: 96 theses, dissertations on the 7 authors; 30 papers.

Manuscripts: From the 7 authors, including:

Lewis — 2 mss and many original poems

Williams — a substantial number of mss presently being cataloged, including a first draft of *Descent into Hell.*

IN1.   INDIANA UNIVERSITY   Director: William R. Cagle
       The Lilly Library of   Hours: 9am-5pm, M-F; 6pm-10pm,
       Indiana University   M-Th; 9am-12N, Sat.
       Bloomington, IN 47401

Collection Title: None

Person to Contact: Ms. Geneva Warner

Location: Lilly Library

Restrictions: None

Index/Catalog: No complete catalog; a brief listing is contained in an exhibition catalog—*An Exhibition on Science Fiction and Fantasy*, Bloomington, IN: The Lilly Library, 1975, illus.

ILL: No

Origin: 1972 — a concerted effort was begun by the late director, David A. Randall, to collect fantasy and science fiction.

Holdings — Magazines:

Primary: NA   Secondary: NA

Subscriptions: None

Title	Prim/Sec	Dates	Condition
AMZ	P	v. 1, no. 1-v.47, no. 6	Original
AMZQ	P	v. 1, no. 1-v. 7, no. 2	”
ASF	P	˙v. 1, no. 1-v. 64, no. 5	”
ASF	P	v. 64, no. 6-v. 75, no. 2	”
FSF	P	v. 1-v. 43	”
WST	P	v. 1, no. 1-v. 45, no. 2	”

In addition to the above, there are many uncataloged titles, including some complete or nearly complete runs of science fiction periodicals in the 1930's and 1940's.

Holdings — Books:

Primary : NA   Secondary: NA

Current: Yes

Specialized: Collection includes a comprehensive Arkham House collection and complete first editions of Wells, Verne, Haggard, Chesterton, Derleth, Lovecraft, as well as some first editions of Poe, Mary Shelley, etc.

Holdings — Miscellaneous:

Manuscripts: August Derleth — over 2000 items (monographs, movie scripts, mss)

Papers: Anthony Boucher and Fritz Leiber

Scripts: Movie and TV scripts

IA1. IOWA COMMISSION   Director: Duane Gerstenberger
      FOR THE BLIND   Hours: 8am-5pm, M-F.
         Iowa Comm. for the Blind Library
         524 Fourth Street
         Des Moines, IA 50309

Collection Title: None

Person to Contact: Duane Gerstenberger

Location: Iowa Commission for the Blind building

Restrictions: Yes; blind and physically handicapped Iowans only

Index/Catalog: No; a brief description of the collection has been published in Neil Barron, "Science Fiction for the Blind," LM 35/36 (April/May 1972) 13, 38.

ILL: Yes, on a very limited basis.

Origin: July 1, 1960 — opening of the library; developed by Dr. Kenneth Jernigan, Director of the Iowa Comm. for the Blind; volunteer braillists and tapists have transcribed much of the collection.

Holdings — Magazines:

Primary: NA   Secondary: NA

Subscriptions: GAL; SFRA

Title	Prim/Sec	Dates	Condition
GAL	P	NA	Original press Braille and talking book disc
SFRA	S	NA	NA

Holdings — Books:

Primary: ca. 3500   Secondary: NA

Current: Yes

Specialized: No

Remarks: Probably the largest collection of science fiction in Braille in the world.

KS1. UNIVERSITY OF KANSAS   Director: Alexandra Mason
         Kenneth Spencer   Hours: 9am-6pm, M-F; 9am-1pm,
            Research Library   Sat. (Sat. hours during 1st and
         Lawrence, KS 66045   2nd semesters only)

Collection Title: ASF Collection
Person to Contact: Alexandra Mason, Spencer Librarian
Location: Closed stacks in Dept. of Special Collections
Restrictions: None; some mss are "on deposit," and users must apply to owners for serious use.
Index/Catalog: For printed material: Separate card file (divided into authors, periodicals, anthologies); card file analyzing anthologies by author and story title; NESFA Index (and others) marked to show periodical holdings. For mss material: Lengthy typed descriptions for most material, filed with descriptions of other mss in the loose-leaf Catalogue IV.
ILL: No
Origin: 1969 — Gift funds from Larry Friesen, KU graduate. Additions: substantial gifts of books, magazines, mss by James Gunn; purchase of John H. Ryley collection in 1971; other gifts. Building of this collection is described in "The Library of the Future: Science Fiction and the Department of Special Collections," *Books and Libraries,* 13:3 (Spring 1976), University of Kansas Libraries, Lawrence, Kansas.
Holdings — Magazines:
Primary: 1884   Secondary: NA
Subscriptions: None; James Gunn donates ASF, FSF, GAL after a year's delay.

Title	Prim/Sec	Dates	Condition

NA; all are original.

Holdings — Books:
Primary: 1166 (30%; 70%)   Secondary: ca. 20
Current: Yes
Specialized: Collection emphasizes Campbell-type sf; includes SFWA Depository
Remarks: Library's general collection contains additional secondary material
Holdings — Miscellaneous:
Manuscripts: Author's archives (drafts, proofs, correspondence, souvenirs) of James Gunn, T.L. Sherred, Lloyd Biggle; Algis Budrys' draft of "Who?" accompanied by Kelly Freas painting. New material periodically received and in process.
SFWA: Gunn's archives include microfilmed minutes of SFWA under Gunn's Presidency.
Ephemera: Gunn, Biggle, and Sherred have given large numbers of fanzines and ephemeral publications picked up at conventions or received in the mail; these are boxed and stored but not cataloged or readily usable.

KS2. UNIVERSITY OF KANSAS   Director: Alexandra Mason
     Kenneth Spencer   Hours: 9am-6pm, M-F; 9am-1pm,
       Research Library   Sat. (Sat. hours during 1st and 2nd
     Lawrence, KS 66045   semesters only)

Collection Title: Stewart Fantasy Collection
    Person to Contact: Alexandra Mason, Spencer Librarian
    Location: Closed stacks in Dept. of Special Collections
    Restrictions: None
    Index/Catalog: Shelf list provides indentification of the Collection
    ILL: No
    Origin: 1965 — bequest of James H. Stewart of Wichita, KS.
    Holdings — Magazines:
        Primary: 310   Secondary: 0
        Subscriptions: None

Title	Prim/Sec	Dates	Condition

NA; primarily a long run of WRT; original

Holdings — Books:
    Primary: ca. 470 (75%; 25%)   Secondary: 0
    Current: No
    Specialized: Collection is basically what Stewart owned, primarily Love-
        craft, Machen, Long.

KY1. CITY OF BOWLING GREEN   Director: William F. Bolte
    Public Library   Hours: 9am-9pm, M-Th; 9am-5pm,
    1225 State Street   F-Sat.
    Bowling Green, KY 42101

Collection Title: ScF Collection
    Person to Contact: Circulation Librarian
    Location: First floor, shelved separately from Fiction.
    Restrictions: None
    Index/Catalog: None
    ILL: Yes
    Origin: ca. 1955 — to meet public interest in science fiction.
    Holdings — Magazines: None
    Holdings — Books:
        Primary: ca. 1300 (95%; 5%)   Secondary: None
        Current: Yes
        Specialized: No; collection is strictly for public interest.

KY2. UNIVERSITY OF KENTUCKY   Director: Paul Willis
    Margaret I. King Library   Hours: (Spec. Coll.): 8am-5pm,
    University of Kentucky Libraries   M-F; 8am-12N, Sat.
    Lexington, KY 40506

Collection Title: Science Fiction Collection
    Person to Contact: Bill Marshall
    Location: Special Collections Department
    Restrictions: Non-circulating
    Index/Catalog: Yes; separate shelf list housed in Spec. Coll.

ILL: For most items
Origin: Gift by University professor who collected them with the goal of giving them to the library.
Holdings — Magazines:
Primary: ca. 525   Secondary: None
Subscriptions: None

Title	Prim/Sec	Dates	Condition
ASF	P	July 1947-Jan. 1974	Original

There are additional titles with scattered, incomplete runs.

Holdings — Books:
Primary: ca. 1500   Secondary: 3
Current: Only by gifts
Specialized: No

KY3. UNIVERSITY OF LOUISVILLE   Director: NA
     Univ. of Louisville Library   Hours: 9am-5pm, M-F; by appoint-
     Belknap Campus   ment
     Louisville, KY 40208

Collection Title: None
Person to Contact: George T. McWhorter, Curator, Rare Book Room
Location: Patterson Rare Book Room
Restrictions: Non-circulating materials to be used under the supervision of Rare Book Curator.
Index/Catalog: Informal inventory lists only.
ILL: Subject to condition of materials
Origin: 1973 — Special purchase of duplicates from the Univ. of California pulp collection; 1974 — Burroughs collection donated by George McWhorter, Curator.
Holdings — Magazines:
Primary: ca. 7000   Secondary: 0
Subscriptions: None

Title	Prim/Sec	Dates	Condition

NA; over 150 titles, including detective, westerns, and general pulp fiction of 20th c.; originals.

Holdings — Books:
Primary: NA   Secondary: 0
Current: Yes
Specialized: Yes. Edgar Rice Burroughs: ca. 2500 items, including first editions, reprints, magazines, movie posters; Curator's goal is to make this the definitive Burroughs collection. Baum/Oz Collection: ca. 100 items, including all but one of the regularly published Oz titles, most of Baum's non-Oz fantasies published under his own name, and many of his pseudonymous titles.

KY4. WESTERN KENTUCKY
      UNIVERSITY
        Helm/Cravens Library
        Bowling Green, KY 42101

Director: Earl Wassom
Hours: 8am-11pm, M-Th; hours
vary on weekends.

Collection Title: None
   Person to Contact: Circulation librarian
   Location: With general collection
   Restrictions: Library is open to the public; circulation to faculty, students,
      and special borrowers.
   Index/Catalog: None
   ILL: Only if item is out of print; with some limitations
   Origin: 1975 — to provide material for a course in the literature.
Holdings — Magazines: None
Holdings — Books: over 200
   Primary: NA (100%; 0%)   Secondary: NA
   Current: Yes
   Specialized: No

LA1. TULANE UNIVERSITY
      Howard-Tilton Memorial
        Library
      New Orleans, LA 70118

Director: (Acting) Dorothy
Whittemore
Hours: NA

Collection Title: Rosel George Brown Collection; and Herman Deutsche
   Collection of Robert Heinlein
   Person to Contact: Ann S. Gwyn, Head, Special Collections
   Location: Special Collections Division
   Restrictions: Non-circulating
   Index/Catalog: Yes; typed inventory for Brown Coll; none for Deutsch
      Coll.
   ILL: No
   Origin: n.d. — gifts by Mrs. Rosel Brown and by Herman Deutsche
Holdings — Magazines:
   Primary: ca. 637 (Brown Coll. only)   Secondary: 0
   Subscriptions: None

Title	Prim/Sec	Dates	Condition
AMZ	P	1956-65	Original
ASF	P	1938-60	”
FAN	P	1952-65	”
FSF	P	1951-69	”
GAL	P	1951-66	”

The above are the longer runs from 36 titles; list available upon request.
   Holdings — Books:
   Primary: 235 (Brown Coll. only)   Secondary: 0
   Current: No
   Specialized: Yes; the Deutsche Collection consists of 31 hardbacks by
      Heinlein, many autographed.

MD1. THE JOHNS HOPKINS
     UNIVERSITY
       The Milton S. Eisenhower
         Library
       Baltimore, MD 21218

Director: David Stam
Hours: (Hutzler Undergrad. Lib.):
8am-12M, M-F; (Spec. Coll): 8:30
am-5pm, M-F.

Collection Title: Science Fiction in the Hutzler Undergraduate Library
   Person to Contact: Shirley Baker, Hutzler Undergrad. Librarian
   Location: Undergrad. Lib.
   Restrictions: Yes; to holders of valid Johns Hopkins' ID
   Index/Catalog: Paperbacks are not listed in any card catalog or index;
      hardbacks are cataloged in the Undergrad. Lib.
   ILL: Only cataloged hardbacks.
   Origin: 1972 — gifts of paperbacks by students and purchase of hard-
      backs by Library
   Holdings — Magazines:
      Primary: ca. 12   Secondary: 0
      Subscriptions: None

Title	Prim/Sec	Dates	Condition
ASF	P	Current issues only	Original
GAL	P	” ” ”	”

   Holdings — Books:
      Primary: 450 (10%; 90%)   Secondary: 0
      Current: Volumes added selectively
      Specialized: No
      Remarks: In addition, the Special Collections Dept. has about 250 vol-
        umes from the 1930's to the 1950's which were a gift from a private
        donor. This collection is not listed in any catalog but may be consulted
        by request in the Spec. Coll. Dept.

MD2. UNIVERSITY OF MARYLAND
     BALTIMORE COUNTY
       University Library
       5401 Wilkens Avenue
       Baltimore, MD 21228

Director: Antonio Raimo
Hours: 1pm-3pm, M-F; by
appointment.

Collection Title: Azriel Rosenfeld Science Fiction Collection
   Person to Contact: Binnie Syril Braunstein
   Location: Special Collections Room
   Restrictions: Non-circulating
   Index/Catalog: Yes; included in the catalog for Spec. Coll. room, with
      the following divisions: shelf list, author/title, subject.
   ILL: No
   Origin: 1973 — gift of sf books and magazines; later purchase of fanzines.
   Holdings — Magazines:
      Primary: ca. 1740   Secondary: ca. 11,050
      Subscriptions: AMZ; ASF; DFSF; EX; FSF; GAL

Title	Prim/Sec	Dates	Condition
AMZ	P	1926-Date	Original
ASF	P	1933-Date	,,
DFSF	S	1975-Date	,,
EX	S	1959-72	,,
FSF	P	1949-Date	,,
GAL	P	1950-Date	,,

Individual information NA on 11,000 fanzines, roughly spanning 1930-72.

Holdings — Books:
Primary: 5000 (40%; 60%)   Secondary: 200
Current: Yes
Specialized: No

Holdings — Miscellaneous:
Artwork: Frank Kelly Freas, Aldo Spandoni
Comics: 400 issues; individual information NA
Letters/Papers: Coslet
Manuscripts: Asimov, Harnes, Kornbluth and Pohl, Monteleone, Freas, Zelazny.
Tapes: Several taped readings.

MA1. BOSTON UNIVERSITY   Director: John Laucus
     Mugar Memorial Library   Hours: 9am-5pm, M-F.
     771 Commonwealth Avenue
     Boston, MA 02215

Collection Title: Special Collections
Person to Contact: Dr. Howard B. Gotlieb, Director of Special Collections
Location: 5th floor, Mugar Memorial Library
Restrictions: Use is confined to library; individual manuscript collections may have specific restrictions set by authors.
Index/Catalog: Each manuscript collection has its own inventory listing all manuscripts and other items in the collection; these are filed separately in Special Collections. The manuscript catalog in Spec. Coll. has a unit card for each collection and entries for letters and/or manuscripts by others. The book collections are cataloged as a unit also.
ILL: Printed matter may be photocopied; no reproduction of mss or correspondence without permission.
Origin: 1963 — Initiated; Contemporary Authors, which includes science fiction/fantasy writers; most materials donated by authors.

Holdings — Magazines:
Primary: NA   Secondary: NA
Subscriptions: None

Title	Prim/Sec	Dates	Condition

NA; individual manuscript collections may contain printed material including original primary and secondary magazines related to the specific author. These magazines appear on the manuscript inventory but are not individually cataloged.

Holdings — Books:
Primary: ca. 500 (40%; 60%)   Secondary: NA
Current: Yes, each author usually sends his latest publications
Specialized: Yes, by individual author: Isaac Asimov, Arthur C. Clarke, L. Sprague deCamp, Samuel R. Delany, Harold L. Goodwin (John Blaine, pseud.), Evan Hunter, Alan E. Nourse, Claude Seignolle, Curt Siodmak, John Vance, H.G. Wells, Jay Williams.
Holdings — Miscellaneous:
Manuscript collections, which correspond to the book collections, may contain holograph and typescript drafts of the author's works, notes, research items, personal, fan, business and professional correspondence, and memorabilia. Collections vary in size from a few items to ca. 100 linear feet of Isaac Asimov.

MA2. HARVARD UNIVERSITY
University Library
Cambridge, MA 02138

Director: NA
Hours: NA

Collection Title: Clarkson Collection
Person to Contact: NA
Location: NA
Restrictions: Yes; the magazines are not available for use.
Index/Catalog: NA; a description of the collection has been published: "The Clarkson Collection of Science Fiction at Harvard," Mark Hillegas, EX, vol. V, No. 1, Dec. 1963, pp. 2-14.
ILL: NA
Origin: 1955 — gift of private collection of Richard W. Clarkson of Baltimore who died in December 1954, in his junior year at Harvard; by his father.
Holdings — Magazines:
Primary: NA   Secondary: NA
Subscriptions: NA

Title	Prim/Sec	Dates	Condition

NA; it includes 136 titles, with complete runs of AMZ, ASF, FSF, GAL, WOI; also includes 52 fanzine titles, with usually one or two issues of any title.
Holdings — Books:
Primary: ca. 2200   Secondary: ca. 200
Current: NA
Specialized: Primarily novels by British and American authors; nearly complete holdings of 58 classic writers; includes some obscure sf and some occult. The secondary holdings include ca. 60 bibliographic items and ca. 140 non-fiction, science-related topics.
Holdings — Miscellaneous:
Comics: Small holdings of scattered issues.
Art: 5 original drawings for covers and illustrations for sf magazines
MSS: 27 mss of sf short stories; reportedly many uncataloged mss, including some important John W. Campbell, Jr. short stories.

MA3. MIT SCIENCE FICTION SOCIETY   Director: Gary Goldberg
     Library   Hours: Vary; usually 4pm-1am
     Room W20-421, MIT   daily during academic sessions
     Student Center
     84 Massachusetts Ave.
     Cambridge, MA 02139

Collection Title: None
     Person to Contact: Gary Goldberg, The Skinner, c/o MITSFS
     Location: 4th floor, MIT Student Center
     Restrictions: Only MITSFS members may check out items; anyone may
     use material on location.
     Index/Catalog: Yes; PINKDEX, a computer listing of all holdings; holdings
     from 1951-65 published in Erwin S. Strauss, comp., *The MIT Science
     Fiction Society's Index to the S-F Magazines, 1951-65*, Cambridge,
     MA: New England Science Fiction Assoc., 1966.
     ILL: No
     Origin: 1949 — sf discussion group formed by Rudolph W. Priesendorfer,
     MIT student; books were donated to initiate the library; MITSFS is a
     student organization and is not part of MIT.
     Holdings — Magazines:
     Primary: ca. 13,700   Secondary: NA
     Subscriptions: ALG; AMZ; ASF; CIN; EX; FAN; FSF; GAL; JIR; LOC;
     OW; SFRE; SFST

Title	Prim/Sec	Dates	Condition

Nearly complete collection from 1920's-Date, all original and bound; contains an infinite number of fanzines.

Holdings — Books:
     Primary: ca. 13,000 (23%; 77%)   Secondary: ca. 150
     Current: Yes; SFWA Depository
     Specialized: Includes about 360 SFWA books; 1250 foreign language col-
     lection, including ca. 1000 Perry Rhodan volumes in German.
Holdings — Miscellaneous:
     Art: Jeff Jones original oil painting
     Correspondence: 1 drawer of MITSFS-author correspondence
     Manuscripts: 1 unpublished John Campbell non-fiction ms.

MI1. EASTERN MICHIGAN   Director: Fred Blum
     UNIVERSITY   Hours: 105 hours, 7 days
       Center of Educational Resources
       Ypsilanti, MI 48197

Collection Title: None
     Person to Contact: A Humanities librarian or the University Archivist
     Location: Open shelves, Humanities Division and special collections.
     Restrictions: Partial
     Index/Catalog: None
     ILL: Yes, books only
     Origin: ca. 1973 — when Marshall Tymn offered the first sf course.

Holdings — Magazines:
Primary: ca. 400   Secondary: ca. 145
Subscriptions: EX; SFBRI

Title	Prim/Sec	Dates	Condition
EX	S	1973-Date	Original
LM	S	No. 3-56	,,
LOC	S	No. 114-53 (incomplete)	,,
		No. 114-168	,,

Substantial runs of ASF; scattered holdings of 14 other journals and fanzines.

Holdings — Books:
Primary: NA   Secondary: 10-12
Current: As far as possible
Specialized: No; we do not collect primary sf books, except for the prize-winning titles.

Holdings — Miscellaneous:
Programs from Chicon, Discon, Loncon, Nycon, Pittcon, Seacon, Tricon, Detroit, 1955.
Progress reports from Baycon, Discon, Seacon, Torcon, Tricon, Westercon, WSF 20th and 24th.

MI2. GRAND VALLEY   Director: Stephen Ford
     STATE COLLEGES   Hours: 8am-12M, M-Th; 8am-
       Zumberge Library   10pm, F; 1pm-5pm, Sat; 1pm-
       College Landing   10pm, Sun.
       Allendale, MI 49401

Collection Title: Science Fiction Collection
Person to Contact: Reference Librarian
Location: Office of the Reference Librarian
Restrictions: Non-circulating
Index/Catalog: None
ILL: No; photocopy available
Origin: Several years ago — gift by a student; subsequent donations

Holdings — Magazines:
Primary: ca. 833   Secondary: ca. 45
Subscriptions: ASF; EX; FSF; GAL

Title	Prim/Sec	Dates		Condition
ASF	P	1935-Date	(incomplete)	Original
EX	S	v. 1-Date	,,	,,
FSF	P	v. 1-Date	,,	,,
GAL	P	v. 1-31	(incomplete)	,,
		v. 32-Date		,,
RQ	S	v. 1-6		,,
WOF	P	v. 1-22	(incomplete)	,,

Holdings — Books:
Primary: NA   Secondary: 12
Current: Fair
Specialized: No

MI3. MICHIGAN STATE UNIVERSITY   Director: Richard E. Chapin
   Mich. State University Libraries   Hours: (Spec. Coll.): 8am-5pm,
   East Lansing, MI 48824   M-F; 9am-1pm, Sat.

Collection Title: None; it is a category of the Popular Fiction Collections
in the Popular Culture Collection.
Person to Contact: Jannette Fiore, Special Collections Librarian
Location: Spec. Coll. Division
Restrictions: Room use only, with identification held while material is
in use.
Index/Catalog: Separate shelf list
ILL: No, but photocopy is available
Origin: mid-1960 — purchased a sf pulp collection
Holdings — Magazines:
Primary: NA; ca. 825 issues   Secondary: NA
before 1960
Subscriptions: AMZ; ASF; FAN; FDN; FSF; GAL; LM; LOC; SFM

Title	Prim/Sec	Dates	Condition
FDN	S	No. 4-Date	Original
LM	S	1971-Date	"
LOC	S	1973-Date	"
SFM	S	v. 1, no. 2-Date	"

Additional information NA; have nearly full runs since 1960 of AMZ, ASF,
FAN, FSF, GAL, WIF.

Includes 2000 fanzines.

Holdings — Books:
Primary: 544   Secondary: NA; with general coll.
Current: Yes; depository for SFWA
Specialized: No
Holdings — Miscellaneous:
Primary material generated by the Clarion Science Fiction Writers Work-
shop which is held at Michigan State Univ. each summer, i.e., type-
scripts of stories by participants.
SFWA Oral History: Vincent Voice Library at Michigan State is the prin-
ciple repository for this project, launched March 1977.

MI4. UNIVERSITY OF MICHIGAN   Director: Frederick H. Wagman
   University Library   Hours: (Rare Books): 10am-12N,
   Ann Arbor, MI 48104   1pm-5pm, M-F; 10am-12N, Sat.

Collection Title: Hubbard Imaginary Voyages Collection
Person to Contact: Harriet C. Jameson, Head, Dept. of Rare Books and
Special Collections
Location: Dept. of Rare Books & Spec. Coll., 7th floor, Graduate Library
Restrictions: Yes; individual must be qualified researcher
Index/Catalog: Shelf list in Dept. office
ILL: No

Origin: 1923 — gift of former University of Michigan Regent, Lucius Lee Hubbard. 1959 — added Defoe collection of George Hough.
Holdings — Magazines: 0
Holdings — Books:

Primary: ca. 3000   Secondary: 0

Current: NA

Specialized: Yes; primarily editions, translations, adaptations, abridgments, parodies, and imitations of *Robinson Crusoe and Gulliver's Travels.*

MN1. CITY OF RED WING   Director: Roger D. Sween
    Red Wing Public Library   Hours: 9am-9pm, M-Th; 9am-5pm,
    225 Broadway   Fri-Sat.
    Red Wing, MN 55066

Collection Title: None
    Person to Contact: Roger D. Sween
    Location: With the general collection; personal collection of fanzines in Librarian's office.
    Restrictions: None on general collection; in-library use on fanzines.
    Index/Catalog: Yes, bibliography of general collection published in *Wing-It!*, 1977.
    ILL: Yes; including fanzines.
    Origin: 1966 — general collection; 1972 — personal fanzine collection.
    Holdings — Magazines:

Primary: ca. 200   Secondary: NA

Subscriptions: AMZ; ASF; DFSF; FAN; FSF; GAL; UNI

Title	Prim/Sec	Dates	Condition
DFSF	S	v. 1, No. 1-Date	Original
UNI	P	v. 1, No. 1-Date	,,
WIF	P	Jan. 1971-Oct. 1974	,,

Information on other titles NA.
Titles and No. on personal collection of fanzines NA.

    Holdings — Books:

Primary: 700 (75%; 25%)   Secondary: 0

Current: Yes

Specialized: No; general collection, seeking designation as a special subject-oriented collection for the regional system.

    Holdings — Miscellaneous:
    Archive for APA 070.4. . . , a publication for librarians who are science fiction fans.

MN2. UNIVERSITY OF MINNESOTA   Director: Alan K. Lathrop
    University Libraries   Hours: 8am-4:30pm, M-F.
    Manuscript Division
    Mineapolis, MN 55455

Collection Title: None
    Person to Contact: Alan K. Lathrop, Curator, Manuscripts Division
    Location: Manuscripts Division
    Restrictions: Yes; k-12 children not permitted; varied restrictions, according to donors' wishes.
    Index/Catalog: Yes; each individual collection of papers is inventoried and these finding aids are available in the repository.
    ILL: No
    Origin: 1972 — acquisition of Gordon R. Dickson papers
    Holdings — Magazines:

Primary: 51		Secondary: 0
Subscriptions: None		

Title	Prim/Sec	Dates	Condition

    31 titles, many single issues, no runs, primarily 1932-49.

    Holdings — Books:

Primary: NA (NA)		Secondary: 0
Current: No		
Specialized: No		

    Holdings — Miscellaneous:
    Individual author collections containing manuscripts, correspondence, copies of publications for the following: Gordon R. Dickson (20 linear feet), Thomas Disch (8 linear feet), Carl Jacobi (3 linear feet), Clifford Simak (8 linear feet).

MN3. UNIVERSITY OF MINNESOTA	Director: NA
Walter Library	Hours: 7:45am-4:30pm, M-F
117 Pleasant Street SE	
University of Minnesota	
Minneapolis, MN 55455	

Collection Title: No separate category within the Kerlan Collection or Hess Collection.
    Person to Contact: Karen Nelson Hoyle, Curator, Kerlan and Hess Collections.
    Location: 109 Walter Library
    Restrictions: Non-circulating
    Index/Catalog: None
    ILL: No
    Origin: 1949 — Irvin Kerlan gave his collection of children's books to the library; 1954 — George H. Hess, Jr., had bequeathed his collection of dime novels, story papers, boys and girls series books, paperbound libraries.
    Holdings — Magazines:

Primary: NA		Secondary: 0
Subscriptions: None		

Title	Prim/Sec	Dates	Condition

Early pulp magazines in which sf stories occasionally appeared (Burroughs in ARGOSY, for example); primarily 1888-1935, for instance:

Title	Prim/Sec	Dates	Condition
ARGOSY	P	1888-89	Original
BOYS FRIEND LIB.	P	1905-39	,,
FRANK READE LIB.	P	1892-98	,,
POPULAR MAG.	P	1905-31	,,

Holdings — Books:
    Primary: 157 (85%; 15%)   Secondary: 0
    Current: Yes
    Specialized: Yes: Kerlan Collection is children's literature; Hess Collection is primarily 19th century popular lit., although certain types of 20th c. publications are added (boys' and girls' series books and periodicals, pulp magazines, paperbound reprints, comics).
    Remarks: The 157 refers to those identified as sf; Kerlan Collection as a whole consists of 28,600 vol.; Hess Collection is over 100,000 items. There may well be unidentified sf items in these two collections.
Holdings — Miscellaneous:
    Manuscripts: 5 relating to sf: Ruth Carlsen, *Ride A Wild Horse,* 1970; Madeleine L'Engle, *A Wind in the Door,* 1973; Louis Slobodkin, *Round Trip Space Ship,* 1968; Mary Q. Steele, *The Journey Outside,* 1969; Adrien Stoutenburg, *Out There,* 1971.
    Illustrations: 2 relating to sf: Paul Galdone, *Space Cat,* by Ruthven Todd, 1952; Louis Slobodkin, *Round Trip Space Ship,* by Louis Slobodkin, 1968.

MS1. UNIVERSITY OF SOUTHERN   Director: Claude E. Fike
     MISSISSIPPI   Hours: 8am-5pm, M-F
         William David McCain Graduate Library
         Southern Station
         Box 5148
         Hattiesburg, MS 39401

Collection Title: Science Fiction Writers of America Collection
    Person to Contact: Henry L. Simmons
    Location: Graduate Library
    Restrictions: Cannot be taken from the collection area.
    Index/Catalog: Separate card catalog by author only.
    ILL: Yes
    Origin: 1969 — contacted SFWA and requested all books sent to them for review; the library is not a Regional Depository for SFWA.
Holdings — Magazines: 0
Holdings — Books:
    Primary: over 500 (5%; 95%)   Secondary: 0
    Current: Yes
    Specialized: No

MO1. SAINT LOUIS UNIVERSITY
 Pius XII Memorial Library
 3655 West Pine Blvd.
 Saint Louis, MO 63108

Director: William Cole
Hours: 7:45am-11:45pm, M-Th;
7:45am-8:45pm, F; 12N-6pm, Sat.
2pm-10pm, Sun.

Collection Title: None
 Person to Contact: Katherine Thorp, Reference Librarian
 Location: With the general collection
 Restrictions: None
 Index/Catalog: None
 ILL: Yes
 Origin: n.d. — to aid students in sf and future studies courses.
 Holdings — Magazines:
  Primary: NA   Secondary: 0
  Subscriptions: ASF; GAL

Title	Prim/Sec	Dates	Condition
ASF	P	1/76-Date	Original
GAL	P	1/76-Date	"

 Holdings — Books:
  Primary: 179 (NA)   Secondary: 30
  Current: When funds permit
  Specialized: No

MO2. UNIVERSITY OF MISSOURI
 ROLLA
 University Library
 Rolla, MO 65401

Director: Ronald G. Bohley
Hours: 8am-10:30pm, M-F; 8am-
5pm, Sat; 2pm-10pm, Sun.

Collection Title: UMR Science Fiction Collection
 Person to Contact: Bryan M. Williams, Librarian
 Location: With the general collection
 Restrictions: Rare or fragile items do not circulate
 Index/Catalog: Card index of short stories by author, title, and motif in
  progress; inventory card index of current acquisitions.
 ILL: Yes
 Origin: 1973 — first sf course offered; collection built through donations
  by alumni.
 Holdings — Magazines:
  Primary: ca. 575   Secondary: ca. 35
  Subscriptions: CTL; EX; SFST

Title	Prim/Sec	Dates	Condition

NA; 26 titles, especially strong in 1950's and 1960's; all original.
 Holdings — Books:
  Primary: ca. 1300 (50%; 50%) Secondary: ca. 200
  Current: Yes
  Specialized: No; includes Arno press Utopia series; especially strong in
  reference.

Holdings — Miscellaneous:
Cassettes: ca. 20 interviews, dramatizations, lectures on sf.

MO3. UNIVERSITY OF MISSOURI   Director: Robert C. Miller
     ST. LOUIS   Hours: 8am-11pm, M-Th; 7am-
        Thomas Jefferson Library   5pm, F; 9am-5pm, Sat; 1pm-
        8001 Natural Bridge Road   9pm, Sun.
        St. Louis, MO 63121

Collection Title: None
    Person to Contact: Reference Librarian
    Location: Reference Collections, Special Collections, and with the general
       collection.
    Restrictions: Reference and Spec. Coll. material does not circulate
    Index/Catalog: None
    ILL: Yes
    Origin: n.d. — primarily purchases
    Holdings — Magazines:
    Primary: 78   Secondary: 26
    Subscriptions: None

Title	Prim/Sec	Dates	Condition

Scattered holdings of 1960's and 1970's of ASF; EX; FSF; GAL.

Holdings — Books:
    Primary: ca. 600 (NA)   Secondary: ca. 150
    Current: Yes; substantial growth planned.
    Specialized: Yes, emphasis on utopia and related fiction.
    Remarks: Books include original publication, microfilm, reprint, and
       proof material.

MT1. UNIVERSITY OF MONTANA   Director: Earle C. Thompson
     University Library   Hours: 8am-11pm, M-Th; 8am-
     Missoula, MT 59812   10pm, F; 10am-6pm, Sat.; 1pm-
                               10pm, Sun.

Collection Title: None
    Person to Contact: Humanities Librarian
    Location: With the general collection
    Restrictions: None
    Index/Catalog: A card file arranged by author is in process.
    ILL: Yes
    Origin: 1972 — gift by John McGilvrey; successive gifts and aid by Leroy
       Berven.
    Holdings — Magazines:
    Primary: ca. 325   Secondary: 15
    Subscriptions: CTL; EX

Title	Prim/Sec	Dates	Condition
AMZ	P	1926-45	Microfilm
AMZQ	P	1928-34	”
CTL	S	1974-Date	Original
EX	S	1975-Date	”
PLA	P	1939-45	Microfilm

Holdings — Books:

Primary: ca. 950 (25%; 75%)   Secondary: ca. 60
Current: No
Specialized: No

NM1. EASTERN NEW MEXICO   Director: NA
UNIVERSITY   Hours: 8am-12N, 1pm-5pm, M-F;
University Library   7pm-9pm, T&TH.
Portales, NM 88130

Collection Title: Special Collections
Person to Contact: Mary Jo Walker, Special Collections Librarian
Location: Spec. Coll. Room
Restrictions: Yes; non-circulating; room use except under special circumstances.
Index/Catalog: Separate author/title catalog for books; checklist for periodicals; collection described in Mary Jo Walker, "Fantastic Tale: Science Fiction at Eastern New Mexico University," EX 14, No. 2 (May 1973), 126-28.
ILL: Yes, subject to condition and availability of material.
Origin: 1967 — gift of Jack Williamson collection; 1970 — gifts of Leigh Brackett and Edmond Hamilton collections; 1971 — purchase of books and magazines.
Holdings — Magazines: ca. 7000
Primary: NA   Secondary: NA
Subscriptions: ASF

Title	Prim/Sec	Dates	Condition
AST	P	1930-76	Original
ERB	S	1960-70	”
FAD	P	1939-53	”
FAN	P	1952-74	”
FATE	P	1948-59	”
FSF	P	1950-75	”
FUT	P	1939-60	”
GAL	P	1950-75	”
MSS	P	1938-52	”
NWB	P	1954-70	”
SFA	P	1956-74	”
SFT	S	1957-68	”
SPW	P	1954-70	”

STL	P	1939-55	"
WIF	P	1952-74	"
WRT	P	1925-74	"

The above titles are the longer runs from a pulp collection of ca. 185 titles and a fanzine collection of ca. 175 titles.

Holdings — Books: ca. 5000
    Primary: NA   Secondary: NA
    Current: Yes
    Specialized: No
Holdings — Miscellaneous:
    Manuscripts: Duplicate mss of Piers Anthony
    Papers: 28 cu. ft. of papers (correspondence, mss, memorabilia) of the following: Leigh Brackett, Edmond Hamilton, Jack Williamson.

NM2. UNIVERSITY OF NEW MEXICO   Director: Dorothy Wonsmos
        Zimmerman Library   Hours: 8am-4:30pm, M-F; 6:30pm-
        Albuquerque, NM 87131   9pm, Wed.

    Collection Title: Day Science Fiction Collection
    Person to Contact: Director of Special Collections
    Location: At present in storage; eventually to be housed in Spec. Coll. Dept.
    Restrictions: Yes; because of the fragile nature of these items, collection will be for research only; researchers must apply to Director of Spec. Coll.
    Index/Catalog: Yes; Donald Day's original card catalog of ca. 20,000 file-cards, but it is still in storage; published version of the Index: Donald Day, *Index to the Science Fiction Magazines, 1926-50* is available.
    ILL: No, only xerox copies
    Origin: n.d. — purchase
    Holdings — Magazines:
        Primary: over 1275   Secondary: 0
        Subscriptions: None

Title	Prim/Sec	Dates	Condition
AMZ	P	1926-50	Original
ASF	P	1930-50	"

The above titles are the longer runs in the collection of 58 American and British titles.

    Holdings — Books: 0

NY1. CITY OF NEW YORK   Director: James W. Henderson
        New York Public Library,   Hours: NA
            Research Libraries
        General Research and Humanities Div.
        5th Avenue and 42nd Street
        New York, NY

Collection Title: None
  Person to Contact: NA
  Location: With the general collection
  Restrictions: None
  Index/Catalog: None
  ILL: No
  Origin: NA
  Holdings — Magazines:
  Primary: NA   Secondary: NA
  Subscriptions: ALG; AMZ; ASF; DFSF; EX; FDN; FSF; GAL; RQ;
    SFRE; SFWA

Title	Prim/Sec	Dates	Condition
ALG	S	n.d.-Date	Original
AMZ	P	n.d.-Date	,,
ASF	P	1960-Date	Microfilm
EX	S	n.d.-Date	Original
FSF	P	1964-Date	,,
GAL	P	1961-Date	,,

Also includes scattered issues of other titles.

  Holdings — Books:
  Primary: ca. 1500 (85%; 15%)   Secondary: ca. 150
  Current: Yes
  Specialized: No. In addition to the 1500 volumes, library has strong 19th
    century collection which would include scientific romances; library
    collects 50-75% of all primary material published and 90% of all sec-
    ondary material on the 19th c.

NY2. ITHACA COLLEGE   Director: Leo R. Rift
     Ithaca College Library   Hours: 8:30am-12M, M-Th;
     Ithaca, NY 14850   8:30am-11pm, F-Sat; 1pm-12M,
                                     Sun.

  Collection Title: None
  Person to Contact: NA
  Location: Majority in Browsing Collection, 4th floor; remainder with
    general collection.
  Restrictions: None
  Index/Catalog: Yes, author file for the Browsing Collection
  ILL: Yes
  Origin: NA
  Holdings — Magazines: 0
  Holdings — Books:
  Primary: ca. 200 (40%; 60%)   Secondary: 0
  Current: NA
  Specialized: No

NY3. SARAH LAWRENCE COLLEGE
    The Library
    Bronxville, NY 10708

Director: Rose Anne Burstein
Hours: NA

Collection Title: None
    Person to Contact: Phyliss Byan, Circulation Librarian
    Location: Lower level library
    Restrictions: NA
    Index/Catalog: None
    ILL: Yes
    Origin: 1969 — gift by German scientist, Friedrich H.A. Brandt.
    Holdings — Magazines:
        Primary: 2000   Secondary: 0
        Subscriptions: None

Title	Prim/Sec	Dates	Condition
AMZ	P	1948-65	Original
ASF	P	1950-69	"
FAN	P	1940-60 (incomplete)	"
GAL	P	1952-69	"
OWS	P	1952-58	"

A few scattered holdings in other titles.

Holdings — Books:
    Primary: 700 (75%; 25%)   Secondary: 0
    Current: No
    Specialized: Yes; about 100 titles in German.

NY4. STATE UNIVERSITY OF
    NEW YORK AT ALBANY
        University Libraries
        1400 Washington Avenue
        Albany, NY 12222

Director: C. James Schmidt
Hours: (Spec Coll.): 8am-5pm,
M-F.

Collection Title: None
    Person to Contact: Marion P. Munzer, Curator, Spec. Coll.
    Location: Spec. Coll.
    Restrictions: Yes; a few books and all periodicals are non-circulating.
    Index/Catalog: Yes, in the Spec. Coll. catalog.
    ILL: Most books may be borrowed; photocopying depends on condition
        of item.
    Origin: 1973 — private donation of periodicals; 1974 — in order to protect
        the books already owned.
    Holdings — Magazines:
        Primary: 527   Secondary: NA
        Subscriptions: AMZ; ASF; FSF; GAL

Title	Prim/Sec	Dates	Condition
ASF	P	1938-Date	Original
BFF	P	1953-55	"
WOT	P	1963-67	"

Also includes scattered issues and short runs of other titles.

Holdings — Books:
Primary: ca. 900 (85%; 15%)　　　　Secondary: NA
Current: Yes
Specialized: No, but includes many biographical tools and special indexes.

NY5. SYRACUSE UNIVERSITY　　　Director: Kenneth J. Oberembt
　　　George Arents Research Library　Hours: NA
　　　Syracuse, NY 13210

Collection Title: Science Fiction Collections
　Person to Contact: Kenneth J. Oberembt
　Location: NA
　Restrictions: NA
　Index/Catalog: Yes; inventory lists for Anthony, Cullum, Galaxy, Gerns-
　　back, Jenkins, Kyle, Laumer, McCaffrey, Silverberg, Wilson, Wollheim,
　　Zelazny; partial inventory lists for Ackerman, Mercury, Pohl. A mimeo-
　　graphed descriptive listing exists: Philip F. Mooney, comp., "Science
　　Fiction Collections in The George Arents Research Library at Syracuse
　　University," Syracuse, NY, 1970.
　ILL: NA
　Origin: NA
Holdings — Magazines: NA
Holdings — Books: NA
Holdings — Miscellaneous:
　Collection consists of the papers (correspondence, mss, diaries, books,
　　periodicals) of 17 sf authors and 2 sf publishing companies.
　Forest J. Ackerman — primarily correspondence, 1930-69; 40 boxes.
　Piers Anthony — correspondence (1962-63), mss, diaries (1951-53);
　　1951-68; 6 boxes. (Restricted)
　Hal Clement — primarily mss, 1965-67; 1 box.
　James Cullum, Jr. — primarily runs of sf periodicals (e.g. AMZ, 1926-
　　66; FSF, 1949-60; TWS, 1936-55); also books, sf convention mater-
　　ials; 1926-66; 125 boxes.
　Hugo Gernsback — correspondence; mss of articles, addresses, and
　　editorials; bound copies of all publications; 2 slide sets; 1952-65;
　　70 boxes.
　Will F. Jenkins — correspondence and mss; 1915-68; 72 boxes.
　Damon Knight — primarily mss, 1964-67; 3 boxes.
　David A. Kyle — Mss, n.d.; 4 boxes.
　Keith Laumer — correspondence (1958-67), and mss; 1958-69; 22
　　boxes.
　Anne McCaffrey — Mss; 1947-68; 5 boxes.
　Larry Niven — Correspondence and mss; 1967-68; 2 boxes.
　Andre Norton — Correspondence and mss; 1965-68; 3 boxes.
　Frederik Pohl — Correspondence and mss; 1961-69; 25 boxes.
　Robert Silverberg — Correspondence and over 40 mss; 1960-69; 22
　　boxes. (Restricted)
　Richard Wilson — Correspondence and mm; 1940-69; 25 boxes.

Donald A. Wollheim — Mss, 1961-64; 3 boxes.

Roger Zelazny — Correspondence and ca. 100 mss; 1954-69; 9 boxes.

Galaxy Publishing Corp. — Complete run of GAL; 200 original illus.; correspondence of Robert Guinn, 1951-60; hundreds of mss; 1951-69; 27 boxes.

Mercury Press — Over 1000 mss; questionnaires; Anthony Boucher's editorial files; some magazines; 1957-69; 45 boxes.

Remarks: All of the above material comes from the 1970 Mooney report which is out of date but does cover most of the collection; no current description exists.

NC1. DUKE UNIVERSITY   Director: Connie R. Dunlap
        University Library   Hours: 8:30am-5pm, M-F; 9am-
        Durham, NC 27706   1pm, Sat.

Collection Title: The Glenn Negley Utopia Collection
Person to Contact: John L. Sharpe III, Curator of Rare Books
Location: Rare Book Division
Restrictions: NA
Index/Catalog: Yes; Separate card catalog of current holdings; Bibliography in press at University of Kansas.
ILL: No
Origin: n.d. — gift of Glenn Negley
Holdings — Magazines: 0
Holdings — Books:
    Primary: 1500 (NA)   Secondary: 0
    Current: Yes
    Specialized: Utopia fiction

NC2. EAST CAROLINA UNIVERSITY   Director: Eugene A. Brunelle
        J. Y. Joyner Library   Hours: 8am-12M, M-Th; 8am-9pm,
        Greenville, NC 27834   F; 9am-5pm, Sat; 2pm-12M, Sun.

Collection Title: None
Person to Contact: Artemis C. Kares, Reference Dept.
Location: With the general collection.
Restrictions: None
Index/Catalog: None
ILL: Yes
Origin: n.d. — to support the curriculum.
Holdings — Magazines:
    Primary: NA   Secondary: 0
    Subscriptions: ASF; GAL

Title	Prim/Sec	Dates	Condition
ASF	P	1948-72; 1974-Date	Original
FSF	P	1950-72	"

GAL	P	1950-71; 1974-Date	"
WRT	P	1940-54	"

Some additional titles with scattered holdings.

Holdings — Books:
Primary: ca. 500   Secondary: 0
Current: Yes
Specialized: No

OH1. BOWLING GREEN STATE UNIVERSITY
Popular Culture Library
University Library
Bowling Green, OH 43403

Director: William L. Schurk
Hours: 8am-5pm, M-F.

Collection Title: None
Person to Contact: William L. Schurk, Head; Nancy Lee, Reference Assistant
Location: Popular Culture Library
Restrictions: Non-circulating
Index/Catalog: Yes; separate card catalog in the Popular Culture Library Room.
Origin: 1968 — to support the courses offered in the English and Popular Culture Departments.
Holdings — Magazines:
Primary: NA   Secondary: 0
Subscriptions: AMZ; ASF; FSF; GAL

Title	Prim/Sec	Dates	Condition
AUT	P	No. 19-65; 67-84	Original
FAD	P	1946-53	"
FAN	P	1952-64 (incomplete)	"
FATE	P	1948-69 "	"
FFM	P	1946-53	"
FUT	P	1950-60	"
ISF	P	1950-58	"
NEB	P	No. 1-41	"
PLA	P	1941-55	"
SFS	P	1953-60	"
SUP	P	No. 27-93 "	"
WIF	P	1952-73	"
WOT	P	1963-70	"
WRT	P	1944-54	"

The above titles are the longer runs from a collection of 45 titles; a large collection of fanzines is not available for use.

Holdings — Books:
Primary: 10 (90%; 10%)   Secondary: 0
Current: NA
Specialized: NA

Holdings — Miscellaneous:
Manuscripts: Located in the Center for the Study of Popular Culture.
Posters: A small number; not available for use.

OH2. CASE WESTERN RESERVE   Director: NA
UNIVERSITY   Hours: NA
University Libraries
Cleveland, OH 44106

Collection Title: None
Person to Contact: Wesley C. Williams, Curator, Special Collections
Location: Special Collections
Restrictions: Yes; collection not accessible to users.
Index/Catalog: None
ILL: None
Origin: NA
Holdings — Magazines: NA
Holdings — Books:
Primary: ca. 2000 (10%; 90%)   Secondary: NA
Current: No
Specialized: NA

OH3. CITY OF CLEVELAND   Director: Ervin J. Gaines
Cleveland Public Library   Hours: 9am-8:30pm, M; 9am-6pm,
325 Superior Avenue   T-Sat.
Cleveland, OH 44114

Collection Title: None
Person to Contact: Head, Popular Library
Location: With the general collection; periodicals in General Reference
Dept. and Periodical Reading Room.
Restrictions: None, with a few exceptions.
Index/Catalog: None
ILL: Yes
Origin: NA

Holdings — Magazines:
Primary: NA   Secondary: 0
Subscriptions: None

Title	Prim/Sec	Dates	Condition
ASF	P	Nov. 1963-Date	Original
FSF	P	July 1970-Date	"

Holdings — Books:
Primary: ca. 2500 (100%; 0%)   Secondary: 0
Current: Yes
Specialized: Yes, works by Lewis Carroll in Children's Room; otherwise,
emphasis is on general circulation.

Remarks: Library contains two specialized collections of interest:
   Treasure Room Collection of Early Children's Books — includes ca. 200 science fiction titles and 1300 fantasy titles, as well as some picture book titles for younger children.
   John G. White Collection of dime novels — this may contain some unidentified sf titles; non-circulating.

OH4. KENT STATE UNIVERSITY

Kent State University Libraries
Kent, OH 44242

Director: Hyman W. Kritzer
Hours: 8am-12N, 1pm-5pm, M-F.

Collection Title: None
   Person to Contact: Dean H. Keller, Curator of Special Collections
   Location: Dept. of Spec. Coll.
   Restrictions: Non-circulating
   Index/Catalog: Brief listing (author and title) in the Dept. of Spec. Coll.
   ILL: No
   Origin: 1968 — gift/purchase
   Holdings — Magazines: 0
   Holdings — Books:
   Primary: ca. 500 (5%; 95%)   Secondary: 0
   Current: No
   Specialized: No

OH5. OHIO STATE UNIVERSITY

Ohio State University Libraries
Columbus, OH 43210

Director: William Studer
Hours: (Spec. Coll.): 9am-5pm, M-F.

Collection Title: None
   Person to Contact: Robert A. Tibbetts, Curator of Special Collections
   Location: Division of Spec. Coll.; remainder with the general collection.
   Restrictions: None
   Index/Catalog: None
   ILL: Yes, generally.
   Origin: 1967 — purchase.
   Holdings — Magazines:
   Primary: NA   Secondary: NA
   Subscriptions: NA

Title	Prim/Sec	Dates	Condition

NA; includes considerable number of American and British titles.

   Holdings — Books:
   Primary: NA (NA)   Secondary: NA
   Current: NA
   Specialized: NA
   Remarks: Includes many primary and secondary volumes housed in the general collection; no statistical information available.

OH6. UNIVERSITY OF DAYTON   Director: Raymond H. Nartker
     University Library   Hours: 8:30am-4:30pm, M-Sat.
     300 College Park
     Dayton, OH 45469

     Collection Title: Science Fiction Writers of America Regional Collection
         Person to Contact: Raymond H. Nartker
         Location: Special Collections Room
         Restrictions: Non-circulating
         Index/Catalog: Yes; shelf list
         ILL: No
         Origin: 1973 — Dr. Joseph Patrouch (Engl. Dept.) asked by Dr. Lloyd
            Biggle, Jr., if the University would be a Regional Depository for SFWA.
         Holdings — Magazines: 0
         Holdings — Books:
         Primary: 205 (100%; 0%)   Secondary: 0
         Current: Yes; books arrive nearly every month.
         Specialized: No

OR1. CITY OF PORTLAND   Director: James H. Burghardt
     Library Association   Hours: 9am-9pm, M-Th; 9am-5:30
         of Portland   pm, F-Sat.
     801 S.W. 10th Ave.
     Portland, OR 97205

     Collection Title: None
         Person to Contact: Ida A. McClendon, Head, Popular Library
         Location: Popular Library, Fiction Department
         Restrictions: None
         Index/Catalog: Yes; an author/title listing on shelf list cards, available at
            the public service desk.
         ILL: Yes
         Origin: n.d. — to be a regular part of fiction collection.
         Holdings — Magazines:
         Primary: NA   Secondary: NA
         Subscriptions: ASF

Title	Prim/Sec	Dates	Condition
ASF	P	1966-Date	Original

         Holdings — Books:
         Primary: ca. 1450 (100%; 0%)   Secondary: ca. 8
         Current: Yes
         Specialized: No

PA1. PENNSYLVANIA STATE   Director: Stuart Forth
     UNIVERSITY   Hours: (Rare Bks): 8am-5pm, M-F.
         Pattee Library
         University Park, PA 16801

Collection Title: None
  Person to Contact: Charles W. Mann, Curator, Rare Books and Special Collections
  Location: Rare Books Room and Spec. Coll.
  Restrictions: Room use only
  Index/Catalog: Yes; Rare Books Room has 2 card catalogs, 1 for cataloged books, 1 for uncataloged materials.
  ILL: Occasionally
  Origin: 1973 — for the SFRA Conference.
  Holdings — Magazines:
    Primary: 3800   Secondary: 0
    Subscriptions: None

Title	Prim/Sec	Dates		Condition
AMZ	P	1928-67	(incomplete)	Original
ASF	P	1934-68	"	"
FAN	P	1952-65	"	"
FFM	P	1939-53	(minus 3 issues)	"
FSF	P	1949-68	(incomplete)	"
GAL	P	1950-68	"	"
STL	P	1939-55		"
TWS	P	1936-54	(minus 9 issues)	"
WIF	P	1952-68	(incomplete)	"
WRT	P	1932-51	"	"

The above are the longer runs from the collection.

  Holdings — Books:
    Primary: 1225 (40%; 60%)   Secondary: 0
    Current: Yes
    Specialized: Includes a strong Utopian collection and an Arkham House collection of 59 vols.

PA2. TEMPLE UNIVERSITY   Director: Arthur T. Hamlin
      Samuel Paley Library   Hours: 8:30am-5pm, M-F.
      Broad and Montgomery Sts.
      Philadelphia, PA 19122

Collection Title: David Charles Paskow Science Fiction Collection
  Person to Contact: Thomas M. Whitehead, Head of Special Collections and Curator of SF Collection.
  Location: Rare Book Room
  Restrictions: Non-circulating; maintained for scholarly and research use.
  Index/Catalog: Yes, a separate author, title, subject and shelf list catalog maintained in the Rare Book Room.
  ILL: No
  Origin: 1972 — gift of Mrs. Jeannette Paskow of the 5000 item collection of her son, David Charles Paskow, Temple graduate.
  Holdings — Magazines: 2880
    Primary: NA   Secondary: NA
    Subscriptions: ALG; ASF; EX; FSF; LM; RQ; SFST

Title	Prim/Sec	Dates	Condition
ALG	S	1973-Date	Original
ASF	P	1926-Date	"
EX	S	1969-Date	"
FAN	P	1926-72	"
FSF	P	1950-Date	"
GAL	P	1950-75	"
LM	S	1973-Date	"
RQ	S	1964-Date	"
SFST	S	1973-Date	"
WRT	P	1951-Date	"

The above are the longer runs from a list of 119 titles, especially strong for 1950-60. Individual information NA on 900 fanzines.

Holdings — Books:

Primary: ca. 4600 (50%; 50%)   Secondary: 70

Current: Yes, through a standing order plan for anthologies, reference works, text books, privately-issued pamphlets.

Specialized: Yes. Collection is strong in 1950-70 period; includes 420 Ace Doubles and 200 sf books from library of Kingsley Amis (primarily review copies, many with his notes). Fantasy generally excluded unless written by an sf author; no juvenile books, comic books, or fanzines added except by gift. An attempt is made to collect all works by authors in mss collection.

Holdings — Miscellaneous:

Art: 2 oil paintings

Manuscripts: Selected mss (1-5 per author) of Michael Bishop, James Blish, A. Bertram Chandler, Miriam Allen DeFord, L. Sprague de Camp, Felix Gotschalk, Robert Silverberg, John Varley, and others. Also mss of historical interest: several stories of John W. Campbell, 3 book mss of John Taine, 13 mss of Edward E. Smith.

Papers: Type and no. NA; collected for the following authors: Ben Bova, Jack Dann, Gardner Dozois, Richard Peck, Tom Purdom, Pamela Sargent, George Zebrowski.

Recordings: 10

RI1. BROWN UNIVERSITY   Director: NA
      John Carter Brown Library   Hours: NA
      Providence, RI 02912

Collection Title: Imaginary Voyages of the Eighteenth Century
    Person to Contact: Thomas R. Adams, Librarian
    Location: NA
    Restrictions: NA
    Index/Catalog: NA; a partial listing published in John Carter Brown
        Library of Brown University, "Imaginary Voyages of the Eighteenth
        Century: An Exhibition of Books from the Collection of the John
        Carter Brown Library," Providence, 1974.

ILL: NA
Origin: NA
Holdings — Magazines: NA
Holdings — Books: NA
  Remarks: A significant collection of two periods of imaginary voyages literature: 1700-30; 1750-1800.

RI2. BROWN UNIVERSITY   Director: Charles D. Churchwell
     University Library   Hours: 9am-4:30pm, M-F.
     Box A
     Providence, RI 02912

Collection Title: Howard Phillips Lovecraft Collection
  Person to Contact: Assistant Librarian, John Hay Library
  Location: John Hay Library
  Restrictions: None on printed material; information available on literary rights.
  Index/Catalog: Yes; separate register of mss items.
  ILL: No
  Origin: 1937 — collection was deposited by literary executor of Lovecraft; additions through gift and purchase.
Holdings — Magazines:
  Primary: ca. 200   Secondary: NA
  Subscriptions: *HP Lovecraft Soc. Journal; Esoteric Order of Dagon; Whispers; Xenophile; Nyctalops; Weirdbook; Macabre.*

Title	Prim/Sec	Dates	Condition
MT	P	1934-35	Original
WRT	P	1923;	Microfilm
	P	1924-54	Original

  Numerous amateur journals (1910-40), containing Lovecraft material.
Holdings — Books:
  Primary: ca. 300 (90%; 10%)   Secondary: ca. 30
  Current: Yes
  Specialized: Lovecraft material.
Holdings — Miscellaneous:
  Manuscripts: Over 4000 Lovecraft items (1894-1960) including over 1400 letters by Lovecraft and over 200 mss of his essays, fiction, poetry (1896-1937); also includes letters to, or about, Lovecraft and essays, fiction, and poetry by his associates including: Robert Hayward Barlow, W. Paul Cook, August William Derleth, Ernest Arthur Edkins, Frank Belknap Long, Samuel Loveman, Maurice Winter Moe, C.L. Moore, E. Hoffmann Price, Clark Ashton Smith, Wilfred Blanch Talman, Elizabeth Toldridge, Donald Wandrei.

SC1. UNIVERSITY OF SOUTH   Director: Kenneth E. Toombs
      CAROLINA   Hours: (Spec. Coll.): 8:30am-5pm,
        Thomas Cooper Library   M-F.
        Columbia, SC 29208

    Collection Title: None
        Person to Contact: Roger Mortimer, Head, Special Collections, H.P. Lovecraft Collection
        Location: Special Collections and with the general collection.
        Restrictions: Yes, for Special Collections material.
        Index/Catalog: No
        ILL: Yes, for general collection
        Origin: NA
    Holdings — Magazines:
        Primary: NA   Secondary: 6
    Holdings — Books:
        Primary: NA; medium-sized core   Secondary: NA
               collection
        Current: Yes
        Specialized: Yes; a complete Arkham House Collection (130 vols.) and a medium-sized Lovecraft collection (44 primary works, including a virtually complete set of first editions; 42 secondary works).
    Holdings — Miscellaneous:
    Manuscripts: One letter from Lovecraft to Frank Belknap Long.

TN1. UNIVERSITY OF TENNESSEE   Director: Florine S. Fuller
      AT NASHVILLE   Hours: 8am-10:15pm, M-Th; 8am-
        University Library   10pm, F; 8am-5pm, Sat; 1pm-
        10th and Charlotte   9pm, Sun.
        Nashville, TN 37203

    Collection Title: SFWA Collection
        Person to Contact: Betty T. Smith, Reference Librarian
        Location: Separate shelving from general collection
        Restrictions: None
        Index/Catalog: None
        ILL: Yes
        Origin: 1970 — a faculty member contacted Science Fiction Writers of America.
    Holdings — Magazines: 0
    Holdings — Books:
        Primary: 171   Secondary: ca. 20
        Current: No; library has received no books from SFWA for 2 years.
        Specialized: Yes; Regional Depository for SFWA.

TX1. CITY OF DALLAS   Director: Lillian Bradshaw
      Central Research Library of   Hours: 9am-9pm, M-F; 9am-6pm,
        the Dallas Public Libraries   Sat.
      1954 Commerce Street
      Dallas, TX 75201

Collection Title: None
  Person to Contact: Ron Boyd, Literature and Language Division
  Location: Literature and Language Division
  Restrictions: None
  Index/Catalog: No
  ILL: Yes
  Origin: 1950's — general collection started in response to public interest;
    1974 — research-level collection initiated.
Holdings — Magazines:
  Primary: NA   Secondary: NA
  Subscriptions: ALG; AMZ; ASF; CTL; DFSF; EX; FDN; FSF; GAL; LM;
    LOC; RQ; SFST; WIF

Title	Prim/Sec	Dates	Condition
ASF	P	1968-Date (incomplete)	Original
FSF	P	1971-Date "	"

The above are the longer runs from 15 titles, most of which are new subscriptions.

Holdings — Books:
  Primary: ca. 2500 (85%; 15%)   Secondary: ca. 50
  Current: Yes
  Specialized: No; library emphasizes "pure" sf, not fantasy or sword and
    sorcery genres.

TX2. SAM HOUSTON STATE   Director: John Nunelee
     UNIVERSITY   Hours: 8am-11pm, M-Th; 8am-
       University Library   5pm, F; 11am-5pm, Sat; 2pm-
       Huntsville, TX 77340   11pm, Sun.

Collection Title: None
  Person to Contact: NA
  Location: Special Collections
  Restrictions: None
  Index/Catalog: None
  ILL: Yes
  Origin: NA
Holdings — Magazines: 0
Holdings — Books:
  Primary: NA (NA)   Secondary: NA
  Current: NA
  Specialized: Yes; a collection of H.G. Wells first editions, including both
    books and pamphlets.

TX3. TEXAS A&M UNIVERSITY   Director: Irene B. Hoadley
       University Libraries   Hours: (Spec. Coll.): 8am-5pm,
       College Station, TX 77843 M-F.

Collection Title: Science Fiction Research Collection

Person to Contact: Evelyn M. King, Asst. Director for Special Collections
Location: Special Collections
Restrictions: Non-circulating; used under supervision.
Index/Catalog: Yes, a computerized printout arranged alphabetically by author; serials holdings available through a computerized printout arranged alphabetically by title; collection described in H.W. Hall, "Announcing the Future: Science Fiction at Texas A&M University," *Texas Library Journal* 50, No. 5 (Dec. 1974), 221-23, 257.
ILL: No; photocopies of most materials are available.
Origin: 1970 — purchase of several small private collections with the encouragement by English faculty to develop collection for teaching and research; 1973 — gift of fanzines by Joanne Burger, former student.

Holdings — Magazines:

Primary: ca. 5500   Secondary: over 5000

Subscriptions: ALG; AMZ; ASF; DFSF; EX; FAN; FSF; GAL; SFST, and others.

Title	Prim/Sec	Dates	Condition
AMZ	P	1926-Date	Original
ASF	P	1930-Date	"
FAD	P	1939-53	"
FFM	P	1939-53	"
FUT	P	1950-60	"
LM	S	1969-Date	"
LOC	S	1970-Date	"
MSF	P	1938-52	"
NWB	P	1946-71	"
PLA	P	1939-55	"
SPW	P	1953-70	"
SSS	P	1940-51	"
STL	P	1939-55	"
TWS	P	1929-55	"
VEN	P	1957-70	"
WRT	P	1923-54	"

The above titles are some of the longer runs of the 138 primary titles and 19 secondary. In addition, there are 5000 issues of unprocessed fanzines. It has been estimated that this massive collection contains 90% of all Am. and Br. sf magazines published from 1923-74.

Holdings — Books:

Primary: 10,000 (30%; 70%)   Secondary: ca. 250
Current: Yes
Specialized: No; collection does include SFWA Depository volumes and is especially strong in books published since 1950.

Holdings — Miscellaneous:

Manuscripts: Avram Davidson Manuscript Collection of Fantasy and Science Fiction contains ca. 3000 pages of mss, letters.

TX4. UNIVERSITY OF TEXAS   Director: F. Warren Roberts
       AT AUSTIN   Hours: 9am-5pm, M-F; 9am-12N,
         Humanities Research Center   Sat.
         Box 7219
         Austin, TX 78712

Collection Title: Lee Huddleston Science Fiction Collection
     Person to Contact: Sally Leach, Associate Librarian
     Location: Humanities Research Center
     Restrictions: Non-circulating
     Index/Catalog: Yes; a collection file describing the holdings; material
         uncataloged but usable.
     ILL: No; photocopying available if condition of material permits.
     Origin: 1967 — gift by Lee Huddleston, Denton, TX.
     Holdings — Magazines:
         Primary: 2050   Secondary: 0
         Subscriptions: None

Title	Prim/Sec	Dates	Condition
AMZ	P	1935-66 (incomplete)	Original
ASF	P	1956-63	”
		1947-55; 1963-76 (incomplete)	”
FAN	P	1954-66 (incomplete)	”
FSF	P	1949-56 ”	” .
		1957-66	”
GAL	P	1950-57; 1959-66	”
STL	P	1940-55 (incomplete)	”
TWS	P	1940-54 ”	”
WIF	P	1952-66	”
WRT	P	1938-54 ”	”

The above is a sampling of the longer runs in 103 titles.

     Holdings — Books:
         Primary: NA   Secondary: NA
         Current: NA
         Specialized: NA

TX5. UNIVERSITY OF TEXAS AT   Director: Fred W. Hanes
       EL PASO   Hours: 8am-12M, M-Th; 8am-5pm,
         University Library   F; 10am-6pm, Sat; 1pm-12M, Sun.
         El Paso, TX 79963

Collection Title: None
     Person to Contact: NA
     Location: With the general collection
     Restrictions: None
     Index/Catalog: No; there is a student-compiled bibliography available.
     ILL: Yes
     Origin: Sf items have always been purchased; 1973 — first sf course
         offered and gifts and donations have increased.

Holdings — Magazines: 0
Holdings — Books:
Primary: ca. 400 (85%; 15%)   Secondary: 4
Current: Yes
Specialized: Includes two reprint series — Garland (50 vols.) and Gregg Press (50 vols.)

UT1. BRIGHAM YOUNG UNIVERSITY   Director: Donald K. Nelson
Harold B. Lee Library   Hours: 7am-11pm, M-Sat.
Provo, UT 84602

Collection Title: Fantasy-Science Fiction Collection
Person to Contact: Elizabeth D. Pope or Blaine Hall
Location: Burroughs Collection in Rare Books; remainder in Humanities Section, 5th Level.
Restrictions: Arkham House, Burroughs, and SFWA are non-circulating.
Index/Catalog: In progress: card index containing entries for authors, titles, subject, illustrators, history, criticism, bibliographies.
ILL: Yes, most items.
Origin: 1964 — purchased collection of Doreal in Colorado, containing many out-of-print items, sf and fantasy, and occult.
Holdings — Magazines: ca. 1769
Primary: NA   Secondary: NA
Subscriptions: AMZ; ASF; EX; FSF; GAL; SFRE; SFWA

Title	Prim/Sec	Dates		Condition
AMZ	P	1945-Date	(incomplete)	Original
ASF	P	1947-Date	"	"
EX	S	1959-Date		"
FFM	P	1946-52		"
FSF	P	1949-Date		"
GAL	P	1950-Date		"
LM	S	1969-72		"
PLA	P	1939-45		Microfilm
		1947-51		Original
RQ	S	1973-Date		"
SFWA	S	1974-Date		"
SSS	P	1940-51		"
STL	P	1940-52		"
TWS	P	1940-51		"
WIF	P	1952-Date		"

The above are the longer runs from a collection of 39 titles.

Holdings — Books:
Primary: 4114 (92%; 8%)   Secondary: 147
Current: Yes
Specialized: Includes an SFWA Regional Depository collection; an Arkham House collection of 93 vols; a Burroughs collection of 49 first editions.

VA1. UNIVERSITY OF VIRGINIA
    Alderman Library
    Charlottesville, VA 22901

Director: NA
Hours: 9am-5pm, M-F; 9am-1pm, Sat.

Collection Title: James Branch Cabell Collection in Clifton Waller Barrett Library.
Person to Contact: Edmund Berkeley, Jr., Curator of Manuscripts.
Location: Manuscripts Department
Restrictions: None
Index/Catalog: NA; Description of the manuscripts in Matthew J. Bruccoli, *Notes on the Cabell Collections at the University of Virginia.* Charlottesville: Univ. of Va. Press, 1957.
ILL: Mss do not circulate; some correspondence has been microfilmed and is available from Manuscripts Dept.
Origin: n.d. – gift of Mrs. Cabell; gift of Clifton Walter Barrett.
Holdings – Magazines: 0
Holdings – Books: 0
Remarks: Rare Book Dept. has two author collections: August Derleth (31 vols.) and Howard P. Lovecraft (14 vols.).
Holdings – Miscellaneous:
Manuscripts: In the combined collection, mss for 38 books (including a first draft of *Jurgen*), several short stories and articles.
Correspondence: In the combined collections, ca. 2000 original items, ca. 800 copies of originals; in addition, there are other uncounted Cabell letters in collections of other authors held in the Manuscripts Department.

VA.2 VIRGINIA COMMONWEALTH
    UNIVERSITY
    James Branch Cabell Library
    901 Park Ave.
    Richmond, VA 23220

Director: NA
Hours: NA

Collection Title: James Branch Cabell Collection
Person to Contact: NA
Location: Special Collections
Restricitons: NA
Index/Catalog: None; collection described in Jean Maurice Duke, "James Branch Cabell's Library: A Catalogue," Diss. Univ. of Iowa, 1968.
ILL: Yes; of duplicate books only; photocopies may be made, depending on condition of material; permission required to copy letters.
Origin: NA
Holdings– Magazines: 250
    Primary: NA   Secondary: NA
    Subscriptions: NA

Title	Prim/Sec	Dates	Condition

NA; about 250 magazine articles by and about Cabell.

Holdings— Books:

Primary: ca. 120   Secondary: 22

Current: NA

Specialized: Yes, books and pamphlets by and about Cabell, including first editions, revisions, and reprints; many autographed.

Holdings — Miscellaneous:

Correspondence: 27 letters, 1921-34.

WA.1 UNIVERSITY OF WASHINGTON   Director: Marilyn Sharrow
   Odegaard Undergraduate Library   Hours: 7:30am-12M, M-Th;
   Seattle, WA 98105   7:30am-10pm, F; 9am-10pm, Sat; 12N-12M, Sun.

Collection Title: None

Person to Contact: Anne Passarelli

Location: Paperbacks in Contemporary Issue Collection; remainder with the general collection.

Restrictions: Open to the public; borrowing restricted to Univ. personnel.

Index/Catalog: Yes; a separate card file with entries under author/editor.

ILL: No

Origin: 1971 — 'Contemporary Issues' SF Collection begun; sf added to general collection when sf course was taught in English Dept.

Holdings — Magazines:

Primary: NA   Secondary: NA

Subscriptions: ASF; EX; FSF; LM; SFST

Title	Prim/Sec	Dates	Condition
ASF	P	1942-53, 1969-Date	Original
EX	S	1959-Date	”
FSF	P	1971-Date	”
LM	S	1969-Date	”
PLA	P	1948-51	”
SFST	S	1973-Date	”
STL	P	1949-52	”

Scattered holdings in 14 additional titles, 1946-52.

Holdings — Books:

Primary: 1100 (25%; 75%)   Secondary: 6

Current: Yes

Specialized: No

Holdings — Miscellaneous:

10 items in the Undergraduate Library Media Center related to sf, mostly taped readings, interviews, records, film.

WI1. BELOIT COLLEGE   Director: H. Vail Deale
   College Library   Hours: 8:30am-11pm, M-Th; 9am-
   Beloit, WI 53511   5pm, F-Sat; 1pm-11pm, Sun.

Collection Title: None
　　Person to Contact: Clyde Peterman
　　Location: With the general collection
　　Restrictions: Non-circulating for non-college patrons.
　　Index/Catalog: None
　　ILL: Yes
　　Origin: 1971 — Clyde Peterman gift of Science Fiction Book Club titles; additional donations by fans; periodicals given by former janitor, Arthur Bolstad.
　　Holdings — Magazines:
　　　　Primary: 712　　　　　　　　　　Secondary: 0
　　　　Subscriptions: None

Title	Prim/Sec	Dates	Condition
ASF	P	1949-73 (incomplete)	Original
FSF	P	1962-72 　　"	"
GAL	P	1962-72 　　"	"
WIF	P	1960-73 　　"	"

The above are the longer runs from the collection of 21 titles.

　　Holdings — Books:
　　　　Primary: 396 (95%; 5%)　　　　Secondary: NA
　　　　Current: Yes
　　　　Specialized: No

WI2. MARQUETTE UNIVERSITY　　　　Director: William M. Gardner
　　　　Memorial Library　　　　　　　　Hours: (Archives): 8:30am-12N,
　　　　1415 West Wisconsin Avenue　　1pm-5pm, M-F.
　　　　Milwaukee, WI 53233

Collection Title: John Renel Tolkien Manuscripts
　　Person to Contact: Paul Gratke, University Archivist
　　Location: Archives
　　Restrictions: Mss are for researchers only; researchers from outside the Univ. are requested to make advance arrangements for use.
　　Index/Catalog: Yes; a card index in the Archives.
　　ILL: No
　　Origin: 1957 — purchase from J.R.R. Tolkien
　　Holdings — Magazines:
　　　　Primary: NA　　　　　　　　　　Secondary: NA
　　　　Subscriptions: NA

Title	Prim/Sec	Dates	Condition
NA			

　　Holdings — Books:
　　　　Primary: NA　　　　　　　　　　Secondary: NA
　　　　Current: NA
　　　　Specialized: yes; published books, articles, and pamphlets relating to Tolkien. The general collection contains standard publications by and about Tolkien for which there is open access.

Holdings — Miscellaneous:
Art: 1 water color by Horus Engels
Manuscripts: Holographs, typescripts, and galleys with holograph correc-
tions by Tolkien, some notes—all on 3 books: *The Hobbit, Farmer
Giles of Ham, The Lord of the Rings* (trilogy); holograph manuscript
with colored pencil illustrations by the author for the unpublished "Mr.
Bliss."
Ephemera: Calendars and placards relating to Tolkien.

WI3. MILTON COLLEGE   Director: Doris Brewster
     Shaw Memorial Library   Hours: 8am-10pm, M-Th; 8am-
     Milton, WI 53563   5pm, F; 1pm-5pm, Sat; 2pm-
                                       10pm, Sun.

Collection Title: SF Collection
     Person to Contact: Jim Hemesath
     Location: First Floor
     Restrictions: None
     Index/Catalog: None
     ILL: Yes
     Origin: 1972 — when sf course was initiated.
Holdings — Magazines:
     Primary: 143   Secondary: NA
     Subscriptions: ASF; FSF

Title	Prim/Sec	Dates	Condition
ASF	P	1969-74; 77-Date	Original
FSF	P	1972-Date	"
SFRE	S	On order	"

Holdings — Books:
     Primary: 185 (75%; 25%)   Secondary: 30
     Current: Yes, in basic titles.
     Specialized: Yes, working toward a complete Barry N. Malzberg collection.

WI4. UNIVERSITY OF WISCONSIN   Director: Edwin L. Hill
     LA CROSSE   Hours: (Spec. Coll.): 8am-5pm,
     Murphy Library   M-F; 1pm-4pm, Sat.
     La Crosse, WI 54601

Collection Title: Skeeters Collection
     Person to Contact: Edwin L. Hill
     Location: Special Collections Room
     Restrictions: Non-circulating; in-room use only.
     Index/Catalog: Yes; separate catalog in Spec. Coll. for Arkham House only.
     ILL: No
     Origin: 1971 — purchase from a dealer.
Holdings — Magazines: 0
Holdings — Books:

Primary: 1000 (100%; 0%)   Secondary: NA
Current: No
Specialized: All are first editions in horror, gothic, fantasy, sf, dated 1890-
  1940's; includes 125 titles in Arkham House coll., many signed.

WI5. UNIVERSITY OF WISCONSIN   Director: William C. Roselle
  MILWAUKEE   Hours: 8am-4:30pm, M-F.
  University Library
  Milwaukee, WI 53201

  Collection Title: None
    Person to Contact: Head, Special Collections
    Location: Special Collections
    Restrictions: Non-circulating
    Index/Catalog: None
    ILL: No; photocopying available
    Origin: 1970 — gift.
  Holdings — Magazines:
    Primary: 715   Secondary: 0
    Subscriptions: 0

Title	Prim/Sec	Dates	Condition
AMZ	P	1926-53	Original
AMZQ	P	1928-34	"
ASF	P	1930-57	"
GAL	P	1975-Date	"
STL	P	1939-53	"
TWS	P	1929-54	"

The above are the longer runs from the collection of 10 titles.
  Holdings — Books:
    Primary: NA   Secondary: NA
    Current: NA
    Specialized: NA

WY1. UNIVERSITY OF WYOMING   Director: Gene M. Gressley
  Division of Rare Books   Hours: 8am-12N, 1pm-5pm, M-F.
    & Special Collections
  Box 3334, University Station
  Laramie, WY 82071

  Collection Title: Each individual manuscript collection named after donor.
    Person to Contact: Research Historian
    Location: Division of Rare Books
    Restrictions: Only as donors have directed
    Index/Catalog: Yes; detailed card catalog by subject and by content of
      each collection; individual collection receipts also serve as indexes.

ILL: No; some items are available by xerox.

Origin: Early 1960's—general acquisitions program.

Holdings — Magazines: NA

Holdings — Books: NA

Holdings — Miscellaneous:

Papers (correspondence, mss, legal and financial material, proofs and publication materials, press releases, clippings, speeches, interviews, art works, photographs) of 8 authors and 1 publishing company:

No. 2358 — Forrest J. Ackerman — 90 boxes, 350 photos.

No. 2256 — Robert Bloch — 44 document boxes, 131 photos.

No. 2946 — Martin Caidin — 35 document boxes.

No. 2684 — Stanton A. Coblentz — 1 document box.

No. 6211 — James Cowan — 1 document box.

No. 3054 — Hugo Gernsback — 1 document box.

No. 2482 — J. Vernon Shea — 8 document boxes.

No. 2119 — Donald A. Wollheim — 13 document boxes.

No. 968 — Ace Books — ca. 1000 sf book publications.

CAN1. UNIVERSITY OF
     NEW BRUNSWICK
       Ward Chipman Library
       P.O. Box 5050
       Saint John, N.B.
       Canada E2L 4LS

Director: Kenneth M. Duff
Hours: 8:30am-11pm, M-F; 9am-5pm, Sat; 2pm-10pm, Sun.

Collection Title: University of New Brunswick in Saint John Science Fiction and Fantasy Collection

Person to Contact: Dennis Abblitt, Assistant Chief Librarian

Location: With general collection and in restricted area

Restrictions: Periodicals and rare items non-circulating.

Index/Catalog: Yes, cardex file for periodicals; PZ classification for sf only; description and sf history included in "Science Fiction and Fantasy Collection," Ward Chipman Library (mimeographed).

ILL: Yes, except for rare items, noncurrent periodicals and SFWA Regional Depository books.

Origin: 1966 — gift of books by Prof. John Grube; expansion under encouragement of Dennis Abblitt, Librarian, and Prof. William Prouty, Head of English.

Holdings — Magazines:

Primary: 4329   Secondary: 1010

Subscriptions: Too numerous to mention — 55 titles, primary and secondary, American and foreign.

Title	Prim/Sec	Dates	Condition
AMZ	P	1926-Date	Original '
ASF	P	1930-Date (incomplete)	"
DFSF	S	1975-Date	"
ERB	S	1960-Date	"

EX	S	1959-Date	,,
FBK	P	1947-51	,,
FFM	P	1939-53	,,
FUT	P	1939-43; 1950-60	,,
GAL	P	1950-Date	,,
ISF	P	1950-58	,,
LOC	S	1968-Date	,,
NEB	P	1952-59	,,
PLA	P	1939-55	,,
SFA	P	1958-63	,,
SFS	P	1953-60	,,
STL	P	1939-55	,,
WRT	P	1931-54; 1973-74 (incomplete)	,,

The above titles are a sampling of the longer runs from this massive collection of sf magazines, fanzines, journals, reviews of 190 titles.

Holdings — Books:

Primary: 5500 (35%; 65%)   Secondary: 180

Current: Yes

Specialized: No, but includes SFWA Depository. Library has an additional 345 sf related books (futurism, cybernetics, etc.)

Holdings — Miscellaneous:

Art: 26 sf art vols.

Cassettes: 3

Manuscripts: 5, primarily Wyndham

Phonorecords: 6

Slides: 240

Theses: 51 (on microfilm)

CAN2. UNIVERSITY OF WINNEPEG   Director: Raymond C. Wright
     University Library   Hours: 8am-11pm, M-F; 9am-5pm,
     515 Portage Avenue   Sat; 12N-8pm, Sun.
     Winnipeg, Man. R3B 2E9
     Canada

Collection Title: Science Fiction Collection

Person to Contact: Helen Muckosky, Circulation Supervisor

Location: Reserve Library

Restrictions: Closed stack; materials must be requested from circulation staff

Index/Catalog: No

ILL: Yes

Origin: 1970 — proposed and initiated by Dept. of English.

Holdings — Magazines:

Primary: NA   Secondary: NA

Subscriptions: None

Title	Prim/Sec	Dates	Condition
AMZ	P	1926-45	Microfilm
AMZQ	P	1928-34	,,

Holdings — Books:
    Primary: 1250 (50%; 50%)   Secondary: 30
    Current: Yes
    Specialized: No; includes complete collections of best known writers
        (Asimov, Bradbury, Clarke, Hamilton, Heinlein, Leiber, Norton, etc.)

CAN3. CITY OF TORONTO   Director: Doris Mehegan
      Spaced Out Library   Hours: 10am-6pm, MTTHF; 9am-
      Toronto Public Libraries   5pm, Sat.
      40 St. George St.
      Toronto, Ontario, M5S 2E4
      Canada

Collection Title: None
    Person to Contact: Doris Mehegan
    Location: 2nd floor of Boys' and Girls' House
    Restricitons: Yes, non-circulating
    Index/Catalog: Yes — subject indexes for fanzines, non-fiction books,
        articles and introductions in anthologies; author-title indexes to short
        stories in anthologies; additional files for tapes, series, foreign publica-
        tions, etc.
    ILL: No; some photocopying available at 10 cents per page.
    Origin: 1970 — Judith Merril donated her personal collection; collection
        has been tripled; 1972 — Mehegan cataloged collection. Main catalog
        complete and publishable.
    Holdings — Magazines: 8600
    Primary: NA   Secondary: NA
    Subscriptions: 56 titles, including pulps, fanzines, and scholarly journals.

Title	Prim/Sec	Dates	Condition
ASF	P	Nearly complete	Original
FSF	P	Nearly complete	,,
GAL	P	Nearly complete	,,
NWB	P	Nearly complete	,,

Information on individual titles NA; an extensive collection, esp. from 1940-
Date; 3000 issues duplicated in microfilm; includes 295 fanzine titles.

    Holdings — Books:
    Primary: 4800 (65%; 35%)   Secondary: 1125
    Current: Yes
    Specialized: Yes; 1) Arkham House Collection, nearly complete (120).
                2) Jules Verne Coll. of 1st ed., Engl. and Fr. (250).
                3) Ace Double coll., nearly complete (200).
                4) Special collections in related areas, such as futurology,
                    fantastic art, Atlantis.
                5) Vertical file of clippings and photocopies (over 200
                    subject headings).

Holdings — Miscellaneous:
Tapes: ca. 220
Records: ca. 12
Manuscripts and Letters: Some; no. and authors NA
Art: 15 framed, 10 originals
Additional items include posters, games, reproductions.

CAN4. QUEEN'S UNIVERSITY
Douglas Library
Kingston, Ontario
Canada

Director: Don Redmond
Hours: 8am-11pm daily; (Spec.
Coll.): 9am-5pm, M-F.

Collection Title: Gothic Fantasy Collection
Person to Contact: Stuart MacKinnon, Special Collections
Location: Pulps and Lovecraft in Spec. Coll.; remainder with general coll.
Restrictions: Spec. Coll. is non-circulating; may be photocopied if not too fragile.
Index/Catalog: Checklist for pulps and pamphlets; separate catalog for remainder.
ILL: Yes; if not too rare or fragile; for use within borrowing library only.
Origin: 1968 — NA; 1970 — purchase of Lovecraft collection; details described in Charles Pullen, "Howard Phillips Lovecraft," *Douglas Library Notes*, vol. xix, nos. 1-2, Autumn 1970, pp. 2-3.
Holdings — Magazines:
Primary: NA
Subscriptions: None

Secondary: 0

Title	Prim/Sec	Dates	Condition

NA; 246 titles, all original, from 1930's-Date; 300-page checklist available at library.

Holdings — Books:
Primary: NA
Current: NA

Secondary: NA

Specialized: Collection of 18th, 19th, 20th century literature to show relationships between gothic, fantasy, and sf. Includes over 59 books by Lovecraft.
Holdings — Miscellaneous:
Manuscripts: Some Lovecraft items, both prose and verse, including information on Arkham House press.

CAN5. UNIVERSITY OF GUELPH
McLaughlin Library
Guelph, Ontario
Canada. NIG 2W1

Director: Margaret Beckman
Hours: 8:30am-12M, M-Th;
1pm-12M, Sat-Sun.

Collection Title: None
Person to Contact: C. Evans, Head, Humanities and Social Science Division

Location: With the general collection
Restrictions: None
Index/Catalog: None
ILL: Yes
Origin: Acquired in process of building the general literature collection;
Dept. of English has donated special funds for 4 years.
Holdings — Magazines:
Primary— 0   Secondary: 40
Subscriptions: SFST

Title	Prim/Sec	Dates	Condition
EX	S	1969-75	Original
RQ	S	1964-74	,,
SFST	S	1976-Date	,,

Holdings — Books:
Primary: 900 (95%; 5%)   Secondary: 30
Current: Yes, to a limited degree
Specialized: No

CAN6. CONCORDIA UNIVERSITY   Director: Paul E. Filion
         Norris Library   Hours: 9am-11pm, M-F; 9am-5pm,
         1435 Drummond Street   Sat; 10am-6pm, Sun.
         Montreal, Quebec
         Canada

Collection Title: None
   Person to Contact: Joseph Princz
   Location: With general collection
   Restrictions: Reference books cannot circulate.
   Index/Catalog: No
   ILL: Yes
   Origin: Usual library selection methods over the years.
   Holdings — Magazines:
   Primary: 0   Secondary: NA
   Subscriptions: EX; SFST

Title	Prim/Sec	Dates	Condition
EX	S	1959-Date	Original
SFST	S	1973-Date	,,

   Holdings — Books:
   Primary: ca. 300   Secondary: ca. 100
   Current: Yes
   Specialized: No; scattered holdings by major authors.

CAN7. McGILL UNIVERSITY   Director: M. Scott
         McLennan Library   Hours: Varied; visitors are en-
         3459 McTavish Street   couraged to write in advance for
         Montreal, Quebec   appointments.
         Canada H3A 1Y1

Collection Title: None
- Person to Contact: A. Cole, Humanities and Social Science Area Librarian and Director of McLennan Library
- Location: McLennan Library
- Restrictions: Circulation privileges only for registered borrowers.
- Index/Catalog: None
- ILL: Yes, except for microfilms, rare and/or fragile items.
- Origin: Conscious development of sf material began about 1975.
- Holdings — Magazines:
  - Primary: NA   Secondary: NA
  - Subscriptions: ALG; ASF; EX; FSF; GAL; HOR; JLN; LM; NEB; OSF; RQ; SFRE; SFWA; WNL

Title	Prim/Sec	Dates	Condition
ASF	P	1973-Date	Original
EX	S	1959-74;	Microfilm
		1974-Date	Original
GAL	.P	1972-Date	"
LM	S	1973-Date	"
RQ	S	1964-Date	"
SFST	S	1973-Date	"

An additional 9 titles, all runs from ca. 1974–Date.

Holdings — Books:
- Primary: Ca. 1000   Secondary: ca. 160
- Current: Yes
- Specialized: No

Holdings — Miscellaneous:
- Cassettes: *War of the Worlds*, Reading, 2 tapes.
- Phonotapes: 10 cassettes, including 4 history, 1 interview, and 6 dramatizations.
- Slides: *Science Fiction: Jules Verne to Ray Bradbury* (3 cassettes and 3 slide trays).

CAN8. UNIVERSITY OF BRITISH   Director: NA
      COLUMBIA   Hours: NA
        University Library
        Vancouver 8, Canada

Collection Title: None
- Person to Contact: Anne Yandle, Head, Special Collections Division
- Location: NA
- Restrictions: Non-circulating
- Index/Catalog: Collection is cataloged by title.
- ILL: NA
- Origin: 1960 — purchase of Thomas Walton collection; brief description in John McKinlay, "The Science Fiction Collection at the University of British Columbia Library," *B.C. Library Quarterly*, April 1971, 34:4, pp. 5-19.

Holdings — Magazines:

Primary: NA		Secondary: NA
Subscriptions: None		

Title	Prim/Sec	Dates	Condition

NA; 380 issues, 30 titles, all original, particularly of 1920's and 30's, including incomplete runs of ASF, FFM, PLA, STL; includes both American and Canadian titles.

Holdings — Books:

Primary: NA; very small	Secondary: NA; very strong
Current: NA	
Specialized: NA	

A SELECTED BIBLIOGRAPHY OF WORKS ON
SCIENCE FICTION & FANTASY COLLECTIONS

Barron, Neil. "Science Fiction for the Blind." *Luna Monthly*, 35/36 (April-May 1972), 13, 38. (IA1)

Bruccoli, Matthew J. *Notes on the Cabell Collections at the University of Virginia.* In *James Branch Cabell: A Bibliography.* Charlottesville: University of Virginia Press, 1957. (VA1)

Catalog of the Wells Collection. In *Catalog of the Rare Book Room, University of Illinois at Urbana-Champaign Library.* Boston: G.K. Hall, 1972. (IL5)

Duke, Jean Maurice. "James Branch Cabell's Library: A Catalogue." Unpublished, Ph.D. dissertation, University of Iowa, 1968. (VA2)

Durham, Philip. "The Huntington Library Collection of Beadle's Dime Novels." San Marino, CA: By the Author, 1954. (CA5)

Hall, H.W. "Announcing the Future: Science Fiction at Texas A&M University." *Texas Library Journal*, 50 (December 1974), 221-223, 257. (TX3)

Hillegas, Mark. "The Clarkson Collection of Science Fiction at Harvard." *Extrapolation*, 5 (December 1963), 2-14. (MA2)

Hyde, Ann. "The Library of the Future: Science Fiction and the Department of Special Collections." *Books and Libraries at the University of Kansas* (Spring 1976), pp. 1-5. (KS1)

John Carter Brown Library, Brown University. *Imaginary Voyages of the Eighteenth Century: An Exhibition of Books from the Collection of the John Carter Brown Library.* Providence: John Carter Brown Library, 1974. (RI1)

McKinlay, John. "The Science Fiction Collection at the University of British Columbia Library." *B.C. Library Quarterly*, 34 (April 1971), 5-19. (CAN8)

Mooney, Philip F. "Science Fiction Collections in the George Arents Research Library at Syracuse University." Syracuse, 1970. (Mimeographed.) (NY5)

Negley, Glenn Robert. *Utopian Literature: A Bibliography.* Lawrence, KS: Regents Press of Kansas, 1978. (NC1)

Newman, John. "America at War." *Extrapolation*, 16 (December 1974), 33-41. (CO2)

————. "Part Two: America at War." *Extrapolation*, 16 (May 1975), 164-172. (CO2)

Pullen, Charles. "Howard Phillips Lovecraft." *Douglas Library Notes,* 19 (Autumn 1970), 2-3. (CAN4)

Randall, David A., Sigmund Casey Fredericks and Tim Mitchell. *Science Fiction and Fantasy: An Exhibition.* Bloomington, IN: The Lilly Library, 1975. (IN1)

Scott, Catherine D. "National Air and Space Museum Library." *The Bowker Annual of Library and Book Trade Information,* ed. Miele, Moore and Prakken. 21st ed. New York: R.R. Bowker, 1976. (DC1)

Walker, Mary Jo. "Fantastic Tale: Science Fiction at Eastern New Mexico University." *Extrapolation,* 14 (May 1973), 126-128. (NM1)

Ward Chipman Library of University of New Brunswick. "Science Fiction and Fantasy Collection, and SFWA Collection." New Brunswick, Nova Scotia [n.d.]. (Mimeographed.) (CAN1)

AUTHOR INDEX

Goodwin, Harold L. — MA1
Gotschalk, Felix — PA2
Griffith, George — CA9
Guinn, Robert — NY5
Gunn, James — KS1

Haggard, H. Rider — CA9, IN1
Hamilton, Edmond — NM1, CAN2
Harness, Charles Leonard — MD2
Harrison, Harry — CA1
Hawthorne, Nathaniel — CA5
Heinlein, Robert A. — CA4, CA10,
    CA11, LA1, CAN2
Herbert, Frank — CA1
Hunter, Evan — MA1

Jacobi, Carl — MN2
Jenkins, William F. — CA9, NY5

Keller, David H. — CA9
Knight, Damon — NY5
Kornbluth, Cyril — MD2
Kuttner, Henry — CA8
Kyle, David A. — NY5

Laumer, Keith — NY5
Leiber, Fritz — CA8, IN1, CAN2
L'Engle, Madeleine — MN3
Lewis, C.S. — IL6
London, Jack — CA5, CA11
Long, Frank Belknap — KS2, RI2,
    SC1
Lovecraft, Howard P. — CA9, IL3,
    IN1, KS2, RI2, SC1, VA1, CAN4

McCaffrey, Anne — NY5
McDonald, George — IL6
Machen — KS2
Malzberg, Barry, N. — WI3
Merril, Judith — CAN3
Merritt, A. — CA9
Monteleone — MD2
Moore, C.L. — RI2
Moore, Ward — CA8
Mundy, Talbot — CA9

Niven, Larry — CA6, NY5
Norton, Andre — NY5, CAN2
Nourse, Alan E. — MA1

Peck, Richard — PA2
Poe, Edgar Allan — IN1
Pohl, Frederik — MD2, NY5
Pournelle, Jerry — CA6
Purdom, Tom — PA2

St. Clair, Margaret — CA8
Sargent, Pamela — PA2
Sayers, Dorothy — IL6
Seignolle, Claude — MA1
Shea, J. Vernon — WY1
Shelley, Mary — CA5, IN1
Sherred, T.L. — KS1
Silverberg — NY5, PA2
Simak, Clifford — MN2
Siodmak, Curt — MA1
Slobodkin, Louis — MN3
Smith, Clark Ashton — CA8, RI2
Smith, E.E. — CA9, PA2
Spinrad, Norman — CA1
Steele, Mary Q. — MN3
Stoutenberg, Adrien — MN3
Sturgeon, Theodore — CA4
Swift, Jonathan — CA5, MI4

Tolkien, J.R.R. — IL6, WI2

Unidentified — AZ1, CA1, CA6,
    CA11, DC2, MA2, MI3, OH1,
    PA2, CAN3

Vance, John — MA1
van Vogt, A. E. — CA8
Varley, John — PA2
Verne, Jules — CA9, CA11, IN1,
    CAN3
Vonnegut, Kurt — CA11

Wells, H.G. — IL5, IN1, MA1, TX2
Williams, Charles — IL6
Williams, Jay — MA1
Williams, Robert Moore — CA1
Williamson, Jack — NM1
Wilson, Richard — NY5
Wollheim, Donald — NY5, WY1
Wright, S. Fowler — CA9
Wyndham, John — CAN1

Zebrowski, George — PA2
Zelazny, Roger — MD2, NY5

MAGAZINE INDEX

ALG — AZ1, CA2, CA9, ID1, MA3, NY1, PA2, TX1, TX3, CAN7

AMZ — AZ1, CA3, CA9, FL1, IL3, IN1, LA1, MD2, MA2, MA3, MI3, MN1, MT1, NM2, NY1, NY3, NY4, NY5, PA1, TX1, TX3, TX4, UT1, WI5, CAN1, CAN2

AMZQ — FL1, IN1, MI1, WI5, CAN2

ASF — AZ1, CA2, CA3, CA7, CA9, CA11, CO1, CO3, DC1, GA1, IL1, IL3, IN1, KS1, KY2, LA1, MD1, MD2, MA2, M12, MI3, MN1, MO1, MO3, NM1, NM2, NY1, NY3, NY4, NC2, OR1, PA1, PA2, TX1, TX3, TX4, UT1, WA1, WI1, WI3, WI5, CAN1, CAN3, CAN7, CAN8

AST — NM1

BFF — NY4

CIN — IL4, MA3
CTL — MO2, MT1, TX1

DFSF — AZ1, CA3, CA9, MD2, MN1, NY1, TX1, TX3, CAN1

ERB — NM1, CAN1
EX — AZ1, CA3, CA7, CA9, CO1, FL1, GA1, IL2, IL4, MD2, MA3, MI1, MI2, MO2, MO3, MT1, NY1, PA2, TX1, TX3, UT1, WA1, CAN1, CAN5, CAN6, CAN7

FAD — FL1, IL3, NM1, TX3
FAN — AZ1, CA3, CO3, GA1, IL3, LA1, MA3, MI3, MN1, NM1, NY3, PA1, PA2, TX3, TX4
FAU — IL3
FBK — CAN1

FDN — CA7, MI3, NY1, TX1
FFM — AZ1, IL3, PA1, TX3, UT1, CAN1, CAN8
FSF — AZ1, CA2, CA3, CA7, CA8, CA9, CA11, CO1, ID1, IL1, IL3, IL4, IN1, KS1, LA1, MD2, MA2, MA3, MI2, MI3, MN1, MO3, NM1, NY1, NY4, NY5, NC2, PA1, PA2, TX1, TX3, TX4, UT1, WA1, WI1, WI3, CAN3, CAN7

FUT — NM1, TX3, CAN1

GAL — AZ1, CA2, CA3, CA9, CA11, GA1, IL1, IL3, IA1, KS1, LA1, MD1, MD2, MA2, MA3, MI2, MI3, MN1, MO1, MO3, NM1, NY1, NY3, NY4, NY5, NC2, PA1, PA2, TX1, TX3, TX4, UT1, WI1, WI5, CAN1, CAN3, CAN7

HOR — CAN7

ISF — CAN1

JIR — MA3
JLN — CAN7

LM — AZ1, CA9, IL1, IL2, MI1, MI3, PA2, TX1, TX3, UT1, WA1, CAN7
LOC — CA3, CO1, GA1, MA3, MI1, MI3, TX1, TX3, CAN1

ML — IL4
MSF — TX3
MSS — NM1
MT — RI2

NEB — CAN1, CAN7
NWB — NM1, TX3, CAN3

OSF — CAN7
OW — ID1, MA3
OWS — NY3

PLA — AZ1, FL1, IL3, MT1,
    TX3, UT1, WA1, CAN1, CAN8

RQ — AZ1, CA7, IL4, MI2, NY1,
    PA2, TX1, UT1, CAN5, CAN7

SFA — NM1, CAN1
SFBRI — CA7, MI1
SFM — MI3
SFRA — IA1
SFRE — MA3, NY1, UT1, WI3,
    CAN7
SFS — CAN1
SFST — AZ1, CA3, CA7, CA11,
    FL2, GA1, ID1, IL4, MA3,
    MO2, PA2, TX1, TX3, WA1,
    CAN5, CAN6, CAN7
SFT — NM1
SFWA — NY1, UT1, CAN7

SPW — NM1, TX3
SSM — GA1
SSS — TX3, UT1
STL — AZ1, CA9, IL3, NM1, PA1,
    TX3, TX4, UT1, WA1, WI5,
    CAN1, CAN8

TWS — NY5, PA1, TX3, TX4,
    UT1, WI5

UNI — MN1

VEN — TX3

WIF — AZ1, CA9, GA1, MI3, NM1,
    PA1, TX1, UT1, WI1
WNL — CAN7
WOF — GA1, MI2
WOT — MA2, NY4
WRT — AZ1, KS2, NM1, NC2,
    PA1, PA2, MI2, TX3, TX4,
    CAN1
WST — FL1, IN1

Marshall B. Tymn

RESOURCES FOR TEACHING SCIENCE FICTION

This bibliography contains articles and handbooks/teaching guides that are directed toward the implementation of science fiction and fantasy in the public schools and universities. Items have been selected on the basis of their usefulness to the teacher, providing either background information or practical teaching suggestions. The scope of the first section, "Selected Articles," is the decade beginning 1967, when the first results of classroom experimentation in the SF field began to be published, and includes selected 1979 articles. The second section, "Handbooks/Teaching Guides," is current, although selective. For ongoing information on teaching science fiction, see "The Year's Scholarship in Science Fiction and Fantasy," published annually in *Extrapolation* by Roger C. Schlobin and Marshall B. Tymn.

A. SELECTED ARTICLES

Akey, Craig. "Getting It Off the Ground." *Wisconsin English Journal,* 18, No. 3 (1976), 9–12.

> Guidelines, with suggested titles, for the teacher with no background who is confronted with a unit on science fiction or futuristics.

Anderson, E. "Three Cheers for Science Fiction." *College Composition and Communication,* 25 (1974), 203–05.

> The use of science fiction in conjunction with composition.

Aukerman, Charles W. "SF in the Classroom: Developing a High School Reading List." *Extrapolation,* 18 (1977), 155–61.

> In response to an attempt to censor Michael Crichton's *The Terminal Man* in a high school curriculum, Aukerman, a newspaper editor, was asked by a local board of education to help develop a science fiction core list suitable for high school consumption. Aukerman shares his criteria for selection and the list he presented to the school.

Baddock, Barry. "SF in the Classroom: A Look at Student Projects." *Extrapolation,* 17 (1975), 29–31.

A report on the wide-ranging and varied student projects pursued in James Gunn's SF classes at the University of Kansas and an analysis of their effectiveness and value.

Barnes, Myra. "Using Science Fiction for Teaching Linguistics." *College Composition and Communication,* 26 (1975), 392–94.

A practical plan for teaching linguistics by using science fiction. Includes recommended readings.

Becker, Muriel. "Start Them Early." *Media & Methods,* 16 (1979), 36–37, 52.

A dozen do's and don'ts for introducing science fiction at the middle school and junior high levels.

Bengels, Barbara. "The Teaching of Science Fiction—Another View." *NPTnews: Newsletter of the Lehigh University Perspectives on Technology Program,* No. 3 (1977), pp. 4–6.

A description of a historically-arranged, undergraduate science fiction course.

Biggle, Lloyd, Jr. "Science Fiction Goes to College: Groves and Morasses of Academe." *Riverside Quarterly,* 6 (1974), 100–09.

A critical evaluation of the academic involvement with science fiction. First presented in New Orleans at the Nebula Awards Banquet, 28 April 1973.

Bingham, Jane M., with Grayce Scholt. "Enchantment Revisited: Or Why Teach Fantasy?" *CEA Critic,* 40 (1978), 11–15.

A plea for the discussion of fantasy as serious literature rather than as "only" literature for children.

Brice, William R. "Extrapolation of Space: Fact or Fiction." *Journal of College Science Teaching,* 7 (1977), 107–10.

The use of science fiction in teaching the solar system in a college-level, introductory astronomy course. Includes a planet-by-planet discussion of methods and a bibliography of short stories.

Burgess, Andrew J. "Teaching Religion Through Science Fiction." *Extrapolation,* 13 (1972), 112–15.

A description of the organization of a "task force" at Case-Western Reserve University to study the possibility of interplanetary communication of religious concepts.

Burke, Michael C. "Free-Fall Sex and Golden Eggs." *Science Teacher,* 45 (1978), 33–34.

A brief essay discussing science fiction with a physics orientation in the high school with passing references to several appropriate films.

Bushmaker, Keith, and Richard Onesti. "Myccane to Mars: Science Fiction in the Nineth Grade Curriculum." *Wisconsin English Journal,* 18, No. 3 (1976), 13–14, 21.

A description of a team-taught unit in science fiction at D.C. Everest High

School that stresses the nature of man and his society. Includes mention of useful texts and visual media.

Cacha, Frances B. "Children Create Fiction Using Science." *Science and Children,* November/December, 1977, pp. 21–22.

Using a variety of science fiction, fantasy, and science readings, Cacha presents a program to stimulate creative writing in children.

Calame, Gerald P. "Science in Science Fiction: A Seminar Course." *American Journal of Physics,* 41 (1973), 184–87.

A description of a seminar course in science fiction offered in the Physics Department at the U. S. Naval Academy. The format of the course consisted of reading stories and then discussing the physics which serve as the scientific background for the story.

Clareson, Thomas D. "Special Topics: English 390." *Extrapolation,* 14 (1972), 64–66.

A description of a science fiction class taught by Professor Clareson at The College of Wooster.

Collins, Robert A. "Extrapolation: Going Beyond the Present." *Media & Methods,* 16 (1979), 22–25.

Defines the process of extrapolation as used by science fiction writers, with illustrations from major works.

Connolly, James F. "The Science Fiction Short Story: Excitement, Adventure, and Discovery." *Exercise Exchange,* 19, No. 2 (1975), 21–22.

A brief description of a unit on the writing of a science fiction short story which the author includes in his SF class at Brockton High School in Brockton, Massachusetts.

Cooper, B. Lee. "Beyond Flash Gordon and 'Star Wars': Science Fiction and History Instruction." *Social Education,* 42 (1978), 392–97.

A class outline for teaching legitimate back-to-basics history and historiography through science fiction. Includes six themes for student projects with recommended readings and a brief list of teaching resources.

Crossley, Robert. "Education and Fantasy." *College English,* 37 (1975), 281–93.

Using undergraduate responses, Crossley analyzes the student reaction to fantasy and postulates that fantasy is divided into two types: the fantasy of recovery and the fantasy of revelation. He concludes that fantasy as a genre and as a teaching tool is irreducible, educational, evocative, thought-provoking, and psychedelic.

Donlan, Dan. "Developing a Reading Participation Guide for a Novel." *Journal of Reading,* 17 (1974), 439–43.

Develops a reading unit around Ray Bradbury's *Fahrenheit 451.*

Dumbleton, Duane D. "Science Fiction and Cultural Understanding." *Trends in Social Education,* 24 (1977), 14–19.

The use of science fiction to teach cultural understanding on the elementary, secondary and college levels. Includes a very selective bibliography of appropriate materials.

Elkins, Charles, and Darko Suvin. "Preliminary Reflections on Teaching Science Fiction Critically." *Science-Fiction Studies,* 6 (1979), 263–70.

Outlines some fundamental problems pertinent to teaching science fiction: critical evaluation of works, characteristics of science fiction, good SF teaching, and the role of the teacher.

Erlich, Richard S. "SF in the Classroom: Strange Odyssey: From Dart and Ardrey to Kubrick and Clarke."*Extrapolation,* 17 (1976), 118–24.

A description of a writing course, "The Literature of Life Sciences," offered at the University of Illinois at Urbana-Champaign that traces the history of "the predatory transition from ape to man." Arthur C. Clarke's *2001* is used in addition to various nonfiction readings.

Friend, Beverly. "Turning Readers into Fans." *Media & Methods,* 16 (1979), 36–37, 53–55.

A listing of science fiction fan magazines and newsletters, conventions, and award programs.

Hillegas, Mark R. "The Course in Science Fiction: A Hope Deferred." *Extrapolation,* 9 (1967), 18–21.

Accuses English departments of an intellectual conservatism, making courses in science fiction difficult to achieve. Among the reasons for this is an anti-scientific stance taken by the discipline as a whole.

Hogan, Patrick G. "Opportunities and Limitations." *Extrapolation,* 13 (1972), 106–11.

An evaluation of the place of science fiction in the college curriculum.

Hollister, Bernard C. "The Martian Perspective." *Media & Methods,* 10 (1973), 26–28ff.

Outlines an anthropological approach to teaching science fiction, citing representative works.

—————. "Paperbacks—Grokking the Future." *Media & Methods,* 9 (1973), 23–27, 57.

Outlines a science fiction class in which various titles are arranged into social science topics.

—————. "Teaching American History with Science Fiction." *Social Education,* 39 (1975), 81–86.

Suggestions for readings, exercises and activities for teaching American history courses in future shock and cultural shock.

Kafka, Janet. "Why Science Fiction?" *English Journal,* 64 (1975), 46–53.

A general justification for using science fiction in the classroom with suggestions for approaches and readings.

Kam, Rose Sallberg. "Science Fiction in the High School." *Extrapolation*, 15 (1974), 140–43.

A description and evaluation of science fiction courses taught on the junior and senior levels at Encina High School.

Kirman, Joseph H. "Teaching About Science, Technology and Society." *History and Social Science Teacher*, 13 (1977), 54–56.

Uses science fiction to explain the effects of science and technology on human affairs. Includes recommendations for various approaches and methods.

Lamb, Janice E. "Space Biology: Bringing the Far Out into Focus." *Science Teacher* (1976), pp. 19–21.

The use of science fiction, particularly Michael Crichton's *The Andromeda Strain,* to introduce space biology into the high school's biology curriculum.

Lamb, William. "Employing Science Fiction: Classroom Environmental Value Clarification." *Journal of Environmental Education*, 6, No. 4 (1975), 14–17.

A justification and plan for creating an environmental value system through the use of science fiction in the classroom.

—————, and Roland B. Bartholomew. "Science Fiction—A Unique Tool for Science Teachers." *Science Teacher*, No. 3 (1975), pp. 37–38.

A brief explanation of how science fiction generates content learning, scientific "feel," attitude and value acquisition, and future preparation in the classroom. Includes a short list of sources for selecting SF short stories for classroom use.

Landers, Clifford E. "Science Fiction in the Political Science Classroom: A Comment." *Teaching Political Science*, 4 (1977), 475–80.

The use of science fiction to introduce the theories of political science.

—————. "Teaching Political Science Through Science Fiction." *Politics*, No. 6 (1976), pp. 17–32.

A discussion of methods and materials in using science fiction to teach political science. Includes an annotated bibliography of pertinent fiction.

Larson, David M. "The Two-Cultures Split and the Science Fiction Course." *NPTnews: Newsletter of the Lehigh University Perspectives on Technology Program*, No. 3 (1977), pp. 1–4.

A description of the use of the undergraduate science fiction course as a means of creating a forum for the connections between the humanities and the sciences.

Lederer, Richard. "Shaping the Dystopian Nightmare." *English Journal*, 56 (1967), 1132–35.

A consideration of the creation of a challenging and stimulating writing project. Quotes from several papers.

Le Guin, Ursula K. "Why Are Americans Afraid of Dragons?" *Pacific Northwest Library Association Quarterly*, 38, No. 2 (1974), 14–18.

A talk given at the 1973 PMLA Conference in Portland, Oregon. An explanation of why fantasy is kept from children, some discussion of it as a force in maturation, and a justification of the necessity of fantasy for children.

Livingston, Dennis. "Science Fiction as an Educational Tool." In *Learning for Tomorrow: The Role of the Future in Education*. Ed. Alvin Toffler. New York: Vintage Books, 1974.

Contends that "the intelligent use of science fiction . . . can not only enhance (a) student's sense of the future, but enliven the imagination and increase the ability to cope with the change and surprises that are likely to be features of the future." Contains a useful bibliography.

—————. "Science Fiction Taught as Futurology." *Extrapolation*, 14 (1973), 152–56.

A science fiction course at Fairleigh Dickinson University entitled "In Search of the 21st Century: SF Images of the Future" uses novels, films, lectures, and simulation exercises as the basis of analyzing science fiction "as a literature of alternate futures."

Lind, Orval A., Jr. "SF as an Undergraduate Course." *Extrapolation*, 15 (1974), 143–48.

A description of an undergraduate science fiction course with student projects and evaluations.

McNelly, Willis E. "Science Fiction and the Academy: An Introduction." *CEA Critic*, 35 (1972), 6–9.

A defense of science fiction as an academic discipline.

Marks, Gary H. "Teaching Biology with Science Fiction" *American Biology Teacher*, 40 (1978), 275–79.

A well-developed plan for the use of science fiction in the high school biology curriculum with a list of activities for students and a valuable bibliography of suggested science fiction readings arranged by biological category.

Mayhew, Paula C. "Science in Science Fiction Mini-Course." *Science Teacher*, April (1967), pp. 36–37.

A description of the author's mini-course, "Science in Science Fiction," which utilizes the works of Fredric Brown, Stanley G. Weinbaum, and Arthur C. Clarke.

Mobley, Jane. "Fantasy in the College Classroom." *CEA Critic*, 40 (1978), 2–6.

Suggests an approach to the teaching of fantasy literature on the college level that stresses fantasy as a key to understanding social insight and responsibility, basic human needs, human behavior, and artistic creation.

Morressy, John. "SF in the Classroom: A First Attempt at Franklin Pierce." *Extrapolation*, 20 (1979), 129–32.

A discussion of the problems associated with organizing a science fiction course at Franklin Pierce College in Rindge, New Hampshire.

Newton, Charles. "Underground Man, Go Home!" *College English*, 37 (1975), 337–44.

A thoughtful reevaluation of the college contemporary literature course with a consideration of the appeal that popular literature and science fiction have for students and a discussion of those themes and characters that most appeal to students.

Ower, John B. "Some Reflections on the College Teaching of Science Fiction." *Journal of English Teaching Techniques* (Fall 1972), pp. 1–10.

Aquaints the reader with some of the problems inherent in organizing a science fiction course; these observations are based on an SF class at the University of Tennessee at Chattanooga.

Parish, Margaret. "Fantasy." *English Journal*, 66 (1977), 90–93.

Responses to Ursula K. Le Guin's Earthsea trilogy by a college professor, a fifth-grade teacher, and a high school teacher; includes an annotated checklist of seventeen series and individual novels for young adults.

Pfeiffer, John. "USAFA: 'English, Special Topics 495': Spring 1971." *Extrapolation*, 13 (1972), 116–18.

A description of a course in science fiction and fantasy that Pfeiffer offered at the United States Air Force Academy.

Pine, Martha, and Ginger Petrafaso. "Science Fiction in the High School." *Extrapolation*, 14 (1973), 149–51.

A thematic, individualized approach is used in this one-semester elective SF course.

Quina, James, and M. Jean Greenlaw. "Science Fiction as Mode for Interdisciplinary Education." *Journal of Reading*, 19, No. 2 (1975), 104–11.

A practical classroom program for the use of science fiction to combine existing and/or speculative disciplines. Includes guidelines and suggestions for single and multidiscipline texts (divided by field) and suggestions for independent research.

Rabkin, Eric S. "Fantasy Literature: Gut with a Backbone." *CEA Critic*, 40 (1978), 6–11.

Suggestions for making the college fantasy literature course more challenging, if still enjoyable, with mention of numerous possible course topics and readings.

Reed, Charlette, and Zenobia Verner. "It'll Never Happen." *English Journal*, 65 (1976), 65–66.

A discussion of a three-week mini-course for ninth to twelfth grade students designed to promote thinking about future life.

Richardson, Carmen C. "The Reality of Fantasy." *Language Arts,* 53 (1976), 549–51, 563.

Points out that fantasy allows children to safely explore the problems of being human in the 1970s.

Reynolds, John C., Jr. "Science Fiction in the 7–12 Curriculum." *Clearing House,* 51 (1977), 122–25.

The results of a survey of 300 teachers in four southeastern states that demonstrates the widespread use of science fiction and fantasy in a variety of themes or approaches. Concludes with a few samples of teachers' comments and an analysis of the data.

Rogers, Chester B. "Science Fiction and Social Sciences." *Social Studies,* 66, No. 6 (1975), 261–64.

Based on the results of a course, "Science Fiction and Politics" and using Isaac Asimov's *The Currents of Space* as a model, Rogers indicates that science fiction has three major assets when allied with social sciences: concern for the future, flexibility of ideas, and interest and readability. Includes a thematically arranged bibliography of fiction and a brief bibliography of critical works.

Roos, Richard. "Middle Earth in the Classroom: Studying J. R. R. Tolkien." *English Journal,* 58 (1969), 1175–80.

A discussion of the literary elements of LOTR with suggestions for teaching it.

Rothfork, John. "Revitalizing the 'Intro to Lit' Course at a Technical Institution." *Freshman English Resource Notes,* 2 (1977), 6.

The use of science fiction to bring new energy to introductory literature classes at a technical institution. A brief list of recommended titles and projects is included.

Schlobin, Roger C. "Preparing for Life's Passages: How Fantasy Literature Can Help." *Media & Methods,* 16 (1979), 26–27, 29, 50–51.

Fantasy literature deals with those issues that are imminent in the lives of all people and that are especially crucial for the growing student.

Schmidt, Stanley. "SF in the Classroom: Science Fiction and the High School Teacher." *Extrapolation,* 17 (1976), 141–50.

Moving from the dual premise that science fiction is fun and a combination of literature and science, Schmidt offers suggestions and guidelines for approaches that "range from incidental use of science fiction in science courses to complete courses focusing on science fiction as a literary craft with scientific speculation as one of its tools." Includes a section on the relationships between science and science fiction with illustrations from the works of Poul Anderson, Hal Clement, Robert A. Heinlein, Isaac Asimov, Arthur C. Clarke, Daniel Keyes, A. E. Van Vogt, Alexei Panshin, and Larry Niven, along with suggestions for critical reading and visual aids.

—————. "Science Fiction Courses: An Example and Some Alternatives." *American Journal of Physics*, 41 (1973), 1052–56.

Discusses types of science fiction courses and a sample course offered at Heidelberg College in Tiffin, Ohio. Includes examples of reading lists and sources of additional information and teaching aids.

"Science Fiction in the Political Science Classroom." *Teaching Political Science*, 3 (1976), 401–12.

An examination of the nature of social science fiction and its usefulness in the political science classroom. Includes a valuable table listing science fiction novels and identifying their politically relevant themes.

Senatore, Margaret. "Besides Just Reading The Book." *Media & Methods*, 16 (1979), 36–37, 53.

Eight ways to channel science fiction interest into other areas of language arts skill development.

Statuti, Jude Anne. "SF in the High School." *Extrapolation*, 17 (1975), 31–34.

A report ón the successful integration of the science fiction course and high school curriculum requirements plus a series of guidelines for "rookie" SF teachers.

Tashlik, Phyllis. "Science Fiction: An Anthropological Approach." *English Journal*, 64 (1975), 78–79.

A brief description of a course combining science fiction and anthropology as it is taught to high school juniors and seniors.

Tate, Janice M. "Sexual Bias in Science Fiction for Children." *Elementary English*, 50 (1973), 1061–64.

Surveys 49 SF works in order to determine the sexual bias of current children's science fiction recommended for grades three through six.

Troutner, Joanne. "Trekking with Science Fiction." *Audiovisual Instruction*, 22 (1977), 46–48.

A report of a media-center-based science fiction program at Jefferson High school in Lafayette, Indiana, which includes an annotated bibliography of science fiction novels popular among high school students.

Tymn, Marshall B. "A Guide to AV Resources in Science Fiction and Fantasy." *Media & Methods*, 16 (1979), 41–43, 56–59.

The most comprehensive listing of science fiction teaching aids ever compiled. Includes an author-title index.

—————. "Science Fiction: Coping with Change." *Media & Methods*, 16 (1979), 18–20.

A rational for using science fiction in the school curriculum and the reason for its current popularity.

Veix, Donald B. "Teaching a Censored Novel: *Slaughterhouse-Five*." *English Journal*, 64 (1975), 25–33.

A general discussion of censorship in the high school followed by a practical method of dealing with its realities, and a justification for teaching *Slaughterhouse-Five* when faced with possible censorship, along with techniques of teaching the novel.

Watkins, William Jon. "How a Science Fiction Writer Teaches Science Fiction." *Media & Methods,* 14 (1977), 22–24.

Brief description of eight approaches to teaching science fiction.

Watson, Ian. "SF Capsules for Art Students." *Foundation,* 5 (1974), 56–62.

A description of an SF art class with an outline and suggestions for modular subject material.

Weinkauf, Mary S. "Breaking the Discipline Barriers: Practical Uses of Science Fiction." *Delta Kappa Gamma Bulletin,* 41, No. 3 (1975), 32–38.

Outlines the reasons why science fiction should be incorporated into the English curriculum in the high school.

Wheatley, Barbara. "Teaching Linguistics Through Science Fiction and Fantasy." *Extrapolation,* 20 (1979), 205–13.

A description of a course entitled *Aspects of Language: The Languages of Science Fiction and Fantasy* developed at the University of Wisconsin-Milwaukee, which utilized SF works as a basis for investigating linguistic questions.

Williamson, Jack. "Science Fiction Comes to College." *Extrapolation,* 12 (1971), 67–78.

A discussion of the increased academic interest in the field, followed by an annotated listing of some 70 courses offered at the University levels during the academic year 1970–71.

Woodcock, John, ed. "Teaching Science Fiction: Unique Challenge." *Science-Fiction Studies,* 6 (1979), 249–62.

A transcription of an MLA Special Session held in New York, December 1978. The participants (Gregory Benford, Samuel R. Delany, Robert Scholes, Alan J. Friedman, and John Woodcock) discuss three issues associated with teaching science fiction: the problem of scientific content, the problem of reading one's first SF book, and the problem of realism.

Zander, Arlen R. "Science and Fiction: An Interdisciplinary Approach." *American Journal of Physics,* 43, No. 1 (1975), 9–12.

A description of an SF course developed by a physicist, a poet, a psychologist, and a literary scholar. The objectives, structure, development, and degree of success are described, and a typical lesson plan for one novel, Walter M. Miller's *A Canticle for Leibowitz,* is included.

Zjawin, Dorothy. "Close Encounters of the Classroom Kind: How to Use Science Fiction in All Subject Areas." *Instructor,* 87 (April 1978), 54–57.

A justification for using science fiction with elementary school children and a discussion of the use of science fiction to stimulate learning in a variety of elementary school subjects: language arts, science, social studies, art, and mathematics.

B. HANDBOOKS/TEACHING GUIDES

Allen, L. David. *The Ballantine Teachers' Guide to Science Fiction: A Practical Creative Approach to Science Fiction in the Classroom.* New York: Ballantine, 1975 (paper).

A useful handbook for the beginning SF teacher with little or no orientation in the field. Contains material on teaching science fiction; categories of science fiction; and analyses of one anthology, *Stellar 1*; one collection by Stanley Weinbaum; and thirteen novels: *Dragonfly* by Anne McCaffrey, *The Ginger Star* by Leigh Brackett, *More Than Human* by Theodore Sturgeon, *The Midwich Cuckoos* by John Wyndham, *Brain Wave* by Poul Anderson, *Childhood's End* by Arthur C. Clarke, *Fahrenheit 451* by Ray Bradbury, *The Space Merchants* by Frederik Pohl and C. M. Kornbluth, *Nerves* by Lester del Rey, *Under Pressure* by Frank Herbert, *Starman Jones* by Robert A. Heinlein, *Rendezvous with Rama* by Arthur C. Clarke, and *Ringworld* by Larry Niven.

Amelio, Ralph J., ed. *Hal in the Classroom: Science Fiction Films.* Dayton, OH: Pflaum, 1974 (paper).

A teacher resource book on how best to use the SF film, with primary emphasis on the humanities class. Contains useful background articles by a number of writers, a filmography, a bibliography of works on the SF film, and a key to film distributors.

Aquino, John. *Fantasy in Literature.* Washington, D. C.: National Education Association, 1977.

A discussion of fantasy literature followed by suggestions for teaching fantasy; limited usefulness.

————. *Science Fiction as Literature.* Washington, D. C.: National Education Association, 1976 (paper).

Treats science fiction as a subject in the language arts curriculum in the public schools. Includes background information, model lesson guides, reading lists, and teaching aids.

Calkins, Elizabeth, and Barry McGhan. *Teaching Tomorrow: A Handbook of Science Fiction for Teachers.* Dayton, OH: Pflaum, 1972 (paper).

Contains a unit on teaching science fiction, an annotated list of 200 recommended novels, and short lists of fan and professional publications, SF organizations, critical works, and other resources. Intended for high school teachers. Badly in need of revision.

Donelson, Kenneth, ed. *Science Fiction in the English Class.* Urbana, IL: National Council of Teachers of English, 1972 (paper).

The October 1972 issue of the *Arizona English Bulletin,* which contains articles on teaching science fiction, including much practical information.

Friend, Beverly. Science Fiction: *Classroom in Orbit*. Glassboro, NJ: Educational Impact, 1974 (paper).

An ambitious attempt to provide the beginning teacher with necessary background on science fiction and fantasy. Includes philosophic justification for SF in the classroom, definitions, short history, major themes, techniques of writing science fiction, SF films and television programs, fandom, and various practical methods of using science fiction in the classroom.

Hollister, Bernard C., and Deane C. Thompson. *Grokking the Future: Science Fiction in the Classroom*. Dayton, OH: Pflaum, 1973 (paper).

This exploration of the key themes of modern science fiction offers ways to approach social issues through the literature of science fiction.

Holtzman, Marcia. *Science Fiction: A Study Guide*. New York: New American Library, 1975 (paper).

Organized around a series of short plot outlines of NAL titles, followed by sample discussion questions, this work is of little value as a resource tool for SF teachers.

Isaacs, Leonard. Darwin to Double Helix: *The Biological Theme in Science Fiction*. London and Boston: Butterworths, 1977 (paper).

Forms the basis for a course designed to examine the manner in which two of the most important developments in modern biology have been reflected in science fiction: evolution and genetic engineering.

McNelly, Willis, ed. *Science Fiction: The Academic Awakening*. Shreveport, LA: College English Association, 1974 (paper).

A CEA Chapbook containing a collection of short essays by scholars, critics, and SF writers. Designed to acquaint the new teacher with the field as a whole.

Millies, Susan. *Science Fiction Primer for Teachers*. Dayton, OH: Pflaum, 1975 (paper).

An overview of the field for the SF teacher, including chapters on the nature of science fiction, its history, major themes, and value. Includes an outline for a semester course and short biographies and canons of SF writers. Especially valuable for the annotated lists of fiction that accompany the various sections.

Paine, Doris M., and Diane Martinez. *Guide to Science Fiction: Exploring Possibilities and Alternatives*. New York: Bantam Books, 1974 (paper).

Designed to stimulate, rather than dictate, the thinking of the beginning high school SF teacher. Has a thematic emphasis and contains a potpourri of information and ideas.

Schwartz, Sheila. *Science Fiction: An Introduction* (cassette). Urbana, IL: National Council of Teachers of English, 1973.

In three especially recorded talks, Schwartz advocates greater use of science fiction in the literature curriculum, furnishes basic information about major SF works, and suggests ways of approaching science fiction in the classroom.

Searles, Baird, et al. *A Reader's Guide to Science Fiction.* New York: Avon Books, 1979 (paper).

A useful introduction to the science fiction field for students and teachers. Contains profiles of 200 major writers and their works, a guide to major series, a listing of the Hugo and Nebula Award winners, a suggested basic reading list, and a concise history of the genre. A necessary acquisition for anyone new to the field.

Spann, Sylvia, and Mary Beth Culp, eds. *Thematic Units in Teaching English and the Humanities.* Urbana, IL: National Council of Teachers of English, 1975 (paper).

One of the fifteen units in this program, "The Future Arrives before the Present Has Left," maintains the format of all units: an overview, general objectives, notes on evaluation, list of materials needed, daily lesson plans, suggested related activities, supplementary reading, bibliography, and selected teaching materials for use in class. Questions for *The Gods Themselves, 2001: A Space Odyssey, Planet of the Apes, Brave New World,* and *The Martian Chronicles.* The *First Supplement* (1977) contains a unit entitled "Is Anyone Out There?" which deals with life on other planets and contains the apparatus for implementing this unit in an eleventh grade SF class.

Whitenight, Cynthis. *Prophecies and Possibilities: The Science Fiction Novel.* 3rd ed. Lawrence, KS: University of Kansas Division of Continuing Education, 1975 (paper).

Teaching units for eight works: *War of the Worlds, The Martian Chronicles, The Andromeda Strain, 1984, I, Robot, Brave New World, Flowers for Algernon,* and *Stranger in a Strange Land.* Each unit contains a discussion of the work, review questions, and writing assignments. Superficial, but some of the material may be of use to the beginning teacher searching for ideas.

C. AUDIO-VISUAL MATERIALS

Alternate World Recordings (148 East 74th St., New York, NY 10021).

Original science fiction and fantasy records, produced beginning 1975.

Aldiss, Brian W., *Frankenstein Unbound,* 1976.
Bloch, Robert, *Gravely, Robert Bloch,* 1976.
Bloch, Robert and Harlan Ellison, *The Life and Future Times of Jack the Ripper,* 1977.
Ellison, Harlan, *Harlan Ellison Reads Harlan Ellison,* 1976.
Howard, Robert E., *From the Hells Beneath the Hells* (read by Ugo Toppo), 1975.
Le Guin, Ursula K., *The Ones Who Walk Away from Omelas,* 1976.
Leiber, Fritz, *Gonna Roll the Bones,* 1976.

Russ, Joanna, *Joanna Russ Interpreting Her Stories,* 1976.
Sturgeon, Theodore, *Theodore Sturgeon Reads,* 1976.

Audio Brandon Films (34 MacQuesten Parkway South, Mt. Vernon, NY (10050).

A science fiction film rental program consisting of seven major titles specifically selected for classroom use. Each film comes with a comprehensive teaching manual. All films were made available in 1978.

Colossus: The Forbin Project.
Fahrenheit 451.
The Illustrated Man.
Invasion of the Body Snatchers.
The Omega Man.
THX 1138.
The Terminal Man.

Ballantine Books (201 East 50th St., New York, NY 10022).

Designed for junior and senior high school science fiction classes, *The Cosmic Classroom* is a tightly coordinated program of paperback novels, cassettes, ditto masters, and *The Ballantine Teacher's Guide to Science Fiction* (1975) by L. David Allen.

BFA Educational Media (2211 Michigan Ave., Box 1795, Santa Monica, CA 90406).

BFA has produced a science fiction film series consisting of four twenty-minute films adapted from actual stories. The series was produced by Bernard Wilets, a leading educational filmmaker. Carefully structured guides help develop lively classroom discussions.

All the Troubles of the World by Isaac Asimov, 1978.
Rescue Party by Arthur C. Clarke, 1978.
The Veldt by Ray Bradbury, 1979.
Zero Hour by Ray Bradbury, 1978.

Caedmon (1995 Broadway, New York, NY 10023).

Caedmon's ever-expanding record and cassette program features selections from the science fiction and fantasy classics as well as recent works.

Anderson, Poul, *Yonder,* 1980.
Asimov, Isaac, *Foundation: The Psychohistorians* (read by William Shatner), 1975.
Asimov, Isaac, *The Mayors from Foundation,* 1977.
Bradbury, Ray, *The Illustrated Man* (read by Leonard Nimoy), 1976.
Bradbury, Ray, *The Martian Chronicles* (read by Leonard Nimoy), 1975.
Burgess, Anthony, *A Clockwork Orange,* 1973.
Clarke, Arthur C., *Childhood's End,* 1979.
Clarke, Arthur C., *Fountains of Paradise,* 1979.
Clarke, Arthur C., *Transit of Earth, The Nine Billion Names of God, The Star,* 1978.
Clarke, Arthur C., *2001: A Space Odyssey,* 1976.

Heinlein, Robert A., *The Green Hills of Earth and Gentlemen, Be Seated* (read by Leonard Nimoy), 1977.

Herbert, Frank, *Battles of Dune,* 1979.

Herbert, Frank, *Dune: The Banquet Scene,* 1977.

Herbert, Frank, *Sandworms of Dune,* 1978.

Herbert, Frank, *Truths of Dune,* 1979.

Kuttner, Henry, *Mimsy Were the Borogroves* (read by William Shatner), 1976.

Le Guin, Ursula K., *Gwilan's Harp and Intracom,* 1977.

Lewis, C. S., *Chronicles of Narnia: Prince Caspian* (read by Ian Richardson), 1979.

Lewis, C. S., *Chronicles of Narnia: The Silver Chair* (read by Ian Richardson), 1980.

Lewis, C. S., *Chronicles of Narnia: Voyage of the Dawn Treader* (read by Anthony Quayle), 1979.

Lewis, C. S., *The Lion, the Witch, and the Wardrobe* (read by Ian Richardson), 1979.

Lovecraft, H. P., *The Dunwich Horror* (read by David McCallum), 1976.

Lovecraft, H. P., *Haunter of the Dark* (read by David McCallum), 1979.

Lovecraft, H. P., *The Rats in the Walls* (read by David McCallum), 1973.

McCaffrey, Anne, *The White Dragon,* 1978.

Merril, Judith, *Survival Ship and The Shrine of Temptation,* 1978.

Shelley, Mary, *Frankenstein* (read by James Mason), 1977.

Silverberg, Robert, *Dying Inside,* 1979.

Stevenson, Robert Louis, *The Strange Case of Dr. Jekyll and Mr. Hyde* (read by Anthony Quayle), 1969.

Stoker, Bram, *Dracula* (read by David McCallum and Carole Shelley), 1975.

Sturgeon, Theodore, *Baby is Three,* 1977.

Sturgeon, Theodore, *The Fabulous Idiot,* 1980.

Tolkien, J. R. R., *The Hobbit and The Fellowship of the Ring,* 1975.

Tolkien, J. R. R., *The Lord of the Rings: The Two Towers and The Return of the King,* 1975.

Tolkien, J. R. R., *Poems and Songs of Middle Earth,* 1967.

Tolkien, J. R. R., *The Simarillion: Of Beren and Luthien* (read by Christopher Tolkien), 1977.

Tolkien, J. R. R., *The Simarillion: Of the Darkening of Valinor and Of the Flight of the Noldor* (read by Christopher Tolkien), 1978.

Verne, Jules, *Journey to the Center of the Earth* (read by James Mason), 1976.

Verne, Jules, *Twenty Thousand Leagues Under the Sea* (read by James Mason), 1976.

Vonnegut, Kurt, Jr., *Cat's Cradle,* 1978

Vonnegut, Kurt, Jr., *Kurt Vonnegut, Jr. Reads Slaughterhouse-Five,* 1973.

Vonnegut, Kurt, Jr., *Welcome to the Monkey House,* 1972.

Wells, H. G., *The War of the Worlds* (read by Leonard Nimoy), 1976.

White, T. H., *The Book of Merlyn* (read by Christopher Plummer), 1978.

White, T. H., *The Book of Merlyn II* (read by Christopher Plummer), 1980.

Center for Cassette Studies (681 Fifth Avenue, New York, NY 10022).

The Center has a large inventory of science fiction cassettee interviews, dramatizations, and critical discussions.

Brunetti, Mendor, *Jules Verne*, 1974. Brunetti, a Verne translator, discusses the problems with the early translations and examines various facets of Verne's work, such as his scientific knowledge, his characterizations, and his affection for the sea and music.

Asimov, Isaac, *Nightfall*, 1972. Dramatization.

Bradbury, Ray, *Marionettes, Inc.* Dramatization.

Brown, Fredric, *The Last Martian*, 1972. Dramatization.

A Conversation with Aldous Huxley, 1972. In an interview shortly before his death, Huxley discusses his career, his novels *Brave New World* and *Island*, and the contemporary problems of overpopulation, poverty, and the social influences of technology.

Cyclic Obsession in Science Fiction, 1975. Four talks by critic Paul Green which survey the development of the science fiction novel from H. G. Wells to contemporary writers.

Dick, Philip, *The Defenders*. Dramatization.

The Egg of Time I-II, 1975. A discussion of the science fiction field-at-large, featuring author/editor Judith Merril.

Fantasy and Reality, 1972. Ray Bradbury explains the relationship between today's reality and science fiction's fantasy, emphasizing that with the aid of the spaceship humans may rediscover the beauty of their life and environment.

Focus on Frederik Pohl, 1974. Pohl discusses the past trends and future directions of science fiction.

Focus on Jack Williamson, 1974. Williamson discusses the last fifty years of science fiction and his feeling that the literature has had an unfortunate effect on attitudes toward scientific and technological progress.

The Future of Science Fiction, 1974. An evaluation of the value of science fiction in the universities.

A Gun for Dinosaur, 1972. Dramatization.

Heinlein, Robert A., *Requiem*. Dramatization.

Hello Tomorrow, 1972. Dramatization.

An Interview with Poul Anderson, 1973. In describing his style of writing, Anderson cites the influence on him of H. G. Wells, Jules Verne, and Joannes Jensen, and his belief that science fiction is a child of the 19th century.

Kurt Vonnegut, Jr., 1975. Vonnegut describes the major experiences of his life and the impact they have had on his professional attitudes and career.

Leiber, Fritz, *Appointment in Tomorrow*. Dramatization.

Leinster, Murray, *The Lost Race*, 1972. Dramatization.

The Man Who Invented Hobbits. Documentary of Tolkien's life and career.

Orwell, George, *1984*. Dramatization.

Pohl, Frederik, *Tunnel Under the World*, 1972. Dramatization.

Power and Science Fiction, 1975. A discussion of militarism and elitism in science fiction, featuring Philip Klass, Judith Merril, and Joanna Russ.

Ray Bradbury as Philosopher, 1974. An optimistic view of the future, contingent on our ability to recognize our own evil.

Robert Silverberg, 1974. The value of science fiction in preparing people for change and in encouraging young people to read is discussed by Silverberg. He also examines the science fiction trend away from gadgetry toward the human condition.

Science Fiction: Its Future, 1973. Isaac Asimov examines science fiction as the literary response to technological change, while Jack Williamson prescribes it as medicine for future shock.

Starkie, Walter, *Dracula & Other Vampires*, 1973. Dr. Starkie traces the vampire legend as an ancient superstition from the literature of Homer to current works.

Sturgeon, Theodore, *Saucer of Loneliness*. Dramatization.

To the Future, 1972. Dramatization.

2001 Revisited, 1975. Arthur C. Clarke discusses the current problems of population control, food shortages, use of leisure time, and pest control as well as the possible future problems of planetary engineering, genetic manipulation, and living on other worlds.

Ursula K. Le Guin: Woman of Science Fiction, 1973. Le Guin discusses her life and work, airs her views on the literary world, and cheers the woman's liberation movement.

Vonnegut, Kurt, Jr., *Report on the Barnhouse Effect*. Dramatization.

Wells, H. G., *The Man Who Could Work Miracles*. Dramatization.

Williamson, Jack, *With Folded Hands*. Dramatization.

Center for Humanities (Communications Park, Box 100, White Plains, NY 10602).

I Couldn't Put It Down: Hooked on Reading-Collection Three (2 carousels of slides/cassettes/records), 1976. Four classic stories of suspense are presented in comic-style format, permitting the use of carefully selected vocabulary to advance the plotlines. Each story is stopped at a crucial moment, motivating students to read the works themselves. Works treated are *Frankenstein, The Strange Case of Dr. Jekyll and Mr. Hyde, Dracula*, and *The Invisible Man*.

Literature of the Supernatural: Worlds Beyond Reason (2 carousels of slides/cassettes/records), 1974. An exploration of literature dealing with supernatural beings. Illustrations from Shakespeare, Hawthorne, Castaneda, Saki, Stevenson, Blackwood, Seabrooke, Wells, and Stoker.

Science Fiction: Jules Verne to Ray Bradbury (3 carousels of slides/cassettes/records), 1974. A survey of the major works and periods of the history of science fiction. Teacher's guide includes complete script, discussion questions, related essay questions and activities, and suggested readings. The most comprehensive introduction to the genre currently available.

Current Affairs (Box 398, 24 Danbury Rd., Wilton, CT 06897).

A series of fifty reading motivation units (filmstrip/cassette), prepared from best-selling curriculum books and their authors. Titles have been carefully chosen by a panel of educators and represent the works of many different publishers. All categories of students are represented: the gifted, reluctant, college-bound, and special education. Each title comes with a hardcover teacher's edition of the work, a teacher's discussion guide, and student evaluation tools. Science fiction works offered in the series are:

Bradbury, Ray, *Dandelion Wine,* 1978.
Bradbury, Ray, *Fahrenheit 451,* 1978.
Bradbury, Ray, *The Martian Chronicles,* 1978.
Keyes, Daniel, *Flowers for Algernon,* 1978.
Orwell, George, *1984,* 1978.
Tolkien, J. R. R., *The Hobbit,* 1978.

Education Audio Visual Inc. (Pleasantville, NY 10570).

Science Fiction and Fantasy (2 filmstrips/cassettes/records), 1976. This program examines the growth of science fiction within the context of the Industrial Revolution, the cult it created, and its recent acceptance as serious literature. The best of the filmstrip introductory programs.

Educational Dimensions Group (Box 126, Stamford, CT 06904).

Classics of Science Fiction (4 filmstrips/cassettes/records), 1975. Evaluates four influential works: *Fahrenheit 451* by Ray Bradbury, *R. U. R.* by Karel Capek, *Childhood's End* by Arthur C. Clarke, and *The Time Machine* by H. G. Wells.

Future Imperfect (2 filmstrips/cassettes/records), 1974. A survey of the anti-utopian mode, concentrating on Aldous Huxley's *Brave New World* and George Orwell's *1984.*

Tales of Time and Space (4 filmstrips/cassettes/records), 1978. Examines four types of science fiction stories for their emphasis on the human consequences of science and technology: "Nightfall" by Isaac Asimov, "First Contact" by Murray Leinster, "Vintage Season" by C. L. Moore and Henry Kuttner, and "Neutron Star" by Larry Niven.

Uncertain Worlds: The Literature of Science Fiction (4 filmstrips/cassettes/records), 1974. Traces the evolution of science fiction literature from pioneers like Verne to Wells through the works of such recognized masters as Asimov, Bradbury, Clarke, and Heinlein.

Everett/Edwards, Inc. (Box 1060, DeLand, FL 32720).

This science fiction cassette program consists of critical discussions by John Hollow on the following works:

Asimov, Isaac, *I, Robot,* 1976.
Asimov, Isaac, *The Foundation Trilogy,* 1976.
Bradbury, Ray, *The Illustrated Man,* 1976.

Bradbury, Ray, *The Martian Chronicles,* 1976.
Burroughs, Edgar Rice, *Gods of Mars,* 1976.
Burroughs, Edgar Rice, *A Princess of Mars,* 1976.
Burroughs, Edgar Rice, *Warlord of Mars,* 1976.
Shelley, Mary, *Frankenstein,* 1976.
Verne, Jules, *From Earth to the Moon,* 1976.
Verne, Jules, *Journey to the Center of the Earth,* 1976.
Verne, Jules, *Twenty Thousand Leagues Under the Sea,* 1976.
Wells, H. G., *The Time Machine.*
Wells, H. G., *The War of the Worlds.*
French, Warren, *An Introduction to H. P. Lovecraft,* (Narrated by French, this covers all of HPL's major writings).

Films for the Humanities (P. O. Box 2053, Princeton, NJ 08540).

Kurt Vonnegut: A Self-Portrait, a 29-minute 16mm film, purchase or rental, produced by Harold Mantell.

Franklin Watts, Inc. (730 Fifth Ave., New York, NY 10019).

Their recent catalogue shows a number of record and tape recordings of science fiction and fantasy stories.

Carroll, Lewis, *Alice In Wonderland.*
Carroll, Lewis, *Alice Through the Looking Glass.*
Grahame, Kenneth, *The Reluctant Dragon* (read by Michael Hordern).
Adams, Richard, *Scenes from Watership Down* (read by Roy Dotrice).
Tolkien, J. R. R., *The Hobbit.*
Verne, Jules, *Journey to the Center of the Earth* (read by Tom Baker).
Wilde, Oscar, *The Happy Prince, The Star Child,* abridged (read by Robert Morley).

Guidance Associates (Communications Park, Box 300, White Plains, NY 10602).

Getting Hooked on Fantasy (filmstrip/cassette/record), 1976. An introduction to fantasy via the works of ten writers of children's fantasy (in order of treatment): *The Phantom Tollbooth* by Norman Juster; *The Lion, the Witch and the Wardrobe* by C. S. Lewis; *Treasure of Green Knowe* by L. M. Boston; *Pippi Longstocking* by Astid Lindgren; *Charlotte's Web* by E. B. White; *The Genie of Sutton Place* by George Seldon; *Half Magic* by Edward Eager; *The Enormous Egg* by Oliver Butterworth; *The Borrowers* by Mary Norton; *The Search for Delicious* by Natalie Babitt; and *The Book of Three* by Lloyd Alexander.

Getting Hooked on Science Fiction (filmstrip/cassette/record), 1976. An introduction to some of the basic themes of science fiction via the works of ten writers (in order of treatment): *The Wonderful Flight to the Mushroom Planet* by Eleanor Cameron; *The White Mountains* by John Christopher; *Dolphin Island* by Arthur C. Clarke; *The Runaway Robot* by Lester del Rey; *Enchantress for the Stars* by Sylvia Louise Engdahl; *Twenty Thousand Leagues Under the Sea* by Jules Verne; *Star Surgeon* by Alan Nourse; *Moon of Three Rings* by Andre Norton; *A Wrinkle in Time* by Madeleine L'Engle;

and *Mrs. Frisby and the Rats of NIMH* by Robert C. O'Brien.

What Is Science Fiction? (2 filmstrips/cassettes/records), 1975. An introductory background program consisting of material on the structure of the SF story and the basic themes of the genre.

Hourglass Productions (10292 Westminster Ave., Garden Grove, CA 92643).

An ongoing series of interviews with science fiction and fantasy writers that promises to become the most comprehensive program of its kind ever produced. Cassettes now available:

An Hour with Fritz Leiber: "The Author and His Works," 1979.

An Hour with Isaac Asimov: "Building a Firm Foundation," 1979.

An Hour with Katherine Kurtz: "An Introduction to the Author and Her Work," 1979.

An Hour with Kathleen Sky: "Comments on Star Trek & Other Matters," 1979.

An Hour with Marion Zimmer Bradley: "A Personal Note," 1979.

An Hour with Randall Garrett: "Magic and Mystery and Lord Darcy," 1979.

Learning Corporation of America (1350 Avenue of the Americas, New York, NY 10019)

The Ugly Little Boy, by Isaac Asimov.

Miller-Brody Productions (342 Madison Ave., New York, NY 10017).

The following filmstrip/cassette/record dramatizations are available:

L'Engle, Madeleine, *A Wind in the Door,* 1977.

L'Engle, Madeleine, *A Wrinkle in Time,* 1974.

Le Guin, Ursula K., *The Tombs of Atuan,* 1979.

National Council of Teachers of English (1111 Kenyon Rd., Urbana, IL 61801).

Science Fiction: An Introduction (cassette), 1973. In three talks Sheila Schwartz advocates greater use of science fiction in the literature curriculum, gives the listener basic information about major SF works, and suggests ways of approaching science fiction in the classroom.

National Film & Video Center (Suite 200, 1425 Liberty Rd., Eldersburg, MD 21784).

The following *Star Trek* episodes are available for sale or rental on 16mm or 8mm color sound: "Space Seed," "Miri," "Shore Leave," "Squire of Gothos," "Menagerie, Pt. I," Menagerie, Pt. II," "City on the Edge of Forever," "Trouble with Tribbles," "Amok Time," and "Cat's Paw." Also available are two reels of *Star Trek* bloopers.

Prentice-Hall Media (150 White Plains Rd., Tarrytown, NY 10591).

Fahrenheit 451 (2 filmstrips/cassettes), 1978. A dramatization of Ray Bradbury's dystopian novel.

Fantasy Sampler (4 cassettes), 1977. Dramatizations of Daphne du Maurier's *Peter Ibbetson*, Mary Shelley's *Frankenstein*, Jules Verne's

Twenty Thousand Leagues Under the Sea, and Oscar Wilde's *The Happy Prince.*

The Isaac Asimov Cassette Library (6 cassettes), 1977. Asimov reads a selection of his own stories with personal commentary: "I Just Make Them Up, See?" "The Feeling of Power," "Someday," Satisfaction Guaranteed," "Living Space," "The Last Question," "Jokester," "The Immortal Bard," "Spell My Name with an S," and "The Ugly Little Boy."

The Ray Bradbury Cassette Library (6 cassettes), 1977. Bradbury reads a series of his best-known stories with personal commentary: "The Lake," "The Smile," "The Foghorn," "The Veldt," "The Crowd," "John Huff's Leavetaking," "Illuminations," "The Illustrated Man," "Marionettes, Inc.," "The Pedestrian," "The Dwarf," "There Will Come Soft Rains," "The Sound of Thunder," and "Fever Dream."

Ray Bradbury Filmstrip Series (6 filmstrips/cassettes), 1977. Bradbury's fiction read against a background of music and sound effects: "The Foghorn," "The Illustrated Man," "The Veldt," "The Dwarf," "The Sound of Thunder," and "There Will Come Soft Rains."

Sci Fi and Time Fiction (3 cassettes), 1977. The program consists of *Science Fiction, the Early Days*, a talk by Isaac Asimov and Frederik Pohl on pre-World War II science fiction; *Conversations with Kurt Vonnegut*, an interview; and *Tolkien and Time Fiction*, a discussion of Tolkien's major works.

Science Fiction: Familiar, Strange, and Possible (6 filmstrips/cassettes/ records), 1977. A six-part investigation of science fiction as a creative interdisciplinary medium. Focuses on the contributions of the genre in interpreting and predicting technological developments and their effects on society. Written and narrated by SF writer Tom Disch.

H. G. Wells Filmstrip Series (3 filmstrips/cassettes), 1978. Dramatization of *The Invisible Man*, *The Time Machine*, and *The War of the Worlds.*

The Works of H. G. Wells (3 cassettes), 1977. Dramatizations of *The Man Who Could Work Miracles*, *The Time Machine*, and *The War of the Worlds.*

Satellite Broadcasting (4101 Conger St., Wheaton, MD 20906).

Radio's Golden Age of Science Fiction (cassette, 8-track/reel-to-reel), 1978. Excerpts from over 100 SF radio shows. The first time such a program has ever been assembled; contains four full hours of selections from such radio classics as *X Minus One, Superman, Buck Rogers, Dimension X, Captain Jupiter, Exploring Tomorrow, Host Planet Earth* (BBC), *Tarzan, 200 Plus, The Hermit's Cave* and *CBS Science Fiction.* Catalog lists extensive collection of full-length programs available.

Society for Visual Education (1345 Diversey Parkway, Chicago, IL 60614).

Science Fiction (4 filmstrips/cassettes), 1977. Classic stories have been adapted into a controlled vocabulary form for slow learners. Designed as a self-contained reading improvement unit: A. Merritt,

"The People of the Pit"; Mary Shelley, "The Mortal Immortal"; Jules Verne, "Off on a Comet"; and H. G. Wells, "The Time Traveller."

Space Wars (4 filmstrips/cassettes), 1978. A multi-media module combining high-interest low-vocabulary reading materials with motivational filmstrips, creative writing exercises, skill exercises, and a variety of stimulating visual and cassette story-builders. The program is a highly flexible and extensive resource for developing reading and writing skills at the junior high and high school level. The focus for much of the program is on H. G. Wells' *The War of the Worlds*, which has been adapted for use here.

Sunburst Communications Inc (39 Washington Ave., Pleasantville, NY 10570).

Encounters with Tomorrow: Science Fiction and Human Values (6 filmstrips/cassettes/records), 1976. A six-part interdisciplinary program that is specifically designed to enrich classes in social studies, science, literature, and humanities. The key to the program is the use of science fiction as a framework for exploring and considering the future human implications of current technological innovations.

University of Kansas Audio Visual Center (746 Massachusetts St., Lawrence, KS 66044).

"The Literature of Science Fiction Film Lecture Series" has interviews and lectures by well-known science fiction writers. The only series of its kind produced on film. The following titles are available for rental:

Early Days of the Science Fiction Magazines, 1975. Jack Williamson is interviewed concerning his early writings, associations with science fiction magazine editors, and formulas used in the early science fiction pulps.

The Early History of Science Fiction, 1973. Damon Knight explores science fiction literature from the mythical voyages of Greek gods to the popular SF pulp magazines of the 1930s.

History of Science Fiction from 1938 to the Present, 1971. Isaac Asimov welcomes viewers into his study to talk about the recent history of science fiction. He discusses the works of various writers, explains the difference between science fiction that is largely fantasy and science fiction based on scientific knowledge, and discusses the three major SF magazines.

Ideas in Science Fiction, 1973. Frederik Pohl traces the maturation of science fiction's current themes from their inception, describing the changes in the ideas for science fiction topics over the past forty years.

An Interview with Clifford Simak: A Career in Science Fiction, 1975. Simak describes his career and how his writing evolved over a period of years. He describes the changes which have occurred in science fiction and some of the writers who have influenced his own work.

Lunch with John Campbell, Jr.: An Editor at Work, 1972. Gordon Dickson and Harry Harrison discuss with Campbell the theme for a new story—and end up with plot, theme, and characters ready to write.

New Directions in Science Fiction, 1971. Harlan Ellison, in response to questions from James Gunn and other seminar participants, describes science fiction as a street fiction, a fiction of the people, with a mission and a message.

Plot in Science Fiction, 1970. James Gunn interviews Poul Anderson on plot. Anderson analyzes the subject in terms of Heinlein's three basic plots: "Boy Meets Girl," "The Little Tailor," and "The Man Who Learned Better." He compares these to classical plots, shows how plot interrelates with theme and character, and illustrates through his own writings how ideas develop into plot and then into story.

Science Fiction and the Mainstream, 1975. John Brunner presents a lecture concerning the styles and techniques of science fiction writers compared with those of other writers. He describes some of the common misconceptions most people have concerning contemporary SF writing.

Science Fiction Films, 1971. Forrest Ackerman analyzes the development of science fiction films according to subject or theme, illustrated with props, artifacts, posters, and photographs from what may be the most extensive collection in the world.

Stranger Than Science Fiction, 1968. One of the films from the CBS "21st Century" series, this shows how yesterday's science fiction has become today's fact.

Theme in Science Fiction, 1975. Gordon Dickson discusses some of the popular themes of science fiction with James Gunn. Differences between mainstream fiction themes and science fiction themes are explained.

INDEX TO RESOURCES

Distributors Code

ARW	Alternate World Recordings	GA	Guidance Associates
ABF	Audio Brandon Films	HP	Hourglass Productions
BB	Ballantine Books	LCA	Learning Corp. of America
BFA	BFA Educational Media	MB	Miller-Brody Productions
C	Caedmon	NCTE	National Council of Teachers
CCS	Center for Cassette Studies		of English
CH	Center for Humanities		
CA	Current Affairs	NFVC	National Film & Video
EAV	Educational Audio Visual		Center
EDG	Educational Dimensions	PHM	Prentice-Hall Media
	Group	SB	Satellite Broadcasting
EE	Everett/Edwards	SVE	Society for Visual Education
FFH	Films for the Humanities	SC	Sunburst Communications
FW	Franklin Watts	UK	University of Kansas

Authors

Ackerman, Forrest (UK)
Adams, Richard (FW)
Aldiss, Brian (AWR)
Alexander, Lloyd (GA)
Allen, L. David (BB)
Anderson, Poul (C, CCS, UK)
Asimov, Isaac (BFA, C, CCS, EDG, EE, LCA, HP, PHM, UK)
Babbitt, Natalie (GA)
Blackwood, Algernon (AWR)
Bloch, Robert (AWR)
Boston, L. M. (GA)
Bradbury, Ray (BFA, C, CA, CCS, EDG, EE, PHM)
Bradley, Marion Zimmer (HP)
Brown, Fredric (CCS)
Brunetti, Mendor (CCS)
Brunner, John (UK)
Burgess, Anthony (C)
Burroughs, Edgar Rice (EE)
Butterwórth, Oliver (GA)
Cameron, Eleanor (GA)
Campbell, John, Jr, (UK)
Capek, Karel (EDG)
Carroll, Lewis (FW)
Casteneda, Carlos (CH)
Christopher, John (GA)
Clarke, Arthur C. (BFA, C, CCS, EDG, GA)
del Rey, Lester (GA)
Dick, Philip K. (CCS)
Dickson, Gordon (UK)
Disch, Tom (PHM)
Du Murier, Daphne (PHM)
Eager, Edward (GA)
Ellison, Harlan (AWR, UK)
Engdahl, Sylvia Louise (GA)
French, Warren (EE)
Garrett, Randall (HP)
Graham, Kenneth (FW)
Green, Paul (CCS)
Gunn, James (UK)
Harrison, Harry (UK)
Hawthorne, Nathaniel (CH)
Herbert, Frank (C)

Heinlein, Robert A. (C, CCS, EDG)
Howard, Robert E. (AWR)
Huxley, Aldous (CCS, EDG)
Juster, Norman (GA)
Keyes, Daniel (CA)
Klass, Philip (CCS)
Knight, Damon (UK)
Kurtz, Katherine (HP)
Kuttner, Henry (C, EDG)
L'Engle, Madeleine (GA, MB)
Le Guin, Ursula K (AWR, C, CCS, MB)
Leiber, Fritz (AWR, CCS, HP)
Leinster, Murray (CCS, EDG)
Lewis, C. S. (C, GA)
Lindgren, Astid (GA)
Lovecraft, H. P. (C)
McCaffrey, Anne (C)
Merril, Judith (C, CCS)
Merritt, A. (SVE)
Moore, C. L. (EDG)
Niven, Larry (EDG)
Norton, Andre (GA)
Norton, Mary (GA)
Nourse, Alan (GA)
O'Brien, Robert C. (GA)
Orwell, George (CA, CCS, EDG)
Pohl, Frederik (CCS, PHM, UK)
Russ, Joanna (AWR, CCS)
Saki [pseud. of H. H. Munro] (CH)
Schwartz, Sheila (NCTE)
Seabrooke, William B. (CH)
Seldon, George (GA)
Shakespeare, William (CH)
Shelley, Mary (C, EE, PHM, SVE)
Silverberg, Robert (C, CCS)
Simak, Clifford (UK)
Sky, Kathleen (HP)
Starkie, Walter (CCS)
Stevenson, Robert Louis (C, CH)
Stoker, Bram (C, CH)
Sturgeon, Theodore (AWR, C, CCS)
Tolkien, J. R. R. (C, CA, FW, PHM)
Verne, Jules (C, EDG, EE, FW, GA PHM, SVE)

Vonnegut, Kurt, Jr. (C, CCS, FFH, PHM)

Wells, H. G. (C, CCS, CH, EDG, PHM, SVE)

Wilde, Oscar (FW, PHM)

White, E. B. (GA)

White, T. H. (C)

Wilets, Bernard (BFA)

Williamson, Jack (CCS, UK)

Titles

Alice in Wonderland (FW)

Alice through the Looking Glass (FW)

All the Troubles of the World (BFA)

An Hour with Fritz Leiber (HP)

An Hour with Isaac Asimov (HP)

An Hour with Katherine Kurtz (HP)

An Hour with Kathleen Sky (HP)

An Hour with Marion Zimmer Bradley (HP)

An Hour with Randall Garrett (HP)

Appointment in Tomorrow (CCS)

Baby Is Three (C)

Ballantine Teachers' Guide to Science Fiction, The (BB)

Battles of Dune (C)

Book of Merlyn, The (C)

Book of Merlyn II, The (C)

Book of Three, The (GA)

Borrowers, The (GA)

Brave New World (CCS, EDG)

Cat's Cradle (C)

Charlotte's Web (GA)

Childhood's End (C, EDG)

Classics of Science Fiction (EDG)

Clockwork Orange, A (C)

Colossus: The Forbin Project (ABF)

Conversation with Aldous Huxley, A (CCS)

Conversation with Kurt Vonnegut (PHM)

Cosmic Classroom, The (BB)

Cyclic Obsession in Science Fiction (CCS)

Dandelion Wine (CA)

Defenders, The (CCS)

Dolphin Island (GA)

Dracula (C, CH)

Dracula & Other Vampires (CCS)

Dune: The Banquet Scene (C)

Dunwich Horror, The (C)

Dying Inside (C)

Early Days of the Science Fiction Magazines (UK)

Early History of Science Fiction, The (UK)

Egg of Time I-II, The (CCS)

Enchantress for the Stars (GA)

Encounters with Tomorrow (SC)

Enormous Egg, The (GA)

Fabulous Idiot, The (C)

Fantasy and Reality (CCS)

Fantasy Sampler (PHM)

Fahrenheit 451 (ABF, CA, EDG, PHM)

Flowers for Algernon (CA)

Focus on Frederik Pohl (CCS)

Focus on Jack Williamson (CCS)

Foundation: The Psychohistorians (C)

Foundation Trilogy, The (EE)

Fountains of Paradise (C)

Frankenstein (C, CH, EE, PHM)

Frankenstein Unbound (AWR)

From the Hells Beneath the Hells (AWR)

Future Imperfect (EDG)

Future of Science Fiction (CCS)

Genie of Sutton Place, The (GA)

Getting Hooked on Fantasy (GA)

Getting Hooked on Science Fiction (GA)

Gods of Mars (EE)

Gonna Roll the Bones (AWR)

Gravely, Robert Bloch (AWR)

Green Hills of Earth and Gentlemen, Be Seated, The (C)

Green Knowe (GA)

Gun for Dinosaur, A (CCS)

Gwilan's Harp and Intracom (C)

H. G. Wells Filmstrip Series (PHM)

Halt Magic (GA)

Happy Prince, The (PHM)

Happy Prince, The, Star Child, The (FW)

Harlan Ellison Reads Harlan Ellison (AWR)

Haunter of the Dark (C)

Hello Tomorrow (CS)

History of Science Fiction from 1938 to the Present (UK)

Hobbit, The (CA, FW)

Hobbit and the Fellowship of the Ring, The (C)

I, Robot (EE)

Ideas in Science Fiction (UK)

Illustrated Man, The (ABF, C, EE)

Interview with Clifford Simak, An (CCS)

Interview with Poul Anderson, An (CCS)

Introduction to H. P. Lovecraft, An (EE)

Invasion of the Body Snatchers (ABF)

Invisible Man. The (CH, PHM)

Isaac Asimov Cassette Library, The (PHM)

Island (CCS)

Joanna Russ Interpreting her Stories (AWR)

Journey to the Center of the Earth (C, EE, FW)

Jules Verne (CCS)

Kurt Vonnegut: A Self-Portrait (FFH)

Kurt Vonnegut, Jr. (CCS)

Kurt Vonnegut, Jr. Reads Slaughter-house-Five (C)

Last Martian, The (CCS)

Life and Future Times of Jack the Ripper, The (AWR)

Lion, the Witch, and the Wardrobe, The (C, GA)

Literature of Science Fiction Film Lecture Series, The (UK)

Literature of the Supernatural (CH)

Lost Race, The (CCS)

Lord of the Rings, The (C)

Lunch with John Campbell, Jr. (UK)

Man Who Could Work Miracles, The (CCS, PHM)

Man Who Invented Hobbits, The (CCS)

Marionettes, Inc. (CCS)

Martian Chronicles, The (C, CA, EE)

Mayors from Foundation, The (C)

Mimsy Were the Borogroves (C)

Moon of Three Rings (GA)

Mrs. Frisby and the Rats of NIMH (GA)

New Directions in Science Fiction (UK)

Nightfall (CCS)

Nine Billion Names of God, The (C)

1984 (CA, CCS, EDG)

Omega Man, The (ABF)

Ones Who Walk Away from Omelas, The (AWR)

Peter Ibbetson (PHM)

Phantom Tollbooth, The (GA)

Pippi Longstocking (GA)

Plot in Science Fiction (UK)

Poems and Songs of Middle Earth (C)

Power and Science Fiction (CCS)

Prince Caspian (C)

Princess of Mars, A (EE)

R. U. R. (EDG)

Radio's Golden Age of Science Fiction (SB)

Rats in the Walls, The (C)

Ray Bradbury as Philosopher (CCS)

Ray Bradbury Cassette Library, The (PHM)

Ray Bradbury Filmstrip Series, The (PHM)

Reluctant Dragon, The (FW)

Report on the Barnhouse Effect (CCS)

Requiem (CCS)

Rescue Party (BFA)

Robert Silverberg (CCS)

Runaway Robot, The (GA)

Sandworms of Dune (C)

Saucer of Loneliness (CCS)

Scenes from Watership Down (FW)

Sci Fi and Time Fiction (PHM)

Science Fiction (SVE)

Science Fiction: An Introduction (NCTE)

Science Fiction and Fantasy (EAV)

Science Fiction and the Mainstream (UK)

Science Fiction: Familiar, Strange, and Possible (PHM)
Science Fiction Films (UK)
Science Fiction: Its Future (CCS)
Science Fiction: Jules Verne to Ray Bradbury (CH)
Science Fiction, The Early Days (PHM)
Search for Delicious, The (GA)
Silver Chair, The (C)
Simarillion: of Beren and Luthien, The (C)
Simarillion: of The Darkening of Valinor and of the Flight of the Noldor, The (C)
Space Wars (SVE)
Strange Case of Dr. Jekyll and Mr. Hyde, The (C, CH)
Stranger than Science Fiction (UK)
Star, The (C)
Star Surgeon (GA)
Star Trek (NFVC)
Survival Ship and the Shrine of Temptation (C)
Tales of Time and Space (EDG)
Terminal Man, The (ABF)
Theme in Science Fiction (UK)
Theodore Sturgeon Reads (AWR)
THX 1138 (ABF)
Time Machine, The (EDG, EE, PHM)
To the Future (CCS)

Tolkien and Time Fiction (PHM)
Tombs of Atuan, The (MB)
Transit of Earth (C)
Truths of Dune (C)
Tunnel Under the World (CCS)
Twenty Thousand Leagues Under the Sea (C, EE, GA, PHM)
2001: A Space Odyssey (C)
2001 Revisited (CCS)
Ugly Little Boy, The (LCA)
Uncertain Worlds: The Literature of Science Fiction (EDG)
Ursula Le Guin (CCS)
Veldt, The (BFA)
Voyage of the Dawn Treader (C)
War of the Worlds, The (C, EE, PHM, SVE)
Warlord of Mars (EE)
Welcome to the Monkey House (C)
What is Science Fiction? (GA)
White Dragon, The (C)
White Mountains, The (GA)
Wind in the Door, A (MB)
With Folded Hands (CCS)
Wonderful Flight to the Mushroom Planet, The (GA)
Works of H. G. Wells, The (PHM)
Wrinkle in Time, A (CA, MB)
Yonder (C)
Zero Hour (BFA)

Appendices

Douglas R. Justus

DOCTORAL DISSERTATIONS IN
SCIENCE FICTION AND FANTASY, 1970–1979

A large body of scholarship in the science fiction and fantasy fields is to be found in Ph.D. dissertations. The following bibliography consists of contemporary dissertations whose *primary focus* seems to be a science fiction or fantasy subject or writer; dissertations dealing with the Gothic or utopian studies are not included. This listing is intended to update the special section on dissertations compiled by Douglas R. Justus which appears in *A Research Guide to Science Fiction Studies*, ed. Marshall B. Tymn, Roger C. Schlobin and L. W. Currey (Garland Publishing, 1977). I have also eliminated the borderline titles from the earlier list.

The major source for this compilation is *Dissertation Abstracts International*, as of August, 1979. For the convenience of the reader who desires a description of individual dissertations, references to DAI are provided.

Aldridge, Alexandra Bertash. "Scientising Society: The Dystopian Novel and the Scientific World View." University of Michigan, 1978; *DAI, 39* (1978), 3560A.

Alterman, Peter Steven. "A Study of Four Science Fiction Themes and Their Function in Two Contemporary Novels." University of Denver, 1974; *DAI, 35* (1974), 2976A.

Barnes, Myra Jean Edwards. "Linguistics and Languages in Science Fiction-Fantasy." East Texas State University, 1971; *DAI, 32* (1972), 5210A. [Reprinted as *Linguistics and Languages in Science Fiction-Fantasy* by Arno Press, 1974.]

Barraford, Nora Mary MacDonald. "The Secular Supernatural." University of Massachusetts, 1976; *DAI, 37* (1977), 5841A.

Berger, Harold Lynde. "Anti-Utopian Science Fiction of the Mid-Twentieth Century." University of Tennessee, 1970; *DAI, 32* (1971), 420A. [Published as *Science Fiction and the New Dark Age* by Bowling Green University Popular Press, 1976.]

Berman, Ruth Amelia. "Suspending Disbelief: The Development of Fantasy as a Literary Genre in Nineteenth-Century British Fiction as Represented by Four Leading Periodicals: *Edinburgh Review, Blackwood's, Fraser's,* and *Cornhill."* University of Minnesota, 1979; *DAI,* 40 (1979), 865A.

Bray, Mary Katherine. "The Outward Sense." University of Colorado, 1973; *DAI,* 34 (1973), 1893A.

Brock, Eleanor Evelyn Huebner. "Projected Societies in American Science Fiction." Ohio State University, 1976; *DAI,* 37 (1977), 5363A.

Burns, Marjorie Jean. "Victorian Fantasists from Ruskin to Lang: A Study in Ambivalence." University of California at Berkeley, 1978; *DAI,* 40 (1979), 265A.

Carter, Albert Howard, III. "Fantasy in the Work of Italo Calvino." University of Iowa, 1972; *DAI,* 32 (1972), 5223A.

Chalpin, Lila. "Dystopia as Viewed by Social Scientists and Novelists." Boston University School of Education, 1977; *DAI,* 38 (1978), 5383A.

Cohen, John Arthur. "An Examination of Four Key Motifs Found in High Fantasy for Children." Ohio State University, 1975; *DAI,* 36 (1976), 5016A.

Cook, Bruce Randall. "Science, Fiction, and Film: A Study of the Interaction of Science, Science Fiction Literature, and the Growth of Cinema." University of Southern California, 1976; *DAI,* 37 (1977), 6810A.

Cornwell, Charles Landrum. "From Self to the Shire: Studies in Victorian Fantasy." University of Virginia, 1972; *DAI,* 33 (1972), 1163A.

Cullinan, John Thomas. "Anthony Burgess' Novels: A Critical Introduction." Columbia University, 1972, *DAI,* 35 (1975), 7900A.

Dailey, Jennie Ora Marriott. "Modern Science Fiction." University of Utah, 1974; *DAI,* 35 (1974), 1095A.

Dimeo, Richard Steven. "The Mind and Fantasies of Ray Bradbury." University of Utah, 1970; *DAI,* 31 (1971), 3541A.

Dockery, Carl Lee. "The Myth of the Shadow in the Fantasies of Williams, Lewis, and Tolkien." Auburn University, 1975; *DAI,* 36 (1975), 3727A.

Dowie, William John, Jr. "Religious Fiction in a Profane Time: Charles Williams, C. S. Lewis and J. R. R. Tolkien." Brandeis University, 1970; *DAI,* 31 (1970), 2911A.

Edelheit, Steven J. "Dark Prophecies: Essays on Orwell and Technology." Brandeis University, 1975; *DAI,* 36 (1975), 308A.

Estren, Mark James. "Horrors Within and Without: A Psychoanalytic Study of Edgar Allan Poe and Howard Phillips Lovecraft." State University of New York at Buffalo, 1987; *DAI,* 39 (1978), 1565A.

Fisher, Vivian Boyd. "The Search for Reality Through Dreams: A Study of the Work of William Morris from 1856 to 1872." Emory University, 1973; *DAI,* 34 (1973), 767A.

Fleming, Linda A. "The Science Fiction Subculture: Bridge between Two Cultures." University of North Carolina at Chapel Hill, 1976; *DAI,* 38 (1977), 1033A.

Flieger, Verlyn Brown. "Medieval Epic and Romance Motifs in J. R. R. Tolkien's *The Lord of the Rings."* Catholic University of America, 1977; *DAI,* 38 (1978), 4157A.

Foster, Mark Anthony. "Write the Other Way: The Correlation of Style and

Theme in Selected Prose Fiction of Ray Bradbury." Florida State University, 1973; *DAI,* 34 (1973), 1906A.

Fraser, Joseph Hugh, Jr. "An Introduction to the Hermetic Novels of Charles Williams." Texas A&M University, 1975; *DAI,* 36 (1975), 2808A.

Friend, Beverly Oberfield. "The Science Fiction Fan Cult." Northwestern University, 1975; *DAI,* 36 (1976), 4475A.

Garr, Alice Carol. "German Science Fiction: Variations on the Theme of Survival in the Space-Time Continuum." University of North Carolina at Chapel Hill, 1973; *DAI,* 34 (1973), 2623A.

Glad, John Peter. "Russian Soviet Science Fiction and Related Critical Activity." New York University, 1970; *DAI,* 31 (1971), 6055A.

Grebenschikov, George Vladimir. "Ivan Efremov's Theory of Soviet Science Fiction." Michigan State University, 1972; *DAI,* 33 (1972), 753A. [Published as *Ivan Efremov's Theory of Soviet Science Fiction* by Vantage Press, 1978.]

Greenlaw, Marilyn Jean. "A Study of the Impact of Technology on Human Values as Reflected in Modern Science Fiction for Children." Michigan State University, 1970; *DAI,* 31 (1971), 5665A.

Hamilton, Seymore C. "Towards a Human View of the Future: A Study of American Science Fiction Short Stories in Popular Magazines 1926-1960." Queens College [Canada] , 1971.

Harms, Jeanne McLain. "Children's Responses to Fantasy in Relation to Their Stages of Intellectual Development." Ohio State University, 1972; *DAI,* 33 (1973), 6234A.

Hein, Rolland Neal. "Faith and Fiction: A Study of the Effects of Religious Convictions in the Adult Fantasies and Novels of George MacDonald." Purdue University, 1970; *DAI,* 32 (1971), 919A.

Herwald, Michelle Hope. "Amazing Artifacts: Cultural Analysis of *Amazing Stories* 1926-1938." University of Michigan, 1977; *DAI,* 38 (1978), 6726A.

Hines, Joyce Rose. "Getting Home: A Study of Fantasy and the Spiritual Journey in the Christian Supernatural Novels of Charles Williams and George MacDonald." City University of New York, 1972; *DAI,* 33 (1972), 755A.

Jackson, Donald George. "The Changing Myth of Frankenstein: A Historical Analysis of the Interactions of a Myth, Technology, and Society." University of Texas at Austin, 1976; *DAI,* 37 (1977), 4664A.

Jacobs, James Swensen. "Lloyd Alexander: A Critical Biography." University of Georgia, 1978; *DAI,* 39 (1978), 3559A.

Jones, Kellie Frances Corlen. "A Pentaperceptual Analysis of Social and Philosophical Commentary in *A Wrinkle in Time* by Madeleine L Engle." University of Mississippi, 1977; *DAI,* 38 (1978), 7325A.

Keller, Edwin Roy, Jr. "Disintegrated Man: A Study of Alienation in Selected Twentieth-Century Anti-Utopian Novels." University of Arkansas, 1977; *DAI,* 38 (1977), 2776A.

Kellman, Martin Hirsh. "Arthur and Others: The Literary Career of T. H. White." University of Pennsylvania, 1973; *DAI,* 34 (1973), 1917A.

Kirlin, Thomas Michael. "H. G. Wells and the Geometric Imagination: A Study of Three Science Fiction Novels in the Nineties." University of Iowa, 1974; *DAI,* 35 (1974), 2276A.

Lang, Leonard Alan. "The Impact of Classical Science on American Literature: The Creation of an Epic American Hero in Science Fiction." University of Minnesota, 1978, *DAI,* 39 (1978), 3665A.

Larson, Ross Frank. "Fantasy and Imagination in the Mexican Narrative." University of Toronto, 1973; *DAI,* 35 (1974), 1108A. [Published as *Fantasy and Imagination in the Mexican Narrative* by Center for Latin American Studies, Arizona State University, 1977.]

Leitenberg, Barbara. "The New Utopias." Indiana University, 1975; *DAI,* 36 (1976), 5282A.

Letson, Russell Francis, Jr. "The Approaches to Mystery: The Fantasies of Arthur Machen and Algernon Blackwood." Southern Illinois University, 1975; *DAI,* 36 (1976), 8047A.

McGuire, Patrick Llewellyn. "Red Stars: Political Aspects of Soviet Science Fiction." Princeton University, 1977; *DAI,* 38 (1977), 1626A.

Mann, Nancy Elizabeth Dawson. "George MacDonald and the Tradition of Victorian Fantasy." Stanford University, 1973; *DAI,* 34 (1973), 3414A.

Mathews, Richard Barrett. "The Fantasy of Secular Redemption." University of Virginia, 1973; *DAI,* 34 (1974), 4211A.

Mazer, Charles Litten. "Orwell's Oceania, Zamyatin's United State, and Levin's Unicomp Earth: Socially Constructed Anti-Utopias." Texas Technical University, 1975; *DAI,* 37 (1976), 957A.

McInnis, John Lawson, III. "H. P. Lovecraft: The Maze and The Minotaur." Louisiana State University, 1975; *DAI,* 36 (1975), 2207A.

Mobley, Jane. "Magic Is Alive: A Study of Contemporary Fantasy Fiction." University of Kansas, 1974; *DAI,* 36 (1975), 881A.

Mogen, David Lee. "Frontier Themes in Science Fiction." University of Colorado at Boulder, 1977; *DAI,* 38 (1977), 2792A.

Mundhenk, Rosemary Karmlich. "Another World: The Mode of Fantasy in the Fiction of Selected Nineteenth-Century Writers." University of California at Los Angeles, 1972; *DAI,* 33 (1973), 5688A.

Nesteby, James Ronald. "The Tarzan Series of Edgar Rice Burroughs: Lost Races and Racism in American Popular Culture." Bowling Green State University, 1978; *DAI,* 39 (1979), 4347A.

Neumann, Bonnie Rayford. "Mary Shelley." University of New Mexico, 1972; *DAI,* 33 (1973), 5689A.

Orth, Michael Paul. "Tarzan's Revenge: A Literary Biography of Edgar Rice Burroughs." Claremont Graduate School, 1974; *DAI,* 35 (1974), 3002A.

Ozolins, Aija. "The Novels of Mary Shelley: From *Frankenstein* to *Falkner.*" University of Maryland, 1972; *DAI,* 33 (1972), 2389A.

Parker, Helen Nethercutt. "Biological Themes in Modern Science Fiction." Duke University, 1977; *DAI,* 38 (1978), 7347A.

Pechefsky, Howard S. "The Fantasy Novels of John Cowper Powys." New York University, 1971; *DAI,* 32 (1972), 4014A.

Petty, Anne Cotton. "The Creative Mythology of J. R. R. Tolkien: A Study of the Mythic Impulse." Florida State University, 1972; *DAI,* 33 (1972), 2390A.

Pierson, Clayton Jay. "Toward Spiritual Fulfillment: A Study of the Fantasy World of George MacDonald." University of Maryland, 1978; *DAI,* 39 (1979), 6148A.

Popescu, Constantin C. "Fantastic Elements in Nineteenth-Century American Prose." University of Wisconsin at Milwaukee, 1973; *DAI,* 34 (1974), 7718A.

Pratter, Frederick Earl. "The Uses of Utopia: An Analysis of American Speculative Fiction, 1880–1960." University of Iowa, 1973; *DAI,* 35 (1974), 468A.

Reddy, Albert Francis. "The Else Unspeakable: An Introduction to the Fiction of C. S. Lewis." University of Massachusetts, 1972; *DAI,* 33 (1972), 2949A.

Rogers, Deborah Champion Webster. "The Fictitious Characters of C. S. Lewis and J. R. R. Tolkien in Relation to Their Medieval Sources." University of Wisconsin, 1972; *DAI,* 34 (1973), 334A.

Rossi, Lee Donald. "The Politics of Fantasy: C. S. Lewis and J. R. R. Tolkien." Cornell University, 1972; *DAI,* 33 (1973), 5195A.

Rothfork, John. "New Wave Science Fiction Considered as a Popular Religious Phenomenon: A Definition and an Example." University of New Mexico, 1973; *DAI,* 35 (1974), 1670A.

Sadler, Frank Orin. "Science and Fiction in the Science-Fiction Novel." University of Florida, 1974; *DAI,* 36 (1975), 883A.

St. Clair, Gloria Anne Strange Slaughter. "Studies in the Sources of J. R. R. Tolkien's *The Lord of the Rings.*" University of Oklahoma, 1970; *DAI,* 30 (1970), 5001A.

Segal, Phillip D. "Imaginative Literature and the Atomic Bomb: An Analysis of Representative Novels, Plays, and Films from 1945 to 1972." Yeshiva University, 1973, *DAI,* 34 (1974), 5993A.

Senf, Carol Ann. "Daughters of Lilith: An Analysis of the Vampire Motif in Nineteenth-Century English Literature." State University of New York at Buffalo, 1979; *DAI,* 39 (1979), 7363A.

Siciliano, Sam Joseph. "The Fictional Universe in Four Science Fiction Novels: Anthony Burgess' *A Clockwork Orange,* Ursula Le Guin's *The Word for World Is Forest,* Walter Miller's *A Canticle for Leibowitz,* and Roger Zelazny's *Creatures of Light and Darkness.*" University of Iowa, 1975; *DAI,* 36 (1976), 8053A.

Sprague, Kurth. "From a Troubled Heart: T. H. White & Women in *The Once and Future King.*" University of Texas at Austin, 1978; *DAI,* 39 (1978), 2302A.

Swann, William Kirk, III. "The Techniques of Softening E. T. A. Hoffmann's Presentation of the Fantastic." Yale University, 1971; *DAI,* 32 (1972), 7009A.

Tropp, Martin. "Mary Shelley's Monster: A Study of *Frankenstein.*" Boston University Graduate School, 1973; *DAI,* 34 (1973), 1871A. [Published as *Mary Shelley's Monster* by Houghton Mifflin, 1976.]

Urgang, Gunnar. "Shadows of Heaven: The Use of Fantasy in the Fiction of C. S. Lewis, Charles Williams, and J. R. R. Tolkien." University of Chicago, 1970.

Vasbinder, Samuel Holmes. "Scientific Attitudes in Mary Shelley's *Frankenstein*: Newtonian Monism as a Basis for the Novel." Kent State University, 1976; *DAI*, 37 (1976), 2842A.

Walker, Steven Charles. "Narrative Technique in the Fiction of J. R. R. Tolkien." Harvard University, 1973.

Warrick, Patricia Scott. "The Cybernetic Imagination in Science Fiction." University of Wisconsin at Milwaukee, 1977; *DAI*, 40 (1979), 253A.

Marshall B. Tymn

SCIENCE FICTION ORGANIZATIONS AND SOCIETIES

One of the distinguishing characteristics of the science fiction field is the tendency of its readers to organize themselves into special interest groups. Besides the hundreds of conventions that occur each year which are attended by thousands of fans, writers, artists, collectors, scholars, and teachers, many of the readers belong to scores of clubs, societies, and organizations. It is my intention here to single out some of the major, active organizations in the United States and in Great Britain.

ACADEMY OF SCIENCE FICTION, FANTASY AND HORROR FILMS

Founded in 1972, the Academy is an organization consisting of individuals devoted to presenting awards of merit and recognition for science fiction, fantasy, and horror films. Publications: *Popcorn* (house organ); awards: The Golden Scroll; information: 334 West 54th St., Los Angeles, CA 90037.

BRITISH FANTASY SOCIETY

Established in 1971, the British Fantasy Society is devoted to the study and discussion of all forms of fantasy in literature, films, and art. Publications: *British Fantasy Society Bulletin* (house organ) and *Dark Horizons*, a fantasy magazine; awards: British Fantasy Award; information: 447a, Porter Ave., Dagenham, Essex, RM9 4ND, UK.

BRITISH SCIENCE FICTION ASSOCIATION

Established in 1958 to promote science fiction activities and to improve the genre's image. Publications: *Matrix* (house organ), *Vector,* and *Tangent*, science fiction magazines; awards: BSFA Award; information: 245 Rosalind St., Ashington, Northumberland, NE63 9AZ, UK.

JAMES BRANCH CABELL SOCIETY

Organized in 1965 to facilitate the exchange of ideas and information on the writings of James Branch Cabell. Publications: *Kalkai: Studies in James Branch*

Cabell, a journal; awards: none; information: 665 Lotus Ave., Oradell, NJ 07649.

AUGUST DERLETH SOCIETY

Organized in 1977 to bring together those persons interested in the works of August Derleth and his circle. Publications: *August Derleth Society Newsletter* (house organ); awards: none; information: 418 East Main St., Sparta, WI 54656.

COUNT DRACULA SOCIETY

Formed in 1962, the Count Dracula Society is devoted to the serious study of horror films and Gothic literature. Publications: *Count Dracula Society Quarterly* (house organ); awards: Ann Radcliffe Award; information: 334 West 54th St., Los Angeles, CA 90037.

FANTASY ASSOCIATION

Affiliated with the British Fantasy Society and the Mythopoetic Society, the Fantasy Association was founded in 1973 to foster communication and the serious exchange of ideas about fantasy literature. Publications: *Fantasiae* (house organ) and *The Eildon Tree,* a journal; awards: none; information: Box 24560, Los Angeles, CA 90024.

FIRST FANDOM

Founded in 1959 "to stimulate and revive interest among older fans." Members must prove "more than a reading interest" in science fiction before 1938. Publications: *Newsletter of First Fandom* and *First Fandom Magazine* (house organs); awards: First Fandom Hall of Fame; information: 3853 St. Johns Terrace, Cincinnati, OH 45236.

FRIENDS OF DARKOVER

Formed in 1975, Friends of Darkover is an organization of persons sharing an interest in Marion Zimmer Bradley's Darkover series of novels. Publications: *Darkover Newsletter* (house organ) and *Starstone,* a magazine; awards: none; information: Friends of Darkover, Box 72, Berkeley, CA 94701.

HYBORIAN LEGION

Organized in 1956, the group is devoted to the study of *Conan,* Robert E. Howard, and heroic fantasy. Publications: *Amra,* a literary magazine, and *Sardonic Worlds,* a fanzine; awards: none; information: Box 8243, Philadelphia, PA 19101.

INSTRUCTORS OF SCIENCE FICTION IN HIGHER EDUCATION

ISFHE is an organization of teachers of science fiction in junior colleges, colleges, and universities. Founded in 1973 primarily to present awards for science fiction writings, which, from the point of view of instructors, seem to be very distinguished works. Publications: none; awards: Jupiter Award; information: English Department, Eastern Michigan University, Ypsilanti, MI 48197.

LOS ANGELES SCIENCE FANTASY SOCIETY

Organized in 1934 as a result of the creation of the Science Fiction League by *Wonder Stories,* the LASFS is the oldest science fiction club in existence. Publications: *De Profundis* (house organ); awards: Forry Award; information: 11513 Burbank Blvd., North Hollywood, CA 91601.

MYTHOPOETIC SOCIETY

Formed in 1967, the society is devoted to the study of myth and fantasy literature, especially the works of J. R. R. Tolkien, C. S. Lewis, and Charles Williams. Publications: *Mythprint* (house organ) and *Mythlore,* a fantasy magazine; awards: none; information: Box 4671, Whittier, CA 90607.

NATIONAL FANTASY FAN FEDERATION

Established in 1941 for the purpose of disseminating information on fan activities and publications, NFFF provides needed services to those new to fandom through its information bureau and in-house publications. Publications: *The National Fantasy Fan* and *Tightbeam* (house organs); awards: none; information: Janie Lamb, Rt. 1, Box 364, Heiskell, TN 37754.

NEW ENGLAND SCIENCE FICTION ASSOCIATION

Organized in 1967 as a serious fan group which has since established itself as a publisher of magazine reference works and convention proceedings. Publications: *Instant Message* (house organ), *Proper Boskonian,* a fan magazine, and the following NESFA Press titles: *The NESFA Index to the Science Fiction Magazines and Original Anthologies* (annual), Boskone books (works by and in tribute to guests of honor at annual Boskones), and various volumes of Worldcon proceedings; awards: none; information: Box G, MIT Branch Post Office, Cambridge, MA 02139.

NEW YORK C. S. LEWIS SOCIETY

Founded in 1969 "for the purpose of bringing together those who have a special enthusiasm for C. S. Lewis." Publications: *CSL: The Bulletin of the New York C. S. Lewis Society,* a journal; awards: none; information: 32 Park, Ossining, NY 10562.

SCIENCE FICTION FOUNDATION

Founded in England in 1971 as a subject discipline within the North East London Polytechnic. The Foundation promotes the use of science fiction in education, and has research facilities for scholars and students. Publications: *Foundation: The Review of Science Fiction,* a journal; awards: James Blish Award; information: North East London Polytechnic, Longbridge Road, Dagenham, Essex, RM8 2AS, UK.

SCIENCE FICTION ORAL HISTORY ASSOCIATION

Organized in 1977 by science fiction writer Lloyd Biggle, Jr. and a group of

Michigan fans, the association is concerned with the recording of important events in the science fiction field and preserving the recordings in official repositories where they will be available for study. Publications: *S.F.O.H.A.* (house organ); awards: none; information: 117 Goodison Hall, Eastern Michigan University, Ypsilanti, MI 48197.

SCIENCE FICTION RESEARCH ASSOCIATION

Founded in 1970 by Professor Thomas D. Clareson and a group of academics interested in promoting the study of science fiction and fantasy. Its programs seek to encourage and develop new scholarship in the field and to make both published and unpublished materials more widely available to students, teachers, and scholars. Publications: *SFRA Newsletter* (house organ); awards: Pilgrim Award; information: Marshall Tymn, English Department, Eastern Michigan University, Ypsilanti, MI 48197.

SCIENCE FICTION WRITERS OF AMERICA

Organized in 1965 by Damon Knight and a group of seventy-five charter members, SFWA is a professional organization of independent writers in the science fiction and fantasy fields. Publications: *Bulletin of the Science Fiction Writers of America* and *SFWA Forum* (house organs); awards: Nebula Award; information: David F. Bischoff, 2004 Erie St., No. 2, Adelphi, MD 20783.

TOLKIEN SOCIETY

Formed in 1969 "to provide a focal point for the many people interested in the works of J. R. R. Tolkien." Publications: *Amon Hen* (house organ) and *Mallorn*, a fantasy magazine; awards: none; information: 9 Kingston Rd., Ilford, Essex, UK.

H. G. WELLS SOCIETY

Founded in 1960 to promote active interest in the life and works of Herbert George Wells. Publications: *Newsletter of the H. G. Wells Society* (house organ); awards: H. G. Wells Award; information: 24 Wellin Lane, Edwalton, Nottingham, UK.

WORLD SF

Organized at the First World Science Fiction Writer's Conference in Dublin in 1976, World SF is a means for professionals in the field to communicate with their colleagues worldwide. Publications: *World SF Newsletter* (house organ); awards: none; information: Elizabeth Anne Hull, William Rainey Harper College, Palatine, IL 60067.

WORLD SCIENCE FICTION SOCIETY

Convened at World Science Fiction Conventions, the society has no formal existence except at these annual gatherings. Governs the Hugo Award rules and the selection of Worldcon sites. Membership is formed from members of current and previous year's Worldcons. Information: annual World Science Fiction Convention committee (various locations annually).

Marshall Tymn

DIRECTORY OF SPECIALTY PUBLISHERS

Although most of the science fiction published today comes from major hardcover and paperback houses such as Doubleday, Harper & Row, St. Martin's, Ballantine, Ace, DAW, and others, a significant number of titles are released each year by a few specialty presses. These small publishers, usually fans with an abiding interest in the SF field, produce beautiful and expensive books, often highly illustrated, in limited editions. These quality collector's editions supply a demand not fully met by the general publishers. Specialty publishers have also supplied the need for research tools by issuing reference works and critical studies for the scholar and researcher. The following listing consists of the major speciality presses active today; volume of output is not a criterion for selection, as some publishers have produced only one or two volumes.

Advent Publishers
Box A3228
Chicago, IL 60690
(criticism, reference)

Algol Press
Box 4175
New York, NY 10017
(criticism)

Ariel Books
845 Third Ave.
New York, NY 10022
(fiction, art)

Arkham House
Sauk City, WI 53583
(fiction, criticism)

The Borgo Press
Box 2845
San Bernardino, CA 92406
(criticism)

Bran's Head Books
91 Wimborne Ave.
Hayes, Middlesex, U.K.
(fiction, criticism)

Burning Bush Press
Box 7708
Newark, DE 19711
(fiction)

Carcosa House
Box 1064
Chapel Hill, NC 27514
(fiction)

Centaur Books
799 Broadway
New York, NY 10003
(fiction)

Russ Cochran
Box 437
West Plains, MO 65775
(fiction)

Gerry de la Ree
7 Cedarwood Lane
Saddle River, NJ 07458
(fiction, criticism, art)

Del Rey Books
201 East 50th St.
New York, NY 10022
(fiction, criticism, reference)

Howard DeVore
4705 Weddel St.
Dearborn Heights, MI 48125
(reference)

Dragon Press
Elizabethtown, NY 12932
(criticism, reference)

FAX Collector's Editions, Inc.
Box 851
Mercer Island, WA 98040
(fiction, criticism, reference)

Ferret Fantasy Ltd.
27 Beechcroft Rd.
Upper Tooting
London SW17, U. K.
(fiction, reference)

Firebell Books
Box 804
Glen Rock, NJ 07452
(reference)

Donald M. Grant
West Kingston, RI 02892
(fiction, reference)

Gregg Press
70 Lincoln St.
Boston, MA 02111
(reprints, reference)

Heritage Press, Inc.
Box 721
Forest Park, GA 30050
(fiction)

House of Collectibles, Inc.
773 Kirkman Rd. No. 120
Orlando, FL 32811

JDS Books
Box 67 MCS
Dayton, OH 45402
(fiction, reference)

Luna Publications
655 Orchard St.
Oradell, NJ 07649

Necronomicon Press
101 Lockwood St.
West Warrick, RI 02893
(fiction, criticism)

NESFA Press
Box G, MIT Branch
Cambridge, MA 02139
(fiction, criticism, reference)

Newcastle Publishing Co.
13419 Saticoy St.
North Hollywood, CA 91605
(fiction)

Norstrilia Press
Box 5195AA
Melbourne, Victoria 3001
Australia

Owlswick Press
Box 8243
Philadelphia, PA 19101
(fiction, criticism)

P. D. A. Enterprises
Box 8010
New Orleans, LA 70182

Pendragon Press
Box 14834
Portland, OR 92214
(fiction, criticism)

Pennyfarthing Press
2000 Center No. 1226
Berkeley, CA 94704
(fiction, reference)

Phantasia Press
13101 Lincoln
Huntington Woods, MI 48070
(fiction)

Purple Mouth Press
713 Paul St.
Newport News, VA 23605
(fiction, reference)

Purple Unicorn Press
4532 London Rd.
Duluth, MN 55804
(reference)

Science Fiction Book Club
245 Park Ave.
New York, NY 10017
(fiction, reference, art)

Silver Scarab Press
500 Wellesley S. E.
Albuquerque, NM 87106
(criticism)

Starblaze Editions
253 W. Bute St.
Norfolk, VA 23510
(fiction, art)

Starlog Press
475 Park Ave. South
New York, NY 10016
(gen. comment, art)

Starmont House
Box 851
Mercer Island, WA 98040
(criticism, reference, art folios)

Oswald Train
Box 1891
Philadelphia, PA 19105
(fiction)

Underwood/Miller
239 North 4th St.
Columbia, PA 17512
(fiction, reference)

Robert Weinberg
15145 Oxford Dr.
Oak Forest, IL 60452
(fiction)

Weirdbook Press
Box 35, Amherst Br.
Buffalo, NY 14226
(fiction)

Whispers Press
Box 1492–W
Azalea St.
Brown Hills, NJ 08015
(fiction)

Roger C. Schlobin

DEFINITIONS OF SCIENCE FICTION AND FANTASY

When Hugo Gernsback first gave birth to the term "scientifiction" over a half-century ago, he spawned not only the name of a literary genre but a veritable dynasty of "definers." It seems every author or critic of science fiction has attempted to sythesize the essential nature of the genre. The principles for selecting the definitions here from the seemingly infinite number available have been to represent as much variety as possible and to present the opinions of major authors and scholars in the field. Such a selection should allow the critic, teacher, librarian, and fan to become aware of the varied approaches to the nature of science fiction and to select those best suited to their needs. Since all definitions quoted here are taken out of context, once the reader's curiosity is piqued, it is strongly recommended that the original source be consulted.

ABERNETHY, FRANCIS E. "The Case For and Against Sci-Fi." *Clearing House,* April 1960, p. 474.

. . . just as science fiction is the manifestation of a rather noble and Faustian desire to know infinity, so it is also a symptom of a neurotic tendency to escape conditions on this earth at this time rather than to try to improve them.

ALDISS, BRIAN W. *Billion Year Spree: The True History of Science Fiction.* Garden City, NY: Doubleday, 1973, p. 8; rpt. New York: Schocken Books, 1974, p. 8.

Science fiction is the search for a definition of man and his status in the universe which will stand in our advanced but confused state of knowledge (science), and is characteristically cast in the Gothic or post-Gothic mould.

ALLEN, DICK. "Introduction." In *Science Fiction: The Future.* Ed. Dick Allen. New York: Harcourt Brace Jovanovich, 1971, p. 3.

Is it any wonder that a new generation has rediscovered science fiction, rediscovered a form of literature that argues through its intuitive force that the individual can shape and change and influence and triumph; that man can eliminate both war and poverty; that miracles *are* possible; that love, if given a chance, can become the main driving force of human relationships?

AMIS, KINGSLEY. *New Maps of Hell: A Survey of Science Fiction.* New York: Harcourt, Brace, 1960, pp. 18, 26; rpt. New York: Arno Press, 1975, pp. 18, 26.

> . . . science fiction is that class of prose narrative treating of a situation that could not arise in the world we know, but which is hypothesised on the basis of some innovation in science or technology, or pseudo-science or pseudo-technology, whether human or extraterrestial in origin.

> . . . science fiction presents with verisimilitude the human effects of spectacular changes in our environment, changes either deliberately or involuntarily suffered.

ASIMOV, ISAAC. "Social Science Fiction." In *Modern Science Fiction: Its Meaning and Its Future.* Ed. Reginald Bretnor. New York: Coward-McCann, 1953, pp. 158–59, 167; rpt in *Turning Points: Essays on the Art of Science Fiction.* Ed. Damon Knight. New York: Harper & Row, 1977, pp. 29, 30, 37.

> Science Fiction is that branch of literature which is concerned with the impact of scientific advance upon human beings. . . .

> . . . I would like to say that my definition applies . . . to . . . "social science fiction."

> Science Fiction is that branch of literature which deals with a fictitious society, differing from our own chiefly in the nature or extent of its technological development.

ASIMOV, ISAAC. "Why Read Science Fiction?" In *3000 Years of Fantasy and Science Fiction.* Ed. L. Sprague de Camp and Catherine Crook de Camp. New York: Lothrop, Lee & Shephard, 1972, p. 10.

> Modern science fiction is the only form of literature that consistently considers the nature of the changes that face us, the possible consequences, and the possible solutions.

BAILEY, J. O. *Pilgrims Through Space and Time: Trends and Patterns in Scientific and Utopian Fiction.* New York: Argus Books, 1947, p. 10; rpt. Westport, CT: Greenwood Press, 1972, p. 10.

> A piece of scientific fiction is a narrative of an imaginary invention or discovery in the natural sciences and consequent adventures and experiences.

BENFORD, GREGORY. " 'Definition.' " In *Science Fiction: The Academic Awakening.* Ed. Willis E. McNelly. Shreveport, LA: College English Association, 1974, p. 57.

SF is a controlled way to think and dream about the future. An integration of the mood and attitude of science (the objective universe) with the fears and hopes that spring from the unconscious. Anything that turns you and your social context, the social you, inside out. Nightmares and visions, always outlined by the barely possible.

BOVA, BEN. "The Role of Science Fiction." In *Science Fiction, Today and Tomorrow.* New York: Harper & Row, 1974, pp. 4–5, 11, 13; rpt. Baltimore: Penguin Books, 1975, pp. 4–5, 11, 13.

They [science fiction writers] try to show the many possible futures that lie open to us.

Science fiction, when it's at its best, serves the function of a modern mythology.

. . . science fiction is the literature of change.

BOYD, JOHN. " 'Definition' " and "What It Means to Write SF." In *Science Fiction: The Academic Awakening.* Ed. Willis E. McNelly. Shreveport, LA: College English Association, 1974, pp. 14, 44.

Science fiction is story-telling, usually imaginative as distinct from realistic fiction, which poses the effects of current or extrapolated scientific discoveries, or a single discovery, on the behavior of individuals of society.

Mainstream fiction gives imaginative reality to probable events within a framework of the historical past or present; science fiction gives reality to possible events, usually in the future, extrapolated from present scientific knowledge or existing cultural and social trends. Both genres ordinarily observe the unities and adhere to a cause-and-effect schema.

BRADBURY, RAY. " 'Definition.' " In *Science Fiction: The Academic Awakening.* Ed. Willis E. McNelly. Shreveport, LA: College English Association, 1974, p. 17.

Science fiction is really sociological studies of the future, things that the writer believes are going to happen by putting two and two together.

BRETNOR, REGINALD. "Science Fiction in the Age of Space." In *Science Fiction, Today and Tomorrow.* Ed. Reginald Bretnor. New York: Harper & Row, 1974, p. 150; rpt. Baltimore: Penguin Books, 1975, p. 150.

Science Fiction: fiction based on rational speculation regarding the human experience of science and its resultant technologies.

BRETNOR, REGINALD. "SF: The Challenge to the Writer." In *The Craft of Science Fiction.* Ed. Reginald Bretnor. New York: Harper & Row, 1976, p. 4.

. . . science fiction and science fantasy, in our own century, emerged as a separate literary stream: to try to cope in fiction—in the imaginations of its authors and its readers—not just with life as it had "always" been but with the world as it promises, or threatens, to become tomorrow, next week, next year, or as it may become if new and unanticipated doors into knowledge or into other worlds suddenly are opened by men using the scientific method and its technologies.

BRUNNER, JOHN. "Science Fiction and the Larger Lunacy." In *Science Fiction at Large: A Collection of Essays, by Various Hands, About the Interface Between Science Fiction and Reality*. Ed. Peter Nicholls. New York: Harper & Row, 1976, p. 103.

At its best, SF is the medium in which our miserable certainty that tomorrow will be different from today in ways we can't predict, can be transmuted to a sense of excitement and anticipation, occasionally evolving into awe. Poised between intransigent scepticism and uncritical credulity, it is *par excellence* the literature of the open mind.

CAMPBELL, JOHN W., JR. "The Place of Science Fiction." In *Modern Science Fiction: Its Meaning and Its Future*. Ed. Reginald Bretnor. New York: Coward-McCann, 1953, pp. 12–13.

. . . science fiction is the literature of speculation as to what changes may come, and which changes will be improvements, which destructive, which merely pointless.

CANARY, ROBERT H. "Science Fiction as Fictive History." In *Many Futures, Many Worlds: Theme and Form in Science Fiction*. Ed. Thomas D. Clareson. Kent, OH: Kent State University Press, 1977, p. 166.

Science fiction's implicit claim to operate by the same rules as historical reality means that it is inevitably speculating about the nature of those rules, implying that some are accidents of our history and subject to change, while others are relatively immutable "laws of history" and "facts of nature."

CLARESON, THOMAS D. "The Other Side of Realism." In *SF: The Other Side of Realism: Essays on Modern Fantasy and Science Fiction*. Ed. Thomas D. Clareson. Bowling Green, OH: Bowling Green University Popular Press, 1971, p. 25.

. . . science fiction, with its freedom to create unearthly worlds as well as to explore and distort time and space, may give new vitality to the dream of human experience.

CLARKE, ARTHUR C. "Science Fiction: Preparation for the Age of Space." In *Modern Science Fiction: Its Meaning and Its Future*. Ed. Reginald Bretnor. New York: Coward-McCann, 1953, p. 198.

It can hardly be doubted that, of all the themes used in science fiction, that of space is by far the most prominent. Indeed to the public the two ideas are now practically synonymous. . . .

CLEAVER, DIANE. " 'Definition.' " In *Science Fiction: The Academic Awakening.* Ed. Willis E. McNelly. Shreveport, LA: College English Association,
1974, p. 53.

More than prophetic fiction science fiction is an extrapolative fiction.
Future or past it basically constructs a parallel world, a world aligned in
the mind with what we are now. Its concern is man and his reaction to any
given environment. Centauri IV or Kalamazoo, technological or pastoral,
human or alien, inner or outer space—science fiction is the immediate
future.

CLEMENT, HAL. "The Creation of Imaginary Beings." In *Science Fiction,
Today and Tomorrow.* Ed. Reginald Bretnor. New York: Harper & Row,
1974, p. 260; rpt. Baltimore: Penguin Books, 1975, p. 260.

... if we travel to Mars in a story, the vehicle must operate either along
physical laws we currently think we know, or at least on more or less
convincing extrapolations of those laws.

CONKLIN, GROFF. "What is Good Science Fiction?" *Junior Libraries* [*Library
Journal*] , 15 April 1958, p. 16.

The best definition of science fiction is that it consists of stories in which
one or more definitely scientific notion or theory or actual discovery is
extrapolated, played with, embroided on, in a non-logical, or fictional
sense, and thus carried beyond the realm of the immediately possible in
an effort to see how much fun the author and reader can have exploring
the imaginary outer reaches of a given idea's potentialities.

DE CAMP, L. SPRAGUE. "Imaginative Fiction and Creative Imagination." In
Modern Science Fiction: Its Meaning and Its Future. Ed. Reginald Bretnor. New York: Coward-McCann, 1953, pp. 153–54.

Therefore, no matter how the world makes out in the next few centuries,
a large class of readers at least will not be too surprised at anything. They
will have been through it all before in fictional form, and will not be too
paralyzed with astonishment to try to cope with contingencies as they
arise.

DEL REY, LESTER as quoted by Thomas D. Clareson. "The Other Side of
Realism." In *SF: The Other Side of Realism: Essays on Modern Fantasy
and Science Fiction.* Ed. Thomas D. Clareson. Bowling Green, OH: Bowling Green University Popular Press, 1971, p. 1.

... science fiction "is the myth-making principle of human nature today."

DICKSON, GORDON R. "Plausibility in Science Fiction." In *Science Fiction,
Today and Tomorrow.* Ed. Reginald Bretnor. New York: Harper & Row,
1974, p. 297; rpt. Baltimore: Penguin Books, 1975, p. 297.

In short, the straw of a manufactured realism with which the sf writer
makes his particular literary bricks must be entirely convincing to the
reader in its own right, or the whole story will lose its power to convince.

FIEDLER, LESLIE A. "Introduction." In *In Dreams Awake: A Historical-Critical Anthology of Science Fiction.* Ed. Leslie A. Fiedler. New York: Dell, 1975, p. 13.

In this sense, all authentic writers of science fiction make prophecies which are *necessarily* fulfilled, subjectively rather than objectively.

FRANKLIN, BRUCE. "Foreword to J. G. Ballard's 'The Subliminal Man.' " In *SF: The Other Side of Realism: Essays on Modern Fantasy and Science Fiction.* Ed. Thomas D. Clareson. Bowling Green, OH: Bowling Green University Popular Press, 1971, p. 199.

We talk a lot about science fiction as extrapolation, but in fact most science fiction does not extrapolate seriously. Instead it takes a willful, often whimsical, leap into a world spun out of the fantasy of the author. . . .

FRANKLIN, H. BRUCE. *Future Perfect: American Science Fiction of the Nineteenth Century.* Rev. ed. London and New York: Oxford University Press, 1978, p. vii.

In fact, one good working definition of science fiction may be the literature which, growing with science and technology, evaluates it and relates it meaningfully to the rest of human existence.

FREDERICKS, S. C. "Revivals of Ancient Mythologies in Current Science Fiction and Fantasy." In *Many Futures, Many Worlds: Theme and Form in Science Fiction.* Ed. Thomas D. Clareson. Kent, OH: Kent State University Press, 1977, p. 64.

. . . because of the undisguised excellence of every one of these [science fiction and fantasy] books they maintain their dual nature to perfection, balanced between the futuristic themes of science fiction—space and time travel, technological advances not yet available to the present world, and the implications of *change in general*—and the ancient, perhaps even "archetypal," interests of mankind in mythological themes like the loss of paradise, the descent of the gods to men, the redemption of fallen mankind, and life after death.

FRYE, NORTHROP. *The Anatomy of Criticism: Four Essays.* Princeton, NJ: Princeton University Press, 1971, p. 49.

Science fiction frequently tries to imagine what life would be like on a plane as far above us as we are above savagery; its setting is often of a kind that appears to us technologically miraculous. It is thus a mode of romance with a strong tendency to myth.

GADDIS, VINCENT H. " 'Definition.' " In *Science Fiction: The Academic Awakening.* Ed. Willis E. McNelly. Shreveport, LA: College English Association, 1974, p. 57.

Science fiction expresses the dreams that, varied and modified, later become the visions and then the realities in scientific progress. Unlike fantasy, they present probabilities in their basic structure and create a reservoir of imaginative thought that sometimes can inspire more practical thinking.

GERNSBACK, HUGO in *Amazing Stories* as quoted by Fielder, Leslie A. "Introduction." In *In Dreams Awake: A Historical-Critical Anthology of Science Fiction.* Ed. Leslie A. Fielder. New York: Dell, 1975, p. 11.

By "scientifiction," . . . I mean the Jules Verne, H. G. Wells, and Edgar Allan Poe type of story—a charming romance intermingled with scientific fact and prophetic vision.

GODSHALK, WILLIAM L. "Alfred Bester: Science Fiction or Fantasy?" *Extrapolation,* 16 (1975), 150.

Realistic fantasy is science fiction. It is based on extrapolation, and the author attempts to project a future world. However, even though the author wishes to give us a realistic projection, his work is basically fantasy; it is not a work about the "real" world as we know it and experience it.

GUNN, JAMES. *Alternate Worlds: The Illustrated History of Science Fiction.* Englewood Cliffs, NJ: Prentice-Hall, 1975, p. 32.

"In science fiction a fantastic event or development is considered rationally."

GUNN, JAMES. "Science Fiction and the Mainstream." In *Science Fiction, Today and Tomorrow.* Ed. Reginald Bretnor. New York: Harper & Row, 1974, pp. 192–93; rpt. Baltimore: Penguin Books, 1975, pp. 192–93.

Pride in humanity has been one of science fiction's most significant attitudes . . . but pride not so much in the qualities a creature must have to survive . . . but pride in the qualities a creature that must survive can develop and sustain in spite of unrelenting adversity.

HEARD, GERALD. "Science Fiction, Morals, and Religion." In *Modern Science Fiction: Its Meaning and Its Future.* New York: Coward-McCann, 1953, pp. 250–51, 255.

Science fiction in the hand of a character-draughtsman can create a new contemporary tension-of-choice, new moral decisions, and so indicate how they may be faced or flunked.

In its [science fiction's] aim it is bound, by its extrapolation of science and its use of dramatic plot, to view man and his machines and his environment as a three-fold whole, the machine being the hyphen. It also views man's psyche, man's physique and the entire life process as also a threefold interacting unit. Science fiction is the prophetic . . . the apocalyptic literature of our particular and culminating epoch of crisis.

HEINLEIN, ROBERT A. "Science Fiction: Its Nature, Faults and Virtues." In *The Science Fiction Novel: Imagination and Social Criticism.* [Ed. Basil Davenport]. Chicago: Advent, 1969, pp. 22–23; rpt. In *Turning Points: Essays on the Art of Science Fiction.* Ed. Damon Knight. New York: Harper & Row, 1977, p. 9.

A handy short definition of almost all science fiction might read: realistic speculation about possible future events, based solidly on adequate knowledge of the real world, past and present, and on a thorough understanding of the nature and significance of the scientific method.

To make this definition cover all science fiction (instead of "almost all") it is necessary only to strike out the word "future."

HERBERT, FRANK. "Science Fiction and a World in Crisis." In *Science Fiction, Today and Tomorrow.* Ed. Reginald Bretnor. New York: Harper & Row, 1974, p. 74; rpt. Baltimore: Penguin Books, 1975, p. 74.

. . . science fiction, in its dealings with crisis for the sake of story, does indicate other avenues open to us.

HERBERT, FRANK. "Science Fiction and You." In *Tomorrow, and Tomorrow, and Tomorrow. . . .* Ed. Bonnie L. Heintz, Frank Herbert, Donald A. Joos, and Jane Agorn McGee. New York: Holt, Rinehart, and Winston, 1974, p. 1.

Science fiction represents the modern heresy and the cutting edge of speculative imagination as it grapples with Mysterious Time—linear or nonlinear time.

Our motto is *Nothing Secret, Nothing Sacred.*

HILLEGAS, MARK R. "Science Fiction as a Cultural Phenomenon: A Re-Evaluation." In *SF: The Other Side of Realism: Essays on Modern Fantasy and Science Fiction.* Ed. Thomas D. Clareson. Bowling Green, OH: Bowling Green University Popular Press, 1971, p. 280.

What is really important about science fiction is that in its various genres it provides an extraordinarily flexible instrument for social criticism, that it is particularly able to deal with problems of life in a new age of science and technology, and that at the same time it is able to reach, because it is a kind of popular lterature, a much larger audience than does most mainstream literature.

HILLEGAS, MARK R., ed. *Shadows of Imagination: The Fantasies of C. S. Lewis, J. R. R. Tolkien, and Charles Williams.* Carbondale: Southern Illinois University Press; London and Amsterdam: Feffer & Simons, 1961, p. xvii.

. . . science fiction is the myth of machine civilization, which, in its utopian extrapolation, it tends to glorify.

KETTERER, DAVID. *New Worlds for Old: The Apocalyptic Imagination, Science Fiction, and American Literature.* Bloomington and London: Indiana University Press, 1974, p. 15; rpt. Garden City, NY: Anchor, 1974, p. 15.

If, at its most exalted level, apocalyptic literature is religious, the concerns of such a literature, at its most popular level, find expression in the gothic mode and especially in science fiction. Clearly, the introduction of the other, the *outré,* whether in terms of supernatural manifestations or creatures from outer space, is going to upset man's conception of his own situation and prompt him to relate his existence to a broader framework. It is the particular function of all worthwhile science fiction to explore the philosophic consequences of any radical disorientation.

KNIGHT, DAMON. *In Search of Wonder: Essays on Modern Science Fiction.* 2nd ed. Chicago: Advent, 1967, p. 4.

What we get from science fiction—what keeps us reading it, in spite of our doubts and occasional disgust—is not different from the thing that makes mainstream stories rewarding, but only expressed differently. We live on a minute island of known things. Our undiminished wonder at the mystery which surrounds us is what makes us human. In science fiction we can approach that mystery, not in small, everyday symbols, but in big ones of space and time.

KNIGHT, DAMON. "What is Science Fiction?" In *Turning Points: Essays on the Art of Science Fiction.* Ed. Damon Knight. New York: Harper & Row, 1977, p. 63.

In an attempt to find out [what science fiction is], I wrote out a list of promising definitions and checked them against works published as science fiction to see how well they matched. Here is the list:

1. Science (Gernsback).
2. Technology and invention (Heinlein, Miller).
3. The future and the remote past, including all time travel stories (Bailey).
4. Extrapolation (Davenport).
5. Scientific Method (Bretnor).
6. Other places—planets, dimensions, etc., including visitors from the above (Bailey).
7. Catastrophes, natural or manmade (Bailey).

LE GUIN, URSULA K. "Science Fiction and Mrs. Brown." In *Science Fiction at Large: A Collection of Essays, by Various Hands, About the Interface Between Science Fiction and Reality.* Ed. Peter Nicholls. New York: Harper & Row, 1976, p. 29.

And what is science fiction at its best but just a 'new tool' as Mrs. Woolf avowedly sought 50 years ago, a crazy protean, left-handed monkey-wrench, which can be put to any use the craftsman has in mind—satire, extrapolation, prediction, absurdity, exactitude, exaggeration, warning, message-carrying, tale-telling, whatever you like—an infinitely expanding metaphor exactly suited to an expanding universe, a broken mirror, broken into numberless fragments, any one of which is capable of reflecting, for a moment, the left eye and nose of the reader, and also the farthest stars shining in the depths of the remotest galaxy?

LUNDWALL, SAM J. *Science Fiction: What It's All About.* New York: Ace, 1971, p. 22.

A simplified definition would be that the author of a "straight" science fiction story proceeds from (or alleges to proceed from) known facts, developed in a credible way. . . .

McCAFFREY, ANNE. "Romance and Glamour in Science Fiction." In *Science Fiction, Today and Tomorrow.* Ed. Reginald Bretnor. New York: Harper & Row, 1974, pp. 278, 287–88; rpt. Baltimore: Penguin Books, 1975, pp. 279, 287–88.

Science fiction, then and to a great extent now, is more cerebral than gonadel.

. . . any science fiction or fantasy tale abounds with Romance and Glamour: The Romance of man with the products of his agile and inventive mind, with his mechanical miracles. The Glamour of the glittering possibilities of the Future, or of Better Planets under Other Stars, has cast an enchantment over the dogmatic reader.

McNELLY, WILLIS E. "Science Fiction the Modern Mythology [Vonnegut's *Slaughterhouse-Five*]." In *SF: The Other Side of Realism: Essays on Modern Fantasy and Science Fiction.* Ed. Thomas D. Clareson. Bowling Green, OH: Bowling Green University Popular Press, 1971, p. 194.

The best science fiction treats of the interface between man and the machine, the human problems issuing from the common boundary of differing disciplines. It considers the human problems affected by an extrapolation of some scientific hypothesis or device.

And like any mythology, science fiction works best on two levels, the objective as well as the subjective. It permits its readers to understand the implications of a hypothesized action, possible invention, or transcendent machine.

McNELLY, WILLIS. "Science Fiction and the Academy: An Introduction." *CEA Critic,* November 1972, p. 9.

The fabric woven by skillful satirists, ironists, or myth-makers enmeshes the reader while it pleases or nets him with its subtlety. Science fiction can instruct while it pleases. The specific social situation is broadened or extended and the tensions which illuminate the stories or new myths may vary: hypocrisy and complacency brother each other; contempt and pity turn upon themselves; folly and stupidity gleam darkly. Indignation breeds the intolerable.

MOORE, ROSALIE. "Science Fiction and the Main Stream." In *Modern Science Fiction: Its Meaning and Its Future.* Ed. Reginald Bretnor. New York: Coward-McCann, 1953, pp. 92, 95.

... science fiction ... is more fun to read than the kind doggedly referred to as "mainstream."

Science fiction ... is any fiction based on extrapolation of or application of any existing or *imaginable* science, or extrapolation from the same.

MOSKOWITZ, SAM. *Seekers of Tomorrow: Masters of Modern Science Fiction.* Cleveland: World Publishing, 1966, p. 7; rpt. Westport, CT: Hyperion Press, 1974, p. 7.

Science fiction is a branch of fantasy identifiable by the fact that it eases the "willing suspension of disbelief" on the part of its readers by utilizing an atmosphere of scientific credibility for its imaginative speculations in physical science, space, time, social science, and philosophy.

NICHOLLS, PETER. "Science Fiction: The Monsters and the Critics." In *Science Fiction at Large: A Collection of Essays, by Various Hands, About the Interface Between Science Fiction and Reality.* Ed. Peter Nicholls. New York: Harper & Row, 1976, pp. 179, 180–81, 182.

First, it [science fiction] is the great modern literature of metaphor. Conventional literature has a limit, set by everyday realism, to the juxtapositions of imagery it can allow itself. Science fiction, which creates its own worlds, has access to new juxtapositions.

The second major strength of SF is related to the first. It is able to incorporate intellectually *shocking* material, partly because it is so preeminently the literature of change, as opposed to mainstream literature, which is the literature of human continuity.

Third, science fiction is the literature of the outsider, in the extreme sense. Traditional realist fiction observes its action from the viewpoint of a partaker. It shares the illusions of the society which produces it. So does all fiction, but it is science fiction which makes the conscious effort, sometimes quite successful, to stand outside, to give us the Martian eye view of affairs.

Fourthly, science fiction allows us to escape, but gives us the choice of escaping into a world where all is not easy.

Fifthly, the freedom of imagery available to the science-fiction writer allows him to derive a potency of effect, whether consciously or unconsciously, from his own hopes and fears, which, in the way of archetypes, are likely to be ours too.

NOURSE, ALAN E. "Science Fiction and Man's Adaptation to Change." In *Science Fiction, Today and Tomorrow.* Ed. Reginald Bretnor. New York: Harper & Row, 1974, p. 119; rpt. Baltimore: Penguin Books, 1975, p. 119.

... [science fiction] deals specifically with change and its impact on human lives.

PANSHIN, ALEXEI. *Heinlein in Dimension: A Critical Analysis.* Chicago: Advent, pp. 1, 2.

Facts and a concern with change are the stuff that science fiction is made of; science fiction that ignores facts and change can be made less frightening and more popular, but inasmuch as it is superficial, stupid, false-to-fact, timid, foolish or dull, it is minor in another and more important way, and it is certainly bad as science fiction.

... its [science fiction's] attraction lies ... in the unique opportunity it offers for placing familiar things in unfamiliar contexts, and unfamiliar things in familiar contexts, thereby yielding fresh insight and perspective.

PHILMUS, ROBERT M. *Into the Unknown: The Evolution of Science Fiction from Francis Godwin to H. G. Wells.* Berkeley: University of California Press, 1970, pp. vii, viii.

... science fantasy involves the rhetorical strategy of employing a more or less scientific rationale to get the reader to suspend disbelief in a fantastic state of affairs.

[This] strategy [is] one of displacing the real world with a fantastic myth that, through the process of displacement, interprets elements of reality.

PHILMUS, ROBERT M. "Science Fiction: From Its Beginning to 1870." In *Anatomy of Wonder: Science Fiction.* Ed. Neil Barron. New York & London: R. R. Bowker, 1976, p. 6.

Whether stated or implicit, the rationale behind the science-fictional "invention" (in the largest, Wellsian, sense) may derive from the natural or the social sciences, the former being generally the more central, or "hard core." It usually entails an imaginative extension or application of scientific theory to account for the invention—the hitherto unknown machine or species or what-not—which impinges upon or altogether displaces mundane reality. Both the invention and its rationale may be more or less essential to the fiction. The more incidental the invention, the closer the story comes to being "re-presentational"; the more dispensable its rationale, the closer the story approaches to supernatural fantasy.

ROSE, LOIS, AND STEPHEN ROSE. *The Shattered Ring: Science Fiction and the Quest for Meaning.* Richmond, VA; John Knox Press, 1970, pp. 19, 24.

Perhaps science fiction is best defined ... by an enumeration of its themes. They can be grouped into the following categories: *technological gim-*

mickry, space travel, future scenarios, and finally, *the exploration of inner space and ultimate meaning.*

. . . the obvious benefit of such sf musing is to summon forth the possible conjunctions between man's actions and the various worlds that may come into being.

SAMUELSON, DAVE. " 'Definition.' " In *Science Fiction: The Academic Awakening.* Ed. Willis E. McNelly. Shreveport, LA: College English Association, 1974, p. 56.

Science fiction is imaginative literature based on extrapolation from contemporary reality, consistent with contemporary scientific assumptions and theory . . . imaginative literature based (at least in part) on extrapolation from present (past, present, and un-) reality, consistent with scientific (quasi-scientific, para-scientific, or pseudo-scientific) assumptions and theory of the present (past, or future, in this or a hypothetical parallel dimension or "time-track").

SCHOLES, ROBERT. *Structural Fabulation: An Essay on Fiction of the Future.* Notre Dame: University of Notre Dame Press, 1975, pp. 29, 102.

Fabulation, then, is fiction that offers us a world clearly and radically discontinuous from the one we know, yet returns to confront that known world in some cognitive way.

That modern body of fictional works which we loosely designate "science fiction" either accepts or pretends to accept a cognitive responsibility to imagine what is not yet apparent or existent, and to examine this in some systematic way.

SCORTIA, THOMAS N. "Science Fiction as the Imaginary Experiment." In *Science Fiction, Today and Tomorrow.* Ed. Reginald Bretnor. New York: Harper & Row, 1974, p. 136; rpt. Baltimore: Penguin Books, 1975, p. 136.

. . . [science fiction has] the humanistic assumption that the laws of nature are amenable to the interpretation of human logic and, more than this, amenable to logical extrapolation.

SPINRAD, NORMAN. " 'Definition.' " In *Science Fiction: The Academic Awakening.* Ed. Willis E. McNelly. Shreveport, LA: College English Association, 1974, p. 56.

Science fiction is fiction which contains a speculative element in its setting, characters, or thematic material; that is some factor which could exist in the past, present, or future, but which does not exist in the present and did not exist in the past according to present knowledge. Fantasy also contains "unreal elements," but these unreal elements cannot, have not, and will not exist according to our present knowledge. The reading of fantasy requires suspension of disbelief on the part of the reader; proper science fiction creates suspension of disbelief in the mind of the reader.

SPINRAD, NORMAN. "Introduction—Modern Science Fiction." In *Modern Science Fiction*. Ed. Norman Spinrad. Garden City, NY: Anchor Books, 1974, pp. 1–2, 3, 6.

Speculative fiction is exactly what the words imply—any fiction containing a speculative element, anything at all written about the could-be-but-isn't.

Science fiction, on the other hand, is a special case of speculative fiction. It's a school of literature, a commercial genre with its own strange history and an attendant subculture. It's all those tacky old pulp magazines and murky-looking paperbacks, but it's also a large body of literature that can hold its own in respectable company. . . .

I have myself coined what I believe to be the only valid definition of science fiction: "Science fiction is anything published as science fiction."

Speculative fiction is the only fiction that deals with modern reality in the only way that it can be comprehended—as the interface between a rapidly evolving and fissioning environment and the resultant continuously mutating human consciousness. Speculative fiction is surfacing into popular culture from every direction because it reflects the conditions of the modern mind. It is the only fiction that confronts and explores the modern zeitgeist and is therefore inherently the literature of our time.

. . . [science fiction is] art flowing from the lives of human beings under evolutionary pressure.

STURGEON, THEODORE as quoted by Lundwall, Sam J. *Science Fiction: What It's All About*. New York: Ace, 1971, p. 117.

. . . "a science fiction story is a story built around human beings, with a human problem, and a human solution, which would not have happened at all without its scientific content."

TOFFLER, ALVIN. "Science Fiction and Change." In *Science Fiction at Large: A Collection of Essays, by Various Hands, About the Interface Between Science Fiction and Reality*. Ed. Peter Nicholls. New York: Harper & Row, 1976, p. 118.

By challenging anthropocentricism and temporal provincialism, science fiction throws open the whole of civilization and its premises to constructive criticism.

WELLS, BASIL. " 'Definition.' " In *Science Fiction: The Academic Awakening*. Shreveport, LA: College English Association, 1974, p. 34.

Science fiction, in its purest sense, should mean entertaining, colorful fiction that either extrapolates what logically, or possibly, will take place in the future, or creates a more or less logical alien culture, or cultures, and records the probable impact upon it by an extrapolated Terran civilization. Successful science fiction, hopefully, brings temporary suspension of disbelief and a sense of identification with either the humans or the likeable or offbeat alien entities involved. Along with this should be the feeling of: WHAT IF? and WHY NOT? The seeds of speculative thought are sprouted—hopefully, the reader is hooked on science fiction. . . .

WILLIAMSON, JACK. "SF Comes to College." *Extrapolation,* 12 (1971), 68.

"Hard" science fiction . . . probes alternative possible futures by means of reasoned extrapolations in much the same way that good historical fiction reconstructs the probable past. Even far-out fantasy can present a significant test of human values exposed to a new environment. Deriving its most cogent ideas from the tensions between permanence and change, science fiction combines the diversions of novelty with its pertinent kind of realism.

WOLFE, GARY K. "The Known and the Unknown: Structure and Image in Science Fiction." In *Many Futures, Many Worlds: Theme and Form in Science Fiction.* Ed. Thomas D. Clareson. Kent, OH: Kent State University Press, 1977, p. 114.

. . . the intellectual basis of much science fiction—this kind of dialectical extrapolation—is more closely related to the emotional basis (the "sense of wonder") than is generally suspected. The process may be summarized somewhat as follows: the known exists in opposition to the unknown, with a barrier of some sort separating them. The barrier is crossed, and the unknown creates the known. But the crossing of the barrier reveals new problems, and this sets the stage for a further opposition of known and unknown. This barrier is crossed, yet another opposition is set up, and so on. The "sense of wonder" grows in part out of the tension generated by awareness of this opposition, and the images of the sense of wonder are those which most strongly reinforce this tension, images that stand at the barrier. The transformations continue until an opposition is arrived at that requires no further transformation or resolution.

WOLLHEIM, DONALD A. *The Universe Makers: Science Fiction Today.* New York: Harper & Row, 1971, pp. 6, 10.

Science fiction is above all a system of ideas. It deals with ideas more than it deals with literary styles. It speculates in futurities and in probabilities.

It is this harvest of wonders, this garden of marvels, this vision of what could be and what could have been that makes science fiction so different and makes its readers marked for life in out-of-the-rut trains of thought.

Science fiction is that branch of fantasy, which, while not true to present-day knowledge, is rendered plausible by the reader's recognition of the scientific possibilities of it being possible at some future date or at some uncertain period in the past.

WYLIE, PHILIP. "Science Fiction and Sanity in an Age of Crisis." In *Modern Science Fiction: Its Meaning and Its Future.* Ed. Reginald Bretnor. New York: Coward-McCann, 1953, pp. 238, 239.

Our science fiction . . . shows a regressive mythological bent; . . . where it evades the rules of science and draws on the imagination without regard to logic or knowledge, it is obsolete.

The proper function of the science-fiction author—the mythmaker of the 20th century—would be to learn the science of the mind's working and therewith to plan his work . . . so it will represent in *meaning* the known significance of man.

CONTRIBUTORS

An award-winning writer, esteemed editor, and maverick literary agent, **Frederik Pohl** entered the field of science fiction when he first opened a *Science Wonder Stories Quarterly* at the age of ten. By the time he was nineteen Pohl was editor of *Astonishing Stories* and *Super Science Stories*. As editor of *Galaxy* and *If* in the 1960s, he shaped the field for most of a decade. As a literary agent Pohl helped to create the market for hardcover science fiction; his *Star Science Fiction* series pioneered the concept of original anthologies. Along with all this Pohl has produced a number of truly memorable works of science fiction. As a writer, he has been praised for his unnervingly real perceptions of the future. His *Man Plus* was awarded the 1976 Nebula, and *Gateway* won the top three awards in the field: the John W. Campbell Memorial Award, the 1977 Nebula, and the 1978 Hugo. *Jem* was the winner of the 1980 American Book Award. Pohl was the first winner of Hugo Awards for both his writing and editing. He has recently published his autobiography, *The Way the Future Was* (Del Rey, 1978) and a book on SF film, *Science Fiction: Studies in Film* (Ace, 1981) with Frederik Pohl IV.

Marshall B. Tymn, an associate professor of English at Eastern Michigan University, has taught science fiction there since 1974, and is director of the annual Conference on Teaching Science Fiction, a national workshop. Dr. Tymn is the author of numerous reference works and articles about science fiction and the literature of fantasy. His publications include *A Research Guide to Science Fiction Studies* (coauthor), *Index to Stories in Thematic Anthologies of Science Fiction* (coauthor), *American Fantasy and Science Fiction, The Year's Scholarship in Science Fiction and Fantasy: 1972–1975* (coauthor), *Fantasy Literature: A Core Collection and Reference Guide* (coauthor), and *The Science Fiction Reference Book*. His bibliographic articles and essays have appeared in *Extrapolation, Choice, CEA Critic, English Journal, Media & Methods, Mosaic, Handbook of American Popular Culture,* and other anthologies. Dr. Tymn is editor of a major critical series published by Greenwood Press, Contributions to the Study of Science Fiction and Fantasy; advisory acquisitions editor for G. K. Hall's Masters of Science Fiction and Fantasy series; and bibliographer for the Taplinger Press Writers of the 21st Century series. He is a former officer of the Science Fiction Research Association and an affiliate member of the Science Fiction Writers of America. Dr. Tymn holds a Ph.D. in American Culture from the University of Michigan. His continuing interest in American literature of the romantic period is reflected in his *Thomas Cole's Poetry* (1972) and *Thomas Cole: The Collected Essays and Prose Sketches* (1980).

Thomas D. Clareson, professor of English at Wooster College (Ohio), has been editor of *Extrapolation,* the pioneer academic journal in the field, since 1959. From 1970 through 1976 Clareson was the first president of the Science Fiction Research Association, who in 1977 gave him the Pilgrim Award in recognition of his contributions to the study of science fiction. His major books in the field include *SF: The Other Side of Realism* (1971), *SF Criticism: An Annotated Checklist* (1972), *A Spectrum of Worlds* (1972), *Voices for the Future I-II* (1976, 1979), and *Many Futures, Many Worlds* (1977). Clareson is general editor for the Greenwood Press microfilm publication of the early SF magazines; he has contributed introductions to a number of the Gregg Press Science Fiction series volumes; and he has published essays in Neil Barron's *Anatomy of Wonder* (1976; revised 1981). Although his major interest has remained with early American SF and fantasy, Clareson has written on such contemporary writers as Clifford D. Simak, Arthur C. Clarke, Gene Wolfe and Robert Silverberg. Most recently, his study of science fiction and the literary tradition appeared in Jack Williamson's *Teaching Science Fiction* (1980). He is at work on a history of early American science fiction and fantasy to be entitled *Some Kind of Paradise.* He is an affiliate member of Science Fiction Writers of America.

Francis J. Molson is a professor of English at Central Michigan University, where he teaches courses in science fiction and children's fantasy. He is a specialist in 19th-century American literature, children's literature, and juvenile science fiction and fantasy. Molson is author of essays on such diverse figures as Emily Dickinson and Francis Finn, and is one of the contributors to *Anatomy of Wonder.* He is preparing a bibliography of children's science fiction for G. K. Hall's Masters of Science Fiction and Fantasy series. Another area of his active interest is ethical fantasy, that contemporary fantasy for young readers that embodies ethical concerns and purposes and may serve as an effective substitute for traditional didactic literature.

Vincent Di Fate attended the Phoenix (now the Pratt-Manhattan Center) for his formal art training, graduated in 1967, taught art for a year, and then quit to work in animated films before beginning his freelance art career in January of 1969. He has worked almost exclusively in the science fiction, astronomical and aerospace art markets ever since and has received numerous awards for his work, including the Frank R. Paul Award and the 1979 Hugo Award for Best Professional Artist. In addition to his art activities, Di Fate writes a column on SF art for *Starship* magazine and has lectured extensively on the history and art of science fiction. He has had a number of one-man showings of his work in both museums and galleries here and abroad. He has several paintings in the Space Art Collection of the Smithsonian's National Air & Space Museum, and he represented the Smithsonian as a NASA artist on the Apollo-Soyuz launch in 1975. In 1979 DiFate taught a special course in science fiction visual concepts for the University of Bridgeport, and he currently has a book of his work in print from Workman entitled *DiFate's Catalogue of Science Fiction Hardware.*

Vincent Miranda began his career in science fiction after working extensively in the visual media as a photo-journalist and cinematographer-scriptwriter for educational television. He helped coordinate and promote science fiction classes in Florida high schools while researching and writing in his specializations, history of fantastic literature, history of the fantastic cinema, and bibliography. As former editor of Curtis Publications, Miranda edited *Fantasy*

Voyages: Great Science Fiction from the Saturday Evening Post. As a researcher he has compiled the most comprehensive bibliography on Damon Knight, which appeared in a special issue of *The Magazine of Fantasy and Science Fiction* in 1977. Miranda is an advisor to the estate of A. Merritt. Since the inception of both Marshall Tymn's Conference on Teaching Science Fiction and the International Conference on the Fantastic in the Arts, Miranda has served on the faculty and staff of each as lecturer and media specialist, mounting exhibits on the literature, film and art of the fantastic from his own considerable collection.

Joseph Siclari has been involved in science fiction fandom since 1965 and has been a fan publisher since 1970. He currently publishes *Fanhistoria*, a magazine devoted to fandom's past, and is the publisher of Harry Warner Jr.'s history of fandom in the 1950s, *A Wealth of Fable.* Siclari is involved in fandom on many levels: he has written reviews and articles for several fan publications, programmed films for several Lunacons and the New York City regional conventions, and served as program director for SunCon, the 35th World Science Fiction Convention. He has taught courses on the history of the horror film and science fiction which were adapted for media use by the Florida State University Cooperative Education Program. Siclari is currently involved in collecting and indexing fan publications.

Harlan Perry McGhan holds a B.A. in Philosophy from Michigan State University and is at work on a Ph.D. in the History and Philosophy of Science from Princeton University. He taught for nine years in the Philosophy Departments of Virginia Commonwealth University and the University of Delaware. At Delaware he offered a course in "Philosophy and Science Fiction." McGhan is currently employed as chief technical writer for one of the Exxon Information System Ventures in California. Although he began reading science fiction at an early age, his systematic interest in the subject of SF awards dates back to an original (unpublished) study of this subject done in 1964. More recently, McGhan has inaugurated an annual survey which attempts to provide exhaustive coverage of the science fiction and fantasy awards and honors given each year. His current project is rumored to be a complete analysis and account, together with a comprehensive index, of all literary awards for the field, from their dim historical beginnings to the present day.

Howard DeVore became involved with science fiction in the mid-1930s, is a member of First Fandom and two amateur press organizations some thirty years old. He served on the original Hugo Award rules committee, as chairman of Detention, the 7th World Science Fiction Convention, and on the committees of many regional and national conventions. DeVore owns one of the largest SF collections in the United States and is a well-known dealer in rare science fiction and fantasy in addition to his involvement in several primary research projects. He is coauthor and publisher of *A History of the Hugo, Nebula, and International Fantasy Awards* and various other nonfiction works.

James Gunn is a professor of English at the University of Kansas and director of the Intensive English Institute on the Teaching of Science Fiction. He has been a science fiction writer since 1948. Among his sixteen SF novels and collections are *The Dreamers, Kampus, The Listeners, Star Bridge* (with Jack Williamson), *This Fortress World, The Joy Makers,* and *The Immortals.* He is president of the Science Fiction Research Association and the former president of the Science Fiction Writers of America. Gunn is the winner of the SFRA Pilgrim Award; producer of the University of Kansas Science Fiction Lecture

Film Series; former chairman of the John W. Campbell Memorial Award; editor of *Nebula Award Stories Ten* and the three-volume historical anthology, *The Road to Science Fiction;* and author of *Alternate Worlds: The Illustrated History of Science Fiction.*

Roger C. Schlobin, an associate professor of English at the North Central Campus of Purdue University, holds a Ph.D. in Medieval Literature from Ohio State University. He is the author of *The Literature of Fantasy: A Comprehensive, Annotated Bibliography of Modern Fantasy Fiction* and *Andre Norton: A Primary and Secondary Bibliography,* as well as coeditor of "The Year's Scholarship in Science Fiction and Fantasy" and coauthor of *A Research Guide to Science Fiction Studies.* Schlobin is the editor of the Starmont Reader's Guides to Contemporary Science Fiction and Fantasy Authors and the forthcoming Garland Reprint Library of Fantasy Classics. His essays and bibliographies have appeared in the *CEA Critic, Media & Methods, Extrapolation,* and other publications. He has recently completed editing an anthology of essays on the aesthetics of fantasy art and literature and is currently at work on a survey of fantasy literature and criticism. He lives in a remote hamlet in Indiana with his sixteen-pound tomcat, Joshua Thunderpussy.

Joseph DeBolt is a professor of sociology at Central Michigan University. His abiding interest in science fiction is reflected in his publications, *The Happening Worlds of John Brunner* (1975) and *Ursula K. Le Guin: Voyager to Inner Lands and Outer Space* (1979). He has also coauthored the chapter on the modern period for *Anatomy of Wonder.* DeBolt is the past president of the Science Fiction Research Association.

Elizabeth Cummins Cogell teaches English at the University of Missouri-Rolla. She has presented several papers on Ursula Le Guin at academic meetings and has published articles on Le Guin's works in *Extrapolation* and other sources. She has just completed *Ursula K. Le Guin: A Primary and Secondary Bibliography* for G. K. Hall's Masters of Science Fiction and Fantasy series. Women in literature and the apocalyptic novel are additional research interests. Cogell is currently serving her second term as treasurer of the Science Fiction Research Association.

Douglas R. Justus, who earned his B. S. at Ball State University and his M.A. at Eastern Michigan University, developed his academic interest in science fiction and fantasy literature during the mid-1970s while adding English certification through Purdue University. Justus contributed the chapter on science fiction doctoral dissertations for *A Research Guide to Science Fiction Studies* (Garland, 1977). He presently teaches English in Highland, Indiana, as well as occasional courses at Purdue North Central University.

INDEX

This index cites significant mention of authors, editors, artists, fans, titles, and events in the development of science fiction. No attempt has been made to index the hundreds of award-winners cited in McGhan's chapter, "The Writing Awards," but all awards are listed. Cogell's chapter on SF library collections contains its own index, as does the audio-visual section of Tymn's chapter on teaching resources. Additional items not indexed are the individual articles on teaching in Tymn's chapter, and the doctoral dissertations compiled by Justus.

A

517